Pan-Africanism and Communism

The Harriet Tubman Series on the African Diaspora

Paul E. Lovejoy and Toyin Falola, eds., *Pawnship, Slavery and Colonialism in Africa*, 2003.

Donald G. Simpson, *Under the North Star: Black Communities in Upper Canada before Confederation (1867)*, 2005.

Paul E. Lovejoy, *Slavery, Commerce and Production in West Africa: Slave Society in the Sokoto Caliphate*, 2005.

José C. Curto and Renée Soulodre-La France, eds., *Africa and the Americas: Interconnections during the Slave Trade*, 2005.

Paul E. Lovcjoy, *Ecology and Ethnography of Muslim Trade in West Africa*, 2005.

Naana Opoku-Agyemang, Paul E. Lovejoy and David Trotman, eds., *Africa and Trans-Atlantic Memories: Literary and Aesthetic Manifestations of Diaspora and History*, 2008.

Boubacar Barry, Livio Sansone, and Elisée Soumonni, eds., *Africa, Brazil, and the Construction of Trans-Atlantic Black Identities*, 2008.

Behnaz Asl Mirzai, Ismael Musah Montana, and Paul E. Lovejoy, eds., *Slavery, Islam and Diaspora*, 2009.

Carolyn Brown and Paul E. Lovejoy, eds., *Repercussions of the Atlantic Slave Trade: The Interior of the Bight of Biafra and the African Diaspora*, 2010.

Ute Röschenthaler, *Purchasing Culture in the Cross River Region of Cameroon and Nigeria*, 2011.

Ana Lucia Araujo, Mariana P. Candido and Paul E. Lovejoy, eds., *Crossing Memories: Slavery and African Diaspora*, 2011.

Edmund Abaka, *House of Slaves and "Door of No Return": Gold Coast Castles and Forts of the Atlantic Slave Trade*, 2012.

Christopher Innes, Annabel Rutherford, and Brigitte Bogar, eds. *Carnival: Theory and Practice*, 2012.

Paul E. Lovejoy and Benjamin P. Bowser, *The Transatlantic Slave Trade and Slavery*, 2012.

Joel Quirk and Darshan Vigneswaran, eds., *Slavery, Migration and Contemporary Bondage in Africa*, 2013.

Hakim Adi, *Pan-Africanism and Communism: The Communist International, Africa and the Diaspora, 1919-1939*, 2013.

PAN-AFRICANISM and COMMUNISM

The Communist International, Africa and the Diaspora 1919-1939

HAKIM ADI

AFRICA WORLD PRESS
TRENTON | LONDON | CAPE TOWN | NAIROBI | ADDIS ABABA | ASMARA | IBADAN | NEW DELHI

AFRICA WORLD PRESS
541 West Ingham Avenue | Suite B
Trenton, New Jersey 08638

First Printing 2013

Book and Cover design: Saverance Publishing Services

Library of Congress Cataloging-in-Publication Data

Adi, Hakim.
Pan-Africanism and communism : the communist international, Africa and the diaspora, 1919-1939 / Hakim Adi.
p. cm.
Includes bibliographical references and index.
ISBN 978-1-59221-915-5 (hard cover) -- ISBN 978-1-59221-916-2 (pbk.)
1. International Trade Union Committee of Negro Workers. 2. Communist International. 3. Pan-Africanism--History--20th century. 4. Communism--History--20th century. I. Title.
HD6305.B56A35 2013
320.53208996--dc23
2012049798

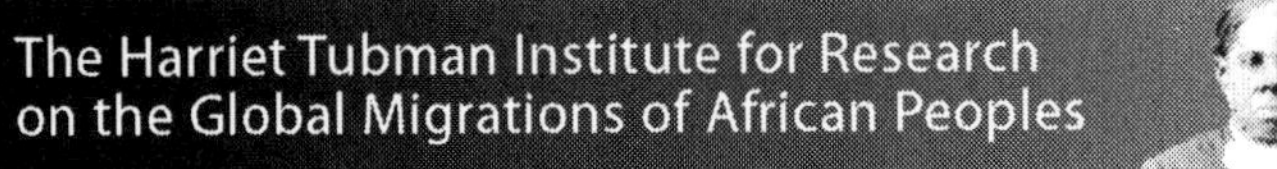

Contents

Acknowledgements

It has been remarked on many occasions that books involving historical research are collective enterprises involving the work not only of the author but also many other individuals and institutions. I would therefore like to take this opportunity to acknowledge all those who have contributed.

I am particularly grateful for the generous support of the British Academy, which provided funds to enable me to visit archives in Moscow. I was able to devote a year to further research and writing courtesy of a British Academy/ Leverhulme Trust Senior Research Fellowship. I would also like to acknowledge the support of the School of Arts and Humanities, Middlesex University, which provided funds enabling me to carry out research in the United States. I must also thank Hugo Frey and the History Department of the University of Chichester, the Harriet Tubman Research Institute, the Canada Research Chair in African Diaspora History at York University, Toronto, and the Major Collaborative Research Initiative Programme, 'Slavery, Memory, Citizenship' of the Social Sciences and Humanities Research Council of Canada for generous financial support which has allowed this book to be published. I extend special thanks to those who supported my funding applications, especially Richard Rathbone, Toyin Falola, Michael West, Francis Mulhern and Paul Lovejoy.

I would also like to thank the staff at the many libraries and archives that assisted my research. I am particularly grateful to Randall K. Burkett and his colleagues at the Manuscripts, Archives and Rare Books Library, Emory University for providing me with a MARBL Research Fellowship and fulfilling several request for documents. Thanks also to library staff at Middlesex University, especially Monica Johnson, who also fulfilled many requests for articles and books. I am also grateful for the assistance of librarians and archivists at the Archives Nationales d'outre-mer, the Bibliothèque Nationale de France, Columbia University, Howard University, the Library of Congress, especially John Earl Haynes, the London School of Economics, the Marx Memorial Library, the National Archives, the Russian State Archive for Social and Political History, the Schomburg Centre for Research in Black Culture, New York University and the Bodleian Library at Oxford University.

Several colleagues have been kind enough to share the results of their research and kwowledge with me and I'm particularly grateful for the continual help and support of my friend Marika Sherwood. Thanks also to Apollon Davidson, Allison Drew, Irina Filatova, Lily Golden, Richard Hart, Leslie James, Doreen Musson, James Spiegler, Margaret Stevens, Maria van Enckevort, Daniel Whittall and Jacob Zumoff. Marika, Allison and Irina were also kind enough to read and comment on draft chapters and I thank them for all their comments and criticisms.

The documentary sources on which this book is based sometimes required translation and I am extremely grateful to those who assisted me in this endeavour. I would particularly like to thank Tomi Adeaga, Emilie Agonstini, Ama Biney, Myrto Konstantarakos, Glwadys Le Goff, Saynab Mahamud, and Nicholay Scherbakov.

My thanks go to all those, some of whom were already friends and some who became friends, who helped with accommodation in France, the United States and Russia, or supported my research in other ways. Special thanks to Nicholay Scherbakov, Olga Malinkovskaya and their family in Moscow, to Souley Hassane and especially Abdou Diallo and the maison du thé in Aix-en-Provence. I also wish to express my gratitude to Nana Asante, Michael Chant, Afua Cooper, Mary Dillard, Donna Forde, Elsa Geneste, Venus Green, Monica Wells Kisura, Lillian Ma, Louise Meriwether, Mary Louise Patterson, and Isaac Saney.

Last, but not least, I would like to acknowledge the critical support of my wife Esther, especially during several years of enforced economic inactivity.

Without the help and support of the above mentioned this book would not have been completed.

Abbreviations

AAC	All-African Convention
ABB	African Blood Brotherhood
AFL	American Federation of Labor
AFTU	African Federation of Trade Unions
ANC	African National Congress
ANLC	American Negro Labor Congress
AWUN	African Workers' Union of Nigeria
BGLU	British Guiana Labour Union
CFAA	Coloured Film Artists Association
CAI	Service de Contrôle et d'assistance des indigènes des colonies Françaises
CDRN	Comité de Défense de la Race Nègre
CGTU	Confédération Générale du Travail Unitaire
CI	Communist International
CP	Communist Party
CPGB	Communist Party of Great Britain
CPSA	Communist Party of South Africa
CPUSA	Communist Party of the United States
CSA	Colonial Seamen's Association
CSLA	Confederación Sindical Latinamiericano
CWIA	Committee for West Indian Affairs
ECCI	Executive Committee of the Communist International
FNETU	Federation of Non-European Trade Unions

GCARPS	Gold Coast Aborigines' Rights Protection Society
HC	Hamburg Committee (of the ITUCNW)
ICU	Industrial and Commercial Workers' Union
IAFA	International African Friends of Abyssinia
IASB	International African Service Bureau
ICDEP	International Committee for the Defence of the Ethiopian People
IFTU	International Federation of Trade Unions
ILD	International Labour Defence
IRA	International Red Aid
ISL	International Socialist League
ISH	International of Seamen and Harbour Workers
ITUCNW	International Trade Union Committee of Negro Workers
JLTU	Jamaica Labour and Trade Union
KUTV	(Russian acronym for) University of the Toilers of the East
LACO	League Against Colonial Oppression
LAI	League Against Imperialism
LCP	League of Coloured Peoples
LDRN	Ligue de Défense de la Race Nègre
LSI	Labour and Socialist International
MOPR	(Russian Acronym for) International Red Aid
NAACP	National Association for the Advancement of Colored People
NLL	National Liberation League
NMM	National Minority Movement
NUS	National Union of Seamen
NWCSA	Negro Welfare, Cultural and Social Association
PCC	Partido Comunista de Cuba
PCF	Parti Communiste Français
RC	Rassemblement Coloniale
RGASPI	Russian State Archive for Social and Political History
RILU	Red International of Labour Unions
SFIO	Section Français de I'Internationale Ouvrière

SLOTFOM	Service de Liaison avec les Originaires des Territoires Français d'Outre Mer
SMM	Seaman's Minority Movement
SPA	Socialist Party of America
SRI	Secours Rouge Internationale
TNA	The National Archives
TUEL	Trade Union Education League
TUUL	Trade Union Unity League
TWA	Trinidad Workingmen's Association
UTN	Union des Travailleurs Nègres
UNIA	Universal Negro Improvement Association
WAYL	West African Youth League
WP	Workers' Party
YCL	Young Communist League

Introduction

In October 1935 George Padmore, the former secretary of the International Trade Union Committee of Negro Workers (ITUCNW), published 'An Open Letter to Earl Browder,' at that time the leader of the Communist Party of the United States of America (CPUSA), in the pages of *The Crisis*. Padmore alleged that:

> The Communist International liquidated the Negro Trade Union Committee, of which I was secretary, in August 1933, without giving me one word of explanation, simply in order not to offend the British Foreign Office which has been bringing pressure to bear on Soviet diplomacy because of the tremendous indignation which our work has aroused among the Negro masses in Africa, the West Indies and other colonies against British Imperialism.[1]

Padmore also made several other allegations, and threatened but did not pursue legal action against his former comrades. In addition, he made the claim that the Communist International (Comintern or CI) was also responsible for 'the suppression of *The Negro Worker* of which I was editor in-chief.'[2]

This attempt at publicly debating the recent history of the ITUCNW and its publication was extraordinary and had first appeared in the African American press the previous summer, accompanied by angry responses from several of Padmore's former comrades.[3] Not only did Padmore make public allegations

1. G. Padmore, 'An Open Letter to Earl Browder,' *The Crisis* (October 1935) pp.302 and 315.
2. Ibid.
3. See e.g., 'Expelled Red Scores Party,' *Amsterdam News*, 16 June 1934; 'Exposure of Communists is Promised,' *Amsterdam News*, 28 July 1934; 'Communists, After 15 Years Make No Headway Among Negroes, Says Padmore,' *Philadelphia Tribune*, 2 August 1934; 'Africans Will Help Padmore,' *Amsterdam News*, 4 August 1934; G. Padmore, 'Padmore Answers Heywood's Slanders,' *Pittsburgh Courier*, 22 September 1934; '"Padmore Belly Crawls," Says Angelo Herndon,' *Negro Liberator*, 8 September 1934; C. Briggs to The Editor, *New Amsterdam News*, 23 July 1934; J. W. Ford, 'James Ford Answers Padmore's Charges,' *Crusader News Agency*, 4 August 1934, George Padmore Collection, Princeton University Library. Also J. W. Ford, *World Problems of the Negro People -A Refutation of George Padmore* (New York, n.d.).

about internal Comintern matters, but within his 'Open Letter' he immediately refuted his own allegations by complaining about criticisms of him made by Otto Huiswoud, who was both his successor as secretary of the ITUCNW and the new 'editor-in-chief' of *The Negro Worker* both of which, according to Padmore, had already been 'liquidated' by the Comintern.[4] When Earl Browder's response was published, some two months later, Padmore's allegations were easily dismissed with Browder querying the timing of the publication of the 'Open Letter', over a year after it had originally been written and coinciding with an attack on the Soviet Union's foreign policy in regard to the Italian invasion of Ethiopia in the pages of *The Crisis*.[5]

Nevertheless, Padmore had made several similar allegations in private as well as in public. In July 1934, for example, he wrote to his friend Cyril Olliviere: 'Last August the Communist International wanted me to close down our activities in order to appease the British Foreign Office, which was raising hell because the Blacks in Africa were beginning to wake up.' According to Padmore's account, he had been left with no choice but to resign.[6] Even lengthier allegations and denunciations of the Comintern, along with copies of a resignation letter addressed to 'the Secretariat Communist Party of USA,' and including even greater detail about internal Comintern affairs had been sent to some newspaper editors.[7] Padmore repeated his allegations over twenty years later in his book *Pan-Africanism or Communism?* There he again claimed that 'the ITUCNW, with which I was associated was liquidated, in keeping with the pro-League of Nations orientation in Soviet foreign policy.'[8] Padmore was, however, reluctant to entirely repudiate his own activities as a leading member of the ITUCNW, although this is the only mention of the Committee in a book largely devoted to condemning the international communist movement and its relationship with Africa and the African Diaspora.[9] Indeed, he seems

4. G. Padmore, 'An Open Letter to Earl Browder.'

5. 'Earl Browder Replies,' *The Crisis* (December 1935) p.372.

6. See Padmore to Cyril Olliviere, 28 July 1934, George Padmore Papers, Schomburg Centre (Sc MG 624).

7. See e.g. G. Padmore, 'Why I left the Communist International Padmore Refutes Lies and Slanders of Communists,' 13 February 1934, and Padmore to Moon, 4 October 1934, George Padmore Collection, Princeton University.

8. G. Padmore, *Pan-Africanism or Communism? The Coming Struggle for Africa* (London, 1956) p.330.

9. Even one of Padmore's close friends, the French Anarchist Daniel Guérin, was critical of aspects of this book, claiming that in it he was 'too indulgent to the *reactionary* anticommunist forces.' See Daniel Guérin to Padmore, 18 September 1956. Le Fonds Daniel Guérin (1904-1988/F RES 688-19), Bibliothèque de Documentation Internationale Contemporaine, Paris.

to have been happy to continue to be associated with *The Life and Struggles of Negro Toilers*, the book that he had written in 1931 under the auspices and based on the political orientation of the Comintern and the ITUCNW.[10]

What is significant is that from the mid-1930s onwards there existed a publicly contested history of the ITUCNW and the Comintern's alleged attempts to 'liquidate' it. Padmore's initial attempt to present his version of events can be explained by his rupture with the Comintern in 1933-34 and his later attempts to establish Pan-Africanism as an ideological means for Africa and Africans to chart a course between East and West during the height of the Cold War and the bi-polar division of the world. The circumstances surrounding the break with the CI as well as Padmore's boast that that the ITUCNW had aroused in Africa, the Caribbean and elsewhere 'tremendous indignation,' will be examined in more detail below. Despite his criticisms of the Comintern, for many years Padmore remained ambivalent about communism and the Soviet Union. Even in his letter of resignation to the CPUSA he stated 'I find myself in no conflict with the fundamental principles of our movement.' In 1945 he was still writing about 'how the USSR solved the National and Colonial problems it inherited from Czarist Russia,' in order to contrast this 'achievement' with the oppressive nature of European colonialism in Africa, and as 'a challenge to the imperialist powers.'[11] However, there was no ambivalence about Padmore's allegations against the Comintern and the ITUCNW, and it is these that seem to have been accepted and repeated without much further investigation in other historical accounts, including Hooker's inadequate biography of Padmore.[12]

Padmore's criticism of the Comintern is, for example, repeated in Kanet's otherwise useful survey on the Comintern and the Negro Question. Although Kanet states that Padmore's allegation concerning the 'liquidation' of the ITUCNW 'is obviously incorrect,' he still agues that 'his basic contention was correct.' In Kanet's view 'the Comintern was ready to sacrifice the revolutionary aspects of the organisation in the interests of Soviet Foreign policy,' and he concludes that 'the failure of the communists to develop strong revolutionary movements in either Africa or the United States among the black population,' was due to 'their dependence on the vagaries of Soviet foreign policy,' or 'a result of

10. This book is listed as one of the author's works in the first edition of *Pan-Africanism or Communism*, just as it is in Padmore's earlier publications. He clearly remained as proud of the book in 1956 as he was in 1934.

11. G. Padmore, *How Russia Transformed Her Colonial Empire - A Challenge to the Imperialist Powers* (London, 1946).

12. J.R. Hooker, *Black Revolutionary – George Padmore's path from Communism to Pan-Africanism* (London, 1967) pp.31-32.

directives from Moscow.' Kanet even suggests that for the Comintern 'little distinction was made between a policy for blacks in Africa and the United States.'[13]

This monolithic view of Soviet and Comintern policy was much in vogue during the Cold War, although more recent historical accounts have shown it be inaccurate.[14] However, as well as being factually inaccurate it also prevented any real understanding of the aims and significance of the Comintern, or the ITUCNW, in regard to Africa and the African Diaspora. Indeed such an approach generally denied that the ITUCNW and the communist movement were trying to address and solve complex economic and political problems that confronted millions of people in Africa and the Caribbean, as well as in the United States, South America, Europe and elsewhere. Moreover, it was an approach that took no account of the fact that for many years several communist parties failed, or for various reasons were reluctant, to fully implement Comintern decisions relating to Africa, the Caribbean and the African Diaspora in general, what was then referred to as the Negro Question. It was this reluctance, and what was then considered an underestimation of the importance of the Negro Question, or even 'white chauvinism,' that led in 1928 to the creation of the ITUCNW. The Cold War approach also largely ignored the conscious participation and agency of African and 'Negro' Communists both within individual communist parties and in the work of the ITUCNW.[15]

A different perspective was perhaps not widely known before the publication of Harry Haywood's famous autobiography *Black Bolshevik* in 1978. Haywood, one of the leading African American Communists of the 1930s, had spent several years studying in the Soviet Union, and was involved in the development of the Comintern's approach to the Negro Question. But although Haywood's fascinating account mentioned many of the other 'Black Bolshe-

13. R. E. Kanet, 'The Comintern and the "Negro Question": Communist Policy in the United States and Africa, 1921-1941,' *Survey*, XIX no.4 (1973) pp.86-122. For a similar approach to the history of the ITUCNW see W. Record, *The Negro and the Communist Party* (New York, 1971) pp.84-86. Padmore's allegations also surface in E.T. Wilson's very informative *Russia and Black Africa Before World War II* (London, 1974) pp.260-261.

14. For more recent accounts of the Comintern's history see e.g. G. Roberts, 'Collective Security and the Origins of the People's Front,' in J. Fyrth (ed.) *Britain, Fascism and the Popular Front* (London, 1985) pp.74-78; T. Rees and A. Thorpe, 'Introduction,' in T. Rees and A. Thorpe (eds.) *International Communism and the Communist International 1919-1943* (Manchester, 1998); M. Worley, 'Courting Disaster? The Communist Disaster in the Third Period,' in M. Worley (ed.) *In Search of Revolution: International Communist Parties in the Third Period* (London, 2004) pp.1-17.

15. 'Negro' was the term widely used at the time and therefore is used here and below to refer to both Africans and those of African origin. For an interesting discussion on the use of the term by the ITUCNW in preference to 'African,' 'West Indian,' and 'Colored' see Padmore to F. Thomson, 5 January 1932, Russian State Archive for Social and Political History (RGASPI) 534/3/754.

viks' in the Comintern's ranks, he said little about the ITUCNW, which he described as 'the first attempt to bring together black workers on a world scale.'[16]

In the last twenty years the opening of the archives of the Comintern in Moscow have provided historians with the material to more thoroughly research the history of the ITUCNW and to present a more accurate account of the Comintern's attempts to find answers to the Negro Question. Several works have now been published which shed some light on the work of individual communist parties, particularly the activities of the Communist Party of South Africa (CPSA) and what eventually became the Communist Party of the United States (CPUSA).[17] The opening up of the archives has now led to three important biographical accounts of the leading members of the ITUCNW, two relating to Otto and Hermina Huiswoud, and one to George Padmore, as well as some new accounts of the ITUCNW.[18] It has also made possible the correction of several factual errors that were repeated in the literature for many years. However, even some of those who have more recently written about the ITUCNW, having consulted the Comintern archives, can still be guilty of uncritically repeating aspects of the old approach. A well-researched article published in 2001 could still maintain that 'the ITUCNW was disbanded by the Comintern in August 1933.'[19]

The archives of the Comintern in Moscow are a vital source for the re-writing of this history, containing reports, articles, correspondence, personal files and other material but they are not the only source. Material from other archival

16. H. Haywood, *Black Bolshevik - Autobiography of An Afro-American Communist* (Chicago, 1978) p.329.

17. For example: M. Solomon, *The Cry Was Unity – Communists and African Americans, 1917-1936* (Jackson, 1998); G.E. Gilmore, *Defying Dixie: The Radical Roots of Civil Rights, 1919-1950* (London, 2008). Also A. Davidson et al (eds.) *South Africa and the Communist International: A Documentary History* [2 vols.] (London, 2003) and A. Drew, *Discordant Comrades: Identities and Loyalties on the South African Left* (Pretoria, 2002).

18. J.M. Turner, *Caribbean Crusaders and the Harlem Renaissance* (Chicago, 2005); M. C. Van Enckevort, 'The Life and Work of Otto Huiswoud: Professional Revolutionary and Internationalist [1893-1961]' (Ph.D. dissertation, University of the West Indies, Mona, Jamaica, 2001) and L.E. James, "'What we put in black and white': George Padmore and the practice of anti-imperial politics" (Ph.D dissertation, University of London, 2012). For recent work on the ITUCNW see e.g. M. Makalani, *In the Cause of Freedom – Radical Black Internationalism from Harlem to London, 1917-1939.* (Chapel Hill, 2011) and the various Comintern Working Papers produced by Holger Weiss and his colleagues entitled *Comintern and the African Nationalism, 1921-1935* and available at http://www.abo.fi/institution/en/Content/Document/document/26026. Accessed July 1, 2012

19. J.A. Miller, S. Pennybacker and E. Rosenhaft, 'Mother Ada Wright and the International Campaign to Free the Scottsboro Boys, 1931-1934, *American Historical Review*, 106/2 (April 2001) pp.387-430 (quotation from p.396 n.25). Leslie James, on the other hand, incorrectly suggests July 1936. James, 'What we put,' p.92

sources, particularly that gathered by the security services in France and Britain, has also proved invaluable, although it cannot always be relied upon for accuracy and some material has been withheld or destroyed. One characteristic of the written sources is that they tend to present a male-dominated picture of events, that is to say of events dominated by men, who appear as the main activists but also the main rapporteurs and interpreters of events. The recent work on Otto Huiswoud has highlighted the fact that his wife Hermina was his indispensable co-worker, particularly when they were both based in Europe from 1934-1937, a key contributor to *The Negro Worker* and a vociferous critic of Padmore. Other scholars have begun to document the important roles played by African American women in the communist movement in the United States.[20] Other women activists, such as Josie Mpama in South Africa and Elma Francois in Trinidad also played leading roles in their respective countries, although not necessarily roles that were central to the history of the ITUCNW.[21] One woman who might claim that role was Padmore's Austrian partner, Frieda Schiff, who played a significant role aiding his work in Hamburg and producing *The Negro Worker* but remains generally completely unknown.

The Comintern and the Negro Question

What was referred to as the Negro Question, or Negro problem, first manifested itself in the United Sates in the nineteenth century in the years following the civil war. It posed itself as a question of how the full emancipation of African Americans would be brought about and how this related to the overall struggle of American workers for emancipation and socialism, at a time when segregation and discrimination, as well as racist violence, were the norm throughout much of the United States. However, it was not a problem that was initially taken up with any vigour by the American members of the International Workingmen's Association, nor those associated with the Second International, even though it is from this period that the first African American Socialists began

20. See e.g. E. S. McDuffie, *Sojourning for Freedom: Black Women, American Communism, and the Making of Black Left Feminism* (Durham, 2011) and L. Harris, 'Running with the Reds: African American Women and the Communist Party During the Great Depression,' *Journal of African American History*, 94/1 (Winter 2009) pp.21-43.

21. See e.g. R. Reddock, *Elma Francois – The NWCSA and the workers struggle for change in the Caribbean in the 1930s* (London, 1988) and M. Roth, 'Josie Mpama: the contribution of a largely forgotten figure in the South African liberation struggle,' *Kleio*, 28/1 (1996) pp.120-136.

their activities.[22] This wholly inadequate response prompted W.E.B. Du Bois to write that 'the Negro problem then is the great test of the American Socialist.'[23]

The great merit of the Comintern was that from its inception in 1919, and initially under the guidance of Lenin, it took up the Negro Question for solution, demanded the liberation of the African and Caribbean colonies and began organising for these aims.[24] This was at a time when even the Pan-African movement of the day, whatever its merits and whether under the leadership of Du Bois or that of Garvey and the Universal Negro Improvement Association (UNIA), had no detailed programme in answer to the problems facing African Americans and others in the Diaspora, nor those facing colonial subjects in Africa and the Caribbean. During the 1920s Du Bois's Pan-African congresses, which had a close relationship with the British Labour Party and several governments in Europe, demanded of the League of Nations racial equality and colonial reforms but had no programme to realise these aspirations and Du Bois was unable to organise any further congresses after 1927. The UNIA had much greater international influence, especially in Africa and the Caribbean, an orientation towards 'race pride and love,' self-help and self-reliance, as well as a clear demand – 'Africa for the Africans at home and abroad.' However, despite its undoubted influence, it had no programme to realise this demand and in the 1920s gradually retreated from its earlier militancy, becoming mired in legal disputes culminating in Garvey's imprisonment and a divided organisation.[25]

During the 1920s, the Comintern's main focus was initially on taking measures to address the Negro Question in the United States, and later in South Africa, two areas where there were established communist parties and the necessity to deal with issues of race and racism in society, as well as within the communist movement. From Lenin's time, however, the Negro Question for the Comintern was related to the struggles of people throughout Africa, the Caribbean and elsewhere to end colonialism and establish the right of all nations to self-determination. In order to fully address the Negro Question the Comintern also had to assist several of the young and inexperienced communist parties to overcome their weaknesses. The CPUSA, for example, was severely handicapped by factional infighting for many years. The Party in South Africa initially had only white members, while the Cuban CP had an extremely

22. P. S. Foner, *American Socialism and Black Americans – From the Age of Jackson to World War II* (London. 1977).

23. W.E.B. Du Bois, 'Socialism and the Negro Problem,' in D. Levering Lewis (ed.) *W.E.B. Du Bois: A Reader* (New York, 1995) p.579.

24. Largely due to wartime conditions, the Comintern dissolved itself in 1943.

25. See e.g. 'Introduction' in R. A. Hill (ed.) *The Marcus Garvey and Universal Negro Improvement Papers*, [vol. X] (London, 2006) especially pp.lxxxiii-lxxxv.

unstable leadership, an irregular press and for several years little contact with the Comintern.[26]

Eventually, in 1928, the decisions of the Comintern and its affiliated labour organisation, the Red International of Labour Unions (RILU or Profintern) led to the creation of the ITUCNW that began to focus not on the United States but mainly on sub-Saharan Africa, the Caribbean and the wider African Diaspora, often in countries where no communist parties existed, or in the imperialist countries where, it was considered, insufficient attention was paid by the existing communist parties to the Negro Question. For the Comintern and the ITUCNW this question was always viewed from an international perspective, as an issue exhibiting some common characteristics even when different policies were necessary for different countries and regions. In this sense, the Comintern can be said to have adopted a Pan-Africanist approach to the issue, directed at the liberation of Africa and the African Diaspora, of all 'Negroes,' and this was itself a consequence of the early focus on the United States, the influence of the African American experience and the important role of African American Communists in shaping Comintern policy.[27] It was evidently also viewed in this way because of the perceived need to combat widespread 'white chauvinism' and the international influence of the 'dangerous ideology' of Garveyism, as well as other more local forms of 'national reformism,' that all exhibited features that were deemed to be inimical to Negro liberation.[28] The Comintern was certainly aware that significant differences existed between social, economic and political conditions in such countries as South Africa, the United States, Cuba and the Gold Coast and accordingly developed differing policies for these different countries. However, a recognition that a Negro Question with some common features needed to be addressed persisted until the late 1930s, when the apparent differences between the problems facing 'Negro workers' in various parts of the world, as well as the international struggle against the rise of fascism and other circumstances led to a change of policy.

The central question, however, remained the same throughout the entire inter-war period – how to organise all those of African descent to liberate themselves in whatever country they inhabited, and in the particular conditions that existed at the time. In addition there were important questions that needed to be addressed concerning the rights of those of African descent in former slave societies such as Cuba and the United States. Were these populations of African

26. On Cuba see B. Carr, 'From Caribbean backwater to revolutionary opportunity: Cuba's evolving relationship with the Comintern, 1925-34,' in T. Rees and A. Thorpe (eds.), *International Communism and the Communist International* (Manchester, 1998), pp. 234-253.

27. It is perhaps significant that the North African colonies were generally not included in the Comintern's conception of the Negro Question.

28. G. Padmore, *The Life and Struggles of Negro Toilers* (London, 1931) pp.124-126.

origin just mainly workers who should join in a general struggle with their compatriots for economic and social emancipation, or did they in some countries constitute nations (albeit of a special type), that should organise themselves to struggle for national rights such as self-determination? In particular, what measures needed to be taken to overcome centuries of racial and national oppression, often existing with legal backing, that had led to 'white chauvinism' not only throughout society and amongst the workers but even in the communist parties? In this regard, the Comintern exerted sustained pressure on all its sections, particularly the parties in the United States and South Africa, as well as those in the major imperialist countries, to put their own houses in order and to be seen as the champions of the rights of those of African descent, including the right of self-determination. It was in these circumstances, and in the struggle to empower the 'Negro masses' and transform society that communist parties in the United States, Cuba, South Africa and elsewhere were also transformed and became recognised as some of the greatest defenders of the rights of Africans and those of African origin. It was in this context that many in Africa and the Diaspora were attracted to a communist movement that was seen to take up the struggle for their rights and liberation as part of a wider struggle to defend and guarantee the rights of all.

The Comintern's approach to the Negro Question developed from Lenin's analysis of imperialism and the importance of the liberation struggles in the colonies as part of a global struggle against imperialism. However, it also developed from Lenin's concern with the particular problems faced by African Americans. For several years it was African American Communists who were seen as the vanguard force within the Comintern, who would also play a leading role in the revolutionary movements in Africa. This approach necessarily had its limitations, although it also reflected the fact that initially 'Negro' Communists who had undergone some training were only to be found in the United States. It was, however, a situation that sometimes led to rapid promotion, even within the Comintern, and placed some African American Communists in a strong position to stress the importance of the Negro Question and contribute to the Comintern's approach to it, a circumstance that certainly helped create the conditions for the founding of the ITUCNW and the Comintern's Pan-Afrianist perspective.

The ITUCNW, a communist organisation with a Pan-Africanist orientation, has perhaps been rather neglected by historians. As a body established under the auspices of the RILU its focus was on organising the 'toiling Negro masses' and particularly with the 'setting up of connections with the Negro workers of the whole world and the unification of the wide masses of the Negro workers on the basis of the class struggle.'[29] It was clearly stated that one of the

29. RGASPI 495/155/53/1.

principal reasons for its formation was the inability of the 'communist parties of the west' to adequately address the Negro Question.[30]

The founding of the ITUCNW was a consequence of the Comintern's concern for the liberation of Africa and all those of African descent but was clearly also informed by the agitation and demands of those in Africa and throughout the Diaspora, both inside and outside the communist movement. The Comintern recognised that the 'Negro masses' were a potentially revolutionary force, but a force that might be diverted into a non-revolutionary path under the influence of Garveyism and other forms of Pan-Africanism, or even conscripted into armies of the major imperialist powers to be used against the revolutionary movement and the Soviet Union. However, the distinction between the revolutionary Pan-Africanist perspective of the Comintern and that of Garveyism and other forms of Pan-Africanism or 'Black Internationalism,' was sometimes not fully appreciated even by the ITUCNW's own supporters and activists. It was a perspective that the Comintern and ITUCNW grappled with for many years before finally abandoning it in 1937.[31]

The ITUCNW was formed at a time when the Comintern was in the process of changing its orientation in order to take account of changing circumstances in the world, especially changing economic and political conditions. According to the CI's analysis, the world was entering a 'third period' in the post-World War I era in which there would be a further global economic crisis, the growing likelihood of 'imperialist wars,' of 'gigantic class battles,' culminating in 'a new revolutionary upsurge.'[32] The Comintern's analysis seemed to have been confirmed, especially by the onset of the Great Depression, the rise of fascism and the preparations for world war that ensued, all of which had global ramifications. The Comintern therefore instructed all its sections to organise and prepare accordingly, to concentrate on building the unity of the workers and to attempt to isolate the influence of Social-Democracy and 'reformism' that might divert the workers' struggles from what the Comintern considered the necessary revolutionary path. The 'third period,' ushered in by the Comintern's Sixth Congress in 1928 was a time when there was a special focus on the Negro Question in general and especially as it posed itself in the United States and South Africa, as well as a concern with the related problem of 'white chauvinism,' both inside and outside the communist movement.

30. RGASPI 534/3/306/25.

31. For a discussion of the relationship between the Comintern's approach and other forms of Black Internationalism see M.O. West, W.G Martin, & F. C. Wilkins (eds.) *From Toussaint to Tupac: The Black International since the Age of Revolution* (Chapel Hill, 2009) especially pp. 1-47.

32. W.Z. Foster, *History of the Three Internationals: The World Socialist and Communist Movement from 1848 to the Present* (New York, 1955) pp.357-358.

However, it was also a period in which conditions were created for some Communists to become increasingly sectarian in outlook and this was perhaps particularly the case within the RILU, another organisation that has been rather neglected by historians.[33] This 'third period' is therefore sometimes presented as one of extremism in the history of the Comintern, where there was an unreasonable turn to the left. It might be said, however, that it was the political and economic conditions and the problems that they caused that were extreme, especially in the colonies, and it was these that the Comintern and the ITUCNW attempted to address. The Comintern also attempted to deal with instances of sectarianism, which isolated the Communists and the communist parties. Many of these problems were only resolved in the period after 1934 when the Comintern was under new leadership (the role of Georgi Dimitrov the Bulgarian Communist and 'hero of Leipzig' was undoubtedly significant) and was able to develop a new political orientation that was formally adopted following its Seventh Congress in 1935. It is ironic that it was in this period that the Comintern was criticised by Padmore and others for allegedly departing from its former militancy in regard to the Negro Question.

In the early 1930s the ITUCNW put most of its emphasis on Anglophone West Africa, attempting to establish workers' organisations in several colonial countries in which a working class was beginning to flex its muscles and trade unions were in the early stages of development but where no communist parties or other organisations representing the majority of the population existed. The ITUCNW also regularly intervened to try and assist the CPSA, and as a consequence established links with individuals and organisations throughout southern Africa. However, most of its work focused on areas in Africa where it had to train and nurture a handful of activists from afar, with extremely limited resources and finances and in the difficult and repressive conditions produced by colonial rule. Even *The Negro Worker* was banned throughout colonial Africa and the Caribbean, as were many other publications, and it had to be smuggled to its readers. The ITUCNW was itself subject to constant harassment and surveillance, especially from 1930 onwards when it established itself in Europe, and its activists were arrested, imprisoned and expelled from Germany, Holland and Belgium. In 1930 the British Labour government even prohibited the ITUCNW from organising an international conference of Negro workers in London and the gathering was forced to move to Hamburg. Nevertheless, the ITUCNW continued to work in the major imperialist countries, not least because the communist parties in such countries were considered by the Comintern to be insufficiently concerned with the Negro Question. In Britain and

33. See R. Tosstorff, 'Moscow Versus Amsterdam: Reflections on the History of the Profintern,' *Labour History Review*, 68/1 (April 2003) pp.79-97. Also W.Z. Foster, *Outline History of the World Trade Union Movement* (New York, 1956) especially pp.271-382.

France, for instance, there were groups of African and Caribbean seafarers and other workers that the ITUCNW attempted to organise in order to strengthen its links and work in the African and Caribbean colonies. In the Caribbean, where a communist party only existed in Cuba (and for a brief period in Haiti), the ITUCNW mainly organised in those areas where there were no parties, especially the British and to a lesser extent the French colonies.[34] The ITUCNW had varying degrees of success in the Caribbean before it was dissolved in 1937, just as the mass labour rebellions erupted throughout the region.

It might appear paradoxical that the ITUCNW concluded its work at the very time that an upsurge occurred in the struggles of the workers in the Caribbean and following the rise in Pan-Africanist sentiment in response to the invasion of Ethiopia by fascist Italy. However, once again changing international conditions, especially the menace of fascism and world war necessitated different tactics and policies from the Comintern that would ensure the maximum unity of the people. In the colonies, for example, the Comintern strove to unite the widest sections of the people in the anti-imperialist struggle, rather than just focusing on the struggles of the workers. At this stage the whole conception of the ITUCNW, essentially an underground organisation with no mass membership was questioned and considered to be no longer appropriate.

The ITUCNW emerged during a period when economic and political conditions left many in Africa, the Caribbean and throughout the African Diaspora with no choice but to struggle against racial violence and discrimination, economic hardship and colonial domination. It was also a period in which many looked to Communism as the means to liberation. In France the communist-led Union des Travailleurs Nègres (UTN) declared: 'Neither the Radicals, nor even the Socialist Party recognise the Negroes' rights to total liberation; only the Communist party has written into its programme Negro rights and aspirations to their political liberty and national independence...it would be unjust not to grant our sympathy to the only political party which is disposed to assist Negroes in their struggle for justice, liberty, and liberation.'[35] Some like Albert Nzula, who became one of the leaders of the CPSA, went even further and stated 'I have come to the conclusion that every right-minded person ought

34. In Martinique a Communist organisation, the *Groupe Jean Jaurès*, had been established as early as 1919 but it remained small and isolated and seems to have had no link with the Comintern or its sections until 1934. R. Ménil, 'Notes sur la développement historique du Marxisme à la Martinique,' *Action – Revue Theoretique et Politique du Parti Communiste Martiniquais,* 13 (1967) pp.17-30.

35. Quoted in J.A. Langley, 'Pan-Africanism in Paris, 1924-36,' *The Journal of Modern African Studies*, 7/1 (1969) pp.69-94.

to be a communist.'[36] It was a period that produced outstanding personalities of African origin who like Paul Robeson were closely connected with the communist movement, while the famous Haitian poet Jacques Roumain, openly declared 'I am a Communist.' It was in this period that the Comintern first called for majority rule, or a 'black republic,' in South Africa and when the Communists first called for a United States (of Soviet Republics) of Africa.

What follows focuses on the Comintern's efforts to grapple with the Negro Question – the question of how to advance the struggle to liberate Africa and the African Diaspora - and particularly on the activities of the ITUCNW, established as a consequence of its Pan-Africanist approach during the inter-war years.

Outline

Part One

Chapter 1 outlines the development of the communist movement's approach to the Negro Question during the period of the First, Second and Third Internationals, as well as the growing yet critical support expressed by many in Africa and throughout the African Diaspora for the revolutionary communist movement. It also traces the Comintern's approach to this question after 1919, a period that culminated with the founding of the ITUCNW in 1928.

Chapter 2 focuses on the momentous decisions taken by the Comintern at its Sixth Congress in 1928 in regard to the Negro Question in the US and South Africa. It highlights the fact that even policies relating to individual countries might still have an important international significance and outlines the influence of the Comintern's approach and policies pertaining to the US especially in Cuba in the inter-war period.

Chapter 3 focuses on the First International Conference of Negro Workers held in Hamburg in 1930. It examines the worldwide preparations for this event, which became a major focus of all the work of the ITUCNW, and its consequences for the ITUCNW and the Comintern. It also traces the early development of the ITUCNW's *The Negro Worker.* Chapters 4 and 5 focus on the activities of the Hamburg Committee of the ITUCNW, established after the Hamburg Conference in 1930 and led first by James Ford, from 1931-1933 by Padmore and then re-established and led by Huiswoud from 1934-1937.

36. Quoted in E. Roux, *Time Longer Than Rope: The Black Man's Struggle For Freedom in South Africa* (Madison, 1964), p.216.

Part Two

Chapters 6 to 10 present case studies of the activities and tasks of the ITUCNW and the major organisations and individuals affiliated to it in five main geographical areas. Chapter 6 focus on the ITUCNW and organisations in France such as the UTN but it also outlines the history of the relationship between the Comintern and earlier organisations such as the Comité de Défense de la Race Nègre. Chapter 7 discusses the attempts to find solutions to the Negro Question in Britain and especially the activities of the Negro Welfare Association. Chapter 8 focuses on the activities of the ITUCNW in the Caribbean. Chapter 9 traces the Comintern's work in West Africa, especially in the British colonies, and Chapter 10 the work of the ITUCNW with the CPSA and organisations led by it, such as the African Federation of Trade Unions. The dissolution of the ITUCNW and some evaluation of the historical significance of the Comintern's approach to the Negro Question are addressed in the final chapter.

Part I

Chapter One

Communism and the Negro Question

The Forerunners

The oppression and exploitation of Africa and the African Diaspora was an important issue for the communist movement even before the twentieth century, as is evident from the writings of Karl Marx and Frederick Engels. In his famous work *Capital* Marx pointed out that along with exploitation of the peoples and resources of America and Asia, the 'the turning of Africa into a warren for the commercial hunting of black-skins, signalised the rosy dawn of the era of capitalist production.'[1] He argued that 'the veiled slavery of the wage-workers in Europe needed for its pedestal, slavery pure and simple in the new

1. Quoted in *Marx and Engels on Colonialism* (London, 1960) p. 258.

world', and here he had in mind chiefly the enslavement of Africans.[2] In his own writing Marx's collaborator Frederick Engels, condemned the 'scramble' for and division of Africa amongst the main European powers at the close of the nineteenth century as simply in the interests of the stock exchange, and supported the anti-colonial resistance that broke out in Egypt in the 1880s.[3] Both Marx and Engels took a keen interest in the struggle against slavery and the slave trade in the United States, as their writings on the subject demonstrate.[4] In regard to the significance of abolitionism for the worker's movement in the United States, Marx famously concluded that 'labour cannot emancipate itself in the white skin where in the black it is branded.'[5]

The attitude of some of their successors in Britain to colonialism in Africa can be judged from the famous *Manifesto of the Socialist League on the Sudan War*, issued by Eleanor Marx, Edward Aveling and William Morris in 1885.[6] In France, Paul Lafargue and others also took a stand against colonial conquest in Africa and elsewhere but many who considered themselves Marxists adopted a position of vacillation.[7] The Second International, which was founded in 1889 by the socialist parties of Europe and North America, was also generally opposed to colonialism, at least in terms of the resolutions passed at its congresses in 1900, 1904 and 1907. However, many individual parties either accepted the colonial policies pursued by the governments of the big powers, or did little to oppose them.[8] During this period Marxism spread to both the American and African continents, however it remained particularly poorly developed in Africa, where it first became significant in Egypt and South Africa.[9]

---

2. Ibid. p.268. See also D. Boersner, *The Bolsheviks and the National and Colonial Question* (Westport, Connecticut, 1994) p.24.
3. *Marx and Engels on Colonialism* p.273.
4. See K. Marx and F. Engels, *The Civil War in the United States* (London, 1938).
5. K. Marx, *Capital – A Critique of Political Economy*, (online edition) vol. 1, ch.10, section 7, p192.
6. Reproduced in *Labour Monthly* (July 1952), 303-307. The Manifesto has been seen as the first anti-imperialist manifesto of the socialist movement in Britain.
7. On Lafargue and other French Marxists see J-P Biondi, *Les Anticolonialistes* (Paris, 1992) pp.59-63.
8. W. Z. Foster, *History of the Three Internationals: The World Socialist and Communist Movements from 1848 to the Present* (New York, 1955) pp.200-203. See also Ercoli's, 'Social Democracy and the Colonial Question,' *International Press Correspondence (Inprecor)*, 4 October 1928, pp.1234-1243.
9. See S. Johns, *Raising the Red Flag: The International Socialist League and the Communist Party of South Africa 1914-1932* (Belville, 1995) and T.Y. Ismael and R. El-Sa'id, *The Communist Movement in Egypt, 1920-1988* (Syracuse, 1990).

The 'Negro Question,' as it became known, was initially primarily concerned with the oppression and liberation of African Americans, and was therefore a question posed first in the United States rather than internationally.[10] There it was a question of how the full emancipation of African Americans would be brought about and how this related to the overall struggle of American workers for social progress at a time when segregation and discrimination, as well as racist violence, were the norm throughout much of the United States. However, even in the United States it was not a major political issue for the members of the International Workingmen's Association, nor those connected with the Second International. Indeed one informed commentator later wrote that 'the American socialist movement almost completely ignored the long-continued shocking persecution' of African Americans.[11] The socialists of the Second International also became increasingly divided over the issue of colonialism and in the period leading up to World War I some of its members, such as the British Labour Party, openly supported European colonial rule in Africa and elsewhere as a form of benevolent 'trusteeship.'[12]

In South Africa, socialism was initially an ideology imported by European migrants although it clearly soon had its African adherents. As early as 1907, the editor of *Izwi LaBantu*, A.K. Soga, who featured articles on socialism in that publication, wrote to the Independent Labour Party in Britain, 'our desire is to educate the intelligent native mind on the principles of Labour and Socialism.'[13] The South African Labour Party, however, formed in 1910 and affiliated to the Second International, concerned itself only with those workers of European origin and based its programme on 'the separation of native and white races as far as possible.'[14] The increasingly militant actions by black workers, especially following the strikes of African mineworkers in 1913, soon forced all who called themselves socialists in South Africa to address the concerns of all workers and the need for their unity. The International Socialist League, formed in 1915 largely in opposition to the South African Labour Party's support for government participation in the First World War, was instrumental in establishing the Industrial Workers of Africa and working with the South African National Congress (ANC) to organise African workers. From this activity several African

10. Similar question were posed elsewhere and *la question noire* certainly existed in France.

11. Foster, *History of the Three Internationals*, p.202.

12. S. Howe, *Anticolonialism in British Politics: The Left and the End of Empire 1918-1964* (Oxford, 1993) pp.44-46.

13. A. Drew, *Discordant Comrades – Identities and Loyalties on the South African Left* (Pretoria, 2002) p.26.

14. Ibid. p.28.

socialists emerged, including T. William Thebedi, subsequently the first African member of the Communist Party of South Africa (CPSA).[15]

Soga was just one of several in Africa and throughout the African Diaspora who took an interest in socialism at the dawn of the 20th century. In Britain, for example, the ideology was evidently of interest to Bandele Omoniyi, an early Nigerian Pan-Africanist, who may even have written a book on the subject entitled *Socialism Examined*.[16] From France, supporters of the Second International had introduced socialist ideas into the French Antilles by the early years of the twentieth century. Peter Clark and the first African American socialists had begun their activities even earlier in the late nineteenth century, and several African Americans were present at the founding convention of the Socialist Party of America (SPA) in 1900.[17] However, for the SPA, an affiliate of the Second International, the Negro Question would be resolved 'when the working class have triumphed in the class struggle,' and Eugene Debs, the leader of the SPA, remarked that the party had 'nothing special to offer the Negro.'[18] It was a view that became entrenched and those African Americans who later were connected with the SPA, such as W.E.B. Du Bois and Hubert Harrison, were critical of its failure to fully address the Negro Question, or to come to terms with chauvinism and racism. Indeed Du Bois wrote that 'the Negro problem then is the great test of the American Socialist.'[19]

Hubert Harrison, the 'Father of Harlem Radicalism' as he is sometimes known, migrated to the United States from the Virgin Islands in 1900, and was the most influential of the early twentieth century Caribbean radicals, someone who managed to combine a defence of socialism, the class struggle and a Marxist critique of capitalism with an adherence to the principle 'Race First,' more commonly associated with Marcus Garvey. Harrison was initially an activist, writer and speaker in the ranks of the SPA, which he joined in 1909, although he became critical of its lingering racism and inactivity on the Negro Question. Following his resignation from the SPA he was also, for a time, connected with the International Workers of the World, before establishing his own organisa-

15. Ibid. p.39.

16. H. Adi, 'Bandele Omoniyi – A Neglected Nigerian Nationalist,' *African Affairs* (1991), 90, pp.581-605.

17. P.S. Foner, *American Socialism and Black Americans: From the Age of Jackson to World War II* (London, 1977) pp.45-57 and 94-100.

18. Ibid. p.114.

19. W.E.B. Du Bois, 'Socialism and the Negro Problem,' in D.L. Lewis (ed.) *W.E.B. Du Bois: A Reader* (New York, 1995) pp. 577-580. See also H. Harrison, 'Southern Socialists and the Ku Klux Klan,' in J. B. Perry (ed.), *A Hubert Harrison Reader* (Middletown, Connecticut, 2001) pp.76-78. For an example of the attitude of the SPA to lynching in the United States see Foster, *History of the Three Internationals*, pp.177-178.

tion, the Liberty League and its publication *The Voice* and then, between 1920 and 1922, editing Marcus Garvey's *Negro World*.[20]

Harrison saw no contradiction between nationalism and internationalism in his approach to politics, described himself as a 'Radical Internationalist,' and was one of the first in the twentieth century to call for a 'coloured internationalism.'[21] He clearly influenced others, including future Communists, Otto Huiswoud, Richard B. Moore and particularly Cyril Briggs, who carried similar views into the African Blood Brotherhood (ABB), from where it seems likely that they subsequently had some influence on both the American Communist Party (CP) and even the Communist International.[22] Harrison's activities also came to the attention of the British Intelligence Services, which referred to him as 'a scholar of broad learning and a radical propagandist,' and 'more effective than any other individual radical.' It was reported that 'his lectures might well be considered as a preparatory school for radical thought in that he prepares the minds of conservative negroes (sic) to receive and accept the more extreme doctrines of Socialism.'[23] Harrison welcomed the Russian Revolution referring to it as 'the first attempt to establish real democracy,' however, long before 1917 he had turned to socialism as the means to analyse American and international capitalism and to chart a way forward to a new society in which racism and national oppression would not hold sway.[24]

For Harrison, socialism represented a step forward, a way to 'lighten the black man's burden,' as he explained in 1911:

> I do not expect the advent of Socialism will at once remove race prejudice – unless it remove ignorance at the same time. But I do

---

20. On Harrison see J. B. Perry, *Hubert Harrison – the Voice of Harlem Radicalism, 1883-1918* (New York, 2009).

21. See W. James, *Holding Aloft the Banner of Ethiopia – Caribbean Radicalism in Early Twentieth Century America* (London, 1998) p.126. See also B. H. Edwards, *The Practice of Diaspora – Literature, Translation, and the Rise of Black Internationalism* (Cambridge, 2003) p.244 and J.A. Rogers, *World's Great Men of Color, Vol. II* (New York, 1996) pp.432-443.

22. Harrison is also cited as influencing Randolph and Owen, Domingo, and even Garvey and with gaining the respect of those sent to spy upon him. See James, *Holding Aloft*, pp.130-133 and J. M. Turner, *Caribbean Crusaders and the Harlem Renaissance*, (Chicago, 2005) p.19.

23. W.F. Elkins, '"Unrest Among the Negroes:" A British Document of 1919,' *Science and Society*, 32/1 (Winter 1968) pp.66-79.

24. Harrison was later connected with the American CP and the American Negro Labor Congress in New York. See Diary entry, November 1918, Box 9 Folder 11, Hubert Harrison Papers, Columbia University and L. Fort-Whiteman to Dr Hubert Harrison, 1 April 1926, Box 1 Folder 52, ibid.

> expect that it will remove racial injustice and lighten the black man's burden. I do expect that it will take the white man from off the black man's back and leave him free for the first time to make of himself as much or as little as he chooses...Socialism is here to put an end to the exploitation of one group by another, whether that group be social, economic or racial. This is the position of Marx, Engels, Kautsky and every great leader of the Socialist movement. It is imbedded in the very fabric of the Socialist philosophy.[25]

Harrison wrote these words at a time when lynching by armed racist mobs was commonplace in the United States, although it was also a period when resistance by African Americans took more militant forms, so his sentiments may well have been shared by many. Over eleven hundred African American men, women and children were murdered by racist mobs between 1900-1914 and many more attacked and wounded. Indeed it was reported that there were at least two such racist murders every week just prior to World War I. This was in addition to the legal segregation and discrimination that occurred throughout the country and particularly in the southern states in the period after 1877.[26] In Africa the violent colonial conquest and division of the continent by the major European imperialist powers was almost complete by the eve of World War I. Atrocities in Africa were also commonplace, the most infamous example being the genocide in what was then called the Congo Free State. Even official Belgian government reports concluded that half of the total population, an estimated 10 million people, had been wiped out in that region between 1880 and 1908.[27] In the Caribbean and South America the enslavement of millions of people of African origin had ended, to be followed by colonial exploitation and other forms of subjugation that continued in the twentieth century. Anti-African racism in this period could be said to be ubiquitous, even in European countries such as Britain and France where a colour bar and other forms of racism were widespread and legal.[28]

By 1917 the theory of Marxism, or Scientific Socialism, had penetrated Africa, the Caribbean and elsewhere. It had also been adopted by some of the leading African American thinkers and activists, including Du Bois, Hubert

25. H. Harrison, 'The Duty of the Socialist Party,' in Perry, *A Hubert Harrison Reader,* p.59.

26. J.H. Franklin and A.A. Moss, Jr., *From Slavery to Freedom: A History of African Americans* (New York, 1994) pp.312-317 and W.Z. Foster, *The Negro People in American History* (New York, 1982) pp.419-422.

27. The best know modern account of the genocide in the Congo is A. Hochschild, *King Leopold's Ghost* (New York, 2006).

28. See P. Ndiaye, *La condition noire – Essai sur une minorité francaise* (Paris, 2008) pp.148-149; H. Adi, *West Africans in Britain 1900-1960 – Nationalism, Pan-Africanism and Communism* (London, 1998) pp. 9-12 and M. Sherwood, *Origins of Pan-Africanism – Henry Sylvester Williams, Africa and the African Diaspora* (London, 2011) pp.28-29.

Harrison, A. Philip Randolph, Chandler Owen, W.A. Domingo and Helen Holman, as well as future Communists, Williana Jones Burroughs, Grace Campbell, Lovett Fort-Whiteman, Otto Huiswoud, and Richard B. Moore.[29] Yet like Harrison, many African American socialists remained dissatisfied with the approach to colonialism, racism and the Negro Question advocated by the SPA. Solutions were also sought to the problems posed by colonialism, racism and other forms of oppression in the new era of imperialism. Marxism might offer a way forward for the workers of the world but could it also provide a solution to the Negro Question, the particular problems faced by those throughout Africa and the African Diaspora, the 'Negroes' seemingly neglected by the 'anti-Negro socialism' of the parties of the Second International?

Lenin, the Russian Revolution and the Communist International

It was Lenin, and the Third Communist International (Comintern or CI) formed in 1919, that sought to clarify Marxism's approach to the Negro Question and to begin to establish a general political orientation for the liberation of Africa and the African Diaspora and for the new international communist movement. The CI was formed as an organisation uniting the new communist parties that were being formed throughout the world inspired by the revolutionary events in Russia. In effect the CI became 'a single universal communist party of which the parties operating in every country form individual section,' with the aim of liberating the working people of the entire world.[30] Lenin's writings certainly contain several references to the status of African Americans, as other writers have pointed out,[31] and some of his work also focuses on the partition

29. Foner, *American Socialism and Black Americans*, pp.266-267 and Turner, *Caribbean Crusaders*, pp.3-59. On Campbell, who has been credited as being 'probably the first black woman to join the Socialist Party; and almost certainly the first black woman to join the Communist Party,' see James, *Holding Aloft*, pp.173-177. On Burroughs see Perry, *Hubert Harrison*, pp.92-94 and L. Harris, 'Running with the Reds: African Amerian Women and the Communist Party During the Great Depression,' *Journal of African American History*, 94/1 (Winter 2009) pp.21-43.

30. Institute of Marxism-Leninism, *Outline History of the Communist International* (Moscow, 1971) pp.89-90.

31. See e.g. Solomon, *The Cry Was Unity*: 39 See also H. Haywood, *Black Bolshevik: Autobiography of an Afro-American Communist* (Chicago,1978) pp. 223-225 and P.S. Foner and J.S. Allen (eds.) *American Communism and Black Americans – A Documentary History* (Philadelphia, 1987) pp. xii-xiv.

and exploitation of Africa and its significance in the epoch of imperialism.[32] But of perhaps even greater significance are the views he and other Bolsheviks developed on the nature of imperialism and what came to be called the 'national and colonial question'.[33]

Lenin's consideration of these issues was very much linked with the practical task of organising revolution in Tsarist Russia, before 1917 a 'prison of nations', in which the vast majority of the population comprised non-Russian peoples who had been forcibly incorporated within the Tsarist empire. Lenin's analysis of the development of capitalism into imperialism led him to stress the important role of all the oppressed nations of Russia in the revolution against Tsarism. However, he also highlighted the important role that all oppressed nations would play in the anti-imperialist struggle, not just those such as the Irish and Poles in Europe, but also the millions of those oppressed by colonial rule in Africa, Asia and elsewhere. As his successor Joseph Stalin later explained, it was Lenin and the Communists 'who first revealed the connection between the national question and the question of the colonies' and who, 'broke down the wall between the white and coloured peoples, between the "civilised" and "uncivilised" slaves of imperialism.'[34] Just as in Russia, where Lenin called for a revolutionary alliance between the working class and the largely non-Russian peasantry, he also called for an alliance between the revolutionary movement of the working class in the advanced capitalist countries and the anti-colonial movements and oppressed peoples in the colonies, to undermine and destroy imperialism. Lenin regarded the revolutionary movement in the colonies as vital in this struggle, since it was there, he argued, that imperialism might well be breached at its weakest link.[35]

Initially, however, it was the revolutionary events in Russia in 1917, rather than Lenin's revolutionary theory, that first had an impact on Africa and the African Diaspora. There was an immediate impact on those Africans who were serving in the armies of the major powers in Europe during World War I. It was reported that revolutionary Russian troops made contact with African soldiers stationed in France, as well as those who were sent to occupy Soviet

---

32. For details of Lenin's interest in Southern Africa see A. Davidson et al. *South Africa and the Communist International: A Documentary History* [vol.1] (London, 2003) p.3. See also *The October Revolution and Africa* (Moscow, 1983) p.20.

33. See e.g. V.I Lenin 'The Socialist Revolution and the Right of Nations to Self-Determination' in *Lenin on the National and Colonial Questions* (Pekin, 1967) pp.1-19 and J.V. Stalin, 'The National Question' in *Marxism and the National and Colonial Question* (London, 1936) pp. 190-199. See also Boersner, *The Bolsheviks and the National and Colonial Question.*

34. Stalin, 'The National Question,' p.112.

35. V. I. Lenin, *Imperialism The Highest Stage of Capitalism* (Pekin, 1975).

Russia in 1918 and 1919. Some of the latter, it was reported, joined the Red Army in Odessa and Sevastopol in 1919 and one was even immortalised in verse.[36] Russia also had its own African Diaspora, including those based in the Abkhazia region of the Caucasus, some of whom were inspired to join the Red Army in the period after 1917.[37] But in the African continent itself it seems that initially the October Revolution made the biggest impact in South Africa, where the International Socialist League had been formed in 1915 and in Egypt where Marxism had been discussed since the 1890s.[38]

The founding of Africa's first communist party, the Communist Party of South Africa (CPSA) in 1921, was inspired both by the Russian Revolution and the emergence of the Comintern, although at the time of its founding it probably had only one African member.[39] One of the leaders of the new party, W.H. Andrews, prophetically wrote: 'The influence of the Russian Revolution is felt far beyond the boundaries of the vast Soviet Republic and probably has even more immediate appeal to the enslaved Coloured races of the earth than to Europeans.'[40] Indeed, even before the formation of the CPSA, South African revolutionaries in the International Socialist League (ISL) were quoting Marx's famous dictum 'Labour cannot emancipate itself in the white skin while in the black it is branded,' and issuing revolutionary leaflets in Sesuto and Zulu.[41]

An African workers' movement that was influenced by socialist ideas was also in evidence in South Africa. The Industrial Workers of Africa was formed by the ISL and militants such as Jimmy La Guma had raised the red flag not only in South Africa but also in the German colony of South West Africa before 1919.[42]

36. *The October Revolution and Africa*, pp.20-21. Boris Kornilov's poem *My Africa* was apparently dedicated to an African officer who died leading a Red Army cavalry regiment. See E. T. Wilson, *Russia and Black Africa Before World War II* (New York, 1974) p.95.

37. A. Blakely, *Russia and the Negro – Blacks in Russian History and Thought* (Washington D.C., 1986) pp. 75-77.

38. J. Derrick, *Africa's 'Agitators' – Militant Anti-Colonialism in Africa and the West, 1918-1939* (London, 2008) p.116. See also Johns, *Raising the Red Flag* and Ismael and El-Sa'id, *The Communist Movement in Egypt.*

39. Johns, *Raising the Red Flag*, pp.111-127. See also, Drew, *Discordant Comrades*, pp. 46-57 and S. Johns, 'The Birth of the CP of South Africa,' *International Journal of African Historical Studies*, Vol. IX, No. 3 (1976) pp. 371-400. The exact status of Thibedi, an African teacher, is a little unclear but by 1921 he was already a member of the forerunner organisation of the CPSA, the ISL, and is generally recognised as the first African member of the CPSA. See Davidson et al, *South Africa and the Communist International*, p.67.

40. Quoted in A. La Guma, *Jimmy La Guma – A Biography* (Cape Town, 1997) p.28.

41. See "The Bolsheviks Are Coming" quoted in *South African Communists Speak* (London, 1981) pp. 38-40.

42. On La Guma who was to become a leading 'Coloured' Communist see chapters two and ten and La Guma, *Jimmy La Guma.*

The *Manifesto* of the CPSA, adopted at its founding conference in 1921, decisively broke with the racial divisions in the South African labour movement and appealed to all workers 'white and black, to join in promoting the overthrow of the capitalist system and outlawry of the capitalist class, and the establishment of a Commonwealth of Workers throughout the world.'[43]

In the United States, the revolutionary events in Russia led to heated debates between W.E.B. Bois and the Jamaican writer Claude McKay in the pages of the National Association for the Advancement of Colored People's *The Crisis*. Similar debates occurred in the pages of Garvey's *Negro World* between McKay and its editor William Ferris.[44] McKay, who had already come into contact with the revolutionary movement in the United States and Britain, was one of several important figures in African American political circles influenced by the October Revolution, which he referred to as 'the greatest event in the history of humanity.'[45] He publicly wondered if Bolshevism, which for McKay was 'the greatest and most scientific idea in the world today' might make the United States 'safe for the Negro.'[46] He opined: 'If the Russian idea should take hold of the white masses of the western world, and they should rise in united strength and overthrow their imperial capitalist government, then the black toilers would automatically be free.'[47] Such views were not uncommon amongst the African American socialists of the day. In 1919, A Philip Randolph and Chandler Owen, two leading African American members of the SPA, who would both remain in that party, proclaimed in *The Messenger* 'The Soviet Government proceeds apace. It bids fair to sweep the whole world. The sooner the better.'[48]

When the Comintern was established it was on the basis of the experience of the revolutionary events of 1917, Lenin's and the Bolshevik's theoretical work and the need for a complete break with the politics of the Second International. The *Manifesto of the Communist International to the Proletariat of the Entire World*, launched in 1919, therefore included a call to the 'Colonial Slaves of Africa and Asia' to rise up against colonial rule. However, it concluded by stating: 'The emancipation of the colonies is possible only in conjunction with the emancipation of the metropolitan working class...The hour of proletarian dictatorship in Europe

43. *Manifesto of the CPSA adopted at the Cape Town conference held on July 30-31 and August 1, 1921*. Ibid p.62.

44. W.E. B. Du Bois, 'The Negro and Radical Thought,' in Lewis, *W.E.B. Du Bois: A Reader* pp.531-534. Also James, *Holding Aloft*, p.165.

45. Quoted in James, *Holding Aloft*, p.166. On McKay's early political career see C. McKay, *A Long Way From Home – An Autobiography* (London 1985) especially pp.73-84 and W. F. Cooper, *Claude McKay: Rebel Sojourner in the Harlem Renaissance* (Baton Rouge, 1996).

46. James, *Holding Aloft*, p.165.

47. Ibid. p.166.

48. Foster, *The Negro People in American History*, p.437.

will also be the hour of your own liberation'[49] This formulation suggested that not all the Bolsheviks understood or shared Lenin's views on the colonial question and the full significance and nature of the anti-colonial struggles.

The Russian Revolution, the founding of the Comintern and the publication of the *Manifesto* immediately exerted an influence on several key figures in the United States, including the members of the Socialist Propaganda League's Harlem branch established by Randolph, Owen and others in New York and including amongst its membership Otto Huiswood, Richard B. Moore and Grace Campbell. Another member, the Jamaican Wilfred Domingo, wrote:

> The question naturally arises: Will Bolshevism accomplish the full freedom of Africa, colonies in which Negroes are the majority, and promote human tolerance and happiness in the United States by the eradication of the causes of such disgraceful occurrences as the Washington and Chicago race riots? The answer is deducible from the analogy of Soviet Russia, a country in which dozens of racial and lingual types have settled their many differences and found a common meeting ground, a country which no longer oppresses colonies, a country from which the lynch rope is banished and in which racial tolerance and peace now exist.[50]

Revolutionary Russia's approach to the 'national and colonial question' was one that would continue to inspire all those concerned with the Negro Question for many years to come. Even George Padmore, who turned his back on the Communist movement in 1933 felt compelled to publish his *How Russia Transformed Her Colonial Empire* over a decade later.[51]

The African Blood Brotherhood

Yet another to be inspired was Cyril Briggs another immigrant from the Caribbean to New York who was the editor of the *Crusader*, launched in 1918 and, in 1919, the founder of the African Blood Brotherhood for African Liberation and Redemption (ABB).[52] Briggs defined himself as 'pro-Negro' while also

---

49. R.V. Daniels (ed.), *A Documentary History of Communism* [vol.2] (New York, 1962), p. 89.

50. Quoted in James, *Holding Aloft*, p.165.

51. G. Padmore, *How Russia Transformed Her Colonial Empire – A Challenge to the Imperialist Powers* (London, 1946).

52. There are now several studies of the ABB see e.g. J. Zumoff, 'The African Blood Brotherhood: From Caribbean Nationalism to Communism,' *Journal of Caribbean Studies*, 41/1-2 (2007) pp.200-226 and M. Makalani, *In the Cause of Freedom – Radical Black Internationalism from Harlem to London, 1917-1939* (Chapel Hill, 2011) pp.45-71.

asserting that 'the Negro's place is with labor.'[53] The ABB established branches or 'posts' throughout the United States and in parts of the Caribbean but its main activities were based in New York, where it included amongst its members Wilfred Domingo, Richard B. Moore, Grace Campbell, and later Claude McKay, Lovett Fort-Whiteman, Otto Huiswoud and Harry Hayward.[54] Its aims included 'immediate protection and ultimate liberation of Negroes everywhere,' and it also envisaged the organisation of a 'worldwide Negro Federation,' and a 'Pan-African army.'[55] Briggs and other members rapidly began to combine elements of Marxist analysis with a 'Race First' approach and Pan-Africanism. Although there were initially attempts to work with Garvey's UNIA, Briggs later wrote that the ABB was established with the aim of 'combating several aspects of the Garvey movement and particularly its "Back to Africa" philosophy.'[56]

In its publications the ABB declared that it was an organisation of 'Race Radicals' and 'Class Radicals'[57] and that its attitude to 'Bolshevism and Communism' was based on 'its belief that all such forces as menace white capitalist control of the world...and the imperialist regimes of Europe should be encouraged by the darker peoples who stand to benefit most by the undermining and destruction of European imperialism and white world domination.'[58] In its

53. Solomon, *The Cry was Unity*, p.8. On Briggs career see R.A. Hill, 'Cyril V. Briggs,' in R.A. Hill (Ed.) *The Marcus Garvey and UNIA Papers, Vol. 1* [Appendix 1] (Berkeley, 1983) pp.521-527.

54. The ABB's influence even spread as far as Britain where in 1921 its literature was confiscated from an African American sailor who landed at Liverpool. 'African Blood Brotherhood Association,' CO 323/883,The National Archives. Kew, UK (TNA).

55. 'Program of the ABB,' *Communist Review*, April 1922, pp.449-454.

56. See C. Briggs to T. Draper, 17 March 1958. Theodore Draper Papers. Emory University, Box 31.The ABB's aims included: 'A Liberated Race; Absolute Race Equality – Political, Economic, Social; The Fostering of Racial Self-respect; Organized and Uncompromising Opposition to Ku Kluxism; A United Negro Front; Industrial Development; Higher Wages for Negro Labor, Shorter Hours, and Better Living Conditions; Education; Cooperation with the other Darker Peoples and with the Class-Conscious White Workers.' *Summary of the Program and Aims of the ABB*, (New York, 1920) RGASPI 515/2/37.

57. The ABB explained that 'the Negro masses are leavened by a large body of Race Radicals and a small but growing body of Class Radicals. The former are Negroes who while roused to action by the thought and action of the wrongs of the race, have not yet recognised the essential class nature of the struggle nor the exact cause and source of their wrongs, which they blame indiscriminately upon the entire white race. They are, however, generally inclined to side with and follow the leadership of the class radicals who, fully cognisant of the value of Race Radicalism for rousing the masses and as a natural and necessary step towards Class Radicalism have not been slow in utilising it and even in helping in its development.' ABB, Supplementary Papers, No.1, (Probably from the Report made by Claude McKay to the CI) RGASPI 495/155/43.

58. ABB, 'Special Membership Bulletin' (n.d. probably 1922) RGASPI 495/155/43.

Program the ABB explained that 'the important thing about Soviet Russia... is not the merits or demerits of the Soviet form of Government, but the outstanding fact that Soviet Russia is opposing the imperialist robbers who have partitioned our motherland and subjugated our kindred, and that Soviet Russia is feared by those imperialist nations and by all the capitalist plunder-bunds of the earth, from whose covetousness and murderous inhumanity we at present suffer in many lands.'[59]

Indeed those who joined the ABB may have been inspired by a variety of factors including dissatisfaction with the SPA. Several were impressed by the opposition of Soviet Russia to the big capitalist powers, the Bolsheviks' efforts to construct a new society, and perhaps especially the fact that they concerned themselves with the national question and anti-racism, as is evident from Domingo's article referred to above.[60] Briggs later explained that in his own case: 'interest in Communism was sparked by the national policy of the Russian Bolsheviks and the anti-imperialist orientation of the Soviet state birthed by the October Revolution.'[61]

Briggs looked forward to a 'Socialist Cooperative Commonwealth,' which would in his view be 'along the lines of our own race genius as evidenced by the existence of Communist states in Central Africa and our leaning towards Communism wherever the race genius has had free play.'[62] In this fashion Briggs and the ABB managed to merge together Pan-Africanist views with elements of socialism just as Hubert Harrison had done before 1917. As a consequence of the revolutionary developments in Russia, however, the ABB moved more in the direction of the socialism of Lenin and the Bolsheviks and, after 1919, towards the Comintern. This new revolutionary approach became increasingly popular during this period. It was evident not just in the ranks of the ABB and the pages of the *Crusader* but also in the pages of the more openly socialist *Emancipator*, which Claude McKay referred to as 'the most brilliant and practical theoretical paper that was ever circulated among the American Negroes,' a publication started by Domingo and Richard B. Moore in 1920.[63]

The Russian Revolution also impacted on the political career of Otto Huiswoud, one of the founder members of the American CP. Huiswoud had arrived in the United States from Dutch Guiana in 1910 and was first introduced to

59. 'Program of the African Blood Brotherhood.'

60. Turner, *Caribbean Crusaders*, pp.75-76.

61. C. Briggs to T. Draper, 17 March 1958. Quoted in R. Hill, 'Racial and Radical: Cyril V. Briggs, The Crusader and the African Blood Brotherhood, 1918-1922,' in *The Crusader* (New York, 1987) p.xxv.

62. Solomon, *The Cry Was Unity*, p.13.

63. Turner, *Caribbean Crusaders*, p.78. C. McKay, 'For A Negro Congress,' n.d. RGASPI 495/155/43/158.

socialism after hearing Harrison speak at a street meeting. He then became a student at New York's famous Rand School of Social Science where he met two Communists, the exiled Japanese revolutionary Sen Katayama and S.J. Rutgers, who was originally from Holland, both of whom subsequently played key roles in the founding of a communist party in the United States and in the work of the Comintern. Huiwsoud joined the SPA and also became associated with the Harlem Caribbean radicals, Briggs, Domingo, Moore and Grace Campbell. In the aftermath of the Russian Revolution he became associated with the left wing of the SPA that in 1919 attempted to establish a communist party. Huiswoud was one of the delegates at the National Left Wing Conference, held in June 1919, and a founder member of the Communist Party of America (CPA), one the of two such parties formed in the United States at the time.[64]

The ABB and the UNIA

The Caribbean and African American socialists in New York were also influenced by some of the early successes of the Jamaican Pan-Africanist Marcus Garvey's Universal Negro Improvement Association (UNIA). Briggs, Harrison, Domingo, A. Phillip Randolph, Garvey and future Communists such as Richard B. Moore all knew each other, initially moved in the same circles and sometimes discussed common problems. Indeed some of the members of the ABB were initially also members of the UNIA or in some way connected with it. One former ABB member later referred to the UNIA as 'the greatest mass movement of Blacks since Reconstruction,' adding, 'there can be no doubt that its influence extended to millions who identified wholly or partially with its programs.'[65] Garvey first established the UNIA in Jamaica but it was re-established in New York in 1916 and soon spread throughout the United States and in many other countries wherever people of African origin were to be found. At its height the movement was said to have a membership of some four million, half of them outside the United States.[66]

Like Pan-Africanists before him, Garvey developed an approach aimed both at Africa and the Diaspora. The UNIA's approach was enshrined in the *Declaration of Rights of the Negro Peoples of the World* adopted at its Conven-

64. On Huiswoud's early career see Turner, *Caribbean Crusaders*, pp.3-74 and M.G. van Enckevort, 'The Life and Work of Otto Huiswoud: Professional Revolutionary and Internationalist (1893-1961),' Ph.D thesis, UWI Mona, 2001, pp.13-28. The two communists parties, the Communist Labor Party and the CPA combined a few months later. Huiswoud was a founder member of the CPA the only organisation that specifically mentioned the 'Negro problem' at its founding.

65. Haywood, *Black Bolshevik*, p.102.

66. James, *Holding Aloft*, p.136.

tion in New York in 1920. This document demanded, amongst other things, an end to discrimination, segregation and other injustices, self-determination for Negroes, 'wheresoever they form a community among themselves,' and 'Africa for the Africans at home and abroad.' The UNIA even refused to recognise the League of Nations because 'it seeks to deprive Negroes of their liberty.' But although the *Declaration* was in many ways an accurate summary of the rights demanded by African Americans, as well as those in the colonics and elsewhere, it did not provide any programme to realise these demands.[67] Garvey encouraged economic self-reliance and 'race pride,' especially pride in Africa and its history, a particularly important aspect of his doctrine at a time of virulent anti-African racism. However, his ideas and the movement he led contained many contradictory elements. His emphasis on 'Race First' and hostility to communism precluded the possibility of alliances with other workers and oppressed people and the UNIA increasingly became identified with the notion of a return to Africa.[68] In his *Philosophy and Opinions*, first published in 1923, Garvey concluded that: 'The future of the Negro...outside of Africa, spells ruin and disaster.' In his view the solution to the problems facing Africa and the Diaspora would be based on a self-reliant approach 'by redeeming our Motherland Africa from the hands of alien exploiters,' and by establishing there 'a government, a nation of our own, strong enough to lend protection to the members of our race scattered all over the world, and to compel the respect of the nations and races of the earth.'[69] It was partly in an attempt to realize this aim that Garvey and the UNIA became involved in dubious economic schemes and even in discussions with the Ku Klux Klan.[70]

The ABB initially hoped to recruit from the UNIA and even to work with it and ABB members attended the UNIA's conventions. At the 1921 convention, the ABB called for a programme for 'the guidance of the negro race (sic) in the struggle for liberation,' to 'raise and protect the standard of living of the negro people,' and to 'stop the mob-murder of our people and to protect them against sinister secret societies of cracker whites, and to fight the ever expanding

67. R. Minor, 'After Garvey – What?' in J. H. Clarke and A. J. Garvey (eds.) *Marcus Garvey and the Vision of Africa* (New York, 1974) pp.165-173.

68. Garvey's anti-communism was expressed in print on many occasions, e.g. in 1923 in 'The Negro, Communism, Trade Unions and his Friend,' and in 1937 in his 'Course of African Philosophy.' See T. Martin, (ed.) *Message to the People: The Course of African Philosophy* (Dover, MA., 1986) pp.134-139.

69. A.J. Garvey (ed.), *The Philosophy and Opinions of Marcus Garvey* (Dover, MA., 1986) pp. 52-53.

70. C. Briggs, 'The Decline of the Garvey Movement,' in Clarke and Garvey, *Marcus Garvey and the Vision of Africa*, pp.174-179. See also R. Minor, 'Negroes Wont Fight Ku Klux Klan, Garvey,' R Hill (ed.) *The Marcus Garvey and UNIA Papers*, vol. 5 (Berkeley, 1987) pp.768-772.

peonage system.' It even called for a federation of the existing 'negro organisations,' in order 'to present a united and formidable front to the enemy,' as well as demanding that Soviet Russia 'be endorsed by the congress.' Not only were these proposals rejected but the ABB denounced as 'traitors and Bolshevist agents,' and expelled from the convention. The ABB and the UNIA took divergent political paths but Briggs and his comrades continued to make efforts to counter the influence of Garveyism.[71]

After Garvey was framed, prosecuted and finally imprisoned and deported for fraud in the mid-1920s the UNIA became increasingly divided and weakened. Nevertheless, Garveyism remained a major influence in the United States, in Africa and throughout the African Diaspora during the 1920s and 1930s. Moreover, its significance and the need to combat its international influence remained a key concern of American Communists and the Comintern during this period. Despite Garvey's well-known anti-communism, the revolutionary events in Russia also had an impact on the UNIA and Garvey welcomed the emergence of Soviet Russia. In 1924 he publicly mourned the death of Lenin in *Negro World*, calling him 'probably the world's greatest man,' and even sent a telegram to Moscow 'expressing the sorrow and condolence of the 400,000,000 Negroes of the world.'[72]

In the early 1920s Briggs and some of the other leading members of the ABB joined the CPA, possibly following an introduction from Claude McKay, although Briggs had evidently been invited to join both communist parties then in existence.[73] The ABB soon became an important provider of Caribbean and African American recruits to the CPA, and later the unified Workers Party (WP). In some cases it acted as a training ground for future African American Communists and a vehicle for disseminating communist ideology amongst African Americans.[74] The political orientation of the ABB naturally also brought it to the attention of the security services in the United States, where its members were immediately categorised as dangerous Bolsheviks. Perhaps more significantly, the Caribbean origins of many members as well as their internationalism meant that they were also of concern to the British security services. Indeed in regard to Briggs's *Crusader*, it was the British who alerted their colleagues in the United States to what they considered a 'very extreme magazine'

71. See C.B. Valentine, 'The Negro Convention,' *The Toiler*, 4/190 (I October 1921) pp.13-14.

72. Quoted in Haywood, *Black Bolshevik*, p. 105.

73. C. Briggs to T. Draper, 17 March 1958. Also Turner, *Caribbean Crusaders*, p.87 and Solomon, *The Cry Was Unity*, p. 9.

74. On Briggs and the ABB see Haywood, *Black Bolshevik*, pp.121-131; James, *Holding Aloft*, pp. 155-184; Solomon, *The Cry Was Unity*, pp.9-17; and Turner, *Caribbean Crusaders*, pp.53-57 and 93-96.

because of its opposition to imperialism, support for Bolshevism and 'abuse of the white man.'[75]

The ABB's Pan-Africanist orientation certainly added a new dimension to existing Marxist approaches to the global Negro Question. According to the ABB's *Program* it was 'the Negroes resident in America – whether native or foreign born – who are destined to assume the leadership of our people in a powerful world movement for Negro liberation...and the United States is destined, until the Negro race is liberated, to become the centre of the Negro World Movement.' Such US-centred views would subsequently have some influence within the American CP and the Comintern.[76] The ABB may also have presented some antecedents for the later Comintern policy regarding the right of self-determination for the 'African American nation.' Even before the Russian Revolution Briggs had been an advocate of a 'coloured autonomous State' with a separate political existence' which might be established in 'one-tenth of the territory of the United States.'[77] He also spoke of African Americans as a 'nation within a nation, a nationality oppressed and jim-crowed, yet worthy as any other people of a fair deal or failing that a separate political existence.'[78] Subsequently he advocated 'the establishment of a strong, stable independent Negro state (along the lines of our race genius) in Africa or elsewhere,' as part of a 'Universal Socialist Cooperative Commonwealth.'[79]

THE COMINTERN AND THE NEGRO QUESTION

In the CI it was V.I. Lenin who initiated discussion on the 'Negro Question' at the Comintern's Second Congress in 1920. In the course of submitting his 'Draft Thesis on the National and Colonial Question,' Lenin, who had already written some remarks on this question in the United States, specifically requested more 'concrete information' on what he referred to as 'very complex problems,' including colonies and 'Negroes in America.'[80] The 'Draft Thesis' itself provided guidelines for the Comintern on the forms of organisation and struggle needed to liberate the colonies but also urged 'that all Communist Parties should render direct aid to the revolutionary movements among the

75. T. Korniweibel, Jr., *Seeing Red – Federal Campaigns Against Black Militancy 1919-1925* (Bloomington, 1998) p.133.

76. 'Program of the African Blood Brotherhood'.

77. T. Draper, *American Communism and Soviet Russia* (New York, 1960) pp.323-324.

78. Ibid. p.323.

79. Solomon, *The Cry Was Unity,* pp.13-14. Briggs thought that such a state might also be established in the Caribbean.

80. Foner and Allen, *American Communism and Black Americans*, pp. xii-xiv.

dependent and underprivileged nations (for example, Ireland, the American Negroes, etc.) and in the colonies.'[81]

Lenin stated that the Comintern must pay particular attention to those 'people oppressed through colonial dependence' who, he pointed out, 'represent 70 per cent of the world's population.'[82] 'Without the control of the vast fields of exploitation in the colonies,' he explained, 'the capitalist powers of Europe cannot maintain their existence even for a short time.' He therefore argued for a united struggle between the workers in the advanced capitalist countries and the oppressed people in the colonial and dependent countries against the common enemy - imperialism. For the communist parties in the imperialist countries there was therefore a need to actively work with and support anti-imperialist movements in the colonies and dependent countries. Similarly, because of the offensive of all the big powers against Soviet Russia, which was in 1920 still defending itself against foreign invasion, there was a need to unite all the anti-imperialist and national liberation movements with the Soviet Union against the imperialist powers. The importance and nature of this struggle meant that the Comintern would even work with 'bourgeois nationalists' in the colonies.[83]

But apart from a lengthy intervention by the American Communist John Reed, who had first submitted his views on the Negro Question to Gregori Zinoviev, the first president of the Comintern, as early as February 1919, there was little further discussion of the subject at the Second Congress.[84] Subsequently the CI did establish a special Negro Commission and announced that a 'Congress of the Negro Peoples of the World,' would 'be convened in the near future' but such a gathering was not convened for a further ten years, until the historic First Conference of Negro Workers was held in Hamburg in July 1930.[85] The CI had at least signalled its intent to find solutions to the 'Negro Question.' The fate of the proposed congress in the interim shows that despite many good

81. V.I. Lenin, *Collected Works*, Vol., 31 (Moscow, 1965) pp.144-151. In addition to Lenin's draft theses there were also supplementary theses drafted by the Indian Communist, M.N. Roy. Both, in slightly amended form, were subsequently adopted by the congress.

82. V.I. Lenin, 'Report to the Second Congress of the CI,' in *Lenin On the United States* (Moscow, 1975) pp.458-468.

83. Foster, *History of the Three Internationals*, pp.300-308. *Outline History of the Communist International*, pp. 85-89. Boesner, *The Bolsheviks and the National and Colonial Question*, pp.80-87.

84. Reed to Zinoviev, 19 February 1919, RGASPI 495/155/1/3. Reed attended the second congress as a delegate of the Communist Labour Party. Foner and Allen, *American Communism and Black Americans*, pp.5-8.

85. From the Small Bureau of the ECCI to Comrades Reed, Fraina, Gurvitch, Jansen and Scott n.d., RGASPI 495/155/1/2.

intentions there were many political and logistical obstacles to overcome before it could be convened.[86]

At the Third Congress of the CI in the summer of 1921 D. Ivon Jones, a delegate from South Africa who had drawn attention to Garvey's UNIA Convention and Du Bois's Pan-African congress, proposed that the Comintern should establish a Colonial Bureau which would be concerned with matters relating to Africa but might also take up the 'Negro question as it surges up in its most frenzied form in America.'[87] He argued that 'Africa's hundred and fifty million natives are most easily accessible through the eight million or so which comprise the populations of South Africa and Rhodesia,' and he concluded 'primitive though they be, the African natives are ripe for the message of the Communist International.'[88]

Following Jones's initiative the congress passed a motion instructing the Executive Committee of the Communist International (ECCI) to pay attention to 'Negro movements and proletarian movements among Negroes.'[89] Subsequently the ECCI established both a Negro Commission and a Negro Bureau but there were allegations that the representatives of the American CP in Moscow were hampering progress on the Negro Question.[90] There were certainly differing view within the CI about how this question should be approached and there were lengthy debates about exactly what kind of question it was. Evidently, it was not simply a 'national question,' or an issue of the self-determination of a nation, but often appeared to be a racial issue. Sen Katayama, by that time a leading member of the CI based in Moscow, appears to have remained the most enthusiastic supporter of the proposed Negro congress but others such as Jones queried the basis on which 'Negroes' from different countries and nations could be brought together and wondered if a 'Negro Race Congress' would be counter-productive.[91] The CI also discussed whether such a

86. See Sen Katayama, 'Action for the Negro Movement Should not be Postponed,' n.d. RGASPI 495/155/17/9-12.

87. On Jones see B. Hirson and G.A. Williams, *The Delegate for Africa – David Ivon Jones 1883-1924* (London, 1995). See Davidson et al, *South African and the Communist International*, p.78. The ECCI's Bureau of Colonial and Semi-Colonial Countries subsequently resolved to create a 'Department of Dominion Countries and Negro Peoples' and to appoint Jones as its head. Ibid., n. 1.

88. Wilson, *Black Africa*. p.126; R. Kelley, 'The Third International,' pp.103-104; S.Johns, 'The Comintern, South Africa and the Black Diaspora,' *The Review of Politics*, 37/2 (1975) p.210.

89. Davidson, *South African and the Communist International*, p.105 note 2.

90. Sen Katayama, 'Action for the Negro movement should not be postponed,' 22 May 1923, RGASPI 495/155/17/9-12.

91. Ibid. Discussion in CI Anglo-Saxon Group Meeting, 10 May 1922. RGASPI 495/155/3/5.

'Negro Congress' should also include North Africans, 'Moors and Egyptians', a consideration which seemed likely to add even further complexities.[92]

The Fourth Congress of the Comintern and the Thesis on the Negro Question

It was at the Fourth Congress of the CI, in 1922, that the Negro Question was first discussed in detail. For the first time two 'Negro' delegates attended the congress and they clearly had a significant impact on its proceedings. Claude McKay, the well-known Jamaican writer and representative of the ABB, was highly critical of what he characterised as the lack of effort devoted to communist activity amongst African Americans but he also highlighted the problems associated with organising in the south of the United States.[93] He argued that the Negro Question was the central problem of the class struggle and confidently asserted 'the Third International will be amazed at the fine material for Communist work there is in the Negro Race.'[94] McKay argued that 'an international movement of the Negro peoples' was developing and he cited the UNIA's conventions and Du Bois's Pan-African congresses as evidence of this trend. Consequently, he considered that it was time for the Comintern to convene a 'Negro conference of representative American, South African, West African and West Indian Negroes of Revolutionary spirit.'[95]

The other delegate was Otto Huiswood, an official representative of the WP and another leading member of the ABB. Huiswoud called for serious attention to be given to the Negro Question, which he said had previously been ignored, and he was subsequently made chairman of the Negro Commission established by the congress. For Huiswoud, the 'Negro question' was, 'another phase of the race and colonial question,' but 'aggravated and intensified by the friction which exists between the white and Black races.' His main focus was on the United States and although he mentioned both the Caribbean and Africa,

92. See 'Remarks on proposal to call a Negro congress at Moscow,' RGASPI 495/155/3/3. No clear definition of what was meant by the term 'Negro' was established, but North Africa was excluded from the CI's concern with the Negro Question that focused on sub-Saharan Africa.

93. *Bulletin of the IV Congress of the CI*, 2 December 1922, pp.21-23.

94. Solomon, *The Cry was Unity*, p.41.

95. C. McKay, 'For A Negro Congress,' RGASPI 495/155/43/156-162. See also RGASPI 515/1/93/97 and 99-105 and C. McKay, 'Report on the Negro Question – Speech to the 4th Congress of the Comintern,' November 1922, *Inprecor*, 5 January 1923, pp.16-17.

he maintained the ABB's view that the United States was the 'headquarters and centre of political thought among Negroes.'[96]

The most important consequences of the deliberations at the Fourth Congress were not just the fact that a Negro Commission was established and a 'Thesis on the Negro Question' agreed, but also that CI policy was established in regard to all 'Negroes' throughout the world, that is for Africa and the Diaspora. This essentially Pan-Africanist approach was maintained by the Comintern for the best part of the next fifteen years. The 'Thesis on the Negro Question,' finally agreed at the congress and probably largely drafted by Huiswoud and other American Communists,[97] declared that 'the penetration and intensive colonisation of regions inhabited by black races is becoming the last great problem on the solution of which the further development of capitalism itself depends.' It argued that, 'the Negro problem has become a vital question of the world revolution', and therefore that, 'the cooperation of our oppressed black fellow-men is essential to the Proletarian Revolution and to the destruction of capitalist power.' It concluded that 'the international struggle of the Negro race is a struggle against Capitalism and Imperialism,' and 'it is on this basis that the World Negro movement must be organised.'[98] This 'World Negro movement' included those in Africa, the Caribbean and South America, as well as the United States. However, it was the US that was seen as 'the centre of Negro culture and the crystallisation of Negro protest.'[99] Huiswoud explained that the proposals of the Negro Commission 'should be carried out by the various sections of the Communist International who have Negroes in their territories or colonies.' The Commission had, he therefore concluded, prepared a proposal for 'work amongst Negroes throughout the world.'[100]

The CI's Pan-Africanist approach to the Negro Question meant that it was now viewed in an international rather than just an American context. This was at least partly a consequence of the view that those of African descent had been the victims of a particular form of racist oppression. It was also based on what seemed to be the emergence of a new awakening and common struggle in the post-war period epitomised by the rapid development of the Garvey movement, the international influence of Du Bois's Pan-African congresses, as well as particular struggles that had broken out in the African continent against colonial rule. The Fourth Congress of the Comintern implicitly recognised this fact by pledging to organise a 'general Negro conference or Congress in Moscow,'

---

96. Foner and Allen, *American Communism and Black Americans*, pp.25-27.

97. Davidson, *South Africa and the Communist International*, p.130.

98. 'Thesis on the Negro Question,' RGASPI 495/155/5/8-11.

99. Ibid.

100. *Bulletin of the IV Congress of the CI*, 2 December 1922, p.20.

and by calling for support for 'every form of Negro movement which tends to undermine or weaken capitalism or imperialism, or to impede its further penetration.'[101] The CI's concern with the Negro Question was also influenced by the fear that African troops might be used as a counter-revolutionary force by one of the major colonial powers, either in Europe or against the new Soviet Union. This possibility was alluded to by several of the speakers including McKay and the Soviet Commissar for War, Leon Trotsky.[102] At the same time there was also a concern to apply Lenin's theses to the African colonies, since these colonies were seen as important 'reserves' for imperialism.

Although Huiswoud maintained that the Negro Commission had considered the 'situations as they actually exist in Africa and America,' the thesis was largely couched in terms that suggested that its main relevance was in connection with the situation facing workers in the United States.[103] Declaring that 'it is to be a special duty of Communists to apply the "Thesis on Colonial Questions" to the Negro problem,' the formulation of the 'Thesis' stressed the need to overcome discrimination and fight for equality, as much, or perhaps even more, than it did the right of colonial peoples to self-determination.[104] Even after it had been re-drafted by the Negro Commission it still retained something of a bias towards the United States. It was certainly seen as being too American in focus by Sidney Bunting, the representative of the CPSA and another member of the Negro Commission. He complained that in regard to organising 'Negro workers,' it had 'nothing to say about the many hundred thousand negroes who are exploited in countries where there are no white unions at all, or hardly any: e.g. West, East and Central Africa, the Congo, West Indies etc.'[105]

The 'Thesis' also presented the view, long held by the ABB, that 'the history of the Negro in America fits him for an important role in the liberation struggle of the entire African race.'[106] Indeed this seems to have been a commonly held view at the time. Israel Amter, another leading American Communist, remarked that 'The American Negro by virtue of his higher education and culture and his greater aptitude for leadership, and because of the urgency of the issue in

101. R. Kanet, 'The Comintern and the "Negro Question": Communist Policy in the United States and Africa, 1921-1941' *Survey* 19/4 (1973) pp.86-122.

102. Wilson, *Russia and Black Africa*, pp.128-129.

103. *Bulletin of the IV Congress of the CI*, 22 December 1922, p.20.

104. Ibid. pp. 8-11.

105. For the official list of the Commission's members see *Bulletin of the IV Congress of the CI*, 12 November, 1922, p.1.

106. Foner and Allen, *American Communism and Black Americans*, p.29. For the redrafted Thesis see *Bulletin of the IV Congress of the CI*, 7 December 1922, pp.8-11.

America, will furnish the leadership for the Negro race.'[107] On this same issue Ivor Jones argued that 'the status of the American Negro cannot be raised without the awakening of Africa, but it is no less true that the European proletariat cannot obtain a real link with Africa except through the more advanced Negroes of America.[108] Such views placed an onus on the American Communists to organise this 'leadership.'[109]

The role of the two 'Negro' delegates at this congress should not be underestimated. Huiswoud played a key role in drafting the 'Thesis,' and chaired the Negro Commission in which both participated. After the congress Huiswoud had the unforgettable experience of meeting with Lenin.[110] Certainly the views of the ABB on the significance of the worldwide Negro movement, its recognition of the influence of Garveyism and the particular vanguard role that African Americans should play seem to have become more significant in the approaches of American Communists and the CI to the Negro Question in this period. That both Huiswoud and McKay made a big impact on the congress, is clear from the letter of 'fraternal greetings and best wishes' sent by Zinoviev through McKay to the 'Negro Workers of America,' as well as from contemporary accounts.[111] Katayama, for example, reported that the two delegates 'made a profound impression on the Congress and the Congress treated the Negro problems with a due respect and consideration and attempted all that the Comintern can do under the circumstances.'[112] McKay not only addressed the congress but also wrote several articles on various aspects of the Negro Question whilst he was

107. Draper, *American Communism and Soviet Russia,* p.328 and p.508 note 42 for similar statements by other American communists. See also 'To the American Negro,' RGASPI 495/155/44/20.

108. Draper, *American Communism and Soviet Russia,* p.328. At least one internal CI document states, 'It will be the duty of the American, West Indian and South African Negroes to lead in the emancipation of the vast native population of Africa. They have a higher culture and are better organised for the huge task. Until the native population of Africa has been liberated from the shackles of western imperialism the Negro race will not be free.' RGASPI 495/155/4/33.

109. See the remarks of Borodin in 'Minute of meeting of Commission appointed by the Orgbureau to prepare and guide the work for the forthcoming World Negro Congress', n.d. RGASPI 495/155/8/1.

110. Rose P. Stokes, 'The CI and the Negro,' in Foner and Allen, *American Communism and Black Americans,* p.31; Turner, *Caribbean Crusaders,* p.107.

111 See James, *Holding Aloft* p.181 and Foner and Allen, *American Communism and Black Americans,* p.31.

112. Sen Katayama, 'Action for the Negro Movement should not be Postponed,' 22 May 1923, RGASPI 495/155/17/9-12.

in Moscow and following his return to the United States.[113] Moscow clearly made a great impression on him and he later wrote that never in his life had he felt 'prouder of being an African.'[114] He was a strong supporter of the call for a 'general Negro conference', but also of the view that the task of organising appropriate delegates for such an event could not just be left to 'the Communist Groups'. He stated that he was particularly opposed to 'the American and South African Parties having an altogether free hand in organising the conference as I do not think they are familiar or class-consciously enough interested in the Negro as revolutionary material.'[115]

Following the Fourth Congress, a Negro Bureau was established by the ECCI, as Huiswoud and the Negro Commission had proposed, [116] and a secretariat established to organise the planned 'Negro Congress,' which was sometimes even referred to as a 'great Pan-African Congress,' that would be convened in order to form 'a great international Federation for the liberation of the Negro peoples, in America and in Africa.'[117] Initially it was planned that the congress would convene in Moscow, but there were some fears that this might prove difficult, and Berlin was also mentioned as a possible venue. One consideration was the fact that any announcement that the gathering would be held in Moscow 'would be met with the most intense and widespread race persecution which in turn would bring great difficulties in reaching the Negro masses.'[118] By 1923 it had been decided instead to hold a conference of 'Negro communists,' to coincide with Fifth Congress of the CI in the spring of 1924. In addition to this gathering, it was also planned to hold an open 'International Negro Conference' either in London, Paris, Berlin or New York. By the end of

113. See e.g. C. McKay, 'Soviet Russia and the Negro,' *The Crisis*, (December 1923) pp.61-65; C. McKay, 'The Racial Question – The Racial Issue in the United States,' *Inprecor*, 21 November 1922, p.817; See also McKay's report for the CI in RGASPI 515/1/93/99-105 and A. Mcleod, (ed.) *The Negroes in America* (London, 1979).

114. McKay, *A Long Way From Home*, p.168.

115. C. McKay, 'For a Negro Congress,' n.d. RGASPI 495/155/43/159.

116. Foner and Allen, *American Communism and Black Americans*, p.32.

117. See RGASPI 495/155/44/27. There also seem to have been plans by the CI to 'start a Negro propaganda paper in America,' and to hold a 'smaller conference' within six months. These plans were not realised. See C. McKay to V. Kolarov, 23 December 1922, RGASPI 515/1/93/92-93 and S. Katayama, 'Action for the Negro Movement Should not be Postponed, n.d. RGASPI 495/155/17/9-12.

118. RGASPI 495/155/44/28.

1923, New York had been established as a likely venue and communist parties were instructed to hold local preparatory conferences 'in all the Negro lands'.[119]

Agreement on the venue and composition of the conference/congress was not however the only problem facing the CI. The 'Negro Question' itself was problematic for the CI and in its documents 'Negroes' were referred to as both a 'race' and a nation and sometimes even 'the Negro race as an oppressed Colonial Nation.' Mention was made of the Negro movement for national liberation, while at the same time greater emphasis seemed to be placed on the 'toiling masses,' and the need for the unity of the Negro workers. In one draft manifesto for the planned congress it was stated: 'The Communist International declares that only by an awakening of the Negro masses of Africa and America to a consciousness of the common bond which binds them altogether as a race, as a race of oppressed people, can they begin the task of Negro emancipation.'[120]

The minutes of the meetings of the CI's Commission 'to prepare and guide the work for the forthcoming World Negro Congress' show similar confusion and disagreement, perhaps compounded by the fact that membership of the Commission, which included British, American and French Communists, did not include anyone of African descent.[121] Indeed, the Commission itself, which was chaired by the Russian Mikhail Borodin, had been belatedly appointed by the ECCI and one of its senior members, Sen Katayama, openly accused the American Party of continually impeding the proposed congress.[122] The South African representative, David Ivon Jones, even suggested that the main focus of such a congress should be Africa. He argued that 'the Comintern could do nothing for the negroes (sic) in America that the American Communist Party could not do,' and asserted, 'the negro question (sic) was a question for the millions in Africa, and that the centre on which attention should be concentrated

119. Letters from the Provisional Secretary for Calling the Negro Conference to Executive Committee CPSA, 23 July and 15 November 1923, in Davidson, *South Africa and the Communist International,* pp.131-133. See also ECCI 'Draft Manifesto on the Negro Question,' RGASPI 495/155/4/16-26.

120. ECCI, 'Draft Manifesto on the Negro Question,' Ibid.

121. The members of the Commission were Borodin, Amter, Katayama, Jones, Gallacher, Hannington, Stewart and Georges Lévy.

122. For Katayama's remarks see 'Action for the Negro Movement should not be Postponed,' 22 May 1923, RGASPI 495/155/17/9-12 and 'Negro Race as a Factor in the coming World Revolution, 14 July 1923.' RGASPI 495/155/17/13-23. Katayama, appears to have seen the entire 'Negro Question' largely in relation to the US. See also Minutes of the Meeting of the Negro Commission held on May 30, 1923, RGASPI 495/155/8/4 and Minute of meeting of Commission appointed by the Orgbureau to prepare and guide the work for the forthcoming World Negro Congress, n.d. RGASPI 495/155/8/1.

was Central Africa.'[123] Following such discussions, it is evident that the Commission was concerned that Africans as well as African Americans should be fully represented at any international gathering that was organised.[124]

A further problem was that although the 'Provisional Secretary for Calling the Negro Conference' communicated with various communist parties, no work in preparation for the event was carried out by these parties.[125] Although much has been made of the monolithic character of the Comintern, the reality was rather different. The body to organise the congress therefore began to take on the responsibility of demanding from various parties that they began some work both in the African colonies and amongst Africans in the metropolitan countries. However progress was slow. The Communist Party of Great Britain (CPGB), for example, admitted with regret and some understatement that 'there is not sufficient contact between the Party in England and the Negro population to warrant us being optimistic of a successful conference in London,' and promised to 'start propaganda among the Negro population,' presumably the first time the notion had been considered even though three of its leaders were members of the Negro Commission. The Executive Committee of the CPGB therefore respectfully suggested the congress should be held in France.[126] In the autumn of 1923 the British, French and other major European parties were instructed to submit reports on their work in the African colonies and amongst 'Negro seamen.'[127] In October the CPGB was again asked what work it had undertaken 'to carry out propaganda amongst the negro (sic) population in the British colonies,' and was specifically asked to take up work amongst African sailors who frequented the 'African Natives' Club' in London as well as in Liverpool, with an aim of also developing work in African ports.[128] There does not appear to have been any response to these enquiries.

123. Minute of meeting of Commission appointed by the Orgbureau to prepare and guide the work for the forthcoming World Negro Congress, n.d. RGASPI 495/155/8/1.

124. Provisional Secretary for Calling the Negro Conference to CEC of the WP [of America], 16 July 1923, RGASPI 495/155/14/1.

125. Letters were sent to the parties of the United States, Britain, France, Belgium, Mexico, Guatemala, Cuba, Holland and Portugal. RGASPI 495/155/1-10.

126. Thomas Bell to Amter, 17 August 1923. RGASPI 495/155/16/2-3. The CPGB was even unable to provide Amter with any information about the Pan-African congress organised by Du Bois and held in London in 1923 and did not publish his article on it 'Pan-African Congress – A Futile Congress'. A. McManus to Amter, 15 March 1924, RGASPI 495/155/27/7.

127. Secretary for Calling Negro Conference to the EC of the CP of France/Portugal/Italy, 15 November 1923, RGASPI 495/14/19.

128. Secretary of Negro Conference to CEC, British CP, 24 October 1923. RGASPI 495/155/14/16.

The following February, the Parti Communiste Français (PCF) was being asked why at its recent congress, 'the question of the Negro was not taken up at all.' The Secretary of the Negro Conference admitted that this omission was 'astonishing in view of the fact that the colored troops are still in France, and that tens of thousands of Negro workers are in France, some of them being used as strike-breakers.' The French Party was again asked 'at least to begin' this work and reminded that 'the Comintern has pointed out to you the necessity of taking up the NEGRO question as a special question and not as part of the colonial problem.'(capitals and emphasis in original)[129] But the PCF, like other parties, was evidently unable to take up the issue with any great success. Amter, the American secretary of the Negro Commission, admitted that hitherto the Negro Question had been treated as 'an American problem,' and that therefore the 'British and French parties have not taken any interest in the question.'[130] As a consequence it was impossible for the CI to convene its 'Negro World Congress.'

The Fifth Congress of the Comintern and the American Negro Labor Congress

At the CI's Fifth Congress in June 1924 the Negro Question was again part of the discussion on the 'National and Colonial question' and once again the communist parties in Britain and France were criticised for their lack of attention to colonial matters.[131] Manuilsky, the head of the Comintern Commission on National and Colonial Questions characterised the CPGB as the representative of a proletariat 'more infected with colonial prejudice than all others in the Comintern,' and pointed to the fact that no statement could be found in which the British CP 'declares itself unequivocally for the separation of the colonies from the British Empire.' He considered this to be particularly serious following the election of Britain's first Labour government and suggested that the CPGB might adopt the slogan 'Hands off the Colonies.' As for the PCF, it was again criticised for having done nothing to organise the thousands of Africans and other colonial subjects resident in France, including the '250,000 blacks' in the French army and for also being reluctant to 'demand the liberation of the colonies.'[132]

129. Secretary of Negro Conference to the CC of the CPF, 20 February 1924, RGASPI 495/155/27/6.

130. Amter to McManus, 31 March 1924, RGASPI 495/155/27/8.

131. Johns, *Raising the Red Flag*, p.210; Haywood, *Black Bolshevik*, pp.225-227.

132. E.T. Wilson, *Russia and Black Africa Before World War II* (London, 1974) p.140; *V Congress of the CI – Abridged Report of Meetings Held in Moscow, June 17 to July 8, 1924*, pp.192-193.

In the discussions that took place on Negro Question in the United States it was evident that various opinions existed. What had to be decided was the precise nature of the problem to be addressed, the character of the oppression suffered by African Americans and how they might liberate themselves. Could African Americans be considered a subject nation, an oppressed race, or simply a particularly disadvantaged section of the American working class? The answers to such questions would dictate the strategy of the WP, which was itself increasing criticised for its weaknesses in regard to the Negro Question. One of these critics was Lovett Fort-Whiteman, the first African American to join the Party and one of its delegates to the Fifth Congress.[133] In an article for the *Communist International* he complained that

> Communist achievements among Negroes are but slight,' a view which provoked an editorial that criticized 'our American comrades of the ruling race,' who 'have not yet been able to approach the Negro question in a right and proper manner.[134]

At the Fifth Congress there were renewed calls for a 'general Negro Conference' and for establishing a 'permanent Negro Commission' with members drawn from the ECCI and the British, French and Belgian parties in order to 'organise propaganda amongst the Negroes.'[135] Following the decision of the congress, a new Negro Commission, which included Fort-Whiteman, was appointed to prepare what was referred to as the 'Negro Workers' Congress,' afterwards the American Negro Labor Congress (ANLC). [136] This congress, eventually to be held in Chicago, would be organised by Fort-Whiteman and the WP and would itself then issue a call to a 'Negro World Congress.'[137]

It is evident that Fort-Whiteman had himself proposed to the CI that the ANLC should be held in Chicago as part of the efforts of African American Communists to make progress on the Negro Question both in the United States

133. Foner and Allen, *American Communism and Black Americans*, pp.69-70. For biographical details on Fort-Whiteman see G. E. Gilmore, *Defying Dixie: The Radical Roots of Civil Rights, 1919-1950* (New York, 2008).

134. Ibid. pp.86-89.

135. 'Report of the Enlarged ECCI,' *V Congress of the CI*, p.283.

136. Fort-Whiteman, who after the Congress remained in Moscow for eight months as a student, thought that the World Congress should be held after the CI's Sixth Congress and should be called 'International Congress of African Races.' 'Some suggestions pertaining to the proposed Negro World Congress to be held in Moscow,' RGASPI 495/155/25/5-8.

137. Decisions of the Negro Commission, 16 January 1925, RGASPI 495/155/30/1-3.

and internationally.[138] In a letter to Zinoviev, he was critical of the inability of the CI to convene a World Congress and of an American CP that 'had made no serious or worthwhile effort to carry the Communist teaching to the great mass of American black workers.'[139] He even claimed that his passage to the Fifth Congress of the CI had been paid for not by the WP but 'by individual Negro communists, inspired by the belief that sending one of their group to Moscow, he might be successful in getting the Comintern to take some practical steps helpful to our work among Negroes both in America and on a world scale.'[140] Not for the last time here was an instance of an individual African American Communist calling on the Comintern to assist in dealing with problems within the WP, but more significantly also urging the Comintern to make advances on the Negro Question in general, as well as suggesting measures to make certain that such advances were made.

The CI was, however, continually hampered by the inactivity and lack of experience of its constituent parties and a tendency to view the Negro Question as a problem to be addressed mainly in the United States. In February 1923, for example, the ECCI had informed the WP that it had been decided 'to request your party provisionally to take care of the propaganda of the negro-movement, and also in general to prepare the ground for the coming negro-congress.'[141] This was a consequence of the fact that the European parties were still unable to make any headway, that the Negro Question clearly was a major concern in the United States, that some within the WP had recognised this, and that there were party members, especially African American ones, who were concerned to make headway on this question. The CPSA, the only other party closely connected with the issue, was still finding it difficult to make any headway amongst the African population and was not in a position to lead the work on the Negro Question. Unfortunately the WP was still hamstrung by factionalism, the legacy of the merger that had led to its creation, as well as by an inability to fully recognise the effects of racism.[142] It was in these circumstances that the Comintern criticised it for 'ignoring the question of racial antagonism,' and for allowing the 'Negro liberation movement in America to take a wrong path.'[143]

---

138. On Fort-Whiteman and the ANLC see Haywood, *Black Bolshevik*, pp.143-147 and Solomon, *The Cry Was Unity*, pp.52-67.

139. Ibid. p.47.

140. Ibid.

141. O. Kuusinen to the CC of the Workers Party of America, 23 February 1923, RGASPI 515/1/164.

142. For Fort-Whiteman's views on these issues see Foner and Allen, *American Communism and Black Americans*, pp.86-87 and L. Fort-Whiteman to Dear Comrades, 8 August 1925, RGASPI 495/155/33/23.

143. Foner and Allen, *American Communism and Black Americans*, p.88.

The 'wrong path' referred to what was considered to be the harmful influence of Garveyism and the 'Back to Africa' slogan that the ABB had hitherto made strenuous efforts to combat, especially through its *Crusader News Service*.[144] It was still thought that there were many members of the UNIA who might respond to the approach of the ABB and the Communists. At the Fourth Congress of the CI, Otto Huiswoud had even spoken of the 'rebel rank and file movement' of the UNIA and concluded that it was 'influencing the Negroes against imperialism.'[145] But the life of the ABB was coming to a close, as many of its leading members, particularly in New York and Chicago, became involved with the WP and the ANLC.[146] The WP attempted to exert some influence on the UNIA through its participation in the UNIA convention held in August 1924.[147] At this major gathering it was able to elaborate the Comintern's position on the Negro Question - the 'right of self-determination of the peoples of Africa' and other colonial peoples, as well for countries such as Haiti and the Dominican Republic which were dominated by US imperialism. However, it also took issue with the UNIA's refusal to condemn the Ku Klux Klan, which created a further breach between the two organisations that was never repaired.[148] Nevertheless, the Comintern continued to be impressed with the strength of the UNIA and recommendations were even made for 'Communist nuclei' to be established 'within its ranks.'[149]

The ANLC, held in Chicago in October 1925, was mainly concerned with the struggles of African Americans, especially with their exclusion from the trade union movement, but it was certainly the intention of the Comintern's Negro Commission that 'all problems of the Negro race in addition to all problems of the Negro workers in America should be discussed,' and that the Congress 'should issue a manifesto to the Negroes throughout the world summoning them to a Negro World Congress.' The Negro Commission also expected that 'a Committee of Action should be elected by the Congress for the organisation of this World Congress,' and that 'the Congress should supply definite instructions to this Committee.'[150] The Negro Commission even envisaged that 'a Negro comrade' might be brought from South Africa to attend and the ECCI instructed the European parties to 'undertake immediately extensive

144. C. Briggs to T. Draper, 17 March 1958, Theodore Draper Papers.

145. *Bulletin of the IV Congress of the CI*, 2 December 1922, pp.18-19.

146. C. Briggs to T. Draper, 17 March 1958 and 'The Most Important Negro Organisations in America and Other Countries,' RGASPI 495/155/34/32.

147. See Foner and Allen, *American Communism and Black Americans*, pp.76-86.

148. Solomon, *The Cry Was Unity*, pp.33-37.

149. 'The Garvey Organisation,' n.d. RGASPI 495/155/34/33.

150. Decisions of the Negro Commission, 16 January 1925, RGASPI 495/155/30/1-2.

work among the Negro colonies in Africa' in connection to the congress and the proposed World Negro Congress.[151]

As if to further emphasise the international significance of the ANLC, the leaders of the Kresintern (or Peasant International) wrote to Fort-Whiteman and the WPA to express the hope that 'in view of the attendance of delegates from the African countries and colonies' the ANLC would also focus on the 'conditions of the Negro peasantry both in America in the colonies.'[152]The 'Call' issued for the ANLC certainly had an international character and placed the struggles of African Americans as 'part of the world-wide stirring of the darker races against European imperialism.'[153] The 'Provisional Committee for Organising the ANLC' included Sahir Karimiji, a 'Fraternal Delegate from Natal Agricultural Workers' in South Africa and E.A. Lynch, 'Fraternal Delegate from West African Seamen's Union,' in Liverpool, but there is no evidence that either attended the congress.[154]

Fort-Whiteman had written that on the occasion of the ANLC 'efforts should be made to rally the Negro races of the world: Africa, America and the West Indies, for a struggle against world Imperialism.'[155] He made contact with Joseph Gothon-Lunion, a leading figure in the Paris-based Comité de Défence de la Race Nègre (CDRN), who he had met at the Fifth Congress of the CI, and invited him to attend the ANLC.[156] Through the PCF Fort-Whiteman tried to make contact with those in the anti-colonial movement in the French colonies in Africa, in order to invite them to what he called 'the World Congress

151. Secretary of the ECCI to the CC of the Workers Party of America, n.d. RGASPI 495/155/32/13. Letters were sent to the parties in Britain, France, Holland, Belgium, Italy, Portugal and Germany.

152. From Orlov, Dombal and Voznesensky to Dear Comrades, 17 September 1925, RGASPI 495/155/32/28-30. In response Fort-Whiteman expressed the hope that the Kresintern would begin work in West Africa, saying that he had a contact in Lagos, Nigeria who wished to organise 'the Peasants in that section of the country.' Fort-Whiteman to Dear Comrade,' 16 April 1926, RGASPI 495/155/37/1-2.

153. Foner and Allen, *American Communism and Black Americans,* p.109.

154. Details from ANLC letterhead. This used for the first time the characteristic figure of an African male worker towering over the Atlantic and breaking asunder chains that stretched across the African and American continents. This image was later extensively used by the ITUCNW and its publication *The Negro Worker*. RGASPI 495/155/33/34. See also 'Committees of ANLC,' n.d., RGASPI 495/155/33/29-33.

155. L. Fort-Whiteman, 'American Negro Labor Congress,' *Imprecor*, 5/67, 27 August 1925, p.983.

156. It appears that Gothon-Lunion was eager to attend but uncertain about the practicalities. See RGASPI 495/155/33/7.

of Negro leaders to be held in Europe in the near future'.[157] He was also already in contact with African students in the United States, including Bankole Awooner-Renner from the Gold Coast, who was soon to be sent to study at the University of the Toiler of the East (KUTV) in Moscow.[158] Fort-Whiteman reported that he intended to send one of his 'strong lieutenants' to London to popularise the Word Congress and that he was attempting to make contact with unnamed 'Negro Nationalist leaders' in Angola.[159] He appears to have believed that 'representatives from the African colonies, Liberia, Dahomey, Ashanti and Abyssinia' would attend the ANLC but it is not clear who he had in mind, and there is no evidence that they attended. He evidently still believed that 'the American Negro worker by reason of his historical experience in such a country as America, where capitalism has reached its highest stage of development, seems well fitted to take the leadership of the Negro Race of the World in its struggle against World Imperialism.' Fort-Whiteman hoped that the ANLC would be the mechanism through which such leadership was exercised.[160]

The ANLC did pass a resolution instructing its national executive committee 'to convene a world congress of our race,' and it instructed the 'American Negro delegates' to 'lay the foundations for a world organisation of the workers and farmers of our race and to make this organisation a leader and fighter in the liberation movements of all the darker-skinned peoples in the colonies of imperialism everywhere.'[161] But despite Fort-Whiteman's efforts, the directives of the CI, which were enshrined in the ANLC's resolutions, and the CI's exhortations to the communist parties in the major imperialist countries in Europe, no world congress was organised, even though there was at least one public reference to a 'World Congress of Coloured Workers' apparently to be held Belgium in March 1926.[162]

Indeed the ANLC was not a great success and in 1927 Fort-Whiteman was removed from its leadership. In 1928 he went to the Soviet Union as a delegate to the Sixth Congress of the Comintern and remained there for the rest of his life.[163]

157. See Ruthenberg to Secretariat, CI, 1 June 1925, RGASPI 495/155/33/6 and e.g. L. Fort-Whiteman to Central Executive Committee, CP of France, 12 December 1925, RGASPI 495/155/33/34.

158. See chapter nine.

159. L. Fort Whiteman to Dear Comrades, 5August 1925, RGASPI 495/155/33/23-24.

160. L. Fort-Whiteman, 'American Negro Labor Congress,' *Imprecor*, 5/67, 27 August 1925, p.983.

161. Foner and Allen, *American Communism and Black Americans,* p. 123.

162. See Johns, *Raising the Red Flag,* p.213.

163. Fort-Whiteman died in prison in the Soviet Union in 1939. See Turner, *Caribbean Crusaders*, pp.227-228 and Gilmore, *Defying Dixie*, p.154.

Although the ANLC was not considered a success and did not immediately lead to an international congress it was another example of the Comintern's efforts to make advances on the Negro Question. The Eastern Department of the ECCI, which had overall responsibility for matters relating to colonies and the Negro Question, envisaged that the Chicago congress would 'connect the struggles of the Negro workers and farmers in the United States with the struggles of the Negro colonials in American possessions such as Haiti,' and 'with those of the African masses and finally with those of all colonial and semi-colonial countries.' Following the ANLC the Comintern still looked forward to a 'world race congress,' and continued to emphasise that 'the connection between the African and American Negro liberation movements is in the common struggle against world imperialism.'[164]

The League Against Imperialism

Although the World Negro Congress was not immediately organised, an International Congress against Colonial Oppression and Imperialism was held in Brussels in February 1927.[165] It was at this congress that the League Against Imperialism and for Colonial Independence (LAI) was founded. The Brussels congress was convened by the League Against Colonial Oppression (LACO), which had been founded by Willi Munzenberg and other German Communists in 1926.[166] LACO presented itself as 'an association of persons of widely different party tendency' but certainly did not hide the leading role played by Munzenberg and other Communists.[167] It was the Comintern's intention that Communists should remain largely in the background as far as the practical organising of the congress was concerned, however, its political orientation was agreed by a commission of the ECCI, with the aim of establishing a permanent organisation 'to support the liberation movement in the colonies.'[168]

Over 170 delegates participated in the congress, representatives from throughout the colonial world, and such personalities as Nehru, Madame Sun Yat Sen, and Albert Einstein. There were also several representatives from Africa and the Diaspora including: Messali Hadj and Hadjali Abdel-kader from the Paris-based L'Étoile Nord Africaine; Carlos Martins from Haiti; Max Blon-

164. Eastern Department of the ECCI, Information Review No. 8, 17 September 1925, RGASPI 495/155/34/73-86.

165. On the Brussels Congress see J. Derrick, *Africa's Agitators*, pp.172-182.

166. W. Munzenberg, 'For a Colonial Conference,' *Inprecor,* 26 August 1926, p.968.

167. W. Munzenberg, 'The First International Congress against Imperialistic Colonisation, *Inprecor*, 4 February 1927, pp.246-247.

168. Secretariat of the ECCI to Munzenberg, 8 July 1926, RGASPI 542/1/3.

court and Camille Saint Jacques represented the Union Intercoloniale in Paris; Lamine Senghor, member of the PCF and Narcisse Danaé represented the CDRN; J.T. Gumede of the African National Congress (ANC) and James La Guma of the CPSA and formerly of the Industrial and Commercial Workers' Union (ICU); and Richard B. Moore, representing the ANLC.[169] William Pickens of the NAACP, George Weston, president of the UNIA and Hubert Harrison had been invited and encouraged to attend the Brussels conference by the ANLC but were unable to do so.[170]

The great significance of the Brussels Congress was that it brought together those who were struggling for national independence in Asia and Africa, those in Latin America and elsewhere who were determined to safeguard their sovereignty, as well as representatives of organisations in the imperialist countries that had a critical attitude towards colonialism or were opposed to it. Both the Indian National Congress and the Guomintang government in China were represented, as were the British Labour Party and Independent Labour Party.[171] Representatives from China, India and Britain, including British Communists, even signed a joint resolution against 'suppression and intervention in the colonial countries.'[172]

Most importantly the Brussels Congress brought together delegates from Africa, the United States and the Caribbean and established its own five member 'Negro Commission', including Bloncourt, Martins and Gumede with Lamine Senghor as chairman and Moore as rapporteur, and devoted a whole session to the Negro Question. Indeed Munzenberg and the other organisers had used the occasion of the congress to make contact with over a hundred nationalists and anti-colonial activists in Africa and throughout the Diaspora. These included those associated with the National Congress of British West Africa such as J.E. Casely Hayford, Kobina Sekyi, H. Bankole Bright and S.R. Wood, as well as union and labour organisers such as Clements Kadalie of the ICU in South Africa and E.A. Richards, the President of the Sierra Leone Railway Workers Union. LACO, and subsequently the LAI, were also in contact with

169. I. Geiss, *The Pan-African Movement: A History of Pan-Africanism in America, Europe and Africa* (New York, 1974), p. 326 and Derrick, *Africa's Agitators,* p. 175. For biographical details of Moore see W. B. Turner and J. M. Turner (eds.) *Richard B. Moore, Caribbean Militant in Harlem: Collected Writings 1920-1972.*

170. See L. Fort-Whiteman to C.E. Ruthenburg, 31 August 1926, RGASPI 515/50/720. According to Fort-Whiteman the WP had long considered sending a party of 'representative Negro intellectuals' to the Soviet Union and had hoped this might be done as part of the 'Brussels Conference arrangement.'

171. W. Munzenberg, 'The First International Congress against Imperialistic Colonisation, *Inprecor*, 4 February 1927, pp.246-247. On the Congress see also Derrick, *Africa's Agitators,* pp.172-182.

172. See *Inprecor,* 17 February 1927, p. 292.

other organisations in Africa, including the Gold Coast Farmers' Association, the Mozambique Railwaymen's Union and organisations in Liberia, French Somaliland, and Madagascar. [173]

Lamine Senghor, who died a few months after the Congress, evidently made a great impression and delivered a speech on behalf of the CDRN in which he declared that 'the Negroes formed the most oppressed and exploited race in the world' and that France was 'civilising' Africa through torture, forced labour and 'at the point of the bayonet.' He took issue with the comments of the Egyptian delegate, Hafiz Ramadan Bey, who had claimed that Egypt had not been colonised, and saluted the struggles of the people of China as 'a good revolutionary example' to all those suffering under colonialism. He concluded by stating that the struggle against imperialism was necessarily a struggle against capitalism and called for the unity of those in the colonies and metropolitan countries so that imperialism could be destroyed and 'replaced by the union of free peoples.'[174] Delegates from other French colonies, including Morocco and the Caribbean also gave speeches condemning colonialism and demanding independence.[175] Bloncourt, for example, spoke of the genocide of the indigenous people perpetrated by French imperialism in Martinique and Guadeloupe, as well as the enslavement and deaths of millions of Africans. He also highlighted the predatory interests of US imperialism in the Caribbean and the importance of the Russian and Chinese revolutions, as well as the anti-colonial struggle in India. He concluded by stating that the Congress was a great inspiration for all those struggling for liberation in the Caribbean.[176]

The 'Common Resolution on the Negro Question,' which included references to the history of Africa, the United States, Latin America and the Caribbean, was introduced and presented by Richard B. Moore of the ANLC and WP. [177] The Resolution concerned itself with 'the emancipation of the Negro peoples of the World,' and was perhaps the most politically developed statement that had been formulated on the question, based no doubt on the experience of those involved in drafting it. It called for complete economic and political

173. 'Report on the Activities of the LAI in the Different Countries – February to May 1927,' RGASPI 542/1/16/31.

174. *Inprecor*, 25 February 1927, pp.328-329 and RGASPI 542/1/69/86-88. Senghor was subsequently elected to the Executive Committee of the LAI but arrested by the French government soon after his return to France. J. A. Langley, *Pan-Africanism and Nationalism in West Africa 1900-1945* (Oxford, 1973) p.305. On Senghor and other activists in France see chapter six.

175. *Inprecor*, 25 February 1927, pp.328-329.

176. RGASPI 542/1/69/60-61.

177. According to one authority the Resolution was 'largely drafted' by Moore. Turner and Turner, *Richard B. Moore,* pp.143-146.

independence for the entire Caribbean including Haiti, Cuba, the Dominican Republic, Puerto Rico and the Virgin Islands and for 'a confederation of the British West Indies'. It concluded with a call for 'a resolute and unyielding struggle' to achieve:

1. Complete freedom of the peoples of Africa and of African origin;
2. Complete equality between the Negro race and all other races
3. Control of the land and governments of Africa by the Africans;
4. Immediate abolition of all compulsory labour and unjust taxation;
5. Immediate abolition of all racial restrictions, social, political and economic:
6. Immediate abolition of military conscription and recruiting;
7. Freedom of movement within Africa and elsewhere;
8. Freedom of speech, press and assembly;
9. The right of education in all branches;
10. The right to organise trade unions.[178]

In order to accomplish these aims Moore proposed 'the organisation of the economic and political power of the people,' in unions and co-operatives, including 'the unionisation of Negro workers,' a struggle against 'imperialist ideology,' and he stressed the importance of 'unity with all suppressed peoples and classes for the fight against world imperialism, as well as the 'organisation and coordination of the Negro liberation movements.'

In addition to this 'Common Resolution' the three representatives from South Africa, Gumede, La Guma and Daniel Colrane of the South African Trade Union Congress also jointly signed a declaration 'on behalf of all workers and oppressed people of South Africa, irrespective of race, colour or creed.' The resolution demanded freedom of speech, assembly and movement, the right to organise trade and unions and other demands for rights. However, perhaps the most significant demand was for 'the right to self-determination through the complete overthrow of the capitalistic and imperialist domination.'[179]

The LAI launched at the Brussels Congress became an important organisation assisting the anti-colonial struggle, especially throughout Africa and parts of the Caribbean and amongst those of African and Caribbean origin residing in Britain and in France. The International Secretariat, led by the representatives of the CI, soon reported that it was trying 'to link up the different organisations of the African Negro movement in order to concentrate the forces of the

178. 'Common Resolution on the Negro Question, Presented to the International Congress Contre The Colonial Oppression & L'Imperialism,' (sic) Brussels, 13 February 1927, RGASPI 542/1/67/45-46.

179. La Guma, *Jimmy La Guma*, p.32.

African Negro fight for emancipation.'[180] Indeed it subsequently attempted to establish an 'African Secretariat' of the LAI, based in South Africa and it was initially hoped that through Communist influence in both the ANC and the ICU these organisations could become 'the centre of a continentally organised Negro movement.'[181] The LAI also worked with the CDRN to make contact with those in the French colonies in West Africa and had apparently established a 'special secretariat' in Dakar. [182]

The Brussels Congress undoubtedly created the conditions for the Comintern to extend its links with the anti-colonial movements in Africa and the Caribbean through the LAI and to unite representatives of some of them around 'the Common Resolution on the Negro Question.' The LAI was another avenue through which to attempt to organise on this question, particularly in countries where the communist parties had been slow to focus on it.[183] The congress was also an opportunity for leading African activists to learn more about the Communist movement and subsequently to become influenced by its ideology. Gumede, for example, declared in Brussels, 'I am happy to say that there are Communists in South Africa. I myself am not one, but it is my experience that the Communist Party is the only party that stands behind us and from which we expect something.'[184] Following the Brussels Congress, Gumede and La Guma spent some time on a speaking tour of Germany and after this both travelled to the Soviet Union to see for themselves the construction of the new Socialist state. La Guma was invited by the CI's Anglo-American Secretariat in order to deliver a report about the South African situation. His visit to Moscow was to prove vital in the development of Comintern policy in regard to South Africa as well as for his own political development.[185] In the winter of 1927 Gumede and La Guma were invited back to Moscow together with E. A Richards and others, by the Society for Promoting Cultural Relations for the Tenth Anniversary

---

180. 'Report of the Activities of the LAI in the different countries, February-May 1927,' RGASPI 542/1/16.

181. In fact Communists such as La Guma had already been expelled from the ICU. See J. & R. Simons, *Class and Colour in South Africa 1850-1950* (London, 1983) p.354.

182. 'Report of the Activities of the LAI in the different countries.'

183. See e.g. the early report of the work of the Belgian LAI in regard to the Congo. 'After the Colonial Conference,' n.d. RGASPI 542/1/30/143-144.

184. Quoted in B. Bunting, *Moses Kotane - South African Revolutionary* (Belville, 1998) p.36. For Gumede's other speeches in Brussels see RGASPI 542/1/69/65-71. For biographical details see R. van Diemel,' *'In Search of Freedom, Fair Play and Justice': Josiah Tshangana Gumede, 1867-1947: a biography.* Available at http://www.sahistory.org.za/archive/search-freedom-fair-play-and-justice

185. See Simons and Simons, *Class and Colour*, pp.389-390 and La Guma, *Jimmy La Guma*, pp.34-42.

Otto Huiswoud and Claude McKay at the Fourth Comintern Congress, 1922, Yale Collection of *American Literature*, Beinecke Rare Book and Manuscript Library, Yale University

Claude McKay speaking in Moscow, Yale Collection of *American Literature*, Beinecke Rare Book and Manuscript Library, Yale University

Josiah Gumede (extreme left), Lamine Senghor (sixth from left) and other delegates at the founding of the LAI, Brussels, 1927, *Public Domain*

The Negro Commission, LAI, Brussels, 1927, *Public Domain*

celebrations of the October Revolution.[186] It was following this visit that on his return to South Africa, Gumede proclaimed 'I have seen the new world to come, where it has already begun. I have been to the new Jerusalem.'[187] Gumede was not alone in voicing such sentiments. The previous year W.E.B Du Bois had spent several months in the Soviet Union. He subsequently wrote: 'I stand in astonishment at the revelation of Russia that has come to me. I may be partially deceived and half-informed. But if what I have seen with my eyes and heard with my ears in Russia is Bolshevism, I am a Bolshevik.[188]

The Founding of the International Trade Union Committee of Negro Workers (ITUCNW)

The founding of the LAI had certainly provided the conditions for an advance in the Comintern's work on the Negro Question but it had still not resulted in the convening of the long-awaited 'international congress of Negro workers.' The task of organising such a gathering and making substantial headway on the Negro Question was to be taken up by the Red International of Labour Unions (RILU or the Profintern), following its fourth congress in March 1928 and after the ninth enlarged plenum of ECCI held in February 1928. The ECCI meeting had stressed the importance of organising 'Negro industrial and agricultural workers of the world,' a formulation that included 'Negroes in Brazil, Colombia, Venezuela and the West Indies.'[189]

The RILU was established in Moscow in 1921 as an organisation of the 'revolutionary class element' of the international trade union movement. Over a third of its 17 million members were based in Soviet Russia but it initially had adherents in Germany, Italy, Britain, France, the United States, Spain, Australia and Poland. It was established in opposition to the International Federation of Trade Union (IFTU), which was based in Amsterdam and closely linked to the Second International. Both were seen by the Comintern as having betrayed international labour during World War I and as being hostile to the Russian Revolution. One of the RILU's principal aims was 'to organise the large mass of workers in the whole world for the abolition of capitalism, the emancipation of the toilers from oppression and exploitation and the establishment of the Socialist commonwealth.'[190] From its inception the RILU was closely con-

186. On Richards and his attempts to travel to the Soviet Union see chapter nine.

187. Quoted in Bunting, *Moses Kotane – South African Revolutionary* p.36. For details of Gumede's reception in Moscow see Haywood, *Black Bolshevik,* pp.214-217.

188. W.E.B. Du Bois, 'Russia, 1926,' in Lewis, *W.E.B. Du Bois – A Reader,* pp.581-582.

189. RGASPI 495/155/53/2.

190. W.Z. Foster, *Outline History of the World Trade Union Movement* (New York, 1956) p.274.

nected with and followed the political orientation of the Comintern, although the two organisations were constitutionally separate. It was eager to organise those workers who hitherto had been left unorganised by the IFTU and was particularly concerned to organise in the 'colonial and semi-colonial' countries. The IFTU, on the other hand had a membership that, as one authority has put it, 'were often lacking in understanding of the anti-colonial struggle, if they did not openly defend colonialism.'[191]

As might be expected, the RILU had also taken an interest in the Negro Question well before 1928. At its third congress in July 1924 it had, as part of the 'Resolution on the Eastern [Colonial] Question,' agreed that 'the negro question has its own peculiarities, demanding special study.' For this purpose it appointed a 'special commission' that was charged with putting 'concrete proposals' before the next RILU congress.[192] In the meantime, the congress resolved that 'the adherents of the RILU in America, South Africa, and in other countries where there are negro workers must immediately commence work among the negro worker masses, endeavouring to secure the fusion of parallel organisations of whites and negroes, wherever such exist.' The congress also stressed the importance of organising 'negro farm workers' in the United States and other countries. [193] The ANLC, held in Chicago in 1925, was a significant attempt to organise amongst all African American workers but progress inside and outside the United States was slow to materialise. In 1926 at a meeting of the Executive Bureau of RILU, Alexander Lozovsky, the RILU general secretary, had criticised both the South African and American CPs for their slow progress in implementing the decisions of the RILU on the Negro Question.[194]

One consequence of the founding of ANLC was the recruitment of James Ford, an African American war veteran and a graduate of Fisk University who became a postal worker in Chicago. Ford joined the WP in 1926, rapidly rose through the ranks of the Party and the Comintern and later became the CP's candidate for vice-president in the 1932, 1936 and 1940 elections in the United States. In 1935 he was elected an alternate member of the ECCI and in 1944 when the Communist Party of the United States of America (CPUSA) was

191. R. Tosstorff, 'Moscow versus Amsterdam: Reflections on the History of the Profintern,' *Labor History Review*, 68/1 (April 2003) pp.80-97.

192. 'Resolution on the Eastern Question,' *The Tasks of the International Trade Union Movement: Resolutions and Decisions of the Third World Congress of the RILU, July 1924* (London, 1924), p.48.

193. 'Resolution on the Eastern Question.'

194. Johns, *Raising the Red Flag*, p. 215.

dissolved he became vice-president of the Communist Political Association.[195] Ford attended the RILU's Fourth Congress as a representative of the Trade Union Educational League (TUEL), the RILU affiliate in the United States, the first African American to attend such a gathering, and was subsequently elected to the RILU's Executive Bureau.[196]

At the RILU congress Lozovsky once again criticised those communist parties that were failing to organise amongst 'Negro Workers.' He stressed that 'the negroes represent an enormous potential revolutionary force and any disregard of the work of organising the negroes is really an echo of the ruling classes' influence.' Lozovsky also criticised those, in the United States in particular, who refused to organise 'independent Negro unions,' a different emphasis from the previous congress, pointing out that 'Racial restrictions and racial prejudices will be the more easily overcome the more speedily the broad masses of the negro proletariat enter the path of the organised class struggle. There must be no putting off or delaying, or else the work or organisation will take place without us and consequently against us.'[197] It was as part of this general criticism that Ford spoke about the 'many weaknesses' in the work of the communist parties of the United States, France, Britain and South Africa and vociferously called for a conference of Negro workers 'to work out immediate practical measures to realise the line established by the Congress in the question of organising Negro workers in the United States and Africa.' [198] In order to facilitate this work the Congress called on its sections in the United States, South Africa, Britain and other countries to fully implement the decisions of the previous congress and in a special resolution the Executive Bureau of RILU was urged to convene a conference of delegates from countries with a 'Negro population' who were attending the Sixth Congress of the CI in July 1928.[199]

This conference, convened as part of an enlarged meeting of the Executive Bureau of RILU, was held at the end of July 1928 and attended by delegates from

195. For further biographical details see B. Lazitch in collaboration with M. Drachkovitch, *Biographical Dictionary of the Comintern* (Stanford, 1986) pp.121-122 and A.W. Berry, 'Introduction' in J.W. Ford, *The Negro and the Democratic Front*, (New York, 1938) pp.13-14.

196. J. Ford, 'Report to the First International Conference of Negro Workers,' Hamburg 1930, in J.W. Ford, *The Communists and the Struggle for Negro Liberation*, (New York, n.d.) p.23 The TUEL was the main means by which American communists organised amongst both black and white workers. See P. Foner, *Organised Labor and the Black Worker 1619-1981* (New York, 1982) pp.163-166.

197. A. Lozovsky, *Report to the 4th Congress of the RILU* (London, 1928) pp.23-24.

198. Johns, *Raising the Red Flag*, pp.216-217. Ford was to repeat his criticisms at the sixth congress of the CI.

199. See Ford, *The Communists and the Struggle for Negro Liberation*, p.24

the American and South African parties who were attending the CI congress, as well as by several African American students who were studying in Moscow, including William Patterson and Harry Haywood.[200] It was preceded by criticisms of the 'Negro work' undertaken by the WP in the Negro sub-commission established by the Anglo-American Secretariat of the ECCI.[201] Many of these issues were also addressed at the Sixth Congress of the CI that preceded the RILU conference.

The meeting of the RILU Executive Bureau concentrated on the question of establishing an International Trade Union Committee of Negro Workers (ITUCNW) and notwithstanding heated discussions, mainly a consequence of continuing disagreements and factionalism in the WP, agreement was reached on Lozovsky's proposals to establish such a body, sometimes initially referred to as 'an International Bureau of Negro Workers.'[202] Ford was made chairman of the ITUCNW, which was initially to have two representatives from the United States and one from South Africa, Guadeloupe, Martinique and Cuba. In time it was hoped to include representatives from Haiti, Portugal's African colonies, the Belgian Congo, Liberia and French Equatorial Africa, as well as from Brazil, Colombia, Venezuela and other countries in Latin America.[203]

Patterson and other argued that one of the main reasons for establishing the ITUCNW was the inability of the 'communist parties of the west' to ade-

200. See RGASPI 534/3/306/58-59. William Lorenzo Patterson (1891-1980) a lawyer in Harlem came in contact with Richard B. Moore and through him was introduced to the campaign to free Sacco and Vanzetti and the WP. He was invited to study at KUTV from 1927 and subsequently became a leading figure in International Labor Defence and the Civil Rights Congress. For an autobiographical account of his life see W. Patterson, *The Man Who Cried Genocide* (New York, 1971). On Haywood (1898-1985) see his autobiography *Black Bolshevik.*

201. See e.g. J. Ford, 'Negro Work in America,' RGASPI 495/155/59/1-14. One consequence of these and many other criticisms was that in November 1928 the Eastern Secretariat of the ECCI established a Negro Bureau, part of which also functioned as the Negro Commission of the Anglo-American Secretariat. RGASPI 495/155/54/6-7. In August 1928 a Negro Bureau or Commission was also established within the Kresinterrn. RGASPI 495/155/56/42-3.

202. RILU's International Bureau of Negro Workers was originally composed of Ford (Chairman), George Slavin (Secretary), La Guma (South Africa), Ducadosse (Guadeloupe) an unnamed Cuban member, as well an additional member from the US. See RGASPI 495/155/53/1. Martinez, the Cuban delegate at the meeting of the Executive Bureau, was critical of the emphasis placed on Cuba specifically and the Caribbean in general, and argued that 'the Negro problem is a problem for the whole of Latin America.' He highlighted the importance of the population of African origin in Brazil, Colombia, Venezuela and the Central American countries. RGASPI 534/3/306/26.

203. RGASPI 534/3/306/58. Minutes of the Meeting of Executive Bureau of RILU, 31 July 1928.

quately deal with the 'Negro Question'. The ITUCNW, he hoped, would 'keep its fingers on the pulse of activity in these countries, advising them on procedure and helping them to form slogans for activities to bring the Negroes into the Communist Party.'[204] The ITUCNW was charged with the 'setting up of connections with the Negro workers of the whole world and the unification of the wide masses of the Negro workers on the basis of the class struggle,' as well as, preparing and convening 'an International conference of Negro workers at the end of 1929.[205] Henceforth, the 'Negro Question' would focus mainly on Negro workers and would be addressed mainly through the activities of the ITUCNW working with the communist parties. In the colonies, where such parties might not yet exist, the ITUCNW would attempt to establish connections between Negro workers and the party in the relevant metropolitan country, in addition to encouraging the workers to organise themselves. The Executive Bureau of the RILU called upon all its affiliates especially those in the 'imperialist countries' of the US, Britain, France and Belgium 'to extend all possible and active help to the work of organising the Negro workers.'[206]

The CI and RILU placed particular importance on the organising of Negro workers at this time for several reasons. Of course, Marxism pointed to the revolutionary nature of the working class itself, as the most resolute opponent of exploitation and the 'gravedigger' of capitalism. Then there was the tremendous growth of a 'Negro proletariat' in the United States, a result of migration from the southern states to the north, creating a revolutionary potential already recognised in the work being undertaken by the WP and TUEL. The growing importance of African and 'coloured' workers was also becoming apparent in South Africa, where the CPSA had also struggled to organise them. There was also the importance of the anti-colonial struggle in general and the potential that existed to develop it in many parts of Africa and the Caribbean. Events in China, India, Indonesia and Egypt suggested that anti-colonial and anti-imperialist struggles would assume even more importance in the coming period, as the economic contention between the big powers intensified and opposition to foreign domination grew. Although workers in Africa might not yet exist in large numbers, outside countries such as South Africa, it was predicted that they would assume a greater importance, alongside peasant farmers, particularly where they were organised by communist parties or, where these did not

204. RGASPI 534/3/306/25.

205. RGASPI 495/155/53/1. The ITUCNW immediately issued an 18-point *Trade Union Programme of Action for Negro Workers*. The first edition of the ITUCNW's publication, *The Negro Worker* was launched on 16 July 1928, i.e. before the meeting of the Executive Bureau.

206. 'Resolution of the Executive Bureau of the RILU on the Programme of the ITUCNW,' RGASPI 534/3/359.

exist, in trade unions and peasant associations. In several African and Caribbean countries, Guadeloupe, Gambia, Sierra Leone, and South Africa, for instance, workers had begun to organise trade unions and even strikes and the RILU wanted to be in a position to assist them. The RILU had already established links with the Sierra Leone Railwaymen's Union, Sabin Ducadosse, a labour activist from Guadeloupe, participated in the RILU's Fourth Congress, while in South Africa the CPSA had begun working within the ICU, which in 1927 had joined the IFTU. An additional factor was the threat of a new war by the big powers against the Soviet Union and the role that conscripted soldiers from the African colonies and elsewhere might again be forced to play in such a war, if not organised to oppose it and fight for their own liberation.

However, the documents of the RILU mention just six reasons for the creation of the 'International Bureau of Negro Workers,' – widespread 'race chauvinism' amongst the workers and even within the 'cells of revolutionary organisations;' the fact that despite several resolutions 'the organisation of Negro workers is being effected at an extremely slow pace;' the inability of the RILU affiliates and particularly the TUEL to commence forming 'independent Negro unions;' concern that such delays 'put millions of the most oppressed slaves of capitalism outside the field of action of the RILU;' that Negro workers 'comprise a huge potentially revolutionary power in the struggle against capitalism;' and the view that that the 'Negro workers' of the world would achieve 'equality with the White workers only through the organised relentless struggle against the whole system of capitalist oppression.' The new Bureau was specifically charged with publishing a 'special bulletin,' and convening an 'international conference of Negro workers.' It was also created to establish 'connections with the Negro workers of the whole world;' with the 'unification of the wide masses of the Negro workers on the basis of the class struggle,' and with 'the creation of independent Negro unions.'[207]

The founding of the ITUCNW was a historic decision of the RILU acting under the political direction of the CI. However, it also reflected the agitation of African American Communists who for several years had been amongst those most critical of the slow progress that was being made on the Negro Question by the communist parties of Britain, France, the United States and South Africa. As Johns points out, Ford and other African American communists maintained an 'aggressive concern' with this issue and it remained a major question at the Sixth Congress of the CI and the congress of the Young Communist International held later in 1928.[208] Within the Comintern a much

207. 'On the RILU International Bureau of Negro Workers,' RGASPI 495/155/53/1. The task of establishing 'independent Negro unions' related in particular to the United States and South Africa where black workers were excluded from existing unions.

208. Johns, *Raising the Red Flag*, p.217.

greater sensitivity had been created about the importance of the Negro Question and what came to be referred to as 'white chauvinism.' This was to be most evident during the deliberations of the Sixth Congress. Since its inception the CI had been grappling to find solutions to what was referred to as the Negro Question but hitherto little concrete work had been undertaken outside the United States and South Africa. Nevertheless, despite very evident weaknesses, it had established itself as the only international organisation committed to the revolutionary overthrow of all forms of oppression, including racism and colonialism. As such it had already been an inspiration to many in Africa and throughout the African Diaspora. The founding of the ITUCNW created a new body specifically designed to overcome any vestiges of 'race chauvinism,' one that would further encourage attempts to organise the vast numbers of workers in Africa and throughout the African Diaspora.

Chapter Two

The Sixth Congress and Self-Determination

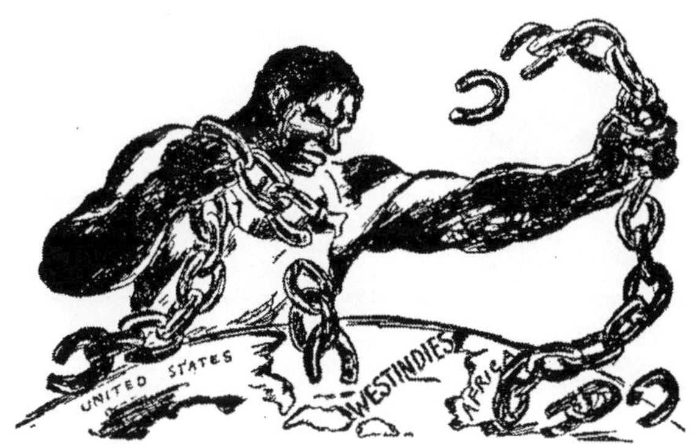

Problems and Preparations

The founding of the ITUCNW occurred in the midst of the Sixth Congress of the Comintern, a congress that was to have a major impact on the CI's approach to the Negro Question especially in two important areas, South Africa and the United States. In these two countries communist parties were pursuing policies that were criticised by the Comintern and by party members, especially black party members, because they were considered to be impeding the development of 'Negro work.' In the WP factional struggles, which had severely handicapped it for several years, were also causing significant problems and compounding the failure to adequately address the Negro Question. The congress also discussed in some detail the important struggles that were developing in many African colonies and stressed the need for the communist parties in the metropolitan countries to find ways to support the emerging anti-colonial movements.

The frustrations of African American Communists had surfaced at previous congresses and were also evident in their attempts to turn to the Comintern for support to overcome inactivity on the part of the WP. There had also been allegations that the Party was too inclined to see the Negro Question simply as an issue that would ultimately be resolved through the class struggle, rather than confronting the actual problems that faced most African Americans. The WP had not yet recognised that overcoming the legacy of slavery would require a liberation struggle by African Americans, especially those in the rural South, distinct from although related to the struggles of the workers. Other major criticisms levelled were that the WP did almost no work amongst African Americans in the southern states, where the vast majority of them lived, and that it had not sufficiently come to grips with 'white chauvinism,' both amongst the workers and in the Party itself. The Comintern and the RILU had made criticisms and at times intervened directly but had often been frustrated both by the ongoing factional struggle and other organisational weaknesses that had undermined the Party's ability to make progress.

The question of what approach to take to African American workers excluded from unions affiliated to the racist American Federation of Labor (AFL) had already become a factional dispute, while the issue of organising in the southern states became part of the factional struggle when the Party's general secretary had expressed the view that work amongst African Americans in the South was largely futile, and that the 'Negro masses' were a 'reserve of capitalist reaction,' a view contested by his opponents.[1] There were, however, many reasons for the apparent slow pace of the WP's work amongst African Americans, and while this work also had some notable successes, there was still an underestimation of the revolutionary significance of the struggle for 'Negro liberation.' The Party's own perspective on its weaknesses was presented in April 1928 just as its approach appeared to be changing. At that time a new Party platform was issued and there were signs that more work would be undertaken in the South. The Central Executive Committee (CEC) declared that: 'the Party as a whole has not sufficiently realised the significance of work among the Negroes. The CEC considers it necessary to educate the whole Party membership on the issues of the Negro work. The work among the Negroes should be

1. H. Haywood, *Black Bolshevik: Autobiography of an Afro-American Communist* (Chicago, 1978) p.255. Also T. Draper, *American Communism and Soviet Russia* (New York, 1960) p.510 n.73.

considered not as a special task of the Negro comrades but as one of the basic revolutionary tasks of every Communist, of the whole Party.'[2]

In regard to the situation in South Africa, the Comintern had not intervened as frequently as it had been required to in the United States. Indeed at the Sixth Congress there were complaints from the delegates of the CPSA that there had been hardly any communication for several years with the Comintern nor with the CPGB.[3] The CPSA had received various resolutions and directives but still appeared to be somewhat out of touch with Comintern policy on colonial, trade union and others matters on which it developed its own policies that were not always in line with the decisions of the CI. Indeed the leaders of the CPSA did not regard South Africa as a colonial or semi-colonial country at all, a position at odds with the line of the Comintern. The CPSA did not fully recognise the need to organise and unite the masses of the people, including those in the rural areas, to wage a struggle to free themselves from the grip of British imperialism but rather viewed South Africa as a country with a growing proletariat, which should be organised to wage a class struggle for socialist revolution. Bunting and other CPSA leaders still adhered to the view that he had expressed in 1922:

> In cases like South, West and East Africa, or the Pacific taken as one unity, or the United States, where a real national liberation movement of the coloured races is hardly practical politics and a peasant movement with any hope of success hardly exists among the coloured peoples, the only revolutionary movement of the subject races is the movement of the workers organised as workers.[4]

The South African labour movement comprised both white and black workers but there were significant differences and often divisions between them. African workers were often largely excluded from certain occupations and paid lower wages even if employed in similar work. South African governments had already introduced laws that openly discriminated against the African majority and attempted to maintain division between black and white workers. In

---

2. J. L. Engdahl, 'The Activities of the American Communist Party Among The Negro Workers and Farmers,' 11 June 1928, RGASPI 495/155/59/47-66 See also P.S. Foner and J.S. Allen, *American Communism and Black Americans – A Documentary History* (Philadelphia, 1987) p.148.

3. S.P. Bunting, 'Statement presented at the Sixth Comintern Congress, 23 July 1928,' A. Drew (ed.) *South Africa's Radical Tradition- A documentary history – volume one 1907-1950* (Cape Town, 1996) pp.77-80.

4. S. Bunting, 'The Coloured Labour Front,' quoted in S. Johns, *Raising the Red Flag – The International Socialist League & The Communist Party of South Africa 1914-1932* (Bellville, 1995) p.205.

these circumstances the leaders of the CPSA felt it was crucial that proletarian unity was built and preserved at all costs. In the past the Party had even concentrated most of its activities on the white workers, although in recent years this approach had been changed. The CPSA had played an important part in the development of Kadalie's Industrial and Commercial Workers' Union (ICU) and in strengthening the African National Congress (ANC). However, in 1926 the former had taken measures to expel the Communists, while the latter could not be relied upon to always follow the lead of the CPSA. The leaders of the CPSA began to despair of both organisations and regarded their 'nationalist tendencies' with 'suspicion and antagonism.'[5] Instead the CPSA had begun to develop its own 'Non-European' trade union centre, whilst waging a less vigorous struggle in the ICU and in the segregated South African Trade Union Council, which included Communists in its leadership, but refused to admit Africans. However, although the CPSA saw itself as a party preparing the proletariat primarily for socialist revolution, rather than an anti-imperialist struggle, it resisted and indeed rejected attempts by the CI to 'Bolshevize' it and organise its members in cells in factories or other work places.[6] In this regard too it went its own way, although as soon became evident, there were significant differences amongst the CPSA leaders on these issues.

In March 1928, at the Fourth Congress of the RILU, the weaknesses of the 'adherents' of the RILU in South Africa, which had allowed the ICU to expel Communists and seek affiliation to the IFTU and which were evident in the divided trade union movement, were highlighted and discussed. The RILU stressed that in South Africa the central problem of the trade union movement was that of organising 'Coloured Labour' and the division that existed between 'white workers and coloured workers.' But it also indicated that this problem had a wider international significance throughout Africa, in the French Antilles, within France and in the United States. It was in this context, and particularly as the RILU stressed the growing importance of Africa, that the work of the CPSA assumed added international importance.[7]

The Comintern was also in the process of changing its orientation in order to take account of changing circumstances in the world, especially changing economic and political conditions. According to the Comintern's analysis, the post-war world was entering a 'third period' in which there would be a further global economic crisis, the growing likelihood of 'imperialist wars' and 'wars of liberation,' of 'gigantic class battles,' culminating in 'a new revolutionary

5. Ibid. p.206.

6. Ibid. p.211.

7. *Report of the Fourth Congress of the RILU* (London, 1928) pp.44-45 and 30-31.

upsurge.'[8] In these conditions it was important that all the communist parties were organisationally and politically prepared, and that factionalism and other weaknesses were eliminated. In the case of the WP, which was still viewed as having the main responsibility to provide leadership to the Comintern's Negro work, it was vital that the Party's approach to the Negro Question should be exemplary. In the case of the CPSA, the only communist party existing in sub-Saharan Africa, it was crucial that it should also set an example, overcome any lingering 'white chauvinism,' genuinely become a party of the majority population in South Africa and lead an anti-imperialist struggle that would also have a profound impact on the rest of the continent. The Sixth Congress occurred at the same time as the congress of the Labour and Socialist International (LSI or Second International) was convening in Brussels. The Comintern lost no time in exposing the resolutions agreed in Brussels, especially those relating to colonialism, and the fact that the LSI in practice rejected the right of self-determination for oppressed countries and nations. The deliberations of the Sixth Congress were therefore of some importance and the resolutions and other decisions which emerged from it in relation to the Negro Question have been the subject of extensive debate and analysis by historians.[9]

In order to assist its deliberations on the Negro Question, the Anglo-American Secretariat of the ECCI, which had responsibility for overseeing the work of the communist parties in the United States and South Africa, established its own special Negro sub-commission to prepare draft resolutions for the congress. The Sixth Congress, acting on a proposal from James Ford, then established its own Negro Commission. Both bodies investigated, discussed and prepared

8. W.Z. Foster, *History of the Three Internationals: The World Socialist and Communist Movement from 1848 to the Present* (New York, 1955) pp.357-358.

9. See especially, Draper, *American Communism and Soviet Russia*, pp.315-357; M Solomon, *The Cry was Unity: Communists and African Americans, 1917-1936* (Jackson, 1998) pp.68-93; J. Turner, *Caribbean Crusaders and the Harlem Renaissance* (Chicago, 2005) pp.154-186 and J & R Simons, *Class and Colour Colour in South Africa 1850-1950* (London, 1983) pp.386-416; Johns, *Raising the Red Flag*, pp.200-230 and A. Drew, *Discordant Comrades: Identities and loyalties on the South African left* (Pretoria, 2002) pp.94-112. Also M. Legassick, 'Class in South African Protest: The South African Communist Party and the "Native Republic" 1928-34,' *Eastern African Studies* XV (July 1973) Syracuse University; R. Kelley, 'The Third International and the Struggle of National Liberation in South Africa,' *Ufahamu*, 15/1-2 (1986) pp.99-120; O. Berland, 'The Emergence of the Communist Perspective on the "Negro Question" in America: 1919-1931 – Part Two,' *Science and Society*, 64/2 (Summer, 2000) pp.194-217; O. Berland, 'Nasanov and the Comintern's American Negro Program,' Ibid. pp.226-228; S. Campbell, '"Black Bolsheviks" and Recognition of African-American's Right to Self-Determination by the Communist Party USA,' *Science and Society*, 58/4 (Summer, 1994) pp.440-470; H. Klehr and W. Thompson, 'Self-determination in the Black Belt: Origins of a Communist Policy,' *Labor History*, 30/3 (Summer, 1989) pp.354-366.

material and had a membership that included a significant number of African American Communists. These 'Black Bolsheviks' were to play a major role in determining Comintern policy on the Negro Question.[10]

The sub-commission of the Anglo-American Secretariat became a forum used by African American Communists to try to overcome what was seen as the harmful approaches to 'Negro Work' of some of the leaders of the American CP. James Ford, for instance, was especially critical of the sectarian methods of the Party, its reluctance to work in the South, its tendency not to pay sufficient attention 'to the position of Negroes as an oppressed minority,' and the fact that there were 'less than 50 Negroes' in the Party. Acting on a request from Richard B. Moore, the head of the ANLC who alleged he had been excluded from the American delegation to the Sixth Congress for supporting such criticisms, Ford even lobbied the Anglo-American Secretariat to hold a special conference of African American Communists in Moscow immediately before the Sixth Congress. He suggested that unless those comrades who he named were invited they would not be sent 'because of their opposition to the present attitude of our Party to Negro work.' He also pointedly asked for an investigation to establish if the 'historical development of Negroes in America' led to the conclusion that 'they constitute a nation,' and demanded 'preparation of plans for a world conference of Negroes' in Moscow in 1929.'[11] This was an early indication that African American Communists would utilise the Sixth Congress in an attempt to overcome problems within the WP and would play a significant role in the deliberations on the Negro Question during the congress.

The Sixth Congress even prompted public complaints from the African American students at KUTV in Moscow to the leadership of the American delegation and the Negro Commission, about the poor and insanitary conditions they endured. They also complained that their studies had no relevance to American circumstances and were not 'touching in any way upon the conditions of Negroes internationally.'[12] It seems that William Patterson (known as Wilson in the Comintern) played a leading role in these protests just as he and the other

10. For an insider's account of these events see Haywood, *Black Bolshevik* pp.228-280. Haywood sat on the Anglo-American Secretariat's sub-commission along with his brother, two other African American students and James Ford.

11. J. Ford, 'Negro Work in America,' 11 May 1928, RGASPI 495/155/59/1-14. For details of Moore's communication to Ford see Turner, *Caribbean Crusaders*, pp. 158-159 and Solomon, *The Cry Was Unity*, pp.68-69. There is no evidence that such a conference took place but those Ford named were Richard B. Moore, Edward L. Doty, Isaac Musey, Lovett Fort-Whiteman and himself. Huiswoud and Briggs were suggested as possible substitutes. Fort-Whiteman and Ford were subsequently included in the American delegation to the congress the others were not.

12. 'American Political Bureau,' n.d., RGASPI 495/155/65/8-9.

African American students would also play a key role in the work of the Negro commissions and subsequent Comintern work on the Negro Question.[13]

The Sixth Congress and the work of the various commissions created the conditions for a thorough examination of the Comintern's approach to the Negro Question but this examination focused on the United States and South Africa, and on the two parties that apparently had the biggest role to play in addressing this question.[14] Even after the founding of the ITUCNW, African Americans were still seen as the vanguard of the 'Negro liberation' struggle, although the CPSA had the largest number of 'Negro' members. In both countries Communists had to address complex issues relating to a majority rural population, establish the precise nature of the struggle for national, social and democratic rights and be clear about the question of self-determination. These were contentious issues and on several occasions protagonists made reference to the Comintern archives and previous resolutions in order to lend weight to one perspective or another.[15] The congress also led to further research on conditions in the African continent,[16] and to the recognition that under the general heading of the Negro Question there were significant variations in local conditions.[17]

James La Guma and the 'Black Republic'

During James La Guma's visit to Moscow in 1927, representatives of the Comintern including its president, Bukharin, made efforts to change the orientation of the CPSA. Hitherto, despite some efforts especially after it had decided on its 'Africanisation' policy in 1924, the Party had found it difficult to attract African members. In early 1927 it was reported that out of a total of four hundred members only fifty were non-white, although African membership grew rapidly in the next two years.[18] There were over 1600 African members in 1928 and at the Party's annual conference in 1929 twenty out of a total of

13. W. Wilson, 'The Question of Students,' RGASPI 495/1555/65/10-11. The students' complaints were subsequently sent to the Political Secretariat of the ECCI by the leaders of the American delegation. RGASPI 495/155/65/1.

14. During the congress the Kresintern also established a 'Commission on Negro Work' the membership of which included Ford, Haywood, Patterson and other African American students. See 'Minutes of Meeting of Kresintern Commission on Negro Work,' 2 August 1928, RGASPI 495/155/56/42-43.

15. See e.g. J.L. Engdahl, 'The Activities of the American Communist Party among the Negro Workers and Farmers,' 11 June 1928, RGASPI 495/155/59/47-54.

16. RGASPI 495/155/63/1-7.

17. 'The Negro Question,' 16 August 1928, RGASPI 495/155/63/14-18.

18. Johns, *Raising the Red Flag*, p.186. La Guma suggested that the CPSA had about one hundred African members at this time.

thirty delegates were Africans.[19] By the time of the Sixth Congress the CPSA had already worked closely with the two most prominent African organisations, the ANC and the ICU, even though Communists including leading figures like La Guma had been expelled from the latter organisation at the end of 1926.[20] However, the general orientation of the Party was still to give primacy to the struggles of the workers, with some bias towards the white workers, even though the majority of the population were neither white nor workers. In short, the CPSA did not fully recognise the importance of organising amongst the African masses, including those in the rural areas, nor fully recognise the nature of the national liberation struggle in which in order to transform South Africa the 'Natives,' especially the workers, would play a leading role.

The CPSA's general orientation had been criticised at earlier congresses, most notably by Claude McKay at the Fourth Congress in 1922. In the course of advocating the convening of an 'International Negro Conference,' McKay had warned against allowing the CPSA, or the WP, to become the main organisers because they were not in his view 'class consciously enough interested in the Negro as revolutionary material.' To support this view he related his first talk with 'comrade Bunting,' who had allegedly told him that 'the natives were a discouraging element to handle,' and who he reported was 'lukewarm about the conference.' Apparently Bunting informed McKay that 'one faction of his party was opposed to the Communists working among the Negroes.' McKay informed Bunting about his own personal contact with an ANC delegation in England and concluded that, 'Comrade Bunting seems to know very little about these native agitators and their work.'[21]

The apparent weaknesses in the political orientation of the CPSA were also evident in its organisational structure. It was not a highly disciplined organisation based on the Comintern's principle of democratic centralism, nor were its basic organisations located amongst the urban or rural workers. In short, it required thorough 'bolshevisation' and, most importantly, a political reorientation. To some degree these weaknesses were exacerbated by limited contact between the CPSA and the Comintern and other parties, although the CPSA and its tasks had long been discussed. However, by 1927 some attempts were being made to solve this weakness too, including the invitation from the Anglo-American Secretariat to James La Guma, to visit Moscow in order to make a personal report on the work of the CPSA.[22]

---

19. Simons and Simons, *Class and Colour in South Africa*, p.406.

20. Ibid., pp. 353-356.

21. C. McKay, 'For a Negro Congress,' n.d. RGASPI 495/155/43/156-162.

22. See 'Proposals of E. Sachs to Comintern,' January 1926 in A. Davidson, et al. (eds.) *South Africa and the Communist International: A Documentary History* [vol.1] *Socialist Pilgrims to Bolshevik Footsoldiers 1919-1930* (London, 2003) p.143-144 and Johns, *Raising the Red Flag*, p.185-199.

During his visit to Moscow, La Guma, a leading 'Coloured' Communist and a leading figure in the ANC, who had also formerly been assistant general secretary of the ICU,[23] delivered his report about the problems facing the CPSA and held discussions with the Anglo-American Secretariat and also the Political Secretariat and the Presidium of the ECCI.[24] La Guma stressed that these problems were how to oppose the South African government's attacks on the African population and how to overcome the 'division between white and black labour.' In particular the question was how to develop a programme that would 'concentrate on the native masses,' and 'rally the workers around the Communist Party.' He added, 'the trouble is that if we formulate a platform to rally black workers there is a danger of alienating the white.'[25] It was during one of the discussions to address this problem that Bukharin, after criticising a draft resolution on South Africa, first suggested that the CPSA should raise and fight for specific demands 'such as a demand for a Negro republic independent of the British empire, or in addition for autonomy for the national white minorities etc.' Bukharin proposed that a committee should be established to draft a new resolution and concluded that 'Overall the CI must say very clearly that in the struggle between the Negroes and the whites that it is on the side of the Negroes.'[26]

Some months later, in July 1927, the Political Secretariat of the ECCI passed a resolution on South Africa that stressed the need to 'reverse the proportion of whites and natives in the Party,' and added that the CPSA 'should do everything possible to help the native comrades into the leadership of the Party.' The resolution also instructed the CPSA to agitate for 'an independent black South African Republic as a stage towards a Workers and Peasants' Republic with full autonomy for all minorities.' However, at the same time it was stressed that the Party should not lessen its work amongst the white population and that its first task was to reorganise itself and 'put forward a political programme of action as a necessary condition to fight for a mass CP of S. Africa.'[27]

This orientation was sometimes subsequently referred to as the Native or Black Republic thesis.[28] Looking back on more recent events in South Africa this does not appear to have been a very inappropriate demand to advance.[29] It

23. On La Guma see A. La Guma, *Jimmy La Guma – A Biography* (Cape Town, 1997).

24. Davidson et al, *South Africa and the Communist International*, p.149 n.1.

25. 'Statement of J. La Guma to Presidium,' ECCI, 16 March 1927, Ibid., pp.151-153.

26. 'Remarks of N. Bukharin to Presidium,' ECCI, 16 March 1927, Ibid., p.155.

27. 'Resolution on South Africa,' 22 July 1927, Ibid., p.161.

28. La Guma, *Jimmy La Guma*, p.36.

29. On the significance of the Resolution for the liberation struggle in South Africa see B. Bunting, *Moses Kotane - South African Revolutionary* (Belville, 1998), pp. 44,48 and B. Bunting, 'Introduction,' in E. Roux, *S.P. Bunting: A Political Biography* (Belville, 1993).

recognised the peculiar semi-colonial nature of the state in South Africa, and that the struggle that had to be waged was essentially an anti-imperialist one, a struggle for national self-determination by the masses of the people, or as it came to be called later in the century 'majority rule,' as the first stage towards establishing socialism in South Africa.[30] Most importantly, it stressed that the CPSA needed to present a programme of demands around which it would rally the people. But most of the leadership of the CPSA, both black and white members, strongly opposed the ECCI's policy, some even dubbing it 'Garvey-ism' and too similar to the slogan 'Africa for the Africans' which hitherto the CPSA had opposed. While others claimed that it would antagonise the white workers, and weaken the unity between them and black workers. Indeed some had no confidence at all in the struggles of the 'Natives.'[31] In response to such views the Comintern explained that:

> Only the driving out of the imperialists and the national liberation of the country will give the Native peoples freedom and opportunity to immediately and radically change their position. So the Native Independent Republic first and foremost means the anti-imperialist revolution, i.e. the driving out of the imperialists and the national liberation of the country...The construction of the socialist society will begin when the peasants, in the conditions of a Native Independent Republic, will themselves become convinced that a really prosperous and happy life is possible only in a socialist society, when together with the workers in the towns, under the leadership of the Communist Party, they will themselves take the matter in hand. Not the immediate building of socialism but the liberation of the country from the imperialist yoke.[32]

When La Guma returned to Moscow at the end of 1927, he reported that the leaders of the CPSA were in general opposed to the Comintern resolution, which was about to be debated at its Sixth Congress, and that they considered that it had been drafted by those 'with an insufficient knowledge of the situation in South Africa, especially "the widespread apathy of the native masses."'[33] At the CPSA's congress it was reported that the Party had made good progress in its work amongst Africans, and three Africans were elected to the CPSA's Central

30. Drew, *Discordant Comrades*, p. 96.

31. See e.g. La Guma, *Jimmy La Guma*, pp.37-42; 'Minutes of Meeting, Executive Committee, CPSA,' 15 March 1928, A. Davidson et al, *South Africa and the Communist International*, pp.177-178 and Roux, *S.P. Bunting* pp.121-122.

32. La Guma, *James La Guma*, pp.40-41.

33. 'Discussion on South Africa, 1 December 1927, Davidson et al, *South Africa and the Communist International*, pp.166-168.

Committee, but the Comintern resolution did not gain overwhelming support and La Guma feared that the CPSA might be split 'on colour lines.'[34] Nevertheless, in Moscow he suggested that the reasons advanced by the CPSA leadership for opposition to the Resolution 'were abundantly refuted by everyday facts.' Indeed he stated that such arguments drove 'the non-European comrades to the conclusion that the Central Executive of the South African Party considers the mass movement of the natives should be held up until such time as the White worker is ready to extend his favour.'[35]

In fact the CPSA did not make any formal response to the Resolution but heated debate within the Party continued in the period leading up to the Sixth Congress in July 1928. Paradoxically this was the very period when the CPSA was starting to make some headway amongst Africans both in urban and even rural areas and hundreds were joining the Party.[36] It had also received strong support from Gumede of the ANC whose visits to Brussels and the Soviet Union led him to speak out in support of the CPSA, the Soviet Union and Communism. At one meeting, for example, he declared to an ANC audience, 'the Bantu has been a Communist from time immemorial.'[37] The Cape Town branch of the ANC echoed Gumede's support for the CPSA and declared that it was 'the only political party that champions the cause of the workers of South Africa irrespective of colour and knows no colour discrimination within its ranks.'[38] However, since the majority in the leadership of the CPSA refused to accept the Resolution, it was thoroughly discussed again within the special Negro Commission established by the Sixth Congress.[39]

The role of La Guma, the first 'Coloured' member of the CPSA to reach Moscow, is an interesting one and he has been credited with being the 'co-author, together with the Comintern, of the "Native Republic" thesis and chief architect of its adoption.'[40] He was certainly seen in this light by some of the leaders

---

34. J. La Guma to V. Demar, 10 January 1928, ibid. pp.173-174.

35. J. La Guma, 'Report on the South African Situation,' quoted in Simons, *Class and Colour in South Africa*, p.395.

36. In 1928 it was reported that the CPSA had 1750 members of whom 1600 were Africans. Editorial note, *South African Communists Speak 1915-1980* (London, 1981) p.80.

37. Simons, *Class and Colour in South Africa*, p.402 and 'Turning Point in African History,' editorial in *The South African Worker*, 2 March 1928, *South African Communists Speak* pp.87-88.

38. 'Workers' Confidence in the CP – Capetown ANC Resolves Support – Answer to Disrupters,' Report in *The South African Worker*, 25 May 1928, *South African Communists Speak* p.88.

39. 'Introduction,' in A. Davidson et al, *South Africa and the Communist International*, p.12.

40. M. Adhikari, 'Introduction,' to La Guma, *James La Guma*, p.10; Simons, *Class and Colour in South Africa*, p.389.

of the CPSA at the time. Edward Roux, for example, even suggested that he was 'a bit of a racialist,' while Sidney Bunting accused him of 'black chauvinism.'[41] It is certainly evident that he was much more than just a go-between in the discussions between the Comintern and the CPSA.[42] He provided evidence to support the drafting of the Resolution and supported it with cogent arguments based on Lenin's views on the struggle against imperialism. He had no doubt been influenced by the discussions that had occurred in Brussels on the Negro Question where, as part of the South African delegation, he had presented a resolution championing 'the right to self-determination through the complete overthrow of capitalism and imperial domination.' This resolution, which championed an anti-imperialist struggle by the African masses, was certainly not based on existing CPSA policy. Similar discussions must also have taken place with other African and 'Coloured' members within the CPSA, especially within the Cape Town branch where Johnny Gomas, another 'Coloured' Communist active in the ANC and ICU, was a leading figure.[43] However, in his initial statement to the ECCI La Guma merely asked for advice about how to implement the decision of the Comintern that the CPSA 'should concentrate on the native masses.'[44] This was the decision taken at the CPSA's third national conference at the end of 1924, which included 'supporting every form of native movement which tends to undermine or weaken capitalism,' and was based on the Cominern's 1922 Thesis on the Negro Question.[45]

The 'Native Republic' thesis itself appears from the documentary evidence to have been first proposed by Bukharin but its precise origins remain unclear and it is quite possible that La Guma played some role in shaping it. Before the Executive Committee of the CPSA, La Guma stated that 'he had suggested that a rallying cry was needed for the workers of S.A.'[46] Once the thesis had appeared La Guma was its most zealous advocate, who not only maintained contact with Petrovsky, the head of Anglo-American Secretariat and Chair of the Negro Commission during the Sixth Congress, but also even made it clear

41. Roux, *S.P. Bunting – A Political Biography*, p.122 and for Bunting's comment Minutes of Negro Commission, 23 August 1928, RGASPI 495/155/56/130.

42. See e.g. S.P. Bunting to E.R. Roux, 5 December 1928, in Drew, *South African's Radical Tradition,*pp.98-101.

43. D. Musson, *Johnny Gomas, Voice of the Working Class – A Political Biography* (Cape Town, 1989) p.47 and Simons, *Class and Colour in South Africa*, p.389.

44. 'Statement of J. La Guma to Presidium, ECCI, 16 March 1927, Davidson et al, *South Africa and the Communist International*, p.153.

45. See e.g. the remarks of William Kalk quoted in 'Editorial note,' *South African Communists Speak* p.80.

46. Minutes of Meeting, Executive Committee, CPSA, 15 March 1928, Davidson et al., *South Africa and the Communist International,* p.178.

that he had no faith in other members of the leadership of the CPSA, including Roux and Bunting, the Party's delegates to the congress.[47] Indeed, La Guma wrote that he intended 'to change the leadership' at the Party's next congress and openly attacked decisions that had already been agreed by the CPSA's Central Committee.[48] Most importantly, according to Haywood, La Guma was not just involved in the discussion that led to the initial thesis but also took part in the work of the sub-commission that developed and reformulated the thesis ahead of the Sixth Congress. That sub-commission, which included Haywood, three other African Americans studying in Moscow and occasionally James Ford, emphasised the importance of the 'agrarian question' and, according to Haywood, even proposed that the CPSA should adopt the slogan 'return of the land to the Natives,' which although it did not appear in the final resolution, somewhat resembled the slogan *Mayibuye iAfrica* that was already becoming popular in South Africa.[49]

Harry Haywood and the Black Belt Thesis

The sub-commission of the Anglo-American Secretariat, which prepared the resolution on South Africa, also prepared the Resolution on the Negro Question in the United States and once again Harry Haywood played a key role. Haywood, born Haywood Hall Jr., was then a thirty year-old African American ex-railroad worker, who joined the CP in the United States in 1925, after joining the Young Communist League (YCL). Here he was following in the footsteps of his brother, Otto Hall, who had previously recruited him into the ABB. In 1926 Haywood was sent to Moscow to study at the University of the Toilers of the East (KUTV) and a year later he became the first black student to be admitted to the more advanced Lenin School. It was as a student, three years after joining the CP, that he took part in the discussions regarding the future orientation and work of both the American and South African communist parties.

According to Haywood's account, he had first been introduced to the concept of 'the right of self-determination for Afro-Americans in the Black Belt, the area of their greatest concentration,' in the southern United States in 1924 when, at the request of the Comintern's president Zinoviev, it had been

47. The other delegate was Rebecca Bunting, a leading member of the CPSA and the wife of Sidney Bunting.

48. See J. La Guma to Petrovsky, 22 August 1928, Davidson et al, *South Africa and the Communist International*, pp.187-188.

49. Haywood, *Black Bolshevik*, pp.235-240.

discussed and then rejected in the YCL[50] It is interesting to note that a focus on the Black Belt may have occurred even earlier. One document dating from around the time of the Fourth Congress of the Comintern referred to the Black Belt as a 'veiled protectorate,' and 'virtually a colonial possession of the United States existing right within its own territory.'[51] In 1928 the thesis was again proposed, this time by a Russian, Nikolai Nasanov of the Young Communist International, who had been that organisation's representative in the United States.[52] Nasanov's thesis was, 'that US Blacks were essentially an oppressed nation whose struggle for equality would ultimately take an autonomous direction and that the content of the Black liberation movement was the completion of the agrarian and democratic revolution in the South – a struggle left unresolved by the Civil War and the betrayal of Reconstruction.'[53] This notion, that African Americans were not just a minority but a 'nation within a nation,' for whom racism was a 'device of national oppression,' and for whom the right to self –determination ('political power in their own hands') in the Black Belt should apply, was gradually and even reluctantly accepted by Haywood, who subsequently became its greatest champion.

For Haywood there was a particular concern to combat the idea that the tradition of nationalism amongst African Americans, that had reached a high point with Garvey and the UNIA, must necessarily be reactionary. This he felt was the thinking of the WP, which argued that the solution to the problems facing African Americans would be found in the class struggle of black and white workers, and which therefore underrated the struggle for what was later called civil rights and full emancipation of those in the South. This latter struggle, Haywood began to argue, had a revolutionary potential of its own and therefore the struggles of African Americans, especially those in the South, were even more important than had hitherto been recognised. [54] In Haywood's new thinking, 'the Garvey movement crystallised in itself the powerful nationalist sentiment of the Negroes,' and Garveyism and other forms of nationalism simply 'expressed the yearning of millions of Blacks for a nation of their own.' Haywood

50. Haywood, *Black Bolshevik*, p.134. The Black Belt was defined as an area that 'has no formal state designation and lacks boundaries, [which] runs through five states and includes 214 counties of which some have a colored population as high as 90 per cent of the total.' H. Haywood, 'The Negro Problem and the Tasks of the United States,' quoted in Foner and Allen, *American Communism and Black Americans*, p.173.

51. J.L. Engdahl, 'The Activities of the American Communist Party among the Negro Workers and Farmers,' 11 June 1928, RGASPI 495/155/59/50.

52. On Nasanov see Berland, 'Nasanov and the Comintern's American Negro Program.'

53. Haywood, *Black Bolshevik*, p.218.

54. Ibid. p.229.

therefore began to argue for a revolutionary nationalism based on the 'right of self-determination in the South, with full equality throughout the country'[55]

Haywood's concern with Garveyism reflected an ongoing concern of the WP that had initially attempted to work with Garvey's UNIA, by the early 1920s the largest African American organisation but also the largest black political organisation anywhere in the world. The ABB had initially believed that it could rival the UNIA, and that its rank and file could be won over to a wider anti-imperialist platform. Efforts to work with Garvey had been initiated by Briggs and the ABB even before their links with the American CP but had not been successful.[56] The efforts of the WP to work with the UNIA begun in earnest when Rose Pastor Stokes addressed the UNIA convention on behalf of the Party in 1921 and continued without any great success for several years. These efforts continued, however, based on the view that there was a latent militancy in Garvey's movement that was being dissipated and which could only be successfully harnessed by the Communists. At the time of the ANLC, held in Chicago in October 1925, Lovett Fort-Whiteman was still urging the WP to 'organise Communist factions' within the UNIA. These he envisaged would 'strive to surround themselves with the working class and poor farmer elements for the purpose of carrying on the struggle to transform the organisation into an organisation fighting for the class interests of the Negro workers in the United Sates.'[57] American Communists' concern with Garvey and the UNIA endured even after 1925 when Garvey was first imprisoned and then deported from the United States.[58] Indeed in 1929 Otto Huiswoud was sent as a delegate of the ANLC to the UNIA convention in Jamaica both to expose the UNIA and to try to recruit 'the Left delegates,' as well as to make 'connections with the trade unions in Jamaica and the local communist elements.'[59] Haywood's concerns therefore reflected the impact that Garvey and the UNIA had on the American CP and many African American Communists, as well as on the

55. Ibid. p.230 and H. Haywood, 'The Negro Problem and the Tasks of the CP of the United States,' quoted in Foner and Allen, *American Communism and Black Americans*, pp.175-176.

56. Solomon, *The Cry Was Unity*, p.26.

57. RGASPI 495/155/34/81. According to one report American Communists even discussed if Garvey should be invited to the Fifth Comintern Congress. See Draper, *American Communism and Soviet Russia*, p.330 .

58. See e.g. R. Minor, 'After Garvey – What?' J.H. Clark, *Garvey and the Vision of Africa* (New York, 1974) pp.165-173; C. Briggs, 'The Decline of the Garvey Movement,' Ibid, pp.174-179 and W.Z. Foster, 'The Garvey Movement: A Marxist View,' Ibid, pp.414-420.

59. RGASPI 495/155/80/49.

Comintern itself.[60] Some Communists believed that the successes of the UNIA showed that the 'Negro masses' were becoming more politically conscious, that even greater results might be achieved with Communist leadership but that the American CP was failing and on occasions refusing to provide this leadership.[61]

When the 'Haywood-Nasanov thesis' was first discussed in the Anglo-American Secretariat's sub-commission, however, no other African American supported it and the issue of self-determination or empowerment was poorly elaborated. The thesis put as much, if not more emphasis on 'the fight against white chauvinism,' indeed this was stated to be the 'central point in the thesis,' and the weakness of the leadership of the Party was that it 'did not see the necessity for fighting against it.' The point was also stressed that the 'Negro masses at the present time are a revolutionary factor,' and that the 'prerequisites of a nationalist movement' existed in the United States. On this basis it was proposed that 'our slogan must be social equality and self-determination.'[62] Perhaps the main characteristic of the discussion that ensued was that it was initially conducted mainly along factional lines, reflecting the on-going struggle that existed in the American CP.[63] The thesis included criticisms of existing party policy and therefore left itself open to the accusation of having been 'drawn up for factional purposes.'[64] Support for it came from those allied with the Foster faction but even they seemed to be unsure about exactly what self-determination entailed, and were content to conclude that 'the Negroes in America are both a racial and national minority.'[65] Factionalism was strongly condemned by Petrovsky, who chaired the sub-commission's meetings. He too considered that the Negro Question was both a national and racial problem and initially argued that 'now is not the time' for the slogan of self-determination. For his part, James Ford

60. For his own experiences and analysis of Garveyism see Haywood, *Black Bolshevik*, pp.101-114. For a summary of the American Party's view of Garvey and the UNIA see W.Z. Foster, *The Negro People in American History* (New York, 1982) pp.442-452; C. Briggs, 'The Decline of the Garvey Movement,' and C. Briggs, 'Briggs Replies to Garvey Editor Who Claims Garveyism and Communism Are Kindred,' in P.S. Foner and H. Shapiro, *American Communism and Black Americans: A Documentary History* (Philadelphia, 1991) pp.83-86.

61. See e.g. S. Katayama, 'Action for the Negro Movement Should not be Postponed,' RGASPI 495/155/17/9-12.

62. 'Meeting of Negro Commission,' 2 August 1928, RGASPI 495/155/56/46-50.

63. 'Discussion at Negro Commission Meeting,' 3 August 1928, RGASPI 495/155/56/53 and 'Statement by Ford at Negro Commission,' 3 August 1928, RGASPI 495/155/56/54-55. Factional activity had been rife in the WPA since its foundation. For some reflections on how this impacted on the Party's approach to the Negro Question see Haywood, *Black Bolshevik*, pp.14-143, 187-191, 246-256. See also Solomon, *The Cry Was Unity*, pp.64-65 and Turner, *Caribbean Crusaders*, pp.114-117.

64. RGASPI 495/155/56/52.

65. 'Meeting of Negro Commission,' 2 August 1928, RGASPI 495/155/56/49-50.

was unenthusiastic about the thesis mainly because he considered it to be part of an academic discussion. He proposed that the sub-commission concentrate on the question of the 'concrete steps' that needed to be taken to develop the Party's influence among 'Negro workers.'[66] William Patterson was rather more supportive but also thought that more practical issues needed discussion.[67] The most surprising intervention came from Nasanov who, according to the minutes, declared 'In the programme of the American party we must include the right of self-determination but at the present time it is not a burning issue.'[68]

The sub-commission sent a resolution to the Negro Commission that emphasised the need for 'self-criticism' within the American CP and a fight against 'white chauvinism,' as well as the need to strengthen 'the Communist movement amongst the Negroes,' and to 'place greater emphasis on the working class character of the Negro work.' It also stressed the need to work in the South, pointing out that 'the peasant question lies at the root of the Negro racial (national) problem.' Opposing the view that characterised the Negro masses as the 'reserve of capitalist reaction' it stressed that the task of the Party was to 'transform these masses of the Negro population into the allies of the working class and the reserve of the revolutionary movement against American imperialism.'

Moreover, the resolution also argued that:

> The Negro question in the USA should be treated as part and parcel of the general international Negro problem. The aim of our work amongst the Negroes should be to organise the USA Negroes as the champions of the international Negro movement against imperialism;' and that 'while fighting the cause of the Negroes as an oppressed race and while underlining the international race character of the Negro movement, the Party must also bear in mind that in the South of the USA there are certain prerequisites which lead to the future development of a national revolutionary movement among the Negroes. The Party must be prepared for this possible development of the Negro movement theoretically and politically.[69]

However, no specific proposals were made on the question of self-determination. The fact that the Negro Question in the US was placed within an international context is noteworthy. It suggests that the policies that the Comintern would put in place to address particular problems within the US and within

66. RGASPI 495/155/56/53-55.

67. RGASPI 495/155/56/92.

68. RGASPI 495/155/56/89.

69. 'Resolution of Negro Commission,' (Draft) 4 August 1928, RGASPI 495/155/56/94-95.

the American CP might also be designed to address problems confronting the 'international Negro movement.'

The Sixth Congress of the Comintern

The Sixth Congress of the Comintern, held in Moscow in July and August 1928, has been interpreted in various ways. Its main significance lies in the fact that it was the first occasion at which the CI was able to present a fully developed political programme that analysed the global political situation and provided practical guidelines for the work of all the communist parties. The congress accepted the view that the post-war years could be divided into three periods. The current 'third period,' it concluded, was one of overproduction in which the capitalist world would become increasingly unstable, leading to economic crises, 'a fresh series of imperialist wars; among the imperialist states themselves; wars of the imperialist states against the USSR; wars of national liberation against imperialism and imperialist intervention, and to gigantic class battles.'[70] Based on this analysis and in these circumstances the Comintern advanced the slogan 'class against class,' in order to guide all the communist parties in what were described as 'maturing conditions for a new revolutionary upsurge.'[71] As the 1920s appeared for some still to be 'roaring', the analysis and conclusions of the CI were contemptuously ridiculed outside the Communist movement at the time. However the economic and political events of the next decade, the Depression, rise of Nazism, fascist invasion of Ethiopia, labour rebellions throughout the Caribbean and eventual outbreak of World War Two, suggest that the CI was perhaps not so far off the mark. In fact, even though the Congress agreed a common programme there were heated debates during its proceedings, and major divisions within many parties. The British delegation, for example, refused to accept the thesis on the colonial question,[72] while the main report delivered by Bukharin, was strongly criticised by many including the members of his own delegation. Indeed the Russian delegation proposed some twenty amendments that almost amounted to a new report and the first public criticism of Bukharin.[73]

It was evident that the Negro Question would be a major issue at the congress, it featured in Bukharin's report and was mentioned by Fort-Whiteman,

70. W.Z. Foster, *History of the Three Internationals: The World Socialist and Communist Movements from 1848 to the Present* (New York, 1955) p.358.

71. J. Stalin,'Disagreements in Regard to the Comintern,' in *Problems of Leninism* (Pekin, 1976) p.346.

72. *Inprecor*, 21 November 1928 p.1529 and 27 December 1928, 1743-1744. See also Haywood, *Black Bolshevik*, pp.272-275.

73. Haywood, *Black Bolshevik*, pp.257-258 and 274.

one of the first speakers at the congress, who addressing the delegates on behalf of 'the Negroes of the United States,' declared 'only the Communist International can free Negroes.'[74] Bukharin stressed the importance of the 'Negro problem' and was critical of those parties that had not paid it sufficient attention, as well as those where there were 'survivals of race prejudice.' This was also seen as a major problem and was alluded to frequently, especially by African American Communists.[75] Bukharin declared that 'even on the Commissions of the Comintern a wrong note is detected when questions concerning the Negro problem are discussed,' an apparent reference to the discussion on South Africa. He added that it was the duty of all to 'fight mercilessly against the slightest manifestation of race prejudice,' and he concluded that the 'Negro problem' needed to be studied not just in regard to North America but also South Africa and elsewhere.[76] His report became an occasion for criticism of the work of individual parties in regard to the Negro Question and, in the case of the WP, for a continuation of factional struggle.[77]

James Ford criticised Bukharin's report for not commenting sufficiently on the colonial question, as it related to Africa and the Caribbean, nor on the factional struggle in the American Party, which he claimed had hampered the 'Negro work.' Ford lamented the fact that although the African American population in the United States was over 12 million, 'we have no more than 50 Negroes in our Party.' He alleged that 'Negro comrades' had been driven out of the Party, and that there was 'evidence of white chauvinism.' Furthermore, he claimed that an investigation of the Comintern archives had revealed at least nineteen resolutions and documents on the Negro Question, but not one of them had been carried out or discussed by the WP. Having established weaknesses in the work of the American Party, Ford then turned his attention to Africa and the Caribbean where, he said, there were millions of 'Negro workers' and 'rumblings of revolt.' There too, he argued, Bukharin should have stressed the need for activity and he called for the delegates of the British, French and American parties to meet at the congress 'in a special commission for the discussion of work among the Negro workers in these colonies.' In conclusion, he predicted 'the next great revolutionary wave will come from the Negro workers, and the exploited workers and peasants of the colonies, in which Negro workers live.' It was 'under the banner of the Comintern,' he suggested, that 'the Negro

74. *Inprecor*, 25 July 1928, p.708.

75. See the document drafted by J. Ford, W. Patterson and A. Sik, 'The Communist Party and Race Prejudice,' n.d. RGASPI 495/155/59/179-186.

76. *Inprecor*, 14 August 1928, p.872.

77. *Inprecor*, 3 August 1928, p.781 and Ibid, 11 August 1928, p.847 and p.851.

workers will be found fighting for the overthrow of capitalism and the downfall of imperialism through the world.'[78]

Others who spoke on the Negro Question in the United States included Jones (Otto Hall) who criticised the factionalism and chauvinism that existed in the American Party but suggested that all the 'Communist Parties in the imperialist countries' needed to address the issue of 'white chauvinism.' He also complained that the 'opportunist attitude' of the WP accounted for the weaknesses in its approach to the Negro Question.[79] The veteran Japanese Communist Sen Katayama, who had been a worker in the US for over twenty years made similar criticisms. He reminded the congress that Lenin 'considered the American Negroes as a subject nation' and also criticised the American Party for its 'criminal neglect of the Negroes.' He urged the congress to seriously consider and decide on a policy for what he called 'Negro problems.'[80]

The Colonial Question and Africa

The question of the liberation of the African continent was discussed is some detail at the congress although mainly from the perspective that the Comintern's work in the continent needed to be strengthened. Otto Kuusinen, one of the leading figures in the Comintern, who presented the main report on the 'revolutionary movement in the colonies,' lamented the fact that there was very little revolutionary activity in Africa and as the delegates from the CPSA were the only representatives from the continent, much of the focus was on South Africa. Bunting suggested that expressions such as 'the return of the country and land back to the black population,' as well as raising the demand for a 'Native Republic' would antagonise white workers.[81] He continued to criticise the Native Republic thesis, and his speech was itself criticised for its reference to South Africa as 'a white man's country.'[82] Roux's interventions, although focused on other parts of the African continent, appear to have been mainly designed to show that South African was very different from the rest of Africa and that a strong nationalist movement for independence would not

78. *Inprecor*, 3 August 1928, pp.772-773.

79. *Inprecor*, 8 August 1928, pp.811-812.

80. *Inprecor*, 11 August 1928, pp.856-857.

81. *Inprecor*, 8 November 1928, pp.1451-1453 and Drew, *South Africa's Radical Tradition*, pp.86-93. See also Haywood, *Black Bolshevik*, pp.269-272.

82. *Inprecor*, 3 August 1928, p.782. See also Drew, *South Africa's Radical Tradition*, pp.77-80. For Bunting's response see *Inprecor*, 21 September 1928, p.1156. For Roux's recollection of this incident and his experience of at the Sixth Congress see Roux, *S.P. Bunting*, pp.118-130.

develop there. He too argued that the Native Republic thesis was inappropriate for South Africa.[83] Rebecca Bunting also made an intervention in which she criticised Bukharin's report for ignoring women and commented that there were few women delegates at the congress. She highlighted the importance of African women workers and demanded that political work amongst women be taken up by the entire Communist Party and not just by women comrades.[84]

The discussion on the colonial question raised many contentious issues about the economic and political consequences of imperialism, the nature of the struggle that needed to be waged against it in Africa and other issues that constituted a significant part of the congress.[85] In the course of the discussion on the colonial question several speakers suggested that the Comintern needed to pay more attention to the anti-colonial movements already in existence on the African continent.[86] Others, such as Lozovsky, pointed out the growing importance of Africa for the colonial powers and the increasing penetration of US and other capital into the continent.[87] The Belgian delegate, Jacquemotte, detailed the growth of capitalist exploitation in the Congo and the corresponding growth of an industrial proletariat in that country and urged much greater joint activity between the communist parties in the imperialist countries and anti-colonial movements in the colonies.[88] It became clear in the course of the Sixth Congress and especially in its Resolution on the Negro Question that henceforth the Comintern would attempt to develop its activities throughout the African continent.

The Comintern's approach to colonialism was in stark contrast to that adopted by the LSI, which meeting in Brussels had recently issued its own resolution on the colonial question. This provided the opportunity for a thorough examination and critique by Ercoli (Palmiro Togliatti), one of the leading figures in the Comintern.[89] He made a major intervention exposing the history of the LSI in regard to colonialism, in which he pointed out that although in the past it had disguised its true aims, it now openly supported colonial rule and opposed the right of self-determination for subject peoples and oppressed

83. *Inprecor*, 11 August 1928, pp.854-855. See also Drew, *South Africa's Radical Tradition*, pp.81-86.

84. See *Inprecor*, 11 August 1928, p.839.

85. See *Inprecor*, 4 October 1928, pp.1225-1233.

86. *Inprecor*, 30 October 1928, pp.1392-1393.

87. *Inprecor*, 30 October 1928, p.1413, also Wilson, *Russia and Black Africa*, pp.173-174.

88. *Inprecor*, 17 October, 1929, p.1317.

89. Ercoli, 'Social Democracy and the Colonial Question,' *Inprecor*, 4 October 1928, pp.1234-1243.

nations. He presented numerous examples highlighting the reactionary role played by the British Labour Party and French Socialist Party.

Although some of the affiliates of the LSI still claimed to be Marxists there were no major discussions on Africa or the Negro Question in Brussels. However, in the material submitted to the Brussels Congress, parties and trade unions were invited to give their views on 'the colonial problem.' A memorandum submitted by the British Labour Party, which was soon to govern Britain's empire for the second time, made clear its views and in regard to the right of self-determination declared: 'In the African territories generally the inhabitants are not yet in a position to govern themselves.' The Labour Party declared that British colonial rule had not yet educated Africans sufficiently for self-government and at the same time had destroyed 'native institutions and native organs.' In a patronising fashion it concluded, 'the sudden abandonment of the Africans would lead to complete anarchy. The policy to be aimed at, therefore, is the preparation as rapidly as possible of the African people for self-government.'[90] The Labour Party also spoke approvingly of colonial rule as 'trusteeship for natives,' declared that the League of Nations mandate system was 'based on the right principles,' and comforted itself with the view that 'it is possible to mitigate the impact of capitalism on the primitive or feudal cultures.'[91] Other parties expressed similar views. The South African Labour Party declared, 'Self-government can only be applied gradually and must depend on the fitness of the native races for such self-government. The form thereof must be such as is best suited to their need and their degree of development.'[92]

The Section Français de l'Internationale Ouvrière (SFIO), the French Socialist Party, mainly favoured the policy of assimilation in regard to the colonial subjects of France but demanded equal rights for those who managed to become French citizens. It expressed its views most forcefully and most clearly in regard to the national liberation struggle then taking place in Morocco and the approach of the Communists by accusing the latter of 'demanding an insane policy *immediate evacuation* of Morocco as of the whole of Northern Africa.' (italics in original) In contrast it declared that: 'The Socialists have rigorously analysed by the light of Marxist principle, these dangerous utopias – dangerous for the cause of civilisation and thus for socialism itself, as well as for the cause of the natives whom it claims to protect and who would thus be thrown with an appalling thoughtlessness into the most bloody and desperate adventure.'[93]

---

90. *The Colonial Problem – Material submitted to the IIIrd Congress of the Labour and Socialist Internationa*l, Brussels, August 1928, p.15.

91. Ibid. p.16.

92. Ibid.p.89.

93. Ibid p.169.

In regard to the Negro Question in the United States, which so occupied the Comintern, little was said. The SPA merely declared that 'with regard to the question of coloured workers, the Party is opposed to their exclusion by the great trade unions of the white workers.[94] As far as the colonies were concerned, the Brussels congress merely demanded some reforms, such as the restriction of forced labour and limiting of taxation, although it also found it appropriate to condemn racial discrimination in industry. But the nature of the reforms was limited and colonialism as an imposed system of exploitation and oppression was not questioned. In regard to land ownership, for example, the congress declared that only land 'not already appropriated by Europeans should be recognised as the property of the native community.'[95] The congress not only approved of the mandates system but actually thought it should be expanded. Its view, that colonies were a trust more for the benefit of the colonisers than the colonised, was perfectly illustrated in its demand for 'the adoption of an open door policy in all the colonies, absolute equality for the trade and industry of all nations and the right of all citizens of all countries to settle in all colonial territories.'[96] Its entire approach to colonial rule, which was essentially one of support, led to representatives from colonial countries walking out of the Brussels congress in protest.[97].

According to James Ford the 'colonial guests' at the LSI congress had declared that:

> Having examined the decisions of the colonial commission of the Socialist Labour International, we have arrived at the conclusion that these decisions in their present form are inconsistent with the equality of nations and with the principle of self-determination and equality of peoples should be applied to all oppressed nations and subject races without any distinction whatever.[98]

Ford condemned the attitude of the Second International which proclaimed that under socialism 'the emancipated proletariat will proceed to emancipate all the oppressed people,' and that therefore there was no need for any struggle 'for the social equality of the oppressed races.' He also condemned the LSI's denial of the right to self-determination on the basis that colonial people were 'not quite fully developed,' as well as the views of the SPA. It was evident that in

94. *Report submitted to the 3rd Congress of the Labour and Socialist International*, Brussels, 5-11 August, 1928, p.150.

95 Ibid. p.176.

96 Ibid. p.178.

97. *Inprecor*, 4 October 1928, p.1243.

98. *Inprecor*, 25 October 1928, p.1345.

regard to colonialism and other matters, stark and significant differences existed between the two internationals.

The Negro Commission

The Negro Commission, originally called for by Ford, was established as a sub-committee of the Colonial Commission of the Sixth Congress and was chaired by Otto Kuusinen, one of the most senior figures in the ECCI. Its membership comprised representatives from several parties including the CPSA and a large delegation from the United States, with five African American members, among them Haywood, Hall and Ford.[99] Although Haywood presented the subsequent debates on the Negro Question in the United States as polemical and especially singles out the opposition of Ford and his brother, the minutes of the Commission meetings suggests that much of the discussion and drafting of the Resolution on the Negro Question in the US was undertaken by smaller sub-committees without major disputes. It was not only concerned with the issue of self-determination but with establishing a clear orientation for the American party's 'Negro work,' particularly in regard to trade unions and the struggle against 'white chauvinism.' Haywood and his brother, as well as Ford were prominently involved in the deliberations, and although Otto Hall remained opposed, the Negro Commission subsequently accepted the thesis on self-determination 'to the point of separation and organisation of a separate state' by a vote of ten to two.[100]

According to the minutes of the Commission there was considerable discussion but surprisingly little disagreement. Haywood emphasised the need to 'recognise the nationalist tendencies among the Negroes,' adding, 'although they are not a nation.' The principle of self-determination was initially proposed by Bittleman, one of the main leaders of the WP, but as a tactical consideration not as the right of a nation. It was accepted by the chairman on the basis that 'when we fight for self-determination in the programme of the American Party, we are fighting against the principle of white chauvinism.'[101] This was formulated as the requirement for the WP to 'fight for the full rights of the oppressed Negroes and for their right to self-determination and against all forms of chauvinism amongst the workers of the oppressing nationality.' After further submissions

99. *Inprecor*, 21 September 1928, p.1156. Although Kuusinen was the chairman the fist session was chaired by the vice-chair, Petrovsky.

100. 'Negro Commission,' 7 August 1928, RGASPI 495/155/56/97-103 and 'Minutes of Negro Commission, 11 August 1928, RGASPI 495/155/56/111-116. Haywood, *Black Bolshevik*, pp.260-268 and Solomon, *The Cry Was Unity*, pp.78-81.

101. 'Negro Commission,' 7 August 1928, RGASPI 495/155/56/97-103.

and discussion the principle of self-determination as formulated was almost unanimously accepted although it was also agreed that the demand for 'social equality' remained the 'central slogan of the party for work among the masses.'[102]

The so-called 'Haywood-Nasanov thesis' was justified on the grounds that it was based on an analysis of the concrete conditions, as well as on some of the views of Lenin, but perhaps it could also be argued that it borrowed something from the ideas that had been advanced by the ABB, Hubert Harrison and others several years before. It was certainly discussed and initially agreed upon in the context of the factional struggle within the WP and the specific problems confronting the Negro work in the United States, especially the neglect of the South and the need to overcome 'white chauvinism.' However, it was economic and political conditions that were initially presented as the cause of 'Negro nationalism', not the fact that African Americans were a nation. In one significant article Haywood used the term 'national minority' but his focus was mainly on the African American 'nationalist movement' and how it might be given revolutionary aims and leadership. Fighting for the rights of African Americans was also seen as important as they were 'to give leadership to the revolutionary struggles of the Negroes of the entire world against imperialism,' a role which was highlighted throughout the deliberation before and during the Sixth Congress, not withstanding the fact that the ITUCNW was also in existence.[103]

The main significance of the deliberations was that the Negro Question was henceforth established as one of the major questions that had to be addressed by the American CP. This included the issue of 'white chauvinism,' which became a major concern not only within the American Party but also throughout the Comintern.[104] Henceforth, a great emphasis was placed on organising in the South of the US, where the majority of African Americans lived in the most oppressive conditions but where almost no work had been undertaken by the Communists.

The centrality of the Negro Question consequently raised the profile of the leading African Americans within the WP and the Comintern.[105] Ford had already been elected to a leading position in the Profintern, Haywood's meteoric rise would continue as he became a key figure in the Negro Bureau established by the Eastern Secretariat of the ECCI, and Huiswoud, who was not even part of the American delegation to Moscow, was elected by the congress as a candidate member of the ECCI. As well as the discussions within the Negro Commis-

---

102. 'Minutes of the Negro Commission,' 11 August 1928, RGASPI 495/155/56/111-116.

103. H. Haywood, 'The Negro Problem and the Tasks of the CP of the United States,' p.172.

104. See e.g. Bukharin's comment at the Sixth Congress that 'survivals of race prejudice are still to be observed in some parties.' *Inprecor*, 11 August 1928, p.872.

105. For the minutes of the Negro Commission meeting of 2 August 1928 see RGASPI 495/155/56/46-50; and 3 August 1928, RGSAPI 495/155/56/52-56.

sion, and in the sessions of the congress, there was also the publication of several major articles in *The Communist International* by Ford, Patterson, Haywood, John Pepper, one of the leaders of the American Party, and Andre Sik, who taught at KUTV and was friendly with the African American students.[106] The articles suggest that in addition to the factional struggle there were also genuine attempts to arrive at a clear understanding of the Negro Question in the US and that for the African American Communists there was a strong desire to advance the 'Negro work' of their Party. As a result of the debates and the urging of these black Communists, the Negro Question had become a major issue for the Comintern.[107] The heated debates and wide-scale discussion also highlighted the fact that significant differences existed between the proponents of contending views. These differences not only concerned the political line within particular parties but on occasions also questioned the CI's entire Pan-Africanist policy. In an article in *The Communist International,* Andre Sik referred to the Resolution on the Negro Question adopted at the Fourth Congress as a 'radical error' and questioned all its main conclusions. He challenged the notion of 'self-determination' and a 'special Negro culture,' as well as the necessity to 'organise a world movement of Negroes' and an 'international organisation of the Negro people.' He even questioned the idea of 'American Negroes' as the 'advance-guard of the emancipation movement of the "entire Negro race."' [108]

The Native Republic Thesis

As regards the Commission's deliberations on the 'Native Republic' thesis for South Africa, these stemmed from the discussions that had been held with La Guma, the proposals subsequently made by the Comintern for the future work of the CPSA and the limited responses that the latter had made. In summary therefore the discussion in the Commission was based on the premise that the CPSA did 'not pay enough attention to the Negro problem, does not sufficiently stand as the champion of the Negroes and does not understand the peculiar relations of forces among the Negroes themselves;' and that the CPSA incorrectly believed that 'it can simply organise the masses of proletarianised

---

106. Foner and Allen, *American Communism and Black Americans,* pp.164-180.

107. See e.g. L. Fort-Whiteman's 'Propositions,' which amongst other things demanded a Negro Bureau of the CI and which stressed 'it is highly necessary that something special be done at this Congress on behalf of Negro work.' RGASPI 495/155/56/96. Also Cardenas's views on Latin America, 'To the Commission on work among Negroes,' RGASPI 495/155/56/108.

108. A. Sik, 'The Comintern Program and the Racial Problem,' in Foner and Allen, *American Communism and Black Americans,* pp.164-166.

Negroes directly into the Party itself.'[109] Regarding the last point, it seems clear that Bunting in particular was reluctant to continue working within the ANC and the ICU and argued that 'the native people' or at least the more militant sections could be drawn into the CPSA.[110]

It soon transpired that there were even differences between the CPSA delegates but after some discussion it was decided that a sub-commission would be appointed to draft a resolution repudiating the arguments of the leadership of the CPSA that were in opposition to the demand for a 'Native Republic.' Two of the three South African delegates, Bunting and Roux, were part of this body along with three Americans including Haywood.[111] For the CPSA delegates the key issue was that the slogan advanced by the CI might lead to an 'eventual race war' which would entail 'clashes with the class solidarity of black and white workers, which it is the Party's task to promote.' The delegation, which was composed of three leading white members who were all opposed to the CI Resolution, continued to argue that the Native Republic slogan would antagonise white workers whose support was important, and that in any case there was no national movement in South Africa. They proposed instead the slogan 'an independent workers and peasants South African republic with equal rights for all toilers irrespective of colour, as a basis for a native government.' In the event that the slogan could not be changed, they proposed that other measures should be taken, including further investigation of South African conditions by 'a real good English Communist.'[112] They eventually admitted that the leadership of the CPSA might have misunderstood the slogan but suggested that one of the problems was that it lent itself to such misinterpretation and that it had been initially introduced because La Guma had misrepresented the facts.[113] They also strongly objected to the way they were being treated and viewed with suspicion by others at the congress and in the Negro Commission.[114] According to Roux, the CPSA delegation was shunned throughout the congress and James Ford even refused to speak to them.[115]

The response they received to such complaints and proposals in the Negro Commission was not entirely unsympathetic. Petrovsky, the chairman of the

109. 'Minutes of Negro Commission,' 11 August 1928, RGASPI 495/155/56/111-116.

110. S. Bunting, 'Some Notes for S. African Delegate's Report to the Negro Sub-Commission,' 9 August 1928, RGASPI 495/155/56/117-128.

111. 'Minutes of Negro Commission,' 11 August 1928, Davidson et al, *South Africa and the Communist International*, p.186. See also RGASPI 495/155/56/111-116.

112. 'The Colonial Thesis on South Africa,' 25 August 1928, in Davidson et al, *South Africa and the Communist International*, pp.188-191.

113. Negro Commission, before 23 August 1928, RGASPI 495/155/56/129-131.

114. Ibid.

115. Roux, *S.P. Bunting*, pp.118-130. For an alternative view see Haywood, *Black Bolshevik*, pp.271-272.

Commission informed them that all their arguments were old ones, and stated that 'we have never thought to give up this slogan which is a fundamental one for us because full rights for the blacks in South Africa means a Native Republic and it cannot be interpreted in any other way.' He added 'there is nothing new and original in this resolution, nothing which is in any way outside the general line put forward by Lenin.'[116]

The new 'Resolution on the South African Question' was drafted and subsequently re-drafted by the Commission with the full participation of Roux and Bunting, indeed Bunting was a member of the Commission's editorial board charged with this task. The new Resolution credited the CPSA with many successes but pointed out that:

> South Africa is a black country, the majority of its population is black and so is the majority of the workers and peasants. The bulk of the South African population is the black peasantry, whose land has been expropriated by the white minority. Seven eighths of the land is owned by the whites. Hence the national question in South Africa, which is based upon the agrarian question lies at the foundation of the revolution in South Africa. The black peasantry constitutes the basic moving force of the revolution in alliance with and under the leadership of the working class.[117]

The Resolution also stressed that in these circumstances the CPSA did not show 'sufficient understanding of the revolutionary importance of the mass movements of the workers and peasants,' and that its opposition to the CI slogan showed a similar 'lack of understanding of the tasks of our Party in South Africa.' It was explained that 'the Comintern slogan of a native republic means restoration of the land to the landless and land-poor population... [but] does not mean that we ignore or forget about the non-exploiting elements of the white population.' Indeed the Resolution stressed the need for the Party to continue to work for the united struggle of the black and white workers who were 'the leaders of the revolutionary struggle of the native masses against the white bourgeoisie and British imperialism.' The CPSA was also required to strengthen the ANC and 'transform it into a fighting nationalist revolutionary organisation.' The Party was also required to 'reorganise itself on the shop and street nuclei basis,' develop 'a special paper in the chief native languages,' and develop a 'native' leadership.'[118] Such was the all-encompassing nature of the new CI Resolution on South Africa.

---

116. Negro Commission, 23 August 1928, RGASPI 495/155/56/129-158.

117. 'Resolution on the South African Question,' in *South African Communists Speak*, pp. 93-97

118. Ibid.

The Negro Commission, in which several African Americans played a significant role, eventually agreed to accept the self-determination thesis although its precise meaning remained contentious.[119] It also gave its support to the Native Republic thesis, despite continued opposition and attempts at amendments from the CPSA delegates,[120]who did however attempt to find ways to work according to the new orientation after the congress.[121] It is interesting to note that the Commission also concluded that 'The Negro question in the USA should be treated as part and parcel of the general international Negro problem. The aim of our work among the Negroes should be to organise the USA Negroes as the champions of the International Negro movement against imperialism.'[122] Thus both the Comintern's Pan-Africanist approach to the Negro Question and its assertion that African Americans should play a leading role internationally were maintained and if anything enhanced by the deliberations during the Sixth Congress.[123] When the Resolution on the Negro Question in the US was finally published in October 1928 this emphasis was also evident:

> The Negro Question in the United States must be treated in its relation to the Negro questions and struggles in other parts of the world. The Negro race everywhere is an oppressed race. Whether it is a minority (USA etc.), majority (South Africa) or inhabits a so-called independent state (Liberia, etc.), the Negroes are oppressed by imperialism. Thus, a common tie of interest is established for the revolutionary struggle of race and national liberation from imperialist domination of the Negroes in various parts of the world. A strong Negro revolutionary movement in the USA will be able to influence and direct the revolutionary movement in all those parts of the world where the Negroes are oppressed by imperialism.[124]

119. 'Minutes of Negro Commission,' 11 August 1928, RGASPI 495/155/56/113

120. See e.g. 'The Colonial Thesis on South Africa,' in Davidson et al, *South Africa and the Communist International*, pp.188-191.

121. See e.g. E.R. Roux to Wolton, 5 September 1928, E.R. Roux to Central Executive CPSA, 25 September 1928 and S.P. Bunting to Roux, 5 December 1928, in Drew, *South Africa's Radical Tradition*, pp.93-101.

122. Negro Commission, 7 August 1928, RGASPI 495/155/56/99. A sub-commission on the Negro Question outside the US and South Africa had also been established and consisted of Kuusinen, Petrovsky and Williams, subsequently Haywood, Ford, Bunting and Cardenas were added. RGASPI 495/155/56/102.

123. See e.g. 'Resolution on Work Among the Negroes of the USA,' 25 August 1928, RGASPI 495/155/49/1-14.

124. Foner and Allen, *American Communism and Black Americans*, p.192.

In regard to South Africa the CI issued two slightly different versions of the Native Republic thesis. In its 'Resolution on the South African Question' the CPSA was instructed to advance the slogan of 'an independent native South African republic, as a stage towards a workers' and peasants' republic, with full rights for all races, black coloured and white.'[125] While as part of the 'Thesis on the Revolutionary Movement in the Colonies and Semi-Colonies' the CPSA was urged 'to put forward the slogan for the creation of an independent native republic, with simultaneous guarantees for the rights of the white minority, and struggle *in deeds* for its realisation.'[126] (italics in original) The issue of the 'struggle in deeds' would become a major one for the CPSA in the years that followed.

The Comintern's approach to South Africa and the United States was summed up in a general resolution on the Negro Question adopted by the Sixth Congress. This pointed out that 'the position of the Negro varies in different countries, and accordingly requires concrete investigation and analysis.' Apart from its focus on South Africa and the US special emphasis was placed on the African colonies. The communist parties in the major imperialist countries were again instructed to 'put an end to the indifference' which they had exhibited, to make every effort to expose the 'bloody exploits' of imperialism and offer every assistance to the anti-colonial movements in the colonies.[127]

Historical Significance

Some historians have tried to suggest that behind the Comintern's approach to the Negro Question in the United States can be detected the invisible hand of Joseph Stalin, or the domination of Moscow. There seem to be several anecdotal links to Stalin. One is Otto Hall's recollection that when he and other African American students met Stalin at the Kremlin, he (Stalin) stated that: 'the whole approach of the American party to the Negro question is wrong. You are a national minority with some of the characteristics of a nation.' Hall also reported that he and the others did not respond favourably to Stalin's suggestion.[128] Another is contained in a letter from Joseph Z. Kornfeder, a member of the American delegation and the Anglo-American Secretariat, to the historian Theodore Draper. Kornfeder claimed that he alerted Bittleman, to 'Stalin's Self-determination Thesis,' before the Sixth Congress took place, in order to give Bittleman's faction

125. *South African Communists Speak,* pp.93-94.

126. Ibid. p.91.

127. Foner and Allen, *American Communism and Black Americans,* pp.196-198.

128. Draper, *American Communism and Soviet Russia,* p.334 and Haywood, *Black Bolshevik,* p.219.

an advantage, and that he had been informed about the thesis by Lozovsky.[129] A third is contained in another letter to Draper from William Kruse, who recalled that while he was a student at the Lenin School he was invited to hear a presentation on the subject of the self-determination thesis, given by a Russian professor, which Stalin also attended.[130] Whatever the truth and reliability of these accounts, it is clear that Nasanov and other Russian Communists played a key role in the discussions, but it is also important not to ignore the wider African American context and in particular the role of Haywood and others. What cannot be ignored are the many heated debates that occurred throughout the Sixth Congress, in the various commissions and in print. Kornfeder's claim certainly suggests that factionalism within the American Party was a key factor in the debates but although Bittleman and his allies were generally more supportive of the Haywood/Nasanov thesis that does not seem to have been a major factor determining the content nor the acceptance of the final Resolution.

The notion of a 'nation within a nation,' was certainly not new and can be found in the writings of Martin Delany in the nineteenth century, and even the demand for self-determination had its precedents in the views of Hubert Harrison and others.[131] As Haywood pointed out, the nature of the struggle unfolding in the United States in the 1920s did have several characteristics of a movement for national liberation, even though, he argued, it was being diverted away from a revolutionary path under the influence of Garveyism. Here again, as Haywood makes clear, Comintern policy drew not only on Lenin's comments suggesting that African Americans might constitute a nation, but also on their own experiences of struggle. It is clear that Haywood drew on and re-evaluated his own experiences of Garveyism in order to develop his analysis of the revolutionary potential of the African American liberation movement and undoubtedly also his experiences in the ABB. The role of Haywood, and other African American students, in debating and developing this new policy is itself significant and shows that within the ranks of the Comintern the influence of African American Communists might be considerable. Haywood subsequently became a member of the ECCI's Negro Bureau, a strong position from which to influence policy within the American CP and elsewhere and with a direct hand in a revised resolution on the Negro Question in the US in 1930.[132] Indeed the

---

129. Kornfeder to Draper, 18 May 1958, Draper Papers 18/24, MARBL, Emory University; Turner, *Caribbean Crusaders*, p.158 and Draper, *American Communism and Soviet Russia*, p.334.

130. Ibid.

131. On Harrison's demand for 'a state or states, in the Union as a homeland for the American Negro,' see J.B Perry (ed.) *A Hubert Harrison Reader* (Middletown, 2001) p.402. See also W.Z. Foster, *The Negro People in American History* (New York, 1982), p.478.

132. Solomon, *The Cry was Unity*, p. 83.

new Negro Bureau of the Eastern Secretariat of the ECCI was a direct consequence of 'the request of Negro comrades' and the emphasis on the Negro Question that existed during the Sixth Congress. It was established in December 1928 in order to 'conduct research, propaganda, and agitation, as well as the building of connection with the negroes.'(sic) In fact it began to monitor the implementation of the decisions of the Sixth Congress and had a particular interest in the American CP, since its members were mainly African Americans, including Ford and Patterson as well as Haywood.[133]

In the 1928 thesis on the Negro Question in the US, what was stressed for the first time was that the 'oppression of the Negro masses', provided the necessary conditions 'for a national revolutionary movement among the Negroes' and that this necessitated that the Communists 'must come out openly and unreservedly for the right of self-determination in the southern states, where the Negroes form a majority of the population'.[134] But it should be stressed that the issue of self-determination was only mentioned in one of twenty-six clauses and that the overall emphasis of the thesis was on the importance of Negro work in general. One clause, for example, was entirely devoted to the issue of 'the Negro woman in industry' and the double oppression they faced but this does not seem to have merited the same attention.[135] It also seems to be the case that in 1928 self-determination meant 'full emancipation,' or what today might be termed empowerment. However, the revised thesis of 1930 laid even greater stress on the necessity of the majority of African Americans in the South having the right to govern themselves, pointing out that in certain revolutionary conditions this could involve secession.[136] It was a thesis around which discussion and controversy would rage for some years with many of the leading African American Communists, such as Huiswoud, Richard B. Moore and Cyril Briggs, initially opposed to it with some even complaining of 'Garveyism'.[137]

The question has been posed as to why there was a need for two theses on the Negro Question in the US, one that emerged from the Sixth Congress in 1928, to be followed by another only two years later. In his autobiography Haywood explained that this was necessitated by the lack of understanding of the 1928 thesis within the American CP and he pointed to the publication in 1930 of an article by Otto Huiswoud, the head of the Party's new Negro Department,

133. 'Draft Resolution on the Organisation of a Negro Bureau Attached to Eastern Secretariat,' 22 November 1928, RGASPI 495/155/54/6-7. See also H. Hayward to the CP of the USA, 30 September 1929, RGASPI 495/155/80/79.

134. *Resolution of the Communist International on the Negro Question in the US*, October 26, 1928.

135. Ibid.

136. *Resolution of the Communist International on the Negro Question in the US*, October 1930.

137. Turner, *Caribbean Crusaders*, pp.168-170.

entitled 'World Aspects of the Negro Question.' This made no mention of self-determination and referred to 'the National-colonial character of the Negro question in Africa and the West Indies and the racial character of this question in the United States.'[138] Huiswoud's article led to a lengthy response from Haywood but the apparent confusion within the WP, which was also connected with the on-going factional struggle, led to significant muscle flexing by the new Negro Bureau in which Haywood and Nasanov played key roles.[139] It seems that it was at the insistence of the Negro Bureau that the ECCI issued a new more detailed *Resolution on the Negro Question in the United States* in 1930.[140]

The 1930 resolution placed much more emphasis on 'the right of self-determination of the Negroes in the Black Belt' and on the peculiar situation of African Americans as 'an oppressed nation,' whose oppression stemmed not just from racism but more importantly from the economic and political legacy of slavery. It was for this reason that the resolution also stressed the importance of 'confiscation of the landed property of the white landowners and capitalists for the benefit of the Negro farmers,' and even the establishment of a 'Negro state' in the Black Belt, which would include a 'white minority.'[141] The resolution made it clear that in the Comintern's view, self-determination included the right to choose separation from the US, although Communists would not in all circumstances be in favour of such separation, nor of 'reactionary Negro separatism' and Garveyism. Although the resolution clearly had international significance, unlike the 1928 resolution it contained no mention of the global Negro Question.[142] According to one source the new resolution with its clarification of the issue of state separation had only emerged after a fierce struggle in

138. Haywood, *Black Bolshevik*, pp.321-325; also Foner and Shapiro, *American Communism and Black Americans*, pp.1-8. Huiswoud subsequently made a self-criticism and announced that he fully supported both CI Resolutions. See O. Huiswoud, 'Report to the Eastern Secretariat on the ANLC Convention,' 19 December 1930, RGASPI 495/155/87/441-445.

139. See e.g. 'Proposals of the Negro Bureau to the American Commission,' 7 May 1929, RGASPI 495/155/70/13-15.

140. Haywood, *Black Bolshevik*, pp.331-338. The ECCI Resolution and Haywood's 'Against Bourgeois-Liberal Distoritions of Leninism on the Negro Question in the United States,' can both be found in Foner and Shapiro, *American Communism and Black Americans*, pp.17-50. For Haywood's views on the 1930 Resolution which suggest that the thesis left room for much further clarification see his speech of 24 November 1930, RGASPI 495/18/810.

141. For Hayward's interpretation suggesting this was not an immediate demand see H. Haywood, 'Some Amendments to My Speech before the American Commission,' n.d., RGASPI 595/155/102/117-122.

142. 'Resolution on the Negro Question in the United States,' in Foner and Shapiro, *American Communism and Black Americans*, pp.36-50.

the Political Secretariat of the Comintern where leading figures had apparently been opposed to changing the 1928 resolution, from which it is claimed Stalin himself had proposed removing all references to 'full separation.'[143] Whether this was actually the case, it is worth noting that the commission that drafted the 1930 resolution included in addition to Haywood, Ford, Patterson, various other American Communists and according to Haywood, 'several Black students' who were based in Moscow at the time.[144]

What had been highlighted in the theses, as has been pointed out, was the right of African Americans to choose their own future, and the fact that African American's desire for liberation had a potentially revolutionary character that should not be under-estimated. At the same time, it provided a new basis for the struggle against racism in the US and 'white chauvinism' and factionalism in the American CP. It also created the conditions for encouraging a new approach and a re-evaluation of African American history and culture.[145] In one historian's estimation, it opened up a new chapter in the history of what had now become the Communist Party of the USA (CPUSA), for the first time allowing Communist ideas to circulate amongst the bulk of the African American population in the South.[146] Indeed in many ways the decisions of the Sixth Congress compelled the American Party to develop and expand its work amongst the African American population of the South, despite the obvious difficulties in so doing. It has now become established that the CPUSA played a crucial role in the struggle in the South, and as one recent scholar has put it the Communists, 'redefined the debate over white supremacy and hastened its end.'[147] Within the Comintern the Negro Question and 'white chauvinism' would certainly not be ignored, particularly in the United States, where African American Communists were more likely to be propelled into leadership positions, but also throughout the ranks of the CI.[148]

Some have also tried to suggest that the new Black Republic thesis was something imposed on South African Communists by a Comintern dominated by Russians, who had other interests, not those of Africans at heart, just as the 'Black Belt thesis' was allegedly imposed on the American CP.[149] Others take a different view and Robin Kelley has argued that 'the Comintern Resolution

143. Klehr and Thompson, 'Self-Determination in the Black Belt, pp.354-366.

144. Haywood, *Black Bolshevik*, p.332.

145. Solomon, *The Cry Was Unity*, pp.86-87.

146. Kelley, *Hammer and Hoe*, p.13.

147. G.E. Gilmour, *Defying Dixie: The Radical Roots of Civil Rights 1919-1950* (New York, 2008) p.6.

148. For some of the consequences in the US see Solomon, *The Cry was Unity*, pp.129-146.

149. See e.g. Johns, *Raising the Red Flag*, pp. 213-214.

reflected the actual struggle of Africans in South Africa as well as Africans in the United States.'[150] Here it is interesting to note the view of a young CPSA member who joined the Party a few days after her arrival from Latvia in 1929. She subsequently wrote:

> The fact that African men and women did not have the right to vote was atrocious to me, and I was a wholehearted supporter of a Black Republic, a democratic Black Republic. It would be black because the majority of the people are black, and the 'Native Republic' slogan inspired in Africans a determination to reject white domination. It was a ray of hope for freedom and equality with other peoples.[151]

Here what is perhaps most important is not to lose sight of the particular problems facing Africans and African Americans in their respective countries, as well as their involvement in developing and adopting theses to address these problems.

Self-Determination in Cuba

Although the Comintern's 1930 Resolution did not specifically mention the global Negro Question, it certainly had an impact outside the United States. In Cuba, the only country in the Caribbean that had a communist party, the thesis on self-determination was adopted and applied during the early 1930s to a region of the Oriente Province. This was considered Cuba's own '*Franja Negra,*' a direct translation of the American term 'Black Belt,' where Afro-Cubans formed ninety per cent of the population. Here the Cuban Communist Party (PCC) supported self-determination to the point of secession, if the population so desired it, as well as championing an anti-racist programme throughout the country.[152] The Party made it clear that it did not necessary advocate secession but supported the right of Afro-Cubans in Oriente to empowerment and to exercise self-government. The Party's view was that such self-government could only be established as a consequence of a revolutionary struggle that confiscated the property of the major landowners and placed it in the hands of all the toilers. Moreover, it also saw the necessity for the removal of US troops and the naval base at Guantanamo, both of which were seen as a 'major instrument of the national oppression

150. Kelley, 'The Third International and the Struggle for National Liberation in South Africa,' p.99.

151. R. A. Simons, *All My Life and All My Strength* (Johannesburg, 2004) p.58.

152. B. Carr, 'Identity, Class, and Nation: Black Immigrant Workers, Cuban Communism, and the Sugar Insurgency, 1925-1934,' *Hispanic American Historical Review*, 78/1 (February, 1998) pp.83-116.

of the black,' as a vital part of this anti-imperialist struggle.[153] In the PCC too it appears that there was resistance from the 'leading comrades' to the introduction of the self-determination slogan because they considered that it did not apply to Cuba. Once again part of the justification for the demand was the existence of a nationalist movement amongst Afro-Cubans, which had been particularly evident in the rebellion of the *Partido Independiente de Color* (PIC) against the Morua Law in 1912 when, it was claimed, one of the main slogans of the rebels had been 'A Negro Republic in the Orient.'[154] But the PCC also thoroughly discussed the 'National Question,' and attempted to ground its practice in the theory on the subject developed by Lenin and Stalin.[155] It declared 'the black question in Cuba is a national question with a strong class component.' Although it seems that sometimes Afro-Cubans in Oriente were referred to as a 'national minority,' at the Party's second congress it was emphatically stated that there was 'the necessity of a greater clarification of the Negro question as a national rather than a "racial" question typified in the slogan for self-determination of the Negroes in the Black Belt of Oriente province.'[156]

The adoption of the self-determination thesis was no doubt influenced by the PCC's links with the Profintern's Caribbean Bureau based in New York, as well as with the American CP, and these connections grew stronger in the 1930s.[157] In 1934, for example, William Patterson secretly attended the convention of the Cuban section of International Red Aid, known as Defence Obrera Internacional (DOI). The DOI was encouraged to follow the PCC's lead in relation to the Negro Question. In regard to Oriente Patterson pointed out:

> There is the Cuban black belt, the homeland of the oppressed Negro nation of Cuba. The existence of democratic rights to these people means in the last analysis the granting to them of the right of self-determination. Defence Obrera Internacional endorsed the demands launched by the party of the working class for the right of self-determination for this group. It accepted the slogan of full social, political and economic equality for Negroes as its own.[158]

153. 'Projecto Resolucion Negra,' n.d. RGASPI 495/105/107.

154. 'Report on work in Cuba and Mexico,' 19 July 1932, RGASPI 495/105/61. On the PIC and the consequences of 1912 see A. de la Fuente, *A Nation For All: Race, Inequality, and Politics in Twentieth Century Cuba* (Chapel Hill, 2001) pp. 66-91. See also 'Report on the Situation of the Negro Race in Cuba,' 3 March 1930, RGASPI 495/155/87/60-66.

155. 'Los Negros En Cuba Cono Nacionalidad Oprimida' 26 September 1932, RGASPI 495/105/64.

156. M. Valencia, 'The Second Party Congress of the Communist Party of Cuba,' *Inprecor*, 15 June 1934, pp.909-910 and de la Fuente, *A Nation For All*, p.192.

157. See e.g. Carr, 'Identity, Class, and Nation,' pp.99 n.9 and 101.

158. W. Patterson, 'The Convention of the Cuban IRA,' *Inprecor*, 14 July 1934, p.1012.

However, such policies were also clearly aimed to deal with local problems and particular weaknesses of the PCC and other Communist-led organisations. The policy placed a particular emphasis on work amongst Afro-Cuban women, for example, pointing out the particularly humiliating oppression that they faced and the lack of Afro-Cuban women in the Party.[159] The Party's programme not only took into account the discrimination faced by Afro-Cubans but also the racism directed at immigrant workers from other Caribbean islands, especially those from Jamaica and Haiti, many of whom worked in the sugar industry. This industry was considered the most 'proletarianized' section of the Cuban economy, a vital area for the PCC where black workers predominated.[160] The province of Oriente contained not only a majority Afro-Cuban population but also about 100,000 migrant Jamaican and Haitian workers, and was seen as one of the most militant regions in the country.

Although the introduction of migrant workers had created some divisions amongst workers even in Oriente, the migrants proved their 'fighting spirit' and the PCC reported that they were in the 'front ranks of the struggle' and joining the Communist-led organisations.[161] In 1933 it was reported that all these 'Negro workers' were not only participating in the general strike but also the occupation of the sugar mills. Moreover, it was noted there was 'an ever growing disposition and will to struggle for their national liberation as well as the struggle for full economic, political and social equality for the Negro.' This revolutionary struggle in Oriente greatly alarmed the press and government in the United States and the Comintern's representative concluded that in his view: 'this is one of the decisive factors in the struggle of the Communist Party and the revolutionary proletariat which will determine the higher struggles of the masses for power.'[162] The Party's concern with the Negro Question was therefore based on the need to develop its work amongst a key section of the working class. It was also concerned to combat racist oppression throughout Cuban society, as well as overcoming 'white chauvinism,' and a lack of Afro-Cuban cadres in the PCC.[163]

---

159. 'Los Negros En Cuba Cono Nacionalidad Oprimida,' 26 September 1932, RGASPI 495/105/64.

160. J. Gomez -The Revolutionary Events in Cuba and the task of the C.P., *Inprecor*, 15 September 1934, pp.884-888; Carr, 'Identity, Class, and Nation,' p.99.

161. 'Report,' 2 December 1933, RGASPI 495/105/68.

162. 'Report of Comrade Bell on the Situation in Cuba,' 3 October 1933, RGASPI 495/155/69. On the mill occupations see B. Carr, 'Mill Occupations and Soviets: The Mobilisation of Sugar Workers in Cuba 1917-1933,' *Journal of Latin American Studies*, 28 (1996) pp.129-158.

163. B. Carr, 'From Caribbean backwater to revolutionary opportunity: Cuba's evolving relationship with the Comintern, 1925-1934' in T. Rees and A. Thorpe (eds.) *International Communism and the Communist International, 1919-43*, (Manchester, 1998) pp.234-53.

It is certainly clear that the PCC had its own weaknesses to overcome in regard to the Negro Question, and one report even claimed that 'one could say that there is no such thing as the Negro question in Cuba.'[164] In 1929 the PCC had referred to the allegedly low cultural level and docility of immigrant Caribbean workers and in 1931 admitted that there were 'practically no negroes in the Party.' In part this seems to have been because of 'white chauvinism' within the PCC. In 1932, for example, it was reported that the Party had not organised dances for youth in Havana because black youth would have participated and that in Santa Clara, Communists had proposed a halt to further recruitment since more than half of their members were Afro-Cuban and if they admitted any more it would deter prospective white members.[165] Within a few years however, the composition of the PCC including its leadership had changed. In 1934 Blas Roca was elected general secretary and Lazaro Pena, an Afro-Cuban, headed the *Confederacion Nacional Obrera de Cuba* (CNOC) the Communist-led national trade union federation.[166]

The Party's concern with the Negro Question extended to the CNOC, which campaigned against all forms of social, political and cultural discrimination against Afro-Cubans.[167] Indeed its orientation was in stark contrast to the trade union federations linked to the Machado regime, which championed immigration controls and attacked migrant Caribbean workers. The Communists while stressing the particular problems faced by Afro-Cubans or Caribbean migrants, also called for the unity of the working class.[168] Indeed the PCC also targeted racism and eurocentrism in all areas of cultural and social life. In 1933, for example, the Party's supporters campaigned against the ban on Afro-Cuban dancing enacted by the authorities in Santiago de Cuba.[169]

It is evident that there was some resistance to the Party's emphasis on the Negro Question and opposition to the thesis of self-determination inside as well as outside the PCC. Nevertheless the Party defended its position and refuted allegations that it was trying to divide the workers.[170] As in the United States, the CPP opposed the separatist policies of Garvey and the UNIA,

164. 'Report of Comrade Juan to the Caribbean Secretariat,' May 1931, RGASPI 500/1/5/40.

165. 'Report on Work in Cuba and Mexico,' 19 July 1932, RGASPI 495/105/61.

166. M. Valencia, 'The Second Party Congress of the Communist Party of Cuba,' *Inprecor*, 15 June 1934, pp.909-910; Carr, 'Identity, Class, and Nation,' pp.100-102; de la Fuente, *A Nation For All*, p.193.

167. This struggle was also necessary amongst some of its affiliates. See 'Report on Work in Cuba and Mexico,' 19 July 1932, RGASPI 495/105/61.

168. de la Fuente, *A Nation For All*, pp.189-190.

169. Carr, 'Identity, Class, and Nation,' pp.100-102.

170. 'Resolution de la Conferencia Nacional PCC,' n.d., RGASPI 495/105/70.

which organised in the country, as well as 'national reformist' trends promoted by Afro-Cubans. It argued that it championed the rights of Afro-Cubans to combat racism and oppose the disunity and mistrust this had caused in order unite the entire working class.[171] The self-determination policy was maintained until the Seventh Congress of the CI in 1935.[172] The adoption of this policy during the early 1930s, as part of the PCC's approach to the Negro Question with its emphasis on mobilising black workers, both native and foreign-born, is generally seen as one of the great successes of the PCC during the period and can be seen as one of the consequences of the Sixth Congress.[173] As one authority concludes, the Comintern's policies on the Negro Question had positive effects in Cuba; 'they turned the struggle for racial equality into a centrepiece of the PCC's work,' and 'highlighted the specificity of racial oppression.' As a result the PCC was seen by many in Cuba as the 'Negro party.'[174]

The Sixth Congress of the Comintern, which ushered in the 'third period' concerned itself with the liberation of the colonies and the right of self-determination not only for colonial inhabitants but also those oppressed in the United States and this emphasis also had important consequences for countries like Cuba and Brazil.[175] The Sixth Congress was clearly a turning point in regard to the Comintern's policy on the liberation of Africans and those of African descent. It called for those in Africa and throughout the Diaspora to be their own liberators, while struggling alongside all working and oppressed people to reclaim their lands and determine their own affairs, and for communist parties everywhere to step up their support for this liberation struggle. Monitoring and encouraging such activity was the new Negro Bureau of the Eastern Secretariat of the ECCI and the Profintern's new ITUCNW.[176]

171. 'Los Negros En Cuba Cono Naciondidad Oprimida,' 26 September 1932, RGASPI 495/105/64.

172. de la Fuente, *A Nation For All,* p.193 and A. Bosse, 'The Cuban General Strike, *Inprecor*, 30 March 1935, p.378.

173. A. de la Fuente, 'Two Dangers, One Solution: Immigration, Race, and Labor in Cuba, 1900-1930,' *International Labor and Working Class History*, 51 (Summer, 1997) pp.30-49 .

174. de la Fuente, *A Nation For All*, p.191.

175. On the Brazilian CP and self-determination see J. L. Graham, 'Representations of Racial Democracy: Race, National Identity and State Cultural Policy in the United States and Brazil.' (Ph.D Thesis, University of Chicago, 2010) especially pp. 33-41 and 47-59.

176. The ITUCNW soon criticised RILU 'adherents' in South Africa and the US for not implementing the decisions of the Sixth Congress. See 'Resolution on the Revolutionary Situation among Negro Workers, March 1930, RGASPI 534/3/499.

Chapter 3

The First International Conference of Negro Workers

The ITUCNW and The Negro Worker

The founding of the ITUCNW in July 1928 was a consequence of the failure of the communist parties of the US, Britain, France, South Africa and other countries to adequately respond to the Negro Question and implement decisions taken by the RILU and the Comintern. These failures were further highlighted and discussed at the Comintern's Sixth Congress and various explanations, including 'race chauvinism' were advanced both to explain the shortcomings and justify the creation of the ITUCNW. The ITUCNW was established with three main aims. The first was 'drawing Negro workers into the trade unions,' as well as creating new 'independent Negro unions' wherever racist practices made this necessary. In addition the ITUCNW was charged with 'setting up connections with the Negro workers of the world,' and the 'unification of the wide masses of the Negro workers on the basis of the class struggle.' The second was concerned with convening the long-awaited international conference of Negro workers and the third with publishing a 'special bulletin' *The Negro Worker*.[1] In addition the Sixth Congress had pointed to the need for the ITUCNW to focus its activities on Africa.

The Negro Worker was published regularly from July 1928 in both English and French, although there were only four editions between July and December 1928. In March 1930 it was announced that there would be two editions each month but very few copies still exist from this period. In January 1931 a new publication *The International Negro Workers' Review* was issued but there were only two editions before a new run of *The Negro Worker* recommenced on a monthly basis from March 1931. Not surprisingly the first edition made much of the growing size and importance of the 'Negro working class' and the problems facing Negro workers, as well as the need for trade union organisation and for the worldwide unity of the working class.[2] It focused almost entirely on the United States and South Africa and contained an article by Lozovsky, the head of the RILU, that was openly critical of the inability of the American CP and the Trade Union Education League (TUEL) to effectively organise amongst '5,000,000 Negro workers' in the US.[3] Subsequent editions expanded the geographical focus and placed increasing emphasis on Africa.

The focus of *The Negro Worker* necessarily reflected the major struggles that were being waged during this period. Chief amongst these was the uprising that broke out in French Equatorial Africa in 1928 but there were also major rebellions in Nigeria and Haiti and strikes or demonstrations in the Gambia, South Africa, Madagascar, Cuba, Barbados and other countries.[4] The uprising in the French Congo, the Kongo-Wara war, and its brutal suppression provoked protests by the Paris-based Ligue de Défense de la Race Nègre (LDRN) and a major campaign throughout 1929 by the French CP in the pages of *L'Humanité* and in the French National Assembly. The war lasted until 1932 and was in

1. 'On the RILU International Bureau of Negro Workers,' n.d. RGASPI 495/155/53/1.
2. 'The Aims and Purposes of The Negro Worker,' *The Negro Worker (NW)* vol.1 no.1 (July 1928) pp.1-3.The first edition was published just before the creation of the ITUCNW and edited by James Ford and Bill Dunne, the American representative in the RILU. Thereafter Ford became the main editor although sometimes assisted by Patterson and others. By 1929 the editorship had passed to George Padmore.
3. A. Lozovsky, 'The RILU and Negro Workers,' *NW*, 1/1 (July 1928) pp.3-5.
4. On Haiti see e.g. J. Wilenkin, 'Dollar Diplomacy in Haiti,' *NW*, 2/6 (December 1929) pp.4-8 'How the Haitian Workers Are Exploited,' *NW*, 3/4 (15 March 1930) p.12. This article announced 'There is a Communist Party starting in Haiti and that will be our leader.'

large part a consequence of the conscription of thousands of Africans who from 1921-1934 were forced to build the Congo-Ocean railway. At least 17,000 died as a result of this system of virtual slavery, which the French government at first tried to conceal.[5] The rebellion that broke out against colonial rule in South Eastern Nigeria, the *Ogu Umunwaanyi* or Women's War, involved thousands of women but was brutally suppressed by the colonial authorities and many were killed or wounded.[6] *The Negro Worker* was quick to highlight the fact that the massacre of over fifty unarmed women had taken place under a Labour government, which it referred to as 'the lackeys of British finance capital,' the same government which had attempted to suppress the strike for trade union recognition in the Gambia.[7] In these circumstances the designation 'His Majesty's Social-Fascist Government' did not appear entirely misplaced.[8] *The Negro Worker* was able to report that 'the revolutionary spirit amongst Negroes is rapidly exerting itself,' and to give numerous examples from Africa, the Caribbean and the United States. Moreover, it also pointed to the need for greater unity, suggesting that this would be an important issue to be addressed at the planned international conference of Negro workers.[9]

A Trade Union Programme of Action for Negro Workers

The basic programme of the ITUCNW was elaborated in *A Trade Union Programme of Action for Negro workers*, drafted by Ford and issued in early 1929, which addressed itself to the 'Negro toiling masses.' They, it declared, 'are subjected both to capitalist exploitation and imperialist oppression – they suffer both as members of the working class and of an oppressed race. In this or that

5. M. Joubert, 'A Negro Rebellion in French Equatorial Africa,' *Inprecor*, 8 February 1929, pp.111-112; S[téphane] R[osso], 'L'Imperialisme Français et les Peuples Nègres d'Afrique,' *L'Ouvrier Nègre*, 2/2, (March-April 1929) pp.13-14; 'Rapport sur la révolte des nègres de l'Afrique Equitoriale française,' 8 February 1929, RGASPI 495/155/77/1-30 and 'Discours du Comrade Kouyaté au Congrés de la Ligue,' *L'Ouvrier Nègre*, N.4 (August 1929) pp.25-28. See also J. Derrick, *Africa's 'Agitators' - Militant Anti-Colonialism in Africa and the West, 1918-1939* (London, 2008), pp.237-241 and R. Nzabakomada-Yakoma, *L'Afrique central insurgée: La Guerre du Kongo-Wara* (Paris, 1986) especially pp.150-154.

6. See E.O. Akpan and V.I. Ekpo, *The Women's War of 1929: A Popular Uprising in South Eastern Nigeria* (Calabar, 1998).

7. G. Padmore, 'Africans Massacred by British Imperialists,' *NW*, vol.2 (December 1929) pp.2-4 and J. Reed, 'The Strike of Negro Workers in Gambia,' ibid, pp.8-9.

8. G. Padmore, 'The Negro Liberation Movement and the International Conference, *NW*, 3/1-2 (January-February 1930) p.3.

9. Ibid.

country the one or the other form of oppression predominates.' But although the *Programme* recognised that there were some differences between the position of the 'Negro toilers' in the United States and those in the colonies, a concrete analysis of these differences was not yet well developed. As might be expected, the *Programme* largely addressed itself to conditions in the United States and South Africa, although other parts of Africa and the Caribbean were mentioned. A key focus was unity 'in the ranks of the labour movement,' the development of a 'united front' both nationally and internationally, although in addition some mention was made of the struggles facing agricultural workers and peasant farmers in Africa and the Caribbean. The *Programme* was based on eighteen demands or aims including: demands for equal pay, an eight-hour day, better housing and social conditions, housing and social insurance, special protection for women and young workers and the right to strike. It also included demands for civil rights, an end to racism and discrimination, the right to vote and the right to self-determination, although this right was only mentioned in regard to South Africa, the Caribbean and the United States. The *Programme* also called for a 'resolute fight' against what it called 'white terrorism' – lynching and state terror and for a fight against class collaboration and 'the influence of the Church and bourgeois and petty bourgeois ideas' including Garveyism and other movements, 'which detract the Negro workers from their fight hand in hand with the international working class, for their emancipation from the yoke of Capitalism and Imperialism.' Lastly the *Programme* alerted 'Negro workers' to the danger of war and war preparations. In particular it pointed out that 'it is almost certain the next war will be directed against the USSR' and it warned that the imperialists were already 'training black armies' both for this coming war and to for use against the workers in such countries as France and China.[10]

The Negro Bureau

The Comintern's approach to the Negro Question had been further developed and the status of the ITUCNW greatly enhanced by the deliberations at the Sixth Congress. As a consequence James Ford expressed the hope that 'special colonial and Negro sections' would be established in communist parties in Africa, the Americas and Europe and that all would cooperate with the new ITUCNW.[11] In fact all the old problems and weaknesses, which had led to the founding of the ITUCNW, remained to be solved. It was in an attempt to tackle some of these problems, particularly in relation to organising in Africa, and as a

10. *A Trade Union Programme of Action for Negro Workers.*

11. 'Resolution on Trade Union Work Among Negroes for the Negro Commission of the 6th Congress of the CI,' RGASPI 495/155/53/2.

result of the 'request of the Negro comrades,' that the ECCI decided in November 1928 to establish a Negro Bureau, which initially was to include members from the United States, South Africa, Cuba and Guadeloupe.[12] The Bureau was to function partly as means of facilitating liaison between the Eastern Secretariat and the Anglo-American Secretariat of the ECCI on the Negro Question. Its functions were 'to conduct research, propaganda and agitation, as well as the building of connections with the Negroes.'[13] It would in time also involve itself with the work of the ITUCNW and was, according to Haywood, its vice-chairman, something of a 'watch-dog committee' in regard to checking up on the decisions of the Sixth Congress.[14] In the summer of 1929 the Negro Bureau was reorganised as the Negro Section of the Eastern Secretariat of the CI but its remit remained extensive and included work with the RILU and the communist parties in the US, South Africa, France, Britain as well as those in Latin America.[15]

The Negro Bureau/Section soon started flexing its muscles and checking on the work of some of the major parties. In early 1929 it wrote to the CPGB, which had resolved during the course of its recent congress to strengthen its work in the colonies, to enquire about what practical work was being proposed for Britain's African and Caribbean colonies and to make its own detailed suggestions. Amongst other things it proposed that the LAI should be encouraged to do more work in regard to Africa, and that the CPGB should initiate work amongst the African and Caribbean population in Britain, as well as in the colonies, especially in relation to training prospective 'Negro' revolutionaries.[16] By the end of 1929 the Negro Section was sending additional requests and proposals to the CPGB, prompted by the 'revolutionary fermentation' in South Africa, Kenya and West Africa. However, it is evident that neither in Britain nor in British colonies were there any major advances. Apart from Johnstone (Jomo) Kenyatta, no African or Caribbean students were ever sent to Moscow from Britain and most of the Bureau's correspondence went unanswered.[17]

---

12. In fact the Bureau seems to have been dominated by American members, including Ford, Patterson and Haywood. It also included the Russian, Nasanov, and some of its meetings were chaired by Robin Page Arnot a leading British member of the ECCI.

13. 'Draft Resolution on the Organisation of a Negro Bureau Attached to Eastern Secretariat.' RGASPI 495/155/54/6-7.

14. Haywood, *Black Bolshevik*, p.281 also H. Haywood, 'The Work of the Comintern Among the Negroes,' 24 October 1929, RGASPI 495/155/77/187.

15. 'Plan of work for the Negro Section of the Eastern Secretariat,' 19 September 1929, RGASPI 495/155/74/18, 27-30.

16. RGASPI 495/155/67/2-6.

17. 'Work of the CPGB in the Negro Colonies,' 21 November 1929, RGASPI 495/155/70/59.

From the documentary sources it is evident the Negro Section functioned as another means of monitoring the 'Negro work' of the communist parties and the LAI. It tried to encourage them to engage in some activity and often worked in tandem with the ITUCNW. In the autumn of 1929, for example, it convened a special conference to check on all the American Party's 'Negro work.'[18] Haywood was not only the vice-chairman of the Negro Section but for a time also chaired the RILU Negro Bureau that had responsibility for the ITUCNW.[19] James Ford also remained a leading member of both bodies and in that capacity in early 1929 he was sent to Europe to meet with representatives of the French, Belgian and German communist parties.

Ford's meetings were designed to explain the work of the ITUCNW and to explore ways of working with the communists parties especially in connection with Africa. It was hoped that the three communist parties would be able to help with contacts in the colonies and, through sympathetic seamen, assist with the distribution of *The Negro Worker*. It was also intended that they would assist in other ways with the ITUCNW's programme, including developing work amongst African and Caribbean workers and students in Europe. However, the meetings merely served to highlight the weaknesses in the 'Negro work' especially in regard to Africa. The Belgian CP was very small and Ford reported that it 'had done very little work in the Belgian Congo,' and had almost no links with Africans, although possibilities existed for distributing *The Negro Worker* and establishing contacts with seamen in the port of Antwerp.[20] The PCF also admitted that it had carried out very little work in Africa or the Caribbean, or even amongst African troops who were at that time being deployed against strikers in France. A lack of suitable cadres was suggested as an explanation for this weakness, although the PCF also claimed to have over a hundred members of African and Caribbean origin and close links with the LDRN. The German CP also had the possibility of making contact with seamen in Hamburg and using those who were supporters of the Party to deliver material to African ports, in addition to holding meetings and carrying out other activities. Nevertheless, Ford's visit to Europe highlighted the weaknesses in 'Negro work,' as much

18. 495/155/67/28-29.

19. Negro section meetings often involved those temporarily in Moscow such as Padmore and Williana Burroughs (Mary Adams) an African American student and later a wartime announcer on Radio Moscow.

20. Measures to strengthen work with 'negro seamen' in Belgium and establish contacts in the Congo were subsequently taken by the Belgian Secretariat of the LAI. RGASPI 542/1/30/143-144.

as the potential that existed to develop it.[21] Subsequently the Negro Section and the ITUCNW began to focus much more on strengthening the work in Europe, especially with the PCF and the LDRN but also with the CPGB. In March 1929 the Eastern Secretariat of the CI announced that it planned to organise its own conference on colonial questions for all the western European communist parties.[22]

Ford's trip highlighted the priorities of the ITUCNW and the Negro Section. In his discussion with the three European communist parties he stressed the increasing rivalry that was developing between the big powers over resources and markets not only in Africa but also in the Caribbean and South America, as well as the attempts to consolidate and exploit existing colonies and the growing danger of a war between the big powers. This situation, he stressed, meant that both 'Negro troops' and the 'Negro proletariat' assumed even greater significance, as did the Negro Question itself.[23] The danger of war and the role of African troops that had been discussed at the Sixth Congress was also highlighted by a public appeal from the ITUCNW to 'Negro toilers' to join the first 'international day of struggle against imperialist war,' commemorated on 1 August 1929, and by efforts to encourage veterans to join the International Ex-Servicemen's Organisation.[24]

The Frankfurt Congress of the League Against Imperialism

The ITUCNW originally considered several different venues for the First International Conference of Negro Workers. Initially it was planned that it would be held in Moscow between July and August 1929, last no more than a week and be limited to fifteen delegates. Subsequently, Berlin was suggested as a venue for a conference to be held 'no later than October 1929'. However, it was

21. 'Report of trip in interest of the work of the ITUCNW of the RILU and the Negro Bureau of the Comintern, and the meeting of the Executive Committee of the LAI,' January 1929, RGASPI 495/155/70/62-68 and 'Report to the Political Bureau of the German Party on the work of the Comintern and Profintern in Negro Work,' 28 January 1929, RGASPI 495/18/889.

22. RGASPI 495/155/80/10-12.

23. 'Report to the Political Bureau and the Colonial Committee of the French Party on Negro Work,' 23 January, 1929, RGASPI 534/3/450.

24. 'Appeal to Negro Toilers to Join in the International Struggle Against Imperialist War,' RGASPI 495/155/76/5-7. See also RGASPI 495/155/70/66-67. Ford had spoken on the involvement of Negro and especially African troops in a future war at the Sixth Congress. He was a veteran of the First World War and a member of the executive committee of the United American Veterans, an organisation established by the American CP.

also envisaged that it might be held elsewhere in Germany, or in another city in Western Europe, and plans were then drawn up for a conference of twenty-five delegates, the largest number representing the United States. Expectations concerning participation were therefore quite modest, although it was hoped that the conference would include two 'Negro seamen,' from British and French ports, an unspecified 'London Students' Organisation,' possibly the West African Students' Union, and a 'Paris Negro group,' probably the LDRN.[25]

The plans for a conference in 1929 were soon shown to be impractical but the holding of the Second Congress of the LAI in Frankfurt, in July 1929, provided the opportunity to discuss the proposed conference in more detail. Ford therefore made the necessary preparation to make sure that a significant number of Negro delegates attended.[26] The Frankfurt Congress facilitated five separate meetings of delegates from a range of key organisations in Africa, America and Europe, who established a 'Negro Delegation' for the duration of the congress.[27] These meetings, convened by Ford and the ITUCNW, elected a Provisional Committee, with Ford as its chairman, to convene the conference which it was planned would now to be held in London in July 1930.[28] It is interesting to note that one of the most zealous supporters of the proposed conference was Sharpurji Saklatvala, the British-based Communist of Indian origin, who attended some of the 'Negro Delegation' meetings. Indeed it was Saklatvala who suggested that the conference should be held in London. His proposal was based on the fact that there were a 'large number of Negroes under the British Empire,' but also because there was the hope that the conference would serve to expose the the new Labour Government, which had taken office in June 1929. Saklatvala subsequently took part in some of the planning meetings for the London conference, as did British members of

25. RGASPI 495/155/53/3.

26. See RGASPI 542/1/30/48.

27. The organisations represented included the ANLC (Mary Adams/William Patterson), NAACP (William Pickens), TUEL (James Ford) and Haitian Society from the US (Henry Rosemond); the Federation of Non-European Trade Union and the Trade Union Congress, from South Africa; the LDRN (Garan Kouyaté); and the Kenyan Kikuyu Central Association (J. Kenyatta). Representatives of British and French trade unions, the Indian National Congress and the All-China Trade Union Federation also participated in these meeting. There were earlier indications that there would be a delegate from the Dominican Republic but there do not appear seem to have been any representatives from Latin America in Frankfurt, although the proposed conference was discussed at the founding conference of the Latin American Labour Federation, held in Montevideo in May 1929. See RGASPI 542/1/30/70 and ITUCNW to Munzenberg, 14 June 1929, RGASPI 542/1/33/7.

28. Ford, who was a member of the Executive of the LAI, had initially argued that the LAI should postpone its congress until after the ITUCNW's conference, at that time scheduled for the autumn of 1929. 'Speech of Comrade Ford at the meeting of the Executive Committee of the LAI,' 16 January 1929, RGASPI 534/3/450.

the LAI Executive such as Reginald Bridgeman and James Maxton, an MP for the Independent Labour Party, who promised his assistance in Parliament.[29]

The LAI congress was notable also for the participation of two Africans, Johnstone (Jomo) Kenyatta of the Kikuyu Central Association and Garan Kouyaté of the LDRN who, along with Mary Adams of the ANLC, were subsequently invited to visit the Soviet Union by the Russian Trade Unions. Kouyaté delivered a major speech to the congress, condemning French imperialism in the Congo and elsewhere and recalled Senghor's participation at the founding congress in Brussels.[30] Kenyatta had only arrived in London from Kenya a few months previously but quickly made contact with the LAI through Ladipo Solanke, of the London-based West African Students' Union (WASU).[31] In Frankfurt Ford set out the views and programme of the ITUCNW, demanded 'complete and unconditional independence' for the African colonies, and stressed that the masses must be the 'driving force' in the liberation movement, while the intellectuals 'must be the servants of the masses.'[32]

The 'Resolution on the World Negro Question' presented by Ford to the congress, was a detailed document prepared by the Negro Bureau. It contained the first detailed analysis of the political situation throughout the African continent including Ethiopia, Liberia, Haiti and the French Congo.[33] Compre-

---

29. 'Report on the Negro Question at the LAI Congress,' RGASPI 534/3/450. See also *Inprecor*, 19 June 1930, p.530. William Patterson and Mary Adams were also members of the initial organising committee.

30. 'Discours du Comrade Kouyaté au Congrés de la Ligue,' *L'Ouvrier Nègre*, N.4 (August 1929) pp.25-28.

31. H. Adi, *West Africans in Britain, 1900-1960- Nationalism, Pan-Africanism and Communism* (London 1998) p.45. The WASU, which regularly received copies of *The Negro Worker*, was specifically criticised in Ford's report to the Congress, for what he referred to as its 'hazy ideas about the liberation of Africa.' Ford had made a similar criticism of the WASU at the meeting of the Executive Committee of the LAI in January 1929. RGASPI 495/155/70/74-76.

32. J.W. Ford, *The Communists and the Struggle for Negro Liberation* (New York, n.d.) pp.9-20. This idea would be presented in an elaborated form in the *Declaration to the Colonial Workers, Farmers and Intellectuals* at the Pan-African Congress held in Manchester and largely organised by Padmore sixteen years later. See H. Adi and M.Sherwood, *The 1945 Manchester Congress Revisited* (London, 1995) p.56. Padmore does not appear to have participated in the Frankfurt congress, although several accounts suggest that he did. See e.g. J.R Hooker, *Black Revolutionary: George Padmore's Path from Communism to Pan-Africanism* (London, 1967) p.13 and I. Geiss, *The Pan-African Movement: A History of Pan-Africanism in America, Europe and Africa* (New York, 1974) p.333. However, Padmore was elected to the provisional organising committee along with others who had not been present in Frankfurt. See *L'Ouvrier Nègre*, N.4.

33. 'Draft Resolution on the World Negro Question,' RGASPI 495/155/72/40-58 and 495/155/74/8.The leading members of this Bureau were Ford, Haywood and Patterson.

hensive in scope, it attacked both 'Negro reformism' and social reformism and amongst other things demanded immediate evacuation of the colonies by the big powers and their complete independence.[34] As Ford later reported, it was discussed for several hours in Frankfurt, largely because of the opposition of William Pickens of the NAACP.[35] The Negro Bureau had voiced its concerns about Pickens, the NAACP and their 'conciliatory reformism' several months before the Congress, when the LAI announced that Pickens would be the official 'reporter' on the Negro Question. Patterson, on behalf of the Negro Bureau suggested that a 'co-reporter,' perhaps a member of the Bureau should also be appointed.[36] Subsequently, however, the Eastern Secretariat's Commission on the LAI seems to have agreed that Pickens should not be asked to act as a reporter but that Ford and La Guma, who was subsequently unable to attend, should fill that role.[37]

Only three years earlier, Pickens had been held in somewhat higher esteem. At the time the WP was still trying to work with organisations such as the NAACP and the UNIA, or at least with some sections of these organisations. In 1926 Fort-Whiteman had written suggesting that Pickens might be one of a party of three intellectuals invited to tour the Soviet Union. He added, 'personally you stand very much in favour in the regard of our Party leaders.[38] Pickens had also been invited to the founding of the LAI in Brussels in 1927, but was eventually unable to attend when the conference was postponed. He subsequently visited the Soviet Union, met with Trotsky and Kalinin, and was impressed by the lack of 'deference and servility' and the absence of 'race and colour prejudice.'[39] When he returned from the Soviet Union he had told the Fourth Pan-African Congress in New York that 'the proletariat, the workers, the producers of the goods of the human society are beginning to sense a common interest in a common cause, and a need for mutual support, - in Moscow, in Hankow, in Paris, and in Passaic [New Jersey].' For some years he maintained

34. Ford's report was also published in *L'Ouvrier Nègre*, N.4 (August 1929).

35. Report on the Negro Question at the LAI Congress,' RGASPI 534/3/450.

36. Draft Letter to the LAI, 25 March 1929, RGASPI 542/1/79/20-22.

37. Minutes of Eastern Secretariat Commission on the LAI, 30 March 1929, RGASPI 542/1/79/27; 9 April 1929, RGASPI 542/1/79/41.

38. Quoted in S. Avery, *Up from Washington: William Pickens and the Negro Struggle for Equality, 1900-1950* (Newark, 1990) p.115. The other two were Hubert Harrison and George Weston of the UNIA. See also L. Fort-Whiteman to C.E. Ruthenburg, 31 August 1926, RGASPI 515/1/720. According to Fort-Whiteman, Pickens had met with both Lovestone and Robert Minor at the Party's National Office.

39. Avery, *Up from Washington*, p.117.

friendly relations with leading members of the American CP and even wrote articles in the Communist press.[40]

At the LAI congress however, Pickens was critical of what he termed Communist 'control of the general machinery and leading policies of the organisation,' and Communist views concerning the revolutionary potential of the 'American Negro.' He was determined to have his say, made his address in German and, as Ford reported, opposed any attacks on the new British Labour government and any criticism of such individuals as Clements Kadalie in South Africa and A. Philip Randolph in the United States. He also opposed demands for an end to colonial rule and stated 'It is extremely futile to call for an immediate evacuation of Africa. That will not be, and it is certain that it would not be good for Africa or for anybody else. The ultimate evacuation of Africa by the military powers is desirable. The immediate evacuation is not only impossible, but undesirable.' As a consequence of such views, and since it was evident that Pickens's anti-imperialism had its limitations, the Negro Bureau suggested that he be expelled from the LAI.[41] Nevertheless, Pickens maintained some contact with the American CP and seems to have given some support to the idea of an international conference of Negro workers.[42]

The London Conference

Preparations for the London conference only seem to have begun in earnest early in 1930 when concrete proposals were made to the RILU Secretariat by the ITUCNW and 'An Appeal to the Negro Workers of the World,' and other articles were published in *The Negro Worker*.[43] In March 1930 the RILU issued a 'Resolution on the present revolutionary situation among Negro toilers,' highlighting the fact that the grave global economic crisis was having a particularly strong impact on the colonies and leading to the increased exploitation and oppression of the 'black toiling masses' throughout the world. This was said to be creating the conditions for 'widespread revolts and rebellions,' and the Resolution particularly highlighted the situation in Africa and the Caribbean and the strikes and other struggles that were taking place in French Equatorial Africa, the Belgian Congo, Madagascar, and Gambia, as well as in Jamaica,

40. Ibid. pp.118-119.

41. Report on the Negro Question at the LAI Congress,' RGASPI 534/3/450. 'Draft Letter to the Communist Fraction of the Anti-imperialist League,' 9 October 1929, RGASPI 495/155/80/81-85.

42. Avery, *Up from Washington*, p.121.

43. RGASPI 495/18/809/27 and *NW*, 3/1-2 (January-February 1930). See also RGASPI 534/3/439/1-2.

Cuba, Trinidad, Venezuela and elsewhere. In these conditions the RILU called on all its 'adherents' to step up their work for both the 'Negro conference' and the RILU's Fifth Congress, which was due to be held in Moscow in August 1930. It also pointed out the need for these organisations to implement the decisions of the Sixth Congress in regard to self-determination in the United States and the demand for a 'Native Republic' in South Africa. As for the preparations for the International Trade Union Conference of Negro Workers, specific tasks were issued for the various countries and regions and the Resolution particularly called on the 'American, English and French comrades to do their utmost to ensure the success of the conference, as it is to be the beginning of the unification of the revolutionary liberation movement of Negro toilers with the revolutionary struggles of the world proletariat.' The Resolution concluded:

> The ever intensified offensive of the imperialists against the world proletariat and in particular against the USSR makes it imperative to shake off the present inertia and to start with more accelerated tempo the organisational work amongst Negro toilers. The Negro Toilers are to play a tremendous role in the future imperialist war and in the class wars of the proletariat. Therefore we must not lose time in drawing them into our ranks and imbuing them with proletarian revolutionary ideology.[44]

However, several communist parties, including the CPGB were unable to shake off the lethargy and passivity that the Resolution characterised as 'the worst signs of right opportunistic deviations.' The CPGB, the prospective host for the London conference, was expected to step up its work, including its activity in African and other colonies and amongst seamen and other 'Negro groups' especially in London.[45] The Negro Bureau had already stressed that events in South Africa, Kenya, and in West Africa indicated 'the presence of deep revolutionary fermentation among the Negroes,' and that they 'urgently confront the CPGB, with the task of beginning serious work in regard to the Negro colonies in both Africa and in the West Indies.' The British CP had also been instructed to consider the possibility of building 'an auxiliary organisation among the Negro population,' to train and create 'Negro cadres,' and to make one member of its Colonial Committee 'responsible for Negro work.' There is no evidence that the CPGB implemented any of these directives.[46]

---

44. RGASPI 534/3/499 The Resolution was particularly critical of the communist parties in the United States and South Africa, which had been slow to implement the decisions of the CI's Sixth Congress but was also critical of all those parties that were still underestimating the importance of the Negro Question.

45. Report of Comrade Ford to the Negro Bureau, 14 November 1929, RGASPI 534/3/450.

46. 'Work of the CPGB in the Negro Colonies,' 21 November 1929, RGASPI 495/155/70/59.

In addition the CPGB and the National Minority Movement (NMM) –the CPGB's trade union organisation, had been given the responsibility of making preparations for the conference and mobilising those in the British colonies to attend but had not taken up these tasks. In February 1930, John Mahon, one of the leaders of the NMM who was asking for more information about the proposed conference and the NMM's obligations, reported that there were few contacts with Negroes apart from those with seamen in various ports and with organisations in the United States. He added that the whole question of colonial work was still being 'considered' and that the NMM was trying to establish a colonial committee.[47] After some criticism and further questioning, Mahon admitted that links existed with organisations in South Africa, Gambia and Trinidad but it was clear that he thought that the LAI and the ITUCNW itself were better placed to send invitations to the colonies and that little work was being done on that front in Britain.[48] In April, Mahon was still reporting that he had very few details about the proposed conference, did not know how many delegates were expected and what kind of venue was required, or if he should contact the Labour government. He did however claim that he had been in touch with the Gambia and expected a delegate from that country.[49] However, later that same month, William Patterson was complaining that when he met the pioneer Gambian trade union leader E.F. Small in Berlin, he knew little about the London conference because neither the CPGB, the NMM, the British section of the LAI, nor Communist circles in Berlin, had given him and other trade union leaders in the colonies any precise details about it.[50] That same month, Harry Pollitt and the leadership of the CPGB were still being asked if they had received any information about the 'Negro Conference' and were instructed to find an alternative venue for it.[51]

E.F. Small was one of the CI's most important contacts in West Africa. Born in Bathurst (now Banjul) in 1890,[52] he was the founder and leader of the Bathurst Trade Union (BTU), which in October 1929 had called a strike against cuts in local seamen's wages and similar cuts and threats of lockouts affecting other workers. The BTU had to fight against the police and the colonial authorities and the indifference of the Labour Government but successfully

47. J.A. Mahon to ITUCNW, 4 February 1930, RGASPI 534/7/48.

48. J.A. Mahon to ITUCNW, 30 February 1930, Ibid.

49. J.A. Mahon to ITUCNW, 7 April 1930, Ibid. Mahon did confirm that some work was being undertaken amongst 'Negro seamen' in Cardiff and that he expected some delegates to attend the conference.

50. Patterson to Haywood, 10 April 1930, RGASPI 495/18/809/86.

51. RGASPI 495/18/809/87.

52. For details of Small's early life see J.A. Langley, *Pan-Africanism and Nationalism in West Africa 1900-1945* (Oxford, 1978) pp.137-139.

won union recognition and even wage increases. The strike was one of the most successful in colonial Africa before 1939, received international attention and prompted the British government to legalise trade unions, in an attempt to keep them out of politics.[53] Small had also been secretary of the National Congress of British West Africa, had links to local farmer's organisations and founded the Gambian co-operative movement. He came into contact with the Labour Research Department (LRD) during this visit to London as part of a delegation of the NCBWA from 1920 to 1921. By 1929 the LRD was led by Communists and along with the LAI, NMM and others supported the BTU's strike and attempted to bring pressure to bear on the Labour Colonial Secretary, Sidney Webb.[54] Small later commented on the importance of this British support: 'This was the first lesson in international solidarity for the Gambian workers,' he stated, 'for the first time they experienced that they can conduct their struggle not only on their own, but as part of the international working class.'[55]

Small therefore had been in contact with Communists in Britain for some time but Patterson lamented the fact that the CPGB had not spoken with him about the proposed conference, nor the possibility of sending young African workers to Moscow for training. The political training of workers from Africa, the Caribbean and elsewhere became one of the most important aims of the ITUCNW, as the CI reasoned that without trained cadres it would be difficult to organise the labour movement in the colonies, especially in Africa. There were also plans for sending Moscow-trained instructors to the 'Negro colonies' because of the difficulty of obtained such 'students' and the urgent need for 'training contingents of Negro revolutionaries.' However, it seems that nothing came of these proposals and the Comintern persisted in its efforts to recruit 'Negro students.[56] Small promised Patterson that three young Gambian trade unionists and two others from the Gambia Cooperative Marketing Board would be able to travel to Moscow and explained that although the British authorities would not grant visas, these would be available from the French in Senegal. Small had himself travelled to Berlin via Senegal and Marseilles.

53. A. Hughes and D. Perfect, 'Trade Unionism in the Gambia,' *African Affairs*, 88/353 (1989) pp.549-572. Also G. Padmore, *The Life and Struggle of Negro Toilers* (London, 1931) pp.91-95.

54. Hughes and Perfect, 'Trade Unionism,' pp.554-555. The LRD published several studies in its 'colonial series' including in 1927 Elinor Burn's *British Imperialism in West Africa*.

55. Minutes of the meeting of the International Secretariat with the Negro friends, 15 October 1930, RGASPI 542/1/40.

56. 'On the Question of Negro Students,' 7 January 1930, RGASPI 495/155/87-3-4 and 'Proposals in regard to sending instructors to the Negro colonies and the establishment of a course of training for such instructors,' 6 November 1930, RGASPI 495/155/87/43-46.

Patterson also met with Joseph Bilé, the Cameroonian leader of the Berlin section of the LDRN, who was the organisation's delegate for the conference and who had also been recommended for training in Moscow.[57] The Berlin LDRN, or *Liga zur Verteidigung der Negerrasse,* had been established by Bilé and Garan Kouyaté in September 1929 following the Frankfurt Congress of the LAI and based on previous work undertaken in Germany. It was created with the support of the International Secretariat of the LAI, and used the LAI's office in Berlin its headquarters. Although modelled on the French LDRN and officially under its leadership, the section also worked closely with the LAI and the German CP, although it was critical of this relationship and the lack of help it received. The thirty or so members of the LDRN in Berlin, including several women, had established some links with the African port workers in Hamburg and maintained contact with their compatriots in the former German colonies of Cameroon and Togo.[58]

The shortcomings evident in the colonial work of the European CPs were particularly serious in regard to Africa where, outside of South Africa it was reported 'the Comintern up to the present time has no connections,' but these weaknesses also existed in the Caribbean and elsewhere.[59] In order to maximise the chances of wide participation, the ITUCNW planned to hold its conference just before the Fifth Congress of the RILU in the expectation that delegates would be sent to both events. It also decided to send some of its main organisers to Africa and the Caribbean in order to make sure that delegates were elected, funds raised and other preparations made for the conference.[60] The key organisers of the conference, Ford, Patterson, Huiswood and George Padmore therefore stepped up their activities in the spring of 1930. Padmore, who had been born Malcolm Nurse in Trinidad in 1902, attended college in the US in Washington D.C. and New York, where in 1926 he first became connected with International Red Aid and then the following year joined the WP. Rising rapidly through the ranks of those connected with the ANLC he worked on the *Negro Champion* and in the Harlem Tenants League and soon became a regular

57. Patterson to Haywood, 10 April 1930, RGASPI 495/18/809.

58. RGASPI 495/155/87/404-408. On Bilé see R. Aitken, 'From Cameroon to Germany and Back via Moscow and Paris: The Political Career of Joseph Bilé (1892-1959), Performer, "Negerbeiter" and Comintern Activist.' *Journal of Contemporary History*, 43/4 (October 2008) pp.597-616.

59. 'The Work of the Comintern Among Negroes,' 24 October 1929, RGASPI 495/155/77/187-192.

60. 'List of Delegates and Agenda of Negro Workers International Trade Union Conference,' 14 November 1929, RGASPI 534/3/408/31. It was originally optimistically hoped that delegates would attend from Central Africa and the Congo where the ITUCNW had almost no contacts.

speaker at local ANLC and Party meetings.[61] In the autumn of 1929 Otto Huiswoud recommended that Padmore should go to Moscow to work with the ITUCNW and the Negro Section of the ECCI. He was soon editing *The Negro Worker* and became one of the principal organisers of the conference.[62]

Patterson had arrived in Berlin at the beginning of April 1930 and was soon joined by Padmore. According to Patterson's report to the RILU Negro Bureau, no work had been done in Berlin nor in the important German port of Hamburg, despite the great possibilities that existed there, and neither the CI's Western European Bureau, nor those connected with the RILU and the LAI knew anything much about the conference. Patterson was of the opinion that more work should be done through the LAI and suggested that not only should the ITUCNW get hold of the addresses of the LAI's African contacts but also that the RILU Negro Bureau and the CI Negro section should ask for a 'Negro comrade' to be based at the LAI in Berlin.[63] However, he reported general 'apathy and passivity,' even *The Negro Worker* had not been distributed amongst the members of the Berlin-based LDNR. When they realised that there were similar problems in Britain, 'nothing being done, less contemplated,' as Patterson expressed it, he and Padmore decided to proceed immediately to London.

In London, Patterson and Padmore met with Small, who had preceded them, and obtained from him addresses of contacts in West Africa. It was decided that both Small, who was returning to Gambia, and Padmore would attempt to recruit delegates for the conference from West Africa. It was feared that at some stage Padmore was likely to face deportation, or some other unforeseen problem, and if this was the case Small would take over. Following discussions with the CPGB, Padmore left for West Africa in mid-April. Patterson continued to try and organise in Britain, meeting with representatives of the NMM, the leadership of the CPGB and the LAI. Here too he reported 'extremely little activity of any kind' and that *The Negro Worker* again went undistributed. Moreover, it appears that no direct links had been established with the Labour government until this time, when after a meeting with Maxton who suggested a direct approach, Patterson wrote to the Labour Home Secre-

61. See e.g. RGASPI 515/116/1533 and 515/116/1535 and for some of Padmore's personal details RGASPI 539/1/28.

62. O. Huiswoud to J.W. Ford, 14 November 1929, RGASPI 515/130/1688. For biographical accounts see L.J. Hooker, *Black Revolutionary, George Padmore's Path from Communism to Pan-Africanism* (London, 1967) and F. Baptiste and R. Lewis (eds.) *George Padmore: Pan-African Revolutionary* (Kingston, 2008).

63. Patterson to Negro Bureau Profintern, 18 April 1930, RGASPI 534/4/330.

tary, C.R Clynes, asking 'whether the British Government will give its sanction for the proposed Conference.'[64]

Earlier in 1930, Patterson had written about some of the 'significant features of the coming Negro workers' conference,' and had particularly highlighted the fact that it signalled 'the internationalisation of the Negro problem.' He argued that such a conference was particularly important at that time because of the intensification of the oppression suffered by 'the Negro masses' all over the world and the possibility to bring to them 'an appreciation of the commonality of interests between their struggles and those of the oppressed toiling masses of other colonies and the struggling proletariat of the "mother" countries."' He thought that not only the nature of the international situation but also the venue of the conference itself would 'be an extremely significant factor in awakening the consciousness of the Negro masses.' He explained:

> Perhaps it is no exaggeration to say that more than one-half of the Negroes in the world are subjects of the British Empire. After almost a century of practice the "civilising mission" of British imperialism offers them as they gaze upon themselves, a picture of almost inconceivable ignorance, degradation and demoralisation. They turn to this conference the better to examine this degrading caricature of the people they should be. What will be the answer of the Labour government to these Negroes of the Empire who ask leave to discuss in London this phase of their problem? To be sure, to the overwhelming mass of them, the British Empire and particularly the Labour Party still stands for justice and fair play... They know nothing of the Empire's economic basis. They know nothing of the position to which this Labour Party committed them in the colonial resolution of the 1928 Congress of the Second International. But recent events in Gambia, Nigeria and Kenya, leave little room for speculation after the nature of the "Labour" Government's answer. The enlightening effect of this answer will be truly tremendous. For this reason the choice of place for the conference was a particularly happy one and the position of the Labour Party enhances the value of the choice.[65]

This analysis suggested that the Labour government was unlikely to support the conference in any way, but while he waited for a response Patterson also endeavoured to advance the work of the ITUCNW, securing from the NMM

64. RGASPI 534/4/330. Maxton agreed that he would pursue the matter in the House of Commons if the Government declined the request. Patterson's letter and the responses of the Colonial Office can be found in (TNA) CO 323/1096/10.

65. RGASPI 'Some significant features of the coming Negro workers' conference.' 495/155/87/28-31.

an agreement on the 'necessity of a Negro...perhaps two' in the NMM delegation to RILU's Fifth Congress. He also met with Jomo Kenyatta although it is not clear if his assessment that Kenyatta was 'an unsafe element' helps to explain why he did not subsequently attend the conference in Germany. Patterson also travelled to Liverpool and Cardiff and met with a 'group of about 30 Negroes,' in London, whom he described as a 'very poor lot,' but including 'very good elements in one or two cases.'[66]

The organising work in West Africa appeared much more favourable, at least according to the report Padmore sent from Sierra Leone at the beginning of May. At that time he had already visited the Gambia, where his papers had been closely scrutinised by immigration officials,[67] and Dakar, Senegal, where he 'also had a little trouble.'[68] So far he had managed to recruit two delegates. He reported that he had plans to travel to Nigeria, Liberia and the Gold Coast, so as to continue to mobilise delegates in West Africa, before his return to London at the end of June. He was evidently pleased that the West African press had published some articles sourced from the ITUCNW and he thought that there 'were good prospects for future work, reporting 'strong anti-imperialist sentiment everywhere.' In short he was enthusiastic and in one letter concluded 'if other sectors respond as W[est] A[frica] conf[erence] will be a huge success.' In another letter from Accra, capital of the Gold Coast, he was similarly optimistic and reported that he had arrived via Takoradi, was travelling on to Lagos, Nigeria, had recruited another delegate from the Mechanics Union and that 'prospects look good.'[69] On the basis of his travels through West Africa and Small's initial contacts, Padmore established important links in the region that he would utilise in coming years, both for his work for the CI and for his later Pan-African endeavours.[70]

In South Africa too there were reports that the preparatory work for the conference was going well. The South African Federation of Non-European Trade Unions held a preparatory conference in Johannesburg in May, both in order to inform workers and to select delegates. It was reported that the conference would also discuss all the other economic and political problems facing

66. WW (W. Patterson) to Negro Bureau Profintern, 18 April 1930, RGASPI 534/4/330.

67. Padmore had already communicated these difficulties to Patterson who in turn wrote to those in the US who had written recommendations for Padmore. Patterson to Lozovsky, Profintern Secretariat, 7 May 1930 RGASPI 534/4/330.

68. According to the French Consulate in Bathurst, Padmore had been prevented from landing in Dakar by the British authorities. See B. H. Edwards, *The Practice of Diaspora –Literature, Translation and the Rise of Black Internationalism*, (London, 2003) p.449.

69. G. Padmore to Dear Comrades, 2 and 12 May 1930, ibid.

70. It is interesting to note the tone used by Padmore in letters to issue what amount to directives to members of the Negro Bureau in Moscow.

African workers in South Africa, including low wages, repressive legislation and all forms of discrimination, which had recently led to protests in Durban and other towns and cities.[71] Preparations for the conference in the United States were carried out from March 1930 mainly through the activities of the Trade Union Unity League (TUUL), and the ANLC, and the election of delegates was organised through affiliated unions. An organising committee, under Ford's direction, was established in New York and propaganda was carried by such publications as the *Daily Worker* and *Labour Unity,* through special 'news releases' in *The Liberator* and the *Crusader News Service*,[72] and even in some of the 'Negro bourgeois newspapers.'[73]

Meanwhile, Otto Huiswood and his wife Hermina were touring the Caribbean attempting to recruit delegates for the conference mainly in Haiti, Jamaica and Trinidad. This mission was less successful. 'This has been a rather difficult task,' Huiswoud wrote to Padmore from Port of Spain, 'because of the very poor contacts we have and the fact that it is very hard to find some very real class-conscious elements. They are either connected with the Garvey movement as is the case in Jamaica, or they have not the slightest concept of what a labour movement is.' Trinidad, he reported, 'is the most difficult place.' This was mostly because of the influence of Cipriani, the leader of the Trinidad Workingmen's Association, and the British Labour Party but also because of the 'vigilance of the British authorities,' and the fact that the ITUCNW had no contacts there.[74] So although Huiswoud thought a delegate was unlikely, and he might have to travel elsewhere, he concluded that with some preparation Trinidad, like the other Caribbean islands, offered good prospects for future work.[75] He had organised in Jamaica in the past, and even established a trade union, and so despite the influence of Garvey and Garveyism was confident that a good delegate from that island had been recruited. In Haiti, Huiswoud was aided by Henry Rosemond, a Haitian activist from the American CP who translated and made introductions for him. Huiswoud thought that their work might secure another delegate for the conference. In fact Rosemond managed to get himself elected as the delegate of the Haitian Anti-Imperialist League, even though he had been directed to find a delegate from amongst the Haitian workers. It took

71. RGASPI 495/155/87/117-118.

72. Ford also wrote an article 'Negro Toilers Initiate International Conference,' outlining some of the preparations made in Frankfurt and the agenda of the Conference, which appeared in *Inprecor*, 19 June 1930, p.530.

73. 'The International Conference of Negro Workers,' 29 July 1930, RGASPI 495/155/87/245.

74. J. Ford, 'Report on the Preparations for the London Conference,' 12 May 1930, RGASPI 534/3/546.

75. O. Huiswood to George, 14 April 1930, RGASPI 534/4/330.

several letters from Ford, a return visit from Huiswood and a further visit from another activist to finally resolve the problem.[76]

It is evident that the ITUCNW had contact with several activists in the Caribbean during this period. In addition to the Huiswouds and Rosemond, there was also Sabin Ducadosse, a trade union organiser in Guadeloupe, from where Ford and the ITUCNW hoped a delegate would be sent to the Conference. The Cuban CP and the trade union federation that it led had also promised to send a delegate, as had the CP in Honduras. Ford was clearly of the opinion that in the Caribbean 'we have made fairly good organisational preparations', but, he added, 'perhaps there has not been sufficient political preparation made with regards to popularising the London conference.'[77]

But what is clear, not withstanding all this activity, is how little preparation had been made for the conference in the past, and how much of the work was left until the few months directly preceding it. In Europe hardly any work had been done, even though communist parties existed there. In West Africa and the Caribbean, where in general no or few parties existed, it was a similar picture, since the French and British CPs had not carried out any work. Even communication between the leading activists and RILU's Negro Bureau in Moscow was difficult to maintain. Both Padmore and Patterson sent organisational requests with their reports but with no certainty that either were received even when sent by hand through sympathetic seamen or other reliable couriers. In June 1930, Patterson complained to Haywood in Moscow that he had heard nothing from him since he began his trip in April.[78]

From Britain Patterson had moved to Paris where he also found that no preparations had been made and no publicity had been released for the conference, 'impermissible sabotage' was the phrase he used to described the situation, not only in relation to the conference but in regard to 'colonial work' in general.[79] The French CP claimed that it had no funds to send anyone to French Equatorial Africa to recruit delegates. Indeed it had not even been aware that Patterson was arriving in France and he reported to Lozovsky, the head of the Profintern, that he was getting no support from the PCF, nor from the Confédération Générale du Travail Unitaire (CGTU - the communist-led trade union centre), and therefore had no funds to travel to Belgium and then back to London.[80] Patterson complained bitterly of the fact that he had uncovered more evidence of the inactivity

76. RGASPI 534/3/546. The situation had been complicated by the fact that Padmore had written a letter apparently supporting Rosemond's election.

77. RGASPI 534/3/546.

78. W. Patterson to Haywood, 24 June 1930, RGASPI 534/4/330.

79. W. Patterson to Haywood, 24 April 1930, ibid.

80. Patterson to Lozovsky, Profintern Secretariat, 7 May 1930, RGASPI 534/4/330.

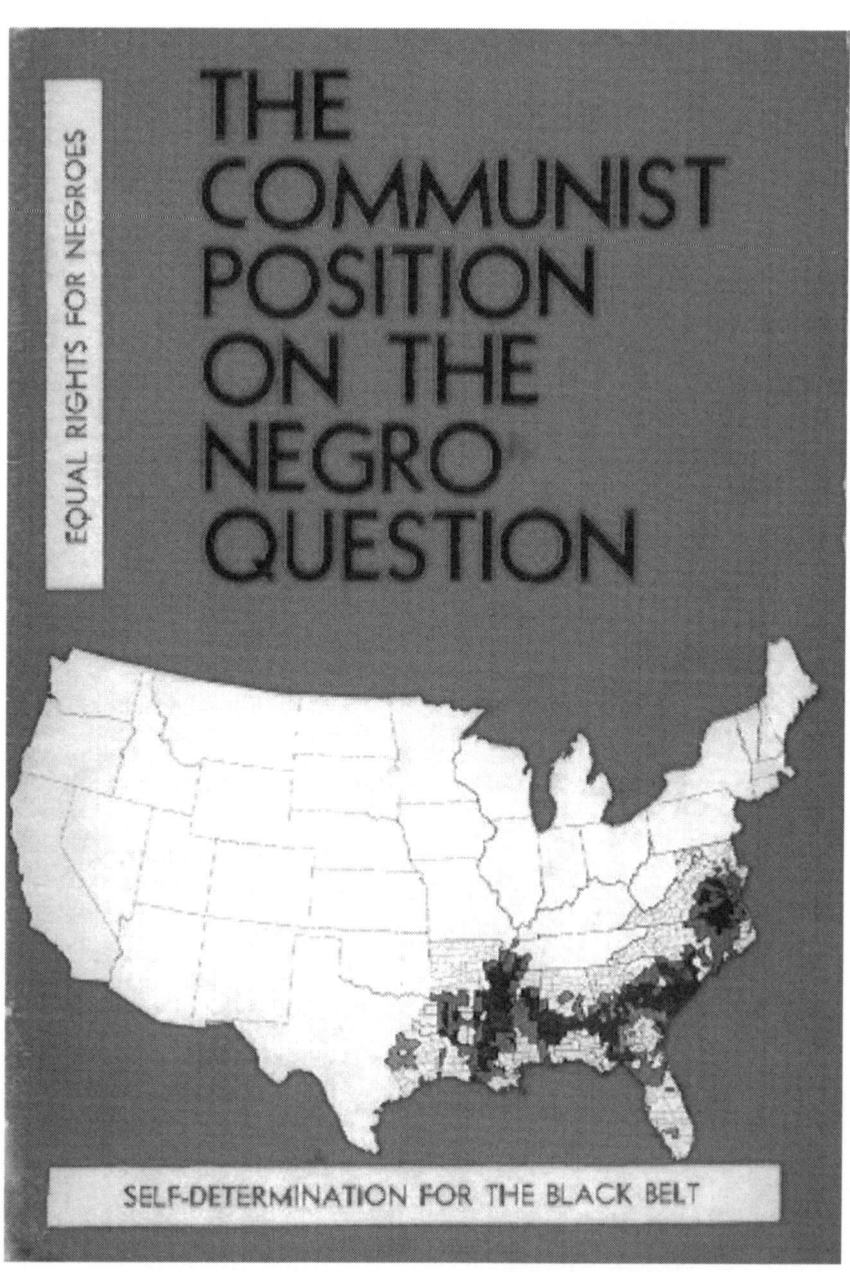

Cover of the Communist Position of the Negro Question (CPUSA, 1934),
From the author's collection

Vol. 3. No 9. 25 Juin, 1930

S O M M A I R E :

I. La Conférence Internationale des ouvriers nègres.

2. Le travail forcé.- SLAVINE.

3. Le Gouvernement Travailliste et les Colonies.

4. Le prolétariat nègre d'Amérique Latine et la Conférence Internationale des travailleurs nègres.- HERNANDES.

5. La différenciation des forces en Afrique Australe.- J. REED.

6. La situation des travailleurs de la Jamaïque.- A. GOLD.

7. La situation des nègres dans les colonies françaises et belges de l'Afrique Centrale.- MICHELSON.

8. La situation des indigènes en Afrique Occidentale.- E.SMITH.

9. La situation des indigènes en Afrique Orientale.- M. K.

L'Ouvrier Nègre, French edition of The Negro Worker, June 1930.
5 SLOTFOM 10, *Archives nationales d'outre-mer, Aix-en-Provence, France*

Delegates at the First International Conference of Negro Workers, Hamburg, 1930,
From the author's collection

A REPORT OF PROCEEDINGS AND DECISIONS OF THE FIRST INTERNATIONAL CONFERENCE OF NEGRO WORKERS

AT HAMBURG GERMANY / JULY 1930

10 cents 3 pence

PUBLISHED BY THE INTERNATIONAL TRADE UNION COMMITTEE OF NEGRO WORKERS
8, Rothesoodstrasse, Hamburg, Germany.

Proceedings of the First International Conference of Negro Workers, Hamburg, 1930,
From the author's collection

Price 5 cents Price 2 pence

THE INTERNATIONAL NEGRO WORKERS' REVIEW

ORGAN OF THE INTERNATIONAL TRADE UNION COMMITTEE OF NEGRO WORKERS, 8 ROTHESOODSTR., HAMBURG, GERMANY

Vol. 1 January 1931 No. 1

CONTENTS

INTERNATIONAL NEGRO WORKERS' REVIEW, 1931, From the author's collection

Workers of the World, unite!

WHAT IS THE INTERNATIONAL TRADE UNION COMMITTEE OF NEGRO WORKERS?

A TRADE UNION PROGRAMME OF ACTION

What is the ITUCNW (1 front cover), *From the author's collection*

What is the ITUCNW (2 back cover), From the author's collection

of the French CP on the Negro Question and its continued 'underestimation of Negro work.' In Paris the Ligue de Défense de la Race Nègre (LDRN) was now several years old but apparently existing in complete isolation from the French CP, which did not even send representatives to its meetings. As a consequence, Patterson concluded, the LDRN instead of having an internationalist orientation 'has now a more confused and racialistic approach to its work.' In Europe, in general, preparations for the conference were greatly hampered by what Patterson described as an 'under-estimation of the importance of colonial work,' which 'generally become in the case of Negro work because of its present stage of development total neglect.' His explanation for this 'total neglect' was that 'all of the CI resolutions on the Negro Question are regarded here as "Open Letters" to the American Party with no reference to our European parties.'[81]

The fact that the resolutions and directives of the CI and RILU remained mere policy documents suggests that the international communist movement was very far from the monolith that is sometimes presented. In the case of 'Negro work' it is clear the western European parties did very little, whatever the reason, and can be said to have largely ignored CI and RILU resolutions, while the parties in South Africa and the United States were often slow or reluctant to act. In addition, as Patterson and others found, there were often very poor communications between the CI/RILU and individual parties and other Communist-led organisations, as well as a chronic shortage of funds. The 'Negro conference,' had taken many years to bring to fruition but its success or failure still ultimately rested on a few dedicated Communists who shouldered the burden of all the final preparations. Patterson, for example, wrote to Moscow asking for instructions, support and funds, but when none arrived used his own initiative and extremely limited resources.

The Preparations for the Hamburg Conference

In May MacDonald's Labour Government announced that it would not permit the conference to be held in Britain, which caused even further organisational problems. It was subsequently announced in the press that the Labour government had given instructions to port officials to monitor the arrival of any 'Negro delegates who may try to enter this country.'[82] Despite his perpetual lack of funds Patterson was forced to return to London to make new arrange-

81. Patterson to Haywood, 24 June 1930, RGASPI 534/3/546.

82. V. Chattopahaya, 'The First International Conference of Negro Workers,' *NW*, Vol.3 – Special Edition (15 October 1930) pp.3-5.

ments.[83] From there he sent further complaints to the RILU's Negro Bureau in Moscow, organised protests by sympathetic MPs, including James Maxton,[84] and prepared articles for the press criticising the Labour government. In one of these articles he argued that the Labour government's refusal had exposed it and the oppressive nature of the British Empire even further in the eyes of the 'Black Masses'. He concluded:

> The Labour Government has said that British democracy does not embrace the black masses of the Empire; that the white workers whose standard of living is being constantly lowered through the ruthless exploitation and oppression of the colonial masses shall not see the alliance with the colonial world as the only way to their emancipation. The Labour Party the standard bearer of British Imperialism says there will be no black workers' conference in London. But the answer of the International Committee of Negro Workers will be to make that answer the basis of the exposure before the black workers and toiling masses who – come what may – will have the first international conference of Negro Workers in July 1930.'[85]

From London Patterson again reported that he 'was borrowing on all sides' but maintained that he intended to return to Paris and then to Berlin to make preparations to hold the conference in Hamburg. On a more positive note he informed his comrades that he had been working closely with the NMM, LAI and the CPGB and had established a 'Negro liberation society' in Britain, perhaps the beginnings of what later became known as the Negro Welfare Association.[86]

---

83. Colonial Office officials who were asked to comment on Patterson's letter to the Home Secretary noted that he managed to combine 'an attack on the conditions in the British colonies and an application for official recognition of this conference.' They were clear that it was a conference organised under the auspices of the Comintern and were therefore hostile to it. One Colonial Office official summed up the general approach by arguing that the conference should be opposed because it 'will be detrimental to the colonies...but also because it would cause the gravest possible offence to the Union of South Africa if it was to be permitted to take place on British soil.' G. Clauson memo, 2 May 1930, (TNA) CO 323/1069/10.

84. In the British parliament only James Marley MP asked question about the banning of the conference. See *Hansard* HC Deb 22 May 1930 vol. 239 cc591-2W.

85 W. Wilson 'The Black Masses and the British Empire,' *Inprecor*, 10/27(5 June 1930), p.498. See also RGASPI 495/18/809/106.

86. Patterson to Negro Bureau, Profintern, 24 May 1930, RGASPI 534/4/330. A week later Patterson asked the Bureau to send a copy of the constitution of the ANLC to Rathbone of the CPGB adding 'we organised new section in England.' Patterson to Negro Bureau Profintern, 30 May 1930, RGASPI 534/4/330.

It seems that it was around this time that meetings were started amongst the black population in Liverpool, mostly seamen but also some who worked ashore in the local sugar refinery. The conditions facing black workers in Britain in this period were oppressive. There had been organised racist attacks against black communities throughout the country in 1919. From 1925 seamen were subject to the Coloured Aliens Seaman's Order, which effectively compelled all 'coloured' seamen to register as aliens, whatever their status and then not only discriminated against them with regard to conditions of work, pay and even residence but also made them subject to police harassment and deportation. In addition a *Report on the Colour Problem in Liverpool and other Ports* had been published which not only attacked the seamen and other workers but also their families, who it was claimed suffered from various genetic defects and constituted a moral danger.[87] Amongst the black community in Liverpool therefore there was growing resentment but this does not seem to have been politically harnessed before April 1930 when organising was initiated by Douglas and Molly Wolton, of the South African CP, who were visiting Britain at the time. The Woltons organised a series of meetings, with the assistance of the local committee of the CPGB, in the course of which it was decided to establish a 'Negro Society' that would affiliate to the LAI. The 'Society' even considered sending a representative to the Negro Workers' conference unaware that the venue had been changed at the last moment.[88]

Patterson returned to Germany at the end of May but it seems that he still received no help in making preparations for the conference from the German CP and only a few days before it was due to commence he finally managed to get assistance from the German section of the LAI. There was also no direct assistance from the Negro Bureaux of the CI and RILU. On the 24 June Padmore arrived in Germany, via London, with four delegates from West Africa. The West African delegates had already been 'followed and harassed by Scotland Yard detectives till their position became intolerable' in London and were then apparently initially denied food and financial assistance, or any other support, by the representative of the German CP.[89] Padmore and the other delegates managed to survive with some assistance from the LAI but by the end of the month he was appealing to the RILU to intervene and remedy the situation.[90] Such were the preparations for the First International Conference of Negro

87. P. Rich, *Race and Empire in British Politics* (Cambridge, 1990) pp.120-135.

88. 'Report of Work among Negroes in England,' RGASPI 496/155/83/53-55.

89. V. Chattopadhyaya, 'The First International Conference of Negro Workers,' *Inprecor*, 25 July 1930, p.635.

90. Padmore to Dear Comrades, 30 June 1930, RGASPI 534/3/546.

Workers. It was a situation that prompted Patterson to remark 'this is a hell of a way of doing things.'[91]

The Hamburg Conference

The *Report of Proceedings and Decisions of the First International Conference of Negro Workers* was subsequently published by the ITUCNW complete with a photo of seventeen of the delegates who finally managed to attend.[92] It was an historic occasion and the fact that it was held at all was, in the circumstances, almost miraculous. As it was, the conference, which was eventually held in the Seamen's Club in Hamburg, started a day later than originally scheduled, on July 7th, because of the late arrival of Ford and the delegates from the United States. Ford reported that 'the Hamburg-German line refused to transport a group of Negro workers.'[93] The African delegates from South Africa were prevented from attending by the actions of the South African government, so Albert Green (E.S. Sachs) represented the Federation of Non-European Trade Unions.[94] Delegates from French, Belgian and, Portuguese colonies in Africa were also prevented from attending although it is unclear to what extent these delegates were preparing to attend. One delegates elected by the Marine Workers Industrial Union in the US did not arrive, nor did elected delegates from Cuba and Panama.[95] However, British West Africa was well represented with two delegates from the Gold Coast, and a delegate from organisations in Nigeria, Sierra Leone and Gambia. The Gambian delegate, Edward Small, represented the Gambia Labour Union, effectively the trade union centre of the colony, which claimed a membership of some 1000 workers and 2,500 farmers. The Nigerian delegate was Frank Macaulay, son of Herbert Macaulay, and a representative of the Nigerian National Democratic Party (NNDP), the first major

91. Patterson to Negro Bureau Profintern, 30 May 1930, RGASPI 534/4/330. The RILU Negro Bureau in Moscow, under Haywood's leadership, continued to make preparations for the conference and for the participation of 'Negro delegates' at the Fifth Congress of the RILU but evidently was not in regular contact with its activists in Europe. See e.g. 'Minutes of the meeting of the ITUCNW of the RILU, 29 May 1930, RGASPI 495/155/83/96-97.

92. Nine delegates were prevented from attending and there were also three 'fraternal delegates.' *A Report of Proceedings and Decisions of the First International Conference of Negro Workers* (Hamburg, 1930).

93. 'RILU Executive Bureau Meeting, 5 August 1930, RGASPI 534/3/490.

94. Joseph Gumede of the ANC was evidently one of those prevented from attending. See *The Crisis*, September 1930, p.312.

95. 'The International Conference of Negro Workers,' 29 July 1930, RGASPI 495/155/87/243-251.

political party in Nigeria.[96] The delegate from Sierra Leone was E.A. Richards formerly the leader of the Railwaymen's Union and Joseph Bilé represented the Berlin section of the LDRN. There were two delegates from the Caribbean, Henry Rosemond and De Leon from the Railway Workers Union of Jamaica. The remaining delegates, including one woman, Helen McClain of the National Needle Workers' Union, represented labour organisation in the United States or the ITUCNW. There is no evidence for the attendance of Garan Kouyaté, nor of Kenyatta, who was a member of the organising committee.[97] In April, Patterson had indicated that he considered Kenyatta 'an unsafe element' following publication in *The Times* and the *Manchester Guardian* of articles in which he had spoken of the Kikuyu Central Association's wish that the peoples of East Africa 'may all march together as loyal subjects of His Britannic Majesty along the road of Empire prosperity.'[98] However, it is still not clear exactly why Kenyatta was unable to attend.

There seems to be only one eye-witness account of the event from a German representative of International Red Aid (MOPR), Willi Budisch, who reported that even on July 7th many of the delegates, including James Ford, had not arrived and so a 'provisional opening of the conference' took place at midday in the Seaman's Club, so that those present could hear the reports of J.A. Akrong, representing the Gold Coast Drivers' and Mechanics' Union and T.S. Morton of the Gold Coast Carpenters' Union, who had to leave almost as soon as the conference opened. They were the most inexperienced of all the delegates and seem to have disappeared without trace after they left Hamburg. There are no known details of their impressions of the conference and their journey to Europe. The conference was then officially re-opened during the evening of the

96. Macaulay later stated that Padmore's visit to Lagos had contributed to attempts by younger members in the NNDP to oust the older leadership and to ask for Padmore's assistance. His own election as a delegate had been part of this struggle to make the NNDP more democratically answerable to its members. Minutes of the meeting of the International Secretariat with the Negro friends, 14 October 1930, RGASPI 542/1/40.

97. According to Dewitte, Garan Kouyaté was not invited to Hamburg, although during the conference he was elected to the Executive Committee of the ITUCNW. The French security services reported that the LDRN was 'very badly informed' about Hamburg and therefore did not make adequate preparations to travel until it was too late. However, in August Kouyaté did travel from Paris to the Fifth RILU Congress in Moscow. See 'Note Sur La Propagande Révolutionaire Interessant Les Pays d'Outre-Mer,' 31 July and 30 September 1930, 3 SLOTFOM 81, Archives Nationale Section Outre-Mer, Aix-en-Provence, France (ANOM). P. Dewitte, *Les Mouvements Nègres en France 1919-1939* (Paris, 1985) pp.203-206 also p.40. The British security services reported that Kenyatta left Britain on 9 July on his way to the Hamburg conference, i.e. after it had concluded. TNA KV2/1787.

98. *The Times*, 26 March 1930. For Patterson's reservations see W. Patterson to Negro Bureau, Profintern, 18 April 1930, RGASPI 534/4/330.

same day by which time fourteen delegates had arrived for what was essentially a reception.[99]

The conference began in earnest on 8th July with the election of the Presidium, an introductory report from Ford and speeches from most of the other delegates. In the evening, when a meeting of the harbour workers took place in the Seaman's Club, the delegates from the conference joined the proceedings and 'fraternisation speeches' were delivered. The next morning the conference concluded after passing several resolutions and most of the delegates left by boat for Leningrad and the Fifth congress of the RILU.[100] However, several of the West African delegates, Small, Macaulay and Bilé, agreed that they would meet in Berlin on their return journey, in order to have more detailed discussion with representatives from the LAI.

The opening speech at the conference was delivered by James Ford who stressed that the delegates were meeting 'at a time of acute crisis of capitalism' when the contention between the big imperialist powers was increasing and there was a growing danger of war. He reminded them that they were concerned not only with the problems facing 'Negro workers' but also those affecting 'the Negro race.' He provided some of the history of the ITUCNW and its creation and detailed the specific problems facing Negro workers throughout the world and the many strike and anti-colonial struggles that had broken out in recent years in Madagascar, Guadeloupe, Gambia, French Equatorial Africa, Nigeria and elsewhere. Lastly he stressed the importance of the Soviet Union, contrasting the lives and status of workers there with other countries, the need to defend it from the machinations of the big powers, as well as the importance of 'the international class struggle against capitalism.'[101]

The other delegates spoke according to their experience. Akrong and Morton the two delegates from the Gold Coast delegates were concerned to ask for support for their fledgling unions, while E.F. Small spoke of ' the need for active resistance against capitalist and imperialist exploitation,' and stated that 'the Gambia workers regard the struggle of the Negro comrades everywhere as their own.'[102] Joseph Bilé explained that the exploitation of Cameroon was no different under the French and British than it had been under the Germans.

99. The MOPR representative could not follow all of the proceedings because of language difficulties. The report originally written in German in July 1930 is contained in RGASPI 534/3/527.

100. In addition to attending the RILU congress there were also plans to hold a special conference of 'Negro delegates to discuss the special problem of trade union work amongst Negro workers.' RGASPI 495/155/83/96.

101. *A Report of Proceedings and Decisions of the First International Conference of Negro Workers*, pp.5-13.

102. Ibid. pp.21-23.

He condemned missionaries as the partners of the imperialists and called for support for 'the Negro workers of Cameroon' to 'win the rights and the independence that belongs to Man and to all races.'[103] The delegates from the United States were often associated with larger more established unions but their concerns often centred on the effects of racism and the compromising actions of the AFL. Helen McClain of the Needle Workers' Union in Philadelphia, the only woman delegate, spoke of the difficulties of organising not only Negro but also Italian workers, as well as the problem of organising in the South where, she reported 'the textile workers in South Carolina were jailed and sentenced for 117 years for organising the white and black together.' She called on the conference to 'draw up a plan' to help these workers establish 'militant and revolutionary unions to fight the capitalist and against discrimination,' and concluded by stating, 'I also call special attention to the position of women workers everywhere.'[104]

The conference concluded with six resolutions and elections to the ITUC-NW's new executive committee. Several of those who had been unable to attend the conference were elected, including Albert Nzula and Moses Kotane from South Africa and Garan Kouyaté of the LDRN. Helen McClain (Jenny Reid) was the only elected female member of the executive. The six resolutions, prepared by the RILU Negro Bureau, were presented to the conference, several of them in major speeches by Padmore, Patterson and Frank Macaulay.[105] These were on: 'Economic Struggles of Negro Workers; The Struggles Against Forced Labour; Against the labour fakirs – the British "labour" government; Against lynching; The Negroes and the War Danger; Negro Workers for International Solidarity.'[106] Finally the conference decided to establish a working bureau to be based in Hamburg under Ford's direction. The Bureau was charged with the following aims and tasks:

Aims

1. To carry on a struggle against the danger of war and the utilisation of Negro soldiers as cannon fodder and to suppress the revolutionary movement.
2. To help the Negro toilers liberate themselves from the imperialist yoke.

103. Ibid. pp.23-25.

104. Ibid. p.20.

105. *NW*, 3/Special Number, (15 October 1930) pp.7-14.

106. *A Report of Proceedings and Decisions of the First International Conference of Negro Workers*, pp.29-40. On the RILU Negro Bureau's preparatory work see RGASPI 495/155/83/96.

3. To fight against racial barriers and white chauvinism that still divide the workers to the advantage of the oppressors and exploiters.
4. To develop a spirit of internationalism amongst the Negro toilers

Tasks

1. To establish and maintain contact with the trade union organisations of the Negro toilers especially on the continent of Africa and to coordinate their actions.
2. To stimulate the organisation of T.U.s in those parts of Africa and the West Indies where war exists (sic).
3. To gather and to give information and other materials relating to the living and working conditions of the Negro workers.
4. To publish papers and periodicals as well as pamphlets and other materials necessary for carrying in propaganda and agitation (sic).[107]

These aims and tasks are themselves significant and clarified the key tasks of the ITUCNW and its Hamburg Bureau, particularly the focus on Africa.

Historical Significance and Assessment

On several occasions during the conference mention was made of the fact that it was an historic occasion, the first time that workers from Africa and the African Diaspora had met to discuss together common problems and how they might be solved and this assessment also appeared in *The Negro Worker*.[108] However, other contemporary assessments were generally quite critical, particularly concerning the way the conference was organised and conducted. The German eye-witness did not have a very favourable impression and noted:

> The preparation and the actual course of the conference left me with the worst possible impression. The speeches and debates were not even taken down in shorthand, although my stenographer from Berlin was present. Comrade Ford was the only one who guided the conference politically. Neither the representative of the League Against Imperialism nor the representative of the Profintern did in any way personally intervene in the debate. Considering that representation at the conference was not bad in regional terms (West Indies, Gambia, Gold Coast, British Africa, North America, South

107. *NW*, 3/Special Number, (15 October 1930) pp.16-17.

108. Ibid. pp.2-3.

> Africa, Cameroon, Sierra Leone etc.) it is a real pity that the conference had been so badly prepared and organised. The more so since a number of delegates made their journey under severe difficulties and had been travelling for weeks in order to come.[109]

Nevertheless, Budisch concluded that if the proceedings of the conference were published it would still be possible to evaluate it positively. Another contemporary account of the conference was by Virendranath Chattopadhyaya, an Indian member of the Secretariat of the LAI and of the German CP.[110] Chatto, as he was known, attended the conference and had also been involved in some of the preparatory discussions during the LAI's Frankfurt congress. His report includes remarks on some of the preparations as well as on the hostile actions of the British and other governments and the harassment of African delegates in London. It seems that he was presenting the views of at least some other Communists when he wrote that 'in spite of these impediments, a more determined effort ought perhaps to have been made to hold the conference in London and thus to challenge the "Labour" Government to use force in suppressing it. This would have even more clearly exposed its true character.'[111]

Chatto also expressed a view about the composition of the conference, arguing that, 'Owing to the absence of the representation from the French colonies, from East Africa, from the Belgian and Portuguese territories, and from the Latin American countries, it was obvious that this first meeting of Negro workers was a mere preparatory Conference, the political importance of which is none the less considerable. The very fact that such a conference was held, and the clear line of policy and action laid down in the resolutions are bound to have a strong influence upon the development of the struggle.' He concluded his article by saying that there was a 'marked difference' between those delegates from the United States 'with a completely proletarian psychology and outlook,' and those from Africa, who he suggested 'have more the of the mentality of the small farmer.' Based on this distinction Chatto made an observation that had important implications for the future work of the ITUCNW. He stated: 'The condition of the problem in Africa necessitates different methods and tactics from those in the USA and there may be a tendency for the Negro workers from the USA to look at the African Negro question too much from the American point of view.' He concluded by asserting, 'nevertheless, it is a gain to the African worker to come into contact with the representatives of the far more

---

109. RGASPI 534/3/527.

110. 'The First International Conference of Negro Workers,' *Inprecor*, 25 July 1930, p.635. This was also included in a special edition of *The Negro Worker* devoted entirely to the Hamburg Conference. See *NW*, 3, (15 October 1930).

111. Ibid. p.636.

advanced Negro proletariat of America. This contact has been achieved by the conference.'[112]

The most detailed assessments of the conference were made by those who had been directly involved in the work to convene it, many of whom met in Moscow shortly afterwards during the RILU's Fifth Congress. At a meeting of the Executive Bureau of the RILU, James Ford pointed to organisational weaknesses in the United States and more significant political weaknesses in the Caribbean, especially in Jamaica and Haiti 'the most developed trade union centres of the West Indies,' where it had been difficult to find the type of working class delegates required. In West Africa too, Ford made clear, there had also been difficulties, 'mainly those of sending comrades... getting Party connections there and organising meetings under the pressure of the watchful British imperialists.' Perhaps the biggest 'political mistake,' in Ford's view was making a formal request to the British government to hold the conference in London, not least because when this request was denied, 'it caused considerable confusion in the plans for holding the Conference.' The change of venue to Hamburg, then added to this confusion. The late arrival in Germany of Ford and the US delegation, caused by the racism of the shipping line that refused to transport them, only added to the organisational problems, as did the inability of the RILU's 'Negro Committee' to take responsibility for organising the conference. Ford was particularly critical of the 'Negro Committee,' which he alleged 'rendered no assistance' in the preparations for the conference and 'did nothing to keep in contact with the preparations for the Conference on the outside.' He also levelled equally serious criticisms the 'Negro Bureau of the CI,' which 'did not react to the political significance of the Conference.' He concluded, 'in spite of the fact that the Secretariat of the ECCI had made a decision for this Conference to be held, no definite instructions were sent out, to my knowledge, to the different parties.'[113]

Ford was also critical of the fact that when he arrived in Germany he was instructed to limit the conference to two days, originally it was planned to last for a week, but the origin of these instructions is not clear. He concluded that despite all the shortcomings and weaknesses, at least the ITUCNW had for the first time made contact 'with large bodies of workers in West Africa and the West Indies,' even if in many cases these were backward elements of the Negro workers who haven't trade union experience.' One of his main conclusions was that much more needed to be done by the CI and RILU to deal adequately with the 'Negro Question,' not least because 'the Communist Parties and revolutionary trade union organisations still maintain their opportunist practices with regard to Negro work. They still, in practice, under-estimate the significance

112. Ibid.

113. RGASPI 534/3/490.

of Negro work. 'This,' he argued, 'was manifested by the fact that practically no assistance was rendered by these Parties in helping us make this Conference a success.'[114] Nevertheless, despite these weaknesses, in his published account of the conference Ford's assessment was overall more positive. He concluded that the main tasks of the conference – bringing together delegates from Africa and the Diaspora; analysing the 'class and race problems of the Negro toilers;' laying the basis for 'stimulating the consciousness and initiative of the Negro toilers, and outlining 'a programme of tasks for developing their movements and bringing them into the International Revolutionary Labour movement,' had largely been achieved.[115]

Other internal evaluations of the conference were more varied. The South African delegate argued that the conference had required much more time to be adequately prepared and he was critical of the fact that there was not even time during it to discuss the resolutions which, he added, were 'written in a mechanical way – even I had to read many of them over and over again to understand their meaning.' He was also critical of the decision to ask the British Labour government for permission to hold the conference in London. He argued that: 'The Conference should have been held in London and it should not have been held in secret on the top floor of the Seamen's Club in Hamburg. Rather that all delegates would be arrested so that we could make good propaganda out of this.' He concluded, 'I thought then that even the South African Communist Party, with all its mistakes, could not have arranged a worse Conference than this was.'[116]

Frank Macaulay, the delegate from Nigeria, was concerned about how those Africans who had travelled to Europe for the first time would be affected by their experiences. He reported how they had been immediately 'surrounded by detectives' demanding to see their passports when they first landed in Liverpool and when they reached London. In both London and Berlin nobody had any information about the conference and it was only through the efforts of Padmore that they had found their way to Hamburg. However, Macaulay thought that despite such problems the 'Negro Conference' could be regarded as the first step towards the formation of trade unions in West Africa and he urged the ITUCNW to seize the opportunity before the British Government took further measure to suppress trade union organisation.[117]

114. Ibid.

115. J.W. Ford, 'The First International Conference of Negro Workers: Its Accomplishments and its Future Tasks,' Hermina Dumont Huiswoud Papers Box 1 Folder 21, TAM 354, Tamiment Library/Robert F. Wagner Labor Archives, New York.

116. Ibid.

117. Ibid.

It was evident that the conference had been hampered by the hostility of the 'capitalists and imperialists and their agents' and the role of the British Labour government was the most blatant example of such hostility. In Chicago meetings held in preparation for the conference had been raided by the police and state harassment had intimidated many in other parts of the United States, as well as in West Africa and Trinidad. In Cuba, Panama and South Africa, state repression had prevented delegates from travelling to Europe. It was even rumoured that the three delegates from South Africa had attempted to board a ship for Europe but had then disappeared without anyone knowing of their whereabouts. Other internal assessments also highlighted the fact that 'the conference preparations had many serious shortcomings,' namely that 'the preparations and the election of delegates was not made on a sufficiently broad enough scale,' especially in the United States and because 'there was not sufficient centralised direction' of the work from RILU and the CI.[118]

There was also considerable criticism levelled at the European communist parties for lack of concern with the conference and the 'Negro Question' in general. In August 1930 a 'Report on Negro Work in France and England commenced by stating:

> It is impossible to make a report on the Negro work of our French and British Parties. To attempt this would be to infer that concrete work in this sphere of Party activity had been accomplished. In the case of the British Party no such assertion can be made, while with reference to our French Party only a little more may be said.[119]

The report was particularly critical because of what it referred to as 'the tremendously favourable objective situation,' brought about by the world economic crisis and the response to it, especially in the colonies. In regard to the Hamburg conference, the French, German and British parties failed to do any work in the colonies, or even amongst the 'Negro workers' in their own countries, little or nothing was mentioned about the conference in the communist press and no delegates attended from France or Britain. Similar criticisms were levied at the CPUSA, the LAI, the Western European Bureaux of the CI and RILU, the Negro Bureau of the ECCI and the ITUCNW itself.[120]

The CPGB, for example, was accused of taking almost no measures to develop its work in the colonies in general, nor to expose the colonial policy of the Labour government, and of 'inexcusable passivity and neglect' in regard to the

118. 'The International Conference of Negro Workers,' 29 July 1930, RGASPI 495/155/87/243.

119. RGASPI 495/155/87/277.

120. 'The First International Conference of Negro Workers and Future Tasks,' 14 August 1930, RGASPI 495/155/87.

Negro Question. It was required to take immediate remedial measures including establishing a 'Negro National Liberation Organisation,' which amongst other tasks would 'struggle against increasing discrimination against Negroes in England.' [121] In a letter to the PCF the vital importance of the colonies as a source of labour and raw materials for French imperialism at a time of the global economic crisis was pointed out and the Party was accused of 'impermissible passivity and inertia,' and 'crass opportunism in Negro work.' It too was required to remedy this situation and charged with stepping up its work in relation to the 'black colonies' and working more closely with the LDRN.[122] As a consequence of all the evident weaknesses there were even more demands for further developing all Negro work, strengthening the Negro Bureau and Negro Section in Moscow, as well as strengthening the work and ideological level of individual communist parties, some of which, it was suggested, still did not understand the importance of the anti-imperialist struggle in the colonies.[123] There were proposals for measures to enable the training of cadres in Africa and the Caribbean and for sending experienced comrades from the communist parties in the major imperialist countries to these areas. There were also calls for work to begin to establish communist parties in Haiti, Jamaica and West Africa.[124]

The meeting of the Executive Bureau of RILU became heated at times and there were different views about which bodies were most responsible for organisational problems and how to correctly assess the significance of the conference. Not withstanding the problems and shortcomings, there had been some successes too, not least the fact that information about the conference and the ITUCNW had spread throughout the world. The composition of the conference although limited in terms of numbers was also solidly based on worker delegates and some, especially those from West Africa, represented important unions and organisations. Some felt that the conference had been highly significant for its militant resolutions, 'the first time that such highly important class principles have ever been laid down by and for the Negro masses.' [125] The conference clearly did much to raise the consciousness of the young trade unions of West Africa and brought both those in Africa and the Caribbean into close contact with the international communist movement and such organisations as the LAI, whose representatives attended the conference. In short the conference was seen as a good place from which to develop the 'Negro work' and

121. 'Draft Letter to the CPGB,' 16 August 1930, RGASPI 495/4/47/20-23.

122. 'Draft Letter to the CC of CPF,' 22 August 1932, RGASPI 495/4/47/28-33.

123. See e.g. 'Negro Work,' 2 August 1930, RGASPI 495/18/810/6-13.

124. 'The International Conference of Negro Workers,' 29 July 1930, RGASPI 495/155/87/243-251.

125. 'The First International Conference of Negro Workers and Future Tasks,' 14 August 1930, RGASPI 495/155/87.

to consolidate and intensify that work in the CI and RILU. The preparatory work, despite all its weaknesses, provided extremely useful experience for the four principle organisers, Ford, Patterson, Huiwsoud and Padmore. Huiwoud and Padmore, in particular, gained valuable contacts and knowledge about the Caribbean and West Africa, and both Ford and Patterson had been able to intervene in the 'Negro work' of several of the key European communist parties, albeit with mixed fortunes. In the course of organising the Hamburg conference, for instance, important steps had been taken to develop work in Britain that continued after the conference.[126] Most importantly, the conference took the decision to fully launch the work of the ITUCNW and to establish its headquarters in Hamburg and there was even discussion about convening the Second International Conference of Negro Workers.[127]

A later assessment concluded that the Hamburg Conference:

> Was of great political and organisational significance and importance as the first attempt to bring together the representatives of the Negro toilers from different parts of the world in order to work out a unified program of action and for laying the basis of the solidified struggle of the Negro toilers. The propaganda and agitation conducted prior to the Conference penetrated into many parts of the Negro world and aroused sections of he oppressed and exploited Negro toilers to the realisation of their conditions and to the necessity for intensifying their struggles against imperialism. The toilers in many of the isolated colonies of Africa through this Conference first learned about the International Revolutionary Movement and the revolutionary struggles of the proletariat and the exploited peasantry.[128]

However, the main consequence of the Hamburg Conference was that it highlighted the important work that the Hamburg Bureau or Committee had in front of it.[129] To some extent it was almost a miracle that the conference had taken place at all and suggests that the Comintern cannot be viewed simply as a great monolith dispensing 'Moscow gold' to its pliant auxiliaries. Even after all the discussions and decisions of the Sixth Congress on the Negro Question, apart from the enthusiasm of the ITUCNW's activists, it appeared that

126. There was even a report in August 1930 that 'an auxiliary organisation has very recently been formed in England.' 'Report on Negro Work in France and England,' 4 August 1930, RGASPI 495/18/810/14-22.

127. *NW*, 3/Special Number (15 October 1930) p.16.

128. 'On the Organisation of the ITUCNW,' 5 September 1930, RGASPI 495/18/810/77.

129. There were also proposals that the Bureau should be based in Berlin with sections in the US, South Africa and the Caribbean.

little had changed. As one document expressed it, in the preparatory work for Hamburg 'the tremendous weaknesses of our Parties and revolutionary trade union movement was glaringly disclosed.'[130] There were therefore many demands for improvement and self-criticism, as well as various proposals concerned with strengthening the work of the ITUCNW. There was even a proposal for a monthly publication in English, French, Spanish and Portuguese.[131]

This historic Pan-African conference is now largely forgotten. It certainly did much to re-launch the work of the ITUCNW and to launch the career of one of its foremost activists, George Padmore. It was Padmore, who following initial work by James Ford, would lead attempts to consolidate the work of the ITUCNW and build its main organising committee in Hamburg from 1931-1933. In 1945, many years later and in very different circumstances, Padmore was the key organiser of a much more well-known Pan-African gathering in Manchester, England. It should not be forgotten that many of the roots of the Manchester Congress can be found in Hamburg, which remains the first ever conference of workers' representatives from Africa and the Diaspora and reflected the Pan-Africanist perspective of the Comintern at that time. The conference presaged the important role that workers would play in the anti-colonial struggles that subsequently broke out in Africa and the Caribbean.

130. 'Resolution on the First International Negro Conference,' 22 August 1930, RGASPI 495/4/47/34-37.

131. 'On the Organisation of the ITUCNW,' 5 September 1930, RGASPI 495/18/810/77.

Chapter 4

The Hamburg Committee

The most important consequence of the 1930 Hamburg Conference was the official public founding of the ITUCNW with a leadership and programme that had been approved by the assembled delegates. Indeed, before the Hamburg Conference there were sometimes references to a 'Provisional' ITUCNW. The conference also highlighted the fact that important differences existed between the conditions and problems facing 'Negro workers' in the United States and those facing the inhabitants of Africa and elsewhere, and that therefore there was a need for different methods of work according to these specific conditions.[1] The conference once again also highlighted the weaknesses in the approach of the European communist parties, as well as other sections of

1. This particular problem was also addressed in the pages of the ITUCNW's publications, see 'The Revolutionary Forces of Africa,' *The International Negro Workers' Review*, 1/1, (January 1931) pp.13-16.

the Comintern, towards colonial work in general and the 'Negro Question' in particular.

The Fifth World Congress of RILU

The political orientation of the ITUCNW was however decided not only on the basis of discussions in Hamburg but also according to the deliberations, resolutions and decisions of the CI and the RILU. The ITUCNW was, after all, essentially a sub-committee of the RILU, established to carry out work amongst 'Negro toilers.' It was sometimes described as 'an organ of the RILU...outwardly reserving its organisational independence in its dealings with the broad masses of Negro toilers.' It was not authorised to establish its own membership, as this would have created 'the impression that the ITUCNW is a Black International conducted on racial lines and not based on the class struggle.'[2] Immediately after the Hamburg Conference, many of the delegates made their way to Moscow in order to attend the Fifth World Congress of the RILU. Seventeen 'Negro delegates' attended the congress, which convened its own 'Negro Commission,' and once again the Negro Question was one of the main agenda items.[3] It was also in Moscow that the first meeting of the new Executive Committee of the ITUCNW was held and subsequently many of the leading figures in the ITUCNW remained in the Soviet Union for some months.

The Fifth Congress of the RILU paid great attention to the effects of the world economic crisis on the workers of all countries but it also devoted special attention to the consequences of the crisis for the 'colonial and semi-colonial countries.' Alexander Lozovsky, the general secretary of the RILU, referred to the 'remarkable activity' of the 'oppressed peoples and oppressed races,' while another speaker noted that even in 'the most backward Negro colonies,' and this referred to Gambia, Nigeria, Haiti and Congo, the anti-imperialist struggle had assumed violent forms.[4] Consequently the RILU concluded that the entire colonial world was in ferment, that this was having a profound effect on the big powers and that therefore the labour movement in the colonial countries, including those Lozovsky referred to as 'our oppressed fellow travellers, the Negro workers,' required the RILU's maximum support. He argued that it was particularly important for the RILU to do more to assist Negro workers in order

2. Resolution on the Organisation and Functions of the ITUCNW, 21 January 1931, RGASPI 495/155/96.

3. On the RILU Congress see also E.T. Wilson, *Russia and Black Africa*, pp.199-202. Based on French sources Wilson claims that there were twenty-five 'Negro delegates.'

4. *NW*, 1/ 4-5 (April-March 1931) p.12. See also *Resolutions of the Fifth Congress of the RILU* (London, 1931) p.42.

to overcome the problem of racism that existed even within the revolutionary trade union movement and that bred 'justifiable suspicion and mistrust.'[5]

The issue of racism and white chauvinism was a key issue at the congress not least because of the infamous incident at the Stalingrad Tractor Works, where Robert Robinson, an African American worker, was the subject of a racist attack from two America workers.[6] The attack led to protests from workers throughout the Soviet Union and subsequently the deportation of the offenders. Lozovsky contrasted this incident with numerous examples of white chauvinism in the United States and it led to the passing of a special resolution by the 'Negro delegates' at the congress, in which they extolled the Soviet Union and resolved to defend it with their lives. Amongst other things the delegates resolved: 'we declare the Soviet Union to be our fatherland. We have seen that the Soviet Union is the only country in the world that has solved racial and national problems. We see here the living example of the right to self-determination in practice.[7]

During the congress Lozovsky called for the ITUCNW to be transformed into an organisation 'with backing among the masses throughout the whole Black Continent, in the US, in Latin America, and in the West Indies.' He concluded by stressing that 'tremendous political importance is attached to the question of organising the Negro workers,' and that only those with 'bourgeois prejudices,' those 'understanding nothing' could fail to see the value of those 'fighting allies' in Africa and elsewhere who were 'seething with hatred against their oppressors.'[8] Indeed the congress concluded that 'the Black Continent has acquired a great significance as an object of capitalist exploitation,' and that increased exploitation as a result of the economic crises was leading to resistance amongst the workers, who had to be organised. The congress resolved in regard to Africa that, 'The principal task in all countries is to organise the industrial proletariat which, in spite of its small numbers, is, nevertheless, to be considered as the basis of the revolutionary anti-imperialist movement.' However, it added that the organisation of agricultural workers especially on large plantations was also vital.[9]

---

5. *NW*, 1/ 4-5 (April-March 1931) p.16. Also *The International Negro Workers' Review*, 1/ 2 (February 1931) pp.15-18.

6. For Robinson's own view on this incident see his autobiography. R. Robinson with J. Slavin, *Black On Red: My 44 Years Inside the Soviet Union* (Washington D.C., 1988) pp.65-75.

7. 'Declaration of the Negro Delegation of the fifth RILU Congress against the white chauvinism of two American workers.' *The International Negro Workers' Review*, 1/2 (February 1931) pp.15-18. See also the letter sent by workers at a factory in Moscow to workers of the Stalingrad Tractor Factory, ibid pp.21-22.

8. *The International Negro Workers' Review*, 1 /2 (February 1931) p.17.

9. *Resolutions of the Fifth Congress of the RILU*, pp.64-66.

James Ford, himself a member of the Executive Bureau of the RILU, reported to the congress on 'work among Negroes', and pointed out how the economic crisis was radicalising millions of 'Negro toilers' throughout the United States, Africa and the Caribbean. He paid particular attention to the significance of the strikes that had occurred in Gambia, Sierra Leone and Dahomey, as well as the recent uprisings in French Equatorial Africa and in Nigeria. He stressed that in regard to Negro workers, the RILU had not done enough and that was why the ITUCNW had been established, both to awaken the 'class-consciousness of the Negro toilers' and organise them to struggle against any vestiges of white chauvinism, particularly in the US and South Africa.[10] Several of the other Negro delegates addressed the congress including Small and Macauley from West Africa, Hernandez (Sandalio Junco) from Cuba and Mary Adams (Burroughs) from the United States. Perhaps it is not coincidental that in the final resolution on Negro workers attention was paid for the first time to the particular problems facing 'Negro women workers.'[11] Attention was also paid to Negro workers in South America, the congress resolutions stressing that they too needed to be recruited into the revolutionary trade unions.

The congress Resolution on Work among Negro Workers noted that they were more likely to bear the effects of the economic crisis. While again criticising the RILU sections in the US, South Africa, Britain, France and Belgian for their well-established weaknesses, it called on the 'class-conscious Negro workers' to realise that 'the responsibility for the many weaknesses and short-comings in the Negro work falls to a great degree to them owing to the fact that it is the direct result of their inertia and lack of initiative.'[12] This was tantamount to a directive to the ITUCNW and its supporters and the congress also resolved to make Africa 'the centre of gravity' for the work of the ITUCNW.[13] It concluded that despite the differences between the various African colonies and the need to organise the agricultural labourers, the central task was to 'organise the industrial proletariat which, despite its small numbers, is nevertheless the main basis of the trade union movement in these countries.' The congress also recognised that this work required trained organisers and in future years the ITUCNW would attempt to provide the appropriate education and training

10. *The International Negro Workers' Review*, 1/2 (February 1931) pp.18-22.

11. *L'Ouriver Nègre,* numéro spécial (1November 1930).

12. *The International Negro Workers' Review*, 1/2 (February 1931) pp.18-19 and *NW*, 1/3 (March 1931) pp.14-15. *Resolutions of the Fifth Congress of the RILU,* pp.159-165.

13. 'Resolution on the work of the Hamburg Committee, 18 October 1931, RGASPI 534/3/668.

both in *The Negro Worker* and by encouraging potential activists in Africa and the Caribbean to study to Moscow.[14]

The visit to Moscow provoked a variety of views amongst the African delegates. Joseph Bilé, for example, appears to have had some negative experiences with the 'bureaucrats of the Comintern' and spoke of the chauvinism that existed between African Americans and Africans. The Gambian delegate, Edward Small, reported that he was disappointed that 'the Negro comrades who were present did not work and discuss together, as this opportunity would have warranted.' He added that, the 'American Negroes' viewed the 'Negro Question' in an entirely different ways from those from Africa. In his view this question could not be solved if it was viewed merely it in terms of class, since he argued that 'Negroes are not only exploited as workers, but also as a race.' He also complained that although in Moscow there had been prolonged discussion about 'lynching and white chauvinism', they had not discussed the 'social problems' faced by the workers. Small had other criticisms, some of which were directed at the Negro Bureau of the RILU, but he acknowledged that the journey to Moscow was 'very instructive and motivating.'[15]

Indeed the delegates travelled throughout the Soviet Union and witnessed at first hand the 'socialist construction' of the new state. Small admitted that they returned 'after gaining many useful impressions and above all with the conviction of how important the Soviet Union is for the Negroes.' The Nigerian Frank Macaulay, on the other hand, stated that the trip to Moscow had helped him realise that not only had Nigeria been isolated from international allies for too long but also that hitherto demands for self-government in Africa had only been directed along constitutional lines. He concluded 'I myself have only realised during my present journey that this method cannot be successful.' He admitted previously knowing little about the Soviet Union but following his visit expressed the conviction that 'Negroes can only be liberated with the help of the Soviet state. For a couple of years we had our hopes pinned on the English Labour Party. However, since the party's recent assumption of power we have become convinced that they are worse than the Conservatives and that we can gain our freedom and independence only with the help of Russia.'[16]

---

14. *NW*, 1/3 (March 1931) pp.28-29. In addition to articles in *The Negro Worker* pamphlets such as Lozovsky's *ABC of Trade Unionism for Negro Workers* were published by the ITUCNW. The preface to the pamphlet appeared in *NW*, 1/7 (July 1931) pp.11-13.

15. 'Minutes of the meeting of the International Secretariat with the Negro friends,' 14 October 1930, RGASPI 542/1/40.

16. Ibid.

James Ford and the Hamburg Committee

Following the discussions at the Fifth Congress it was decided that the ITUCNW should establish an operational base in Hamburg and from November 1930 James Ford took up the responsibility of directing the work of what came to be called the Hamburg Committee (HC). The Committee's immediate aims were to popularise the deliberations of the Hamburg Conference as well as the Fifth Congress and reports on both soon appeared in *The Negro Worker*. In addition five thousand copies of a report of the conference were produced and distributed in Africa, the United States, the Caribbean and Europe. The dissemination of the report and other literature was often the work of seamen in the main European ports of Hamburg, London, Rotterdam and Antwerp. Reports of the conference also appeared in the international communist press and it was publicised through special meetings in several countries and regions including: South Africa, West Africa, the United States, France, Germany and Panama. In Hamburg meetings were even held on board ships and included white as well as black seamen.[17] Ford re-established contact with several of the ITUCNW's executive committee members and main supporters in the United States, the Caribbean and Africa, including Edward Small and E.A. Richards in West Africa and Albert Nzula and others in South Africa.[18] They were all asked to submit reports 'on the conditions of Negro workers in their countries' and instructed to establish local sub-committees to undertake agitation and propaganda work on behalf of the ITUCNW.[19] However, there were many difficulties and some weaknesses in this work and therefore constant advice, encouragement and criticism from the RILU Negro Bureau in Moscow.[20] This Bureau was reorganised under Padmore's chairmanship in the period after the Fifth Congress, with the general aim of directing the organisation of 'the Negro workers in Africa, North and Latin America and the West Indies,' and with the authority to give directives to the appropriate RILU sections 'so that the Negro workers might be able to organise themselves especially in the colonies of British, French and Belgian imperialism in Africa.'[21] Gradually, however, the ITUCNW was

17. See especially *NW*, 1/4-5 (April-May 1931).

18. See Ford to the Secretariat, CPSA, 3 January 1931, J.W. Ford Papers, Tamiment Library, New York.

19. 'Report to the European Secretariat of RILU on the ITUCNW,' 31 January 1931, RGASPI 534/3/669. Ford reported that initially he had heard nothing from East Africa and the Caribbean. See also 'Plan of work and Immediate Tasks of the ITUCNW at Hamburg,' 28 February 1931, RGASPI 534/3/668.

20. See e.g. Padmore to Ford, 8 and 13 February 1931, RGASPI 534/3/668.

21. 'Plan of Work of the Negro Bureau of RILU,' 31 December 1930, RGASPI 534/1/164/4-5.

removed from any responsibility for work in the US and instead concentrated more on 'those sections of the black world where there are no parties or official sections of the RILU,' although also on South Africa where although a communist party existed the RILU section remained extremely weak.[22]

For the distribution and dissemination of literature, and for maintaining international communications, sympathetic seamen were vital. This was obviously one of the main reasons why Hamburg had been chosen as the European base of the ITUCNW. It was at this time not just the main German port but also the centre of the Comintern's Western European Bureau, as well as the centre of its maritime activity and the headquarters of the International of Seamen and Harbour Workers (ISH), founded in October 1930.[23] One of the ways in which the ISH distinguished itself from the existing International Transport Federation, was that whereas it claimed that the latter 'kindles racial hatred... for the benefit of capital,' the ISH stated that it based 'all its work on the extermination of racial hatred and of the abolition of the rupture existing between working conditions of white and coloured seamen.'[24] The relationship between the ISH and the ITUCNW was a close one and they shared the same premises at 8 Rothestroodstr, near the Hamburg docks, which was also the base of the International Seamen's Club.

From Hamburg and other ports seamen of all nationalities were used as couriers for CI propaganda material and correspondence and one of Ford's first tasks was to establish as many reliable contacts of this sort as possible. He had already initiated this work during his earlier visit to Hamburg and discussions with the German CP in 1929. At that time Ford reported that there were almost three hundred Communist seamen on the ships that docked in Hamburg and regular contact with African ports. It was envisaged that through such means it might even be possible to smuggle people out of the African continent without the need of passports.[25] Seamen from many nations were engaged in this work. Chinese seamen were particularly useful couriers for material to and from South Africa, while it was reported that a German seaman managed to establish a useful contact in Panama. In Hamburg Ford began organising amongst African seamen, both ashore and on board the mainly German, English, Dutch and

22. Padmore to B.D. Amis, 2 January 1932, RGASPI 534/3/754.

23. See G. Minsk, 'The Founding of the International of Revolutionary Seamen and Harbour Workers,' *Inprecor*, 16 October 1930, p.992, also 'Resolution on the colonial work of the sections of the ISH in imperialist countries,' in TNA MT 2084.

24. E. Kitten, 'The International of Seamen and Harbour Worker,' *RILU Magazine*, January 1931, p.21.

25. 'Report of the trip in the interests of the ITUCNW and the Negro Bureau of the RILU, and the meeting of the Executive Committee of the LAI,' 14 February 1929, RGASPI 534/3/450.

American ships that visited the port. He held political education classes, conducted work in the bars frequented by seamen and tried to encourage them to frequent the port's International Seamen's Club, where he displayed literature, hung a 'wall paper' and a map 'showing the extent of the developing struggles of the Negroes in Africa etc.' He even arranged meetings and a dinner for black seamen with their counterparts on ships from the Soviet Union.[26] Amongst the African seamen the aim was not just to recruit them as couriers but also to encourage them to read and discuss the ITUCNW's literature and to try to make further contacts in Africa. Ford managed to establish small groups of 'Negro seamen' on more than a dozen ships and was able to successfully encourage the seamen to overcome divisions based on nationality and other factors that were being exacerbated by the shipowners.[27]

Similar work was begun in Britain, Belgium, Holland and France and was aided by the activity of the ISH, in which Ford also played a key role.[28] In Britain, Ford eventually made contact with the newly formed Negro Welfare Association (NWA) and its secretary Arnold Ward, and he was also in communication with Harry O'Connell, a seaman and activist from British Guiana based in Cardiff. In France it was Tiemoko Garan Kouyaté, the secretary-general of the Ligue de Défense de la Race Nègre (LDRN), who became most actively involved in the work of the ITUCNW and was encouraged to undertake more work amongst seafarers.[29] The LDRN had already established contacts in some French colonies in Africa through its publication *La Race Nègre* and it also organised in French ports such as Bordeaux and Le Havre. After meeting with Ford in Germany in the summer of 1931, Kouytaté became particularly active in Marseilles where he organised mainly amongst African seamen in collaboration with the French section of the ISH, the Fédération Unitaire des Marins, and the CGTU – the revolutionary trade union opposition affiliated to the RILU.[30] Kouyaté organised meetings and encouraged the African and other colonial seamen to unite with their European comrades and join the ISH, but he also spoke of the need for colonial independence and the significance of developments in the Soviet Union and attempted to establish a school for illiterate

26. See 'Report of the Work of the ITUCNW (Hamburg) Covering the Period from December 1930 to September 15 1931,' RGASPI 534/3/669 and Ford to Padmore, 6 August 1931, RGASPI 534/3/668.

27. 'Report of the Work of the ITUCNW,' 2 October 1931, RGASPI 534/3/669.

28. See 'Plan of Work and Immediate Tasks of the ITUCNW at Hamburg,' 28 February 1931, RGASPI 534/3/668.

29. The most important source for background material on Kouyaté remains P. Dewitte, *Les Mouvements Nègres en France, 1919-1939* (Paris,1985).

30. 'Note sur la propagande révolutionnaire interessant les pays d'outre mer,' 31 July 1931, 3 SLOTFOM 71, Archives Nationales d'Outre-Mer (ANOM), Aix-en-Provence, France.

seamen. He claimed to be organising amongst soldiers as well as seamen, and it was during a demonstration in Marseilles on August 1st, which the Comintern had declared 'International Day of Struggle against Imperialist War,' that he was arrested and subsequently sentenced to forty-five days in prison.[31] Kouyaté's arrest temporarily halted the Hamburg Committee's plans to establish a sub-committee in Marseilles, which it had been hoped would 'strengthen work and connections in the French colonies.'[32]

The activities conducted from the Seamen's Club in Hamburg, as well as the work of the ISH, were closely monitored by the security services of several countries. The links between the ISH and the National Minority Movement (NMM) in Britain, as well as Communist activities relating to British ships, seamen or colonies were, for example, closely monitored by the British government and by the Special Branch of the Metropolitan Police. The British government paid particular attention to monitoring the activities of the ITUCNW and 'Negro seamen' in British, colonial and European ports, who it suspected of acting as couriers or being engaged in other subversive activities.[33] Evidently the work of Ford and the activities of the ISH were of some concern to the British government, which worked closely with the Shipping Federation, an organisation established at the end of the nineteenth century to safeguard the class interests of the British shipowners. The Special Branch and other agencies noted that ISH activists in Hamburg, Liverpool and other ports coordinated their activities particularly in relation to African seamen and it was not uncommon for the ISH in Hamburg to recruit these seamen for the NMM. It was also noted that Ford maintained close contact with the British-based Indian Seamen's Union led by Saklatvala, no doubt as part of his overall responsibility for the colonial work of the ISH, and that *The Negro Worker* was being widely circulated in British and West African ports. From this period therefore the British authorities took measures to disrupt the activities of the ITUCNW, especially when it attempted to organise on board ships. They had already begun to confiscate copies of *The Negro Worker* found on ships heading for the colonies, as well as

31. 'Report of Work of ITUCNW,' 2 October 1931, RGASPI 534/3/669. See also 'An appeal to the Black Soldiers of France,' *NW*, 1/9 (15 September 1931) pp.5-8. See also Kouyaté's 'Black and White Seamen Organize to Struggle,' *NW*, 1/12 (December 1931) pp.19-20. Also Note sur la propagande révolutionnaire, 30 September 1931, 3 SLOTFOM 71, ANOM.

32. 'Concrete Proposals on Report of Work of Hamburg Committee,' 10 June 1931, RGASPI 534/3/668 and 'Report on Work of ITUCNW,' 2 October 1931, RGASPI 534/3/669.

33. TNA MT9/2084.

those found in the possession of couriers.[34] Ford concluded that even when he was harassed and interrogated by the German police this was on behalf of the British authorities.[35]

The Negro Worker

The Negro Worker, with its characteristic front cover showing an African worker breaking free from his chains, was the main regular publication of the ITUCNW throughout its existence. Padmore, who became the chairman of the RILU Negro Bureau, claimed that the continual use of this image on all ITUCNW literature 'will help to establish a certain familiarity amongst the workers for our literature and at the same time convey the idea that only the workers themselves can break their chains.'[36]

The Negro Worker temporarily became *The International Negro Workers' Review* for the first two editions of 1931 before it reverted back to its original and more appropriate title. The title *The Negro Worker,* it was explained, 'expresses more clearly and definitely the central aim and idea of our Committee, that is, that it is only by the organisation and leadership of the workers, the Negro toilers, can the Negro masses successfully carry on the struggle for their freedom and emancipation.' The aims of the publication did not change and *The Review* was also clearly intended to be both a forum for discussion and an organiser. The first editorial explained: 'It is our aim to discuss and analyse the day to day problems of the Negro toilers and connect these up with the international struggles and problems of the workers.'[37]

The main aims of the ITUCNW also remained the same with a firm focus on providing 'a picture of the life and struggles of the Negro workers,' including agricultural workers, and on helping to establish revolutionary trade unions throughout Africa, the Caribbean and elsewhere. It was considered that there was a need to combat the isolation of Negro workers and so an emphasis on utilising *The Negro Worker* to help raise their 'international outlook,' by providing information about the international labour movement and 'the successful building of socialism in the Soviet Union.' In addition, the ITUCNW had the

34. TNA MT9/2084. For some details of the Indian Seaman's Union see M. Sherwood, 'Lascar Struggles Against Discrimination in Britain 1923-45: The Work of N.J. Upadhyaya and Surat Alley,' *The Mariner's Mirror*, 90/4 (November 2004) pp.438-455.

35. Ford to Padmore, 30 April 1931, RGASPI 534/3/668.

36. Padmore to Ford, 25 February 1931, RGASPI 534/3/668.

37. *The Review* initially had an editorial board of Ford, as editor in chief, and George Hardy and Walter Albert of the ISH, the aim being to draw the latter two individuals 'into active Negro work.' See Padmore to Ford, 8 February 1931, RGASPI 534/3/668.

aim of enlightening its readers about the dangers of 'Negro bourgeois nationalism' by which it meant the ideas and activities of Garvey, Kadalie in South Africa and A. Philip Randolph in the United States.[38]

The ITUCNW also made every effort to explain that not only did the Negro Question have different features in Africa, the Caribbean and the United States, but also that conditions within Africa might also vary from region to region.[39] At the same time it pointed out what was common for Africa and the Diaspora, in particular a need for the organisation of workers in order to resist the deteriorating economic conditions resulting from the global Depression. The Hamburg Committee stressed the fact that 'Negro toilers' were amongst those most affected by the economic crisis, unemployment and overproduction and by what it saw as an accompanying increase in racial oppression on the one hand and 'Negro reformism' on the other. It was these economic struggles that were emphasised at the time as the means to wage 'an uncompromising fight against imperialism,' and for self-determination. Anti-imperialism was therefore an issue that often appeared in the pages of *The Negro Worker* and other publications as an economic and political question requiring a struggle by the workers against existing conditions organised and led by 'powerful revolutionary trade unions.'[40]

Approximately one thousand copies of *The Negro Worker* appeared on a monthly basis in both English and French throughout 1931.[41] It was widely distributed in Africa, especially the British and French colonies in West Africa and in South Africa, where the largest single consignment of one hundred and fifty copies were despatched. Copies were also disseminated throughout the American continent (Ford reported that copies were being translated into Portuguese by Communist seamen from Brazil), as well as in Europe and even in Australia.[42] The ITUCNW also distributed hundreds of mimeographed copies of particularly significant articles from *The Negro Worker* and other relevant pamphlets and propaganda material. These included Stalin's *The Year of Great Change,* as well as Ford's *The Negro and the Imperialist War of 1914-1918* and

38. *The International Negro Workers' Review,* (January 1931) p.3.

39. T. Ring, 'The Revolutionary Forces in Africa,' *The International Negro Workers' Review,* (January 1931) pp.13-16.

40. *The International Negro Workers' Review* 1/2 (February 1931) p.11.

41. The French edition sometimes carried different articles.

42. Ford to Padmore, 31 July 1931, RGASPI 534/3/668. Also 'Report on work of ITUCNW (Hamburg) covering the period from December 1930 to September 15, 1931,' RGASPI 534/3/669.

Padmore's *The Life and Struggles of Negro Toilers* and *Negro Workers and the Imperialist War - Intervention in the Soviet Union.*[43]

The Life and Struggles of Negro Toilers, commissioned by the RILU, apparently written in three weeks and published at the end of 1931, was perhaps the most important of the ITUCNW publications.[44] It was widely distributed and publicised and also published in French as *La Vie et les luttes des travailleurs nègres.* The book was guided by the Comintern's Pan-Africanist approach to the liberation of Africa and the Diaspora, or in Padmore's words the '250 million Negroes in the world...scattered throughout various geographical territories,' the vast majority of whom were 'workers and peasants.' It was written chiefly to enlighten workers in the major imperialist countries and to 'indicate in a general way the tasks of the proletariat in the advanced countries so that the millions of black toilers might be better prepared to carry on the struggles against their white imperialist oppressors and native (race) exploiters, and join forces with their white brothers against the common enemy – World Capitalism.' Padmore explained that 'in the present crisis of world capitalism' the imperialist powers were 'turning their attention more and more to Africa and other black semi-colonies (Haiti, Liberia), which represent the last stronghold of world imperialism,' in order to 'unload the major burden of the crisis on the shoulders of the black colonial and semi-colonial masses.' He concluded that 'the general conditions under which Negroes live, either as an national (racial) group or as a class, form one of the most degrading spectacles of bourgeois civilisation.'[45]

In this book Padmore described not just the nature of the historical and contemporary 'oppression of Negro toilers' but also some of the most recent struggles waged in Africa, the Caribbean and the United States. He also devoted considerable attention to the likelihood of a future 'imperialist war' and armed attacks of 'the capitalist states against the Soviet Union,' as well as the historical recruitment of black troops to participate in such conflicts. He also stressed the need for both black and white workers to rid themselves of the ideas and prejudices of their rulers, of racism and reformism, and here he particularly singled out Garveyism as a 'hindrance to the mass Negro struggle for liberation against American imperialism.' He called on both black and white workers to recognise that their struggles for liberation were interrelated and called on them to support the programme of the RILU and CI. In this context he reminded the

43. Two lesser-known pamphlets by Padmore were published during the early years of the ITUCNW, *Africa the Land of Forced Labour* and *Haiti, An American Slave Colony*. For the difficulties involved in producing such publications see RILU Negro Committee to the Secretariat, 15 July 1931, RGASPI 534/3/668. Also 'Report on Work of the ITUCNW,' 2 October 1931, RGASPI 2 October 1931.

44. 'To The Secretariat,' 15 July 1931, RGASPI 534/3/668.

45. G. Padmore, *The Life and Struggles of Negro Toilers* (Hollywood, 1971) pp.5-7.

workers of the imperialist countries of the famous words of Marx, 'labour in the white skin cannot free itself while labour in the black skin is enslaved.'[46]

The Work of the Hamburg Committee

Ford was almost solely responsible for the work of establishing the Committee in Hamburg and making all the necessary contacts in Germany as well as other countries. His main initial tasks were to establish connections with seafarers and other workers in Africa and the Caribbean. However, he was also, until November 1931 when he left Hamburg, editor-in-chief of *The Negro Worker*,[47] for a time directly involved in a struggle for higher wages organised by black seamen in Hamburg, and found that he was sometimes overwhelmed by his other responsibilities with the LAI and with leading the colonial work of the ISH. On one occasion he was asked to travel to Austria on behalf of the LAI and the International Friends of the Soviet Union, even though he protested that he already had too much work to do in Hamburg. In the course of this trip he was arrested and deported back to Germany.[48] On another occasion he appeared with Kenyatta at the International Conference on African Children held in Geneva organised by Save The Children.[49] He also had very little money, lacked adequate support from the ISH and the German representatives of the RILU and CI and was often harassed by the German police. [50] He even complained that Albert Walter, the German leader of the ISH, would not even allow him office space and was afraid that if there were too many 'Negroes' in the Seamen's Club the police might close it down. [51] In one report Ford even claimed that he found 'definite expressions of unfriendliness on the part of some of the comrades to the Negro seamen who came to the Club' and that he 'had to become very sharp' with some of them, while in another he speaks about the need to 'breakdown the bourgeois influence' and 'general impression' that 'Negroes, Chinese and Indians are nothing but 'niggers, coolies etc.'[52] Although

46. Padmore, *The Life and Struggles of Negro Toilers.*

47. In November 1931 Padmore became both the chief editor of *The Negro Worker* and responsible for the work of the ITUCNW in Hamburg.

48. Ford to Padmore, 6 August 1931, RGASPI 534/3/668.

49. *NW*, 1/7 (July 1931) pp.8-10. On Kenyatta's appearance see J. Murray Brown, *Kenyatta* (London, 1973) p.153.

50. Regarding Ford's financial difficulties see e.g. Ford to Padmore, 7 February 1931, RPASPI 534/3/668.

51. See Ford to Padmore, 30 April 1931; Padmore to Middle European Secretariat, Berlin, 18 July 1931, and Padmore to Walter, 21 July 1931, RGASPI 534/3/668.

52. Ford to Padmore, 30 April and 6 August 1931, RGASPI 534/3/668.

Padmore tried to remedy this state of affairs from Moscow, he faced similar problems when he arrived in Hamburg.[53]

Ford was still extremely critical of what he referred to as the 'non-cooperation' of the local sections of the RILU especially those in Europe, such as the NMM and the CGTU, which made the work of the ITUCNW so much more difficult. In one report, for example, he explained that he often met with African seamen who lived in England but when he forwarded their details the Seaman's Minority Movement (SMM) failed to visit and make contact with them.[54] Nevertheless, in July 1931 on the basis of the work already undertaken, the RILU Secretariat decided to attempt to establish sub-committees of the Hamburg Committee in Marseilles, Cape Town, New York and Liverpool to enable the recruitment of cadres in these countries that might later be trained to work in the colonies. But although this decision was taken, little or nothing was done to implement it.[55] The ITUCNW proposal for a second international conference was also soon dropped as it became clear that work on the African continent and in the Caribbean was also developing slowly.[56]

Although Ford had the support of the Negro Section of the CI and the RILU Negro Bureau/Committee, the other key figures involved with the work of the ITUCNW, Padmore and Huiswoud, were initially based in Moscow and were engaged in other additional work and responsibilities.[57] The RILU Negro Committee was itself concerned with a considerable amount of work, including monitoring the activity of all the trade union organisations that were engaged with the Negro Question and issuing detailed directives in order to strengthen this work. It was weakened still further in 1931 by the redeployment of three of its members, including its designated vice-chairman, Hernandez (Sandalio Junco), who had been responsible for work in Latin America and parts of the Caribbean.[58]

One of the other key concerns of the RILU Negro Bureau, in the period after the Hamburg Conference, was the international campaign in relation to the 'Scottsboro Boys,' nine African American youths who were facing the death

53. See e.g. Padmore to Walter, 21 July 1931, RGASPI 534/3/668.

54. 'Report of the Work of the ITUCNW,' 2 October 1931, RGASPI 534/3/669.

55. Resolution on the Work of the Hamburg Committee, 18 October 1931, RGASPI 534/3/668.

56. Concrete Proposals on Report of Work of Hamburg Committee, 10 June 1931, RGASPI 534/3/668. The Caribbean sub-committee of the RILU, based in New York, was subsequently charged with acting as a sub-committee of the ITUCNW with responsibility for the Caribbean and Latin America.

57. The RILU Negro Bureau was sometimes known as the RILU Negro Committee.

58. See e.g. Minutes of the Negro Committee of the RILU, 25 May 1931, RGASPI 534/3/668. Huiswood to RILU Secretariat, 2 April 1931, ibid. On Junco see also chapter eight.

penalty after being found guilty of trumped-up charges of the rape of two white women in Alabama.[59] The Scottsboro case has been referred to as 'one of the great defining moments of the twentieth century' but its global significance was largely a consequence of the campaign organised by the Comintern and its organisations, especially International Red Aid, (IRA but sometimes known by its Russian acronym MOPR) which had already declared itself a supporter of the struggles of the Negro masses against oppression and for liberation.[60] The campaign involved all the parties and bodies of the Communist International and the Negro Committee of the RILU. It was the Negro Committee that from May 1931 shouldered the responsibility of assisting the MOPR to develop the international campaign.[61] The campaign was of major importance for the ITUCNW, not only in its own right but also because it might help to 'mobilise the mass of Negro workers to join the revolutionary trade union movement.'[62] In Hamburg Ford held discussions about the Scottsboro case with African seamen as part of his work to encourage them to organise for their own demands and they joined in sending a protest letter to the Governor of Alabama.[63] Subsequently the case regularly featured in the pages of *The Negro Worker* and the Hamburg Committee issued special appeals in order to further develop the international campaign. In France, where the LDRN launched a new publication, the *Cri des Nègres* in the summer of 1931, the Scottsboro case appeared on the front page of the first edition.[64]

Perhaps the major weakness of the Hamburg Committee was that initially it made little headway in Africa, which had been declared 'the centre of gravity' of its work. The Committee did make numerous contacts amongst seamen and other individuals but had limited influence amongst workers and their organisations in the colonies, and was not yet able to directly influence their struggles. Ford complained that this lack of influence was partly because of interference

59. See J.A. Miller, S. Pennybacker and E. Rosenhaft, 'Mother Ada Wright and the International Campaign to Free the Scottsboro Boys, 1931-34, *American Historical Review* (April 2001) 6/102, pp.387-430 and W.T. Howard (ed.) *Black Communists Speak on Scottsboro* (Philadelphia, 2008).

60. The MOPR was founded in 1922 and based in Berlin. It provided financial and legal support for Communists, anti-fascists and others facing legal prosecution or state harassment. See 'The Origins of International Red Aid,' *Inprecor*, 7 March 1928, p.262.

61. See e.g. 'Minutes of the Negro Committee of RILU,' 21 and 25 May 1931, RGASPI 534/3/668.

62. 'Concrete Proposals on Report of Work of Hamburg Committee,' 10 June 1931, RGASPI 534/3/668.

63. *NW*, 1/6 (May 1931) p.11.

64. See e.g. *NW*, 1/7 (July 1931) pp.3-4 and 'Note sur la propagande révolutionnaire,' 30 September 1931, 3 SLOTFOM 71, ANOM.

by the British government. Indeed, in Sierra Leone the postal authorities had told Richards that they would not deliver any mail to or from the Hamburg Committee, while in the Gold Coast Morton and Akrong who had attended the Hamburg Conference reported that they were both facing persecution. [65] The RILU and its Negro Committee made efforts to overcome these difficulties but here again the weaknesses of the communist parties and local sections of the RILU in Britain and France had an adverse impact on their work.

A strong connection did exist with South Africa, through the work of the CPSA and its affiliates, in particular the Federation of Non-European Trade Unions led initially be Ben Weinbren and subsequently by Albert Nzula,[66] that distributed *The Negro Worker* and established contacts in other parts of southern Africa. Other connections were established in East Africa and elsewhere on the continent through the work of the LAI. One of the most promising areas of work was West Africa, where the ITUCNW had consolidated its connections with some key individuals in the course of convening the Hamburg Conference. In the spring of 1931 there was further consolidated when the ITUCNW agreed to a request to co-opt E.A Richards, from the Sierra Leone Railway Workers' Union, onto its executive committee.[67] On the basis of this connection Ford despatched a thousand copies of 'An Open Letter to the Workers of Sierra Leone,' in which he emphasised the importance of building the Union and the need for it to take the lead in organising the peasants, the unemployed and other workers, as well organising and fighting against all forms 'capitalist exploitation.'[68] In addition, Ford had established some links with African seamen from Sierra Leone and Liberia, the most prominent of whom was Ebenezer Foster-Jones, one of the leaders of the Freetown-based United Seamen's Club, a social and welfare organisation originally formed in 1923, which represented the seamen in talks with their employers. Foster-Jones, a former policeman turned seamen who had managed to organise a committee of 'negro seamen' under the auspices of the British-based SMM on board one of the ships

65. 'Resolution on the Work of the Hamburg Committee' and Ford to Dear Comrades, 14 August 1931, RGASPI 534/3/668. Also 'Report on Work of ITUCNW,' 2 October 1931, RGASPI 534/3/669.

66. Nzula initially suggested that the Federation should be a sub-section of the ITUCNW a suggestion that Ford rejected. See Report to European Secretariat of RILU on Activities of the ITUCNW at Hamburg, 21 February 1931, RGASPI 534/3/669.

67. See Ford to all members of the executive committee of the ITUCNW, 21 April 1931, RGASPI 534/3/669.

68. RGASPI 534/6/23/2-8 and *NW*, 1/9 (September 1931) pp.17-19 A similar letter was sent to the British Guiana Labour Union and the workers of British Guiana. See *NW*, 1/8 (August 1931) pp.9-13.

sailing from West Africa to Europe, became for a time a courier for the ISH and a significant activist for the ITUCNW. [69]

Padmore and the Hamburg Committee

After nearly a year in Hamburg Ford was required to return to work in the United States and it was evident that the work of the Hamburg Committee was still poorly developed.[70] It had managed to send some directives to trade unions in Sierra Leone, as well as British Guiana, and had contact with individuals in West and South Africa, the Caribbean and Central America, although these were not considered to be extensive. To a large extent advances, especially in the Afrian and Caribbean colonies, depended on the national sections of the RILU in Britain and France. These were required to 'make a radical change in their activities among the colonial workers,' and to 'give systematic and constant assistance to the work in the colonial countries particularly supporting the activities of Hamburg Committee.' Progress also required more trained cadres to take up the work of the ITUCNW and although this also partly depended on the work of the RILU sections, the HC began to take its own measures to recruit potential students who could be sent to Moscow for training.[71]

In November 1931 George Padmore arrived in Hamburg to replace Ford, and immediately set to work to reorganise the work of the ITUCNW and *The Negro Worker*, to gain the full support of the representatives of RILU and the CI in Germany and to establish stronger connections with the ITUCNW's supporters in Africa and the Caribbean, as well as in France, Germany and Britain. He also began to make some contacts in Belgium that the RILU Negro Bureau intended to utilise to develop links amongst the Congolese workers in Antwerp and through them with their compatriots in the Belgian Congo.[72] Padmore also began to make more strenuous efforts to recruit potential students, particularly those from Africa, who might be sent to the Soviet Union for political train-

69. Ford to Padmore, 20 April 1931, RGASPI 534/3/669. See also Foster-Jones, 'Situation of Native Workers in Sierra Leone,' *NW*, 1/4-5 (April-May 1931) pp. 3-5. The activities of Foster-Jones, in Britain, at sea, and in West Africa were closely monitored by the British security services. See e.g. Sir Vernon Kell to G. Clauson, 2 November 1931, TNA M9/2084.

70. One account suggests that Ford was recalled following a police raid on the premises of the HC. J. Valtin, *Out Of The Night* (New York, 1941) pp.308-309.

71. 'Resolution on the work of the Hamburg Committee,' 18 October 1931, RGASPI 534/3/668.

72. Some of this work appears to have been successful. See Lukuta te, 'Atrocities in the Congo,' *NW*, 2/7 (July 1932) pp.7-9.

ing.[73] His first report from Hamburg suggests some criticism of Ford, who it was claimed had failed to send out thousands of pamphlets and other ITUCNW publications, including 'the whole French edition' of *The Negro Worker,* and had left the office of the HC in a state of chaos.[74]

On his arrival in Germany Padmore also found a major crisis within the ranks of the LDRN in Berlin. Its leading figure, Joseph Bilé, who was also a member of the German CP, was nearly destitute and facing charges levelled at him by another member of the League, while the organisation itself was splitting into squabbling factions. Padmore strongly supported Bilé, although he also proposed that that the LDRN in Berlin should be closed down, and suggested that he should be sent to Moscow to be trained for future political work in Africa.[75] Factional struggles had also split the LDNR in France and Padmore suggested that the LAI might assist in helping to resolve some of the problems by taking responsibility for the political orientation of the organisation in both France and Germany.[76]

The precise orientation of Padmore's work had been decided by the RILU Secretariat, following discussions based on Ford's reports. The Secretariat's Resolution of October 1931 noted that the HC had made some progress but concluded that it had not done enough to make 'Africa the centre of gravity of our work' and it was called on to widen its contacts and 'intensify' its organisational work.[77] In particular, the Resolution called for the HC to establish and develop workers' organisations in Africa and the Caribbean, always taking into account the differences that existed between individual colonies. In some places, such as Nigeria and Barbados, this might mean forming trade unions where none currently existed. In others, such as Sierra Leone and Jamaica where unions did exist, the task was to provide revolutionary orientation and leadership. The Resolution also paid special attention to 'Indian and other alien immigrant workers' in the Caribbean, and demanded that they should also be organised and that 'any tendencies of segregation must be strongly combated.' It also stressed the importance of work amongst the unemployed and seamen and dockers, as well as demanding that the Committee put into effect the decision to establish sub-committees.

---

73. Padmore to E. Small, 20 November 1931, Padmore to Comrade Adolf (ISH) 10 December 1931 and Padmore to Comrade Minor, 16 December 1931, Padmore to Ward, 17 December 1931, Padmore to Kouyaté, 29 December 1931, RGASPI 534/3/668. Also Huiswoud to Padmore, 11 January 1932, RGASPI 534/3/753.

74. Padmore to Dear Comrades, 16 November 1931, RGASPI 534/3/668.

75. Padmore to Comrade B, 17 December 1931, RGASPI 534/3/668.

76. Padmore to Dear Comrades, 16 November 1931, RGASPI 534/3/668.

77. Resolution on the work of the Hamburg Committee, 18 October 1931, RGASPI 534/3/668.

The Resolution reiterated the fact that the HC was an auxiliary of the RILU with particular responsibilities for work amongst 'Negro workers' and for popularising the struggles of these workers in the metropolitan countries and in the Soviet Union. In this regard, and for all the Committee's work, it stressed the importance of *The Negro Worker*. This publication had to concern itself with both the everyday struggles of Negro workers and the international situation, such as the threat of war and imperialist intervention against the Soviet Union. It was also reiterated that the HC did not have the responsibility for organising directly in Britain or France, only for encouraging links between the national sections of the RILU and Negro workers in those countries. In regard to the work in the United States, the ITUCNW no longer had any responsibility. As Padmore explained in one of his letters, 'the leading comrades in M[oscow] have decided that our committee is not expected to direct the work of the Negro movement in the USA in view of the fact that our party and the TUUL [Trade Union Unity League] as well as the LSNR [League of Struggle for Negro Rights] are making considerable headway in this field. We are to concentrate our attention on those sections of the black world where there are no parties or official sections of the RILU.'[78] The national sections of RILU therefore had to be encouraged to work with the HC to organise Negro workers themselves, as well as assisting those in the colonies. Ultimately the aim was to have sections of the RILU in Africa and the Caribbean and in developing all this work the HC not only had to work with the RILU sections but also with the LAI, ISH, MOPR and other auxiliaries of the Comintern. Clearly such important work could not be left to one or a few people and the Resolution called for more cadres and the training of 'advanced Negro workers,' both from the metropolitan countries and the colonies.[79]

In this connection Padmore tried, unsuccessfully, to arrange for both Arnold Ward of the NWA and E. Foster-Jones to travel from Britain to Moscow for training at the same time as Johnstone Kenyatta. But he was thwarted both by a lack of funds, as well as the reluctance of the LAI and CPGB to assist him.[80] He also continued to try to arrange for Kenyatta and P.G. Mockerie, another representative of the Kikuyu Central Association who had been sent to London, to travel to Moscow despite Kenyatta's well-known political unreliability. Kenyatta still occupied a unique position as one of the few East Africans who was in close contact with the Comintern but that did not prevent Padmore from publicly as well as privately reprimanding him on several occasion, even informing him that the other 'Negro comrades' were ashamed of his constant political vacil-

78. Padmore to Amis, 2 Jauuary 1932, RGASPI 534/3/754.

79. Resolution on the work of the Hamburg Committee, 18 October 1931, RGASPI 534/3/668.

80. See Padmore to Dear Comrades, 12 June 1932 and 16 June 1932, RGASPI 534/3/755.

lation and close connections with the Quakers.[81] Kenyatta, for his part, rebutted such allegations, suggesting that his public statements had been distorted in the press. He claimed to have broken with the Quakers, who had provided some of his education during his sojourn in Britain, since he had 'found out that they are just as bad as other exploiters and oppressors of our mother land,' and he asked Padmore what more he could do to prove that he also wanted to 'free Africa from white imperialist rule.'[82] Whether Padmore was convinced or not, Kenyatta left London for Berlin in the summer of 1932 and then travelled onward to Moscow where he studied at KUTV for a year.[83] Although the RILU had developed a 'correspondence course' that could be utilised for training trade unionists in the colonies, the question of students continued to be a major preoccupation for the ITUCNW, with Padmore insisting that those recruited should return to their countries of origin and not remain in Europe.[84] At the close of 1932 he reported that there had been several successes in this work and that it was the first time such a large number of Africans had been sent to the Soviet Union for training.[85]

By 1932 the ITUCNW operating from both Hamburg and Moscow had established global connections that it now sought to consolidate.[86] A 'plan of work' drawn up for the first six months of that year shows that the Committee was working with organisations, or planning activities, in France, Jamaica, Haiti, South Africa, Guadeloupe, Holland (including the Dutch Antilles), Germany, Porto Rico, Belgian Congo, Britain, and West and East Africa.[87] Padmore personally corresponded with supporters and potential supporters throughout Africa, the Caribbean, the Americas and Europe. He worked diligently to establish and consolidate contacts, largely through the dissemination of *The Negro Worker* and other publications of the ITUCNW, and continually wrote to check up on the delivery of such publications and to make sure that those who received them were actually distributing them. On other occasions he would attempt to enlist even quite recent contacts. He encouraged one correspondent in Basutoland by explaining that the ITUCNW wanted to free Africans

81. Padmore to Kenyatta, 6 May 1932 and 1 June 1932, RGASPI 534/6/23.

82. Kenyatta to Padmore, 9 June 1932, RGASPI 534/7/74.

83. Murray-Brown, *Kenyatta*, p.162.

84. 'Practical Decisions on the Discussion of the ITUCNW,' 23-26 May 1932, RGASPI 534/3/753.

85. Report of the Work of the Hamburg Committee for the Period 1931-32, RGASPI 534/3/753.

86. O. Huiswoud, 'The Revolutionary Trade Union Movement Among Negro Workers,' *RILU Magazine*, 2/3 (15 February 1932) pp.212-216.

87. Plan of Work of the ITUCNW for February to July 1932, 1 February 1932, RGASPI 515/234/3038.

from 'white imperialism' and instructed him to send reports of conditions in his country and establish a branch of the ITUCNW. Padmore informed him that he would then send a programme and a 'charter' that would give him 'full authority to be connected with the parent body.'[88]

However, it is clear that Padmore also continually attempted to direct some of the 'Negro work' in the United States, France, Britain and elsewhere even though this was not his responsibility. On many occasions, for example, he wrote detailed letters to Ward and other members of the NWA in London, as well as to Party or YCL members in the United States, suggesting how they should carry out their work and sometimes criticising the local CP. Drawing on his own experience as a student activist at Fisk University he wrote to one comrade to point out the importance of carrying out political activity amongst the youth and students, even when conditions were not entirely favourable. In this regard he recalled that he and four other managed to organise the 'biggest student strike ever pulled off in the South,' which lasted some nine months and 'was nothing less than a revolution.' He used the same experience in order to criticise the past and current mistakes and concluded, 'unfortunately the [Young Communist League] YCL in those days was so "left" that they were unable to see any revolutionary potentialities among Negro students. We did not put our emphasis on the working class intellectual but on the working class youth. Had we then understood the national question we would have realised that the Negro students are the allies of the revolutionary movement, potentially, and not, as Lovestone would have us believe of the counter-revolution.'[89] 'You see comrade,' he wrote on another occasion to the same correspondent, 'history is not waiting upon us. While certain comrades are sleeping on the job, the Garveyites and our enemies are wide awake...Although our work is chiefly concerned with Africa and the colonies we wish we could get into contact with the comrades who are assigned to do Negro work in the States. Perhaps our relationship with America would be stronger. For when we write [to] leading organs we get no reply.'[90]

Britain and the NWA

Padmore paid special attention to the newly formed NWA, led by the Barbadian Arnold Ward, but he also corresponded with other Caribbean activists in Britain included Harry O'Connell, a seafarer from British Guiana based in Cardiff, Jim Headley, a Trinidadian seamen temporarily resident in London,

88. Padmore to M.C. Motebang, 1 April 1932, RGASPI 534/4/755.

89. Padmore to E.L. Beone, 1 June 1932, RGASPI 534/3/755.

90. Padmore to Beone, 16 February 1932, RGASPI 534/3/753.

as well as Foster-Jones and others in Liverpool.[91] The NWA had been established in rather mysterious circumstances early in 1931 and although James Ford had corresponded with Ward, he knew little about the organisation and did not manage to develop a close relationship with it. In September 1931 he still referred to Ward as 'a Negro comrade working with the LAI and carrying on work for the Hamburg Committee,' without making any reference to the NWA. [92] Although the NWA was initially established as a worker's organisation the NMM in Britain knew little about it. It was therefore instructed by the RILU to 'acquaint itself with the work of the Negro Workers' Welfare Association, drawing its attention to the need to set up better connections with the Hamburg Committee.' During most of its early life, however, the NWA remained closely connected with and affiliated to the LAI.[93]

One of Padmore's main tasks was to encourage the ever-pessimistic Ward and to make efforts to establish the NWA as the affiliate of the ITUCNW in Britain. At first he envisaged that the NWA could be organised with the help of the SMM and he encouraged Ward to organise meetings in all the major ports in Britain in order to commence agitation amongst black workers but also as the means to establish maritime couriers to Africa and the Caribbean. He explained to Ward that if he accepted the task of establishing 'a section' of the ITUCNW this would be to educate the 'coloured workers' but also 'to educate the English workers and get them to agitate more in (sic) behalf of freeing the colonies in Africa, the West Indies, etc.'[94]

From November 1931 Padmore maintained regular contact with Ward, sending him instructions and receiving reports of the NWA's meetings and activities. On occasions Padmore would also compose messages of greeting to be presented to the meetings of the NWA, which outlined the ITUCNW's analysis of the international situation, the dangers facing black workers and the programme of action that the NWA was encouraged to adopt. In one of his earliest messages of this type he stressed the importance of fighting for what he called 'simple, common place, every day issues,' and highlighted the case of the well-known black boxer, Len Johnson who, because of the colour bar in British boxing, was prevented from fighting for a British title. Padmore urged the

91. See e.g. Padmore to Ward, 17 December 1931, RGASPI 534/3/668; Padmore to O'Connell, 5 January 1931, RGASPI 534/3/754; Headley to Padmore, 7 March 1932 RGASPI 534/3/754 and William Brown to Padmore, 25 June 1932, RGASPI 534/3/755.

92. See e.g. Ward to Ford, 2 September 1931, RGASPI 534/7/50 and 'Report on Work of the ITUCNW (Hamburg) Covering the period from December 1930 to September 15, 1931,' RGASPI 534/3/669.

93. 'Concrete Proposals on Report of Work of Hamburg Committee,' 10 June 1931, RGASPI 534/3/668.

94. Padmore to Ward, 17 December 1931, RGASPI 534/3/668.

NWA, 'when such outrages occur your organisation should be the first to raise a protest through public meetings, calling upon the class-conscious white workers in England to form a united front with you in exposing the sham British democracy.' He concluded by stressing that only if the NWA took up the fight against 'such outrages' could it hope to 'win the support of all the coloured workers not only in London, but wherever they happen to be in England'. He explained, 'only in this way will your colonial brothers feel that they have worthy friends in you, uncompromising fighters against British imperialism, in the very citadel of these capitalist exploiters.'[95] On other occasions Padmore would criticise the actions, or inactivity, of the NWA or the content of its meetings, but he always attempted to encourage them to become more organised and politically active.[96]

However, because he was not only in touch with Ward but also trying to organise others in Britain at the same time, problems sometimes arose. The SMM had been encouraged by the RILU to establish a 'sub-committee,' which was led by Jim Headley and was, as Padmore put it, 'working in connection with the coloured seamen in London.' The SMM's 'committee of militant coloured seamen' led by Headley had first met in London in 1930. The SMM had been instructed to 'organise the Negro seamen in London and other ports' and, in order to achieve this, it had been advised to 'form the Negro seamen into groups or committees in order that they may discuss their own problems and take part in the general activities of the seamen's union.'[97] It is not yet clear how Headley came to lead this committee, the formation of which seems to have been prompted not just by RILU directives in general but more particularly by the work of the ITUCNW in preparation for the Hamburg Conference. It appears that this committee had been re-established with the support of the RILU Negro Bureau, which had agreed that Headley should continue to lead it.[98]

Padmore feared that there might be a conflict of interests between Headley's committee, which also included amongst its leading members Chris Jones (Braithwaite) another Barbadian activist, and the NWA and therefore he wrote to Ward concerned that there might be a danger of 'splitting up into too many organisations.' He proposed that the two organisations should merge but that Headley's committee should become 'the Seamen's section of the new united organisation,' with special specific tasks such as, 'trying to get all coloured seamen not only to join the organisation of the coloured people but also to enrol in the SMM, so that they will be able to carry on their economic struggles

95. Padmore to the NWA, 14 February 1932, RGASPI 534/3/754.

96. See e.g. Padmore to Ward, 27 February 1932, RGAPI 534/3/754.

97. Padmore to Ward, 7 March 1932, RGASPI 534/3/754 and RGASPI 534/7/48/170-171.

98. Huiswoud to Padmore, 11 January 1932, RGASPI 534/3/753.

with the white seamen.'[99] He explained that 'our Committee is only interested in one thing, and that is – the SMM must organise the coloured seamen, - not into any special Negro union, but together with the white seamen into one revolutionary union. This is our principle, which we will not compromise with. About the methods of doing this we give you a free hand, we have no fixed rules for this.'[100] Ward seems to have had no prior knowledge that Headley was organising within the SMM but he was clearly not impressed. He felt that the NWA in conjunction with the LAI, rather than the SMM was more likely to 'do work for Negroes,' and he urged Padmore to come to Britain so that they could discuss and resolve the matter.[101]

Padmore eventually travelled to England in the spring of 1932 and was able to meet with Ward, Headley and others and to speak at Scottsboro campaign meetings. The 'Negro work' of the SMM in Cardiff was not as developed as Padmore desired and he signalled his intention that the ITUCNW should start to organise amongst black workers in Cardiff, just as it did in Liverpool and London. O'Connell was subsequently elected as one of the SMM delegates to the ISH congress in Germany, which he attended a few weeks later.[102] Throughout this period Padmore continued to encourage O'Connell, in one letter he wrote:

> Always keep in mind that we are not doing anything for anybody, - we are doing it for ourselves. What Negroes do not always seem to understand is that they are the most oppressed people in world and that if they want freedom they have got to fight for it. They are always waiting for somebody to give it to them as a gift. We know better than this. The road to freedom is a hard road full of disappointment, difficulties, etc. etc. But we cannot turn back. We have got to make the journey.[103]

The Scottsboro Case

The Scottsboro case continued throughout the early 1930s and as before the RILU Negro Bureau and the Hamburg Committee played a key role in

99. Padmore to Ward, 28 February 1932, RGASPI 534/3/754.

100. Padmore to Ward, 7 March 1932, RGASPI 534/3/754.

101. Ward to Padmore, 1 March 1932, RGASPI 534/3/754.

102. At the ISH Congress the ITUCNW organised its own 'Negro Workers' conference at which O'Connell was asked to report on 'Negro work in England.' See 'Programme for the Negro workers Conference,' n.d., RGASPI 534/3/753.

103. Padmore to O'Connell, 12 June 1932, RGASPI 534/3/755.

coordinating the international campaign.[104] This intensified during early 1932 after the Supreme Court of Alabama upheld the death sentence and then the Supreme Court of the United States, under immense international pressure, decided to review the sentences. It was in these circumstances that supporters of the IRA in Germany invited Ada Wright, the mother of two of the accused, to embark on a speaking tour of Germany and subsequently much of Western Europe. As part of the campaign the ITUCNW published numerous articles on the case in *The Negro Worker*, including one by Maxim Gorky, as well as a pamphlet *The Scottsboro Case in America*.[105] Supporters of the ITUCNW, including Joseph Bilé in Berlin, the LDRN in France and the NWA in Britain were heavily involved in Ada Wright's extensive tour. Despite efforts by the British and some other governments meetings and other protest actions were organised in Berlin, Vienna, Budapest, Brussels, Paris, and many towns and cities in Britain.[106] In Hamburg Ada Wright even addressed the delegates at the World Congress of Seamen, while in Britain Padmore spoke on behalf of the ITUCNW at meetings organised as part of her tour in London, Cardiff and Liverpool.[107] The campaign also had significant support in Africa and the Caribbean, where protest actions were reported in several countries including South Africa, the Gold Coast, Nigeria and Cuba.[108] One consequence of all this work was that that the MOPR, with the ITUCNW's assistance, established a 'Negro Department' and began to develop its work in Africa.[109]

The Work of the Hamburg Committee

In his report to the RILU Secretariat on the HC's work during 1932, Padmore claimed to have established 'thousands of new connections' in the Gambia, Senegal, Sierra Leone, Gold Coast, Nigeria, South Africa, Belgian Congo, Kenya, Uganda and Tanganyika, as well as in Jamaica, Haiti, Barbados, Trinidad, Grenada, St Lucia, the Virgin Islands, Bermuda, British Guiana,

104. IRA Executive to ITUCNW, 9 June 1932, RGASPI 534/3/755.

105. M. Gorky, 'Capitalist Terror in America,' *NW*, 2/1-2 (January-February 1932) pp.13-16, see also O. Huiswoud, 'Stop the Scottsboro Murder,' *NW*, 2/4 (April 1932) pp.30-31.

106. J.L. Engdahl, 'Scottsboro Campaign in England,' *NW*, 2/8 (15 August 1932) pp.18-20. In Berlin the Nazis called for Ada Wright's arrest and expulsion. NW, 3/4-5 (April-May, 1933) p.1.

107. On the Scottsboro campaign in Britain see RGASPI 539/3/307.

108. Report on the Work of the ITUCNW, December 1932, *NW*, 2/6 (June 1932) pp.9-11 and Huiswoud to Padmore, 7 February 1932, RGASPI 534/3/753. J. Donbrowski, 'The Scottsboro Case,' *NW*, 2/11-12 (November-December 1932) pp.25-27 and 'Awakening of African Women,' *NW*, 4/8-9 (August-September 1933) pp.12-14.

109. IRA Executive to ITUCNW, 9 June 1932, RGASPI 534/3/755.

Panama and British Honduras. He also claimed that hundreds of contacts were established in the United States, England, and France, while reporting that up until 1931 the HC only had in total about 60 contacts. In Britain alone he claimed to be organising 'over 600 Negroes' through sub-committees organised in London, Cardiff and Liverpool.[110] Padmore also asserted that on the basis of some of these individual contacts, trade union groups and committees had been established in Senegal, Madagascar, Haiti, Cameroons, Liberia, Guadeloupe, Conakry, Jamaica, St Lucia and Panama.[111] Certainly an organised group existed in Guadeloupe, but evidence of such groups or large numbers of contacts in other places is less obvious and there seem to be few signs of the much sought after worker correspondents for *The Negro Worker*.

Padmore also mentioned links with what he referred to as 'working class organisations,' such as the African National Congress, the Nigerian Workers' Union, the Gold Coast Native Workers' Association, the Georgetown Stevedores' Union and the Trinidad Workers' Association. Evidently he had established some of these new contacts through the dissemination of *The Negro Worker* that, as he himself admitted, was distributed free in the early part of 1932 in order to gain more subscribers. As a consequence, according to Padmore's account, the circulation had increased considerably from a thousand to five thousand copies a month. However, on many occasions copies of *The Negro Worker* and other literature did not arrive at their intended destinations because of interception and confiscation by the colonial authorities, so the quantity of literature produced and distributed is not necessarily a guide to the exact extent of the ITUCNW's international network. But Padmore even managed to put the actions of the colonial authorities in a positive light, pointing out that the banning of *The Negro Worker* in many colonies 'is the best indication that our organ is meeting with popular support.'[112]

Nevertheless, despite many advances there were still significant problems and the RILU continued to criticise its adherents in Britain, France, South Africa and the United States, as well as the ISH, for failing to give adequate support to the Hamburg Committee. The RILU Secretariat pointed out, for instance, that 'the organisation of Negro seamen in the motherlands and colonies' should be carried out by the ISH, while the Hamburg Committee should pay more attention to the mass unemployment that existed in the colonies and other economic questions, as well as the problem of training cadres. The Hamburg Committee

110. Report of the work of the Hamburg Committee for the period 1931-1932, RGASPI 534/3/753.

111. Ibid.

112 Ibid.

was also tasked to strengthen *The Negro Worker*, and there were even proposals that it should be published in Spanish and Portuguese.[113]

Padmore and Kouyaté

In the course of his work in Hamburg, Padmore significantly strengthened links with Kouyaté and other activists in France.[114] Following the split in the ranks of the LDRN, a new organisation, the Union des Travailleurs Nègres (UTN), was established in Paris in 1932 with branches in several French ports, including Rouen, Bordeaux, Le Havre and Marseilles. The *Cri des Nègres,* which existed almost as a French-language edition of *The Negro Worker* following the decision to end the publication of *L'Ouvrier Nègre,* was widely distributed throughout the French colonies and had its production costs subsidised by the ITUCNW.[115] Although it was not always published on a monthly basis, it had a circulation of about 3000 copies, a third of which were sent to contacts in the colonies, including those in Dakar, Djibouti, Madagascar, Guadeloupe Martinique, as well as Haiti. In addition Padmore's *The Life and Struggles of Negro Toilers* and *Imperialist War Intervention in the Soviet Union* were translated into French and plans were made for their distribution throughout the French colonies in Africa.[116] In both Djibouti and Martinique communist groups were in existence, although these were not affiliated to the French CP and there is no evidence that the Hamburg Committee was in direct contact with them. In Guadeloupe, Sabin Ducadosse remained a key activist and it was almost certainly from his circles that the *Cri* received letters asking for support and directions from a group of workers in Guadeloupe.[117]

Indeed the origins of the *Cri des Nègres* can be found in the wish of Padmore and the RILU Negro Bureau to establish a French publication that reflected 'the economic situation of the Negro workers' but was not entirely dependent on the CGTU and PCF.[118] The attempts to circumvent the weaknesses of the

113. Resolution on the Report of the Work of the Hamburg Committee, n.d. RGASPI 534/3/753.

114. See e.g. Padmore to Marcel, 21 March 1932, RGASPI 534/3/754/180.

115. Report of Paul, 21 October 1932, 3 SLOTFOM 53, ANOM. See also B.H. Edwards, *The Practice of Diaspora –Literature, Translation, and the Rise of Black Internationalism* (London, 2003) especially pp.241-306.

116. Padmore to S. Rosso, 17 March 1932, RGASPI 534/3/754/171-173.

117. 'Preliminary verification of the fulfilment of the RILU Secretariat decisions on the work of the Hamburg Committee,' 14 March 1932, RGASPI 534/3/730. See Special Report by Kuyatte(sic) n.d. RGASPI 534/3/753.

118. Edwards, *The Practice of Diaspora*, p.263. See also O. Huiswoud to CGTU Colonial Commission, 16 February 1932, RGASPI534/3/754.

French CP in colonial matters, were not unprecedented and in part were the raison d'etre of the ITUCNW, but the close collaboration of Padmore and Kouyaté, that has been seen as one increasingly emphasizing 'race-based organising,' created some of the conditions that ultimately led to the expulsion of both from the Communist movement.[119]

Padmore did everything he could to support and encourage Kouyaté and the two of them corresponded soon after Padmore's arrival and then met and worked closely together following the ISH's World Congress of Seamen held in Hamburg in May 1932.[120] On occasions Padmore also travelled to Paris to speak to Kouyaté and other members of the UTN.[121] Padmore remained critical of the lack of support provided by the PCF and the CGTU and he became increasingly involved with the work of the UTN and its secretary general, encouraging Kouyaté to act when the PCF and CGTU were slow or reluctant to take up 'Negro work' but also indirectly supporting Kouyaté's continual attempts to keep the *Cri des Nègres* independent of total PCF control.

When Padmore wrote to Kouyaté from England in May 1932 it was to encourage him in this direction and also to insist that he was most determined to conduct work in 'l'Afrique noire.' Padmore was critical of the fact that this work had been neglected by his predecessor, James Ford, who he claimed had been more interested in America, but he was also critical of the CGTU and the British CP, because, according to him, the former was mainly interested in North Africa, while the latter had no interest in Africa at all. Padmore therefore proposed that in future he and Kouyaté should work together in regard to French colonies in Africa and the Caribbean. In particular he reiterated what he had previously told Kouyaté, not to wait for the CGTU to take action but to take things in hand himself and to establish a French section of the ITUCNW. To assist him Padmore planned to write to ask the RILU to instruct the CGTU to provide suitable premises, while he thought that the RILU itself might provide Kouyaté's salary. In short, he wanted Kouyaté and the French section to be responsible for all 'Negro work' in France and its colonies and even in the Belgian Congo and for it to act independently of the PCF and CGTU.[122] However, Padmore's encouragement of Kouyaté occurred just at the time when the PCF was attempting to exert greater control over the UTN and the *Cri des Nègres* and when Kouyaté appeared to be acting independently even of his comrades in the UTN. It was a course of action that added to allegations of the

119. Edwards, *The Practice of Diaspora*, p.264.

120. Padmore to Kouyaté, 1 February 1932, RGASPI 534/3/754. Practical Decisions on the Discussions of the ITUCNW, 23-26 May 1932, RGASPI 534/3/753. On Kouyaté's participation at the congress see 'World Congress of Seamen,' *NW*, 2/6 (June 1932) p.24.

121. Reports of Paul and Joe, 7 October 1932, 3 SLOTFOM 53, ANOM.

122. Padmore to Kouyaté, 6 May 1932, RGASPI 534/3/755.

George Padmore, Courtesy of Marika Sherwood.

ORIGINAL COVER OF GEORGE PADMORE'S THE LIFE AND STRUGGLE OF NEGRO TOILERS, From the authors collection

James W. Ford (left) and Garan Kouyaté (right) pictured with Willi Munzenberg founder of the LAI. From Arbeiter Illustrierte Zeitung, summer 1931, from the author's collection

William L. Patterson at a Scottsboro demonstration. From *Arbeiter Illustrierte Zeitung*, summer 1931, from the author's collection

Otto Huiswoud in the 1930s.
Hermina Dumont Husiwoud Photographs Collection, Tamiment Library, New York University

embezzlement of funds eventually led to his expulsion from the PCF and the UTN in September 1933, and therefore significantly compromised Padmore's own position.

The Demise of the Hamburg Committee

The HC was unable to advance its work in certain regions because of the lack of cooperation from the local sections of the RILU. This was certainly the case in Antwerp, where Padmore reported no headway had been made in contacting seamen from the Congo and where he was attempting to get help from France to aid 'the Belgium comrades, whose work on the colonial front reflects many weaknesses.'

The RILU noted some achievements in regard to the numerous contacts that had been established but also that even where links had been established they were seldom consolidated, and that as a result it was not possible for the ITUCNW to exercise political leadership in Africa or the Caribbean. It was clear that many of the shortcomings were due to the inability of the ISH and the RILU sections to seriously engage with 'Negro work.'[123] The HC's work was also hampered by numerous police raids on its office and activists in Hamburg and on its maritime couriers. Even the police attacks carried out by the German government were, according to Padmore, inspired by the governments of Britain, France and the other colonial powers.[124] Similar hostile activities continued to occur in the colonies, where seamen couriers were harassed and *The Negro Worker* and other literature were confiscated. Literature was routinely confiscated by the authorities in South Africa, for instance, and in many colonies banned altogether.[125]

Padmore also had to overcome the problem that he was working alone in Hamburg, alhough he was supported by Huiswoud and the RILU Negro Bureau in Moscow, and worked in conjunction with other Comintern bodies. As he explained to an enquiry from MOPR, 'usually all our organisations appeal to the Negro Committee, which despite its pretentious name is only one man, to give them assistance on every campaign.'[126] Despite such problems Padmore appears to have been attempting to extend the work of the Hamburg Committee and even to develop its independence, sometimes beyond its official remit. He certainly wished to recruit another activist, almost certainly Kouyaté, to

123. Resolution on the Report of the Work of the Hamburg Committee, December 1932, RGASPI 534/3/753.

124. 'Our First Anniversay,' *NW*, 2/1-2 (January-February 1932) pp.2-3.

125. See J. Gomas to Padmore, 4 November 1932. RGASPI 534/3/756.

126. Padmore to Dear Comrade, 28 February 1932, RGASPI 534/3/754.

join him in organising the work of the Committee. He also proposed that the ITUCNW should be able to recruit individual members and demanded that it should have the right to independently select and send students to Moscow, rather than under the auspices of other organisations such as the LAI. He also clearly wished to have a larger 'independent budget,' which might to allow him and Kouyaté to travel throughout Europe, as well as additional funds that could be spent in the colonies.[127]

Padmore's plans might just have been overambitious, on one occasion for example, he wrote that he was trying to carry out the slogan 'a Negro workers' committee in every port in every country!' On another he planned to bring some twenty-five delegates from Africa and the Caribbean to the congress of International Labour Defence (ILD), held in Moscow in November 1932, at least partly with the aim of holding a meeting of the ITUCNW soon afterwards.[128] Indeed, he proposed that what he began to term the Hamburg Bureau might consider calling 'a wide united front Congress of Negro Toilers,' a second international conference, a proposal that does not seem to have been accepted by the RILU Negro Bureau.[129] It is also possible that he was fearful that the RILU would 'liquidate' the Hamburg Committee if it did not produce results. He certainly wrote in such terms to Kouyaté not long after he had arrived in Hamburg, suggesting that the Committee only had a year to disprove the view that it was impossible to 'organise Negroes in the colonies.' He suggested to Kouyaté that they needed to work like 'devils' and that their work had to be a 'living response to those comrades who underestimate the revolutionary capacities of the black race.'[130] There is no other indication of the ITUCNW's imminent 'liquidation,' and Padmore does not appear to have confided such fears to anyone else.

Expulsion and Relocation to Paris

The police raids that hampered the work of the HC at the beginning of 1932 intensified after Hitler came to power in Germany at the beginning of 1933. Hitler's subsequent attack on the German CP, which followed soon afterwards, led to Padmore's arrest, brief imprisonment, and subsequent deportation

127. Practical Decisions on the Discussion of the ITUCNW, 23-26 May 1932, RGASPI 534/3/753.

128. This congress was attended by delegates from British Guiana, Trinidad, the United States, South Africa, Nigeria, Liberia and Kenya. Delegates from Senegal and Madagascar were prevented from attending by the colonial authorities. See T. Jackson (Albert Nzula) 'The ILD and the Negro Peoples,' *NW,* 3/2-3 (February-March 1933) pp.9-12.

129. Resolution on the Report of the Work of the Hamburg Committee, December 1932, RGASPI 534/3/753. See also Padmore to Kouyaté, 1 February 1932, RGASPI 534/3/754.

130. Padmore to Kouyaté 1 February 1932, RGASPI 534/3/754.

to Britain by the Nazi regime in February 1933.[131] The Nazis collaborated with the British authorities regarding his deportation and the British Consulate in Hamburg even delayed his departure for a few days because the ship that the German authorities intended to use was also carrying fifteen seamen from the Soviet Union. When Padmore embarked for Grimsby he was accompanied by the British police who thoroughly searched and interrogated him when he arrived in England. Although the police appeared to be unaware of exactly who he was, the British and German authorities had already taken measures to make sure that he could not dispose of five large trunks that contained names, addresses and literature including *The Negro Worker*. Padmore's own report of his deportation was almost light-hearted and even triumphant in places, since he viewed the great concern shown by the British authorities as evidence of the success of the ITUCNW's activities in Africa. Although he admitted that he had not been able to dispose of all incriminating material, his assertion that when the police raided, 'the "deck" was cleared for action,' and material 'safely deposited' was clearly at variance with the facts.[132] Both the German and the British authorities secured names and addresses of contacts and other material and the work of the Hamburg Committee was severely disrupted.

Padmore was under police surveillance throughout the rest of his brief stay in England but with the aid of Arnold Ward he managed to obtain some money and left for France the same day he arrived in Grimsby. He then made his way to Paris, where he lodged with 'an Indo-Chinese comrade' introduced to him by Kouyaté, as the latter was too well known for Padmore to stay with him. From Paris he made efforts to continue the work of the HC, warning contacts not to write to Hamburg, 'as everything is being confiscated that goes there.' To his comrades in Moscow he wrote, 'I am handicapped for lack of a typewriter and more important still, stationery and stamps,' and he added 'I have absolutely no money... I have no possibility to live much less work.' The absence of financial support to continue his work led him to allege that 'there is no phase of work that is being sabotaged more than Negro work,' a view that later came to dominate his thinking. Overall, however, he remained optimistic and informed his comrades that despite the expulsion 'we are marching forward and not all the devils in hell will stop us. When once a Negro's eyes are opened they refuse to shut again.'[133]

131. 'Fascist Terror Against Negroes in Germany,' *NW*, 3/4-5 (April-May, 1933) pp.1-3.

132. Padmore to Dear Comrade, 6 March 1933, RGASPI 534/3/895. See also British Consulate General to Foreign Office, 21 February 1933, TNA FO 372/2910.

133. Padmore to Dear Comrade, 3 March 1933, RGASPI 534/3/895.

He clearly intended to make France his base, to use the office rented by the 'French Negro Sub-Committee' and to use the printer of *Le Cris des Negres* to produce *The Negro Worker.* Although he predicted it would 'take a few weeks to get things properly re-organised,' and lack of finance held up publication he anticipated that distribution of *The Negro Worker* could still continue by sea. He also wrote of his intention to stay in the background and only 'operate through the local committee,' adding optimistically, 'with my presence here our French work will be greatly strengthened.'[134] In this connection he continued to seek payment and support for Kouyaté, who was already under growing suspicion by the PCF, claiming that if this was not forthcoming Kouyaté might have to give up his political activities and look for a job and that 'the consequences for our work will be serious.'[135]

One of most significant aspects of Padmore's correspondence with Moscow at this time was his announcement regarding work in the Caribbean. He had taken it upon himself to send 'Comrade H,' almost certainly Jim Headley, from England to Trinidad because, as he put it, 'the Americans are not interested in this work.' He even innocently enquired whether $50 a month could be sent to 'Comrade H' so that he could begin his activities. Padmore was evidently also in contact with de Leon, who had attended the Hamburg Conference, recently 'organised a union of 200 members,' in Jamaica and to whom he planned to send 'directives.'[136]

In April Padmore received a message from Moscow explaining some of the proposals for new methods of work. The ITUCNW had temporarily been renamed the 'International Committee for Mutual Aid to Negro Workers' and Padmore was instructed to work less openly so as 'not to leave so many traces of yourself.' In this regard he was forbidden to speak at public meetings and instructed to build an 'active group' around him through which he could continue his work. He was also criticised for several perceived weaknesses and the message made very clear that his old method of work, especially acting on his own initiative, was no longer to be tolerated. Amongst other things he was told:

> It is important to stress here the absolute necessity of collective work and not individualistic business relationships. In this respect there is much to be required of you in the way of quitting some of inclinations in this direction. You have a good opportunity for collective work now, make use of it. On the same basis of comradely criticism we must draw your attention to the fact that it is the general opinion that you are not entirely blameless in regard to the incidents in the

134. Padmore to Dear Comrade, 6 March 1933, RGASPI 534/3/895.

135. Padmore to Dear Comrade, 3 and 6 March 1933, RGASPI 534/3/895.

136. Padmore to Dear Comrade, 6 March 1933, RGASPI 534/3/895.

> other place. We advise you comradely to treat our proposals in this letter seriously and avoid further complications...
>
> We want to draw your attention to the question of selection of students. It is intolerable for you to send people that you don't know. And we find ourselves in a difficult position in regard to your last choice. It is not only this case but as a rule you have no right to send people whom you have not thoroughly investigated from every aspect.
>
> We are rather astonished at your information that you have sent somebody to the W[est] I[ndies] on your own account. We would like to know what reason you had to send this person on your own initiative. Whose advice did you act on? It is true the American comrades have been passive in this respect but it is wrong to send somebody whom we don't know and whom you also probably don't know well, on such responsible work...
>
> The WI affair and the student affair show that you have not orientated yourself correctly in accordance with our requirements and our special situation.

The letter concluded by urging Padmore to make more use of both 'the French comrades' and the NWA in Britain for his work and warned him to only send communications through trusted channels. Finally the letter stressed, 'writing private letters to your friends is your own affair, but we don't recommend you to mention anything concerning the work as it may have very serious consequences both for yourself and for us. We are convinced you will consider our proposals seriously and utilise them to conduct your work in such fashion as to avoid previous mistakes.' [137]

It was from Paris that Padmore prepared the next few editions of *The Negro Worker*, although from April 1933 a post office box in Copenhagen was given as the publication's new public address. At first his presence was not widely known, even by the members of the UTN, and by July 1933, when he first appeared openly at UTN meetings, Kouyaté was already facing accusations of misconduct and was appearing before the Control Commission of the PCF.[138] By the following month Padmore's own circumstances had changed. When Otto Huiswoud arrived in Paris in mid-August it was in order to inform him that he had been relived of his duties.

The reason for the change in Padmore's role has been little understood and it is his version of events, including the alleged 'liquidation' of the ITUCNW and his resignation in protest that has become established as historical fact. The

137. J. to Padmore, 22 March 1933, RGASPI 534/3/895.

138. Réunion de la fraction communiste nègre de l'UTN, 24 July 1933, 3 SLOTFOM 53, ANOM.

documentary evidence presents a rather different version of events. The activities of the Hamburg Committee had been severely damaged by the actions of the Nazi regime in Germany, the acquisition of contact details and other material by the British and German authorities and Padmore's expulsion and reappearance in Paris. Padmore and the ITUCNW were also compromised by the activities of Kouyaté and would almost certainly have been further compromised by permanent relocation to Paris as police agents had already infiltrated the UTN. There were clearly also concerns about Padmore's own recent conduct, as well as financial concerns about the future of the ITUCNW. It was in these circumstances that the RILU despatched Huiswoud to Paris to see how the work of the ITUCNW and the publication of *The Negro Worker* might be continued.

According to Padmore's account, Huiswoud arrived from Moscow and instructed him to 'close down' the HC, however he acknowledged that a meeting was called to discuss the work of the Committee, which would have been unnecessary if his version of events was completely accurate.[139] Huiswoud certainly did convene a meeting with Padmore and several of the leading French comrades including Stéphane Rosso of the UTN, Julien Racamond of the CGTU and Henriette Carlier (Eva Neumann), a representative of the Comintern working with the PCF's colonial commission.[140] However, this gathering was not to discuss the 'liquidation' of the HC but rather how it might be re-established in the new circumstances.

At the meeting Huiswoud spoke mainly about the financial viability of *The Negro Worker* and the former HC and whether the cost and organisation of both could become the responsibility of the colonial commission of the CGTU. Linked to this question was the issue of whether the work of the ITUCNW could be based in Paris, or should be located elsewhere. Since the CGTU was still being criticised for its weaknesses in regard to colonial matters, some surprise was expressed that it was being considered for such a responsibility. Padmore, in particular, reminded the meeting that the ITUCNW had been established because of the weaknesses of the RILU sections in France, Britain and elsewhere, and he asked why the RILU was effectively relieving him of his duties without offering any explanation or discussing the matter with him first. However, the other participants had no doubt that the questions were being posed not in an attempt to criticise Padmore and certainly not to 'liquidate' the ITUCNW, but rather to find ways of improving and developing the ITUCNW's work and funding in very difficult circumstances. Nevertheless, they were forced to agree with Padmore's assessment that neither the ITUCNW nor *The Negro Worker* could be

139. Padmore to the Secretariat, CPUSA, 3 February 1934, George Padmore Collection, Box 1 Folder 2, Princeton University.

140. Réunion pour la discussion sur le comité international des nègres, 23 August 1933, RGASPI 534/3/895.

successfully organised by the CGTU. Huiswoud added that he had personally spoken with Lozovsky and had been assured that there was no political criticism of Padmore, but it was felt that he had been away from political activity in the United States for a long time and that was not seen as 'a good thing.' Padmore voiced his general agreement with the discussion concerning the inability of the CGTU to take any responsibility for the work of the ITUCNW and remarked that in his view the RILU should have posed the question of how to strengthen the work of the Committee. However, he accepted that it had the right to transfer its cadres but added that he had heard rumours that Kouyaté had been relieved of his duties because he was suspected of being a police agent and was concerned that the same accusation might also be levelled at him. Racamond assured him that there was no question of Kouyaté's involvement with the police.[141]

Padmore later wrote that it was after attending this meeting that he wrote his 'Au Revoir' in the August/September edition of *The Negro Worker*, announcing that he was relinquishing his position as editor and that the journal was facing bankruptcy. He still called on the subscribers for continued support so that the new editor could 'overcome the present financial difficulties,' and 'carry on the militant traditions of *The Negro Worker* – the only international voice of the Negro Peoples.'[142]

Husiwoud sent a report of the meeting to the RILU, pointing out that the CGTU could not be tasked with any responsibility for the ITUCNW nor *The Negro Worker*. He recommended that another individual be found to lead the work and suggested that Bordeaux, Antwerp or one of the Dutch ports might be suitable as the European headquarters of the ITUCNW. He also emphasised that the work required adequate and regular funding and proposed a monthly budget of 5000 francs. However, he pointed out that in order to economize it would be necessary to cut the number of copies of *The Negro Worker* and that since 'all the technical work of the Committee and the journal has hitherto been done by the wife of comrade P[admore],' it would also be necessary to factor in this cost and that of hiring an office. He even went so far as to remind the RILU that the funds for the next issue of *The Negro Worker* 'must be available immediately.' Here too there was no sense that the ITUCNW or *The Negro Worker* were being 'liquidated' but it is certainly clear that the decision concerning how they were funded and organised was in the hands of the RILU.[143]

It may well be that the RILU took some time to make its decision and temporarily suspended the activities of the ITUCNW, certainly the discussions about its

141. Réunion pour la discussion sur le comité international des nègres, 23 August 1933, RGASPI 534/3/895.

142. 'Au Revoir,' *NW*, 4/8-9 (August-September 1933) p.18.

143. Report of Edwards, 13 September 1933, RGASPI 534/3/895. 'Padmore's wife' was presumably his Austrian partner Fredricke 'Frieda' Schiff.

re-launching continued throughout the winter of 1933.[144] It is also not clear what further discussions Padmore had with Huiswoud and Albert Nzula, the acting chairman of the RILU Negro Bureau during this period. According to Helen Davis, Huiswoud's wife, Padmore had refused to listen to advice from Huiswoud, or criticism and warnings about 'police agents' from French comrades, including Henriette Carlier.[145] In February 1934, in his resignation letter to the CPUSA, Padmore alleged that Nzula, who had died of pneumonia in Moscow the previous month, 'was not even paid the courtesy to be consulted' about the future of the ITUCNW but there is no evidence to suggest that the two corresponded while Padmore was in Paris. Whatever the exact circumstances, Padmore believed that his redeployment meant that the ITUCNW had effectively been 'liquidated,' that 'the Negroes have been thrown to the "wolves" and that he had been treated badly, without even a word from Lozovsky, 'whom he loved as a father.'[146] He saw a conspiracy to 'sabotage' the Comintern's 'Negro work,' for which he blamed 'bureaucrats' such as Alexander Zusmanovich, a Russian who had become a leading figure in the RILU's Negro Bureau.[147]As a consequence he refused to accept that he had to continue his work as a member of the CPUSA and return to the United States. Indeed, as early as June 1933 a police agent in Paris reported that Koutayé had let slip that Padmore did not want to remain in France and had plans to go to Liberia and organise there.[148] What was worse, even after Kouyaté had been expelled from the UTN and the PCF, Padmore continued to associate with him and even shared the same address.[149]

No doubt Padmore was greatly disturbed by his own changed circumstances, perhaps even 'utterly overcome' as one of his friends reported several years later.[150] However, whatever his views regarding his redeployment and the future of the

144. See e.g. Minutes of the Combined Meeting of the Negro Bureau, 17 November 1933, RGASPI 534/3/895.

145. H. Huiswoud, 'Otto Eduard Huiswoud,' p.29, Huiswoud Papers, Tamiment Library.

146. Padmore to the Secretariat, CPUSA, 3 February 1934 and Report of Ferrat, 21 April 1934, RGASPI 517/1/1652/19-21.

147. Padmore to the Secretariat, CPUSA, 3 February 1934. It is not clear exactly why Padmore singled out Zusmanovich. The latter recalled some years later that Padmore was arrogant, that there were several complaints that he was stubbon from other Communists in Hamburg and that his political approach was questionable. R. Italiaander, *Schwarze Haut Im Roter Griff* (Dusseldorf, 1962) p.62. However, in 1935 Zusmanovich himself came under suspicion and was expelled from the Comintern.

148. Report of Agent Paul, 2 June 1932 and Report of Joe, 18 April 1932, 3 SLOTFOM 53, ANOM.

149. On the events leading to Kouyaté's expulsion see the following chapter.

150. N. Cunard, 'For Dorothy,' November 1959, Nancy Cunard Papers, University of Texas at Austin

ITUCNW he made the situation worse by his continued support for Kouyaté, even refusing to testify about him before the leaders of the PCF, and his refusal to cooperate with his comrades and return to Moscow or the United States.[151] The situation was gradually made still more difficult by the disquiet in Comintern circles regarding Padmore's increasingly public criticisms of the CI's approach to the ITUCNW and the Negro Question, as well as other concerns, such as his support for the 'Save Liberia Movement,' being proposed by William N. Jones, editor of *The Afro-American*.[152] Padmore's general attitude can be judged from the letter he wrote at the time to the British Communist Hugo Rathbone, in which he defends his support for Jones in order to 'save Liberia from imperialist intervention and annexation,' and from the reports of two interviews conducted in March 1934 by André Ferrat, a leading member of the PCF and head of the Party's colonial commission.[153] By this time the RILU had decided to re-establish the Europe-based committee of the ITUCNW and Huiswoud had returned to Paris from Moscow to begin the preparations and to again remonstrate with Padmore. It was after Huiswoud's return, in February 1934, that Padmore wrote his resignation letter to the CPUSA but even during December 1933 he and Kouyaté were already planning a 'World Negro Congress' with Padmore acting as secretary of the 'workers and peasants section.'[154] In February 1934 the International Control Commission of the Comintern had already discussed Padmore's expulsion, so the meetings with Ferrat constituted a last attempt to resolve matters.[155]

Ferrat reported that Padmore still claimed that he was 'with the Comintern,' agreed with its programme and 'always considered himself a Party member,' but that he continued to accuse the RILU of 'liquidating' the ITUCNW, and complained of the methods used against him by what he referred to as the RILU 'bureaucracy.' When asked why he did not return to the United States as instructed Padmore advanced several excuses, which ranged from his British citizenship and alleged prohibited entry status, to lack of money, he apparently subsisted in France on money sent by his parents. In response to questions about

151. Réunion de la fraction communiste nègre de l'UTN, 26 February 1934, 3 SLOTFOM 33, ANOM.

152. F. Ruettan, 'Black America's Perception of Africa in the 1920s and 1930s,' MA Thesis, Seton Hall University (2009) pp.31-32. See also A. Ward to Patterson, 14 November 1933, RGASPI 534/3/895.

153. Report of Ferrat, 21 April 1934, RGASPI 517/1/1652/19-21, also Padmore to Ferrar, 4 March 1934, RGASPI 495/270/798 and Padmore to Rathbone, 9 January 1934, RGASPI 495/64/132.

154. Report of Moise, 3 February 1934, 3 SLOTFOM 53 and Note sur la propagande révolutionaire, 31 December 1933, 3 SLOTFOM 68, ANOM.

155. J. M. Turner, *Caribbean Crusaders and the Harlem Renaissance* (Chicago, 2005), p.214 and M. G. van Enckevort, 'The Life and Work of Otto Huiswoud: Professional Revolutionary and Internationalist (1893-1961),' Ph.D Thesis, UWI, Mona (2001) p.112.

contact addresses and other ITUCNW material, he claimed to have nothing that he had not already given, or was about to give to Huiswoud. Since Padmore declined to return to the US to continue his political work with the American CP, Ferrat suggested that that he went to Moscow to resolve matters there but this he was also reluctant to do. It was evident that he saw himself not simply as a member of the CPUSA who had been tasked with developing a particular aspect of the work of the Comintern, but rather as the leading representative of 'Negro workers' internationally who was responsible for safeguarding the Comintern's 'Negro work' from its 'bureaucracy.' He put it to Ferrat that if the Comintern wished to discuss re-establishing the 'Negro work,' it only had to send someone and organise a meeting in Paris to discuss the subject just as it had the previous August. In short, Padmore wished to set conditions in order to agree to any proposal made to him and even made it clear that he did not accept the expulsion of Kouyaté. He insisted that he would not travel to Moscow alone but only with two others who, according to him, 'would represent the Negro workers,' J. B. Marks from South Africa and Cecil Hope from New York.[156] In fact Padmore initially tried to insist that Kouyaté should also accompany him, until the absurdity of proposing somebody who had been expelled was pointed out to him. Since neither Marks nor Hope were in Europe, Ferrat continued to encourage Padmore to return to Moscow but he declined do so before consulting with 'his comrades' in South Africa, Trinidad, New York and London who he claimed he would be representing in Moscow. Although Padmore promised to inform Ferrat of 'his comrades' decision and send a report about other matters there is no evidence that he did. His work with the Communist movement had effectively ended and as he had refused to act according to the discipline of the communist party on 20 March 1934 his expulsion by the Comintern was made public.[157]

Although Padmore had persistently refused to act in the disciplined way expected of a Communist, the Comintern's International Control Commission presented several other reasons for his expulsion including his refusal to sever his connection with Kouyaté, his support for the financial schemes of the *Afro-American* and the Liberian government and for carrying out work which 'undermined the class unity of the toiling masses.'[158] In addition to these activities the

156. It is not clear why Padmore chose these two 'representatives' nor what correspondence he had with them. Hope, a Barbadian member of the CPUSA, continued to support Padmore but had his own differences with that Party which subsequently led to his expulsion in 1934. See *Amsterdam News*, 20 October 1934, p.15. Marks was one of the leaders of the CPSA who studied at KUTV from 1933-1934.

157. Report of Ferrat, 21 April 1934, RGASPI 517/1/1652/19-21. See also 'Statement of the International Control Commission,' 20 March 1934, RGASPI 495/261/4718.

158. Padmore's connection with the Liberian financial scheme are also criticised by Ward in a letter written to enquire about what had become of him. Ward to Patterson, 14 November 1933, RGASPI 534/3/895.

ITUCNW, which also expelled Padmore, highlighted his refusal to 'hand over the contacts and other properties of the Committee.'[159] Later editions of *The Negro Worker* carried more extensive articles condemning Padmore and even found evidence of his 'Negro nationalism' in previous editions.[160] Nevertheless, although there was undoubtedly evidence for all the charges against Padmore, it is noticeable that his refusal to accept the discipline of the communist party went entirely unmentioned.

Padmore's explanation for his resignation from the communist movement is rather more curious. He submitted his letter of resignation to the CPUSA at the beginning of February 1934, evidently because he had been informed that his expulsion was imminent, and subsequently released it to the African American press. In it he again claimed that the ITUCNW has been liquidated and that the RILU had refused to discuss this decision with him, again defended Kouyaté and made the accusation that 'Negro work' has 'been systematically sabotaged.' According to Padmore's account, it was only after his resignation that the CI hurriedly despatched Huiswoud to re-start *The Negro Worker*.[161] His later assertion that he resigned because the Comintern 'was called upon not only to endorse the new diplomatic policy of the Soviet Government, but to put a brake upon the anti-imperialist work of its affiliate sections and thereby sacrifice the young national liberation movement in Africa and Asia,' appears to have been added some years later and then embellished by others.[162] Certainly in August 1933 there was no indication of a change in Soviet Foreign policy towards Britain or France, nor in the line of the Comintern. The policy of collective security was not formally adopted in the Soviet Union until December 1933 and its entry into the League of Nations did not occur until 1934.[163] Major changes in Comintern policy did not occur in this period before its new leadership was established in April 1934.[164]

---

159. See 'Expulsion of George Padmore from the Revolutionary Movement,' *NW*, 2/4 (June 1934) pp.14-15 and 'The Struggle for the Independence of Liberia,' ibid., pp.9-13.

160. See e.g. H. Davis, 'The Rise and Fall of George Padmore as a Revolutionary Fighter,' *NW*, 4/4 (August 1934) pp.15-17 and 21.

161. 'Why I Left The Communist International – Padmore Refutes Lies and Slanders by Communists.' George Padmore Collection, 1/2, Princeton University.

162. Quoted in J.R. Hooker, *Black Revolutionary: George Padmore's path from Communism to Pan-Africanism* (London, 1967) pp.31-32. See also e.g. C.L.R. James, 'Notes on the Life of George Padmore,' in A. Grimshaw (ed.) *The C.L.R. James Reader* (London, 1992) pp.288-295.

163. G. Roberts, *The Soviet Union and the Origins of the Second World War* (London, 1995) pp.9-15.

164. G. Roberts, 'Collective Security and the Origins of the People's Front,' in J. Fyrth (ed.) *Britain, Fascism and the Popular Front* (London, 1985) pp.74-88.

Chapter 5
The ITUCNW Re-established

The ITUCNW in Antwerp

The expulsion of George Padmore and the HC from Germany by the Nazi regime in 1933 and the subsequent expulsion of Padmore from the leadership of the ITUCNW and from the ranks of the international communist movement, created both a crisis and hiatus in the work of the ITUCNW. It took several months before a new committee, initially based in Antwerp and publicly known as the Crusader News Agency, was re-established in April 1934 by Otto Huiswoud and his wife Helen Davis (Hermina Huiswoud).[1] Huiswoud, who had led the RILU Negro Bureau had the necessary experience to undertake the task of re-establishing the work of the Committee and the publication of *The Negro Worker* after the disruption caused by the expulsion of Padmore. Davis, born in

1. 'Report of the ITUCNW,' 25 October, 1935, RGASPI 495/14/60/36-47.

British Guiana in 1905 also played a crucial role, as Huiswoud had indicated that it would be difficult to carry out the required tasks alone.[2] She had joined the American CP in 1928, two years after her marriage to Huiswoud. By that time she had already been a member of the ANLC and the Young Workers League and later worked and studied at the Lenin School in Moscow. From 1934 until its demise Helen Davis was one of the main contributors to *The Negro Worker* and worked alongside her husband to re-establish the ITUCNW in Europe.[3]

The ITUCNW also suffered the loss of Albert Nzula, who died from the consequences of alcoholism in January 1934.[4] Nzula, the first African general secretary of the Communist Party of South African, had played a leading role the work of the RILU Negro Bureau during the latter part of the period he was in Moscow. He first arrived in the Soviet Union in August 1931 and worked at KUTV where he collaborated with two Russian specialists also connected with the ITUCNW, Ivan Potekhin and Alexander Zusmanovich[5], to produce a book entitled *The Working Class Movement and Forced Labour in Negro Africa*, published in Russian in 1933.[6] The book presents a comprehensive survey of economic and political conditions in Africa during the Depression years and is an indictment of the colonial system imposed by the major imperialist powers. It also points to the many resistance struggles that were breaking out all over the continent and examines the significance of the African trade union movement, as well as the programme and role of the ITUCNW. Despite Nzula's prominent position in Moscow, it is not yet clear what role he played in the discussions regarding re-establishing the ITUCNW in Europe or Padmore's expulsion.[7] The RILU Negro Bureau was also reorganised during this period and effectively merged with the Negro Commission of the CI under the direction of Zusmanovich. For the first time since 1928 there do not appear to have been

2. Report of Edwards, 13 September 1933, RGASPI 534/3/895.

3. J.M. Turner, *Caribbean Crusaders and the Harlem Renaissance* (Chicago, 2005), especially pp.5-7 and 123-124.

4. See RGASPI 495/279/52. For further biographical details on Nzula see chapter ten.

5. According to the Russian historian Apollon Davidson, Zusmanovich was officially deputy chairman of the RILU Negro Bureau from 1929 until December 1933. However, it seems evident that he played a leading role until his expulsion in 1936.

6. This book was edited by Robin Cohen and re-published in English as A. T. Nzula, I.I. Potekhin and A.Z. Zusmanovich, *Forced Labour in Colonial Africa* (London, 1979) For further biographical information on Nzula see Cohen's introduction pp.1-19 and R. Edgar, 'Notes on the Life and Death of Albert Nzula,' *International Journal of African Historical Studies*, 16/4 (1983) pp.675-679. A short obituary appears in *NW*, 4/1 (May 1934) p.9.

7. See G. Padmore to Secretariat CPUSA, 3 February 1934, George Padmore Collection, Princeton University Library.

any 'Negro' Communists in Moscow who played a key role in the leadership of the ITUCNW.[8]

Padmore's expulsion was followed by his 'campaign of slander' and public recrimination that lasted several months. Articles denouncing him appeared in *The Negro Worker* and other publications, while Padmore, mainly through the African American press, publically attacked various individual Communists, and more harmfully the CI, which he accused of sabotaging 'Negro work' as part of an alleged rapprochement between the Soviet Union, Britain and France. [9] The ITUCNW was also confronted with other difficulties because Padmore refused to hand over contact lists and other material belonging to the HC and he remained in communication with some of the ITUCNW's most important contacts in the colonies, amongst whom he continued to spread some confusion. [10] In addition, Huiswoud complained about the 'lack of technical help' from the Comintern, which did not immediately make available its lists of contacts and addresses, nor the literature that was necessary to continue the Committee's activities, and for some time he was therefore preoccupied with re-establishing communication with contacts and other preparatory work. He did, however, immediately re-start the publication of *The Negro Worker,* which appeared regularly from May 1934.[11] The resumption of publication was announced with a message of regret to its readers. The suspension of publication, the first editorial explained, had been due to 'serious technical difficulties, editorial shortcomings and the necessity to change our location.' In addition, it called for the active support all its readers in order that the journal became 'a powerful instrument to mobilise and organise the downtrodden Negro toilers

8. H. Weiss, 'The Collapse and Rebirth of the ITUCNW, 1933-1938. Part One - From Hamburg via Paris to Antwerp and Amsterdam, 1933-1935.' Comintern Working Paper 24/2011, pp.38-39.

9. See e.g. 'Expelled Red Scores Party,' *Amsterdam News*, 16 June 1934; 'Exposure of Communists is Promised,' *Amsterdam News*, 28 July 1934; 'Communists, After 15 Years Make No Headway Among Negroes, Says Padmore,' *Philadelphia Tribune*, 2 August 1934; 'Africans Will Help Padmore, *Amsterdam News*, 4 August 1934; G. Padmore, 'Padmore Answers Heywood's Slanders,' *Pittsburgh Courier*, 22 September 1934; 'A Betrayer of the Negro Liberation Struggle,' NW, 4/3 (July 1934) pp.6-10; H. Davis, 'The Rise and Fall of George Padmore as a Revolutionary Fighter,' *NW*, 4/4 (August 1934) pp.15-17; '"Padmore Belly Crawls," Says Angelo Herndon,' *Negro Liberator*, 8 September 1934; C. Briggs to The Editor, *New Amsterdam News*, 23 July 1934; J. W Ford, James Ford Answers Padmore's Charges, *Crusader News Agency*, 4 August 1934, George Padmore Collection, Princeton University Library. Also J.W. Ford, *World Problems of the Negro People -A Refutation of George Padmore* (New York, n.d.).

10. 'Report of the ITUCNW' and Wallace-Johnson to Huiswoud, 1 June 1934, RGASPI 495/64/138. See also Padmore to Critchlow, July 1934, in TNA KV2/1787.

11. As editor Huiswoud used the alias Charles Woodson.

for the struggle against our oppressors and for our complete emancipation.'[12] Huiswoud reported that he planned to produce 'special' issues of *The Negro Worker* for those colonial countries where it was banned, which he still referred to as 'the crosses,' an indication that the journal continued to be disguised as a missionary tract. Other plans included the publication as a small pamphlet of the 'Open Letter' to the Liberian Workingmen's Association, which had appeared in the May 1934 edition of *The Negro Worker*, although Huiswoud indicated that this would only be possible if he received suitable contacts from those Liberians who were studying in Moscow.[13]

Making progress in other areas was more difficult. Although Huiswoud prepared some material for distribution in the Congo and was trying to make contacts through the Belgian CP, that Party had still not established strong connections with the Congolese seamen, or other Congolese workers who were living in Belgium. Huiswoud reported that 'the main trouble is that the responsible people do not pay the slightest attention to this question and have up to date not even been able to form a functioning colonial commission.'[14] His attempts to encourage the Dutch CP to develop its colonial work were equally unfruitful and he was also concerned about the work in France where he declared, there was an 'absolute necessity' for help to be given to publish the *Cri des Nègres*, and where he and the French comrades had worked out together 'a plan of activities,' but then he had heard nothing more. He was initially more optimistic about Britain where he was in contact with the LAI and the NWA and planned to develop 'work among the Negro seamen.'[15] Following the Nazi takeover, the International Secretariat of the LAI had been moved from Germany to Britain and was led by Reginald Bridgeman. Huiswoud and Bridgeman began to collaborate in order to try and develop the work of the LAI and ITUCNW in Belgium and the Belgium Congo.[16]

In July 1934 Huiswoud travelled to England to attend the 'Negro in the World Today' conference organised by the League of Coloured Peoples (LCP)

12. *NW*, 4/1 (May 1934) pp.1-2.

13. Edward to Dear Friends, 9 June 1934, RGASPI 534/3/986. During his time in Antwerp Huiswoud produced five regular and two special editions of *The Negro Worker*. During this period for security reasons the official correspondence address for *The Negro Worker* remained in Copenhagen.

14. Edward to Dear Friends, 9 June 1934, RGASPI 534/3/968.

15. Ibid.

16. RGASPI 542/1/61/32-33 and see also "The Situation in the Belgian Congo – Statement of the LAI,' *Inprecor*, 26 January 1934, p.87.

and to meet with the LAI and NWA.[17] Although the NWA actively participated in the conference, submitting a resolution calling 'for a joint struggle of Negro and white workers to defeat imperialist exploitation and for the complete national independence of the Negro masses,'[18] Husiwoud was concerned that it was not as strong as he had been led to believe. It had, he reported, 'only about 30 members in London and the activities carried on are very sporadic and ineffective.'[19] However, he was able to draft a new NWA programme concentrating on seamen in Cardiff, where the ITUCNW had the support of 'about 200 colonial seamen in the unemployed movement,' through whom he hoped to 'more firmly establish our connections with the colonies direct.' It was on the basis of this new programme that Huiswoud optimistically announced, 'a turn in our work is to be observed in England.'[20] In Holland he could also report some slow progress, as in both Amsterdam and Rotterdam there were 'a number of colonial workers who are beginning to make the necessary contacts with colonial seamen from the different countries.' In Belgium too some progress was made with Congolese seamen and Huiswoud announced that they were taking 'small numbers of *Le Cri des Nègres* and other material.' As a consequence he planned to hold regular meetings and to produce a bulletin focusing on their interests.[21] A few months later *The Negro Worker* reported that not only had the *Cri des Nègres* reached the Belgian Congo but also that the local Belgian press was demanding that it should be banned.[22]

During the next few months Huiswoud was able to report an improvement in communication with contacts in Africa and the Caribbean, especially in the Gold Coast and Trinidad and as a result he was hopeful that 'organisational work,' which he characterised as 'the main weakness in our work,' would soon be improved.[23] As always the Committee's work was hampered by poor communication with Moscow as well as a lack of articles and other materials. The sedition laws and other repressive legislation in the colonies were also an impediment but Huiswoud reported that *The Negro Worker* was getting through to the colonies

17. Also in attendance at the conference were NWA members Arnold Ward, Harry O'Connell and Jomo Kenyatta. For the NWA resolution see *NW*, 4/5 (September 1934) p.22. See also *The Keys*, 2/2 (October-December 1934) p. 21.

18. H. Huiswoud, 'Otto Eduard Huiswoud - Early Years and Political Parties,' Huiswoud Papers, Box 1, File 24, Tamiment Library, New York.

19. Edward to Dear Friends, 26 July 1934, RGASPI 534/3/986.

20. Edward to Dear Friends, 23 August 1934, RGASPI 534/3/986.

21. Ibid.

22. *NW*, 4/8 (December 1934) p.24.

23. Edward to Dear Friends, 23 August 1934, RGASPI 534/3/968.

even by post, and that there were new requests for subscriptions.[24] The work in West Africa was also hampered by the political unreliability of some of the local activists and the personal struggles that sometimes broke out between them.[25] Nevertheless, some progress was made, especially in the Gold Coast where Isaac Wallace-Johnson, who was a member of the executive of the ITUCNW and the editorial board *The Negro Worker* and led the West African Youth League, was the most important activist. There seems to have been some uncertainty about Wallace-Johnson amongst some in the RILU but although he was not always reliable he remained loyal despite Padmore's attempts to detach him.[26] He was a frequent correspondent in *The Negro Worker*, which published his poems as well as letters and articles, and was clearly seen as a threat by the colonial authorities.[27] Huiswoud continually attempted to strengthen Wallace-Johnson's political activities in West Africa, sometimes offering public advice and criticism in the pages of *The Negro Worker*.[28]

From Antwerp the Huiswouds were in a good position to travel all over Western Europe and were even able to visit family and take a seaside summer holiday in Holland in the summer of 1934. At the end of August they were invited to Brussels for a meeting with an official from the British Colonial Office whom they had met in London the previous month.[29] The nature of the meeting remains a mystery but the following day they were arrested and briefly imprisoned, the offices of *The Negro Worker* closed down, its resources confiscated and its publication banned. According to *The Negro Worker*, the attempt of 'the slave drivers' to prevent its publication was 'an attempt to deprive the Negro toilers of their journal, which leads the battle against the whole barbarous-system of exploitation, police and soldier terrorism, lynching, exorbitant taxation and confiscation of peasant and communal lands, forced labour and peonage. It is an effort to destroy the organ that aids in the organisation of trade unions among Negro workers that fights for relief for the unemployed, that mobilizes the workers and peasants of all races and nationalities to fight for the

24. On the impact of the sedition law in the Gold Coast see *NW*, 4/5 (September 1934) pp.1-2 and 4-7, also Huiswoud to Dear Comrades, 23 August 1934, RGASPI 534/3/986.

25. See references to such problems between 'Robert' and Daniels' in Letter to Dear Otto, 21 February 1935, RGASPI 495/155/102.

26. Ibid., and Wallace-Johnson to Huiswoud, 1 June 1934, RGASPI 495.64/138.

27. Many of Wallace-Johnson's poems were published in *The Negro Worker*. Se e.g. 'Das sdrarstwuiet,' *NW*, 4/6-7 (October-November 1934) p.15, see also W. Daniels, 'Development of Fascist Terror in the Gold Coast,' *NW*, 4/5 (September 1934) pp.4-7.

28. See e.g. the special West African issue, *NW*, 5/6 (June 1935). Amongst other things this edition contained detailed directions for the Gold Coast's trade unions.

29. Huiswoud, 'Otto Eduard Huiswoud,' p.32.

national independence of the colonial toilers and to struggle against imperialist exploitation, slave oppression and war.'[30]

The Huiswoods were told that the British government was behind their arrest and it seems likely that, as Husiwoud later wrote, they were betrayed by 'a certain individual,' and were subsequently deported to Holland.[31] Helen Davis managed to conceal the September edition of *The Negro Worker* that was ready for the press and, as a new office in Amsterdam was quickly found and they retained lists of contacts, the publication and distribution of the journal was not interrupted.[32] However, the Belgian authorities had access not only to contact lists but also to some of Huiswoud's plans, correspondence and other material, which were soon also in the possession of the French and British authorities. The arrest of the Huiswoods was yet another example of the difficult conditions in which the ITUCNW operated. It also shows that their activities were taken very seriously by the intelligence services of the imperialist powers. Although the work of the Committee continued it was forced to operate clandestinely, while its enemies were in a stronger position to disrupt its work and to maintain surveillance on its leading activists.[33]

The ITUCNW in Amsterdam

In Amsterdam the Huiswoods encountered many of the same difficulties they had experienced in Antwerp and once again they had to develop 'an entirely new apparatus' for the Committee's work. Communication with Moscow was sporadic and not always helpful, especially when demands from the centre were unrealistic. There was a particularly impatience to find 'students,' from Africa and the Caribbean who could be trained in Moscow for future revolutionary activities in the colonies, an indication that there was a recognition that Negro Question could not be addressed solely, or even mainly, through the work of the ITUCNW. In one letter Huiswoud was instructed 'it is necessary to literally mobilise everything that can be mobilised to send the greatest possible number,'

30. 'The Negro Worker shall not be silenced,' *NW*, 4/6-7 (October-November 1934) pp.1-2.

31. 'Report of the ITUCNW,' also Huiswoud, 'Otto Eduard Huiswoud,' pp.34-37. Huiswoud provided a slightly different account of his arrest in a statement to the Comintern in 1937. On that occasion he suspected that his arrest might have been due to his Belgian 'technical helper' who was known to the police, a 'spy at the printing shop,' or a West African student returning from KUTV who had been arrested and was unreliable. He also claimed that the police found 'nothing incriminating.' O. Huiswoud, 'Statement,' 5 May 1937, RGASPI 495/557/668.

32. Turner, *Caribbean Crusaders*, pp.214-5.

33. 'Renseignement,' 4 October 1934, 3 SLOTFOM 111, ANOM.

in another that such recruitment 'should be your central task now.'[34] Huiswoud recognised 'the crying need for reinforcements,' but although he was continually told that money was not a problem he seems to have had no funds to facilitate such recruitment.[35] One letter from the RILU Negro Bureau demanded that he obtain from the NWA 'five or six people from the African colonies,' and from France 'five or six people from the French African colonies' who could be trained and then sent back to Africa. The RILU in Moscow claimed that it was 'bombarding' the British and French CPs about this matter but admitted to Huiswoud, 'evidently without your interference nothing will come of it.' Eventually Huiswoud was told that in order to secure the trainees it had been decided that he 'should go to Bridgeman and Ward and select the necessary people on the spot,' and he was instructed to adopt a similar approach in France.[36] Responding to such demands with some impatience Huiwoud replied, 'Regarding the question of securing new forces, we realise the importance of this question quite well, but with the existing conditions, it is not as easy as it may seem.' In France there was evidently some action taken and several workers from Africa and the Caribbean were mobilised. However, Huiswoud made little headway in London and concluded that nothing would be done unless 'a very strong message' about the whole matter was sent to Harry Pollitt and the leadership of the CPGB.[37]

As had been the case for many years, overcoming the inaction of the local communist parties remained a major problem for the ITUCNW, even though it was this weakness that was its *raison d'etre*. The situation in Britain, where Huiswoud reported that the NWA 'merely flounders around,' was a good example. He even urged the NWA to take action against racism in the pages of *The Negro Worker* and hoped that political activity amongst the seamen, who were facing a racist campaign from the National Union of Seamen and were a vital link with the colonies, would be intensified.[38] However, the NWA did not implement the agreed plan and Huiswoud bemoaned the many problems that existed and the fact that there were 'no trained Negro forces to give leadership to the work.'[39] In

34. Letter to Dear O, 4 December 1934, RGASPI 495/155/102, also My Dear Friend from Your Dear Friend, 3 October 1934 and Dear Comrade from Helen, 11 November 1934, RGASPI 495/64/138 and Zunsmanovitch to Huiswoud, 5 September 1934, RGASPI 495/64/138.

35. Huiswoud to Dear Friends, 24 June 1935, RGASPI 495/155/102.

36. Letter to Dear Otto, 21 February 1935, RGASPI 495/155/102.

37. Husiwoud to Dear Comrades, 11 April 1934, RGASPI 495/155/102. Pollitt was the general secretary of the British CP.

38. *NW*, 4/5 (September 1934) pp.1-3.

39. Husiwoud to Dear Comrades, 11 April 1934, RGASPI 495/155/102. In this period Husiwoud even made direct appeals for action to the NWA in the pages of *The Negro Worker*. See *NW*, 4/5 (September 1934) p.3.

his view the main reason for this was 'the almost complete lack of attention paid to colonial work (particularly Africa) on the part of the highest circles. Thus the leadership is devolved on the shoulders of a few good and willing Negro comrades, but who are untrained.' He was also critical of the LAI, although admitting that the only cooperation he did get was from that quarter, he pointed out that 'their whole approach is of a very passive nature and they fail to develop mass action around burning issues.' He concluded, 'we are convinced that serious steps must be taken to effect a change in this situation. This is bringing about a situation of discontent among Negro comrades who continually complain to us about it.'[40] A further weakness in Britain was the inability of the CP to send a single African or Caribbean Communist for training in the Soviet Union, a situation which led Huiswoud to conclude 'frankly, our opinion is that there has been no effort to secure anyone, while we are sure that there is a great possibility to do this.'[41] These and other problems led to his persistent calls for a meeting in Moscow but this did not occur until the autumn of 1935.[42]

In the interim Husiwoud worked to re-establish regular communication with contacts throughout Africa and the Caribbean, although in his view the ITUCNW's work was still handicapped by its illegal nature and the fact that despite various attempts there was no safe address that would enable direct contact and communication. Meanwhile he continued to encourage those in Europe to further develop their activities. In France he noted some improvements in the regularity and content of the *Cri des Nègres* but in regard to the Paris-based UTN he lamented, 'there is nothing to speak of in so far as concrete organisational activities is concerned...the existing organisation is composed of a handful of people who do nothing actually to build up a movement.' Huiswoud continued to regularly publish *The Negro Worker* and its distribution slowly expanded, especially in South Africa. There were evidently still weaknesses since the editor wrote most of the articles and there were few local correspondents. Huiswoud had written several letters to Ford, Haywood and others in the United States requesting articles and materials, especially in regard to the Caribbean, but he received few responses and none of the publications of the CPUSA.[43] Nevertheless, *The Negro Worker* continued to carry articles and reports reflecting the problems facing African American workers and to call for support and subscriptions in the United States, even though it was not required to organise there. In its pages there were often efforts to contrast the endemic racism in the US, as well as France, Britain, with the anti-racist measures that

40. One such complaint was sent from Arnold Ward, see Ward to Huiswoud, 26 June 1935, RGASPI 495/155/102.

41. Huiswoud to Dear Friends, 24 June 1935, RGASPI 495/155/102.

42. Turner, *Caribbean Crusaders*, p. 217.

43. Huiswoud to Dear Friends, 24 June 1935, RGASPI 495/155/102.

had been taken in the Soviet Union and some incidents had an international significance such as the arrest and persecution of the African American Communist Angelo Herndon.[44] *The Negro Worker* also reported on the continued international campaign surrounding the Scottsboro case. In addition to demonstrations and rallies in the US, protests were also organised in Haiti and Cuba, while in several places including the Gold Coast, British Guiana and Trinidad, special Scottsboro committees were established, as well as close connections with MOPR.[45]

The report that Huiswoud submitted in the autumn of 1935 claimed that the ITUCNW had 'been able to establish a considerable influence among a large section of the colonial workers,' although the only examples mentioned were the appeals for assistance received from the NWA and the British Guiana Labour Union. He pointed to contact with workers' organisations and unions in Sierra Leone, the Gold Coast, Gambia, and Liberia in West Africa and with individuals in Mombasa in East Africa. While in South Africa links existed with the Cape Town Stevedore's Union and the illegal Dockworker's Union in Durban. In the Caribbean, in addition to links with the British Guiana Labour Union, Huiswoud had also made contact with workers in Dutch Guiana. In Holland, he communicated with the exiled Surinamese activist Anton de Kom, although it appears to have been difficult for them to meet, and with the Surinamech Arbeiders Bund.[46] In Trinidad the ITUCNW had links with a group of twenty communists who were active in a range of organisations and unions, including the Negro Welfare, Cultural and Social Association, which reportedly had a hundred members.[47] In Europe the Committee's contacts were mainly in Britain and in addition to the NWA, included the recently formed Colonial Seaman's Association in London, the Colonial Seamen's Committees in Cardiff and Liverpool, and the Coloured National Mutual Social Club in North Shields.[48]

Husiwoud maintained that through letters and appeals and the formulation of specific demands and suggestions it had been possible for a number of these organisations to 'follow more or less closely the line and program of the Committee in its trade union, unemployed and anti-war work.' In particular he cited

44. *NW*, 4/5 (September 1934) p.30.

45. See e.g. E. Owens, 'Lynch Terror in the USA,' *NW*, 4/1 (May 1934) pp.5-8 and Report of the ITUCNW.

46. Huiswoud, 'Otto Eduard Huiswoud,' p.37. See also A. De Kom, 'Starvation, Misery and Terror in Dutch Guyana,' *NW*, 4/2 (September 1934) pp.19-20.

47. In Trinidad the Committee also had links with ten workers in the oil fields, three unemployed workers councils and a tenants' league. See 'Proposals on the work of the ITUCNW,' 29 October 1935, RGASPI 495/155/101/28.

48. Report of the ITUCNW.

recent strikes and campaigns against unemployment and war in British Guiana, Trinidad, Liberia and Kenya, and claimed that the slogans and demands used were 'precisely those worked out by the Committee for these organisations.' [49] He also commented approvingly on the 'high level of struggle' that existed and the fact that the ITUCNW had recently published two thousand copies of its pamphlet, *How to Organise And Lead the Struggle of the Negro Toilers*.

The other main work of the Committee, the regular publication and distribution of *The Negro Worker* had also met with some success. The ITUCNW had continued to develop its own networks for the distribution of the journal, especially in order to reach those colonies where it was banned. Most of the two thousand copies were sent through maritime couriers, or re-sent from agents in Europe and the United States. Over three hundred copies were sent directly by sea to West Africa and another hundred by the same method to South Africa. As to the content of *The Negro Worker,* Huiswoud reiterated his criticism of the 'lengthiness and dryness of the articles,' which may have been more than self-criticism since many of the articles had become contributions from the RILU in Moscow, which appears to have accepted his criticism.[50] Husiwoud claimed that these characteristics were connected with the journal's 'tendency to be narrow and practically limited to the trade union phase of our work,' perhaps a recognition that an emphasis solely on Negro workers needed to be reassessed. His aim was to make the journal more popular and broad in appeal and he again bemoaned the 'almost total lack of worker correspondents' and absence of 'continuous and systematic educational feature articles.' Nevertheless there was evidence of its growing popularity amongst sections of the workers and since a legal address had been established in Copenhagen and the distribution networks strengthened, letters and financial contributions were gradually being received.[51]

Huiswoud's report concluded by detailing with what he considered the most serious weaknesses in the ITUCNW's work, its illegal and clandestine nature, which made it difficult to correspond with contacts and to become an organising centre. He also complained that the ITUCNW was politically isolated even from the CI and RILU, had limited contact with the ISH and LAI and lacked trained cadres to undertake its work. In order to improve and strengthen its influence Huiswoud proposed that the ITUCNW should become an open legal organisation; that it should be able to affiliate other organisations, as well as individuals, so as to provide greater leadership; and that affiliation should be based solely on agreeing with the Committee's programme. The aim in short

49. Ibid.

50. Letter to Dear Otto, 21 February 1935, RGASPI 495/155/102.

51. The Copenhagen address has led some historians to believe that the ITUCNW was located in Denmark.

was that the ITUCNW should change its character and become a mass organisation, or at least an organisation with mass membership, and a mass readership of *The Negro Worker.* To achieve these new aims and establish a new Committee, Huiswoud called for a conference of some of its 'most active co-workers from the colonies in the metropolitan countries.'[52]

Huiswoud also claimed that as a consequence of the Committee's influence it had been possible to 'destroy whatever influence Padmore previously had or tried to secure amongst our supporters, so that today he has practically only access to the Negro bourgeois press for his campaign of slander against the CI and the Soviet Union.' This seems to be a rather optimistic view of events, since although it was possible to eliminate support for Padmore's in the circles of the ITUCNW he was very much at the centre of Pan-African activity in Britain and France and still retained contact with activists in Africa and throughout the Diaspora.[53]

Fascism and War

One of the most important issues that the ITUCNW continually stressed was the growing threat of fascism and war. Indeed one of the principal slogans during this period was 'Unite under the banner of *The Negro Worker* against Hunger, Oppression and War. For the Liberation of Africa! For the Liberation of the Negro Peoples!' The ITUCNW concerned itself not only with the increasing impoverishment and repression in the colonies but also the activities of the fascist powers and the drive for a new world war. After the Nazi coup in Germany many more articles appeared exposing and condemning the growing contention of the imperialist powers over counties such as Liberia and Ethiopia (or Abyssinia as it was then often called), Japanese aggression against China and Nazi Germany's demands for a re-division of existing colonies.[54] In August 1934, *The Negro Worker* was entirely devoted to the threat of a new world war, the war preparations of the major imperialist countries and the likelihood of a new war of intervention against the Soviet Union. In an open call to 'the Negro Peoples of the world,' the ITUCNW called on Negro workers to fight to prevent war. It argued that ' only the toiling masses can put a stop to the

52. Report of the ITUCNW.

53. In one of his letters to Kenyatta in July 1934 Padmore provided the addresses of ITUCNW activists Kolli Tamba in Liberia and Wallace-Johnson in the Gold Coast although he clearly knew that, as with all Kenyatta's mail, it was intercepted by the Special Branch of the London Metropolitan Police. TNA KV2/1787.

54. See e.g. 'The Struggle of the Independence of Liberia,' *NW*, 4/2 (June 1934) pp.9-13.

schemes of the militarists, war profiteers and capitalists. A united working class can prevent the wholesale slaughter of the people.'[55]

It was in this context that an article entitled 'Fight for the Freedom of Abyssinia' appeared in the September 1934 edition of *The Negro Worker*, warning that the only state in Africa which had preserved its independence through military victory was facing imminent invasion by one or several of the imperialist powers. According to the ITUCNW, 'the independence of Abyssinia was never more menaced than at present, it was never more necessary than it is now to direct the attention of the toiling masses of the imperialist countries and of Abyssinia itself to the fact that the imperialists are now doing everything in their power to capture Abyssinia with provocatory methods and with arms.' As evidence to support this prophetic warning, the article detailed not just the rivalry in the region between Britain, France, Italy and Japan, but also the border disputes, policing operations and other provocations instigated against Ethiopia by Britain and Italy since 1932, as well as the secret agreement dividing Ethiopia into spheres of influence made by these two powers in 1925. The article left the reader in no doubt that military intervention by one of the imperialist powers was imminent, but it also gave an indication of Ethiopia's significance for the ITUCNW and what was then referred to as the Negro World. Following the infamous Wal Wal incident in November 1934, the ITUCNW immediately issued an appeal, calling on 'the working class and intellectuals to protest against the acts of war provocation of fascist Italy in forcibly occupying Abyssinian territory.' The appeal, which was addressed to 'the Black and White Toilers,' explained that 'Abyssinia' had for a long time been coveted by the imperialist powers, and called for solidarity with the 'Abyssinian toilers'. It concluded that 'only united working-class action can save Abyssinia from imperialist slavery.'[56]

From that time onwards, the ITUCNW through *The Negro Worker*, called for the defence of Ethiopia's sovereignty and independence and condemned Italy's aggression and the connivance and appeasement policies of Britain, France and the other major powers. Ethiopia's resistance against fascist aggression became a major international *cause célèbre* for Africans and the African Diaspora as well as for the Communist International, which mounted a major campaign in Ethiopia's defence and, in September 1935 following its Seventh Congress, called on the Labour and Socialist International to unite and take joint against fascist aggression.[57] Amongst those in Africa and the Diaspora, Ethiopia occupied a special

55. *NW*, 4/4 (August 1934) pp.1-2.

56. ITUCNW, 'Protest Against Italian Occupation of Abyssinian Territory,' *Inprecor*, 22 December 1934, p.1723.

57. See e.g. Report of the Presidium of the ECCI, 26/9/1935, RGASPI 495/2/229/28-32; Theses on the Struggle Against War in Abyssinia, 11 March 1935, RGASPI 495/4/339/26-30 and Resolution of the ECCI, 15 February 1936, RGASPI 495/2/235/59.

place as a symbol of African independence and self-determination alongside Liberia and Haiti. Kwame Nkrumah, who had recently arrived in Britain at that time, later recalled that when he first heard of the Italian invasion 'it was almost as if the whole of London had suddenly declared war on me personally,' and the *Gold Coast Spectator* reported: 'The Gold Coast man, down to the schoolboy, knows he has everything in common with the Ethiopians.' When riots broke out in the British colony of St Kitts in the Caribbean in 1935, a former colonial governor of Uganda attributed them to 'the rise of feelings of racial antagonism' occasioned by 'the attack of white power on the only remaining Negro nation,' and warned of even more dire consequences if such attitudes should spread to Africa. Fascist Italy's aggression was therefore widely seen as an attack on all Africans and resulted in heightened anti-colonial consciousness and activity.[58]

The Comintern viewed the attack on Ethiopia as major step in the build-up to a new world war, it vigorously supported Ethiopia's struggle for independence, and condemned fascist Italy's warmongering even before the full-scale invasion of October 1935. The various organisations linked to the Comintern, or in which Communists played a leading role, were also actively involved. The International Secretariat of the LAI, for example, issued a statement condemning the 'imperialist ambitions' of Italy in Ethiopia and elsewhere in East Africa in December 1934, shortly after the Wal Wal incident.[59] Not surprisingly the ITUCNW was an even more zealous defender of Ethiopian independence and sovereignty and regularly reported on the conflict in every issue of *The Negro Worker*. In early 1935 it also carried the Communist Party of Italy's *Appeal* to 'Italian workers, soldiers and sailors to organise themselves in opposition to the invasion.'[60]

The full-scale invasion of Ethiopia by Italy in October 1935 signalled a crucial stage in the drive towards a new world war and demonstrated the lengths that the fascist powers would go to in order to re-divide the world in their interests. The invasion also highlighted the weakness of the appeasement policies of Britain and France in particular and the difficulty of maintaining 'collective security,' the peace policy favoured by the Soviet Union, which became increasingly inoperative because of the rivalries existing between the major powers. The

58. K. Nkrumah, *The Autobiography of Kwame Nkrumah* (London. 1957) p.22. See also J. E. Harris, *African American Reactions to War in Ethiopia 1936-1941* (London, 1994) and B. Davidson, *Let Freedom Come – Africa n Modern History* (London, 1978) p.181. See also S.K.B. Asante, *Pan-African Protest: West Africa and the Italo-Ethiopian Crisis 1934-1941* (London, 1977) and R. G. Weisbord, *Ebony Kinship – Africa, Africans and the Afro-American* (London, 1973) especially pp. 89-115.

59. Statement Issued by the International Secretariat of the League Against Imperialism; 'Imperialism in Abyssinia,' in *Inprecor*, 22 December 1934, pp.1722-3.

60. For the *Appeal* see *NW*, 5/2-3 (February-March 1935) pp.5-6. *The Negro Worker* regularly reported on the invasion and Ethiopian resistance from December 1934 See 'Activities of the ITUCNW on the Italo-Abyssinian Conflict,' RGASPI 495/14/60/10-13.

invasion of Ethiopia was itself a consequence of the contention between the big powers, but also exacerbated the rivalries between them, and compounded the grave economic crisis that already had the whole world in its grip. It created even more instability and uncertainly in the world, dealt a body blow to the credibility of the League of Nations, and contributed to an intensification of the economic and political crisis in Europe and to the crisis that was engulfing the colonial world, which called into question the colonial system itself.[61]

Throughout 1935 Ethiopia remained of major concern for the ITUCNW and *The Negro Worker* accordingly provided its readers with a constant stream of articles outlining both the historical background to the growing crisis as well as its contemporary significance as the precursor to world war. It particularly highlighted those aspects of the situation in the Horn of Africa which impacted most on African and colonial affairs or which touched on wider issues of racism. It did not fail to report, for example, the remarks of Italy's Assistant-Secretary for Colonies, who spoke of the 'necessity of solidarity of the European colonial powers in maintaining Africa as the national reserve of the white race,'[62] or the fact that the imperialist powers were attempting to divide up 'the last remaining independent part of Africa'. But at the same time it also emphasised the need for workers of all countries to fight in support of Ethiopia's independence and presented its readers with the 'Hands off Abyssinia' appeal of the Communist Party of Italy, which demanded the 'evacuation' of Libya, Eritrea, Somaliland and all colonies which are under the heel of Italian imperialism.'[63] In many of its early articles, *The Negro Worker* also made much of the need for the Ethiopian people themselves to 'organise their forces to struggle against the semi-feudal system of exploitation and slavery imposed upon them by the native Abyssinian rulers and landowners.' It argued that is was in part 'the policy pursued by the Abyssinian ruling class and reactionary church leaders of playing one imperialist power of against another' that would lead to the loss of Ethiopia's independence.[64] In the course of the conflict this approach changed as the Comintern sought to strengthen and unite all possible forces against fascism.

The Soviet Union and Ethiopia

It was in these circumstances that in May 1935 George Padmore, in an article published in the NAACP's *The Crisis,* alleged hat the Soviet Union had initially refused to support Ethiopia at the League of Nations, following the Wal

61. E. Burns, *Abyssinia and Italy* (London, 1935) pp.114-117.

62. *NW*, 5/1 (January 1935) p.1.

63. *NW*, 5/2-3 (February-March 1935) pp.5-6.

64. Ibid. p.4 and *NW*, 5/1 (January 1935) p.2.

Wal incident, because of a change in its foreign policy occasioned by its recent rapprochement with France and a concern to defend the status quo in Europe.[65] Padmore explained the Italian invasion, at least in part, in racial terms and by inference alleged that the Soviet Union had become part of the 'united front of white Europe against black Africa'.[66] The article was widely publicised in the African American press and because of Padmore's influence and former position, it also had a much wider international significance.[67] Padmore's article was not commented upon in *The Negro Worker*, although his approach seemed to confirm the assessment made of him by the Comintern at the time of his expulsion, but in July 1935 William Patterson published a response.[68] Patterson took particular exception to Padmore's attempt to present the Ethiopian conflict as 'a struggle of white against black,' a view which he argued denied the fact that in Italy and internationally there was growing support for the 'struggle for national independence of a dependent black country.' Patterson's article was also a plea for a 'united front of Negro and white' on the Ethiopian and other issues and he argued that Padmore was deliberately creating confusion about the allies of 'Abyssinia and of the Negro people,' as well as on the nature of fascism, and the growing contention between the big powers. Not surprisingly, he also objected to Padmore's characterisation of the Soviet Union, the inference that Japan, 'a colored nation,' was somehow a friend to Ethiopia, and to his assertion that there was a 'united front of white Europe against black Africa.' Patterson urged that 'the Negro peoples the world over must fight for the real national independence of the Negro states, Abyssinia, Liberia and Haiti,' spoke of the struggle for an 'independent South African Native Republic,' and of the struggle for African American self-determination. He concluded by stating the 'road to the salvation of Abyssinia and the liberation of the Negro people' lay in the struggle against world imperialism both at home and abroad.

For Patterson and others there was a clear recognition of the symbolic importance of Ethiopia and its significance throughout Africa and the Diaspora. However, they also recognised the need to link the struggle for Ethiopia's independence with the struggle against fascism and war, and as a means to draw the 'Negro masses' into the struggles of the working and oppressed people internationally. The concern was that the outrage felt by the 'Negro world' in relation to Ethiopia would be diverted into 'utopian channels' and 'impractical avenues,' or into anti-white sentiment, something that Patterson and others

65. In May 1935 the Soviet Union and France signed a Pact of Mutual Assistance.

66. G. Padmore, 'Ethiopia and World Politics,' *The Crisis*, May 1935, pp.138-139 and 156. See also M. Naison, *Communistm in Harlem During the Depression* (New York, 1984) p. 156.

67. See e.g Arnold Ward to Huiswoud, 26 June 1935, RGASPI 495/155/102.

68. William L. Patterson, 'Negro Reforms, World Politics, and Ethiopia,' *Inprecor*, 6 July 1935, pp.743-745.

asserted would be strengthened by the views of Padmore and other 'Negro reformers.'[69] However, a few months later the CPGB's *Labour Monthly* published a 'Hands off Abyssinia' article by Kenyatta and openly acknowledged that he was the secretary of a new organisation, the International African Friends of Abyssinia (IAFA).[70] *Labour Monthly* did not mention what the CPGB clearly knew, that this 'All-Negro organisation' was led by Padmore and C.L. R. James, at that time a leading Trotskyite critic of the Comintern. It was indeed a time when a united front against fascism and in defence of Ethiopia was being established. Nancy Cunard writing from Moscow in September 1935 captured the mood when she wrote, 'the eyes and the thoughts of the world are focused on Ethiopia.' She reported her own recent experience of UTN and LAI meetings in Paris and meetings and other protest actions of the LAI, IAFA and NWA in London.[71] At its annual conference in October the NWA, with some justification could declare that 'a mighty movement of solidarity is growing day by day throughout the world in support of the Abyssinian people in their struggle for independence.'[72]

The attitude of the Soviet Union towards Ethiopia has been interpreted in various ways by historians but it was based not only on its desire to stop fascist aggression in Africa but also on a foreign policy which aimed to stop such aggression internationally and prevent the outbreak of a new world war. Moreover, the Soviet Union, which was still mindful of the invasion of its territory by Britain, France and their allies in 1918, recognised that the major European powers remained hostile to its continued existence and that Nazi Germany openly coveted its territory. In these circumstances it aimed to oppose fascist aggression and maintain peace in Europe for as long as possible and to preserve its own sovereignty and territorial integrity by advocating and adopting a policy of collective security, that is attempting to establish a system of alliances to prevent aggression especially in Europe.[73] In order to pursue these aims it joined the League of Nations in 1934 and was given a permanent seat on the Council of the League.[74] It signed non-aggression pacts with Italy, in 1933, and

69. William L. Patterson, 'The Abyssinian Situation and the Negro World,' *NW*, 6/5 (June 1935) pp.16-19 and *Inprecor*, 11 May 1935, pp. 542-543.

70. *Labour Monthly*, 17/9 (September 1935) pp.532-536.

71. N. Cunard, 'For Abyssinia,' Nancy Cunard Folder, Claude Barnett Papers, Box 198.

72. Annual Conference of the NWA, 20 October 1935.

73. The best general summary of the foreign policy of the Soviet Union during this period remains W.P. and Z. Coates, *World Affairs and the USSR* (London, 1939), especially pp. 46-85. Cf. J. Haslam, *The Soviet Union and the Struggle for Collective Security in Europe, 1933-39* (London, 1984) pp.60-80.

74. On the Soviet Union's entry to the League of Nations see F.P. Walters, *A History of the League of Nations, Vol. II* (London, 1952) pp.579-586.

with France in 1935, as well as with other countries, and even had significant economic and trade links with Italy. It aimed to use its links with both France and Italy, which both had contradictions with Germany, to keep the latter isolated in Europe. However, the Soviet Foreign Minister, Maxim Litvinov, was the first representative of the League of Nations to openly criticise Italy's actions towards Ethiopia in a speech made in September 1935 and thereafter the Soviet Union, which had also made clear its opposition to 'the system of colonies, to the policy of sphere of influence, to anything pertaining to imperialistic aims,' became the most vocal critic of Italian aggression.[75] After the Italian invasion of October 1935 it opposed an arms embargo on Ethiopia and implemented economic sanctions and even supported further sanctions against Italy. Together with Rumania, it also proposed an embargo on the export of oil, coal, iron and steel to Italy, if the other producing countries would do likewise. In fact no such agreement was reached, not least because the most significant country exporting oil to Italy, the United States, would not be bound to maintain sanctions since it was not a member of the League of Nations and without its support any sanctions were meaningless. Nevertheless, the Soviet Union's oil exports to Italy declined during the period of the war, while shipments of iron ore, manganese and chromium were immediately stopped.[76] The Soviet Union strongly condemned the Hoare-Laval proposals from the British and French governments, which amounted to a colonial partition of Ethiopia and continued to criticise the inactivity and policies of appeasement of certain member countries of the League.[77]

When, in July 1936, it seemed that the Italian occupation of Ethiopia was a *fait accompli* and the League abandoned economic sanctions against Italy, Litvinov argued that all members of the League had to accept 'responsibility and blame' but added, 'I have to declare that the Government that I represent here, from the very beginning of the Italo-Ethiopia conflict, took up a perfectly clear and firm position, arising by no means from its own interests or its relations with the belligerents, but solely from its conceptions of the principle of collective security, of international solidarity, of the Covenant of the League, and of the obligation imposed on it by that Covenant.'[78] It is interesting to note that in September 1936 the Soviet Union opposed the exclusion of the Ethiopian delegation from

75. F. Hardie, *The Abyssinian Crisis* (London, 1974) p.95.

76. Lowell R. Tillett, 'The Soviet Role in League Sanctions Against Italy, 1935-36,' in *The American Slavic and East European Review* (1956) Vol.15, pp.11-16.

77. Max Beloff, *The Foreign Policy of Soviet Russia, 1929-41* [Vol.2] (London, 1955) pp.199-204.

78. M. Litvinov, 'Speech on the Indivisibility of Peace and the Strengthening of Collective Security Delivered at the 16th Assembly of the League of Nations, July 1st, 1936,' in M. Litvinov, *Against Aggression – Speeches* (London, 1936) p.35.

the Assembly of the League and even as late as 1939 when the question of the legal recognition of Italian sovereignty over Ethiopia was brought before the League of Nations Council by Britain, opposition was led by the Soviet Union, which continued to withhold any recognition of the Italian conquest.[79]

Hands off Abyssinia

In the summer of 1935 the ITUCNW issued its own call to build 'Hands off Abyssinia Committees' in 'all working class organisations,' addressed to 'the toilers of the metropolis and the colonies,' and 'the workers of all races and nationalities.' According to the ITUCNW, the central task of these committees was not just to highlight the threat of war in Ethiopia but also to connect it 'with the struggle against their own oppressors'. The ITUCNW declared that the struggle for Ethiopia's independence should be linked with 'the struggle against fascism and war, with the fight for the release of class war prisoners, with the fight for the release of the Scottsboro boys and Angelo Herndon, with the fight for self-determination and independence of the colonial toilers.'[80]

The analysis of the CI and ITUCNW was that fascism threatened not only Ethiopia but also the entire world and in *The Negro Worker* and elsewhere there were repeated warnings that another world war was on the horizon. Although Italy, Germany and Japan were routinely condemned, the ITUCNW and CI also condemned the actions of France and Britain and their contention and collusion with Italy.[81] It called on all working people to step up their struggles against the manoeuvres of the imperialist powers, as part of the struggle to defend Ethiopia's independence and to call for the 'Stoppage of all war material to Italy; Raising the embargo on arms to Abyssinia so that she can obtain adequate means to defend herself; Abrogation of all agreements and treaties dividing Abyssinia into spheres of influence. Surrender of all imperialist interests in Abyssinia; Complete integrity and independence of Abyssinia,' as well as several other demands including the imposition of League of Nations sanctions against Italy.[82]

These demands formed an important part of the worldwide struggle in support of Ethiopia at the time. Many examples of the breadth of this international struggle were reflected in the pages of *The Negro Worker*, which carried reports highlighting its internationalist character and the unity that existed between black and white workers, as well as emphasising the important role

79. Beloff, *The Foreign Policy of the Soviet Union*: 204. See also 'The League Decision on Abyssinia,' *NW*, 6/9 (November 1936) pp.3-4.

80. *NW*, 5/7-8 (July-August 1935) pp.3-5.

81. See e.g. J. Cohen, 'British Imperialism and Abyssinia,' *Inprecor*, 13 July 1935, pp.756-757.

82. 'An Appeal,' *NW*, 5/9 (September 1935) p.2.

that was being played by the 'Negro masses'. A prominent example of the internationalist character of the campaign was the International Conference for the Defence of the Abyssinian People, which was held in Paris in September 1935, organised by the International Committee for the Defence of the Ethiopian People. (ICDEP) The ICDEP was affiliated to the World Committee Against Fascism and War, the chairman of which was the well-known French writer, Henri Barbusse. Both organisations were linked to the French section of the LAI. On behalf of the World Committee, Barbusse presented a memorandum to the League of Nations demanding the evacuation of Italian troops from Africa and a peaceful conclusion of the conflict that safeguarded Ethiopian independence. Both the World Committee and the ICDEP worked together to attempt to coordinate support for Ethiopia. [83] Over one hundred and fifty different organisations were represented at the Paris conference including several from Italy, as well as the ITUCNW and over thirty representing 'colonial and national minority peoples' many of them based in France.[84] The conference adopted a declaration, addressed to the League of Nations, calling for the defence of Ethiopia's independence and sent a delegation, which included a representative of Ethiopia, to Geneva to deliver it. The conference also adopted a programme of action and established an international bureau to facilitate stronger coordination of the many protest actions that were taking place.[85]

In October 1935 Communist organisations and parties in South Africa, Egypt, Algiers, Tunis, Palestine, Syria, Iraq and Italy on behalf of 'the Negro and Arab peoples' had signed a joint declaration in support of Ethiopia.[86] The following May an International Conference of Negroes and Arabs was held in Paris, convened by the French LAI and based on the united front that had been established in defence of Ethiopia even amongst former rival African, Arab and Caribbean organisations.[87] The ITUCNW again participated alongside the French and Italian CPs, the UTN, James Ford representing the National Negro

83. See e.g. 'Activities of the Amsterdam-Pleyel World Committee Against the Italian-Fascist War in Africa,' *Inprecor*, 7 September 1935, pp.1131-1132.

84. 'International Conference in Paris in Defence of Abyssinia,' *NW* 5/9 (September 1935) pp.3-4. The Provisional Committee for the Defence of Ethiopia was represented by James Ford, the LSNR by Benjamin Careathers. See James W. Ford, *The Communists and the Struggle for Negro Liberation* (New York, n.d.) p.29.

85 *NW* 5/9 (September 1935) pp.3-4 and Adami, 'The International Conference for the Defence of the Abyssinian People,' *Inprecor*, 14 September 1935, p.1140. The delegation to Geneva included Messali Hadj, the well-known fighter for Algerian independence.

86. 'Hands off Abyssinia,' *Inprecor,* 5 October 1935, pp.1253-1254.

87. See *NW*, 6/1 (March 1936) p.10 and 'International Conference on Abyssinia,' *NW*, 6/3-4 (May-June 1936) pp.3-5. The organisation of the conference was led by the Communist Léo Wanner, one of the leaders of the French LAI. See also 'Conference International des Noirs et des Arabes,' 3 SLOTFOM 41, ANOM and *Inprecor*, 15 February 1936, p.246.

Congress in the United States, the LAI, several organisations from Britain including the LCP and African Churches Mission, as well as organisations representing the Surinamese in Holland, the Association of Haitian Writers and Journalists and many other organisations based in France, including the LDRN, the Etoile Nord-Africaine and the Union Nationale Malagache. Although there seems to have been some doubt expressed by the Comintern, and within the French CP, about the advisability of holding such an event, partly no doubt because of the rapidly changing political situation in France, the conference was seen as a success. It adopted several resolutions addressed to the League of Nations condemning fascist aggression, demanding that the League refused to recognise any annexation of Ethiopian territory and that sanctions were applied to Italy. It also demanded an end to colonial rule, called on the Popular Front government in France to immediately extend 'democratic liberties' to all French colonies, and pledged that 'Negroes and Arabs would continue to fight together' until their aspirations were realised.[88]

The ITUCNW and the participants at the conferences in France stressed the importance of mass action to oppose fascist aggression. They no doubt had in mind the strike action organised by the port workers of Cape Town and Durban, who refused to load ships with provisions for the Italian army, following an appeal by the CPSA. The protest action in South Africa was particularly significant because it was an example of the united efforts of black, white and 'coloured' workers. It is interesting to note that the appeal from the Durban Communist Party Committee to the 'harbour workers of South Africa' concluded with a special plea to the 'Native dockworkers of South Africa.' They were told:

> Remember it is your fellow black Africans of Abyssinia upon whom Mussolini is making war. The independence of Africa's only remaining black state must be dear to your hearts. You have it in you power to help your fellow Africans against the Italian imperialists...Refuse to send food to Mussolini's soldiers. Demand that the food be kept here to feed the starving people of South Africa. By defending Abyssinia you will be striking a blow against all the white robber imperialists of Africa and bring nearer the day when the black man in South Africa shall also be free.[89]

88. Report of R. Adami, 20 May 1936, RGASPI 495/20/830 also *NW*, 6/3-4 (May-June 1936) pp.3-5. Also *Inprecor*, 23 May 1936, p.659.

89. 'Refuse to Ship Goods to East Africa,' *NW*, 5/9 (September 1935) pp.5-6. African workers in South West Africa took similar strike action. Protests were also organised by Greek and French seamen.

The Negro Worker explained to its readers that the actions taken by workers in South Africa and elsewhere had particularly aroused the fear 'of the British exploiters and their press' who, it was argued 'correctly see in these manifestations an expression of the hatred of the Negro toilers against all imperialist slavery.'[90] By October 1935, *The Negro Worker* had carried reports off protests throughout the United States, in Britain, Belgium, Greece, Holland, France as well as in several colonial and semi-colonial countries including South Africa, Liberia, Egypt, India, Trinidad, St Lucia and British Guiana. Of particular significance were those protests in which Africans and those of African descent played a leading role. In Holland, for example the Union of Surinam Workers sent a protest resolution to the Italian government and formed an Ethiopia support committee. In British Guiana, several organisations sent resolutions to the governor, the British government and the Emperor of Ethiopia.[91] The British Guiana Labour Union, for instance, sent a cable to Haile Selassie stating: 'The Negroes of British Guiana hail your declaration that you will defend your Empire to the last man against foreign aggression.' While the 'crew of Negroes' on the *S.S. Holmlea*, sailing from England, declared that they were 'alive to the war threat of fascists and imperialists against coloured people in Africa,' and that they fully supported 'the proposals of the World Committee Against Fascism and War.' Their resolution concluded: 'We also declare, in the event of this ship being loaded with war material of any description to immediately approach the shore trade unions, dockers etc. to stop the ship from sailing.'[92]

The Negro Welfare, Cultural and Social Association

Some of the most significant protest actions occurred in areas where the ITUCNW exercised some influence, such as South Africa and British Guiana, or where Communists were organising such as Haiti, Martinique and Cuba. They occurred internationally but particularly in Africa and Caribbean countries including Trinidad, where the newly formed Negro Welfare, Cultural and Social Association (NWCSA) played a leading role. The NWCSA was formed in 1934 to fight for the economic political and social rights of the working class and the 'oppressed Negro people.' It seems to have emerged from the Unemployed Workers' League which had been founded earlier by Elma Francois, a domestic worker originally from St Vincent and Jim Headley, a seamen who for several years had been in contact with the ITUCNW and who may have been 'sent' back to Trinidad from Britain by Padmore, just before the latter's

90. *NW*, 5/9 (September 1935) p.12.

91. See e.g. 'Monster May Day Rally in British Guiana,' *NW*, 5/7-8 (July-August 1935) p.28.

92. *NW*, 5/7-8 (July-August 1935) pp.12-13.

expulsion from Hamburg. The role of the ITUCNW in the founding of the NWCSA is not entirely clear but Huiswoud and Headley were clearly in contact and discussing the need for a 'sound revolutionary organisation' in Trinidad. Another early member of the NWCSA was Rupert Gittens, later a leading trade union figure in Trinidad, who had been deported from France in May 1934 for activities carried out in conjunction with the French CP.[93]

The NWCSA's approach was to link the Ethiopian conflict with the problems facing working people in Trinidad.[94] In its propaganda much was made of the imperialist system and the nature of colonial oppression facing the people of both countries, including the prohibition against political protests introduced by the colonial government after one NWCSA-led demonstration.[95] In a leaflet advertising a mass meeting and addressed to 'all interested in the welfare of the Negro peoples,' the NWCSA pointed out that the preparation for fascist Italy's attack on Ethiopia came 'at the same time with the attack on the general living standards of the Negro peoples throughout the world. In the West Indies, in Trinidad Negro youth and adults walk the streets for months unemployed, with no unemployment relief, many existing in state of semi-starvation.' (sic) The leaflet concluded, 'the people of Trinidad must protest against this attack on the standard of living of the Negro people. Protest against any attack on the Abyssinian Negro peoples.'[96] Commenting on the prohibition on assembly another leaflet pointed out that ' In the eyes of Imperialists, this attack against our freedom of association, our social rights, goes hand in hand with the attack against our education, our living standards which are becoming daily like that of the natives of Africa.'[97]

In 1935 the NWCSA sent out several protest resolutions, including one to Mussolini demanding 'Hands off Abyssinia,' and another to the League of Nations calling for the unconditional withdrawal of Fascist Italy from Ethiopia and condemning 'the policy of World Imperialism for the dividing up of

93. See R. Reddock, *Elma Francois: The NWCSA and the workers struggle for change in the Caribbean in the 1930s* (London, 1988) and R. Reddock, *Women, Labour and Politics in Trinidad and Tobago* (London, 1994) pp.108-111 and 135-140. See also K. Yellington, 'The War in Ethiopia and Trinidad 1935-1936' in K.A. Yellington and B. Bereton (eds.) *The Colonial Caribbean in Transition: Essays in Post-emancipation Social and Cultural History* (Gainesville, 1999) pp.189-225. On Gittens expulsion see 'Note sur la propagande révolutionaire,' 18 June 1934, 3 SLOTFOM 75, ANOM. See also *NW*, 4/5 (September 1934) p.28 and 4/6-7 (October-November 1934) pp.4-6.

94. For the actions of the Dockers' Union in Trinidad which refused to load or unload Italian ships see *NW*, 5/11 (December 1935) p.28.

95. K. Yellington, 'The War in Ethiopia and Trinidad,' p.207.

96. RGASPI 495/14/60/14.

97. RGASPI 495/14/60/16.

Abyssinia.' It also addressed a protest to the Colonial Secretary in London demanding the 'immediate withdrawal' of the prohibition on assembly, which the NWCSA viewed as 'something unable to offer any solution towards the problems of the people.' [98] Thereafter the NWSCA remained at the forefront of anti-colonial protests in Trinidad and subsequently played a leading role in the labour rebellion that broke out in the summer of 1937.[99]

'Has the African a God?'

The other area in which the ITUCNW exerted a major influence during this period was West Africa, or more precisely the Gold Coast, where Isaac Wallace-Johnson, who had migrated from Nigeria, was its leading contact and activist. He led several important struggles in the Gold Coast in the early 1930s and by 1935 was organising amongst miners and other sections of the workers, as well as more generally in opposition to the introduction of repressive legislation, such as the so-called Sedition Bill that sought to muzzle the press and to prevent the importation of publications such as *The Negro Worker*.[100] He was also a prolific journalist and skilled orator who was viewed with concern by the colonial authorities not least because of his well-known connection with the international Communist movement, as well as his influence throughout British West Africa and the wider African Diaspora. [101] In 1934 he began establishing the Gold Coast section of the West African Youth League (WAYL), an organisation with a clear anti-colonial orientation that was affiliated with the ITUCNW and concerned itself with every major economic and political issue in the Gold Coast, as well as internationally.

The WAYL played a significant role in agitating amongst the population of the Gold Coast in support of Ethiopia, and as elsewhere opposition to fascism was also an expression of the general hostility to colonial rule and the devastat-

98. RGASPI 495/155/101/42-44.

99. Reddock, *Elma Francois*, pp.28-50.

100. On Wallace-Johnson's political career L. Spitzer and L. Denzer, 'I.T. A Wallace-Johnson and the West African Youth League,' *The International Journal of African Historical Studies*, 6/3 (1973) pp.413-452. See also S. Shaloff, 'Press Controls and Sedition Proceedings in the Gold Coast, 1933-39,' *African Affairs*, 71/284 (1972) pp.241-263 and Asante, *Pan-African Protest*, especially pp.107-135.

101. Sir Arnold Hodgson, the Governor of the Gold Coast, wrote to Sir Cecil Bottomley at the Colonial Office asking him to suggest 'some plan whereby I could get rid of Wallace-Johnson,' whom he referred to as 'in the employ of the Bolsheviks and ...doing a certain amount of harm by getting hold of the young men for his "Youth League."' Sir A. Hodson to Sir C. Bottomley, 14 January1936, (TNA) CO 96/731/1. See also 'Sedition Craze,' *NW*, 5/9 (September 1935) p.20.

ing economic crisis that was particularly felt in the colonies. In October 1935, together with the Ex-Servicemen's Union, the WAYL held a rally at which over a thousand people gathered at the Palladium in Accra where, it was later reported, over five hundred of the participants volunteered to go and fight in Ethiopia's defence. Subsequently an Ethiopia Defence Committee was established and an appeal for funds launched in the local press. The Committee was established to educate 'the masses' not only on all matters relating to the invasion but also 'on matters of racial and national importance.'[102] The WAYL declared the 9th-18th November 1935 an 'Ethiopia week,[103] and raised funds 'in aid of distressed Ethiopians' that were then forwarded to the Ethiopian legation in London. For its part, the Ex-Servicemen's Union addressed a resolution of protest to the secretary-general of the League of Nations, the House of Commons and the War Office. The Resolution was especially designed to concentrate the minds of Britain's rulers and demanded: 'Unless Great Britain sees that justice is rendered to Ethiopia according to the Covenant, the Gold Coast Ex-Servicemen's Union will never take arms to defend European nations in conflicts which may arise out of their diplomatic bargainings.' *The Negro Worker* encouraged other colonial ex-servicemen's organisations to emulate what it called this 'splendid example.' It concluded that they too must 'recognise the treacherous role played by the British Imperialists in the Abyssinian Affair, which has served to whet the appetite of Fascist Germany for colonies in Africa, and may be the cause of another war instigated by them.'[104]

Most importantly Wallace-Johnson used the invasion of Ethiopia as a means to attack the whole colonial system and to present the view that the African was the equal of the European. In articles in the local press and in his many speeches he attacked what he regarded as the hypocrisy of so-called 'western civilisation.' On one occasion he declared, 'The Italo-Abyssinian war is destined to prove to the African masses that Europe with all its civilisation is still enshrined in barbarism and that Western civilisation is sheer mockery. It is also destined to prove to the African masses that Religion, especially Christianity as it has been introduced by the whiteman to the blackman is a heinous mass of deception.'[105] His most famous article on this subject was entitled 'Has the African a God,' and was published in the *Morning Post* in May 1936. 'Has the African a God' was prompted by the Italian invasion of Ethiopia but it also raised more general

102. Spitzer and Denzer, 'I.T. A Wallace-Johnson,' p.440.

103. See L. Denzer, 'I.T.A Wallace-Johnson and the West African Youth League: A case study in West African Nationalism.' University of Birmingham, Ph.D Thesis, 1977, pp.113-116. See *NW*, 5/11 (December 1935) p.17.

104. *NW*, 6/5 (July 1936) p.24.

105. Quoted in Denzer, 'I.T.A Wallace-Johnson, pp.115-116 and Spitzer and Denzer, 'I.T. A Wallace-Johnson,' p.435

issues about colonial rule and the religious ideas accompanying it. Wallace-Johnson wrote that 'the European' believed 'in the god whose name is spelt *Deceit*,' and he continued 'Ye "civilised" Europeans, you must "civilise" the "barbarous" Africans with machine guns. Ye "Christian" Europeans, you must "Christianise" the "pagan" Africans with bombs, poison gases, etc.' His aim was to expose the 'civilising mission' not only of fascist Italy but also of Britain by linking the invasion of Ethiopia with colonial rule and repressive legislation in the Gold Coast and elsewhere. In conclusion he called on Africans to 'follow his example and worship Ethiopia's God,' in other words to rely on their own traditions and reject eurocentrism. It was what *The Negro Worker* called 'a frank and truthful exposure of the methods of imperialist rule.'[106]

The colonial authorities had been waiting for an opportunity to arrest Wallace-Johnson and took advantage of the publication of the article to raid his home, where they discovered incriminating material from the LAI and NWA and evidence that he was the author of the article.[107] He was arrested, charged with sedition and subsequently found guilty of this offence and fined fifty pounds.[108] The whole case became something of a *cause célèbre* both in the Gold Coast and in Britain where the LAI caused questions to be raised in Parliament and supported Wallace-Johnson when he decided to appeal to the Court of the Privy Council.[109] In the Gold Coast the case no doubt contributed to the rapidly growing membership of the WAYL, which amounted to over five thousand organised in twenty two separate branches by the end of 1936.[110]

The many campaigns, resolutions and protests were precisely those envisaged by Lorenzo Gault (William Patterson) when in the pages of *The Negro Worker* he called on the supporters of the ITUCNW to 'set the Negro world

106. Spitzer and Denzer, 'I.T. A Wallace-Johnson,' p.442. An extract from the article was also published in *The Negro Worker*, *NW*, 6/6-7 (August-September 1936) pp.1-2. See also *NW*, 6/5 (July 1936) p.27.

107. Colonial Office officials noted that Governor Hodson had initially felt that Wallace-Johnson's activities could be dealt with by 'broadcast propaganda' but subsequently become much more concerned. G. Creasy note, 27 February 1936, (TNA) CO 96/731/1. Hodson subsequently demanded more powers and voiced his concern that the press was 'controlled by the Red element.' Shaloff, 'Press Controls and Sedition Proceedings in the Gold Coast, 1933-39,' p.255.

108. Spitzer and Denzer, 'I.T. A Wallace-Johnson,' pp.442-445. See also 'Gold Coast Raid and Arrest,' *NW*, 6/5 (July 1936) p.27, 'Persecution on the Gold Coast,' *NW*, 6/6-7 (August-September 1936) p.1, and 'Wallace Johnson fined' *NW*, 6/9 (November 1936) p.27. Nnamdi Azikiwe, the editor of the *Morning Post* was also charged with sedition.

109. Wallace-Johnson ultimately lost the appeal but the Gold Coast government had to pay for it.

110. *NW*, (December 1936) p.3. See also Denzer, 'I.T.A Wallace-Johnson,' pp.145 for different figures that still indicate a significant increase.

aflame with a "holy" war for the continued independence of Abyssinia.' Patterson argued, 'the ultimate independence of the Negro world will be immeasurably influenced by the character of the struggle waged for the preservation of the independence of Abyssinia,' and 'the loss to Abyssinia of its nominal independence can only throw the liberation struggle of the Negro world as a whole back many years.' Although he may have overstated the case, there is no doubt that Italy's intervention in Ethiopia did contribute to a much wider crisis of colonialism and forced the colonial powers, principally Britain and France, to justify their colonial possessions. Italian aggression and the collusion of the other big powers also created the conditions for a more strident anti-colonialism throughout Africa and the Diaspora. Patterson's article takes account of this fact and warns that Italy's demand for colonies is being echoed by Germany, and that from such demands Liberia too is under threat. Although he recognised the class contradictions that existed in Ethiopia, Liberia and other nominally independent countries such as Haiti, rather than emphasising such differences, as in the past, he urged a united front of the entire 'Negro world,' so as to 'take advantage of the instability of the imperialist world's hold upon its colonies.'[111] The article was one of several indications that the Comintern was changing its orientation, in regard to the struggle against imperialism, and responding to the changing situation in the world. The united front that had developed over Ethiopia was just one of the important factors that led to the new orientation which was further discussed, elaborated and confirmed during the Comintern's Seventh Congress in July and August 1935.

The United Front and the Seventh Congress of the Communist International

It is evident that well before the Seventh Congress Huiswoud and the RILU recognised that the ITUCNW needed to broaden its focus so as to strengthen the anti-imperialist as well as the trade union character of its work.[112] This new approach reflected a change that was apparent in the work of the ITUCNW from the latter part of 1934.[113] It was in many ways a consequence of the aggression against Ethiopia, other aggressive acts by the fascist powers during the 1930s, and the growing anti-fascist and anti-imperialist sentiment that developed throughout the world in this period. The demand for a united

111. L. Gault, 'An End to Empire-Building,' *NW*, 5/9 (September 1935) pp.8-9.

112. See e.g. Huiswoud to Dear Friends, 24 June 1935, RGASPI 495/155/102.

113. Paradoxically this new emphasis was accompanied by a new series of articles in *The Negro Worker* entitled 'Organisational Points' which was concerned with questions of trade union organisation. See e.g. *NW*, 4/5 (September 1934) pp.16-19.

front of workers, and other sections of the people, against the growing threat of fascism, and therefore in practice a greater unity between Communists and a wide range of individuals and organisations was particularly evident in the popular front movements of Spain and in France but it was also very evident in the movement to defend Ethiopia. In the African and Caribbean colonies too there was a growing sense of unity not only as a result of the economic crisis but increasingly also in relation to the growing demands for self-government. The unity that was developing, especially in Europe, amongst workers' organisations and trade unions led to a reappraisal of the role of the CI and RILU, and therefore also of the ITUCNW, especially after the RILU, in early 1935, approached the International Federation of Trade Unions (IFTU) and called for a united international trade union movement.[114] This 'new tactical orientation,' and the need for the broadest unity against the danger of fascism and war, was the main theme of the deliberations and resolutions of the Comintern's Seventh Congress in 1935. In practice this resulted not only in a much greater emphasis on the need for a united front against fascism, but also on an anti-imperialist front in the colonial countries that could draw 'the widest masses' into a struggle not just for workers' rights but also 'against imperialist exploitation, against cruel enslavement, for the driving out of the imperialists, for the independence of the country.' It meant that in all countries the Communists had to concern themselves not just with the interests of the working class but in addition with those of the whole people, and that new relationships had to be formed with other forces such as the members of the Second International, the IFTU and various nationalist organisations in the colonies.[115]

The Comintern had consistently opposed both Italian aggression and the appeasement policies of Britain, France and the other big powers and support for Ethiopia was also strongly voiced at the Seventh Congress. It was particularly evident in the speech of the leader of the Italian CP, M. Ercoli (Togliatti), in which he pointed out: 'the war of fascism against the last free native state in Africa will evoke a reaction and indignation throughout black Africa, in all the Arab countries and in Mohammedan India.' Ercoli added that fascist aggression would draw the peoples of Africa into 'the anti-imperialist revolution,' and he assured the CI that in contrast to previous pronouncements, 'if the Negus of Abyssinia, by shattering the aggressive plans of fascism, helps the Italian proletariat to strike a death blow at the regime of the blackshirts, no one will reproach

114. See e.g. G. Dimitrov, 'The Working Class Against Fascism,' *Report of the Seventh World Congress* (London, 1935) pp.49-54 and 'Toward Trade Union Unity,' *NW*, 5/5 (May 1935) pp.10-11.

115. 'Resolution on the Report of Comrade Dimitrov,' *Report of the Seventh World Congress*, p.16.

him with being "backward"'.[116] Shortly afterwards, the CI even took the step of appealing to the Labour and Socialist International (LSI) to join it in opposing Italian aggression in Ethiopia, and in the struggle for peace, and proposed 'an international united front of proletarian action'.[117] The LSI, and in particular the British Labour Party, rejected this appeal, but the CI still expressed the hope that individual 'social-democratic parties' might still join with communist parties in a united front. It continued to express the view that it was only the 'independent and united mass action of the workers and all honest adherents of peace,' that could both move the League of Nations to take any action and successfully win the struggle to avert a new world war.[118] The LAI, and other organisations closely associated with the CI, also called on the working people and all the anti-imperialist forces in the world to mobilise themselves in support of Ethiopia's independence.[119]

Although the CI continually stressed that the Ethiopian struggle was part of a worldwide struggle against fascism and war, there is no doubt that amongst Communists from Africa and the African Diaspora, Pan-African considerations also remained important. In his speech at the Seventh Congress, James Ford made it clear that 'the Ethiopian situation is not a separate, isolated, "African" question, but has world-wide significance,' and he concluded: 'The international proletariat must regard the struggle of Ethiopia as a just war, as a national defensive war, and support the Ethiopia people.' However, at the same time, Ford recognised the symbolic significance of Ethiopia for Africans. 'Only Ethiopia,' he explained, 'which had retained its unity, its culture and its governing power for centuries, was able, through heroic and successful battles to retain its independence.' He therefore informed the congress that 'In the United States the American Negroes are seething with indignation against this attack on the Ethiopian people. In like manner, the toiling masses from South to North Africa, groaning under the heavy yoke of imperialist domination, are awakening to the call of battle for defence of the independence of Ethiopia,' and he

116. M. Ercoli, 'Report on the Preparations for Imperialist War and the Tasks of the CI,' 13 August 1935, *7th Congress of the CI – Abridged Stenographic Report of Proceedings* (Moscow, 1936).

117. J. Degras, *The Communist International 1919-1943- Documents* [Vol. 3] (Oxford, 1965) pp.378-382.

118. Ibid. p.382. See also M. Ercoli, The Italo-Ethiopian War and the Tasks of the United Front,' in *The Communist International*, Vol. XII Nos. 23-24 (20 December 1935) pp.1568-1579 and K.Gottwald, 'The Italo-Ethiopian War, United Working Class Action and the Position of the Second International' in *The Communist International*, Vol. XII Nos.21-22 (5 November 1935) pp.1456-1466.

119. See e.g. International Secretariat of the League Against Imperialism and for National Independence, *Abysinnia* (London: n.d) p.19.

called on the British Communists to 'help develop the movement which is now growing among the Negro population of London and in the British colonies.'[120]

In order to discuss changes in the international situation and CI policy as they affected the 'Negro Question' a conference of 'Negro delegates' was held during the Seventh Congress, as well as meetings between what was now referred to as the CI 'African Section,' and several communist parties.[121] The work of the ITUCNW was again discussed and recognised as having been both correct and in many cases successful. Its activities in conjunction with the NWA in Britain and the UTN in France were favourably mentioned, as was the work to establish contacts in Africa and the Caribbean and to publish regular revolutionary literature. However, the meeting was more critical of the work of the European and US communist parties, noting that the tasks placed before them by the Sixth Congress of the CI 'were not carried out to the necessary extent.' [122] These parties were specifically criticised for not having allocated 'responsible comrades to be in charge of the work amongst Negroes and in the colonies.' A much greater emphasis was now placed on the 'national liberation struggle of the Negro toilers,' and the communist parties were obliged to adopt several measures to remedy the previous unsatisfactory situation including: establishing definite political connections in the colonies, recruiting colonial students for training in Moscow, collecting literature and writing articles relating to 'the anti-imperialist movement ' in the colonies and maintaining 'regular connections' with the ITUCNW.[123] Other specific demands were also made of the parties in Britain, France, Belgium and Portugal but although there was evidence of some progress the criticisms and demands made of the communist parties were very similar to those that had led to the formation of the ITUCNW in 1928. [124]

Although it was recognised that the work carried out by the CPUSA on the 'Negro Question,' in the United States had improved, it too was criticised for its lack of cooperation with the ITUCNW and its poor work in relation to the Caribbean and Africa. It was especially criticised for not taking sufficiently robust measures to counter the activities of Padmore, who it was claimed had 'spread rumours through various papers of the Negro bourgeoisie that the

120. J.Ford, 'Defense of the Ethiopian People' in *The Negro and the Democratic Front* (New York, 1938) pp.159-160.

121. See untitled reports 8 October 1935, RGASPI 495/155/102, 19 August 1935, RGASPI 495/14/60/17-21 and 4 September 1935, RGASPI, 495/14/60/34-35. These reports suggest meetings were held chiefly with the CPUSA and the South African, French, British, Cuban, Brazilian and Portuguese parties.

122. Report of meeting (no title), 19 August 1935, RGASPI 495/14/60/17.

123. RGASPI 495/14/60/18.

124. RGASPI 495/14/60/20-21.

Comintern had dissolved the Negro Committee because it (the CI) is not interested in work amongst Negroes.' The American Party, it was felt, had the means to rebut such rumours and to 'expose the treachery' of Padmore but had not done so effectively.[125] In relation to Africa and the Caribbean, the CPUSA was tasked with organising those of African and Caribbean origin in the United States and it seems that this was part of the impetus for the creation of the Jamaican Progressive League in New York in 1935.[126] The CPUSA was also required to do more to send revolutionary literature to the colonies, publish articles on the anti-imperialist struggles in the colonies and develop an exchange of articles and experience between *The Negro Worker* and *The Liberator*, the publication of the League of Struggle for Negro Rights. *The Liberator* was itself required to carry 'sharper exposures' against Garveyism and 'international Negro reformism' as well as stronger polemics against Padmore. Indeed at the end of 1936 *The Negro Worker* itself carried a series of articles by William Patterson entitled 'Helping Britain to Rule Africa,' which were a critique of Padmore's new book, *How Britain Rules Africa*.[127]

The conclusions that emerged from these meetings suggest that some of Huiswoud's concerns had been heeded, but perhaps more importantly they demonstrate that it was the weaknesses of the communist parties that were again recognised and criticised, and further attempts made to remedy them. Consequently the work of the ITUCNW and *The Negro Worker* was to be continued but with a different focus. The ITUCNW would henceforward, 'co-ordinate the anti-imperialist Negro work of the various Parties' by facilitating an exchange of all the parties' experience of such work mainly through *The Negro Worker*. It was suggested that 'this shall be a means of stimulating and quickening the anti-imperialist Negro work as a whole and on an international scale.'[128] In Africa and other areas where communist parties did not yet exist, the ITUCNW was given the task of liaising with all those ready to protest against 'imperialist persecutions and discriminations against the Negro peoples' (sic) in order to bring them into contact with 'existing anti-imperialist organisations.' At the same time it was to publicise and coordinate work between what were referred to as the 'National Negro Congresses' that were being proposed and in some cases organised in the United States, South Africa, Cuba and Brazil, so as to prepare the conditions

125. RGASPI 495/14/60/18.

126. See W. Domingo's letter in *NW*, 7/1 (January 1937) p.15 and W. Adolphe Roberts, 'Self-Government for Jamaica,' *NW*, 7/5 (May 1937) pp.18-19. See also R. Hart, *Rise and Organise: The Birth of the Workers and National Movements in Jamaica 1936-1939*, (London, 1989) p.23.

127. See *NW*, 6/10 (December 1936) pp.7-11; 7/1 (January 1937) pp.8-9 and15; and 7/2 (February 1937) pp.12-13, 16.

128. Untitled Minutes, 4 September 1935, RGASPI 495/14/60/34.

for an International Negro Congress.[129] Those leading these congresses were also reminded of the need to relate all their work to the 'struggle for the National Independence of Abyssinia.' The National Negro Congress subsequently held in Chicago in February 1936 called for the organising of such an international congress, the main purpose of which would be 'to mobilise the Negroes internationally to defend Ethiopia, to fight against recognition of the fascist imperialist claim to domination over the Ethiopian people.'[130]

The ITUCNW was to remain under the guidance and control of the CI and RILU but was to be located where it could maintain a legal existence. As a consequence of the 'broadening' of the tasks of the Committee,' *The Negro Worker* was also instructed to 'maintain a broad united front appeal.'[131] Evidently this was a major change of focus for the ITUCNW, one that reflected both the criticisms made by Huiswoud and others but also the new orientation of the CI following its Seventh Congress, which now placed much more emphasis on creating in the colonial countries 'an anti-imperialist united front of the broadest masses of the population.' The opposition to the invasion of Ethiopia in the US and some other countries had also shown the possibility of developing a 'united front' in the imperialist countries too, even where some suspicions continued to exist between black and white workers.[132] Although it appeared that following these meetings the future direction of the ITUCNW had been settled, a number of different proposals emerged which all centred on what future form the ITUCNW and work related to the 'Negro Question' should take. It was evident that the future of the ITUCNW was far from settled and that there was still a strongly expressed view that in the new circumstances it was no longer the kind of organisation that was required.

The ITUCNW in Paris

In November 1935, and while the future of the ITUCNW was still being discussed, the Huiswoods re-established a legal office for the Committee and

129. 'International Negro Liberation Committee,' 31 October 1935, RGASPI 495/155/102. On the National Negro Congress in the US see Solomon, *The Cry Was Unity* pp.301-304 and Haywood, *Black Bolshevik* pp.457-462.

130. J. W. Ford, 'Build the National Negro Congress Movement,' *Communist*, 15 (June 1936) p.560. Also 'Special Discussion Material on the Negro Question,' RGASPI 495/14/36/55. On the National Negro Congress in the US see also the article by H. Newton in *NW*, 6/3-4 (May-June 1936) pp.22-27.

131. Untitled Minutes, 4 September 1935, RGASPI 495/14/60/35.

132. On this point see e.g. the example given by J.Ford in his speech to the 7th Congress of the CI, 'The Struggle for Peace and the Independence of Ethiopia,' in J.W. Ford, *The Communists and the Struggle for Negro Liberation*, (New York, n.d.) pp.41-47.

The Negro Worker in Paris, taking advantage of the favourable political conditions created by the new Popular Front government and the work of the International Committee for the Defence of Ethiopia.[133] The ITUCNW was now operating in a new era where the growing threat of fascism and world war was the principal concern and this was recognised and addressed in numerous articles as well as a special 'Anti-Fascist Issue' of *The Negro Worker*.[134] There was a continued focus on the war in Ethiopia and the growing contention between Nazi Germany and the major imperialists powers over the control of African colonies.[135] In January 1936 the ITUCNW called on 'the Negro organisations and Negro press' to forward resolutions to the League of Nations opposing any return of colonies or mandated territories to Nazi Germany. It also continued to focus on the struggles of workers in those areas where it had the most organised support, particularly in South Africa, the British West Indies and the United States.[136] Huiswoud made greater efforts to develop the ITUCNW as an 'international coordinating centre' that could offer support and guidance to the developing struggles around the world by calling for trade union and other organisations to affiliate to the ITUCNW. Two appeals related to this issue were published in *The Negro Worker*, although they seem to have gone unheeded, and another issued calling for increased financial support, for subscriptions and greater distribution of the journal.[137] But the ITUCNW, which had for so long had a clandestine existence, found it difficult to take full advantage of its new circumstances and to establish many new adherents. Plans to hold a small conference for a few delegates from the colonies to broaden the Committee were not realised and Huiswoud reflected that this had further harmed the Committee's prestige.[138]

The ITUCNW's new legal status in Paris did enable it to establish direct contact with several organisations and in some cases to offer 'practical advice.' In South Africa it had close links with the South African Railway and Harbour Workers' Union and the Cape Town Stevedoring Workers' Union, as well as the

133. Joyce Moore Turner, *Caribbean Crusaders*, p.217 and van Enckevort, 'Life and Work of Otto Huiswoud,' p.125 .

134. *NW*, 6/9 (November 1936).

135. *The Negro Worker* carried several articles on Germany's demand for a general re-distribution of colonies. See e.g. H. Davis (H. Huiswoud), 'Hitler Germany Demands Colonies,' *NW*, 6/2 (April 1936) pp.12-22; R. Bridgeman, 'Britain and the System of Colonial Mandates,' *NW*, 6/3-4 (May-June 1936) pp.6-9, 34; and C. Woodson (O. Huiswoud) 'No Colonies to Hitler,' NW, 6/9 (November 1936) pp.5-10.

136. *NW*, 6/3-4 (May-June 1936) p.27.

137. 'An Appeal to the Negro Workers and Toilers,' *NW*, 6/2 (April 1936) pp.18-20; *NW*, 6/3-4 (May-June 1936) pp.3-5 and 'Aid Your Journal,' *NW*, 6/10 (December 1936) .

138. Report on the Activities of the ITUCNW,' January 1937, RGASPI 495/14/87/1.

National Liberation League and the All-African Convention. In addition it had established a close relationship with the WAYL. In the Caribbean it maintained close ties with the NWCSA in Trinidad, the British Guiana Labour Union, and the Dock Workers' and Bakers' Unions in Dutch Guiana. In Europe it maintained its links with the NWA and several other organisations in Britain, but also had links with the Surinaamache Arbeiders Bund in Holland and the UTN in France.[139] Huiswoud also claimed to have 'more or less steady connections' with various other unions and organisations in South and West Africa and the Caribbean, as well as 'a definite influence' amongst 'the Negro press of the colonies.'[140] It is however noticeable that no links are reported with organisations in Latin America, even though developing links in this area had once been a stated goal. In general the most important connections of the ITUCNW were in the Anglo-Dutch world.

During 1936 the two thousand copies of *The Negro Worker*, which continued to be banned in many colonies, were more widely distributed than before, particularly in South Africa, which accounted for twenty per cent of the total. The bulk of the copies were however still sent to the United States. The publication clearly aimed to have a broader, more popular appeal and since the ITUCNW now had a legal headquarters, letters, financial contributions and subscriptions also began to increase. [141] Although there were improvements in the overall style and content of the publication Huiswoud was still concerned about the shortcomings which, he wrote, were a consequence of not receiving 'sufficient live material from the colonies written in the midst of activities and struggles taking place.'[142] In Huiswoud's view, the ITUCNW was an organisation that was merely limited to issuing *The Negro Worker* and other forms of propaganda. It was, he thought, still much too narrow in focus and he concluded, 'the specific features and character of the developing liberation movements in the colonies precludes a trade union committee from functioning as a co-ordinating force, giving assistance, advice and leadership to the growing anti-imperialist movements.'[143] In his view what was now taking place in the colonies, accelerated by events in Ethiopia, was a growing anti-colonial struggle,

139. In Britain the ITUCNW also worked with 'Coloured Seamen's' committees in London, Cardiff and Liverpool and with the Coloured National Mutual Social Club in North Shields.

140. Report on the Activities of the ITUCNW, January 1937, RGASPI 495/14/87/1 also Proposals on the Work of the ITUCNW, 29 October 1935, RGASPI 495/155/101/28. In regard to the press, Huiswoud specifically mentioned the *Gold Coast Spectator*, *Provincial Pioneer* and the *British Guiana Tribune.*

141. Huiswoud reported that the 2597 francs had been remitted for *The Negro Worker* in 1936.

142. Report on the Activities of the ITUCNW, January 1937, RGASPI 495/14/87/54.

143. Report on the Activities of the ITUCNW, January 1937, RGASPI 495/14/87/49.

and in particular demands for democratic rights and self-government. There were now broadly based protest movements and press campaigns, in which intellectuals and others were taking part, 'united front activities' and a variety of organisations that were essentially anti-colonial even if their leadership might be conservative.[144] These could only be 'guided and directed,' he argued, if a suitable organisational form was established. In his view, 'our present major task is to further stimulate and give aid in the development and growth of the National Liberation movement organisations in the colonies and to propagate and help bring about united front actions and the unity of these organisations.'[145] In order to do this Huiswoud argued that a new programme of aims and concrete demands was required. In particular this should stress the demands for self-government and a greatly extended franchise, as well as an end to discrimination and the colour bar in employment and pay, trade union membership, social life and land ownership. Free compulsory education must also be demanded, including facilities for higher education, as well as new social legislation and an end to discriminatory taxation.[146]

In order to develop a broad anti-colonial movement that fought for such demands and a new ITUCNW that could provide political leadership, Huiswoud made several proposals in the period after the Seventh Congress. He initially tried to incorporate comrades from the UTN and RILU onto the Paris-based Committee, hold another international conference to establish a new ITUCNW executive committee and strengthen the contacts of the ITUCNW in South America and the US.[147] Then there was a proposal to form 'an International Negro Liberation Committee' based in Paris, which would also have an open legal status and would operate in addition to the ITUCNW. It was proposed that this Committee would act as 'a coordinating centre of the struggles of the Negro (Black) peoples,' and would publish 'a united front anti-imperialist organ to be known as the *Black Man's World*.' The only condition for affiliation to this Committee would be 'willingness to struggle for the national independence of Abyssinia and against all those imposing any position of inequality or inferiority either socially, politically or economically upon Negro peoples.'[148]

It is clear that Huiswoud and others were grappling with the problems that posed themselves in the rapidly changing political circumstances, as well as the

144. In this context Huiswoud mentioned several organisations including the Aborigines Rights Protection Society in the Gold Coast; the West African National Congress, which was still active in Sierra Leone and the Gold Coast and the Negro Progress Convention in British Guiana.

145. Report on the Activities of the ITUCNW, January 1937, RGASPI 495/14/87/51.

146. Ibid.

147. 'Proposals,' 10 November 1935, RGASPI 495/155/101/38-39.

148. International Negro Liberation Committee, 31 October 1935, RGASPI 495/155/102.

new orientation and guidelines that had emerged from the Seventh Congress. He certainly began to pay much more attention to the fact that significant differences existed between conditions in different continents and countries and that it might now be more appropriate to organise nationally rather than through an international body with a Pan-African focus. However, he concluded, 'this would perhaps be correct if in the colonies there was already a revolutionary movement to take the initiative and actively aid in this direction. But with the exception of South Africa there is no such movement or forces in any of the colonies.'[149] He still considered that it was necessary to 'establish an international co-ordinating committee of the Negro Liberation movements,' and in his view, 'it is obvious that the present ITC of NW could not fulfil this purpose.' He therefore proposed establishing a provisional committee comprised of 'well-known and influential individuals' mainly from existing organisations in West and South Africa, the US and the Caribbean, which through *The Negro Worker* and by other means should agitate in order to 'stimulate action in the colonies' and work to establish a new permanent body which would aid the work of existing organisations through advice and appropriate publications. In some ways this new organisation would build on the successful experience of the ITUCNW, which provided advice for trade union and other organisations and which had also been successful in establishing and encouraging the activities of the 'Hands off Abyssinia' Committees.[150]

However, no quick decision about the future of the ITUCNW or the proposed International Negro Congress was made. In part this was because the RILU was itself being phased out as efforts to establish a united front in trade union matters gathered pace. The Comintern established a Special Commission to reorganise trade union work and this Commission also began to investigate and discuss 'international Negro work,' and asked for proposals from all those involved. There were certainly some who proposed that in the new circumstances the ITUCNW and *The Negro Worker* should be discontinued and that whatever form the future work might take it should be based in the United States.[151] As for the International Negro Congress, this was discussed not only by Huiswoud, Ford, and Patterson but also by Dimitrov and other leaders of the CI throughout 1936 and 1937 and differing views expressed as to when it should occur. Was there a need for a preparatory meeting first in Paris, and should the congress itself be held in Europe or the US in conjunction with the planned

149. Report on the Activities of the ITUCNW, January 1937, RGASPI 495/14/87/51.

150. Report on the Activities of the ITUCNW, January 1937, RGASPI 495/14/87/52.

151. Commission of Trade Union Reorganisation, 22 May 1936, RGASPI 495/20/428.

Second National Negro Congress in Philadelphia?[152] Some of the deliberations suggest that those involved were grappling with how an international forum, or any other body, could adequately deal with the varying conditions that existed in the US, Africa and the Caribbean etc., as well as the 'special and common racial oppression and hindrances' that had created common sympathies and 'a common desire of the Negroes everywhere...to struggle against fascism, for democratic rights, peace and against war.' James Ford, for example, who seems to have taken a leading role in the discussions relating to the ITUCNW in this period, suggested that the recent congresses in the US, South Africa, Brazil and Cuba, in addition to 'the rapid radicalisation among Ethiopian people,' and the 'emerging youth movement in Nigeria,' established the basis for such an international gathering. However, he saw this as a means to create a wider unity of the anti-fascist and anti-imperialist forces internationally and hoped that somehow the initiative would 'emerge from non-communists, with the Communists playing a relatively small outward role.[153] But the international congress was never held and despite the unprecedented level of activity produced by the invasion of Ethiopia and other fascist aggression, as well as other factors, it appeared that the Comintern's Negro work, so much a feature of the 'Third Period' might be drawing to a close in the new period of the popular front.

---

152. See e.g. Letter of 16 April 1936, RGASPI 534/3/1103/16-17 and J. Ford, 'Proposals for an International Negro Conference,' 15 April 1937, RGASPI 495/20/428. The Philadelphia Congress was eventually held in October 1937. See E.O. Hutchinson, *Blacks and Reds: Race and Class in Conflict* (East Lansing, 1995) pp.170-174 and 'Information on the Second National Negro Congress USA,' 3 January 1938, RGASPI 495/14/113/1-5.

153. J. Ford, 'Proposals for an International Negro Conference,' 15 April 1937, RGASPI 495/20/428.

Part II

Chapter 6

Pan-Africanism and Communism in France

Building on the pioneering studies of James Spiegler and J. Ayo Langley there is now a significant body of work on the relationship between the international communist movement and the various Pan-African organisations that emerged in France in the inter-war period. However, there is still surprisingly little analysis of the complexity of the relationship that developed between, the Comintern, the PCF, and their African and Antillean activists and sympathisers.[1]

1. See J. Spiegler, 'Aspects of Nationalist Thought Among French-Speaking West Africans 1921-1939,' DPhil, Oxford, 1968; J.A. Langley, *Pan-Africanism and Nationalism in West Africa 1900-1945* (Oxford, 1973): Also P. Dewitte, *Les Mouvements Nègres en France 1919-1939* (Paris, 1985); Olivier Sagna, 'Des pionniers méconnus de l'indépendence: Africains, Antillais et lutttes anti-colonialistes dans la France de l'entre-deux-guerres 1919-1939,' Thèse de doctorat, Paris, 1987; J. Derrick, *Africa's 'Agitators' – Militant Anti-Colonialism in Africa and the West, 1918-1939* (London, 2008); J. A. Boittin, *Colonial Metropolis: The Urban Grounds of Anti-Imperialism and Feminism in Interwar Paris* (London, 2010), especially pp. 77-111; B. H. Edwards, *The Practice of Diaspora: Literature, Translation and the Rise of Black Internationalism* (London, 2003) especially pp.241-306.

Most of the work on the French Pan-African organisations connected to the PCF has been based on the reports of the Service de Contrôle et d'assistance des indigènes des colonies Françaises (CAI) later known as the Service de Liaison avec les Originaires des Territoires Français d'Outre Mer (SLOTFOM) the intelligence gathering section of the French Ministry of Colonies, which was connected with the police and other security agencies. The Ministry of Colonies developed a network of spies and agents provocateurs in response to activists and organisations originating from French colonies and from the early 1920s recruited agents capable of monitoring and interfering in the activities of African and Antillean organisations in France and overseas. In many cases the agents were existing members of such organisations, or managed to infiltrate them, and in some cases agents were specifically employed to combat communist influence. [2] The successful work of the CAI\SLOTFOM has provided historians with a wealth of information on the relationship between the PCF/CI and Pan-African organisations in the inter-war period but it is not always completely reliable and obviously presents information in a rather one-sided way. Since the opening of the archives of the Communist International it is possible to provide a fuller and hopefully more nuanced picture of the aims of the CI and in particular the role and influence of the ITUCNW in relation to the Negro Question in France.

During the 1920s the PCF was one of the first communist parties to organise amongst those from Africa and the Caribbean but it was often out of step with even its closest supporters and because, in addition, it also lagged behind the expectations of the CI, it was subject to almost constant criticism from both quarters. The relationship between the CI and African and Caribbean activists in France was further complicated and undermined by the infiltration and other subversive activity of agents of the French state, some of whom became leaders of those organisations closest to the PCF, and by the fact that these organisations, for a variety of reasons, wished to maintain an autonomous relationship with the PCF. The ITUCNW, created specifically to strengthen the 'Negro work' of the PCF, as well as other communist parties, therefore operated in very difficult conditions. Its intervention sometimes further complicated rather than fully resolved the relationship between the PCF and African and Caribbean activists in France. Nevertheless, despite these difficult circumstances advances were made. Communist activity continued to be seen as a threat by the French colonial authorities and by the end of the 1930s exerted a significant influence amongst sections of the African and Caribbean population in France and in some French colonies.

2. Sagna, 'Des pionniers méconnus,' pp.142-168.

The Union Intercoloniale

The founding of the PCF in 1920, following the creation of the new revolutionary international communist movement, soon attracted activists originating from France's colonies in Africa, the Antilles, and South East Asia, including Nguyen Ai Quoc, the future Ho Chi Minh. These activists were particularly impressed by the CI's demand for self-determination and an end to colonial rule, which it was declared, would be achieved by the united struggle of the colonial masses and the workers of France. Under the influence of the CI the PCF began to take up the colonial question, whereas the French Socialist Party largely ignored it. Nguyen no doubt spoke for many colonial activists when he declared that it was only as a result of the CI and Lenin's 'Colonial Thesis' that 'our comrades have begun to talk about the colonies.'[3]

The colonial question was especially important in France, which had colonial possessions throughout the world and also, as a consequence, probably the largest African and Caribbean population in Europe at the time. Precise figures are scarce but it is estimated that there were at least eight thousand African factory workers, seamen and dockers and probably an equal number from the Antilles, in addition to the many students and professionals and the thousands who had been recruited into the French army and were living in French cities such as Marseilles, Le Havre, Bordeaux and particularly Paris.[4] The experience of the war and its aftermath radicalised the African Diaspora in France, just as it did elsewhere. Increasingly those from Africa and the Antilles opposed the indignities they suffered in France, as well as the perpetuation of colonial rule and the *indigenat*, the policy of assimilation, and the methods that continued to be used to recruit African troops into the French army. Those politicians who claimed to be representatives of the colonies, such as Gratien Candace and Blaise Diagne, also came under attack as it became clear that their personal advancement would not lead to progress for the colonies, nor for those from the colonies living in France.[5] In these circumstances many activists from Africa and the Antilles, some of them former combatants in World War I, gravitated towards the PCF and in 1921 united to form the *Union Intercoloniale* (UI).[6]

3. Quoted in S. Quinn-Judge, *Ho Chi Minh – The Missing Years* (London, 2003) p.32.

4. J.A. Boittin, 'The Language and Politics of Race in the Late Third Republic,' *French Politics, Culture and Society*, 27/2 (Summer, 2009) pp.23-46. Cf. Sagna, 'Des Pionniers Méconnus,' pp.13-31 and Edwards, *The Practice of Diaspora*, p.3.

5. Langley, *Pan-Africanism and Nationalism*, pp.288-289.

6. 'Note of Agent Désiré,' 13 November 1924, 3 SLOTFOM 3, Archives Nationales d'Outre Mer (ANOM) Aix-en-Provence, France. Dewitte, *Les Mouvements Nègres* p. 97. See also Spiegler, 'Aspects of Nationalist Thought,' p.81.

The UI proclaimed that it was an organisation that had as its goal 'the liberation of the oppressed from the forces of domination, and the realisation of love and fraternity.'[7] It declared that it was opposed to the imperialist exploitation of the colonies and aimed to struggle to end the slavery and injustices that existed not only in the colonies but also in France. Its early members, who were mainly but not all Communists, included those from Madagascar, Algeria, Réunion, Martinique, Guadeloupe, Haiti and French West Africa, as well as those from South East Asia. It was closely linked to the PCF and generally communist-led, which gave the PCF the opportunity to provide training and an introduction to Marxism for several key activists from the Antilles and Africa. Stéphane Rosso, the UI's treasurer from Guadeloupe for example, joined the PCF and became one of the Party's main Caribbean activists in Paris throughout the 1920s and 1930s. Max Clainville-Bloncourt, a lawyer from Guadeloupe who soon became the leading figure in the UI, was also a member of the PCF's *Comité d'Etudes Coloniale.* This body, which was established at the PCF's first congress in 1921 to study and take action on the colonial question as it affected France and the French colonial empire, also had the responsibility of providing communist leadership for the work of the UI.[8] Tiémoko Garan Kouyaté, who originated from what is today Mali and later worked closely with the ITUCNW, also joined the UI. However, its most celebrated African member was undoubtedly the Senegalese war veteran Lamine Senghor who joined the Union and the PCF in 1924. Through the UI's members and its publication *Le Paria,* which was labelled dangerous and subversive by the French colonial authorities, the PCF also made some initial contact with the colonies.[9]

The creation of the UI was certainly a consequence of the influence of the new CI and its revolutionary politics. The call of the CI for the colonial masses to unite with the workers of France for the liberation of the colonies struck a chord with those from the colonies sojourning in France and was stressed by CI representatives at the PCF's third congress in January 1924.[10] No other political organisation proposed such a radical solution to the colonial question, which implicitly acknowledged the equal importance of the demands and struggles of colonial subjects, as well as their human equality. The UI also worked closely with the CGTU, and other communist-led organisations, but at the same time attempted to maintain some independence from the PCF and an uneasy rela-

7. Dewitte, *Les Mouvements Nègres*, pp. 100-101.

8. 'Union Intercoloniale,' 3 SLOTFOM 3, ANOM. See also Derrick, *Africa's 'Agitators'* p.127 and C. Liazu, *Aux Origines Des Tiers-Mondismes: colonisés et anticolonialistes en France, 1919-1939* (Paris, 1982) p.229.

9. 'Note of Agent Désiré,' 13 January 1925, 3 SLOTFOM 63, ANOM; Spiegler, 'Aspects of Nationalist Thought,' p.85; Langely, P*an-Africanism and Nationalism*, pp.293-294.

10. NPR, 31 January 1924, 3 SLOTFOM 101, ANOM.

tionship developed between Party and Union. The PCF was certainly aware of the importance of anti-colonial activity but particularly in its early years it was weakened by factional activity, a variety of internal problems and its practice often did match its theory. As a consequence, it was criticised by the leading Communists in the UI, most notably and vociferously by Nguyen, for underestimating the importance of the colonial question.[11]

The CI also criticised the PCF's weaknesses and tried to assist the Party to strengthen and 'bolshevize' itself. In 1922, at the Fourth Congress of the CI, the PCF was encouraged to pay far more attention to the colonial question and to conduct more propaganda in the colonies. The *Thesis on the Negro Question* discussed at this congress also highlighted the importance of Africa for 'French post-war imperialism.'[12] Africans were being exploited in the colonies, where the use of forced labour and other forms of oppression were commonplace, and they were still being recruited into a French army that was increasingly deployed in France, currently occupying the Ruhr and might in the future again be used to attack the Soviet Union. French imperialism was condemned as an 'oppressor of the Negro,' and the CI's growing concern with the global 'Negro Question' meant that the PCF was also expected to take up this question for solution.[13]

For a time the CI had even considered holding the proposed World Negro Conference in Paris, where it thought favourable conditions for such a gathering existed.[14] However, in February 1924 a representative of the CI wrote a critical letter to the Central Committee of the PCF highlighting the 'astonishing' fact that 'the question of the Negro was not taken up at all' at the Party's recent congress and pointing out that the CI stressed the necessity of 'taking up the Negro question as a special question and not as part of the Colonial problem.' It is clear that this issue had been fully discussed with the leaders of the PCF while they were in Moscow but that insufficient progress had been made. The letter concluded by stressing that as no reports of any work on the Negro Question had been received from the PCF, the CI now expected that it should at least begin this work.[15]

---

11. 'Projet de Résolution sur le Communisme et les Colonies,' December 1921, 3 SLOTFOM 3, ANOM. See also B. H. Edwards, 'The Shadow of Shadows,' *Positions: East Asia Cultures Critique*, 2/1 (2003) pp.11-49.

12. RGASPI 495/155/5/8.

13. 'Draft Manifesto on the Negro Question,' 1923, RGASPI 495/155/4/23 also RGASPI 495/155/14/19.

14. Provisional Secretary for Calling the Negro Conference to the PCF, 27 July 1923, RGASPI 495/155/14/3.

15. Secretary of Negro Conference to the Central Committee of the PCF, 20 February 1924, RGASPI 495/155/27/6.

In response to such criticisms the PCF's delegation to the Fifth Congress of the CI in 1924 included not only Nguyen but also UI activist Joseph Gothun-Lunion, a law student from Guadeloupe who addressed the congress on behalf of the UI and colonial subjects in France.[16] At the Fifth Congress even the leaders of the CI were criticised for their lack of attention to the colonial question, while the PCF was condemned for its continuing 'social imperialism.'[17] Gothon-Lunion enthusiastically condemned French imperialism and evidently made an impression in Moscow where he was photographed sitting on the Tsar's throne, and where both he and Nguyen, who strongly condemned inactivity on the colonial question by the European communist parties and the PCF in particular, were photographed with Leon Trotsky.[18] Gothon-Lunion took the opportunity of his visit to Moscow to establish connections with the ECCI, held meetings with its leaders and subsequently utilised these connections in order to make further criticisms of the PCF.[19] While in Moscow he not only explained the aims and concerns of the UI, which included the demand that black students be sent to Russia for training, but also proposed that the CI step up its activities in order to achieve the independence of the African and Caribbean colonies and the 'total liberation of the oppressed black race.' He clearly expressed more faith in the Comintern than in the PCF and even envisaged the future creation of a 'black socialist republic.'[20] What is significant is that from this early period African and Caribbean activists in France had developed a Pan-African perspective within the UI and that they established a direct link to the CI and in future often attempted to bypass the much-criticised PCF.

Following the congress the PCF took further measures to address the criticisms levelled against it. A Central Colonial Commission replaced the Comité d'Etudes Coloniale, with a special sub-committee focusing on Africa and the Caribbean that included amongst its members Rosso, Bloncourt, Gothon-Lunion and Lamine Senghor, who soon emerged as the most prominent African activist.[21] Senghor was born in Senegal in 1898 and came from a family of peasant farmers. He seems to have had little in the way of formal European

16. Dewitte, *Les Mouvements Nègres*, p.106. For Gothon-Lunion's speech to the congress see RGASPI 495/155/20/7.

17. D. Boesner, *The Bolsheviks and the National and Colonial Question 1917-1928* (Westport, 1957) p.161.

18. *The Workers Monthly*, (December 1924) p.53.

19. See e.g. J. Gothon-Lunion to Manuilsky, 26 March 1927, RGASPI 495/155/40/1-2 and 'Report since the Fifth Congress,' RGASPI 517/1/276/15-21.

20. 'Rapport sur la question Nègre en particulier et les colonies en general,' RGASPI 495/155/20/24-31 and 'Développement de notre rapport,' RGASPI 495/155/20/7-21.

21. 'Note of Agent Désiré,' 3 January 1925, 3 SLOTFOM 37, ANOM; Liauzu, *Aux Origines*, p.229.

education, but he worked for a time for a colonial trading company before being enlisted in the French army in 1915. He fought on the Somme, was wounded and gassed and subsequently awarded the *Croix de Guerre*. After being demobilised he returned to France in 1921 and worked as a postal clerk before joining the UI, PCF and the CGTU in 1924.[22] Almost immediately he became an indefatigable activist and in 1925 both he and Bloncourt stood unsuccessfully as PCF candidates in the Paris municipal elections.

But despite the activity of Senghor and others, which appears impressive when compared to the lack of activity in Britain in the same period, the work of the PCF on the Negro Question was considered extremely weak and solely limited to Paris. The CI was particularly concerned that no action was being taken in regard to the large numbers of African troops still being recruited into the French army and deployed not only in African and other colonies but also against 'the proletariat of France and Germany.'[23] The African and Antillean members of the UI, on the other hand, alleged that the PCF was ignoring the Negro Question, or paying too much attention to important events in North Africa, such as French intervention against the forces of Abd el-Krim in the Rif War in Morocco.[24] The inexperienced and divided PCF appears to have made further errors in connection with the ECCI's request for support for the ANLC held in Chicago in October 1925.[25] Here the documentary sources provide somewhat contradictory accounts but it is evident that the PCF was either unable or unwilling to pay the fares of the UI delegates, including Senghor, who was encouraged to work his passage to the United States.[26]

Whatever the precise facts, this incident was perceived as part of a general hostile attitude on the part of the PCF in regard to the Negro Question. It led to mounting criticism from both Senghor and Gothon-Lunion and in October 1925 the former even threatened to resign from the Party.[27] The latter wrote several critical reports to the ECCI attacking what he saw as the PCF's non-bolshevism, and

22. Dewitte, *Les Mouvements Nègres*, p.127.

23. 'Draft Manifesto on the Negro Question,' (1923) RGASPI 495/155/4/23.

24. Gothon-Luion, 'L'UIC et la Guerre du Maroc,' 25 October 1925, RGASPI 517/1/276/22; *Les Cahiers du Bolchevisme,* 30 June 1926, pp.1421-1423 and 31 July 1926, pp.1606-1608.

25. Secretariat of the ECCI to the Central Committee of the PCF, n.d. RGASPI 495/155/32/14.

26. Dewitte, *Les Mouvements Nègres*, p.111. Senghor was in fact in a dire financial position and had asked the PCF to assist him to find work. 'Note of Agent Désiré,' 25 October 1925, 3 SLOTFOM 63, ANOM.

27. Note of Agent Désiré, 27 October 1925, 3 SLOTFOM 63, ANOM.

this dissatisfaction certainly contributed to his involvement with Senghor in the creation in March 1926 of the Comité de Défence de la Race Nègres (CDRN).[28]

The Comité de Défence de la Race Nègre

The CDRN was the culmination of dissatisfaction with the PCF but it also represented a trend in the declining UI towards establishing national sections, or organisations with a narrower focus. Senghor had previously been asked to form a Senegalese section of the UI, but he had clearly decided that a new Pan-African focus was required even though significant differences existed between the political rights permitted in the Antilles but denied in the African colonies.[29] In addition to Senghor, who became the president of the CDRN and Gothon-Lunion, who became secretary-general, the CDRN's other leading members included Rosso, who became treasurer and Kouyaté who would subsequently emerge as one of its principal leaders.

It is to be noted that this organisation and its successors chose to employ the word *Nègre* (capitalised but still a more derogatory term than the closest English equivalent Negro) rather than the terms *noir* (black) or *homme du couleur* (men of colour). The aim was to distinguish themselves from those assimilated individuals, who would have been uncomfortable with the term *Nègre*, to reject the attempts of French colonialism to divide and rule and to emphasise the nature of their common oppression as Africans. The use of the word *Nègre* was therefore an act of self-definition and self-liberation in much the same way as the use of the term Black would be in the 1960s.[30]

The CDRN declared that it would introduce a new 'positive element into the Negro Question – the affirmation of the Negro personality,' perhaps an early mention of what would later emerge as the basis of *Nègritude*, while it also subscribed to the view that 'the interests of each will be safeguarded in the defence of the general interest.'[31] It started by emphasising its independence from the PCF and soon reported that it had attracted hundreds of adherents in France and in the colonies.[32] However, by the end of 1926 its perilous financial situa-

28. J. Gothon-Lunion, 'A l'Executif toute la Verité – Rapport sur la question Nègre en France,' 18 July 1926, RGASPI 495/155/36. On Senghor's leading role see Dewitte, *Les Mouvements Nègres*, pp. 112-113; 130-147 and Derrick, *Africa's* 'Agitators', pp. 216-218.

29. Note of Agent Désiré, 22 April 1926, 3 SLOTFOM 24, ANOM.

30. See L. Senghor, 'Le Mot "Nègre,"' *La Voix des Nègres*, January 1927, p.1 and Boittin, 'The Language and Politics of Race.'

31. Langley, *Pan-Africanism and Nationalism*, p.301.

32. Note of Agent Désiré, 22 April 1926, 3 SLOTFOM 24, ANOM and RGASPI 495/155/36/2.

tion led to a rapprochement with the Party, which offered a substantial subsidy to support a recruitment tour of the provinces and a new publication *La Voix des Nègres,* the first edition of which appeared in January 1927.[33] The CDRN, largely as a result of the indefatigable efforts of Senghor, soon established 'sections' in Marseilles, Nice, Le Havre, and Bordeaux, building on work already initiated by the UI, and drew wide support in Paris, as well as the French colonies in African and the Antilles.[34]

The CDRN's relationship with the PCF remained problematic but it retained strong ties with the Comintern. Gothon-Lunion, for example, wrote to the ECCI to denounce the PCF and to declare that he was confronting both 'French imperialism and the colonising communists of this country.'[35] The CI was requested to direct its 'generous attention to Negro workers of the world,' and informed that the CDRN had posthumously made Lenin '*président d'honeur perpetual.*'[36] However, it appears that Senghor remained close to the PCF and the police reported that he regularly spoke at PCF meetings to condemn French colonial rule.[37] The CDRN was certainly viewed by the French authorities as an organisation in which there were a significant number of Communists and from its inception was under the surveillance of the CAI/SLOTFOM.[38] Within the CDRN state agents were specifically employed to combat communist influence.[39]

In February 1927 many of the leading activists from France, including Senghor and Bloncourt and Saint Jacques from the UI, attended the founding conference of the LAI held in Brussels. At this conference Bloncourt spoke eloquently of the crimes of French imperialism in the Caribbean, but also of the dangers of US imperialism in the region.[40] Senghor's speech on behalf of the CDRN was a fierce attack on imperialism in general and French imperialism in particular. He declared: 'The Negroes have slept to long. But beware Europe! Those who have slept long will not go back to sleep when they wake up. Today the blacks are waking up.' He concluded by stating:

---

33. RGASPI 495/155/41/1-4.
34. Spiegler, 'Aspects of Nationalist Thought,' p.117.
35. RGASPI 495/155/36/4.
36. *Humanité*, 30 March 1926. Other honorary presidents included Danton, Toussaint L'Ouverture, Booker T. Washington, William Wilberforce and Abraham Lincoln. 'Aims and Constitution of the CDRN,' 4 July 1926, RGASPI 517/1/468/35-44.
37. Report of meeting, 18 November 1926, 3 SLOTFOM 37, ANOM.
38. Note of Agent Désiré, 19 March 1927, 3 SLOTFOM 24, ANOM.
39. Sagna, 'Des pionniers méconnus,' pp.142-168.
40. 'Speech of Bloncourt,' RGASPI 542/1/69/60-61.

> The imperialist oppression which we call colonisation at home and which here you term imperialism is one and the same thing. It all stems from capitalism... Therefore those who suffer under colonial oppression must join hands and stand side by side with those who suffer under the imperialism of the leading countries. Fight with the same weapons and destroy the scourge of the earth, world imperialism! It must be destroyed and replaced by an alliance of the free peoples. Then there will be no more slavery.[41]

Senghor was subsequently elected to the general council of the LAI and he and Bloncourt were both elected to the executive committee of the French section. They and Saint Jacques had been part of the Negro Commission established during the congress, which also included the South Africans La Guma and Gumede and Richard B. Moore from the United States.[42] Senghor's outspoken assault on French imperialism led to his arrest and brief imprisonment soon after his return to France, before both domestic and international pressure secured his release. In France the CDRN and the UI jointly campaigned for his release and raised money to support his wife and family.[43] Senghor's imprisonment subsequently led to a serious deterioration of his fragile health that was soon to prove fatal.

Kouyaté and the Ligue de Défense de la Race Nègre

Senghor was ultimately unable to retain unity within the CDRN, which was beset by major financial problems, as well as political differences, including rivalry between Africans and those from the Antilles, exacerbated by the activities of agents provocateurs.[44] Senghor, Kouyaté, Rosso and others left the organisation and with PCF support formed the Ligue de Défense de la Race Nègre (LDRN) in May 1927.[45] The LDRN like the CDRN took an uncompromising position in opposition to French colonialism. It was established to 'work for the revolutionary education, organisation and complete emancipation of the entire Negro race,' and from June 1927 produced a new publication entitled *La Race Nègre*.[46] The LDRN utilised seamen to distribute its publication through-

41. RGASPI 542/1/69/86-88.
42. Liauzu, *Aux Origines*, p. 36 n.55.
43. Report of 23 March 1927, 3 SLOTFOM 3, ANOM; *La Voix des Nègres*, March 1927 also Langley, *Pan-Africanism and Nationalism*, p.305.
44. Note of Agent Désiré, 17 March 1927, 3 SLOTFOM 24, ANOM.
45. Note of Agent Désiré, 24 May 1927, 3 SLOTFOM 24, ANOM.
46. 'Report,' 29 September 1930, RGASPI 495/155/87/396.

out French West Africa, as well as in the Caribbean, and so from its inception established a presence on the African continent that greatly concerned the colonial authorities. They issued alarmed reports that the LDRN had established branches in Senegal, Dahomey and Cameroun, had been responsible for demands for independence and even uprisings in French Congo and other parts of French Equatorial Africa.[47] The LDRN was also in touch with the press in West Africa and the French Antilles, and from early 1929 endeavoured to recruit students from both regions to be sent to the Soviet Union for political training.[48] As a result of its activities in France and overseas the LDRN came under close government scrutiny. Several agents infiltrated the organisation, meetings and mail were monitored, while publications such as *La Race Nègre* were banned in the colonies and copies sent by clandestine means were regularly intercepted and confiscated.[49]

Senghor's untimely death from tuberculosis in November 1927 cut short his leadership of the LDRN. However, in the space of a few years he had established two important organisations and a political orientation that was to remain a major influence throughout the next decade. An adherent of the CI, he sought a measure of autonomy from the PCF and attempted to combine Pan-Africanist concerns with Communism and internationalism. He sought the unity of the 'Negro race' and was in touch with organisations throughout the Diaspora but evidently made special efforts to establish contacts and organise branches on the African continent. He also placed a special emphasis on organising in the ports and amongst seafarers and they became the vital link between Europe, Africa and the Caribbean and the couriers of *La Race Nègre*.[50]

After Senghor's death leadership of the LDRN passed to Kouyaté who was born in Ségou in what is today Mali in 1902. He was educated locally and taught in Côte d'Ivoire before in 1923 gaining a government scholarship to study in France at the *Ecole Normale* in Aix-en-Provence. He was however soon expelled from that institution, apparently for his political activities, and made his way to Paris where he worked as a clerk and joined the UI and then the CDRN. Under his leadership the LDRN again initially attempted to assert some independence from the PCF, and even searched unsuccessfully for alternative sources of funding from amongst others Marcus Garvey and Du Bois and the NAACP. Neither Garvey nor the NAACP provided such funds and when Garvey

47. Spiegler, 'Aspects of Nationalist Thought,' pp.125-133 and Edwards, *The Practice of Diaspora*, p.254.

48. 'Note sur la propagande révolutionaire,' (hereafter NPR) 31 March 1929, 3 SLOTFOM 81, ANOM.

49. See e.g. NPR, 28 September 1930, 3 SLOTFOM 134, ANOM and 'La LDRN proteste contre le saisies de son journal,' *Humanité*, 31 January 1929, 5 SLOTFOM 3, ANOM.

50. See C. McKay, *A Long Way From Home - An Autobiography* (London, 1985), p.278.

visited Paris in October 1928 he completely ignored Kouyaté and the LDRN.[51] Indeed, during this period Kouyaté contacted a range of potential funders, from the LAI to John Harris of the Anti-Slavery and Aborigines Rights Protection Society in London.[52] He was also in contact with a many other individuals and organisations including Ladipo Solanke and the London-based West African Students' Union, and South Africans Clements Kadalie and Josiah Gumede.[53]

Throughout its existence the LDRN attempted to combine a fervent Pan-Africanism with certain aspects of the internationalist and revolutionary orientation of the CI. It demanded self-determination and political independence, was opposed to euro-centrism and the allegedly 'civilising mission' of France and was a strong advocate of the idea of a '*personalité Nègre*' a concept which would later be further elaborated by the *Nègritude* movement.[54] Like the CDRN, however, it contained elements and personalities that could be in contradiction with each other, including those who were supporters of the PCF and those opposed to it. Kouyaté was certainly amongst those closest to the PCF but also one of the strongest advocates of the LDRN's autonomy.[55] There were also sometimes tensions between Africans and those from the Antilles and a balance had to be kept between these two constituencies.[56] Kouyaté even claimed that the post of president of the LDRN was always reserved for 'an African national revolutionist' in order to avoid the election of anyone 'ideologically assimilated by French democracy,' a euphemism for those from the Caribbean who came from elite family backgrounds.[57] The opposing forces remained together until 1931 when the LDRN split into two rival organisations.

The LDRN's relationship with the PCF was evidently one which divided its membership and it is clear that there was something of a struggle to decide the orientation of the organisation, with Stéphane Rosso, a member of the PCF's Colonial Commission, rather than Kouyaté acting as the Party's most active supporter but both functioning as part of a minority 'Communist fraction' amongst the majority of the LDRN's members. During 1928, for example, one of the key issues discussed in the pages of *La Race Nègre* was the proposal from LDRN member André Beton, a lawyer from Guadeloupe, to establish a

51. R.A. Hill (ed.) *The Marcus Garvey and UNIA Papers, [vol.10] Africa for the Africans, 1923-1945* (London, 2006) pp.422-424.

52. Dewitte, *Les Mouvements Nègres*, p.178.

53. See copy of Solanke to Kouyaté, 27 August 1927 in Report of Agent Desiré, 3 SLOTFOM 24, ANOM and NPR, January 1928, 3 SLOTFOM 81, ANOM.

54. Spiegler, 'Aspects of Nationalist Thought,' p.149.

55. Ibid. p.164.

56. NPR, 31 March 1933, 3 SLOTFOM 68, ANOM.

57. 'Report,' 29 September 1930, RGASPI 495/155/87/398-399.

'Negro bank,' drawing on finance from Africa and the African Diaspora, which it was suggested would enable the self-financing of political activity. This again was an idea closer to the economic ventures of Garvey than it was to the revolutionary politics of the CI.[58]

However, during the same period the LDRN could declare its allegiance to the CI in the most open way. In the October 1928 edition of *La Race Nègre*, following the Sixth Congress of the Comintern, it declared:

> The Second International has betrayed the cause of the colonial peoples...The socialists in Brussels have proved that they have no intention of interfering with any of the prerogatives of the governing bourgeoisie. They have accepted colonisation as a *fait accompli*... On the other hand, the Communist International claims and demands the complete and absolute independence of the colonial peoples. It rejects the theory of the superiority of white over black, and works for universal brotherhood. It supports all the national liberation movements, and thus brings out into the open the clear realities of the true Wilsonian formula of the peoples ' right of self-determination. In such conditions, it is not difficult for Negroes to judge and to make their choice...they recognize unanimously that the Communist International is the only true defender of the oppressed peoples.[59]

At the start of 1929, probably as a consequence of the intervention of James Ford and the ITUCNW, the LDRN was again offered and accepted financial support from the PCF for the publication of *La Race Nègre*, which had barely appeared during the previous year.[60] It was certainly Ford's recommendation that 'the paper that was started by the comrades in Paris be revived and issued regularly,' and from this period mention of the LDRN and the problems facing those in the French colonies appeared in the pages of *L'Ouvrier Nègre*, the French language edition of *The Negro Worker*.[61] However, in this period the politics of Kouyaté could be considered just as close to the Pan-Africanism of Garvey, or Du Bois, as they were to the politics of the CI. In the letter he wrote to Du Bois in April 1929, for example, Kouyaté referred not only to the anti-colonial struggle and the independence of Africa and the Caribbean but also declared

58. Dewitte, *Les Mouvements Nègres*, pp.179-181.

59. Quoted in Langley, *Pan-Africanism and Nationalism,* p.308. It appears that Rosso was the author of this article entitled 'Bruxelles et Moscou.'

60. NPR, 31 January 1929, 3 SLOTFOM 81, ANOM.

61. Ford, 'Recommendations to Negro Bureau,' n.d. RGASPI 495/155/70/61 and see e.g. [S][R]osso, 'L'imperialisme Français et les peoples Nègres d'Afrique,' *L'Ouvrier Nègre (ON)*, March-April 1929 and 'Discourse de comrade Kouyaté,' *ON*, August 1929.

that the LDRN aimed to build a 'great Negro state in Black Africa,' and would accept support from various sources to realize its aims. He particularly stressed the need for Pan-African support and on this basis called on the NAACP to help finance the LDRN. [62] At the same time he sought the political support of the LDRN's contacts throughout North and West Africa and continued to attempt to combine, in his own fashion, the politics of Pan-Africanism and Communism.[63]

The ITUCNW and the Negro Question in France

Although the CI had been concerned about the anti-colonial activities of the PCF during the early years of its existence, that concern increased following the Sixth Congress of the CI and the founding of the ITUCNW in mid-1928. It was originally intended that there should be a representation from the French colonies within the ITUCNW and in the Moscow-based Negro Bureau, but these posts were never filled.[64] From the time of its creation the ITUCNW's publication, *The Negro Worker*, was also published in French as *L'Ouvrier Nègre* but it initially included very few articles that focused on France or the French colonies.[65] The ITUCNW and the Negro Bureau stepped up their work and interventions in France in preparation for the International Conference of Negro Workers, eventually held in Hamburg in 1930 and the PCF also responded to the decisions of the Sixth Congress by making some efforts to strengthen its colonial work. From November 1928 it published a monthly internal *Bulletin Coloniale,* while the following year Jacques Doriot, at that time the head of the PCF's Colonial Commission, published a book, *Les Colonies et le Communisme* which sought to demonstrate the PCF's concern with this issue. Nevertheless, the PCF's successes remained limited and its influence outside North Africa was probably most evident in Madagascar even after the arrest and imprisonment of its two leading activists.[66]

In January 1929 James Ford travelled to Europe on behalf of the ITUCNW and the CI's Negro Bureau and held a series of meetings with the leading members of the PCF and the CGTU in an effort to improve the Party's 'Negro work.' Although there is no record of a specific meeting between Ford and the

62. See Kouyaté to Du Bois, quoted in J-P Biondi and G. Morin, *Les Anticolonialistes 1881-1962* (Paris, 1992) p.180. See also Dewitte, *Les Mouvements Nègres*, pp.191-192.

63. Dewitte, *Les Mouvements Nègres*, p.191-192.

64. 'Minutes of meeting of Negro Section of Eastern Secretariat,' 4 October 1929, RGASPI 495/155/67/28.

65. See RGASPI 495/155/46/1.

66. E.T Wilson, *Russia and Black Africa before World War II* (London, 1974) pp.229-230.

LDRN, it is evident that Kouyaté and Ford met in Paris as well as later that year in Frankfurt.[67] Certainly during 1929 the ITUCNW became more familiar with the particular problems that existed in France. The picture that emerged from Ford's meetings was that the PCF had undertaken no work in the sub-Saharan African colonies, despite the fact that there were about '100 Negro' Party members, and that links existed and could be established through the LDRN and other organisations. In addition, very little work had been carried out in the Caribbean. Ford therefore suggested that the PCF should at least produce some material to be distributed amongst the 'native troops of the French imperialists,' as well as distributing *L'Ouvrier Nègre* and publishing other anti-colonial material including the decisions of the Sixth Congress.[68] As for the LDRN, the representatives of the PCF characterised its membership as mainly composed of those from the Caribbean who had a 'social-democratic outlook,' and as a result it had not been utilised. It was suggested that in order to achieve success Communists, and preferably African Communists, should be sent to Africa but it does not appear that that the PCF envisaged that it was responsible for this task. A little work had been undertaken in the Caribbean by the PCF in conjunction with Sabin Ducadosse, a trade unionist who had attended the 1928 RILU congress and was subsequently one of the founders of the communist movement in Guadeloupe. However this activity, which was financially supported by the PCF, was limited to Ducadosse's work within his own union in Guadeloupe rather than throughout the French Antilles. Ford reported that there was also support in France for the idea that somebody should be sent to the Caribbean from the Party in the US, but again this work was not a priority for the PCF.[69]

When Ford met with the Colonial Commission of the PCF, which included some African and Antillean members, he was promised that henceforth the PCF would take all kinds of measures, including running 'special courses on the Negro question' in its Party School, and that within a few months ten 'Negro comrades' would be sent to Moscow for training.[70] In regard to the LDRN, the PCF was apparently struggling to gain influence. In short, there were significant numbers of African and Caribbean activists in France but poor political leader-

67. Kouyaté subsequently referred to meeting with Ford and others in Paris. See 'Report on the Activity of the French CP Among the Negroes,' 16 September 1930, RGASPI 495/155/87/361-365.

68. J. Ford, 'Report on trip in interest of the work of the ITUCNW of the RILU and the Negro Bureau of the CI, and the meeting of Executive Committee of the LAI,' RGASPI 495/155/70/62. The PCF's 'Agit-Prop Director' doubted that this work could be achieved 'with the limited forces at his disposal.'

69. Ford, 'Report,' RGASPI 495/155/70/62-64.

70. Ibid.

ship from the PCF on the Negro Question in general and consequently also within the LDRN.[71]

Ford submitted a report and proposals 'on Negro work' to the PCF emphasizing the importance of making some headway in the African colonies and also amongst African troops in France. In addition the PCF was expected to make and maintain contact with organisations in the colonies and 'Negro organisation and groups in France;' establish contact with 'colored seamen'; prepare material for and disseminate *The Negro Worker*; give particular attention to the training of students in Paris for colonial work and select students to be sent to Moscow for further training. In order to develop all of this work the PCF was required to 'set up a special committee on Negro work.'[72] The aim was also to strengthen the LDRN, to regularise and improve *La Race Nègre* and to develop work in the ports of Marseilles and Bordeaux.[73] But internal CI documents written several months later suggest that no substantial progress had been made because the PCF continued to underestimate the importance of such work, or for various reasons was unable to carry it out.[74]

Kouyaté and the Liga zur Verteidigung der Negerasse

In July 1929 Kouyaté attended the Frankfurt congress of the LAI, where he made an impassioned speech against French imperialism. He vowed, 'we will do everything to coordinate, centralise, unify the national emancipation movements of the Negroes of black Africa' and, as if to emphasise his own Pan-African conception he added, 'the national emancipation movement of the Negroes of Africa and the Negro movement for political and social emancipation in America will mutually support each other.'[75] He was subsequently elected to the General Council of the LAI as the representative for all France's African and Caribbean colonies. He also participated in the discussions held by the ten-member 'Negro Delegation' assembled at the congress by Ford and Patterson of the ITUCNW.[76] One of the main reasons for the ITUCNW assembling

71. Ibid.

72. J. Ford, 'Report to the Political Bureau and the Colonial Commission of the French Party on Negro Work,' 23 January 1929, RGASPI 495/155/70/69-71.

73. 'Plan of Work for the Negro Section of the Eastern Secretariat,' 16 September 1929, RGASPI 495/155/74/27-28.

74. See e.g. a letter from Paris complaining about the weaknesses of the PCF in North Africa. RGASPI 495/155/80/54-57.

75. Edwards, *The Practice of Diaspora,* p.254.

76. Ford, 'Report on the Negro Question at the LAI Congress,' 5 October 1929, RGASPI 495/155/77/184-186.

this 'delegation' was to discuss the proposed International Conference of Negro workers, planned for July 1930, but in addition those assembled also debated at length on a report and resolutions on the 'World Negro Question' prepared by the Negro Bureau and delivered by Ford.[77]

This report, which was some nineteen pages long, included a detailed analysis of the role of French imperialism in Africa and in particular a resolution on the ongoing uprising in the Congo. Ford called for complete independence for the West African colonies, for the LAI to fight for the rights of Africans to organise and he condemned all manifestations of labour exploitation, which he referred to as 'forms of slavery.' In regard to the Congo, Ford condemned French imperialism, which he said had reduced the population of the colony from 9 million to 2.5 million in less than twenty years. He also took the opportunity to condemn the French Socialist Party which he accused of 'concealing the true facts surrounding the uprising and its suppression,' while at the same time he saluted the 'unmatched heroism and courageous struggle ' of the Congolese people. Lastly, he called on the French workers to demand the evacuation of the Congo, the return of all expropriated land and its full independence.[78]

There can be little doubt that this gathering had a strong impact on Kouyaté who following the congress visited Berlin, where in September of that year he assisted in establishing a German branch of the LDRN, the *Liga zur Verteidigung der Negerasse* (LVN), led by its secretary Joseph Bilé, a Duala from Cameroun and a member of the German Communist Party (KPD).[79] The LVN was founded with some thirty members, including five women, and planned to establish sections in Hamburg, Munich and Frankfurt. It initiated some activities amongst African dockworkers in Hamburg but was prevented from further developing its work by lack of funding from the LDRN and the LAI.[80]

The main aims of the *Liga* were: 'The Liberation of the Negro race in all aspects and by all means and with the genuine solidarity of manual workers and the intelligentsia of the whole world,' and 'to seize the national independence of the Negro people of Africa and to establish a large modern state.' Both of these formulations suggest the hand of Kouyaté.[81] In practice the *Liga* attempted to build an organisation of all African workers in Germany and through correspondence and other means to begin to organise the 'working masses' in the former German colonies of

77. 'Memo on Negro Work for Month of May, 3 May 1929, RGASPI 495/155/74/8.

78. 'Draft Resolution on the Word Negro Question,' 4 June 1929, RGASPI 495/155/72/40-58.

79. On Joseph Bilé and the Berlin LDNR see R. Aitken, 'From Cameroon to Germany via Moscow and Paris: The Political Career of Joseph Bilé (1892-1959), Performer, "Negerbeiter" and Comintern activist,' *Journal of Contemporary History* (2008), 43/4, pp.597-616.

80. 'Brief Progress Report on the LVN,' 30 September 1930, RGASPI 495/155/87/404-408.

81. Aitken, 'From Cameroon to Germany,' p.601.

Togo and Kamerun, which after World War I were mainly controlled by France.[82] Through Bilé and the Berlin branch of the *Liga* copies of *La Race Négres* and other anti-colonial and revolutionary literature was smuggled into West Africa, especially to Cameroun.[83] The *Liga* also wished to send some young Africans to Moscow in order that they might return to the continent as trained activists.[84]

It seems that Kouyaté had been establishing links in Germany for some time, mainly through the distribution of *La Race Nègres* and with the support of the KPD and the German section of the LAI. According to a report by the French Colonial Ministry, he also maintained contacts in Belgium and in Britain where, it was reported, Kenyatta and others were attempting to establish a branch of the LDRN with the support of the WASU. While in Belgium, the *Union Congolaise* was apparently in talks with seamen and miners regarding establishing a 'Belgian section' in Brussels.[85]

Following his visit to Frankfurt, Kouyaté was invited to visit the Soviet Union by the General Council of the Russian Trade Unions, along with Kenyatta and Mary Adams of the ANLC.[86] Kouyaté's subsequent work and stronger support for the politics of the CI were evidently influenced by this journey, which included extensive travel within the Soviet Union and discussions with the RILU and the Negro Bureau. By the time that he returned to Paris to take part in a LDRN protest meeting on Haiti at the end of the year Kouyaté was already exhibiting, on the surface at least, much greater loyalty towards the CI, as well as extolling the virtues of the Soviet Union. He informed the LDRN that he would like to see a government such as existed in the Soviet Union established throughout Africa, and was convinced that with the support of the LAI Africa would be independent within ten years.[87]

The PCF and the LDRN

Following the Frankfurt congress, William Patterson on behalf of the ITUCNW was sent to Paris to investigate what he referred to as 'the very unsat-

82. After World War I, the former German colonies were administered by France and Britain as 'mandated territories' under the auspices of the League of Nations. Kamerun had in fact been partitioned by France and Britain and was incorporated into their respective colonial empires.

83. Aitken, 'From Cameroon to Germany,' p.604.

84. 'Brief Progress Report on the LVN.'

85. NPR, 31 December 1929, APA 10367, Archives Nationales du Cameroun. I am grateful to Robbie Aitken for this reference.

86. RGASPI 495/155/77/184.

87. NPR, 7 November 1929, 3 SLOTFOM 81, ANOM and Dewitte, *Les Mouvements Negres*, p.193.

isfactory Negro work of our French party,' since the PCF had not even managed to send any students to KUTV, as Ford had been promised at the beginning of the year. Again it seems likely that Patterson's intervention, which had been discussed at Frankfurt with Ford and others, had also been prompted by discussion with Kouyaté. Patterson held discussions in Paris for two weeks on 'Negro work' with the PCF, the LAI and Stéphane Rosso, whom he described as the 'acting head' of the LDRN. During that time a detailed programme was established including 'immediate work among the Negro troops in and around Paris.' In addition, Patterson reported that he discussed with 'Negro students' the possibility of study in Moscow. In short he thoroughly discussed all those matters of concern to the CI.[88]

The inability of the PCF to take the Negro Question seriously, or to make headway on it, were seen as particularly important at this time because of continuing CI fears about the use of African troops against French workers and potentially against the Soviet Union, but also because there appeared to be good conditions for agitating amongst the tens of thousands of African soldiers stationed around Paris, who had to endure longer terms of service, worse conditions and lower pay than other French soldiers, as well as amongst the growing black population throughout France.[89]

PCF weaknesses also manifested themselves in the LDRN, which had the possibility to recruit new Party members but, the CI reported, was 'apparently overlooked by our French comrades.' The CI was particularly eager that the LDRN should re-establish regular communication with the branches that Senghor had managed to establish in West Africa. Within the LDRN the Communists were in the minority, even though they constituted an important part of the main leadership. As such their task was to strengthen their influence amongst the majority who were described as 'Nationalists.' The latter were said to 'dream of the establishment of a Negro state or of several Negro states patterned after the democracies of Europe,' and also to have the belief that 'Negroes must work for their liberation by their own efforts, independent of any political party.' This tendency, a CI report asserted, needed to be combated and the Communists had to show that 'no Negro movement has any chance of success unless it is backed up by the general action on the part of the international proletariat.' As Kouyaté embodied both the Communist and the 'nationalist' tendencies, it is clear that matters were far from straightforward, but for all its weaknesses the LDRN included those considered to be 'the anti-imperialist Negro elements'

88. Report by W. Wilson (William Patterson), 31 October 1929, RGASPI 495/155/80/95-96.

89. 'Negro Work of the French Party,' 30 September 1929, RGASPI 495/155/70/51-56.

and had as a main slogan: 'Complete Independence of the Colonies,' which was seen as a reflection of Comintern influence.[90]

The limited influence of the PCF was also reflected in the political orientation of *La Race Nègre*, which nevertheless remained a banned publication in the French colonies.[91] In order to develop the CI activities in France's African colonies and the anti-colonial movement against French imperialism it was considered necessary to strengthen the content and distribution of *La Race Nègre*, and this meant improving the work of the PCF, CGTU and LDRN, and firmly establishing the latter in the main French ports. Unfortunately the LDRN suffered from a lack of trained leaders as well as a lack of funds. One member from the Caribbean had been sent to Moscow for training but many more trained cadres were needed if significant progress was to be made in Africa. At one stage Kouyaté announced that he also intended to study in Moscow, but as this course of action would have left the *Ligue* without its general secretary it was not pursued.[92] The lack of contact and communication with Africa was cited as one of the reasons why the PCF and CI had little direct knowledge of the very significant events occurring in the French Congo.[93]

War in The Congo

The weakness of the PCF in regard to Africa was highlighted by its response to the major anti-colonial uprising that broke out in the Congo towards the end of 1928. The Gbaya revolt, or Congo-Wara war as it is sometimes known, initially broke out in French Congo in May 1928 and spread throughout French Equatorial Africa. Its outbreak was a result of the exploitation carried out in the region by the French colonial government who used the forced labour of tens of thousands of African men, women and children to construct the Congo-Ocean railway in the interests of the major French monopolies and to enable the French government to more rapidly transport its African troops to North Africa and Europe. The insurrection was also a response to the exploitative policies of the forty or so monopoly companies granted concessionary rights to extract ivory and rubber throughout the region by means of forced labour. It is estimated that at least 30,000 lost their lives in the construction of the railway, tens of thousands more at the hands of the monopolies, and protests had been

90. Report on the League for the Defence of the Negro Race. RGASPI 495/18/810.

91. RGASPI 495/155/70/53-54.

92. Report on the League for the Defence of the Negro Race. RGASPI 495/18/810.

93. RGASPI 495/155/70/53-54. See also 'Questions et réponses, RGASPI 495/155/77/14-17.

made in France even before the revolt, which was not finally eradicated until 1932. The Congo-Ocean railway was officially opened two years later.[94]

In February 1929, Henri Barbé, one of the leaders of the PCF and a member of the Political Secretariat of the ECCI, had submitted a report on the revolt in which he highlighted the fact that the anti-colonial work of the PCF had hitherto been limited to the North African colonies, or to responding to major international events elsewhere, and it had no links with or information about the Congo. Barbé proposed intervention by the CI to encourage the PCF to strengthen its anti-colonial activities.[95] Despite Barbé's pessimistic report, the PCF and the LDRN mounted a considerable campaign in connection with the events in the Congo. Indeed one historian goes as far as to say that these constituted the most important of all the anti-colonial activities organised in France in connection with the rebellion. In February 1929 the LDRN, with PCF support, organised a meeting in solidarity with the insurgents and several articles appeared in the *La Race Nègre*, much to the concern of the colonial authorities.[96] Many articles also appeared in the *L'Humanité,* the publication of the PCF, throughout the first part of 1929, which called on the workers of France to support the Congolese people in their struggle against imperialism and for the independence of their country.[97]

But the PCF was unable to send any of its cadres to the Congo during this period and discussions held within the Negro Bureau suggest that despite some significant actions in regard to the Congo insurrection, no substantial progress had been made on 'Negro work' by the PCF, which was called upon to take seriously the task of establishing branches of the LDNR, workers organisations and even communist parties in the colonies. The PCF was instructed that 'specific attention must be focused toward building the Communist fraction within the League,' and that efforts should be made to bring *La Race Nègre* 'more directly under the control of the Communist fraction.' In order to carry out these tasks the Colonial Commission of the PCF was instructed to establish a 'strong Negro sub-section which will have as its specific task the coordination and direction of the Negro work of the French and Belgian Parties.' Furthermore it was suggested that if possible a 'Negro comrade should be put in charge and

94. Derrick, *Africa's 'Agitators'*, pp.237-240.

95. 'Rapport sur la révolte des nègres de l'Afrique Équatoriale française,' 8 February 1929, RGASPI 495/155/77/2-30.

96. The authorities drafted detailed rebuttals of the allegations made in the *Cri des Nègres*. See e.g. Governor-General, French Equatorial Africa to Minster of Colonies, 17 June 1929, 5 SLOTFOM 3, ANOM.

97. K. Nzabakomada-Yakoma, *L'Afrique Centrale Insurgée: La guerre du Kongo-Wara 1928-31* (Paris,1986), pp.150-154.

the work should be organised as to draw in all active Negro comrades.'[98] The inability of the PCF to make headway on such proposals was seen as evidence of a 'white chauvinism' that needed to be combated if there was to be progress in work both in the colonies and amongst the African Diaspora in France.[99]

The CI and the ITUCNW continued to be concerned about events in the Congo, especially with the insurrection that broke out in the Belgian Congo in 1931. The Belgian CP had been seen as much weaker than its French counterpart but it held demonstrations in Belgium, had at least one Congolese Party member, was able to engage in some organising of 'revolutionary groups' in the Congo and was apparently making plans for developing the nucleus of a communist party in the Congo.[100] The Eastern Secretariat of the CI, working with the RILU's Negro Bureau, intervened to strengthen the Belgian Party's work by drafting a programme for a 'Congo People's League for Freedom.' This aimed to provide an orientation for the revolutionary groups already existing in the Congo and was intended for translation into local Congolese languages.[101] The Negro Bureau, under the leadership of Otto Huiswoud also proposed a programme of agitation among African workers based in Antwerp and discussed sending George Padmore to coordinate the PCB's 'Negro work.'[102]

The Syndicats Nègres

In late 1929, in response to criticisms make by the ITUCNW and CI, the PCF did establish it own *Commission Nègre*, which included Kouyaté and a few other members of the LDRN, but this body did not function effectively for some time and at least one LDRN member even refused to participate in it. At the beginning of 1930, Kouyaté was sent to establish sections of the LDRN amongst the seamen and dock workers in Bordeaux, Marseilles and Le Havre, many of whom were facing unemployment, but he ended up also establishing independent unions of black workers, *'syndicats Nègres'* contrary to the line and

98. 'Proposals for the Negro Work of the French Party,' 7 October 1929, RGASPI 495/155/70/57-58.

99. 'Questions and réponses,' RGASPI 495/155/77/14-17.

100. On the Communist Party of Belgium and the subsequent insurrection in the Belgian Congo see 'Notes on the Situation in the Belgian Congo,' 1 Januray 1932, RGASPI 495/155/99/1-10; 'Report on the Situation in the Belgian Congo and the Tasks of the CPB,' 8/31 December 1931, RGASPI 495/155/99/27-40 and 'Draft Directives to PCB on Colonial Work of the Party,' 3 April 1932, RGASPI 495/155/100/12-17.

101. 'Dear Comrades,' 17 May 1932, RGASPI 495/155/100/25-26 and 'Programme d'action de la Ligne du Peuple du Congo pour la Liberté,' 5 May 1932, RGASPI 495/155/100/18.

102. Huiswoud to Padmore, 11 January 1932, RGASPI 534/3/753.

instructions of the PCF and the CGTU which had been fully discussed with him before he left Paris.[103]

Initially these unions met with some support from the mainly African mariners. Several hundred attended a meeting in Marseilles and almost a hundred joined in Bordeaux, many of them recruited after successful negotiations with the shipping companies led to the employment of more black seamen. The unions were built on earlier work that had been carried out by Senghor and to some extent by the CGTU itself, which had established an International Seamen's Club in Marseilles, vividly described by Claude McKay, but does not seem to have carried out any recruitment amongst black workers.[104] However, Kouyaté's initial success was temporarily hampered by the activities of the police, 'the reformists,' that is the Confédération Générale du Travail (CGT), by financial problems and even by national divisions amongst the seamen.[105] Kouyaté's unions were eventually condemned as divisive by the PCF and 'counter-revolutionary' by the CGTU.[106] The programme of the ITUCNW and the RILU called for the 'opening up of the unions to all workers regardless of race and colour.' However, where a colour bar existed the ITUCNW demanded that 'special unions of Negro workers must be organised.'[107] It seems that Kouyaté and the majority in the LDRN simply felt that the CGTU were not organising the seamen and that this was sufficient justification for organising separate unions in the ports, although Kouyaté may have envisaged his unions eventually joining the CGTU.[108]

Kouyaté's action was initially criticised and condemned at a meeting of the PCF's *Commission Nègre* in April 1930.[109] However, when Rosso attempted to criticize him at a meeting of the LDRN in May 1930, all the members present supported Kouyaté, once again demonstrating the problems faced by the PCF in developing its Negro work with the *Ligue* whilst its members were determined to retain their autonomy and act independently.[110] Within the CI it was again

103. 'Réunion de la Commission Nègre,' 2 April 1930, RGASPI 495/18/809/96-97. See also NPR, 31 January 1930, 28 February 1930.

104. Spiegler, 'Aspects of Nationalist Thought,' p.169. McKay, *A Long Way From Home*, pp.278-279.

105. 'Report on Work of the ITUCNW (Hamburg) Covering the Period from December 1930 to September 15, 1931,' 2 October 1931, RGASPI 534/3/669.

106. NPR, 31 May 1930, 3 SLOTFOM 81, ANOM and Dewitte, *Les Mouvements Nègres*, pp.197-206.

107. ITUCNW, 'Trade Union Programme of Action for Negro Workers,' 11 March 1929, RGASPI 495/155/74/5.

108. NPR, 31 March 1930, 3 SLOTFOM 81, ANOM.

109. Réunion de la Commission Nègre, 2 April 1930, RGASPI 495/18/809/96-97.

110. Report of Joe, 4 May 1930, 3 SLOTFOM 24, ANOM.

concluded that the problem stemmed from the 'complete under-estimation of the necessity and importance' of this work by the PCF. While recognising the difficulties facing the PCF's Colonial Commission, the CI strongly criticised the lack of interest and planning and the inactivity of its cadres.[111] As for Kouyaté, he was characterised in one CI report as someone who claimed to be a Communist while exhibiting hostility to the PCF and conducting anti-Communist propaganda. Kouyaté, it was claimed, had given the LDRN a 'Negro nationalist' character and had encouraged the belief that the 'Negro race' could liberate itself without the support of the communist party. He allegedly spoke of liberation but without 'indicating or developing the social and political forms' necessary for such liberation. The report therefore indicated the necessity of destroying Kouyaté's harmful influence within the LDRN, although at this stage there was no condemnation of Kouyaté himself.[112]

Kouyaté's involvement with the syndicats Nègres and his subsequent criticism by the PCF has been seen as one of the main reasons why he did not attend the Hamburg conference of the ITUCNW in July 1930, even though he was elected to its leadership in his absence. However, it is more likely that he was prevented from attending on account of the poor organisation of the ITUCNW, LDRN and the PCF. The LDRN was planning to send a delegation of Kouyaté and two workers. It knew that the venue for the conference had been changed from London to Hamburg, since William Patterson had been in Paris in late June, but appears to have been ignorant of its exact date until after the conference had taken place.[113] The PCF was certainly criticised by the ITUCNW for its lack of assistance to the LDRN and no other delegates attended the conference from France, or from the French colonies.[114]

However, the activities undertaken to organise the Hamburg conference meant that Patterson spent some time in Paris during the early summer of 1930 and was again able to report on the weaknesses of the PCF and the LDRN, which he described as having a 'confused and racialistic approach to its work.' Indeed his hope was that the conference would play a role in addressing some of the obvious weaknesses and he strongly recommended establishing a European base for the ITUCNW, so that it could intervene more directly to strengthen work in France and elsewhere in Europe.[115]

111. 'Rapport sur le Travail Nègre dans le PCF,' 12 May 1930, RGASPI 495/18/809//98-101.

112. Ibid. Also Report of Joe, 4 May 1930, 3 SLOTFOM 24, ANOM.

113. Reports of Paul, 12 June and 12 July 1930, 3 SLOTFOM 24, ANOM.

114. RGASPI 534/3/490. The ITUCNW had intended to recruit delegates from French Equatorial Africa but had been unable to. WW (Patterson) to Dear Comrades, 29 April 1930, RGASPI 534/4/330.

115. Patterson to Hayward, 24 June 1930, RGASPI 534/4/330.

Kouyaté's Report

Although Kouyaté did not participate in the Hamburg Conference he did travel to Moscow to speak and take part in the Fifth Congress of the RILU in August 1930. Once again criticism was made of the inactivity of the RILU sections in France, Britain and Belgium since it was claimed that they 'maintained practically no connections with the labour movement of the Negro colonies.' It was pointed out that the Hamburg Conference of the ITUCNW had not only exposed the weaknesses that existed in these countries but 'showed up also the complete under-estimation and opportunist attitude towards the question of the political significance of the Negro workers for the world revolutionary movement.'[116] This criticism, again aimed principally at the communist parties of Britain, France and Belgium, occurred not only during the congress but also in the meetings of the ITUCNW that were held in Moscow at the same time. One report on this issue claimed 'It is impossible to make a report on the Negro work of our French and British Parties. To attempt this would be to infer that concrete work in this sphere of Party activity has been accomplished.'[117] What was continually highlighted was not only the necessity of such work but also the increasingly favourable conditions for carrying it created by the opposition to the worsening economic crisis.

In regard to the LDRN, the PCF was criticised for having 'capitulated before the nationalist ideology of this organisation and [having] failed to carry out a stubborn ideological struggle for the political line of the Party or the economic policy of our revolutionary trade unions.' In short the LDRN had been allowed to become an arena of conflicting political ideas and aims because the PCF had not paid it sufficient attention. As for the *Liga* in Berlin, it had been treated the same way by the KPD. Although such 'auxiliary organisations' were potentially important links between the communist movement and the colonies, the PCF had 'shamefully neglected' *La Race Nègre* and work in the ports that would facilitate the development of these links. With regard to trade unions, it was stressed that 'there must be no separate unions but organisation along the line of the IV Congress of the RILU.' The RILU concluded that 'the French Party has left it [this work] to the League for the defence of the African race with very unfavourable results.'[118]

Kouyaté presented his own report to the ITUCNW that was also highly critical of the PCF. According to his account, since the death of Senghor there

116. *Resolutions of the Fifth Congress of the RILU* (London, 1931) pp.161-161.

117. Report on the Negro Work in France and England, 4 September 1930, RGASPI 495/155/87/277-285.

118. Ibid.

had been 'no effective work among the Negroes,' a criticism that must have reflected on his own activities as much as those of others, and very little support for the LDRN.[119] He had apparently asked the PCF for 'moral and material support,' in order to agitate amongst African troops based in France, to send activists to Congo to report on the revolt and 'to organise anti-imperialist resistance,' but without success. He claimed that the PCF no longer even sent speakers to LDRN meetings, while it was entirely his own initiative to send an LDRN activist to Moscow for training. In short, Kouyaté claimed that the PCF was negligent in colonial matters in general, and on the Negro Question in particular, and had done nothing to organise communist parties in the colonies as the CI had instructed. In his view, the PCF had forgotten that the revolution in France, the defence of the Soviet Union, the movement against imperialist war, and the anti-colonial struggles were interconnected and partly dependent on effective agitation amongst the African troops of the French army. He also pointed out that the LDRN with its limited financial resources could not, without additional financial support, organise both amongst black seamen and troops at the same time. He also proposed re-organising the PCF's Colonial Commission in order to made sure that its secretary and the majority of its members were from the colonies, but also hinted that 'many sympathizing Negroes' would prefer to join the Comintern rather than the PCF.[120]

It is however unclear how much of Kouyaté's report should be taken at face value. He claimed, for example, that 'ever since its foundation the League has unreservedly condemned Garveyism, which brightened the way for Yankee imperialism,' a statement that was as clearly untrue as his claim that for nearly three years he had been 'working to put the Ethiopians on their guard against a race solidarity which is dangerous in every respect.' While his championing of a 'union of Black Soviet Republics' was certainly not something that was ever proposed by the CI. He also claimed that the LDRN local sections were being formed not only in Brussels, Antwerp and London but also throughout the French colonies in Africa, including Madagascar, as well as in Belgian Congo, Haiti and Morocco. According to Kouyaté, the LDRN already had soldiers and even officers amongst its membership. Only a lack of financial resources and the weaknesses of the PCF, he claimed, had prevented even more successful activity.[121]

It seems that Kouyaté sometimes presented what he thought his audience wanted to hear, such as his hope that the work of the LDRN might eventually 'make of the Negroes a Red Army of Blacks.' As for his work amongst seamen,

119. Report on the Activity of the French Communist Party Among the Negroes, RGASPI 495/155/87/361-365.

120. Ibid.

121. Report, 29 September 1930, RGASPI 495/155/87/396-402.

little was mentioned in the report, although he did claim to have established a 'cultural commission on board every vessel' with the aim of translating material from *The Negro Worker* and the *La Race Nègre* into African languages.[122] He even boasted about the *Ligue's* 'political police system' established to combat espionage, but since so much information about the LDRN was recorded by members who were police spies, this would appear not to have been as effective as Kouyaté envisaged and claimed.[123]

The Split in the LDRN

Little further detail exists regarding Kouyaté's stay in Moscow, although he does seem to have taken an interest in the children of a Togolese woman in Baku, who had once been a circus performer but had since fallen on hard times.[124] On his return he passed through Germany and held a series of meetings with the communist leadership of the LAI in Berlin, along with the three other Africans who had travelled to Moscow to participate in the RILU congress, Edward Small from Gambia, the Nigerian Frank Macaulay and Joseph Bilé. He was also able to discuss further arrangements for sending students for training in Moscow and plans to strengthen the work of the LAI in France but was unable to secure any additional financial support for his own activities.[125] Interestingly his main political contribution to these meetings was his advocacy of the unity of all 'Negroes' and the creation of one federal Pan-African republic in Africa. In this regard he spoke of the artificial borders created by the imperialist powers but also his view that a divided Africa could not survive economically. However, his views were not supported by the other Africans who argued that in the anti-colonial struggle the key issue was for the independence of individual colonies.[126] When he returned to France he was enthusiastic about the support that the LAI and the RILU might offer, and recounted at some length the story of how the Soviet workers and government had defended Robert Robinson, a Jamaican from the United States working in Moscow, from the racism of other American workers. Kouyaté had been impressed by his experiences and was full of praise for the Soviet Union.[127]

122. Report, 26 September 1930, RGASPI 495/155/87/400-403.

123. Ibid.

124. Rapport, 30 September 1930, RGASPI 495/18/810/88-90.

125. 'Letter No. 2,' 7 December 1930, RGASPI 495/155/90/78-81.

126. 'Minutes of the meeting of International Secretariat with the Negro friends,' 14 October 1930, RGASPI 542/1/40/72.

127. Report of Joe, 20 November 1930, 3 SLOTFOM 24, ANOM.

Unfortunately Kouyaté's enthusiasm for the Soviet Union and for the LAI occurred at the very time when some in the LDRN became even more concerned about the organisation's political orientation and closeness to the communist movement. In part such sensitivity, which ultimately led to a major conflict, was caused by the attacks launched by the millionaire fascist, François Coty. Coty's newspaper, *L'Ami du Peuple,* had printed a series of articles exposing and naming African and Antillean activists in Paris who were allegedly in the employ of Moscow.[128] Kouyaté responded in the *La Race Nègre* but the accusations, which appear to have been based on the evidence of police spies, created fear within the ranks of the LDRN and heightened sensitivity concerning links with the PCF. These circumstances exacerbated disagreements about the political orientation of the LDRN, and particularly *La Race Nègre*, that stirred up by Coty culminated in a struggle between Kouyaté, and those who were more sympathetic to the CI, and those members who desired greater autonomy and followed the lead of the organisation's Senegalese president Emile Faure.[129]

In the course of this dispute the publication of *La Race Nègre* was temporarily suspended and when it resumed, in April 1931, competing editions appeared published by the two rival factions. By February 1931 the LDRN had in fact split into two organisations both of which hurled accusations against the other. Kouyaté was also accused of misappropriating funds and Faure, who provided much of the finance for the LDRN, *La Race Nègre*, and even Kouyaté's visit to Moscow, began legal proceedings and eventually obtained a court ruling that gave his minority faction legal ownership of the *La Race Nègre* and the right to use the name of the organisation.[130] The majority of the members, led by Kouyaté and Rosso supported a revolutionary anti-imperialist orientation and they began to prepare the ground for a new publication, *Le Cri des Nègres*. The first edition of this new paper, which remained in publication until 1936, appeared in the summer of 1931 under the editorship of Isidore Alpha, a Communist from Guadeloupe.[131]

128. See e.g. 'Contre le communisme,' *L'Ami du Peuple,* 27 January 1930, 28 May 1930 and 29 May 1930; NPR, 28 February 1930, 3 SLOTFOM 81, ANOM.

129. *La Race Nègre*, February 1930; *L'Ami du Peuple*, 1 February 1931; Report of Paul, 25 November 1930, 3 SLOTFOM 24, ANOM and Spiegler, 'Aspects of Nationalist Thought,' pp.176-178.

130. 'Aux Travailleurs Nègres,' *Humanité*, 16 April 1931; 'Report of Claude,' 15 June 1931, 5 SLOTFOM 3, ANOM.

131. See Edwards, *The Practice of Diaspora*, pp.259-261 and Dewitte, *Les Mouvements Nègres,* pp.210-216.

Ford and Kouyaté

With the LDRN in a state of implosion Kouyaté travelled to Germany, in June 1931, to participate in a meeting of the executive committee of the LAI. There he was taken under the wing of James Ford, who was evidently anxious to make contact with him following a report by the ISH of unsatisfactory work amongst seamen, 'especially the Negroes' in France.[132] The ITUCNW, recognizing the vital role that seamen played as couriers now considered that Kouyaté despite previous problems, might lead a sub-committee based in Marseilles 'to direct the work in the French colonies.'[133] Ford was also encouraged by Kouyaté's criticism of the PCF during the LAI meeting and the latter was invited to Hamburg for further discussions.

In Hamburg Kouyaté and Ford met with representatives of the ISH, held meetings with seamen on board several ships and planned future work amongst the seamen in Marseilles. Ford wrote to Padmore of the 'great possibilities for work in Africa,' and the need to monitor the work in Marseilles and make certain that Kouyaté obtained 'real help and cooperation.' Thus the ITUCNW remained hopeful regarding Kouyaté's future activities, partly no doubt because Kouyaté reported on his previous work in such a way as to exclude himself from criticism. The ITUCNW clearly recognised his potential and wished to strengthen the work of the LDRN in Marseilles so as to further develop its activities in France's colonies.[134] In spite of the weaknesses of the LDRN and the PCF, the former had already established a distribution network for its publications in the Caribbean as well as West Africa.

Padmore therefore also did his best to support Kouyaté and the LDRN from Moscow. Following the decisions of the Fifth RILU Congress and based on Ford's report he wrote on behalf of the Negro Bureau to complain that the CGTU had not responded to previous correspondence and to demand that it made use of Kouyaté's talents, especially in the ports, and worked to develop a '*solide organsation révolutionaire*,' that could also play its role in the colonies. Padmore also explained that it had been decided to assist Kouyaté to produce a publication that better reflected the economic as well as the anti-imperialist struggles of Negro workers. From the start, therefore, the *Cri des Nègres* had the financial and political

132. 'Report to European Secretariat of RILU on Activities of the ITUCNW at Hamburg,' 21 February 1931, RGASPI 534/3/668.

133. Padmore to Ford, 17 March 1931, RGASPI 534/3/668.

134. Ford to Padmore, 31 July 1931, RGASPI 534/3/668.

support of the ITUCNW, and rather than removing the influence of Kouyaté as had been previously suggested, the ITUCNW's intervention strengthened it.[135]

Kouyaté suddenly found himself with influential supporters in the ITUCNW, no longer totally dependent on the PCF and rid of his former opponents in the LDRN. He was to assume national responsibilities with a position in the Colonial Commission of the CGTU, and from July 1931 he began to organise amongst the largely African workers in Marseilles as a representative of the ISH, the ITUCNW and the CGTU. Kouyaté was now clearly implementing the programme of the HC, which had resolved to establish 'sub-committees' amongst seamen and dockers not only in Marseilles but also in Capetown, New York and Liverpool, as 'the best avenue to reach the Negro masses in the different countries.'[136] The 'reformist' French Seamen's Federation affiliated to the CGT at this time openly stated 'we refuse to consider the natives of the colonies French citizens having the right to work on our ships,' so Kouyaté's main aim was now to encourage those unions he had earlier created to join the revolutionary CGTU.[137] He was briefly imprisoned for forty-five days during the course of this work in August 1931, but continued organising in Marseilles following his release. This work went well and it was reported that in one meeting alone Kouyaté was able to recruit over seventy seamen from 'the reformist trade union' for the International Seamen's Club. This assessment was corroborated by police agents who reported a significant increase in recruitment to the LDRN and the CGTU in Marseilles, Rouen, Le Havre and other ports.[138] The LDRN now issued several pamphlets urging the unity of black and white workers and presenting detailed demands for black workers in France and in the colonies. It was now able to utilize seafarers to distribute over a thousand copies of the *Cri des Nègres* in the colonies.[139]

Padmore and the *Cri des Nègres*

After Padmore arrived in Hamburg to take over from Ford in the autumn of 1931, greater efforts were made to support Kouyaté and the LDRN. Padmore

135. Padmore to the Colonial Committee of the CGTU, 21 July 1931, 3 SLOTFOM 31, ANOM: Dewitte, *Les Mouvements Nègres,* pp.285-286.

136. 'Re. the work of the Colonial Commission of the CGTU and its connection with the sub-committee in Marseilles.' 26 December 1931, and 'Resolution on the Work of the Hamburg Committee.' 18 October 1931, RGASPI 534/3/668.

137. 'Negro Marine Workers! Organise and Fight Against Exploitation!' 5 November 1931, RGASPI 534/3/668.

138. 'Report on the Work of the ITUCNW (Hamburg), 2 October 1931,' RGASPI 534/3/669; Note of Victor, 31 December 1931, 3 SLOTFOM 111, ANOM.

139. 'Aux travailleurs Nègre de France et des colonies,' 10 November 1931, 3 SLOTFOM 111, ANOM.

planned to personally contribute to the *Cri des Nègres*, and wrote to Kouyaté outlining a plan of work.[140] The latter continued his activities in Marseilles, where Padmore noted a 'marked improvement' and in other ports where branches of the LDRN, and later the Union des Travailleurs Nègres (UTN), were established and where he continued to work under the auspices of the ITUCNW, the CGTU and the *Syndicats Unitaire des Marins*. Kouyaté's activities were not limited to encouraging union organisation amongst the seafarers, however, he also encouraged opposition to a new imperialist war, explaining to the seafarers that if such a war broke out their main responsibility was to refuse to serve and instead to fight for the freedom of the colonies.[141]

Evidence that the *Cri de Nègres* was making an impact came from Guadeloupe, where a strike of agricultural workers had broken out in 1930. In the autumn of 1931 a group of workers from the island began writing to the *Cri* stating that they supported the slogan of 'class against class' and asking for further guidance.[142] Such successes, there were for example also letters from Guineé, Cameroun and Martinique, prompted the RILU Negro Bureau to encourage the CGTU's Colonial Commission to increase its role in the editing and political development of the paper and led to a lengthy 'Lettre à la Guadeloupe' in the pages of the *Cri des Nègres*.[143] This was seen as being particularly important at a time of increasing resistance to the effects of the worldwide economic crisis and the RILU considered that the paper should explain to workers how to organise against exploitation both in France and the colonies. It was also expected to highlight the needs and demands of the unemployed, including combating the chauvinism of the CGT, which was 'setting French workers against foreign and colonial workers.' Attention also needed to be paid to the anti-colonial struggle and the continuing attempts of the French government to recruit Africans into a 'huge professional black army.' In this regard there was criticism of the CGTU which had resolved 'that the use of black troops in military conflicts must be forbidden,' a demand which was characterised as pandering to racism, instead of actually organising amongst the African troops to mobilize them to 'turn their guns on their exploiters and oppressors.'[144]

In short the *Cri de Nègres* was expected to play the part of an organiser concerned with the 'day-to-day life of the Negro workers,' but also capable of

140. Padmore to Dear Comrades, 16 November 1931, RGAASPI 534/3/668.

141. 'Réunion au Club International des Marins,' 15 July 1932, 3 SLOTFOM 46, ANOM.

142. 'Premliminary Verification of the Fulfilment of the RILU Decisions of the Work of the Hamburg Committee,' 14 March 1932, RGASPI 534/3/754. Also Huiswoud to Padmore, 11 January 1932, RGASPI 534/3753.

143. *Le Cri des Nègres*, (April-March 1932).

144. Negro Committee of RILU to CGTU Colonial Commission, 16 February 1932, RGASPI. 534/3/754 Also see Dewitte, *Les Mouvements Nègres*, pp.288-290.

enlightening them about the international situation and the struggles of workers in other countries, especially the Soviet Union. Throughout its existence the *Cri des Nègres* carried regular reports on the Scottsboro case, the situation in Haiti, developments in the Soviet Union and China as well a regular reports and analysis of events in the French colonies. Its work became even more important when the publication of the *Ouvrier Nègre* (the French edition of *The Negro Worker*) was suspended in 1932 and it is evident that at least in Guadeloupe some saw it as the only worker's paper.[145] With these aims in mind the Negro Bureau criticised lengthy articles 'which do not bring the specific conditions of national exploitation and oppression to light.' It demanded that work must be undertaken to develop worker correspondents especially in the colonies, and that the CGTU established a special commission to develop the paper which the ITUCNW/Negro Bureau would support.[146]

As a result of the success of his work, in May 1932 Kouyaté travelled to Hamburg as the leader of a delegate of the CGTU to attend the ISH congress. In addition he was able to consult with Padmore and deliver a report on work in France and the French colonies to the conference of the ITUCNW held at the same time.[147] According to Kouyaté's account there were only twelve 'active Negro Party members' in Paris, in addition to sympathizers in Dunkirk and Rouen, but through the LDRN good connections now existed with contacts in Dakar, Conakry, Grand Bassam and other places in West Africa where LDRN branches had formerly existed. Contacts also existed in Djibouti, where there was also a small communist group and in Guadeloupe and in Martinique, where the LDRN was in touch with Jules Monnerot and the *Groupe Jean Jaurès*.[148]

It is evident that the activities of Kouyaté in French ports and the links that might be established between the LDRN, the Comintern and potential supporters particularly in Africa greatly alarmed the French colonial authorities. They reported that numerous leaflets and other propaganda were being sent to Africa and believed that the PCF was spearheading efforts to establish a trade union organisation throughout the French colonies in West and Equatorial Africa. Indeed, it was reported that such an organisation with over two hundred members was already in existence in Dakar and in contact with the CGTU.[149] The French authorities concluded that Kouyaté's dispatch to Hamburg at the

145. Practical Decisions on the Discussion of the ITUC, 23-26 May 1932, RGASPI 534/3/753. 'Lettre de la Guadeloupe,' *Le Cri des Nègres,* 1/4-5 (November-December 1931) p.3.

146. Negro Committee of RILU to CGTU Colonial Commission, 16 February 1932, RGASPI. The ITUCNW subsequently supplied articles for the paper.

147. 'Programme for the Negro workers conference,' n.d. RGASPI 534/3/753.

148. 'Special Report by Kouyaté,' n.d. RGASPI 534/3/753.

149. Minister of Colonies to Governor General, French West Africa, 18 May, 1932; Report of Désiré, 1 February 1932; Report of Victor, 19 April 1932, 3 SLOTFOM 31, ANOM.

head of a CGTU delegation that included two other Africans, from Marseilles and Rouen, as well as several other colonial seamen, indicated that significant organising efforts were occurring in Africa and other French colonies.[150]

It is, however, difficult to know exactly how widely the *Cri des Nègres* was distributed and before 1934 it only appeared as a quarterly publication. Certainly the French colonial authorities did their best to intercept and confiscate copies sent to the colonies According to Kouyaté, a total of three thousand copies were distributed in France and throughout Africa and the Antilles. Some were sent to the colonies via the French ports or distributed in other ways, and one hundred and fifty were sent to subscribers.[151] However, at a meeting of the Communist 'fraction' in the LDRN held in early 1932 there was general agreement that there were no such subscriptions and Kouyaté himself reported that copies of the paper remained unsold in Le Havre and Bordeaux. Furthermore, he was doubtful if the copies sent to the colonies had arrived.[152]

In order to further develop the work in France, Padmore encouraged Kouyaté to act when the PCF and CGTU were slow or reluctant to take up 'Negro work' but also indirectly supported Kouyaté's continual attempts to keep the *Cri des Nègres* independent of total PCF control. He wrote to Kouyaté to encourage him in this direction and also to suggest that it was Padmore himself who was most determined to conduct work in 'black Africa.' Indeed Padmore shared with Kouyaté his criticisms of the CGTU, the PCF and even the CPGB concluding that their weaknesses were the reason why so little progress had been made in the colonies. He therefore proposed that in future they should work together in regard to France's colonies in Africa and the Antilles. In particular, he told Kouyaté to establish a French section of the ITUCNW of which he would be secretary.[153] To assist him Padmore planned to write to ask the RILU to instruct the CGTU to provide premises, while the RILU itself, perhaps through the auspices of ISH, might provide Kouyaté's salary. He naturally also encouraged Kouyaté to continue with the production of the *Cri des Nègres,* which he hoped would become the French equivalent of *The Negro Worker*. In short he wanted Kouyaté and the proposed French section of the ITUCNW to be responsible for all 'Negro work' in France, its colonies and in the Belgian Congo and to act independently of the PCF and the CGTU.[154]

150. Report of Agent Thomas, May 1932, 3 SLOTFOM 31, ANOM.

151. 'Special Report by Kouyaté,' n.d. RGASPI 534/3/753.

152. 'Fraction Défense Race Nègre,' 11 February 1932, RGASPI 495/155/99/53.

153. Padmore to Kouyaté, 6 May 1932, RGASPI 534/3/755.

154. Ibid.

The Union des Travailleurs Nègres

When the French courts declared that Faure's faction was the only legitimate owner of the name and assets of the LDRN, Kouyaté and his comrades were forced to launch a new organisation, the *Union des Travailleurs Nègres* (UTN) in June 1932.[155] The UTN presented itself as an association for the 'mutual aid and cultural development,' of black workers and intellectuals in unity with the workers 'of all races and all nationalities.'[156] It aimed to carry on the work initiated by Senghor, provided some medical and legal support, especially for the unemployed, and attempted to organise and politicise African and Antillean workers, students and other residents in France. It also aimed to agitate amonst individuals and organisations in the French colonies, such as *L'Amicale des Anciens Marins* in Dakar, as well as those in French-speaking countries including Haiti and the Belgian Congo.[157] The new secretary-general was the Malagasy Communist, Thomas Ramananjato, while Kouyaté was given the position of assistant-secretary. The activities of the UTN were compromised from its inception, since Ramananjato and other leading figures were agents in the employ of the Ministry of Colonies.[158]

Whatever Kouyaté's official position he remained the leading activist in the UTN and was one of the main speakers at the mass meeting organised by the Secours Rouge Internationale (SRI) in June 1932 as part of the Scottsboro campaign. Over five thousand people came to see and hear Ada Wright, the mother of two of the 'Scottsboro Boys,' who had come to France as part of a European tour organised by International Labour Defence. The SRI, which had already established a section in Madagascar and continued to give legal and other support to activists in that country, also took the leading role in France on the Scottsboro campaign. Throughout 1932 it organised numerous meetings about the case and even established its own Section des Travailleurs Nègres. Evidently the campaign, which was also widely publicised by the PCF, had a major impact in France especially amongst the Antillean students who in the same year published the famous manifesto *Légitime Défense*.[159] The UTN, and Kouyaté in particular, played a key role in many of the SRI rallies and sent its

155. NPR, 30 June 1932, 3 SLOTFOM 64, ANOM.

156. Statutes of the UTN, 3 September 1932, 3 SLOTFOM 136, ANOM.

157. Report of Joe, 27 June 1932, 3 SLOTFOM 53, ANOM.

158. Sagna, 'Des pionniers méconnus,' pp.142-168.

159. L. Kestletoot, *Black Writers in French: A Literary History of Negritude* (Washington D.C., 1991) pp. 15-17 and 49-55.

own delegation to protest to the US ambassador.[160] Amongst its other activities during this initial period, the UTN also managed to send two delegates to the World Congress against War held in Amsterdam in August 1932.[161]

The production of the *Cri des Nègres* remained one of the new organisation's main activities but it still struggled to find the necessary funds and launched a series of fundraising events for this purpose. Financial problems, which also impeded the acquisition of new premises, led to recrimination and suspicion within the organisation, particularly after the expulsion of one of its leading members, Narcisse Danaé, who was accused of being a police agent and of embezzling funds.[162] The content of the *Cri des Nègres* was strengthened by the submission of articles from students and others in Moscow, and from various members of the PCF but most were written by members and supporters of the UTN, including those in the colonies. Many articles concentrated on exposing examples of colonial oppression, unemployment and the effects of the worldwide economic crisis, the increasing threat posed by fascism, in addition to articles relating to the international communist movement.[163] The finance for the production of the *Cri des Nègres* was mainly provided by Padmore, who visited Paris and attended meetings of the UTN and SRI in October 1932.[164]

In addition to providing finance for the *Cri des Nègres*, Padmore became the UTN's greatest champion. He described it as a 'sub-section' of the HC and even accused the CGTU of being opposed to its creation, an approach which he claimed 'greatly handicapped' the work among 'the Negroes of France and the colonies,' and which was subsequently also criticised by the RILU Secretariat.[165] The *Cri des Nègres* evidently lost subscribers because of its irregularity, but police reports suggest that even if it was not distributed in large numbers, its dissemination was widespread. It retained subscribers and contacts in Madagascar, Dahomey, Dakar, Côte d'Ivoire and elsewhere in West Africa, including Togo and Cameroun, where there were demands for the creation of local

160. Report of Paul, 9 and 16 October 1932, Report of Joe, 3 November 1933, 3 SLOTFOM 53, ANOM.

161. Report of Joe, 24 October 1932, 3 SLOTFOM 53, ANOM.

162. Report of Joe, 20 June 1932 and 17 October 1932, 3 SLOTFOM 53, ANOM. Danaé rejected the accusation and in a letter to another member denounced Ramananjato as well as Kouyaté. Danaé to Alpha, 18 November 1932, RGASPI 517/1/1318/132-137.

163. See e.g. *Le Cri des Nègres*, (January-February 1933), which also contains a letter from the Negro Welfare Association in London.

164. Report of Joe, 23 September 1932 and 7 October; Report of Paul 21 October 1932, 3 SLOTFOM, 53 ANOM.

165. 'Report on the work of the Hamburg Committee for the period 1931-1932,' December 1932 and Resolution on the report of the work of the Hamburg Committee,' n.d. RGASPI 534/3/753.

branches of the UTN, and even in the Gold Coast and Liberia. The UTN also had links with the Caribbean, including Jamaica, Haiti and Cuba and significant support in the France ports. By the end of 1932 it was reported that it had established branches in Marseilles, Le Havre, Bordeaux, Rouen and Dunkerque, and its strong support among mariners was utilised to distribute the *Cri* and ITUCNW publications throughout the French colonies.[166]

However, the UTN still faced considerable difficulties. Its publications had to be smuggled by sea into the colonies, sometimes hidden inside other publications, and were often intercepted by the police and colonial authorities. There was growing internal unrest in the organisation and it cannot be discounted that some of this was caused by agent provocateurs, since there were two state agents amongst its leaders. In the face of the difficulties some members resigned. At one stage Stéphane Rosso was accused of having been too close to suspected police agent, Narcisse Danaé, and was said to be planning to resign in order to establish a solely Caribbean anti-imperialist organisation.[167] Public meetings were also poorly attended and to remedy this situation the UTN began to organise dances and social events in order to regain support and to find a new source of badly needed funds, a decision that also led to some dissension.[168]

Kouyaté remained publicly supportive of the PCF but still expressed his dissatisfaction with the lack of finance provided for work in the African colonies, a criticism that appears to have been accepted by the Party.[169] He was reported to be considering resignation from the PCF when it was suggested that as part of his work with the CGTU he became a full-time official of the communist-led Seamen's Federation and relocate to Rouen, a move which would have made it difficult to maintain an active leadership role within the UTN in Paris.[170] The success of Kouyaté's work amongst seamen coincided with a decline in the other activities of the UTN and this was a problem that the PCF's Colonial Commission attempted to resolve at the end of 1932, with the support of the leading Communists in the UTN, Rosso, Isidore Alpha and Pierre Kodo-Kossoul, who was also employed as an agent of the Ministry of Colonies.[171]

---

166. Report of Joe, 14 October 1932: Report of Joe, 25 November 1932; NPR, 31 October and 30 November 1932, 3 SLOTFOM 53, ANOM; Report on the work of the Hamburg Committee.

167. Report of Paul, 11 November 1932, 3 SLOTFOM 53, ANOM.

168. Report of Paul, 6 November 1932, 3 SLOTFOM 53, ANOM.

169. Report of Paul, 4 November 1932, 3 SLOTFOM 53, ANOM.

170. Réunion de la fraction communiste de l'UTN, 14 December 1932, 3 SLOTFOM 53, ANOM.

171. Report of Paul, 27 December 1932, 3 SLOTFOM 53, ANOM, also 'Fraction de UTN,' 14 December 1932, RGASPI 517/1/1318/160-162.

The PCF's Colonial Commission seems to have belatedly recognised that work in the African colonies had tremendous potential. This view was partly the consequence of the success of the SRI in Madagascar, where a local section with over four hundred members had been formed, and partly a response to the continuing criticism of the *Cri des Négres* and the PCF's under-estimation of the colonial question by the CI and the ITUCNW.[172] Consequently the PCF now decided to strengthen all its work, particularly in Africa, and in particular to improve the regularity, format and content of the *Cri des Nègres*. But Kouyaté and the Communist 'fraction' within the UTN responded negatively to demands by the PCF's Colonial Commission that the Party should take more control of the publication. They argued that since the fraction was part of the Colonial Commission, further PCF control was unnecessary, while Kouyaté argued such control would be contrary to the UTN's constitution and would lead to resignations, as not all its ordinary members were Party sympathisers.[173]

The arguments of the fraction were not without merit but Kouyaté seems to have had other concerns. His reliance on Padmore and the ITUCNW for funds and support for the *Cri des Nègres* allowed him some autonomy from the PCF and the CGTU, indeed this seems to have been Padmore's intention, and this he was not prepared to relinquish. Padmore continued to advance funds for the *Cri des Nègres* and Kouyaté therefore continued to believe that the 'Negro work' in France would be largely directed by the ITUCNW under the auspices of the RILU, a view that was given added credibility when he announced that he had received an invitation to meet with Lozovsky, the general secretary of the RILU, in Hamburg in February 1933, a meeting that became impossible after the Nazi takeover.[174] The Nazi coup in Germany led to the arrest and deportation of Padmore and the expulsion or exit of many others of African origin. These circumstances, together with Nazi demands for the return of its former African colonies and a real prospect of a new inter-imperialist war heightened anti-fascist activity in Paris, and led the UTN to call for a united anti-fascist response by all the African and Antillean organisations.

There was, however, a division in the UTN between Kouyaté, who wished to maintain autonomy from the PCF and work even more closely with Padmore and the ITUCNW, and the Union's other Communist leaders, loyal to the PCF and largely ignorant of Kouyaté's close relationship with Padmore. The PCF's Colonial Commission was opposed to Padmore's efforts to install Kouyaté as a representative of the ITUCNW in Paris, believing that the latter was not fit for the task. Indeed following critical reports of his activities in Marseilles and Paris

172. Report of Victor, 29 May 1932, 5 SLOTFOM 23, ANOM.

173. NPR, 30 November, 31 December 1932 and 31 January 1933, 3 SLOTFOM 68, ANOM.

174. Report of Paul, 27 January 1933, 3 SLOTFOM 53, ANOM.

the Party began to investigate his activities more thoroughly.[175] It also managed to get him to agree that the *Cri des Nègres* should be organised separately from the UTN and that the Union should develop a new bulletin.[176] After Padmore's expulsion from Germany and when it seemed that the future of the ITUCNW might be in some doubt, Kouyaté did propose that a new publication, less openly Communist in orientation, should be established as part of a plan to unite several of the African and Antillean organisations in Paris. Since the organisations of students from Martinique, Guadeloupe and West Africa had expressed a wish to work with the UTN, this proposal initially found favour with the UTN's leadership.[177] However, these proposals were made at the same time as the continued non-appearance of the *Cri des Nègres* and when there was an apparent lack of funds to publish it, which prompted questions by the PCF and the CGTU that Kouyaté refused to answer. His reluctance to explain matters led to allegations that he was misappropriating funds, followed by his suspension from the PCF while further enquiries were made.[178] Padmore, who stayed in Paris during this period, although he had no specific directive from the CI to do so, remained close to Kouyaté and clearly planned to work with him to re-establish the ITUCNW and *The Negro Worker.* However, by July 1933 he found himself working with the UTN to organise a new editorial board for the *Cri des Nègres*, from which Kouyaté was excluded, and investigating the Union's finances. When a new edition of the *Cri des Négres* appeared in August 1933 it was thanks to financial support from the PCF.[179]

In the course of discussions between the PCF and the leaders of the UTN it became apparent that the funds supplied by the RILU for the publication of the *Cri des Nègres* and advanced by Padmore to Kouyaté on a regular basis since its creation, had not always been used for that purpose, and had also been kept secret from the other leaders of the UTN. It also became evident that Kouyaté's previous reluctance to allow the PCF to supervise the publication of the *Cri* was not only concerned with maintaining its political independence but also with maintaining his private financial arrangements with Padmore. Kouyaté had dominated all aspects of the UTN's affairs and when challenged in the presence of Padmore was unable to account for the fact that it had absolutely no

175. Section Coloniale, 14 January 1933, RGASPI 517/1/1504/27-28 and 'A la commission des cadres,' 11 January 1933, RGASPI 495/270/5182/19-20.

176. RGASPI 517/1/1575/36-37.

177. Report of Joe, 30 June 1933 and 11 August 1933, 3 SLOTFOM 53; NPR, 30 June 1933, 3 SLOTFOM 68, Report of Paul, 23 June 1933, 3 SLOTFOM 34, ANOM.

178. Report of Paul, 13 June and 6 and 11 July 1933, 3 SLOTFOM 34, ANOM.

179. Réunion de la fraction Communiste Nègre de l'UTN, 24 July 1933, 3 SLOTFOM 53, ANOM.

funds.[180] When summoned before the PCF he refused to give an account of his actions, nor fully explain the finances of the *Cri des Nègres* and he subsequently refused to hand over the names of its subscribers. He then announced that he was much more concerned with the movements in the colonies than he was with *'le mouvement nègre en France.'*[181] He arrogantly declared that nothing could be achieved in France without his involvement and that he was about to launch two new publications focusing on Africa and so required information relating to the distribution of the *Cri des Nègres* for his own work. Although he professed to have no money, he also announced that he was planning a new organisation and a World Negro Congress and to this end, it was reported, was working closely with Padmore and others. His behaviour, and failure to provide any explanation for his actions, led to an initial suspension by the CI and finally to his expulsion from the PCF in September 1933.[182]

Kouyaté was also asked several times by the UTN to explain his behaviour. His only response was a lengthy letter proclaiming his innocence and love for the 'race,' warning about the allegedly unscrupulous nature of the CI and PCF and claiming that the latter and the CGTU owed him money. He even threatened to sue the UTN before the 'bourgeois correctional tribunal' if any defamatory articles were printed about him in the *Cri des Nègres*. To add to the conflict he scheduled the inaugural meeting of the organising committee of his World Negro Congress at exactly the same time as the planned general assembly of the UTN to which he had been summoned. That meeting, held in November 1933 voted almost unanimously to expel him.[183]

Although it must have been clear to Padmore that Kouyaté had acted improperly and certainly without the knowledge of his comrades, since at a UTN meeting he also complained about his conduct, the two remained steadfastly close, united by their previous joint activity as well as a growing opposition to the PCF and CI.[184] In August 1933 Padmore began to face problems of his own but during the meeting held in Paris that month to discuss the future of the ITUCNW he does not seem to have made any attempt to defend Kouyaté, although he did make it clear that after his deportation he had expected to establish a new '*secretariat collectif*' in Paris with Kouyaté and Rosso. He did however question the rumour he had heard that Kouyaté had been suspended because

180. Réunion du bureau d l'UTN, 27 July 1933, 3 SLOTFOM 53, ANOM.

181. Kouyaté to Merlin, 14 August 1933, RGASPI 534/3/895.

182. Report of Paul, 30 September 1933, 3 SLOTFOM 53, ANOM; Dewitte, *Les Mouvements Nègres*, pp.304-309.

183. Kouyaté to the General Assembly of the UTN, 4 November 1993; Report of Joe, 6 November 1933, 3 SLOTFOM 53, ANOM; J.M. Turner, *Caribbean Crusaders and the Harlem Renaissance* (Chicago, 2005) pp.212-213.

184. Report of Joe, 8 September 1933, 3 SLOTFOM 53, ANOM.

he had become a police agent, a suggestion that was strenuously denied by the leading PCF member present.[185] Even after Kouyaté's expulsion, Padmore continued to work with him and was one of the key figures attempting to convene a World Negro Congress in Paris or London in the summer of 1935, alongside René Maran, Emile Faure and some of Kouyaté's former adversaries from the LDRN. It is interesting that Padmore wrote to Du Bois on UTN notepaper to enlist his support for this 'Negro World Unity Congress,' which never took place, and he seems to have linked the organising committee with various plans to raise money to aid Liberia well before his own expulsion.[186]

The expulsion of Kouyaté followed by the evasive behaviour of Padmore created a major problem for the CI and principally for the PCF, which may even have had ramifications amongst some of the students Kouyaté had sent to Mosocw.[187] Padmore's refusal to return either to Moscow or the United States, as well as his refusal to stop working with Kouyaté and start cooperating with the PCF eventually led to his expulsion by the CI in February 1934. After this occurred, partly as a consequence of his continued ties to Kouyaté and support for the Liberia scheme, he still used Kouyaté as an intermediary when he met with André Ferrat, head of the PCF's Colonial Commission the following month.[188] However, Padmore gave no details of his former activities with Kouyaté to the PCF and when the CI subsequently asked Stéphane Rosso what he knew of Padmore, he was only able to reply that Padmore was close to Kouyaté, not the UTN, and that consequently he knew nothing about their activities.[189] Long after his expulsion Kouyaté in a defiant letter to the CGTU declared that the communist movement had sacrificed not only Padmore and himself, but also Chris Jones in England, Cecil Hope in the US, Sandalio Junco from Cuba and others for initiating 'new colonial politics,' and that because of its highhanded methods had lost the support of the masses of colonial activists in France.[190] But unlike the others he named, Kouyaté like Padmore played a significant role in the Comintern's 'Negro work,' developing the influence of the LDRN and the

185. Réunion pour la discussion sur Le Comité International des Nègres, 24 August 1933, RGASPI 534/3/895.

186. J. R. Hooker, *Black Revolutionary: George Padmore's Path from Communism to Pan-Africanism* (London, 1967) pp.39-40. Others involved with this project included the former Cuban Communist Perez-Medina. 'Extracts des deliberations et des decisions initial des reunions,' 4 and 9 December 1933, SLOTFOM 34, ANOM.

187. 'La vie des camarades Nègres à Moscou,' 24 September 1934, 3 SLOTFOM 53, ANOM.

188. Padmore to Dear Comrade, 4 March 1934, RGASPI 495/270/7981/8.

189. Report of Paul, 25 February 1934, 3 SLOTFOM 53, ANOM.

190. Kouyaté to the Secretariat, CGTU, 13 July 1934, RGASPI 517/1/1652/32-33. It seems that Jones resigned shortly after joining the CPGB and was not expelled.

"l'Union Intercoloniale"

Association des Originaires de toutes les Colonies

SIÈGE : 3, Rue du Marché-des-Patriarches, 3
PARIS (V^e)

VENDREDI 17 OCTOBRE 1924, à 20 h. 30
Salle des Sociétés Savantes
8, Rue Danton - PARIS (6e)
Métro : Saint-Michel - Tramways : Montrouge-Gare de l'Est

GRAND
MEETING PUBLIC

sur le

Fascisme dans les Vieilles Colonies
La Politique Coloniale du Bloc des gauches

ORATEURS INSCRITS :

J. LAGROSILLIÈRE
Ancien Député de la Martinique

André BERTHON
Député de Paris

G. SAROTTE
de l'U. I. C., Avocat à la Cour d'Appel

M. BLONCOURT
de l'U. I. C., Avocat à la Cour d'Appel

HADJALI
de l'U. I. C.

N'GUYEN THE TRUYEN
de l'U. I. C.

S. STEFANY
de l'U. I. C., Avocat à la Cour d'Appel

Imp. G. SAUVARD, 61, Rue Pascal, PARIS (13e)

POSTER OF THE UNION INTERCOLONIALE, OCTOBER 1924,
3 SLOTFOM 3, *Archives nationales d'outre-mer, Aix-en-Provence, France*

Première année N° 1. LE NUMÉRO : 50 CENTIMES JANVIER 1927

LA VOIX DES NÈGRES

ORGANE MENSUEL DU COMITÉ DE DÉFENSE DE LA RACE NÈGRE

Rédaction, Administration : 43, rue du Simplon PARIS (18e)

ABONNEMENTS — France et Colonies ... 3 » 6 » — Etranger ... 4 » 7 »

A TOUS NOS FRÈRES !
A TOUS LES NEGRES DU MONDE !
A TOUS LES HUMANITAIRES DU MONDE !
A TOUS CEUX QUI S'INTERESSENT A LA RACE NÈGRE !

Le Comité de Défense de la Race Nègre :

Considérant que parmi les déshérités de la terre d'Afrique :

La Race Nègre qui forme la cinquième partie de la population du Globe, est la plus humiliée de toutes les races humaines ;

Que les centaines de millions d'hommes qui la composent sont un immense monde opprimé;

Que toutes les nations africaines, anéanties au cours des siècles, doivent se relever et refleurir afin de réoccuper leur place dans les conseils de tous les peuples;

Considérant que l'expérience démontre que l'émancipation des nègres sera l'œuvre des nègres eux-mêmes, que la lumière, le progrès et le colonialisme sont incompatibles ;

Que le premier principe de la dignité humaine est qu'elle est faite pour tous les hommes;

A l'honneur de vous informer qu'il a pris l'initiative de publier à Paris LA VOIX DES NÈGRES.

Nous faisons un pressant appel à toutes et à tous. [illegible]

Ce qu'est notre Comité de Défense de la Race Nègre

Certains journaux français et étrangers ont demandé à plusieurs reprises ce qu'était le « Comité de Défense de la Race Nègre ». Pour satisfaire leur curiosité, notre secrétaire général a eu deux fois l'occasion de déposer sur les bureaux de l'agence Havas, à Paris, une *déclaration officielle du Comité* (juillet 1926) et un ordre du jour voté par notre assemblée générale du 31 octobre 1926 à Paris, mais nous constatons avec regret que ces quêteurs de nouvelles ont préféré garder le silence plutôt que de publier ces deux notes.

Cependant, quelques journaux français ont voulu, le 1er novembre dernier (le lendemain de notre assemblée générale), à tout prix, donner des renseignements (à leur façon) à leurs lecteurs sur ce qu'ils croyaient être notre Comité. *L'Echo de Paris* s'est fait plus particulièrement remarquer; ce journal nous gratifie d'un esprit de pur nationalisme français en publiant : « Les nègres sont des Français et veulent servir la France... » (?). Or, rien n'est aussi faux que cette affirmation! Les nègres ne sont d'aucune nationalité européenne et ne veulent servir les intérêts d'aucun impérialisme contre ceux d'un autre impérialisme.

Au sein du Comité de Défense de la Race Nègre, il n'y a pas de distinction entre les races humaines. Pour ne pas salir cette noble œuvre, nous refusons catégoriquement de servir les ambitions d'une nation colonisatrice quelconque, car nous serions toujours les victimes, en fin de compte!

Les jeunesses nègres, réunies au sein du Comité de Défense de la Race Nègre ont la ferme volonté de suivre la voie que leur ont tracée les milliers de nègres conscients et de blancs humanitaires qui n'ont pas hésité devant le sacrifice de leur vie, de leur fortune et, très souvent, de leur liberté, pour la libération totale et l'émancipation de la race nègre. Ils sauront donc être solidaires les uns des autres pour mener la lutte contre le régime spécial auquel leur race est soumise, sans toutefois perdre de vue que tous les blancs ne sont pas des impérialistes ni tous des colonisateurs. Ils feront au contraire voir à l'univers qu'ils savent combien leur sort est lié avec celui des milliers de travailleurs [illegible] et [illegible] des nations européennes.

Les jeunesses patriotes de Nice (Alpes-Maritimes), à leur assemblée générale du 6 novembre dernier ont consacré tout leur temps sur la nécessité d'étendre leur propagande sur les *réservoirs d'hommes*, c'est-à-dire sur les colonies françaises. Ah! Quel retard! Ils ne songent pas que les nègres savent maintenant [illegible]

THE FIRST EDITION OF *LA VOIX DES NÈGRES*, PUBLICATION OF THE COMITÉ DE DÉFENSE DE LA RACE NÈGRE, JANUARY 1927, 3 SLOTFOM 111, *Archives nationales d'outre-mer, Aix-en-Provence*, France

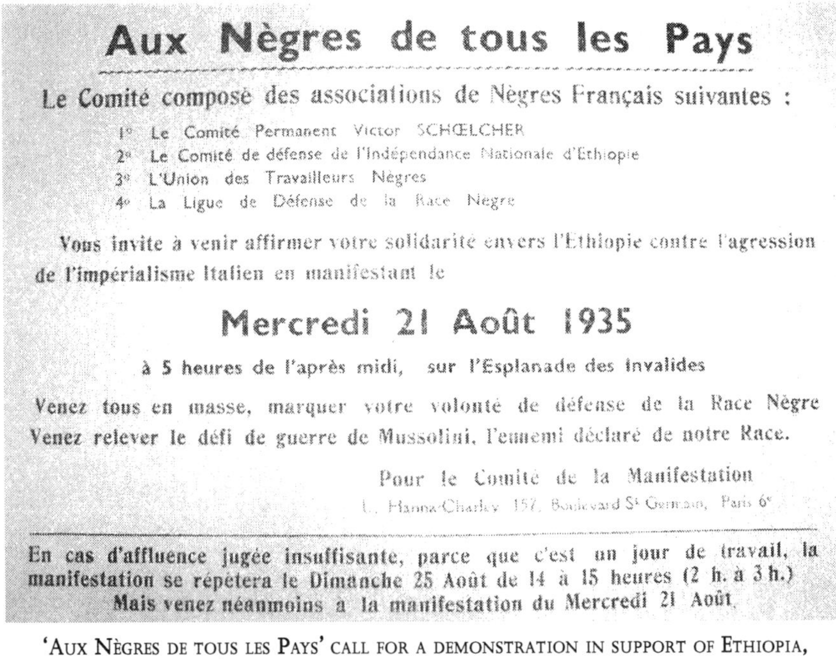

Aux Nègres de tous les Pays

Le Comité composé des associations de Nègres Français suivantes :

1° Le Comité Permanent Victor SCHŒLCHER
2° Le Comité de défense de l'Indépendance Nationale d'Ethiopie
3° L'Union des Travailleurs Nègres
4° La Ligue de Défense de la Race Nègre

Vous invite à venir affirmer votre solidarité envers l'Ethiopie contre l'agression de l'impérialisme Italien en manifestant le

Mercredi 21 Août 1935

à 5 heures de l'après midi, sur l'Esplanade des Invalides

Venez tous en masse, marquer votre volonté de défense de la Race Nègre
Venez relever le défi de guerre de Mussolini, l'ennemi déclaré de notre Race.

Pour le Comité de la Manifestation
L. Hanna-Charley 157, Boulevard St Germain, Paris 6e

En cas d'affluence jugée insuffisante, parce que c'est un jour de travail, la manifestation se répétera le Dimanche 25 Août de 14 à 15 heures (2 h. à 3 h.)
Mais venez néanmoins à la manifestation du Mercredi 21 Août.

'AUX NÈGRES DE TOUS LES PAYS' CALL FOR A DEMONSTRATION IN SUPPORT OF ETHIOPIA, AUGUST 1935, 3 SLOTFOM 43, *Archives nationales d'outre-mer, Aix-en-Provence*, France

Ada Wright during the Scottsboro campaign in Glasgow, 1932.
Courtesy of Irene Brown and Herald Times Group, UK

Demonstration in Cardiff, Wales, 1935. *People's History Museum Manchester, UK*

UTN, sending several students to Moscow and re-establishing important links with seafarers in the French ports and amongst those in West Africa.

Towards a United Front

Despite Kouyaté's claims, the UTN continued its work with the support of the PCF and the re-established ITUCNW led by Otto Huiswoud, although the political influence of the latter seems to have been negligible. It also continued the publication of the *Cri des Nègres,* which was regularly published nearly every month from 1934 to early 1936 and distributed throughout Francophone North and West Africa, the Antilles and even Britain, where Kenyatta appears to have been the main contact. The publication now carried articles in Malagasy and Duala, as well as French, a development that was to continue throughout the remainder of its existence.[191] However, its financial problems continued and it took some time to clear the debts left by Kouyaté and for the PCF to regularise its subsidy.[192] Apart from the distribution of the *Cri,* the UTN slumped into a period of inactivity and was clearly handicapped by continuing police and government repression, and the activity of some its leading members who were agents of the government. Joseph Ébelé, a Camerounian, who was already under suspicion, even joined Kouyaté and Padmore to assist in planning their World Negro Congress before becoming UTN secretary-general in 1935.[193] There were in addition other internal problems, including a continued lack of a permanent base, or even a regular meeting place, and renewed complaints about the way in which the PCF failed to adequately support colonial activists.[194]

Huiswoud's return to France in early 1934 to restart the work of the ITUCNW and to enquire into the previous activities of Padmore, led to renewed efforts by the PCF and the UTN to solve the problems confronting the 'Negro work' in France. It also gave Rosso the opportunity to impress on Huiswoud the importance of the *Cri des Négres*, especially in Africa, and the fact that funding from the ITUCNW was still needed for its publication.[195] However, Huiswoud reported that although he had discussed in detail plans for the future work of the UTN little came of them and the evidence suggests limited contact with the ITUCNW until he relocated to Paris at the start of 1936.[196] The UTN

191. Spiegler, 'Aspects of Nationalist Thought,' p.192.

192. Report of Paul, 22 January, 31 January and 27 February 1934; Réunion de la fraction communiste nègre d l'UTN, 25 February 1934, 3 SLOTFOM 53, ANOM.

193. Report of Moise, 3 February 1934, 3 SLOTFOM 53, ANOM.

194. Report of Paul, 9 January and 25 February 1934, 3 SLOTFOM 53, ANOM.

195. Report of Paul, 3 March 1934, 3 SLOTFOM 53, ANOM.

196. Huiswoud to Dear Friends, 24 June 1935, RGASPI 495/155/102.

did, however, maintain extensive contacts with organisations and individuals in West Africa and the Antilles, and was strongly supported by the associations of students from the Antilles in France. It eventually managed to establish a new headquarters and, at the suggestion of the PCF, again began to organise maritime workers in Marseilles and other ports and in order to increase its membership issued appeals to African and Caribbean workers in Paris.[197] The *Cri des Nègres* continued with its exposure and condemnation of the oppressive nature of colonialism in Africa and the Caribbean and included several installments of a 'Manifesto' to the peoples of Senegal and the Sudan by the mysterious Ligue pour l'indépendence du Sénégal.[198] In its publication and in public meetings the UTN stressed the dangers of fascism, and the possibility that recent events in Germany might also occur in France. It also began an extensive campaign following the brutal assassination of André Aliker, one of the leading Communists in Martinique, in January 1934.[199]

Aliker, who had been the editor of *Justice,* published by the Communist *Groupe Jean Jaurès* in Martinique, often signed his articles 'the eye of Moscow.' In fact the *Groupe* seem to have had little if any contact with Moscow and limited contact with the PCF. However, links had existed between the UTN and the *Groupe*, founded by Jules Monnerot and others in 1919, which had also previously been in contact with the LDRN.[200] Aliker had organised the workers in Martinique and as editor had exposed a major financial and political scandal involving Eugène Aubérry, perhaps the wealthiest man in Martinique, which also implicated and exposed French colonial rule on the island. The campaign in *Justice* had been supported by the UTN but had led initially to attempts to bribe Aliker. When these failed there were several attempts on his life but he had been able to name Aubérry as the likely organiser of these attempts before his assassination. Following his death, the UTN, PCF and SRI established the

197. NPR, 31 October 1934, 3 SLOTFOM 77, ANOM. In May 1934 the French authorities expelled the Trinidadian activist Rupert Gittens from Marseilles. Gittens had been in France for over five months, had communist publications in his possession and was clearly connected with the local branch of the PCF. However his activities in France remain a mystery. NPR, 18 June 1934, 3 SLOTFOM 75, ANOM.

198. For differing view on this organisation see Dewitte, *Les Mouvements Nègres*, pp.310-312 and Sagna, 'Des pionniers méconnus,' pp.705-713. For the Manifesto see *Le Cri de Nègres*, (November-December 1933), Ibid., (January 1934) and Ibid., (April-May).

199. Report of Moise, 24 March 1934, 3 SLOTFOM 53; 'Un Crime Politique à la Martinique,' *Le Cri des Nègres*, (January 1934).

200. For some details on the history of the Groupe Jean Jaurès see R. Menil, 'Notes sur la development historique de Marxisme à la Martinique,' *Action: revue théorique et politique*, vol. 13 (1967) pp. 17-30.

Comité de défense d'André Aliker but despite a lengthy campaign in France, as well as in Martinique, nobody was ever convicted of Aliker's assassination.[201]

During 1934 the *Cri des Nègres* was placed on a firm financial footing thanks to the support of the PCF, however there was still resistance from the UTN to attempts by the PCF to make it a more openly communist publication. In 1935 there was even a threat that the financial support of the PCF would be withdrawn and that Rosso might resign because of the dispute.[202] The print run increased substantially from three thousand to five thousand copies and it managed to maintain an extensive coverage of events in many countries. In the edition of November 1934, for example, there were articles on the problems facing seafarers in Marseilles, the anti-fascist struggle in France and the prospect of a new world war, in addition to articles on Senegal, Madagascar, Haiti, Ivory Coast, French Guyana, Liberia, French Equatorial Africa and Haiti. The UTN evidently maintained close ties with several activists in Haiti, and the *Cri des Nègres* regularly carried articles condemning the continued repression and interference of the US in the country, which were then republished in the Haitian press. [203] The colonial authorities still attempted to prevent the penetration of the paper into the African colonies but according to reports the paper was sold openly in Martinique, much to the concern of local officials.[204] One of the most celebrated news items was the election victory in May 1935 of UTN member Felix Merlin. Merlin, who stood as a Communist, became a municipal councillor, deputy mayor and subsequently mayor in the Paris suburb of Epinay.[205]

The anti-fascist struggle in France, where the threat of fascism was of major concern during this period, was raised to a new level at the beginning of 1934 with joint action by the PCF and the French Socialist Party (SFIO), including a general strike called by the two trade union centres, the CGT and the CGTU. These events and the support for such tactics by the CI a few months later signaled the start of new approach to the 'united front against fascism,' and subsequently to the creation of the Popular Front, the political union of the PCF, SFIO and Radical Party.[206] In keeping with the growing sentiment for united action the UTN also began to work more closely with other individuals and organisations. Many of these were linked to the PCF, such as the

201. RGASPI 517/1/1652/14 and A. Nicolas, *Histoire de la Martinique de 1849 à 1939* [Vol. 2] (Paris, 1996) pp.218-230.

202. NPR, 28 February and 18 April 1935, 3 SLOTFOM 72, ANOM.

203. *Le Cri des Nègres*, (November 1934).

204. Fort-de-France Police Report, 8 October 1935, 3 SLOTFOM 136, ANOM.

205. *Le Cri des Nègres*, (June 1935). Merlin was subsequently invited by the CPUSA to assist with its election campaign in Harlem. See also *NW*, 5/7-8 (July-August 1935) p.29 and Turner, *Caribbean Crusaders*, p.223.

206. E. Mortimer, *The Rise of the French Communist Party, 1920-1947* (London, 1984) pp.226-240.

World Committee Against Fascism and War, the LAI, with which the UTN now shared premises, the *Comité de la liberation des Nègres de Scottsboro* and the campaign led by the SRI protesting against the arrest of activists in Haiti.[207] UTN members were, for example, part of the delegations that were sent to the SFIO, and to such personalities as René Maran and Gaston Monnerville in an attempt to build a united front for the Scottsboro campaign.[208] These activities culminated in early 1935 with the joint actions that were organised following the Italian invasion of Ethiopia.

ETHIOPIA

Fascist Italy's aggression against Ethiopia at the end of 1934 and then its invasion of that country in 1935 led to an unprecedented united front involving all the Paris-based African and Caribbean organisations, even those that hitherto had been in conflict. It also led to wider unity between these organisations and others that voiced their opposition to fascist aggression, colonialism and imperialist war. It was during this period for example that the UTN began to work closely with Paulette Nardal, a key literary figure from Martinique and one of the few women active in the organisation.[209] Although some have downplayed the role of the UTN in this period, by responding to the call of the ITUCNW and condemning fascist Italy's aggression in the January 1935 edition of the *Cri des Negres*, it was probably one of the first organisations to protest. It then rallied others, including the LDRN, and the following month participated in a protest meeting organised by the World Committee against Fascism and War, which under the leadership of the LAI subsequently created the International Committee for the Defence of the Ethiopian People. (ICDEP).[210] Thereafter many protest events were organised by the UTN in conjunction with others and Ethiopia's defense became very much a *cause célèbre*.[211] It certainly provided the UTN with the opportunity to expound on the nature of fascism, the dangers it posed in France and in the colonies, and the need to support the Popular Front. It was also the initiative of the UTN that played a key role in strengthening the growing Pan-African unity and a united front of all the African and Caribbean

207. On the arrest of Jacques Roumain and other Haitian activists see *Le Cri des Nègres*, (March-April 1935).

208. NPR, 31 August and 30 September 1934, 3 SLOTFOM 77, ANOM.

209. See Boittin, *Colonial Metropolis*, pp.133-171.

210. Spiegler, 'Aspects of Nationalist Thought,' pp.238-239; Réunion de bureau de l'UTN, 16 February 1935 and 'Travailleurs Nègre de Paris au secours de l'Abyssinie,' 3 SLOTFOM 70, ANOM; RGASPI 495/64/153.

211. See e.g. NPR, 30 June 1935, 3 SLOTFOM 72, ANOM.

organisations. In July 1935 the UTN called for such a united front and in early August invited the LDRN to participate in *'action commune'* along with all the *'organisations Nègres'* of Paris. Shortly afterwards the UTN, LDRN, the *Comité Permanent Victor Schoelcher* and the *Comité de Défense de l'Indépendence Nationale d'Ethiopie* organised two demonstrations that called on the *'Nègres'* of all countries to show their solidarity with Ethiopia.[212]

In January 1936 the ICDEP, led by the well-known French Communist Léo Wanner, called for an 'international conference of Blacks and Arabs.'[213] The organisers of the conference took account of the solidarity movement in support of Ethiopia that was developing in Africa, the Diaspora and elsewhere. The aim of the conference was not only to further develop support for Ethiopia, but also to highlight the wider issue of colonial rule and strengthen the French and international movements for colonial independence.[214] The UTN, and especially Rosso and Ramananjato, played a prominent role in the preparations for the conference, where they again united with the LDRN and many other organisations. Originally scheduled to take place in Marseilles the conference finally took place in Paris in April 1936 and established contact between African, Caribbean and Arab organisations throughout the world.[215] It was another manifestation of the widespread sentiment for the unity of all organisations opposed to fascism, war and imperialist aggression so prevalent at the time.

The Popular Front

The UTN also participated in the *Association pour la défence et l'émanicipation des peuples colonisés* founded under the political direction of the PCF in March 1936, that initially included the *Etoile Nord Africaine* and the Neo Destour parties. Following the election of the Popular Front government in May 1936, which the PCF supported but did not join, the Association remained opposed to French imperialism and its members, including the UTN, demanded from the new government a variety of reforms, including an end to forced labour, freedom of the press and assembly, and equal rights for all throughout France and it colonies, designed to hasten the independence of the

212. NPR, August-September 1935, 3 SLOTFOM 72; Commission pour la défense du peuple Ethiopien, 3 SLOTFOM 43, ANOM and 'Pour la défense de l'Abyssinie,' *Le Cri des Nègres*, (September 1935).

213. 'A nos frères Noires et Arabes pour la défense du peuple Ethiopien,' January 1936, 3 SLOTFOM 43, ANOM.

214. Note sur la conference des Noires et des Arabes, n.d., 3 SLOTFOM 43, ANOM.

215. Bulletin du Comité du Coordination des associations Noires et Arabe de Paris, (No.1) 3 SLOTFOM 43, ANOM.

colonies, which remained their main aim.[216] The united front of African, Caribbean and Asian organisations was further developed early the following year when the UTN participated with others to found the *Rassemblement Coloniale* (RC), of which Ramananjato was vice-president, Emile Faure secretary-general and Messali Hadj president. The RC was established as a coalition to provide mutual aid and support for all organisations of French colonial subjects, whether in France or the colonies and was initiated by Nguyen The Truyen of the *Rassamblement des Indochochinois en France.* It grew out of common concerns, the actions and inaction of the Popular Front government in relation to colonial matters, and was often strongly critical of that government.[217] The RC also continued to support Ethiopia and was still discussing what further measures it could take on that issue as war loomed in 1939.[218] The UTN apparently resigned from the RC in December 1937 but it seems to have rejoined the following year following the opening of its new headquarters. It therefore appears that there was no essential change in the anti-colonial politics of the UTN during this period, not withstanding the fact that a Popular Front government had temporarily taken office, and even though its political stands were sometimes greatly at variance with those of the PCF. The campaign opposing fascist aggression against Ethiopia provided the opportunity not only to condemn Italian fascism but also to discuss and condemn the oppressive colonial policies of France and Britain, as well as the preparations that were being made for a new world war.

The transfer of the ITUCNW's headquarters to Paris in 1936 significantly strengthened its relationship with the UTN. Huiswoud continued to work with the UTN until he left Paris in 1938, even though its relationship with the PCF appears to have continued to be an uneasy one. In April 1936, for example, Rosso, Alpha and Julians, three of the leading Communists in the UTN wrote a letter of complaint to the CI, claiming that the PCF was attempting to create organisational separation between the UTN's African and Caribbean members.[219] The PCF claimed that the complaint was without any foundation but it is noteworthy that it was made not through Huiswoud but rather through James Ford, who the previous year had traveled to Paris to speak to the UTN about the decisions of the CI's Seventh Congress.[220]

---

216. Report of Meeting, 26 June 1936, 3 SLOTFOM 43, ANOM.

217. See e.g. the report of Faure's speech in England by L. Seleau, 'The French colonies under the Popular Front,' *International African Opinion*, 1/2 (August 1938) p.5. Also J. E. Genova, 'The Empire Within: The Colonial Popular Front in France, 1934-1938,' *Alternatives*, 26/2 (2001) pp.175-209.

218. Congrès Intercoloniale, 9 April 1937 and Note, February 1939, 13 SLOTFOM 1, ANOM

219. RGASPI 495/14/36/2-4 and Sagna, 'Des pionniers méconnus,' p.714.

220. 'Note,' n.d., 3 SLOTFOM 72, ANOM; RGASPI 495/14/87/62-63.

Huiswoud's arrival in Paris also coincided with the suspension of the publication of the *Cri des Negrès*, which after lengthy discussion only re-appeared in a less elaborate form in 1938.[221] The ITUCNW and *The Negro Worker* were both terminated in 1937 but the latter's short-lived successor, *World Wide News – a bulletin on world events and information concerning the Negro people,* was also briefly published in Paris. Thereafter the Huiswoods remained in the city and together with Jacques Roumain, the exiled Haitian Communist leader, continued to support and participate in the work of the UTN, even during its collaboration with the RC and disagreements with the PCF.[222]

It is interesting to note that it was in this period, when the dissolution of the ITUCNW was being discussed and with war on the horizon that some important advances were being made in the French colonies, partly encouraged by the conditions created by the impact of the Popular Front government. In July 1936 it was reported that a communist organisation, closely linked with the PCF had been formed in Dakar, Senegal, with both African and European members. Some of the Africans were former students in Moscow, where activists from French West Africa and the Antilles continued to receive training.[223] While in Martinique, indirectly influenced by the CI, the PCF and the UTN, a merger took place in 1935 between the *Groupe Jean Jaurès* and *Front Commun*, a group of students and young workers recently returned from France. The new organisation, which styled itself the *Région Communiste de la Martinique*, was not initially recognised by the PCF. Four years later as the *Fédération Communiste de la Martinique* it was affiliated to the CP, by 1945 was the strongest political party on the island and included amongst its leading members Aimé Césaire, the new mayor of the capital and one of four deputies elected to the French National Assembly.[224] Despite the many difficulties and setbacks that occurred in connection with their relationship with the CDRN, LDRN and UTN, the Comintern and the ITUCNW had created some of the conditions for the birth of communist movements in the French colonies in West Africa and the Caribbean.

221. Sagna, 'Des pionniers méconnus,' p.715.

222. See e.g. Meeting commun du RC et de l'UTN, 15 March 1938, 2 SLOTFOM 2, ANOM.

223. Sagna, 'Des pionniers méconnus,' pp.715-721 and RGASPI 495/155/102/75. The period of the Popular Front government apparently also created the conditions for several French Communists to seek employment in West Africa. See R. S. Morgenthau, *Political Parties in French West Africa* (Oxford, 1964) pp.22-27.

224. Nicolas, *Histoire de la Martinique* p.241. Similar developments took place in Guadeloupe where a Parti Communiste Région Guadeloupe was launched in 1944.

Chapter 7

The Negro Welfare Association and the Negro Question in Britain

The ITUCNW and the Founding of the Negro Welfare Association

Although there is some evidence to suggest that the Communist Party of Great Britain (CPGB) recruited its first African member, Mohamed Tuallah Mohamed, a Cardiff-based Somali, in the early 1920s, in general it paid little attention to Britain's African and Caribbean population before the last years of that decade.[1] It fared little better in the African and Caribbean colonies and only had strong connections with South Africa, as a consequence of its relationship with the CPSA. With the exception of tenuous links with the trade unionists Edward Small in the Gambia and Vivian Henry in Trinidad, it appears to have had very few other African or Caibbean connections before the late 1920s, even though representatives of the CPGB played a leading role in the CI's Colonial and Anglo-American Commissions, which had direct responsibility for the Negro Question. On many occasions, the CI, its Negro Bureau, and the Profintern found it necessary to reprimand the CPGB for not taking up this important work with sufficient vigour. As late as 1930 the CPGB's 'Negro work' was described as a 'record of the most inexcusable passivity and neglect.' [2]

The Sixth Congress of the CI in 1928 declared that it was 'the special duty of the Communist Parties in the metropolitan countries to put an end to the indifference which they have exhibited', in regard to the growing mass movements in the colonies and 'instead to afford energetic support both in the imperialist centres and the colonies themselves to these movements.'[3] The ITUCNW was established that same year precisely in order to encourage such activities in regard to the African and Caribbean colonies and it is evident that both before and after the Hamburg Conference in 1930 its leading activists, and the Negro Section of the ECCI, did all they could to bring about a turn in this work. In August 1930, when the CPGB was again criticised for the lack of progress it had made 'in the sphere of Negro work' and anti-colonial activity in general, the Party was instructed to take several measures to address 'white chauvinism' which manifested itself in 'the long continued "under-estimation" of Negro work.' It was specifically instructed to organise a 'National Liberation Organisation along the lines of "League for the Defence of the Negro Race" (France).' This organisation, it was instructed 'must have as its task the struggle against increasing discrimination against Negroes in England, activising (sic) and drawing those Negro elements who find no place in industry, and as a con-

1. M. Sherwood, 'Racism and Resistance: Cardiff in the 1930s and 1940s,' *Llafur*, 5/4 (1991) p.65, see also M. Squires, Communists and the Fight Against Racism During the Class against Class Period 1928-33,' *Communist Review*, (Summer 2000), pp.12-19 and M. Sherwood, 'The Comintern, the CPGB, Colonies and Black Britons, 1920-1938,' *Science and Society*, 60/2 (Summer 1996) pp.137-163.

2. See e.g. 'Draft letter to the CPGB, 16 August 1930, RGASPI 495/4/47/20-21.

3. *The Revolutionary Movement in the Colonies* (London, 1929) p.58.

sequence are not attracted by the Trade Union Movement and the activity of our Party, directly into the liberation struggles of the Negroes internationally.'[4]

The CI and the ITUCNW were particularly eager to organise amongst Britain's well-established African and Caribbean population, which by the early twentieth century numbered several thousands.[5] There had already been some attempts at self-organisation by seafarers and other workers in the major ports, such as the National African Sailors and Fireman's Union, founded in Liverpool in 1920.[6] For the CI it was crucial that seamen, especially those from the colonies, were effectively organised because they were such a vital link and conduit for information between the Comintern and Britain's colonial subjects in Africa and the Caribbean. Political activity amongst seamen was also important for the CI because they were the target of attacks launched by the British government, shipping companies and the reactionary National Union of Seamen (NUS).[7] It was largely African and Caribbean seamen and their families who had been subjected to racist attacks during the riots that had occurred in many British cities in 1919.[8] Following the riots some seamen were deported, while those remaining were subjected to discrimination under the Aliens Acts of 1919 and 1920, the openly racist Special Restriction (Coloured Alien Seamen) Order of 1925 and, later in 1935, by the British Shipping (Assistance) Act.[9] Such legislation made in more difficult for African and Caribbean seamen to find employment, attempted to force down their wages and deny them the unemployment benefits paid to white seamen and aimed to create divisions amongst all seamen. The poverty faced by the seamen, and their families, was accompanied by a campaign of racist slurs in the press and elsewhere by politicians, leading trade unionists and police chiefs. [10]

There were also significant organisations of students and intellectuals in London and elsewhere, such as the West African Students' Union (WASU), through whom contact could be established with activists and anti-colonial

---

4. See e.g. 'Draft letter to the CPGB,' 16 August 1930,' RGASPI 495/4/47/20-23, also 'Negro Work,' 2 August 1930, RGASPI 495/18/810; 'Report on Negro Work in France and England,' 4 August 1930, ibid.; 'Resolution on the First International Negro Conference,' 19 August 1930 Ibid.

5. P. Fryer, *Staying Power – The History of Black People in Britain* (London, 1984) p.296.

6. L. Tabili, *"We Ask For British Justice" Workers and Racial Difference in Late Imperial Britain* (London, 1994) p.157.

7. See e.g. the LAI's *Colonial News*, 1/2 (April 1934) pp. 4-5.

8. J. Jenkinson, *Black 1919 – Riots, Racism and Resistance in Imperial Britain* (Liverpool, 2008).

9. 'British Colonial Seamen Face Destitution and Deportation,' *NW*, 5/6 (June 1935) p.31.

10. See P. Rich, *Race and Empire in British Politics*, (Cambridge, 1990) pp.120-144 and Tabili, *We Ask For British Justice* .

organisations in Britain's colonies.[11] Some efforts in this direction were made after the founding of the LAI in 1927 but it seems that major attempts to make a breakthrough can be linked with the ITUCNW and its plans for a conference of Negro workers, originally scheduled to take place in London in July 1930.[12] These plans were thwarted by Ramsey MacDonald's Labour government but the work to convene this conference led to a flurry of activity and the arrival in Britain of some of the leading members of the ITUCNW including George Padmore and William Patterson.[13]

The Negro Bureau of the CI and the ITUCNW had stepped up work in Britain in connection with the Negro Question in the latter part of 1928. Early the following year, in a report to the Bureau, James Ford recommended that a 'special letter' be sent to the CPGB in regard to: 'a) work amongst coloured seamen; b) work in Africa and the colonies; c) work amongst Negro groups in England especially London.'[14] But despite this and other correspondence, little progress was made and Patterson bemoaned the lack of preparatory work for the conference by the CPGB and its trade union organisation, the National Minority Movement (NMM), when he arrived in London in April 1930. 'Nothing being done, less contemplated,' was how he summed up the situation but his concern can perhaps also be understood by noting that he had already written to the CPGB's *Daily Worker* to complain about its use of the word 'nigger,' and to suggest that the term Negro should be capitalised.[15]

Patterson's arrival in Britain allowed him to participate in some activities to remedy the situation and may have led to the emergence of a new communist-led organisation. Subsequently, in conjunction with the CPGB, the NMM and the LAI, he claimed to have established a 'Negro Liberation Society.'[16] Nothing more is known about this organisation but it seems to have been one of a number of attempts to overcome the weakness of the CPGB's 'Negro work.'[17] In the same year in London, under the auspices of the Seamen's Minority Move-

11. See H. Adi, *West Africans in Britain: Nationalism, Pan-Africanism and Communism* (London, 1998).

12. 'On the Convening of the First International Conference of Negro Workers,' RGASPI 495/155/53; also Secret Report on Communist Party Activities in Great Britain Among Colonials, 22 April 1930, Hodgkin Papers.

13. (TNA) CO 323/1096/10.

14. Report of Comrade Ford to the Negro Bureau, 14 February 1929, RGASPI 534/3/450, and Draft Letter to CPGB, 18 August 1930, RGASPI 495/425/28-31.

15. WW (W.Patterson) to the Negro Bureau, Profintern, 14 April 1930, RGASPI 534/4/330 and Paterson to the Editor, 5 March 1930, RGASPI 495/155/90/59-61.

16. W. Patterson to Negro Bureau, Profinern, 24 May 1930 and 30 May 1930, RGASPI 534/4/330.

17. Squires, 'Communists and the fight against racism,' p.15.

ment (SMM), formed by the NMM in 1929, a 'committee of militant coloured seamen' had been established led by Jim Headley from Trinidad and the Barbadian Chris Jones (Braithwaite), a former organiser for the NUS.[18] The activists of the SMM's 'coloured' committee agreed to organise on board ships in the London docks and to take with them what was referred to as 'Negro literature,' presumably the publications of the ITUCNW.[19]

As early as 1923 the CPGB had been instructed by the Comintern to organise amongst seamen in Liverpool and London, with the aim of also developing work in African ports, but it does not appears to have done so with great success.[20] In early 1930 the NMM admitted that it had 'few contacts with Negroes,' and was generally ill- prepared to assist in organising the ITUCNW conference in London.[21] At the RILU's Fifth Congress, in August 1930, the NMM was criticised for its 'weakness and isolation,' directed to strengthen its colonial work, and to assist the ITUCNW and workers in the colonies. It was also instructed that 'the toiling Negroes, Arabs and Hindus employed in Britain must be organised,' and 'any semblance of white chauvinism – the tool of British imperialism – must be put down.'[22] It was only in response to such demands and as a consequence of the ITUCNW's conference, that the SMM's work began in earnest in the latter part of 1930.

Patterson's work in Liverpool seems to have been continued after his departure both by local party member F.C. Moore and by Douglas and Molly Wolton, two of the leaders of the CPSA, who arrived in Britain in the summer of 1930 en route to Moscow. The hundreds of black workers living in Liverpool in this period faced many problems. Most of the male population were seamen facing discrimination relating to their employment from the Shipping Federation as well as the NUS. In addition, the wives and families of the seamen and other workers were also subjected to a campaign of racism and harassment, most notably after the publication that year of the semi-official *Report on an Investigation into the Colour Problem in Liverpool and other Ports.* Amongst other things, this report explained the social and economic conditions of what were

18. Sherwood, 'The CPGB and Black Britons,' p.153; also Tabili, *We Ask for British Justice,* pp.81-82 and Secret Report on Communist Party Activities.

19. SMM Report of Second Meeting of Committee of Militant Coloured Seamen, 30 November 1930, RGASPI 534/7/48/170.

20. Secretary, Negro Conference to CPGB, 24 October 1923, RGASPI 495/14/19.

21. Sherwood, 'The CPGB and Black Britons,' p.143; J. Mahon to the ITUCNW, 4 February 1930, RGASPI 534/7/48.

22. Resolution of the 5th RILU Congress – The NMM of Great Britain: Positions and Tasks, RGASPI 495/100/710.

referred to as 'half-caste' children in terms of eugenics and viewed the relationships that produced them as evidence of a serious moral problem.[23]

It was evidently in response to such issues that a series of meetings were held in Liverpool in the spring and early summer of 1930 with the participation of seamen, students and factory workers from Nigeria, Sierra Leone, Gambia, Cameroon, Liberia, Jamaica, Haiti, Cuba, Barbados, British Guiana and the United States. Over eighty attended the first meeting and although one report claimed that the Wolton's 'South African experience' was an important catalyst, the role of Patterson and the ITUCNW should not be ruled out, not least because the first meeting was reportedly held in April before the Woltons arrived in England. Whatever the precise details, it seems likely that the original initiative may not have come from within the CPGB. The meetings led to the founding of a 'Negro Society' in Liverpool, affiliated to the LAI, which initially aimed to send a delegation to the ITUCNW conference due to be held in London.[24] Subsequently, Moore, writing from Moscow and having discussed matters with Douglas Wolton, recommended that 'one or preferably two Negro comrades should be chosen from those we have got into contact with and sent over here for at least a year in order to attend the Lenin School or the Eastern University.' The aim was to provide training 'so that they will be able to carry on work among Negro seamen, establish and maintain contacts with Africa, or wherever they go, and to do some organising work among Negroes.' For this reason Moore, who was evidently also in touch with Patterson, suggested that if possible those selected should either be seamen, or former seamen.[25] However, none of those recommended were ever sent to Moscow and it is unclear what happened to those who had taken the initial step to organise in Liverpool.

A few months after the Liverpool meeting, Frank Macaulay came to Britain after attending both the Hamburg conference of the ITUCNW and the Fifth Congress of the RILU in Moscow. Macaulay arrived in October 1930 and remained long enough to participate in the national conference of the British section of the LAI in London the following February. He spent much of his time in Liverpool, where he stayed with his brother, spoke at several meetings and even wrote an article for the *Daily Worker* about the problems facing black workers and their families in the city.[26] He also made contact and held meetings with black workers in other towns and cities including London, Cardiff and Barry, and was evidently extremely active throughout his stay.

23. Rich, *Race and Empire*, p.132.

24. D. Wolton, 'Negroes in England,' *Umsebenzi*, 11 July 1930; Report of Work Amongst Negroes in England, 27 August 1930, RGASPI 495/155/83/53-55.

25. F.C. Moore to Dear Comrade, 26 August 1930, RGASPI 495/155/90/73.

26. *See Daily Worker (DW)*, 25 October 1930 and 17 February 1931, p.3.

One of these meetings, held late in the evening with 'negro seamen' in the 'Negro quarter of the docks area' in Cardiff, gives some indication of Macaulay's concerns and impact. According to an NMM report, Macaulay had 'a very remarkable approach to the workers and he was listened to very attentively.' Most of the meeting was conducted in what the report refers to as 'native languages' and even after it had concluded Macaulay spent the rest of the night with the seamen. What was said in English seems to have worried the local representatives of the NMM who reported that 'the line pursued was that of establishing a kind of Negro Workers' organisation.' Although it was difficult for them to say what kind of organisation this might be, they evidently had misgivings and, despite the fact that the seamen were apparently enthusiastic, the local NMM accused Macaulay of pursing a 'very narrow and separatist' approach.[27]

It seems unlikely that Macaulay was acting directly on behalf of the ITUCNW, since the latter had very little knowledge of his activities. He subsequently informed James Ford that he had organised a 'Welfare Association' in Liverpool, and it seems more likely that he was working in conjunction with the LAI.[28] Certainly the Liverpool branch of the LAI, led by the CPGB, was particularly active at this time and in early 1931 initiated an enquiry into the condition of the '300 Negroes,' who it claimed were living in the city and working as seafarers. Apparently much was learned, not only about the oppressive working conditions on the shipping lines but also about the lives of those living under colonial rule in West Africa, and the branch even announced that it could provide a speaker on the 'Negro question' for other organisations. At its first national conference, in London in February 1931, the LAI reported that during the previous December 'a Negro comrade conducted a campaign on behalf of the League among Negroes and other workers in Liverpool and Cardiff, where there was some support from Miners' Lodges and individuals.'[29] The following year the LAI claimed that a branch of the 'Negro Welfare Association' in Liverpool had originally functioned with 'upwards of 30 members,' while Padmore later claimed that this Liverpool branch was definitely established by Macaulay but 'died with his departure.' The evidence certainly points to Macaulay and the LAI being involved in the creation of a 'Negro welfare' organisation in Liver-

27. 'Re. 'Seamen' 31 January 1931, TNA M9/2084.

28. See e.g. G. Padmore to Ford, 17 March 1931, RGASPI 534/3/668. See also Report to European Secretariat of RILU on Activities of the ITUCNW at Hamburg, 21 February 1931, RGASPI 534/3/669. Ford wrote to the Minority Movement in Britain asking for more details.

29. Report of the National Conference of the LAI (British Section), February 1931, p.15, Reginald Bridgeman Papers, University of Hull, DBN/1A.

pool, although it is not clear how this was connected with the previous work of Moore, the Woltons and Patterson.[30]

It is also unclear if the creation of an organisation in Liverpool led directly to the creation of the Negro Welfare Association (NWA) in London in 1931. Described by the *Daily Worker* as 'a militant organisation of Negro workers,'[31] the NWA was an affiliate of the British Section of the LAI and was probably formed during or just after its first conference, held in February 1931. Its first secretary, Arnold Ward, was soon being referred to as 'Comrade Ward of the Negro Welfare Association,' and it was he who proposed the 'Resolution on the Negro Question,' at this conference.[32] Ward, who was born in Bridgetown, Barbados in 1886, was reported to have lived in Trinidad between 1903-1906. From 1907 to 1915 he resided in Germany, where he presumably found employment as a seaman, and where he was interned during World War 1, before being sent to Britain as 'medically unfit'. When he first became connected with the LAI is unclear and a police report even maintained that he did not become a member of the CPGB until 1932. [33] He certainly did not attend the ITUCNW's Hamburg conference and it not yet possible to judge the accuracy of his letter, written in 1935, in which he claimed he had been active in politics in Britain 'for the last 20 years.' [34] He was, however, a regular and effective speaker not only at NWA meetings and rallies but also at those organised by the LAI and the CPGB[35] and at the LAI's second conference in 1932 he was elected to its executive committee. As 'one of the principal Negro agitators' in Britain during this period, he corresponded with activists of African origin throughout the world, and it is worth recalling that Paul Robeson credited Ward with at least some of the responsibility for encouraging his first visit to the Soviet Union.[36]

The LAI had been concerned with the Negro question since its creation in 1927. The British Section, under the leadership of Reginald Bridgeman but led politically by the CPGB, tended in many circumstances to act as the anti-colonial organisation of the communist movement in Britain. Since the NWA

30. *DW*, 20 February 1931, p.3 and Ibid., 18 March 1931, p.3. See also Squires: *Communists and the Fight against Racism*. LAI (Berlin) to Padmore, 15 June 1932, and Padmore to Dear Comrades, 16 June 1932, RGASPI 534/3/755.

31. *DW*, 22 August 1932, p.1.

32. See *DW*, 17 February 1931, p.3. Ward himself wrote to Padmore in March 1932 that the NWA had been started 'about a year ago.' Ward to Padmore, 1 March 1932, RGASPI 534/3/754.

33. See (TNA) CO 295/606/4.

34. See Ward's letter to Wallace-Johnson reproduced in *Vox Populi*, (5 October 1935) p.8.

35. See *DW*, 14 February 1931 p.2 ; (TNA) MEPO 2/3057; and J. Bellamy and J. Saville (eds.) *Dictionary of Labour Biography Vol. Vll* (London, 1984), p.44.

36. M.B. Duberman, *Paul Robeson*, (London, 1989) pp.627-8 n.59.

worked in tandem with the LAI, and since Bridgeman led the work of the LAI and was chairman of the NWA, it is sometimes difficult to see where the activities of one organisation ended and the other began.[37] Whatever its role in the NWA's creation, the ITUCNW had no connection with the new Association before the summer of 1931.[38] Indeed, in February 1931 Padmore confided to Ford that the ITUCNW knew little about the NWA 'except that we understand that it was organised by the C.P. and the M.M,' and instructed him to write to London to obtain some information about it. [39]

The NWA was certainly not a completely 'Negro' organisation, and was more accurately described by Ward, as 'a fighting organisation of class conscious, anti-imperialist Negro and white workers in London,' led by the CPGB and its sympathisers, such as Bridgeman, as well as Hugo Rathbone and Ben Bradley, who both served as members of the Colonial Committee of the CPGB. [40] The executive committee of the NWA soon also included Chris Jones, Trinidadians A.C Rienzi (formerly Krishna Deonarine) and Jim Headley, and Rowland Sawyer from Sierra Leone, but the fact that its chairman and some of its leaders were not of African or Caribbean origin certainly created problems throughout its history.[41] The aims of the NWA, however, made clear its orientation and included: '(working) for the complete liberation and independence of all Negroes who are suffering from capitalist exploitation and imperialist domination,' and endeavouring 'to analyse, expose and combat capitalist exploitation and oppression in Africa, the West Indies, the other Negro colonies as well as in the USA.'[42]

Ward and the NWA established contact with the ITUCNW in mid-1931 but a close working relationship was not consolidated until November, soon after Padmore had arrived in Hamburg.[43] From that time onwards there was a close relationship between the two, maintained largely through regular correspondence. Padmore considered the NWA a 'section' of the ITUCNW, made several suggestions regarding its work and general orientation and received regular reports of the Association's meetings and other activities. He was also responsible for re-drafting much of its programme and for linking the NWA

37. From 1933 Bridgeman also led the International Secretariat of the LAI.

38. The NWA was in contact with Padmore by the summer of 1931. See NWA to Padmore, 15 June 1931, RGASPI 534/7/50.

39. See e.g. Padmore to Ward, 17 December 1931, RGASPI 534/3/668 and Padmore to Ford, 25 February 1931, RGASPI 534/3/668.

40. *The Negro Worker (NW)* 2/9-10 (September-October 1932) p.22.

41. See Ward to Padmore 15 June 1932, RGASPI 534/7/50.

42. Report of the International Secretariat of LAI, 1935.

43. For early correspondence see Ward to Padmore, 15 June 1931, and Ward to Ford, 2 September 1931, RGASPI 534/7/50.

with Headley and others who were associated with the SMM. Padmore also maintained individual contact with other leading members of the NWA in Britain including Harry O'Connell in Cardiff and Jomo Kenyatta and did his best to encourage them to persist in their work. He also made strenuous efforts to arrange for Kenyatta, Headley and the Liverpool-based Sierra Leonean seamen Foster-Jones, to go to Moscow to study.[44]

Colonial Seamen

The Comintern focused great attention on organising amongst seamen and several, O'Connell, Jones and Headley for example, became leading activists in Britain. Another, the Sierra Leonean Rowland Sawyer, began his political career as a courier of ITUCNW and LAI literature from London to Jamaica and then became a member and later secretary of the NWA.[45] Foster-Jones was also utilised by CI and the ITUCNW as a courier, transporting letters and propaganda material from Europe to West Africa. The importance of seamen can also be judged from the extensive surveillance carried out by the British security services on African and Caribbean seafarers, who were thought to be in contact with the CI, as well as on the activities of the ITUCNW and other communist-led organisations in the ports.[46] Those seafarers discovered smuggling communist literature into West Africa were routinely fined and those suspected of 'subversive' activity were likely to be dismissed by the shipping companies.

In October 1930 the RILU established the ISH which announced that it based all its work 'on the extermination of racial hatred and the abolition of the rupture existing between the working conditions of white and coloured seamen.' It instructed the SMM, its affiliate in Britain, to recruit Negro seamen as equal members and also attempted to provide some guidance for its work. The SMM's 'committee of militant coloured seamen,' had been established in London, but SMM activists evidently operated in Liverpool and Cardiff, the other main ports with the largest established African and Caribbean communities and possibly even in Glasgow.[47] Headley had the main responsibility for London, where he was also involved with the work of the International Sea-

44. Padmore to Dear Comrades, 12, 15 and 16 June 1932, RGASPI 534/3/755. On Foster-Jones see chapter nine.

45. 'Communism and the West Indian Labour Disturbances,' (TNA) CO 295/606/4.

46. Headley to Padmore, 15 June 1932, RGASPI 534/3/755; Vernon Kell (MI5) to G. Clauson (Colonial Office), 2 November 1931, (TNA) MT9/2084 and CO 323/1164/14.

47. Sherwood, 'The CPGB and Black Britons,' pp.153-154; 'Resolution on the British Seaman's movement and the tasks confronting the SMM, June 1931,' (TNA) CO 323/1164/14.

men's Club, while Harry O'Connell in Cardiff and William Brown in Liverpool were also key SMM organisers.

Reports from the ITUCNW suggest that although work amongst seafarers had commenced there were noticeable weaknesses. From Hamburg Ford complained about lack of cooperation from the SMM, its limited connections with colonial countries and its failure to even make contact with African seamen whose names had been forwarded, or who arrived in British ports.[48] The RILU's Negro Bureau also kept a close watch on the activities of the SMM's committee in London, since initially there were some reservations that it might become a 'separate coloured organisation,' but there is little evidence of coordinated activity between Headley, O'Connell and Brown. The main problem remained the general weakness of the SMM, which continued to provide poor leadership. On several occasions the ITUCNW intervened to attempt to strengthen the 'Negro work' of the SMM, sometimes in response to calls for assistance from Britain, and Padmore made sure that leading activists such as Headley were also incorporated within the NWA.[49] The RILU continued to call for greater efforts to be made to organise colonial workers in Britain's ports and therefore Padmore paid special attention to this issue when he visited Britain in the spring of 1932, travelling to Cardiff and Liverpool to confer with O'Connell and Brown. However, even after Padmore's visit and some attempts at the reorganisation of the SMM, Brown continued to send pessimistic reports from Liverpool. He admitted having 'a lot of trouble' organising the 'coloured seamen,' largely because of their previous experiences of racism, but also because some were critical of the ITUCNW's condemnation of Marcus Garvey.[50] Frustrated by the lack of progress and cooperation, it seems that Padmore made efforts to organise independently of the SMM in both Liverpool and London and threatened to do the same in Cardiff.[51]

The ITUCNW and the ISH regularly issued appeals to 'Negro Seamen and Dockers,' to join the ISH, to visit the international seamen's clubs, which provided revolutionary literature and a place for discussion, to oppose any war preparations, especially against the Soviet Union, and in 1931 called for participation in the congress of the ISH to be held in Hamburg the following year.[52] Both Ford and Padmore were involved with the work of the colonial section

48. J. Ford, 'Report of the Work of ITUCNW (Hamburg) Covering the period from December 1930 to September 15, 1931, 2 October 1931,' RGASPI 534/3/669.

49. Padmore to Thomson, 5 January 1932, RGASPI 534/3/754; Huiswoud to Padmore, 11 January 1932, RGASPI 534/3/753; Headley to Padmore, 15 June 1932, RGASPI 534/3/755.

50. W. Brown to Padmore, 3 July and 28 August 1932, RGASPI 534/3/756.

51. Sherwood, 'The CPGB and Black Britons,' p.155.

52. See e.g. *NW*, April 1932, pp.20-24 and *RILU,* No.1 (January 1931) p.22.

of the ISH, so the main impetus for its work in Britain still came from the ITUCNW, which sometimes worked through the NWA, and key activists such as Harry O'Connell, if necessary bypassing the SMM. Padmore was, however, critical of the ISH's limitations, found it difficult to work with its German head, Albert Walter and its British representative, George Hardy, and complained that its initial plans to establish seamen's clubs in Dakar, Freetown, Cape Town and the Caribbean had not been realised.[53] Political work amongst seamen was also continually handicapped by the political differences that existed on how best to organise and the lack of leadership from the CPGB. In 1932, after visiting England, Padmore declared that its was a 'damned disgrace' that there were 'so many colonial Negroes' in Britain, 'some of them even in the Party,' yet they were not sufficiently organised and not one ever sent to Moscow for training.[54]

One of the most important 'colonial Negroes,' Harry O'Connell, was by the early 1930s already a seasoned organiser, who may have arrived in Cardiff from British Guiana as early as 1910. Politically active since the mid-1920s he was connected with the seamen's union before he became a leading organiser for the SMM with responsibility for its colonial work.[55] He was arrested several times for his activism and during the Second World War was forcibly removed from one ship and then banned from working on all British ships on the grounds of 'national interest.'[56] O'Connell corresponded with Padmore from late 1931 and in April 1932, after the latter's visit to Cardiff, was elected as an SMM delegate to the ISH congress, which was held in Hamburg the following month. There he spoke on 'Negro work' in Britain, and held discussions with Padmore, Kouyaté and other delegates on the programme of the ITUCNW.[57] It is evident that both Padmore and O'Connell, who was referred to as 'leader of the colonial seamen in England,' in the pages of *The Negro Worker*, were dissatisfied with the work of the SMM in Cardiff and Padmore promised that the ITUCNW would provide some assistance. Indeed at the ISH congress O'Connell spoke scathingly of the SMM's 'political confusion and opportunist tactics,' which he claimed had alienated the hundreds of 'Negro, Arab and Somali seamen' who had once rallied behind it.[58]

---

53. Padmore to Thomson, 5 January 1932; Padmore to Mahon, 13 January 1932, RGASPI 534/3/754; R. Italiaander, *Schwarze Haut Im Roter Griff* (Dusseldorf, 1962) p.63.
54. Padmore to Dear Comrade, 12 June 1932, RGASPI 534/3/755.
55. For some brief biographical details regarding O'Connell see M. Sherwood, 'Racism and Reisistance: Cardiff in the 1930 and 1940s,' *Llafur*, 5/4, (1991) pp. 51-71.
56. See *Hansard*, HC Deb 23 January 1941 vol. 368 cc332-3W.
57. 'Programme for the Negro Workers' Conference,' RGASPI 534/3/753.
58. See *NW*, 2/6 (June 1932), p.24.

It was in an attempt to try and reorganise the SMM that the ISH sent Richard Krebs to Britain in the summer of 1932.[59] However, Krebs's arrival created even more instability and uncertainty as he attempted to limit the influence of Padmore and the ITUCNW and expel the leading black activists. Chris Jones was expelled from the leadership of the SMM because of his employment with the NUS and other alleged misdemeanours, including lending money to impoverished seamen and charging extortionate rates of interest. Krebs also attempted to expel O'Connell and sent less than enthusiastic reports concerning Headley. He also made efforts to place new activists in charge of colonial work and concluded 'the older element must disappear if we wish to make progress.'[60] Krebs's activities had some impact on Jones but they do not seem to have greatly affected Headley or O'Connell.[61] Most importantly the SMM itself was not effectively reorganised and was subsequently dissolved in early 1933. The ITUCNW and the NWA continued to make attempts to organise in Britain's ports, where African and Caribbean workers and their families confronted a range of problems including poverty, unemployment and racism. In Cardiff, for example, it was officially declared that African and Caribbean men 'needed less to live on than white men.'[62] In a letter to *The Negro Worker* O'Connell highlighted some of the problems facing Cardiff's unemployed black population and called on the 'coloured and white workers of Cardiff,' to unite and fight against all forms of racism and for equal unemployment pay. He concluded by arguing that 'as long as the British slave masters' were able to play off one section of the working class against the other, they would 'be able to rob and exploit both alike.' [63]

Welfare Activities

The pages of *The Negro Worker* often carried articles condemning racism in Britain and the actions of the Labour Party and trade union leaders, which it argued, were aimed at creating divisions between black and white workers. Race prejudice, *The Negro Worker* stated, was widespread in Britain and affected not just black seamen and workers but also students and intellectuals. It is interesting to note that although the ITUCNW applauded the efforts of the LAI in bring-

59. For Krebs notoriously unreliable and mainly fictional account of this mission see J. Valtin, *Out of the Night* (New York, 1941) pp.321-328.

60. Krebs to Walter, 3 September 1932, (TNA) KV2/1102.

61. Headley was affectionately remembered in H. Rosen's *Are You Still Circumcised? East End Memories* (Nottingham, 1999) pp.121-122. I'm obliged to Gemma Romain for this reference.

62. See Harry O'Connell's article 'Race Prejudice in England,' in *NW*, 3/4-5 (April-May 1933) pp.24-25. See also 'Smash the Attack on Colonial Seamen,' *NW*, 4/3 (July 1934) pp.1-3.

63. *NW*, 3/4-5, April- May 1933: 24-5.

ing individual cases to light and petitioning the government, it also pointed out that 'only the organised protest of the British working class will force the hands of the imperialists and their lackeys to put an end to these chauvinist outrages.'[64]

The attacks on black workers and the hardships they faced during this period also extended to their families. As Arnold Ward expressed it, 'their children are treated as outcasts and "aliens" and they cannot get a decent job. Thus the hardships of hunger, misery and squalor combined with segregation make life for our little ones as hard and sorrowful as it is for their parents.'[65] One of the most important aspects of the NWA's work, therefore, was for the welfare of children. The NWA was one of the organisations that attempted to provide some support for 'coloured' children in London, most of whom it was reported, 'pass their childhood in the dark and damp slum areas.'[66] It appears to have been the first to organise and raise funds for annual seaside outings, which began in the summer of 1932 with a trip to Southend, a well-known resort on the Essex coast a few hours travel from central London.[67]

Scottsboro

The first major political issue taken up by the NWA was the Scottsboro campaign, launched in Britain in the summer of 1931, as part of the international campaign to save the lives of nine African American youths who had been convicted and sentenced to death or life imprisonment in Alabama on trumped-up charges of rape.[68] Ward was at the forefront of efforts by the NWA, the LAI and the International Labour Defence (ILD) in Britain to free the nine youth, and he spoke at several campaign meetings in 1931.[69] In the spring of the following year, when Padmore arrived in Britain to speak for the Scottsboro campaign, he reported that 'Negro workers are taking up a definitely revolutionary attitude

---

64. *NW*, 2 /3 (March 1932) pp. 2-3.

65. *NW*, 2/9-10 (September-October 1932) p. 22.

66. *NW*, 4/6-7 (June-July 1933) p.32.

67. The League of Coloured Peoples also organised such outings from the summer of 1933. See *The Keys*, 1/2 (October 1933) p.24. One of the features of the NWA outings was that they were financed by the Association and its supporters and appeals for funds were sometimes issued in *The Negro Worker*. See e.g. *NW*, 4/6-7 (June-July 1933) p.32.

68. S. D. Pennybaker, *From Scottsboro to Munich: Race and Political Culture in 1930s Britain* (Princeton, 2009) pp.16-66 and *"We Were Framed" – The First Full Account Published in England of the Trials of the Nine Scottsboro Boys*, (London 1934).

69. *NW*, 1/10-11 (October-November 1931) pp.36-37.

on this case'.[70] The NWA enlisted the support of Indian workers and several celebrities, including the heiress Nancy Cunard, the daughter of Sir Bache and Lady Maud Cunard, who later became an active member of the Association as well as a supporter of the campaign.[71] She helped to arrange publicity for the case in the mainstream press in Britain and launched a fundraising and publicity campaign amongst her friends and associates in the United States.[72]

Ward and the NWA subsequently held several successful meetings in conjunction with the ILD and CPGB and spoke at Scottsboro rallies and demonstrations in London.[73] The campaign intensified in June 1932 in connection with the visit to Britain of Ada Wright, the mother of two of the convicted youths.[74] At first the NWA complained that it was being excluded from her welcoming ceremony, which led Padmore to express some critical comments to the ILD, but subsequently Ward even deputised for Mrs Wright, who was initially denied a visa to enter Britain, and spoke at major Scottsboro rallies in Liverpool, Dundee and Glasgow.[75] When the visa ban was finally lifted, Ward spoke at all the major rallies, alongside Ada Wright, in London, Bristol and Scotland. He generally spoke on behalf of 'Negro workers', and the rallies were often chaired or addressed by other NWA members such as Chris Jones and Jim Headley.[76] The NWA continued this work and in 1933 helped establish the London-based Scottsboro Defence Committee, of which Kenyatta was joint secretary.[77] In 1935 the executive of the NWA was elected en masse to the Scottsboro Defence Committee.[78] It was this Committee, through its links with the MP Eleanor Rathbone, that put pressure on the government to make a statement about the introduction of the Criminal Code Amendment Bill in the Gold Coast. The proposed Sedition Bill, as it was known, was originally

70. Padmore to the Bureau of the ISH, 24 March 1932, RGASPI 534/3/754 and also Padmore to Dear Comrade, 14 June 1932, RGASPI 534/3/755.

71 *NW*, 4/8 (December 1934) p.4.

72. Padmore to Dear Comrades, 14 June 1932, RGASPI 534/3/755; Ward to Padmore, 31 March 1932, RGASPI 534/3/754.

73. See e.g. *NW*, 2/8 (15 August 1932) p.20.

74. Squires, 'Communists and the Fight Against Racism,' p.15; see also J.L. Engdahl, 'Scottsboro Campaign in England,' *NW*, 2/8 (15 August 1932) pp.18-20 and *DW*, 21 June 1932, p.2.

75. See Padmore to Dear Comrade, 14 June 1932, RGASPI 534/3/755 and Ward to Padmore, 15 June 1931, RGASPI 534/7/50; *DW*, 22 June 1932, p.2. For detailed information on the Scottsboro campaign in Britain see RGASPI 539/3/307.

76. See e.g. *DW*, 8 July 1932, p.1.

77. *We Were Framed*; 'London Scottsboro Resolution,' *NW*, 6/1 (March 1936) p.12.

78. Secretary's Report to the AGM of the NWA, 20 October 1935. RGASPI 515/301/3943.

believed to be an attempt to prevent agitation related to the Scottsboro case in the Gold Coast.[79]

Nancy Cunard met Padmore in Paris in November 1932 and soon afterwards began regularly attending meetings of the NWA, promising her financial support for a proposed Negro welfare club and bookshop in London.[80] She continued to play a significant role in the Scottsboro campaign and Defence Committee; organising fundraising events and even holding meetings at her home. She also became a member of the executive committee of the NWA until 1933 when it appears that she quarrelled with Bridgeman over NWA policy and resigned from the organisation. It seems likely that differences arose over the inability of the NWA to organise and recruit new members, and the fact that the organisation was led by white rather than black members. Cunard, with the support of some other leading members of the NWA, notably Chris Jones, then began organising rival meetings at her home. At one such meeting, which was attended by thirty-five 'persons of colour,' it was agreed to establish a 'London Coloured Committee' of the ILD, chaired by Jones and with Cunard as its treasurer, although this body did not survive long.[81]

The Scottsboro campaign in Britain had a great unifying impact. It made a deep impression amongst workers, to judge from the pages of the *Daily Worker*, which carried reports of the many meetings and union branch resolutions throughout the country.[82] The NWA also organised many fundraising events during this campaign and was able to call on the support of the famous African American Paul Robeson, who contributed his services and made generous financial contributions.[83] Although Ward claimed that the campaign 'made the Negroes think', the NWA's thinking was not always in line with that of the ITUCNW.[84] In the autumn of 1934, for instance, there was criticism of a

79. 'Scottsboro Trial,' LAI, 26 February 1932, Bridgeman Papers (DBN 25/4) University of Hull.

80. See M. Joanniu, 'Nancy Cunard's English Journey,' in *Feminist Review*, 78 (2004) p.158 and J. R. Hooker, *Black Revolutionary – George Padmore's Path From Communism to Pan-Africanism*, (Pall Mall Press, 1967) p.27; Special Branch report, 13 December 1932, (TNA) MEPO 38/9.

81. Special Branch Report, 9 June 1933, MEPO 38/9; other members of this committee included Robert Broadhurst, Beresford Gale and Anthony Papafio. Its creation seems to have been supported by at least two English Communists, including Thomas Henry Wintringham; A. Ward to W. Patterson, 18 July 1933, RGASPI 515/206/3373; Col. Kell to McSweeney, 12 December 1933, (TNA) KV 2/1787.

82. See e.g. *DW*, 9 July 1932, p.4; 11 July 1932, p.2; 12 July 1932, p.2; 14 July 1932, p.2; and 19 July 1932, p.2.

83. For details of one of Robeson's financial contributions see Duberman, *Paul Robeson*, p.629 n.7.

84. Ward to Patterson, 19 July 1933, RGASPI 515/260/3373.

resolution adopted by the NWA-organised Scottsboro rally in London's Hyde Park, which had been attended by several thousand people and addressed by Amy Ashwood Garvey and other speakers. On that occasion *The Negro Worker* felt obliged to point out that, 'the lynching and oppression of Negroes is not because of "colour prejudice,"' as the NWA had suggested, 'but arises out of the whole system of national oppression of the Negro masses.' [85]

THE NWA AND THE COLONIES -WEST AFRICA

The NWA's support of the Scottsboro campaign had an impact not only in Britain but also in West Africa where Isaac Wallace-Johnson was active in the Gold Coast on its behalf.[86] Overcoming considerable obstacles, including police harassment, he worked alongside the Ex-Servicemen's Association and others to publicise the campaign and established a fundraising committee.[87] Wallace-Johnson, who originated from Sierra Leone, was a labour leader, journalist, and anti-colonial activist who organised in Nigeria and Sierra Leone as well as the Gold Coast.[88] Through Padmore and the ITUCNW, he was put in touch with Ward, Headley and others in London in early 1932.[89] That same year he studied in Moscow (alongside Kenyatta), joined the executive committee of the ITUCNW and subsequently became a member of the editorial board of *The Negro Worker*.[90] Following a police raid on his home in Lagos in the autumn of 1933, he moved to Accra and it was in the Gold Coast that he first established the WAYL in 1934. His activities in West Africa led to his arrest on several occasion and contributed to the passing of anti-communist legislation throughout Britain's West African colonies. In 1936 he was convicted for sedition, following the publication of his famous article 'Has the African a God.'[91]

---

85. *NW*, 4/ 6-7 (October-November 1934) p. 7-9.

86. It appears that ILD material from the US was sent to West Africa through the NWA. See A. Ward to W. Patterson, 6 March 1934, RGASPI 515/273/3482.

87. L. Denzer, 'Isaac Wallace-Johnson and the West African Youth League: A case study in West African Nationalism.' Ph.D dissertation, University of Birmingham, 1977, p. 72. See also *NW*, 4/2 (June 1934) p.29 and W. Daniels, 'Development of Fascist Terror in the Gold Coast,' *NW*, 4/5 (September 1935) pp.4-7.

88. For details of some of the correspondence that passed between the NWA and Wallace-Johnson regarding the Sedition Bill in the Gold Coast see *Vox Populi*, (5 October 1935) pp.8-9.

89. See e.g. Wallace-Johnson to Ward, 30 April 1932, RGASPI 534/3/755.

90. Wallace-Johnson to Padmore, 3 August 1932, RGASPI 534/3/756.

91. L. Spitzer and L. Denzer, 'I.T.A. Wallace-Johnson and the West African Youth League,' *International Journal of African Historical Studies*, 7/3 (1973) pp.413-452. See also E.T. Wilson, *Russia and Black Africa Before World War II* (New York, 1974) pp. 243-253.

Wallace-Johnson was undoubtedly the most prominent of several supporters of the NWA in West Africa, who collaborated on a range of anti-colonial issues. Through Padmore and the ITUCW the NWA also made contact with Kobina Sekyi, a leading political figure in the Gold Coast and a representative of the Gold Coast Aborigines' Rights Protection Society (GCARPS) and the Gold Coast Farmers' Association, who visited London in the summer of 1932.[92] Wallace-Johnson maintained a close connection with the NWA and the LAI throughout the 1930s and through them with sympathetic Members of Parliament (MPs) in Britain. When the colonial authorities raided his premises in Lagos searching for copies of *The Negro Worker* and other 'seditious publications' he immediately contacted his friends in Britain. It only took two days from the time of his arrest for Bridgeman to write to the Colonial Office demanding information and similar letters soon followed from the Labour Party and TUC.[93] Wallace-Johnson subsequently sought the aid of the NWA in regard to a case of public flogging in Nigeria, which enabled Bridgeman to contact the MP James Maxton, and this matter was also subsequently discussed in Parliament. As a result the Colonial Secretary was forced to assure MPs that no such atrocities would occur again.[94] In 1934 Wallace-Johnson sought NWA support in connection with his campaign following the Prestea mine disaster in the Gold Coast, in which over forty miners lost their lives.[95] In the same year he was a key speaker at one of the NWA's most successful meetings on the theft of African land by the settlers and colonial government in Kenya.[96]

Wallace-Johnson also worked closely with Ward and the LAI to protest against the 'obnoxious Bills' that were being introduced into the Gold Coast in the 1930s, especially the Criminal Code Amendment Ordinance, generally referred to as the Sedition Bill, introduced into the colony in 1934. The Ordinance made it a criminal offence punishable by up to three years imprisonment for an African to be found in possession of 'any newspaper, book or document' which the colonial governor had prohibited. It was also an offence to publish, sell or be in possession of any material containing 'seditious words or writing.'[97] The Ordinance was condemned by the ITUCNW and LAI as an attempt to

92. S. Rhodie, 'The Gold Coast Aborigines Abroad,' *Journal of African History*, 6/3 (1965) pp.385-411.

93. LAI to the Colonial Secretary, 11 October 1933, (TNA) CO 593/195/4.

94. *Hansard*, HC Deb 01 June 1933 vol. 278 cc2061-2 and HC Deb 14 June 1933 vol. 279 cc153-4.

95. Denzer, 'Isaac Wallace-Johnson and the West African Youth League,' p.88.

96. NWA Secretary's Report to the AGM, 20 October 1935, RGASPI 515/301/3943.

97. 'Report of the International Secretariat of the LAI,' 1934, p.3.

stifle agitation connected with the Scottsboro campaign but also to prevent the importation of literature from organisations such as the ITUCNW.[98]

In order to justify the introduction of this legislation, the Colonial Secretary, Sir Cunliffe Lister, had quoted from one ITUCNW publication which demanded that 'the Negro masses must therefore rise up as the tide of the revolutionary front and use the arms which the white oppressors put in their hands not to shoot down their class brothers in the Soviet Union,' and referred to it as 'filth' which could not be tolerated.[99] *The Negro Worker,* on the other hand, compared the Sedition Bill with the actions of the Nazis in Germany.[100] Some of Arnold Ward's advice to Wallace-Johnson and views on organising opposition, particularly his call for local 'protest meetings against the ordinance,' were subsequently made public and published in the Gold Coast press, while in Britain, through the influence of the LAI, several MPs contacted the Colonial Office, or asked questions and proposed amendments to the Bill in Parliament.[101]

In 1935 Wallace-Johnson was instrumental in re-establishing contact between the NWA/LAI and the delegation of the GCARPS, which took its protest against the Sedition Bill to Britain. Contact between the NWA and GCARPS had temporarily faltered but that year the NWA/LAI were able to launch a national campaign to publicise the grievances of the GCARPS delegation, which the Colonial Office initially refused to recognise or meet. This campaign was partly waged during the general election campaign in the autumn of 1935 and the LAI and National Council of Civil Liberties, which targeted the Bassetlaw constituency of the Colonial Secretary, Malcolm MacDonald, certainly contributed to his electoral defeat.[102] Ward and Bridgeman had previously also sought to assist another delegation from the Gold Coast, led by Nana Sir Ofori Atta and Dr Nanka Bruce, but their offers of support had largely been

98. I. Wallace-Johnson, 'A Letter from the Gold Coast,' *NW*, 4/5 (September 1934) pp.26-27. See also R. Bridgeman, Scottsboro' Trial, 26 February 1934, Bridgeman Papers (DBN) 25/4, University of Hull. It seems that Wallace-Johnson initially alerted the Scottsboro Defence Committee and LAI about the proposed Bill in February 1934. According to one source over 1100 copies of *The Negro Worker* were being imported into the Gold Coast. S.Shaloff, 'Press Controls and Sedition Proceedings in the Gold Coast 1933-39,' *African Affairs*, 71/284 (1972) p.251.

99. Quoted in Shaloff, 'Press Controls and Sedition Proceedings,' p.250.

100. *NW* 4/5 (September 1934) pp.1-2.

101. See I. Wallace-Johnson, 'The Gold Coast Independent and Myself (Part V),' *Vox Populi*, (5 October 1935) pp.8-9 and *Hansard* HC Deb, 30 October 1934, vol. 293 cc113-137.

102. *NW*, 6/10 (December 1936) p.17. See also L. Denzer, 'Isaac Wallace-Johnson and the West African Youth League': 84-85. On the ARPS delegation to Britain see Rohdie, 'The Gold Coast Aborigines '

declined.[103] Through the NWA/LAI, the GCARPS delegation made contact with a range of political organisations and parliamentarians in London and eventually remained in Britain for three years. So useful was their visit that Ward suggested to Samuel R. Wood, one of the delegates, that a permanent body should be established in London to represent African interests.[104]

Ward was himself a regular speaker at meetings throughout the country, and particularly in London where he often spoke on the subject of 'British imperialism in Africa.' At one such meeting in 1933, he told the members of the Southgate Labour Party that 'fascism was nothing new to Africa,' and he was able to detail the economic exploitation and denial of basic rights that existed in Britain's African colonies, as well as African demands for trade unions, an end to unfair trading practices and for self-determination.[105] The NWA also maintained close links with the WASU in London, the main African organisation in Britain at the time. The WASU had previously been contacted by James Ford in late 1928 or early 1929, and supplied with copies of *The Negro Worker*; however, at the second congress of the LAI Ford criticised the organisation for its political naivety.[106] Despite such criticism the NWA and the LAI provided a means for the WASU and organisations and individuals in West Africa to ensure that grievances relating to colonial rule were regularly raised in Parliament by sympathetic MPs.[107] The NWA and LAI also worked with the WASU over other grievances such as the campaign to expose and boycott the government hostel in London known as Aggrey House.[108]

Kenyatta and East Africa

The NWA maintained links with East Africa during this period through Johnstone (Jomo) Kenyatta, who had made contact with the LAI and the CPGB almost as soon as he arrived in Britain in 1929. Kenyatta participated in the Frankfurt conference of the LAI in 1929, where he became part of the organising committee of the ITUCNW's Hamburg Conference and from where he first proceeded to Moscow.[109] The only evidence that he subsequently participated

103. For Ward's view see his letter reproduced in Wallace-Johnson, 'The Gold Coast Independent and Myself.'

104. S. Rohdie, 'The Gold Coast Aborigines,' p.404. Ward made similar suggestions to the WASU. See Ward to Solanke, 16 January 1935, Solanke Papers, University of Lagos, Box 11/4.

105. 'A Native Speaker Addresses Southgate Labour Party,' *Wood Green Sentinel*, 23 November 1933.

106. See Adi, *West Africans in Britain,* p. 45.

107. Ibid.

108. Ibid. pp.57-62.

109. Report of the Negro Question at the LAI Congress, 3 October 1929. RGASPI 534/3/408.

in the Hamburg Conference comes from the British security services, since he is not mentioned in this connection in any of the Comintern documents.[110] In Frankfurt Kenyatta had met Garan Kouyaté and they appear to have remained in contact thereafter. In late 1929 the French Colonial Ministry noted that *La Race Nègre*, the journal of the LDRN, had even reported that 'Professors Nathaniels and Kenyatta were organising an English section' of the LDRN with the help of the WASU.[111] From what is known of the WASU at this time it seems an unlikely claim, although Ladipo Solanke, the Union's secretary-general, was also in contact with Kouyaté. It is not impossible that Kenyatta and others were organising within the WASU, but at the present time there is certainly no evidence to suggest the creation of an English section of the LDRN. However, Kenyatta was closely involved with the NWA from its earliest days and in one of his letters to Padmore he claimed that he had been instrumental in establishing it.[112]

In 1933, after several unsuccessful attempts, Kenyatta again travelled to Moscow and became the only African or Caribbean resident from Britain to study at the University of the Toilers of the East (KUTV). As a consequence of his time in Moscow the authorities in Kenya and London suspected that Kenyatta was the link between the international communist movement and anti-colonial elements in Kenya and, on the basis that he was sometimes described as the East African editor of *The Negro Worker*, concluded that he was receiving funding from the ITUCNW.[113] However, although Kenyatta travelled to the Soviet Union, appeared on many platforms for the NWA, wrote articles for *The Negro Worker* and such openly communist publications as *Labour Monthly,* he was seldom relied upon by his comrades and even the security services distrusted his statements. Edwin Mofutsanyana, a long-serving member of the CPSA, referred to Kenyatta as 'the biggest reactionary I have ever met.' While he was in Hamburg Padmore criticised him several times and Kenyatta was forced to defend himself against charges of political unreliability.[114] He was certainly in close touch with Padmore during this period, with

110. See (TNA) KV2/1787.

111. Many thanks to Robbie Aitken for this reference from the Yaoundé archives. The report presumably refers to R.C. Nathaniels, a folklorist and historian from the Gold Coast.

112. Kenyatta to Padmore, 9 June 1932, RGASPI 534/7/74.

113. See Col. Vernon Kell (MI5) to McSweeney (Colonial Office) 6 August 1932, (TNA) KV 2/1787.

114. See e.g. Special Branch report, 6 December 1933, (TNA) KV 2/1787. For a rather negative report on Kenyatta while he was a student in Moscow see I. Filatova, 'Indoctrination or Schoarship? Education of Africans at the Communist University of the Toilers of the East in the Soviet Union, 1923-1937,' *Paeagogica Historica*, 35/1 (1999) p.61; see also Kenyatta to Padmore, 9 June 1932, RGASPI 534/7/74; and R. Edgar, 'Notes on the Life and Death of Albert Nzula,' *Journal of African Historical Studies*, 16/4 (1983) pp.678-679.

Nancy Cunard sometimes acting as an intermediary in unsuccessful attempts to avoid police interception of their letters. After Padmore came to London, following his expulsion from the Comintern, they worked closely together in various organisations. However, Kenyatta maintained his membership of the NWA and ties with the CPGB even while he was a leading member of such organisations as the International African Friends of Abyssinia (IAFA), the Pan-African Federation and the International African Service Bureau (IASB). It was as honorary secretary of the IAFA, led by Padmore and C.L. R. James, that Kenyatta wrote the article 'Hands off Abyssinia' for *Labour Monthly* in September 1935. The precise relationship between the IASB and those connected with the NWA/LAI is far from clear. Ward, Bridgeman and subsequently Peter Blackman all maintained contact with the IASB, and the security services even alleged that Bridgeman and Bradley of the LAI were involved in the discussions to establish it. In February 1937 Padmore unsuccessfully attempted to nominate Kenyatta to serve on the LAI's executive committee during elections held at its annual conference.[115]

Despite his limitations, Kenyatta provided the NWA and the ITUCNW with first-hand knowledge of Kenyan and East African affairs that could be utilised both in meetings and articles. His article 'An African Looks at British Imperialism,' published in *The Negro Worker* in 1933 is a good illustration.[116] In it he attacks the arbitrary plunder of African land in Kenya and makes what must be one of the earliest demands for 'complete self-rule.' Subsequently, the NWA and ITUCNW, together with the LAI, issued a joint statement protesting against the Native Land Trust (Amendment) Ordinance, which amongst other things allowed the colonial government in Kenya to licence the mining of gold in land which only a few years previously had been designated for 'Native' use only. These protests were accompanied by a more general campaign which included a major article in *The Negro Worker* and questions in Parliament that exposed once again the fact that colonial rule was nothing more than the legalised appropriation and exploitation of the land and other resources of Africa.[117]

THE CARIBBEAN

The NWA also had links with anti-colonial organisations and individuals in the Caribbean, sometimes maintained by individual members such as Headley

115. Kenyatta was also joint editor with Padmore of the PAF's little known publication *Voice of Africa*. See various Special Branch reports in (TNA) KV2/1787 and KV2/1838.

116. See e.g. 'An African Looks at British Imperialism,' *NW*, 3/1 (January 1933) pp.18-22.

117. 'To our brothers in Kenya,' *NW*, 4/8-9 (August-September 1933) pp.19-25. For an example of parliamentary questions see *Hansard*, HC Deb 07 February 1933 vol 274 cc 26-30.

and O'Connell. It also regularly held meetings and passed resolutions on political issues in the region, such as the banning of *The Negro Worker* in Trinidad in 1932, or in response to the government-appointed West Indies Closer Union Commission of the same year, despatched to the Caribbean in order to investigate the possibility of a federation.[118] The NWA used the bans imposed on *The Negro Worker* to expose the lack of democracy throughout Britain's colonies in Africa and the Caribbean, as well as in Britain itself.[119] In 1933 it organised a meeting and passed a resolution condemning the new trade union legislation that was being introduced into Trinidad and Tobago in an attempt to further curtail existing limited trade union rights.[120]

In the early 1930s, the Trindadian A.C. Rienzi, who had formerly been one of the leading figures in the Trinidad Workingmen's Association (TWA), was also a member of the NWA executive, while he was a law student in London.[121] In February 1932 he organised an NWA meeting and invited Cipriani, the leader of the TWA, to be the main speaker, despite the fact that they had been political adversaries in Trinidad. Since Cipriani had already become discredited and his activities were regularly condemned in the pages of *The Negro Worker*, it was an invitation that did not find favour with Padmore, who learned of it from the pages of the *Daily Worker*. Padmore wrote to Ward to complain that had he known in advance that Cipriani was to speak under the auspices of the NWA, he would 'have made a trip to London in order to challenge this fellow to a public debate.'[122] For Padmore, Cipriani was 'an out and out imposter, demagogue and racketeer' who, 'has not yet organised one strike in ten years.'[123] *The Negro Worker* subsequently published a report of the meeting, although it gave greater prominence to the resolution adopted by those who attended. This condemned the colonial policy of the National Government in Britain and the British Labour Party and declared that only when the 'workers and peasants are organised on a class basis and prepared by revolutionary action to overthrow their imperialist oppressors, will they ever achieve the freedom of the West Indian islands from foreign domination.'[124]

---

118. For the ITUCNW/NWA resolution see *NW*, 3/1 (January 1933), p.7.

119. NW, 2/6 (June 1932), pp.16-17. Regarding question asked in the House of Commons on this issue see *Hansard*, HC Deb 01 June 1932 vol 266 cc 1150-1.

120. *NW*, 4/8-9 (August-September 1933) p.26.

121. On Rienzi see K. Singh, 'Adrian Cola Rienzi and the Labour Movement in Trinidad, 1925-1944,' *Journal of Caribbean History*, 16 (November 1982) pp.11-35.

122. Padmore to Ward, 27 February 1932, RGASPI 534/3/754.

123. Padmore to Ward, 7 March 1932, RGASPI 534/3/754.

124. See *NW*, 2/4 (April 1932), p.19.

Despite such sentiments the NWA appears to have paid little further attention to the Caribbean, despite the fact that Ward and several other leading members were from the region, until the late 1930s when Peter Blackman, another Barbadian, became secretary. This may have reflected the ITUCNW's strong focus on Africa, but even after the first major strikes broke out in the Caribbean in 1935, the NWA was not particularly active until 1938 when it participated in the formation of the Committee for West Indian Affairs.[125]

Internal Problems

Despite the breadth of the NWA's activities there were many problems and weaknesses confronting the organisation almost from its inception. Ward's great quality was that he persevered, but it is clear that he sometimes faced immense difficulties as an organiser and activist because of his limited experience and the relatively little help he received from the LAI and the CPGB. Moreover, he was always pessimistic and constantly complaining even when the NWA had some success.[126] The support of the ITUCNW was clearly important but after the expulsion of Padmore and the HC from Germany early in 1933, the frequency of correspondence between Padmore and Ward sharply decreased. The NWA was further handicapped by the resignation of Cunard and Jones and it was in this period that Ward turned to William Patterson, at that time head of the ILD in the United States, for advice and support. That he did so perhaps suggests that he felt more able to discuss the NWA's problems with a fellow black Communist in another continent than he did with his comrades in the CPGB. At one stage in 1933 Ward even suggested that Patterson issue an appeal 'asking the Negroes to unite and work together' and convene a meeting to unite all those in Britain connected with the NWA. In the same letter he suggests that perhaps the CPUSA, or even the Comintern, might intervene and send help in the form of an experienced 'CP Negro Woman.' Ward complained that 'our forces here' are 'so scattered and divided' and concluded, 'I could write you pages of hardships the Negroes suffer here. I have been talking and arguing with the men to come together and let us try and do something that would benefit the whole, and help the CP who is working for us all but my pleading always falls on deaf ears.'[127]

---

125. See Blackman to Gillies (Labour Party), 16 November 1938, Labour History Archives and Study Centre LP/WG/BWI/87.

126. See e.g. Ward to Padmore, 31 March 1932, RGASPI 534/3/754; also A. Ward, 'The Negro Situation in Britain,' *NW*, 4/6-7 (October-November 1934) pp.7-9.

127. Ward to Patterson, 19 July 1933, RGASPI 515/260/3373. Headley later returned to Britain and spoke at IASB meeting on Caribbean affairs in October 1937. (TNA) KV2/1787.

Patterson's reply indicated that although he discussed Ward's correspondence with the leaders of the CPUSA he still thought that Padmore would be the best person to help. However, he made several insightful remarks to Ward: 'Perhaps your approach to the Negro workers in Great Britain has been of too general a character. They have not been able to appreciate the benefits that would result to them personally were they to link themselves up with our organisation. I believe that if you come to them with a concrete program dealing with their immediate demands that there are tremendous possibilities of drawing them into the struggle.' In addition he encouraged Ward to work with colonial seamen, so as to take advantage of their links with their countries of origin for the dissemination of literature. He concluded his letter by instructing Ward: 'You must take the initiative in this work. It is for you to relentlessly push the leading comrades there, stressing the importance of this work and outlining its tremendous possibilities. I am certain that if you discuss the possibilities in this work and draw up a program of action with Padmore, Rathbone and others, the leading comrades there will react immediately and definitely. Remember that the Party is your Party.'[128]

The ITUCNW's own internal problems and Padmore's expulsion from the Communist movement in early 1934 prevented this course of action. However, even before his expulsion it seems that Padmore had unilaterally decided to encourage Headley to leave Britain and return to Trinidad and Ward was extremely critical of his actions as well as his 'Liberian scheme.'[129] He later remarked that following his expulsion Padmore 'told his story in such a way that some of the comrades here believe it, and in my opinion, still support him... he has done a lot of harm here – he has sown the seed of dissension among the colonials here.' Ward confided to Patterson that in his view the CPGB was 'too weak' to deal effectively with the situation but concluded, 'Padmore will soon fade out, of this I'm sure.'[130]

Huiswoud, the NWA and Colonial Seamen

Padmore, of course, did not just 'fade out' and it appears that many of the other problems facing the NWA continued. It did not even convene an annual general meeting for two years, but did continue with its activities and meetings and formed closer ties with both the main African and Caribbean organisations in London, the WASU and the LCP. In 1934 it was invited to join the WASU's Africa House Defence Committee and during the same year joined with the

128. Patterson to Ward, 11 August 1933, RGASPI 515/260/3373.

129. Ward to Patterson, 14 November 1933, RGASPI 534/3/895/122.

130. Ward to Patterson, 6 March 1934. RGASPI 515/273/3482.

LCP to organise a very successful conference, 'The Negro in the World Today,' held in London at which it received overwhelming support for a motion on the nature of the struggle against imperialism.[131] Amongst other things the resolution declared:

> the Negro peoples can best achieve their own emancipation by allying themselves with the subjected sections of the peoples of all other countries in an international struggle to end the colonial system and the oppression which is its inevitable consequence and by supporting all struggles for national independence. For only in this manner will the Negro people, like those exploited in all other countries, win through to complete independence and freedom.[132]

Shortly before the conference Huiswoud, who was leading the work of the re-established ITUCNW, also managed to re-establish regular contact with the NWA. In June of that year he wrote to Moscow to report that he expected that there would soon be 'a programme and a plan of action for the Association and work among the Negro seamen.'[133] The following month he travelled to London to meet with Ward and the NWA and to participate in the conference. Huiswoud's report to Moscow on this occasion stated that the NWA 'is not what has been reported to be,'(sic) and he concluded by stating ' we have, therefore, worked out a programme for concentration among the seamen and through the building of groups among them create the basis for the development of the Association. Through this and other activities, we hope to make the necessary connections with the colonies.'[134]

Initially Huiswoud was optimistic about the possibilities of the NWA's future activities; reporting that as far as Europe was concerned, 'a turn in our work is to be observed in England,' and confidently reporting that the NWA was moving 'away from abstract agitation to concrete practical organisational work.'[135] The concentration of this work was among the colonial seamen in Cardiff where, Huiswoud reported, 'we have about 200 seamen in the unemployed movement,' and 'contacts are now being made with the working colo-

131. For further details on the WASU see Adi, *West Africans in Britain*, pp. 58-62; on the LCP's conference see *The Keys*, 2/2 (October-December 1934) p.21.

132. See *NW*, 4/5, (September 1934) p. 27 .

133. Edward to Dear Friends (Ludwig and Alexander [Lozovsky]?), 9 June 1934, RGASPI 534/3/986.

134. Edward to Dear Friends, 26 July 1934, RGASPI 534/3/986.

135. Edward to Dear Friends, 23 August 1934, RGASPI 534/3/986; at this time Huiswoud also openly appealed to the NWA and LAI in the pages of *The Negro Worker* to start organising to make racial discrimination illegal in Britain. *NW* 4/5 (September 1934) p.3.

nial seamen in order to more firmly establish out connections with the colonies direct.'[136] Certainly conditions in Britain were favourable for organising amongst the seamen, who were being viciously attacked in the publications of the NUS and the Labour Party.[137] The NWA now declared:

> To aid in the organisation of the Negro marine workers in the metropolis and in the colonies is the central task of the association. To achieve this it is necessary to commence and carry on in conjunction and cooperation with the ISH, a systematic campaign of agitation, propaganda and distribution of literature among the Negro marine workers. Contacts must be established with the Negro dockers and seamen in all the important ports in England. Meetings with the marine workers should be held to discuss their working conditions and grievances and together with them, demands and a program of action should be worked out. To successfully carry out this task it will be necessary to select some of the most important ships and docks as concentration points for activities. Only in this way can the first steps be made towards the organisation of the Negro transport workers and establishing the influence of the Association among the decisive sections of the Negro workers.[138]

The language of this resolution suggests that it came from outside the NWA, possibly from Huiswoud himself. The work with seamen proceeded slowly, however, and the NWA's activities were mainly limited to issuing resolutions and appeals, some of which Huiswoud felt compelled to publicly criticise.[139]

The NWA was certainly in no position to provide the five or six students for training in Moscow that were demanded in early 1935 by the RILU Negro Bureau.[140] To this request Huiswoud could only respond that he had been told that such forces could not be found in London and although he had suggested that a search should be made outside of the capital he felt that would be necessary to write about the matter to Harry Pollitt, the leader of the CPGB, fearing that otherwise nothing would be done about it.[141] In fact nothing was done and

136. Edward to Dear Friends, 23 August 1934, RGASPI 534/3/986. Harry O'Connell reported that a 'Rank and File Committee' had been established in Cardiff at this time. See *NW*, 4/6-7 (October-November 1934) pp.19-20.

137. See e.g. 'Smash the Attacks on Colonial Seamen,' *NW*, 4/3, July 1934, p.1.

138. 'Communism and the West Indian Labour Disturbances,' (TNA) CO 295/606/4.

139. See A. Ward 'The Negro Situation in England,' *NW*, 4/6-7 (October-November 1934) pp.7-8. For Huiswoud's criticism of a speech by Kenyatta see 'British Slave Rule in Kenya,' *NW*, 4/6-7 (October-November 1934) pp.12-14.

140. Zusmanovitch to Huiswoud, 21 February 1935, RGASPI 495/155/102.

141. Huiswoud to Dear Comrades, 11 April 1935, RGASPI 495/155/102.

Huiswoud reported that there was not much that was encouraging in regard to the NWA because 'they are not getting support from responsible quarters.' Even the plan of work which he had prepared 'was never utilised or put into effect.' In Huiswoud's view the issue of unemployment, which he referred to as the 'burning question at present among the colonial seamen,' was not being taken up by the NWA and he complained that the organisation was paralysed by personal bickering and the fact that 'they have no trained Negro forces to lead the work.'[142]

Although Huiswoud maintained that without such leadership the NWA would continue to flounder, his criticism was pointedly levelled at what he referred to as 'the higher circles,' a clear reference to the leaders of the CPGB, who he claimed were responsible for 'the almost complete lack of attention paid to colonial work (particularly in Africa).' In fact the CPGB had delegated much of this work to the LAI, but according to Huiswoud, the LAI also failed to 'develop mass action around burning issues.' He complained that he had made proposals for such action in regard to the colour bar, the invasion of Ethiopia, the problems facing colonial seamen and other issues but 'they offer all kinds of reasons why mass action cannot be developed.' In early 1935 the NWA did issue a Call to 'African and West Indian dockers' to demand the boycotting of ships that refused to employ 'Negroes' but this was at the time when the British government introduced major subsidies, under the British Shipping (Assistance) Act, for shipping companies which employed solely 'British' crews.[143] Husiwoud concluded that the situation was now so serious that it had led to 'discontent amongst the Negro comrades,' and several complaints.[144]

In one such letter of complaint Ward highlighted many of the problems affecting the NWA, including the continued influence of Padmore and the inactivity of the LAI, the CPGB and other affiliated organisations. Apparently Ward and Saklatvala, who appears to have become the former's closest comrade and greatest support, had for some time been urging Bridgeman and the LAI to take up work amongst seamen, but unfortunately it had not advanced far beyond what Ward referred to as 'a letter to the press.'[145] Saklatvala subsequently commented that he had noticed 'certain defects among the British Party members on the Asiatic, African and colonial problems.' In 1934, after visiting Soviet Central Asia and witnessing how the Communist Party of the Soviet Union dealt with such issues, he concluded that in Britain there was 'a tendency to treat the colonial problem as a mere side issue and as nobody's problem in

142. Ibid.

143. See *NW*, 5/2-3 (February-March 1935) pp.25-26.

144. Huiswoud to Dear Friends, 24 June 1935, RGASPI 495/155/102.

145. Ward to Huiswoud, 26 June 1935, RGASPI 495/155/102.

particular.' Saklatvala made it clear that his criticisms related not only to work in the colonies but also to work in Britain amongst students and seamen. In this regard he pointed out 'many things happen among the colonial seamen in the East End of London and members of the Party and of the unemployed workers' movement, living right in the locality know nothing about it.'[146]

According to Ward, the problems facing 'coloured seamen' in London, where there were fewer ships, and therefore no alternative maritime employment, were quite different to those that existed in other ports such as Liverpool, Cardiff and South Shields. In London seamen would just look for work ashore, at that time mainly as film and stage extras, and as a consequence, Ward claimed, when spoken to about unemployment and the Seamen's Union, 'we hardly get any response from them.' This comment reflects badly on Ward rather then the ex-seamen because, as he explained, those working in the film industry had recently formed a union, the Coloured Film Artists Association (CFAA). Although he was dismissive of its corrupt leaders, clearly those forced into the entertainment industry were also eager to organise themselves. Ward subsequently joined the executive of the CFAA, which had over four hundred members and it later worked closely with the NWA.[147]

O'Connell persisted with his attempts to organise opposition to the racism, unemployment and other economic problems faced by the maritime community in Cardiff, although he too was critical of the lack of support offered by the CPGB.[148] In 1935 a Coloured Seamen's Committee was established under his leadership, but it is interesting to note that it represented Malayan and Arab seamen as well as those from Africa and the Caribbean. It fought for the seamen's rights and against government and trade union attempts to create divisions between white and 'coloured' seamen.[149] Such activism on behalf of the seamen led to questions in Parliament and subsequently an investigation and report by the LCP. During the same period O'Connell also actively campaigned in support of Ethiopia and was arrested and fined for his attempts to encourage the seamen to picket the Italian consulate.[150] The extent of his influence can perhaps be judged by the comments of Harold Moody, the president of the LCP, who in 1935 told the *Western Mail*, 'the coloured people of Cardiff are mainly Communists, simply because no one else has seen fit to give them a helping

146. S. Saklatvala, 'A Few Thoughts on Party Work,' RGASPI 495/100/938.

147. Ward to Huiswoud, 26 June 1935, RGASPI 495/155/102. The CFAA was registered as a 'Friendly Society in 1939. See (TNA) FS 27/294.

148. J. E. Jones, 'The Anti-Colonial Politics and Policies of the CPGB: 1920-1951,' Ph.D Thesis, University of Wolverhampton, 1997, p.163.

149. 'Coloured Seamen's Struggle Against De-nationalisation Memorandum,' *NW*, 5/9 (September 1935) pp. 10-12.

150. *NW*, 5/11 (December 1935) p.25.

hand.'[151] Two years later, in 1937, O'Connell was still writing of the problems facing those in Cardiff, but he also reported that a Colonial Defence Association had been successfully organised with a membership that was increasing on a daily basis.[152]

In 1935, the NWA and other organisations including the LAI, LCP and India Swaraj League were involved in establishing a Colonial Seamen's Association (CSA). [153] The chairman of the CSA was Chris Jones and Roland Sawyer, the secretary of the NWA, became a member of its executive committee.[154] According to the Association's secretary, the Indian Communist Surat Ali, the CSA was established as, 'the expression of the discontent existing among the colonial seamen and its aim was to redress their grievances.'[155] It held its first annual conference in November 1936 attended by over fifty workers and passed resolutions condemning discrimination against colonial seamen and the openly racist Shipping (Assistance) Act of 1935.[156] In February 1937 it was one of the first organisations to respond to an appeal from the ITUCNW to protest against any proposal to return colonies or mandated territories to Germany. In a letter sent to the League of Nations and Britain's Foreign Secretary it demanded, 'that the Colonial People be given full democratic rights to determine their own destiny and to bring about their national emancipation from the present imperialist domination which dwarfs their manhood by starving the masses and by curtailing their civil liberties.'[157] The CSA is an example of the increasing unity that could exist during this period, when it was possible for those of different political persuasions to work together for common goals. The ITUCNW was certainly in contact with the CSA and the Coloured Nationals Mutual Social

---

151. See Sherwood, 'Racism and Resistance,' and *The Keys,* 3/2 (October-December 1935) pp.15-24. Moody is quoted in N. Evans, 'Regulating the Reserve Army: Arabs, Blacks and the Local State in Cardiff, 1919-45,' in K. Lunn (Ed.) *Race and Labour in Twentieth Century Britain* (London, 1985) p.98.

152. *Colonial Information Bulletin* 11, 15 September 1937, p.10. See also *Africa and the World,* 1/1 (6 July 1937) p.10. For another mention of the CDA's activities in Cardiff see, *Colonial Information Bulletin* 16, 30 November 1937, p.9. See also O'Connell's letter on behalf of the CDA to Moody, in *The Keys,* 6/1 (July-September 1938) p.5.

153. *NW,* 7/2, February 1937:4 and M. Sherwood, 'Lascar Struggles Against Discrimination in Britain 1923-45: The Work of N.J. Upadhyaya and Surat Alley.' *The Mariner's Mirror*, 90/4, November 2004: 438-455. See also 'Colonial Seamen Organise,' *NW,* 5/9 (September 1935) p.22.

154. 'Communism and the West Indian Labour Disturbances,' 1 June 1938, (TNA) CO 295/606/4.

155. Sherwood, 'Lascar Struggles,' p.443.

156. 'Colonial Seamen's Conference,' *NW,* 7/2 (February 1937) p.4. See also C. Jones, 'Britain's Coloured Seamen,' in *The Keys,* 5/1 (July-September 1937) pp.17-18.

157. 'No Colonies to Hitler,' *NW,* 7/3 (March 1937) pp.1 and 7.

Club, established in 1934 by African, Caribbean, Indian, and Malay seamen in South Shields.[158]

The 1935 Constitution of the NWA

In 1935, at its first annual general meeting for two years, the NWA attempted to solve some of the many problems that it faced. In his welcome address Bridgeman, the Association's chairman, was the first of several speakers to point out that as a result of the Italian invasion of Ethiopia, not only had war 'broken out in Africa' but also as a consequence of this conflict, and the international situation in general, 'the peace of the whole world is in danger.' He stressed that in these circumstances the NWA had the responsibility to exert all its efforts in defence of the Ethiopian people and also to assist 'the Negro peoples,' throughout Britain, the British Empire and elsewhere in the world, who were daily 'being victimised in many different ways,' and 'looking to Britain for support in their struggle against foreign aggression, land robbery and exploitation.' It was necessary, Bridgeman concluded, to strengthen the NWA 'to a much greater degree than we have been able to do hitherto.'[159]

The 1935 Conference therefore aimed to lay the foundations of a 'really powerful' organisation and the participants openly discussed what they considered to be the NWA's main problems and weaknesses. One obvious impediment was the fact that after four years it was still small, poorly supported and not widely known. At the conference it was announced that there were only fifteen NWA members and one participant declared that he had not heard of it before attending the meeting. However, the chief explanation for such weaknesses, according to its leaders, was that the NWA needed to be totally 'under Negro leadership.' Indeed Bridgeman argued that there was a lack of support because 'coloured peoples look at an organisation started by white men with extreme circumspection,' because the NWA was viewed as 'merely an English bunch, and because the lack of coloured leadership has hindered our membership.' This was one reason why a new constitution was proposed. This did not advocate 'an exclusively Negro body,' but an organisation 'of which the officers and a majority of the Executive Committee will be Negroes.'[160] In fact the new constitution offered 'associate membership' to those now referred to as 'Non Negroes,' who were henceforth prevented from serving as officers.

158. See *NW*, 5/7-8 (July-August 1935) pp.35-37 and *NW*, 5/9 (September 1935) p.23; Report of the Activities of the ITUCNW, January 1937, RGASPI 534/3/1103. In 1935 Saklatvala spoke at the Social Club to denounce the Shipping Assistance Act.

159. Report of the Annual Conference of the NWA, 20 October 1935, RGASPI 515/301/3943.

160. Ibid.

It is not yet clear what prompted this constitutional change, or how much it was influenced by the decisions of the CI's Seventh Congress. It seem likely that it had been discussed internally for some time, but whether the impetus for the change came from existing members, the CPGB, or the ITUCNW it is difficult to say. Certainly some members, including O'Connell, spoke in favour of maintaining white officers, while other leading members such as Rowland Sawyer and Kenyatta expressed a contrary view. The second major change to the constitution was perhaps also prompted by the recent CI congress, by the need for a less sectarian approach, and to attempt to develop a united front amongst African and Caribbean organisations. In Bridgeman's words 'there had been attached to the existing constitution a political construction which suggested that the NWA was extremist,' and therefore prevented people from joining.[161] Now the language used to describe the NWA's aims and objectives also had to be changed, so that it would 'be more acceptable to the masses of the workers,' could 'present a milder front' and not be charged with 'communist affiliations.' At the very time that there was increasing militancy throughout the world, especially in Africa and the Diaspora, and some growing sympathy for the international communist movement, references to 'capitalist exploitation and imperialist domination,' and 'colonial oppression,' were to be removed. In addition, the new constitution made no mention of the struggle for independence of the colonies at all, although the NWA continued to declare that it stood 'for the national liberation of all Negroes.' Its aims now appeared rather vague and merely committed the organisation to 'render assistance to all Negroes here and whenever possible abroad, on all social, political and economic questions.'[162]

As a result of these constitutional changes, which were accepted 'without dissent', Ward became the new chairman, Rowland Sawyer, secretary, and Eileen Tracey, treasurer.[163] Ben Bradley, who was newly elected to the NWA executive committee, would soon become the leading figure in the CPGB's colonial committee, the body that had the responsibility of overseeing the work of the NWA. Bridgeman and CPGB member Hugo Rathbone also remained on the NWA's executive committee. Eileen Tracey had been a member of the executive committee of the NWA since 1933 but nothing more is known about her. Sawyer had been one of the leading figures in the NWA since 1932. He was born in Freetown, Sierra Leone in 1888, although he may have also lived in the Gold Coast, and was employed as a seaman. It seems that he was interned in Wiesbaden, Germany, during World War I but released on medical grounds and arrived in Britain in 1915. Soon afterwards he was in contact with Hubert

161. Report of the Annual Conference.

162. 'Draft Aims and Objects and Rules and Regulations of the NWA.' Cf. 'Report of the International Secretariat of the LAI, 1935. Reginald Bridgeman Papers (DBN/25).

163. *NW*, 5/11 (December 1935) pp.8-9.

Harrison's Liberty League for Negro Americans in New York but between 1917 and 1932 nothing is known of his life. In 1932 he was employed as a fireman on board Elder and Fyffes ships to Jamaica and in that capacity he became connected with the NWA, ITUCNW and LAI and used his position to transport LAI and ITUCNW literature to Jamaica. He continued his life as a seafarer, according to the security services, becoming a CPGB member in 1934, and in the following year one of the leaders of the CSA.[164] In 1940 Sawyer co-wrote a play, *Colour Bar,* about the life of an African student in London in the late 1930s who attempts to combat the everyday racism he faces and eventually becomes a Communist.[165]

The three resolutions passed at the conference, on Ethiopia, West Africa and Britain, give a clear indication of the NWA's main concerns at that time. The lengthy discussion and resolution on the situation facing black people in Britain suggests that the key tasks of the Association had become much more focused. At the previous Annual General Meeting, held in 1933, many of the leading members had emphasised that the main aims were simply 'to build up contacts with the workers' organisations in the colonial countries, and at the same time to work to obtain the support of white workers for the objects of the Association.'[166]

Harry O'Connell presented the statement on 'Negro Problems in Britain,' in which he highlighted the terrible conditions of unemployment and racism facing the black population of Britain, conditions that had been made worse by the recent British Shipping Assistance Act. [167] O'Connell estimated that there were about four thousand men 'of Negro origin' in Britain and that most were unemployed. The 'theatrical and amusement professions,' he claimed, 'provide the only, but most irregular sources of income for a small minority.' In conclusion he spoke of the need for a strong organisation to oppose racism and to 'put the facts before British workers' in order to 'get their solidarity in a united campaign.' He called for the NWA to establish branches not just in London but also in Cardiff, Liverpool and South Shields, 'wherever there are large numbers of Negroes.' Rowland Sawyer, who spoke in support of the statement, stressed the need for 'a much wider organisation of Negroes in order to fight effectively for their rights.' [168]

164. 'Communism and the West Indian Labour Disturbances,' MI5 Report, 6 January 1938, (TNA) CO 295/606/4. At the present time MI5 is refusing to release any further information on Sawyer or any others connected with the NWA.

165. A. M. Bagshaw and E. Sawyer, *Colour Bar* (London, n.d.).

166. NWA Secretary's Report for Presentation to the AGM, 20 October 1935. RGASPI 515/301/3943.

167. Statement on Negro Problems in Britain, NWA October 1935.

168. Report of Annual Conference of the NWA, 20 October 1935. RGASPI 515/301/3943. On the Shipping Assistance Act see Tabili, *"We Ask For British Justice,"* p.158.

S.R. Wood, the secretary of the delegation of the GCARPS, proposed the resolution on West Africa. It seems likely that the NWA had consulted with Wood and other West Africans, including the WASU, which was represented at the conference by its secretary-general, Ladipo Solanke. The resolution was therefore an authoritative document, incorporating the views of West Africans engaged in the anti-colonial struggle and their allies in Britain. In short, it protested against the increasingly autocratic nature of colonial rule, such as the banning of LAI and ITUCNW publications, and what was referred to as 'open fascism' in some colonies. The conference therefore demanded 'the full and unrestricted right of organisation for all African workers, the right of assembly and the right of free press, as well as the abolition of the tyrannical laws and ordinances which discriminate between white and black workers; and the freedom of all political prisoners.' The resolution declared, 'that there is no possibility of reforming imperialist control of the colonies,' and it demanded 'the complete national independence of all African territories now subject to foreign control with the full unfettered opportunity for each nation to determine its own system of government.'[169]

The final resolution, moved by Jomo Kenyatta, was in support of 'the heroic people of Ethiopia,' who were 'being forced to bravely defend the independence of their country against the invasion of Italian imperialism.' The NWA and its members, especially those in Cardiff, had played an active role in the protests against the fascist invasion, and in London there were joint actions with the IAFA. The conference resolution condemned all attempts by the big powers to carve up Ethiopia and expressed the view that the struggle of the Ethiopian people symbolised the struggles of those in the colonies fighting for liberation. It recognised that the struggle over the future of Ethiopia had become a major international issue, the 'beginning of a new world war,' as one participant expressed it, and a clear example of the danger represented by fascism. The Conference therefore demanded collective sanctions against Italy under the auspices of the League of Nations and immediate assistance for the defence of Ethiopia. Kenyatta also reiterated the need for the NWA to work with the LCP and the IAFA, yet another example of the sentiment for a united front so evident in this period.[170]

A New Lease of Life?

Despite the urgings of Huiswoud and the resolutions of 1935 it is difficult to establish exactly how the NWA strengthened its activities thereafter. It clearly

169. Resolution on West Africa, Annual Conference of the NWA, 20 October 1935, RGASPI 515/1/3943.

170. Resolution on Abyssinia, Annual Conference of the NWA, 20 October 1935. See also *NW*, 5/11 (December 1935) p.9.

participated with other organisations such as the LCP, and particularly the IAFA, in the mass opposition to the invasion of Ethiopia.[171] Kenyatta's 'Hands off Abyssinia,' which appeared in the CPGB's *Labour Monthly* in September 1935, was written while he was the secretary of the IAFA as well as a member of the NWA.[172] It continued its work to develop the CSA and the Scottsboro Defence Committee and was also part of the reception committee established by African and Caribbean organisations to welcome the Ethiopian emperor, Haile Selassie, into exile in Britain in 1936.[173] The British security services even reported that Ward was temporarily expelled from the NWA leadership and from the CPGB in April 1936 for failing to implement the agreed changes in the work of the NWA, but there is at present no further information to corroborate this report.[174] Certainly Ward remained a 'corresponding editor' of *The Negro Worker* throughout this period, and he and Sawyer both continued to play leading roles in the LAI. This was a time when Padmore and his allies, such as Chris Jones, Ras Makonnen and Kenyatta stepped up their attacks on the LAI, partly on the grounds that there were too few representatives from Africa and the Caribbean in its leadership, but also because they objected to the fact that the LAI remained under the political leadership of the CPGB. At the LAI conference in February 1937 it was even reported that Ward and Makonnen actually came to blows.[175]

The NWA survived the dissolution of LAI and the ITUCNW in 1937. In April of that year the Secretariat of the CPGB issued a circular to all Party District Committees reminding them that the struggles in the colonies must receive 'serious attention' and that this had not hitherto been the case. District Committees were instructed to make one comrade responsible for colonial work and the CPGB's Colonial Committee announced that it would now issue a *Colonial Information Bulletin* on a regular basis. As a result of the dangerous international situation, the growing contention between the big powers, the Italian invasion of Abyssinia, the role of colonial troops in the Spanish Civil War, the CPGB now placed more emphasis on work in the colonies and amongst all those connected with the colonies living in Britain. Rather than underestimating the importance of the colonial question, for which it had

171. See B. Bush, *Imperialism, Race and Resistance: Africa and Britain 1919-1945* (London, 1999) p.258.

172. *Labour Monthly*, (9 September 1935) pp.632-636.

173. Robert A. Hill (ed.) *The Marcus Garvey and Universal Negro Improvement Association Papers,* (Berkeley, 1983), vol. 7, p. 695 n.8; *NW*, March 1936, p.12.

174. 'Communism and the West Indian Labour Disturbances,' (TNA) CO 295/606/4.

175. India Office Records (IOR) L/P&J/12/275, British Library.

hitherto been criticised, the CPGB now saw its solution as vital in the struggle against fascism and war.[176]

One of the key issues highlighted in the CPGB circular was the need to agitate in the growing peace movement against appeasement and the 'proposals for a redistribution of colonial spheres of influence and an extension of the mandatory system of colonial rule' which were being advocated by the appeasers in response to Nazi Germany's demands for colonies. In opposition to such demands the CPGB made clear its position, which was to support 'the right of colonial peoples to freedom' as well as more immediate demands for 'Civil Liberties and Democratic Rights.'[177] This orientation was evident in the speech given by Arnold Ward to the National Peace Council's 'Peace and the Colonial Problems' conference in 1935 in which he condemned those who sought peace in Europe at the expense of those in the colonies, who he pointed out, 'have no voice in the transfer of their countries,' and 'no voice in the selling of their raw materials, though they have to produce them.' Moreover, Ward asserted that contrary to the view of the imperialists 'black people' were quite capable of 'governing themselves in the interest of their own people.'[178] The possible transfer of the colonies was to become a key issue in the years leading up to the outbreak of war, as is clear from the 'Appeal To All Negro Organisations' issued by the ITUCNW in January 1937.[179]

In a statement on 'Peace and the Colonial Question' issued in June 1938 the CPGB linked the success of the anti-colonial struggles with that of the movement against war and declared, 'every advance of the colonial peoples towards their freedom strengthens the front of the peoples for peace all over the world, and weakens imperialism, the cause of war.'[180] At the same time, it presented a 'Charter of Rights for Colonial People,' including universal suffrage, free education, trade union rights and other freedoms, which it argued should be demanded and fought for by the 'Labour and Peace Movements' in Britain. The CPGB's new colonial policy aimed to build unity on this question as part of its efforts to establish an alternative to the 'pro-fascist policy' of the National Government in Britain, to establish a Popular Front movement in Britain to strengthen the international movement against imperialism and war. The new policy was also evident in the joint statement on colonialism issued by the CPGB, Independent Labour Party and Socialist League in 1937. The CPGB

176. Circular from CPGB Secretariat to all District Party Committees, 16 April 1937, (TNA) CO 323/ 1517/1; *Colonial Information Bulletin (CIB)*, 1 June 1938, pp.2-5.

177. Circular from CPGB Secretariat, 16 April 1937.

178. Quoted in R. P. Dutt, *World Politics 1918-1936* (London, 1936) pp.190-191.

179. *NW*, 7/2 (February 1937) p.3.

180. *CIB*, 1 June 1938, pp.1-5.

supported the strikes and rebellions that were taking place throughout Britain's colonies in the Caribbean, and even sent a Party delegation to a meeting at the Colonial Office, as well as participating alongside the NWA in the 'Peace and Empire' conference convened by the India League and the Scottish Peace Council held in Glasgow in 1938.[181]

At the Fifteenth Congress of the CPGB, in September 1938, a further statement on the colonial question was issued which condemned the latest repressive measures enacted throughout the empire, supported the anti-war struggles and demands for independence of the Indian people, and the strikes and demonstrations throughout the Caribbean. The statement declared that for 'the colonial people' there was 'very little difference between Italian and German fascism and British imperialism,' and refuted what it referred to as 'lying propaganda' that the CP was 'asking the colonial peoples to support Imperialism in a war situation.' The congress made clear that the CP had 'not departed from its fundamental demand with regard to the colonies,' which it reaffirmed, 'is the right of complete independence.'[182]

The NWA therefore took a strong stand over Nazi Germany's demand for a re-division of colonial territories and demanded that in the struggle against fascism, the position of the colonies and the role of the colonial peoples should not be ignored. It continued to demand colonial self-government, which it stressed, was also the 'key to world peace.' It also warned that fascism and war might be unleashed against the struggles of those in the colonies and the workers in Britain, that for this and other reasons they had a common struggle and that therefore the workers in Britain must support anti-colonial demands as part of a broader anti-fascist offensive. It declared that 'none of the handicaps at present placed on the colonial peoples are inevitable, and that the evils now existing in the world – the perpetual threat of war, the malnutrition, illiteracy, disease and chronic poverty of colonial countries – can be eliminated by the united efforts of the workers and peace-loving peoples the world over.'[183]

The importance of the colonial question for the CPGB contributed to a new lease of life for the NWA, as did the organisation's new leadership. In 1937 Peter Blackman, another Barbadian and a former missionary in West Africa, joined the NWA and later the CPGB. Blackman, who was born in Barbados in 1909, arrived in Britain in 1933 and studied Theology in St Augustine's College, Canterbury. For a short while he worked in the Gambia as a missionary, but soon resigned because of a crisis of faith and because he 'would not tolerate discrimination on principle between workers who together ostensibly

181. *NW*, 7/2 (February 1937) p.4.

182. *CIB*, 30 September 1938, pp.6-7.

183. NWA, Annual General Meeting, 28 January 1939.

are out to spread the gospel of love and brotherhood.'[184] Two months after joining the NWA and CPGB, in November 1937 shortly after his return from West Africa, Blackman was co-opted onto the NWA executive committee and then appointed its chairman. The following year he became a member of the CPGB's Colonial Committee with some responsibility for what were referred to as 'Negro matters.'[185]

Blackman's role was to visit those areas where there were significant black communities, such as Manchester, Liverpool and North Shields, on behalf of the CPGB, and there is some evidence that he was also trying to unite several of the 'coloured organisations in England.' Indeed following Ward's initial demand there were other calls for such unity in the years leading up to the outbreak of war, and in 1936 the LCP had called for a 'conference of all Negro organisations in the country.' The CPGB clearly supported such a proposal and a committee to convene what subsequently became the 'African Peoples, Democracy and World Peace' conference was soon established, comprising the LCP, NWA, Gold Coast Students' Association and CFAA.[186] The initiative also had the support of O'Connell who wrote to Harold Moody on behalf of the Colonial Defence Association, 'We believe it is very important at this stage for the complete unification of all the coloured peoples of Britain.[187] Certainly the NWA, LCP and other organisations increasingly worked together during this period, although Padmore and the IASB continued to attack the CPGB's colonial policy. Blackman organised amongst seamen in East London, apparently trying to re-establish seamen's clubs in Poplar, as well as in Liverpool, North Shields and possibly elsewhere.[188] He quickly cultivated contacts with all the key African and Caribbean activists in Britain, becoming a significant figure in the LCP and the editor of *The Keys*. In January 1939, Moody asked Blackman to become the League's secretary, despite his political views, and apparently even wrote of a possible merger between the LCP and the NWA.[189] Certainly during this period the LCP worked closely with the NWA, and even the CPGB, and there were several attempts to establish a united front between

184. I'm grateful to Marika Sherwood for this information, originally supplied by the Senior Archivist from the Dean and Chapter of Canterbury, 1 June 1994.

185. Annual Report, NWA, December 1937-December 1938; Blackman apparently parted company from the CPGB in 1939 only to rejoin in 1947.

186. CPGB Colonial Committee, 21 February 1936, RGASPI 495/14/360a/2.

187. *The Keys*, 6/1 (July-September 1938) p.5. The following year the LCP claimed that it was working to unify 'coloured organisations' in London. *The Keys*, 7/1 (July-September 1939) p.7.

188. See letter from Ben Bradley to Manchester District Communist Party, 10 November 1937, (TNA) KV 2/1838.

189. Moody to Blackman, 1 January 1939, (TNA) KV 2/1838.

all the African and Caribbean organisations. On the eve of war, in July 1939, the 'African Peoples, Democracy and World Peace' conference finally took place. Speakers included the future Labour Colonial Secretary, Creech Jones, several Labour MPs, Padmore, and many others.[190]

There is some indication that Blackman did not have strong communist convictions, and that he had some differences with the CPGB. His commitment to the CPGB was certainly not as durable as that of Desmond Buckle, who became the new secretary of the NWA in 1939. Buckle originated from the Gold Coast but had come to Britain to be educated when still a young child. He had formerly been the leading figure in the Gold Coast Students' Association but joined the NWA and CPGB in 1937 and remained a Party member until his death in 1964.[191] Blackman and Buckle led the NWA at a time when major rebellions were breaking out in the Caribbean and the NWA played an important role, fundraising, liaising with trade unions and anti-colonial organisations in the Caribbean and holding public meetings to enlighten people in Britain about the developing struggles. The anti-colonial struggle in the Caribbean provided an opportunity for the NWA to organise its own meetings and to speak at over sixty meetings held by other organisations in 1938. In July 1937 Paul Robeson was the main performer at an NWA event called in solidarity with the rebellion in Jamaica, which was attended by nearly a thousand people. When the government established the Moyne Commission to investigate the causes of the rebellions, the NWA gave evidence to it and joined with the LCP and IASB to submit a joint memorandum.[192]

The NWA was also instrumental in forming the Committee for West Indian Affairs (CWIA), which was established following a meeting in the House of Commons in November 1938. The CWIA's chairman was the future Colonial Secretary Arthur Creech Jones and it included amongst its members other Labour MPs as well as trade unionists from Britain and the Caribbean. Blackman, who was honorary secretary, and Bridgeman were also members, as was Harold Moody. The CWIA was formed for the purpose of 'giving publicity to conditions in the West Indies, to make representations to Government

190. *The Keys*, 7/1 (July-September 1939) pp.4-5.

191. See e.g. Blackman to R. Bridgeman 30 December 1940, DCL 99/1, NCCL Papers, University of Hull and Special Branch Report, 2 February 1949, (TNA) KV 2/1838. On Buckle see H. Adi, 'Forgotten Comrade? Desmond Buckle: An African Communist in Britain,' *Science and Society*, 70/1 (2002) pp.22-46.

192. Ibid. See also *The Keys*, 6/2 (October-December 1938) p. 15. The NWA, LCP and IASB also jointly submitted a memorandum to the government's Commission of Inquiry regarding a possible union of Nyasaland with Northern and Southern Rhodesia. However, the collaboration was not without its difficulties and apparently on one occasion Padmore and Blackman almost came to blows.

Departments, and to give other such help to the West Indian people as can be mobilised in this country.[193] It called on the Trade Union Congress to give more support to trade unions in the Caribbean and their demand for social and political reforms.[194] It also campaigned over the imprisonment of the Barbadian activist Ulric Grant and was involvwed in the defence campaign of the Trinidadian labour leader Uriah Butler, who had begun an appeal to the Privy Council after his arrest and imprisonment by the colonial government.[195]

The NWA therefore continued with its role as a propagandist and pressure group, sometimes working with other organisations to hold meetings and submit resolutions and letters to the press, sometimes directly involved in the creation of new organisations such as the CSA and the CFAA. It also continued to develop its links and activities with individuals and organisations in Africa and the Caribbean, and to disseminate revolutionary publications in the colonies through the many seafarers that left British ports.[196] Although the NWA outlived the LAI and the ITUCNW it does not appear to have survived long during the war, although as yet it not clear why or when its activities ceased.[197] Certainly its leading figures such as Blackman, especially Buckle continued their political activities and during the war and Blackman became noted for his wartime poems 'My Song Is For All Men' and 'Stalingrad'.

Although the NWA evidently had many weaknesses, it took up the difficult task of organising amongst African and Caribbean workers and communities in Britain, while its call for mass economic and political struggle in the colonies in order to achieve 'complete independence' was far in advance of most other political organisation in Britain during the early 1930s. As in other countries, its weaknesses were a reflection of those of the Communist Party and it was these that the ITUCNW endeavoured to address. It is ironic that it was when the ITUCNW and the LAI were dissolved that the CPGB began to place more emphasis on the African and Caribbean colonies and the NWA and it is

193. Blackman to W. Gillies (Imperial Committee of the Labour Party), 16 November 1938. W. Gillies Papers (WG/BWI/87) Labour History Archive and Study Centre. (My thanks to Marika Sherwood for this reference.) The CWIA worked closely with the British TUC and the Labour Party and attempted to link both with the new trade union and anti-colonial movements in the Caribbean, such as the Oilfield Workers Union in Trinidad and the Peoples' National Party in Jamaica. Other members of the CWIA included D.N. Pritt K.C., Kola Rienzi, Desmond Buckle and Cecil Belfield Clarke.

194. Minutes of the TUC Colonial Advisory Committee, 22 December 1938. TUC Collections- Marjorie Nicholson Papers, London Metropolitan University (972.9).

195. NWA, Annual General Meeting, 28 January 1939.

196. See A.G. Watkis (General-Secretary, the Coloured Nationals Mutual Association, North Shields) to Blackman n.d. (TNA) KV 2/1838.

197. See O'Connell to Blackman, 30 January 1940, (TNA) KV 2/1838.

perhaps in the period leading up to the Second World War that the NWA had some of its greatest successes Certainly it was the call made by Arnold Ward in 1935 for unity amongst the African and Caribbean organisations in Britain that was gradually taken up by others, most notably by George Padmore, during the war years. The call of the CPGB for a Charter for Colonial Peoples had a similar impact and by the end of the war was the universal demand of all the main African and Caribbean organisations in Britain.

Chapter 8

The ITUCNW in the Caribbean

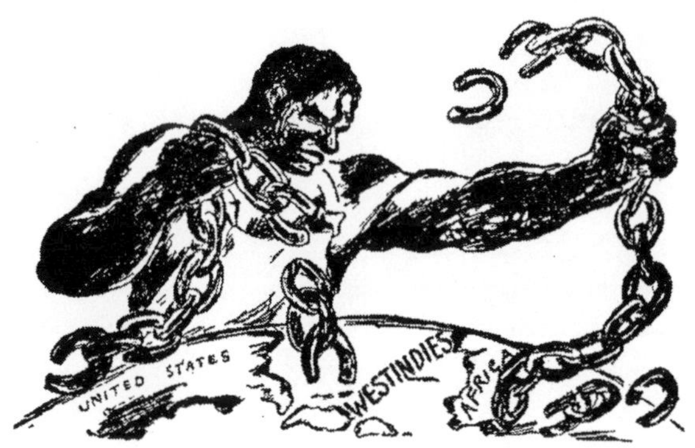

The revolutionary events in Russia and the founding of the Comintern also had an impact on the Caribbean region, which by 1919 was completely dominated by the major imperialist powers. Political control of the Caribbean islands was mostly in the hands of Britain, although France, Holland and the United States also had colonial possessions. By 1919 the United States was emerging as the dominant economic and military power in the region, a dominance expressed by its annexation of Puerto Rico, intervention in Cuba, Nicaragua and Panama, as well as by the invasion of Haiti in 1915 and the Dominican Republic the following year. Opposition to US intervention, as well as to continued colonial rule and economic impoverishment became the key political issues confronting the region in the period following World War I.

The early twentieth century was also a period that witnessed the emergence of trade unions and broad-based political organisations throughout the

Caribbean region. In Trinidad, for example, the Workingmen's Association was formed in the last years of the nineteenth century, while the Labour Congress in Cuba was even older.[1] However, it took several years for workers' organisations to be formed and legally established. In the British West Indies, for example, trade unions were not legalised until after World War I, and in some British colonies not until the 1930s. Under the repressive regimes in such countries as Cuba and Haiti workers' organisations, especially those with communist affiliations, were suppressed. In Haiti in 1936 the government went as far as to outlaw 'any profession of communist faith, oral or written, public or private.'[2] The colonial governments of Britain and France not only attempted to stifle the growth of workers' organisations but also banned and confiscated what they considered to be 'seditious' literature such as *The Negro Worker* and the *Cri des Nègres.* Nevertheless, workers and other sections of the population in the region organised themselves and began to flex their political muscles. The post-World War I period was ushered in by strikes, riots and other protest actions in Trinidad, British Honduras, Jamaica and Grenada.

It was in these circumstances and from a variety of sources that the population of the region were introduced to the revolutionary doctrine and anti-colonialism of the Comintern. The first openly Communist organisation was probably the Groupe Jean Jaurès, formed in Martinique in 1919 by Jules Monnerot and others following a split amongst the members of the Parti Socialiste on the island. The Groupe began the regular publication of its newspaper, *Justice,* even before the creation of the Communist Party in France, but there appears to have been limited contact with the Comintern before the mid-1930s.[3] The PCF and the CI also established links with Guadeloupe, most importantly with the worker activist Sabin Ducadosse, and several activists from the Antilles joined communist-led organisations in France and the PCF itself during the 1920s, including Max Clainville-Bloncourt, Joseph Gothon-Lunion and Stéphane Rosso. Gothon-Lunion, a Paris-based activist from Guadeloupe attended the Comintern's Fifth Congress in 1924 as part of the PCF delegation. Bloncourt and others from the French Antilles attended the founding congress of the LAI in Belgium in 1927, where he spoke on the conditions created by French imperialism in Guadeloupe and Martinique and was one of three Caribbean

1. R. Hart, 'Origins and development of the working class in the English-speaking Caribbean area 1897-1937,' in M.Cross and G. Heuman (eds.) *Labour in the Caribbean* (London, 1988) pp.43-79; A. de la Fuente, 'Two Dangers, One Solution: Immigration, Race, and Labor in Cuba, 1900-1930,' *International Labor and Working-Class History,* 51 (Spring 1997) pp.30-49.

2. M. J. Smith, *Red and Black in Haiti: Radicalism, Conflict and Political Change, 1934-1957* (Chapel Hil, 2009) p.22.

3. R. Ménil, 'Notes sur la development historique du Marxisme à la Martinique,' *Action – Revue Théoretique et Politique,'* 13 (1967) pp.17-30.

members of the committee that drafted the 'Common Resolution on the Negro Question.'[4] Through these activists and their organisations, the UI and CDRN, transnational links where established between the Comintern, the PCF and the French Antilles even before the creation of the ITUCNW in 1928.[5]

The CPGB, on the other hand, appears to have paid little attention to the Caribbean before the late 1930s and outside of the French colonies much of the initiative for communist activity in the early 1920s was placed in the hands of the WP in the United States. It might be considered that such activity would have been strengthened by the close relationship that developed between the Party and the members of the ABB, many of whom like the organisation's founder Cyril Briggs were of Caribbean origin. The ABB's publication, the *Crusader*, maintained something of a Caribbean focus and was evidently distributed and read throughout the Caribbean, not just in Anglophone countries such as Trinidad where it was banned by the colonial authorities in 1920.[6] However, the WP initially made little headway in the Caribbean despite encouragement and criticism from the Comintern, although it paid much more attention to the region, and particularly Haitian and Puerto Rican affairs, following criticism at the Fifth Congress of the CI in 1924 and the founding of the All-American Anti-Imperialist League (AAAIL) early the following year.[7] In 1926 the WP was working with activists in Puerto Rico, such as J. N. Sager one of the leaders of the AAAIL, who were making efforts to establish what in 1927 became the Communist League of Porto Rico in order to pave the way for the creation of a communist party on the island.[8] The following year the WP sent Cyril Briggs to the Caribbean, although his precise mission remains a mystery. The most important development in the region was undoubtedly the founding of the Partido Comunista de Cuba (PCC) in 1925. However, in the early years of its existence the PCC remained an illegal organisation, suffering from severe repression with many of its leading members in prison or exile. Consequently it initially had a limited focus on the Negro Question until the intervention of the CI and the RILU in 1930.[9]

4. 'Discours de Bloncourt, délégué des Antilles,' RGASPI 542/1/69/60-61; J.M. Turner, *Caribbean Crusaders and the Harlem Renaissance* (Chicago, 2005) p.146.

5. See chapter six for further details.

6. M. Stevens, 'The Red International and the Black Caribbean: Transnational Radical Organisations in New York City, Mexico and the West Indies, 1919-1939,' Ph.D Thesis, Brown University, 2010, pp.50-57.

7. Stevens, 'The Red International and the Black Caribbean,' pp.77-78.

8. 'Statement by the Communist League of Porto Rico,' 6 March 1927, RGASPI 542/1/19/32-33 and Stevens, 'The Red International and the Black Caribbean,' pp.147-155.

9. See chapter two and B. Carr, 'From Caribbean backwater to revolutionary opportunity: Cuba's evolving relationship with the Comintern, 1925-34,' in T. Rees and A. Thorpe (eds.) *International Communism and the Communist International, 1919-1943* (Manchester, 1998) pp.234-252.

The Negro Question in Latin America and the Caribbean

From its foundation in 1928 the ITUCNW endeavoured to extend its influence in the Caribbean and also initially in Latin America, although throughout the 1930s its main focus remained on Africa. Even though some of its key activists were from the region, most notably Padmore and Huiswoud, it was only with some difficulty that contacts were gradually established and consolidated. The *raison d'etre* of the ITUCNW was to find ways to overcome the apparent inability of the communist parties, especially those of the US, Britain and France, to take up their responsibilities in regard to the Negro Question. These weaknesses certainly manifested themselves in regard to the Caribbean, while other difficulties, including the precise character of the issues posed by the Negro Question in the region, surfaced in relation to the CI's work in Latin America.

The ITUCNW was initially established with a proposed membership of six, two representing the 'Negro workers of the United States' and one from Cuba, Martinique and Guadeloupe, in addition to a member from South Africa. Subsequently it was envisaged that membership would be extended to include those representing other parts of Africa, as well as Haiti and 'those countries of Latin America where there are considerable numbers of Negro workers (Brazil, Colombia, Venezuela, etc.)'[10] There is no information about which organisations might have supplied the proposed representatives from Martinique and no evidence that the RILU had any links with the Groupe Jean Jaurès. Sabin Ducadosse, who was in contact with the CI, perhaps from as early as 1926, was nominated as the representative from Guadeloupe, although it does not appear that he ever fulfilled this role.[11] The representative from Cuba during the initial phase of the ITUCNW's activities was Sandalio Junco, an Afro-Cuban and a leading trade unionist and Communist whose party name was Hernandez. Subsequently, the ITUCNW focused its activities mainly on the Caribbean and apart from Huiswoud had no other leading members who originated from South America.

In July 1928 at the meeting of the RILU Executive Bureau, at which the ITUCNW and the Negro Bureau were founded, Ricardo Martinez, a Venezuelan Communist who was to play a leading role in Latin America, criticised the resolution on the creation of the ITUCNW and the report of Lozovsky, the RILU secretary-general, because in his view both placed too much emphasis

10. Minutes of Meeting of Executive Bureau of RILU, 31 July 1928, RGASPI 534/3/306.

11. 'On the RILU International Bureau of Negro Workers,' 1928, RGASPI 495/155/53/1. Ducadosse appears to have attended the Fourth RILU Congress and through the PCF had been allocated two thousand francs for work in the Caribbean. 'Report on trip in interests of the ITUCNW,' RGASPI 534/3/450.

on the Caribbean.[12] 'The Negro problem is a problem for the whole of Latin America,' he declared, pointing out that there were more people of African descent in Brazil than in the entire Caribbean. He also rejected a specific focus on Cuba, pointing out that this was only mentioned because a communist party existed there, a fact that he suggested only proved that insufficient work had been undertaken in other countries. In addition, he stressed the importance of establishing contacts in Haiti, which he described as 'a wholly Negro republic,' and a country where US troops had been stationed for many years. He concluded his remarks by stressing that 'Negro work' was 'a continental problem and it should be undertaken as such.'[13]

There were, however, differences of opinion on the importance of the Negro Question in Latin America and how it should be addressed. At the Sixth Congress of the CI in August 1928, at which there was a significant focus on Latin America, Cardenas a delegate from Colombia, made a submission to the Negro Commission in which he declared 'there is no race hatred in Latin America towards the Negroes and the law provides the same rights for blacks and whites.' Although he acknowledged that 'the Negro workers of Latin America are more exploited than the whites,' and 'constitute a first class revolutionary force,' he accepted that not many of them were to be found in the trade unions and 'Party organisations.' He concluded that this was partly due to the fact that they were 'the most backward sections of our workers and peasants.' In his view this discrepancy could be addressed if the communist parties worked more systematically but he added, 'I do not think it necessary to organise the Negro workers separately from the whites in Latin America.'[14] There is no doubt that it was difficult to make generalisations about the Negro Question in Latin America, or even in individual countries. In Cuba, for instance, racism was a major problem, alongside the antagonism that existed between native and foreign-born workers, many of whom were migrants from other Caribbean islands. However, Afro-Cubans were not only strongly unionised in certain sectors of the economy but also often played leadership roles.[15]

The responsibility for organising black workers in the Caribbean and Latin America rested not just with the ITUCNW, or the US, British and French parties, but also with the Confederación Sindical Latinamiericano (CSLA), which was formed in 1929 in Montevideo under the auspices of the RILU. At its founding congress Sandalio Junco gave a major presentation on the

12. The Resolution only mentioned the Negro workers of the US, Africa and the Caribbean.

13. Meeting of the Executive Bureau Profintern, 31 July 1928, RGASPI 534/3/306.

14. 'To the Commission on Work Among Negroes,' 9 August 1928, RGASPI 495/155/56/108-109.

15. A. de la Fuente, 'Two Dangers,' pp.30-49.

Negro Question in Latin America to loud applause, although the issue had not originally been on the congress agenda.[16] However, his comments were based mainly on the Cuban experience and included not just the hardship faced by Afro-Cubans but also the situation facing migrant workers from such countries as Jamaica and Haiti, moreover Junco made no mention of the ITUCNW. Thus, although the presentation contained accounts of the historic struggles of enslaved Africans in Palmares and St Domingue, it suggested that hardly any work had been undertaken in Latin America outside of Cuba, where a Union of Workers of the Antilles had been established especially for Jamaican and Haitian migrant workers. Consequently the main resolutions of the congress stressed the need to recruit Negro workers into the new revolutionary trade union movement and to convince them to take their place amongst the other workers. At the same time, the congress proposed that various actions should be taken against any form of racial discrimination, as well against 'reformism' and Garveyism. The CSLA also resolved to work closely with the TUUL, indeed a sub-commission of the CSLA was established in New York, which had some responsibility for the Caribbean region and for work amongst expatriates in the US.[17] The congress therefore marked the start of work on the Negro Question in Latin America and created the conditions for planned work in several countries including Brazil.[18] What was evident was that unlike the US there were no plans to establish separate Negro workers' organisations in Latin America and it was left to Junco to liaise between the ITUCNW and the CSLA. Indeed he temporarily held the position of vice-chair of the RILU Negro Bureau with responsibility for Latin America and the Francophone Caribbean.[19]

Early in 1930 Junco, on behalf of the RILU Negro Bureau, presented a draft programme for work to be undertaken in the French and Spanish-speaking Caribbean, as well as in Latin American countries such as Colombia, Venezuela and Brazil. The aim was to encourage the affiliates of the RILU to organise specifically amongst Negro workers, especially those on plantations, and to combat any manifestations of racism that excluded them from certain trades, or from trade unions. There was to be a particular emphasis on organising agricultural workers who were 'imported' from such countries as Haiti, Jamaica and Guadeloupe. Most importantly the programme called for a struggle against any signs

16. Junco was to become one of the leaders of the Trotskyism in Cuba. Forced in to exile abroad in 1928 he was expelled from the PCC soon after his return to Cuba in 1932.

17. S. Junco, 'The Problem of the Negro Race and the Proletarian Movement,' 24 June 1930, RGASPI 495/155/87/150.

18. 'Report on the Situation of the Negro Workers in Brazil,' 4 September 1930, RGASPI 495/155/87/322-324.

19. 'Plan of Work of the Negro Bureau of RILU,' 31 December 1930, RGASPI 534/1/164/4-5.

of 'white chauvinism' or the 'underestimation of work among Negroes.' It was notable that one of the proposals suggested that in order to oppose such tendencies as Garveyism it was 'necessary to raise the slogan of self-determination, linking it up with the immediate demands raised by the Negro population throughout all countries.'[20] Here self-determination does not seem to have been connected with the rights of nations, nor with the rights of colonial populations. It was perhaps on this basis that the 'slogan of self-determination' was subsequently also employed in Cuba and Brazil.

It is difficult to assess to what extent this plan to organise amongst Negro workers was implemented, but efforts where made to contact the CSLA, the CGTU and the LDRN in France, the Brazilian Confederation of Labour and others, including the New York sub-commission through which it was intended contact could be made with immigrant workers from Haiti, Panama, the Dominican Republic, Colombia and elsewhere. Of particular interest is the fact that it was proposed that a Spanish edition of *The Negro Worker* should be published, although there is no evidence that this was ever produced.[21]

Huiswoud and Garvey

The first major initiative of the ITUCNW in the Caribbean seems to have been the two visits made by Otto Huiswoud to the region, first in 1929 and again in 1930. Huiswoud's first mission was to attend the Sixth International Convention of the Negro Peoples of the World organised by Garvey's UNIA, held in Jamaica in August 1929. Huiswoud was sent to Jamaica as an official delegate of the ANLC but in fact as the representative of the ITUCNW. Although it considered that the UNIA was undergoing a 'complete disintegration, ' the ITUCNW also accepted that 'the ideology of Garveyism' still exerted some influence and was 'a hindrance to the mass Negro struggle for liberation.'[22] Huiswoud's aim therefore was to 'show up the policy of the UNIA' and to try to organise 'the Left delegates' around the programme of the ITUCNW.' His other task was 'to get connections with the trade unions in Jamaica and the local Communist elements.'[23]

20. 'Plan for Organising the Negro Workers of Haiti, Santo-Domingo, Panama, Colombia, Venezuela, etc.' 13 January 1930, RGASPI 495/79/114/1-5.

21. Ibid.

22. G. Padmore, *The Life and Struggles of Negro Toilers* (Hollywood, 1971) pp.125-126; also N. Nasonov, 'Garveyism – A Reactionary Utopia,' 13 July 1932, RGASPI 495/155/99/72-90.

23. 'Excerpt from Letter from America,' 12 July 1929, RGASPI 495/155/80/49.

The Comintern's approach to the Caribbean had been further elaborated at the founding congress of the League Against Imperialism (LAI) in Brussels in1927. On that occasion Richard B. Moore, the delegate of the ANLC, had been one of the leading figures involved in the drafting of the Resolution on the Negro Question that stated:

> For the Republic of Haiti, Cuba, Santo Domingo and for the peoples of Porto Rico and the Virgin Islands, we must demand complete political and economic independence and the immediate withdrawal of all imperialist troops. For the other Caribbean colonies we must likewise demand and obtain self-government. The Confederation of the British West Indies should be achieved and the Union of all these people accomplished.[24]

This clearly demanded more than the UNIA, although at the Convention, where much of the focus was on Jamaican politics, Garvey did demand 'representation in the Imperial Parliament for a larger modicum of self-government' in Jamaica, as well as 'protection of Native labour.' However, Garvey's record as a supporter of the workers' struggles had received a setback earlier in 1929 when he had encouraged striking Jamaican dock workers to return to work.[25]

At the Convention Huiswoud made a lengthy intervention 'challenging Garvey's theories and his sincerity,' and, according to his own account, made a significant impact on the participants. He managed to outline the programme of the ANLC, publically criticised Garvey, and 'denounced his "back to Africa" and business schemes.'[26] As a consequence, Garvey challenged him to a public debate on whether 'the Negro Problem can be solved only through International Labor Cooperation,' which was held in front of an audience of three thousand people in Kingston's Edleweiss Park. During the debate Garvey reportedly presented himself as a firm supporter of capitalism, arguing: 'If we dare to destroy the capitalists, we are going to destroy the means of getting some of the good

24. 'Common Resolution on the Negro Question,' quoted in W.B. Turner and J.M Turner (eds.) *Richard B. Moore, Caribbean Militant in Harlem: Collected Writings 1927-1972* (Bloomington, 1992) pp.144-146. It is interesting to note that following the congress the CDRN in France also demanded a Caribbean federation in the pages of *La Voix des Nègres*. See M. van Enckevort, 'The Life and Work of Otto Huiswoud: Professional Revolutionary and Internationalist (1893 - 1961)' Ph.D Thesis, (UWI, 2001) p.56 n.97.

25. 'Marcus Garvey Holds First Political Meeting at Cross Roads,' 9 September 1929, in R. Hill et al (eds.) *The Marcus Garvey and UNIA Papers, vol. 7* (London, 1991) pp. 328-344 and O.E. Huiswoud, 'Report on the UNIA Convention,' August 1929, RGASPI 500/1/5/54-60. See also A. Gold, 'La situation des travailleurs de la Jamaique,' *L'Ouvrier Nègre*, 25 June 1930, pp.16-19.

26. See ' Proposed leaflet for distribution Garvey Convention,' n.d., RGASPI 515/1/1842.

things in life,' and 'there is nothing enslaving labor, but labor itself.' For his part, Huiswoud outlined the nature of capitalist exploitation, not failing to mention the contemporary imperialist exploitation of Africa and the Caribbean. He concluded that 'the Negro problem was definitely a class problem.'[27]

Following the debate Huiswoud's views were published in the local press and several UNIA members approached him seeking to form new trade unions.[28] He subsequently held several meetings for this purpose, with hundreds of workers attending, and established a number of local committees as well as an organising committee of what he suggested should be called the Jamaica Trades and Labour Union.[29] The chairman of the organising committee was also vice-president of the Kingston branch of the UNIA. By the time Huiswoud left the island he reported that the Union had recruited two hundred members representing the dockers, masons, sugar boiler workers, dressmakers and office workers.[30]

In the wake of such a successful visit Huiswoud recommended that someone should be sent immediately to continue the work he had started. In his view 'the workers are rapidly attaining political consciousness,' and 'are ready to be organised.' He concluded that 'it is our communist duty to immediately tackle this situation and build a strong movement in the West Indies.' He suggested that the ITUCNW or the TUUL should take responsibility for this work, but he also thought that the LAI, as well as the CPGB supported by the RILU and the CI, should be involved.[31] However, there is no evidence that this work was continued before Huiswoud's return to Jamaica the following year in connection with the preparations for the Hamburg Conference.[32]

27. O.E. Huiswoud, 'Report on the UNIA Convention,' August 1929, RGASPI 500/1/5/54-60.

28. For a report of the debate see 'How can the Negro Problem be solved,' *The Daily Gleaner*, 15 August 1929, p.10. Also Hill, *The Marcus Garvey and UNIA Papers*, p.344 n.1.

29. Post suggests that a union with this name had been in existence since 1907. See K. Post, *Arise Ye Starvelings: The Jamaican Labour Rebellion of 1938 and its Aftermath* (The Hague, 1978) p.4.

30. O.E. Huiswoud, 'Report on the UNIA Convention,' August 1929, RGASPI 500/1/5/54-60. See also van Enckevort, 'The Life and Work of Otto Huiswoud,' pp. 50-53; J. M. Turner, *Caribbean Crusaders* p.139 and Turner and Turner, *Richard B. Moore*, p.55.

31. O.E Huiswoud, 'Report on the UNIA Convention,' August 1929, RGASPI 500/1/5/54-60. Huiswoud made similar comments in the *Daily Worker*. See van Enckevort, 'The Life and Work of Otto Huiswoud,' p.54.

32. In 1930 aborted plans were discussed to send Moscow-trained 'instructors' to the Caribbean. See 'Proposals in Regard to Sending Instructors to the Negro Colonies and for the Establishment of a Course for the Training of Such Instructors in Moscow,' 20 May 1930. RGASPI 495/155/86.

The Hamburg Conference

The work of the ITUCNW in Latin American countries and the Caribbean was intensified as part of the preparations for the International Conference of Negro Workers in the summer of 1930. It was expectated that delegates would attend from Cuba, Panama and from Honduras, where Martinez was charged with overseeing the arrangements, as well as from Trinidad and Guadeloupe.[33] James Ford was in contact with the National Labour Confederation of Cuba, under the leadership of the PCC, while in Honduras Martinez had apparently 'selected a Negro delegate' who was also 'Secretary of the Party there.'[34] Conditions were seen to be favourable because preparations were also being made to bring delegates from Latin America to Moscow for the Fifth Congress of the RILU. However the only delegate who eventually managed to attend the Conference, which eventually took place in Hamburg, was from Jamaica; no other countries from the Caribbean or Latin America were represented.

During the preparatory period for the Hamburg Conference the ITUCNW's main organiser in the Caribbean was Otto Huiswoud, who travelled widely in the region with his Guyanese wife Hermina (Helen Davis). Huiswoud was initially given a mission to visit Jamaica and Trinidad but subsequently was also directed to visit Haiti in order to liaise with Henry Rosemond, a US-based activist of Haitian origin. Eventually, during a trip lasting some four months, the Huiswouds also visited Barbados, British and Dutch Guiana, Curaçao, Cuba, Colombia, and Venezuela, although very little is known about most of their activities.[35]

Rosemond was a member of the ANLC, a leading figure in the New York branch of the Haitian Patriotic Union, vice-president of the new Furrier's Union, and officially a member of the preparatory committee for the Hamburg Conference who had previously attended the Frankfurt conference of the LAI. He had been in Haiti since the previous December, almost certainly in connection with the uprising against US military occupation that had occurred at that time.[36] He had already established a branch of the LAI in Haiti, so evidently he was a

33. The Panamanian delegate was reportedly arrested. See J. Ford. 'The First International Conference of Negro Workers and future tasks,' RGASPI 495/155/290-296.

34. J. Ford, 'Report on the Preparations for the London Conference,' 12 May 1930, RGASPI 534/3/546.

35. Turner, *Caribbean Crusaders*, p.153. It is not clear to what extent these visits were also on behalf of the ITUCNW. In Cuba it was reported that the Huiswood's fell foul of the authorities and were forced to leave. See Post, *Arise Ye Starvelings*, p.5.

36. See J. Wilenkin, 'Dollar Diplomacy in Haiti,' *The Negro Worker (NW)* Vol. 2 No.6 (December 1929) pp.4-8. On Rosemond's and the Worker's Party involvement with Haiti see M. Stevens, '"Hands of Haiti" Self-determination, Anti-imperialism, and the Communist Movement in the United States, 1925-1929,' *The Black Scholar*, 37/4 (Winter 2008) pp. 61-70.

regular visitor, but as he had left the US in some haste he was uninformed about the preparations for the London/Hamburg conference, hence Husiwoud's visit. The Haitian branch of the LAI was reportedly 'composed exclusively of the intellectuals and upper class groups of Haiti,' so Huiswoud's mission was also to make sure that a delegate was elected and sent to Europe from the ranks of the workers. In fact Huiswoud failed in this mission because Rosemond managed to get himself elected as the delegate, much to the displeasure of James Ford and the other leading members of the ITUCNW. Subsequently Rosemond was instructed to stand down although this instruction was contradicted by a letter from Padmore which, written in ignorance of all the facts, appeared to endorse his election. It took several letters from Ford, and a further visit by Martinez before the matter was resolved. Consequently no delegate from Haiti arrived at the conference, an illustration of the difficulties which the ITUCNW experienced developing its work in the Caribbean mainly from outside the region.[37]

Huiswoud's mission in Haiti was also handicapped by his 'lack of knowledge of French,' he had to use Rosemond as an interpreter, and the fact that the Haitian government had placed restrictions on public meetings. The political situation was also unfavourable because of the ITUCNW's focus on workers, whereas most Haitians, including the executive committee of the local LAI, focused on what Huiswoud rather disapprovingly referred to as the 'Nationalist cause,' seemingly without reflecting on its significance. This was a period of rising opposition to the US occupation and the collaborationist government of Louis Borno and most Haitians, including even future Communists such as Jacques Roumain, espoused nationalist politics. Husiwoud reported that 'nothing could get a hearing except the question of evacuation of the American occupation, the election of a Legislative Assembly and the overthrow of Borno.'[38]

The ITUCNW's analysis of the international situation concluded that the struggles of the workers and people in the Caribbean region were on the rise. In addition to the revolt in Haiti, there was also increasing unrest in Venezuela, where the government had banned further immigration from the Caribbean. In Jamaica there had been a series of strikes by dockers and transport workers and the colonial government had been compelled to disband the locally recruited army regiment and replace it with British troops. [39] There were also signs of unrest in Trinidad, British Guiana, Barbados and Grenada. For the RILU there

37. J. Ford, 'Report on the Preparations for the London Conference,' 12 May 1930, RGASPI 534/3/546.

38. Louis Borno, President of Haiti (1922-1930) during the period of US occupation was forced from office in May 1930. Earlier that year *The Negro Worker* published a letter from a 'Haitian Worker' suggesting that 'there is a Communist Party starting in Haiti and this will be our leader.' *NW*, 4/3 (March 1930) p.12.

39. See 'Jamaican Dockers Demand 8 Hour Day,' *NW* 4/3 (March 1930) pp.13-14.

was also the question of how to organise and work with such organisations as the Trinidad Labour Party and Workingmen's Association that were clearly under the influence of the British Labour Party. Should this task be the responsibility of the NMM in Britain, the TUUL in the US, or the CSLA?[40]

From Haiti Huiswoud returned to Jamaica in order to find a delegate for the Hamburg Conference from the Jamaica Labour and Trade Union (JLTU). Since the Union was, in Huiswoud's view 'mainly composed of Garveyites,' he admitted that 'securing the right type of individual' posed some problems. In addition he reported that 'Marcus [Garvey] tried to influence his members to select an outstanding leader of his organisation,' but Huiswoud managed to thwart this attempt. He eventually reported that 'we selected a railway worker, who, while he is a Garveyite, is one of the best workers in the union and has some understanding of the class struggle.' However, he admitted that they might have selected a better delegate.[41] In fact De Leon, the delegate who was initially described as a 'railway worker' travelled to Europe as the only representative from the Caribbean. He was reported to be a 'produce dealer' and declared, 'I am no bolshevik or Communist, never was and never will be.' After the Conference Ford disparagingly referred to him as a 'petty trade union official.' However, Huiswoud's second visit to the island consolidated links with the JLTU, which established closer contact with the ITUCNW.[42]

In Trinidad, Huiswoud's activities were impeded by the intervention of the colonial authorities. He was reportedly told by a police inspector 'We wont have any of your damn foreign agitators come in here and make trouble among our workers.'[43] Huiswoud wrote to Padmore from Port of Spain admitting that his task in the Caribbean had been difficult one 'because of the very poor contacts we have and the fact that it is hard to find some real class-conscious elements. They are either connected with the Garvey movement, as is the case in Jamaica, or they have not the slightest concept of what a labor movement is.' Trinidad, Huiswoud concluded, was 'the worst of the islands' and 'the most difficult place, for we have no real contacts.' His task was made more difficult by the fact everything was dominated by Cipriani, the Mayor of Port of Spain and founder of the Trinidad Labour Party, with whom it was apparently impossible to cooperate. Huiswoud also had a poor opinion of the local agent of the *Liberator*, the publication of the ANLC, who was supposed to be leading the

40. 'Resolution on the Recent Revolutionary Situation Among Negro Toilers,' RGASPI 534/3/499.

41. Huiswoud to Padmore, 14 April 1930, RGASPI 534/4/330.

42. Post, *Arise Ye Starvelings*, p. and 5 and J. Ford, 'Report on the Preparations for the London Conference,' 12 May 1930, RGASPI 534/3/546.

43. Turner, *Caribbean Crusaders*, p.153.

opposition to Cipriani but who, according to Huiswoud had 'not the slightest concept of trade unionism.'[44]

While Huiswoud was in Trinidad, Ford tried unsuccessfully to send him instructions to proceed to Guadeloupe to meet with Sabin Ducadosse. Ducadosse had written to Ford at some length complaining that he had not received any communication from Moscow. His only source of information appears to have been *The Negro Worker*, from where he and others had heard about the Conference. He also sent a report of the major agricultural strike that had taken place in Guadeloupe in February 1929, in which several workers had lost their lives. Ford had hoped that Ducadosse might be able to travel to the US, from where he could be despatched to Europe. However a chronic shortage of funds, due to the costs of the legal fees of those involved in the strike, meant that it was impossible to send a delegate from Guadeloupe to the Hamburg Conference.[45]

Huiswoud's view was that such short visits to the Caribbean were of very limited use when there were few contacts and little preparation. 'One of the things that must be done immediately,' he concluded, 'is a definite plan for activities in the West Indies and the training of a few people to do this work... The West Indies is not Europe or the USA. Here it means pioneer work, for there are no organisations or class conscious elements to begin with.' But he also thought that conditions were 'extremely fertile' and that there was 'an awakening on the part of the masses' that needed proper guidance and organisation.[46]

The absence of delegates from the Caribbean and Latin America in Hamburg meant that the struggles of the workers in these areas were barely mentioned, except during De Leon's speech focusing mainly on the hardship facing Jamaica's workers, and the introductory remarks of Ford, who commented on the recent and bloody clashes in Guadeloupe. The Conference resolutions provided a general political orientation and raised general economic demands but provided little in the way of guidance for the workers of the Caribbean or Latin America. The ITUCNW's new executive committee included only one representative from the region, G. Reid of the JTLU, although provision was made for representation from Haiti and Latin America, 'as soon as the Committee gets in touch with the Negro working class organisations in these parts of the

44. Huiswoud to Padmore, 14 April 1930, RGASPI 534/4/330.

45. J. Ford, 'Report on the Preparations for the London Conference,' 12 May 1930, RGASPI 534/3/546. It should be noted that Ducadosse was refused a passport to travel to the congress of the Latin American Federation of Trade Unions held in 1929. S. Junco, 'The Problem of the Negro Race and the Proletarian Movement,' 24 June 1930, RGASPI 495/155/87/150.

46. Huiswoud to Padmore, 14 April 1930, RGASPI 534/4/330.

world.'[47] It is not surprising, therefore, that in the aftermath of the Hamburg Conference some criticisms were made about the lack of preparation. These and the wider issue of organising in the Caribbean and Latin America were discussed by a special conference of 'Negro delegates' that met in Moscow shortly after the Hamburg Conference as part of the Fifth Congress of the RILU.[48]

At the Fifth Congress there were several significant speeches from the 'Negro delegates', including Junco, who spoke on the Negro Question in Latin America and the Caribbean.[49] However, the Congress concluded that 'in the West Indies and in the Latin–American countries, the organisation of the Negro workers into the class trade unions has practically not even been started.'[50] Criticisms were also again levelled at the adherents of the RILU in the major colonial countries and their 'complete under-estimation and opportunist attitude towards the question of the political significance and organisation of the Negro workers for the world revolutionary movement.[51]

Various plans were discussed for strengthening the work of the ITUCNW in the Caribbean and Latin America, including establishing its own sub-committee and publishing *The Negro Worker* in Spanish and Portuguese.[52] But such proposals came to nought, although MOPR, which had participated in the Hamburg Conference, did establish a Caribbean Secretariat and expressed its resolve to develop its work in this region and throughout Latin America.[53] In general, however, it seems that little was accomplished before the setting up of the HC of the ITUCNW and even then there were few advances before Padmore and Huiswoud compiled a substantial report on the region in January 1931.

The Hamburg Committee and the West Indies

The HC, established under the direction of James Ford, found it difficult to make headway in the Caribbean, although in its first year of existence it did make contact with the British Guiana Labour Union (BGLU), the first workers' organisation to be established in Britain's colonies in the region, and

47. *A Report of Proceedings and Decisions of the First International Conference of Negro Workers* (Hamburg, 1930) and 'Election of Executive Committee,' *NW*, 3 (15 October 1930) p.16.

48. 'Minutes of the meeting of the Trade Union Committee of Negro Workers of the RILU,' 29 May 1930.

49. *L'Ouvrier Nègre*, (November 1930) pp.29-31.

50. *Resolutions of the Fifth World Congress of the RILU* (London, 1931) p.161-162.

51. Ibid.

52. 'On the Organisation of the ITUCNW,' 5 September 1930, RGASPI 495/18/810/77.

53. 'Resolution on the IRA Work among the Negroes,' 11 November 1930, RGASPI 495/14/810/97-102.

planned to develop links in Trinidad, Jamaica, British Honduras and Haiti.[54] By this time the focus of the ITUCNW had been narrowed and largely excluded Latin America, while Haiti, and the Spanish-speaking islands increasingly came under the jurisdiction of the CSLA and the RILU's New York-based Caribbean sub-committee. This remained independent of the ITUCNW despite proposals that it 'simultaneously perform the functions of a sub-committee of the Hamburg Committee for the West Indies and Latin America.'[55] The ITUCNW also lost the services of Junco, who had been sent to the Lenin School in Moscow, with the result that the work of the ITUCNW in Latin America and Haiti was somewhat weakened.[56] The HC thereafter began to focus almost exclusively on the British West Indies, although on occasions it also communicated directly, or through the organisations in France, with those in Haiti and the French Antilles.

The first major initiative was a 'Report on the West Indies' submitted to the ECCI by Huiswoud and Padmore of the RILU's Negro Committee in January 1931. Here too the main focus was the British West Indies, although conditions in Haiti, the US Virgin Islands and Curaçao also warranted a special mention. The main aim was to outline the economic exploitation and political oppression in the islands, as well as the rivalry that existed between the major imperialist powers in the region and the report was accompanied by a leading article in *The International Negro Workers' Review*.[57] According to the authors of the report:

> The Negro masses in the West Indies are just as viciously exploited as the natives of Africa or the black toilers in the Southern parts of the United States of America. The exploiters are not only the foreign imperialists, but the native bourgeoisie and the landlords, who are equally as ruthless in their suppression of the broad toiling masses, as the foreign blood suckers, for in no section of the Black World are class lines more rigidly drawn than in the Caribbean colonies.[58]

54. 'Concrete Proposals on Report of Work of Hamburg Committee,' 10 June 1931, RGASPI 534/3/668. and 'Report on the Work of ITUCNW (Hamburg),' 2 October 1931, RGASPI 534/3/669. On the BGLU see R.J. Alexander and E. M. Parker, *A History of Organized Labour in the English-speaking West Indies* (Westport, 2004) pp.341-342.

55. 'Concrete Proposals' and Padmore to Ford, 17 March 1931, RGASPI 534/3/668.

56. Padmore to the Secretariat, RILU, 2 April 1931, RGASPI 534/3/668.

57. 'Imperialism in the West Indies,' *The International Negro Workers' Review*, 1/1 (January 1931) pp.16-20; 'Report on the West Indies,' 24 January 1931, RGASPI 495/155/98/1-6 The Report also contains a short section on Garveyism, noting its decline but also that it still had influence amongst the workers, especially in Jamaica. RGASPI 495/155/98/26.

58. 'Report on the West Indies,' RGASPI 495/155/98/1-6.

The report highlighted the fact that the Depression was having a major impact on the Caribbean and that consequently favourable conditions existed for organising amongst the workers. The existence of the JTLU, established as a result of Huiswoud's visits, but with only two branches and a few hundred members, was presented as one example of the readiness of the workers to 'put up an organised fight against imperialist domination and exploitation.'[59]

Another example was the BGLU, which had been formed in January 1919 by Hubert Critchlow. Often referred to as the father of trade unionism throughout the Anglophone Caribbean, Critchlow, a dockworker by trade, became active in the worker's movement as early as 1905. He not only established the BGLU but was also a leading figure in the labour movement throughout Britain's Caribbean colonies and the convenor of the first West Indian Labour Conference held in 1926. By the early 1930s the BGLU, which in its early years attracted thousands of members, participated in strikes and demonstrations and had its own monthly publication, was declining and under the influence of the British Labour Party. The ITUCNW, however, recognised that after the election to office of a Labour government in Britain in 1929, many illusions about that party would be shattered and that this would provide good opportunities for its future work in British Guiana.[60] It also pointed to the fact that the workers in British Guiana would require more assistance from the NMM in Britain.[61] It was in these circumstances, and having already made contact with the BGLU, that in August 1931 the ITUCNW decided to send its 'Open Letter' to all the workers of British Guiana, those of African and Indian origin, appealing to them directly to build and strengthen the BGLU.[62]

It seems likely that Padmore's and Huiswoud's Report, although limited in scope, was written in connection with the decision of the ECCI to initiate 'trade union activities' in the British West Indies based on a proposal from the CI's Negro Bureau, a proposal that recognised the importance of both the workers' movement and the anti-imperialist struggle. The ECCI proposed to initiate work amongst West Indian seamen and dock workers, referred to as 'the leading element among the West Indian proletariat,' through the opportunities available to activists of the US-based Marine Workers' Union, both in the Caribbean and in the International Seamen's Clubs in American ports. It was suggested that 'the first steps towards the organisation of revolutionary unions and towards the penetration of the reformist trade unions,' could be taken in this way. The

59. 'Report on the West Indies,' RGASPI 495/155/98/16-19.

60. Ibid.

61. O. Huiswoud, 'Imperialist Rule in British Guiana,' *NW*, 8/1 (August 1931) pp.3-5.

62. 'What Must Be Done In British Guiana – An open letter - Issued by the ITUCNW To all Workers of British Guiana,' *NW*, 8/1 (August 1931), pp. 9-13.

immediate aim was to establish a West Indian Marine Workers' Union through cooperation between the ITUCNW, the RILU's Caribbean sub-committee and the International Marine Workers' Union. This involved establishing an International Seamen's Club in a 'leading port' and then sending 'West Indian members of the CPUSA' to Jamaica and Trinidad. The aim was 'to develop organisation among the plantation and industrial workers, and peasantry, with the object of forming revolutionary unions and peasant leagues, also towards the formation of Communist groups.' The proposals also included launching a 'mass paper' in Port of Spain or Kingston, and establishing local committees of the LAI in US cities where there was a large Caribbean population, such as New York and Philadelphia. These committees would support the paper, make 'contact with the struggles of the workers and peasants in the West Indies,' and support 'the National Liberation Struggles of the West Indian masses.'[63]

The stated purpose of the 'mass paper' was significant, its aim was to wage a struggle against Garvey, who it was thought was now centring his activities in the Caribbean, as well as against the influence of the British Labour Party and the Second International. However, it was also intended to 'mobilise the plantation and industrial workers and peasantry' of the Caribbean,' for the struggle against British and US imperialism.'[64] The relationship between the anti-imperialist struggle and that of the working masses did not receive further analysis but it seems evident that what was envisaged was the organisation of a broader anti-colonial movement that did not just include the workers, hence the proposed involvement of the LAI.

However, there is no indication that this work was ever taken up by the CPUSA and the TUUL, which had overall responsibility for its implementation, even though the Secretariat of the RILU adopted a special resolution on work in the Caribbean in June 1931.[65] James Ford wrote a further report on the Caribbean as he left Hamburg to return to the US at the end of 1931. He admitted that in Jamaica there was 'merely a skeleton' of the JTLU remaining and that in Trinidad the ITUCNW had only managed to 'establish some individual contacts,' reportedly because 'we have carried on no activities whatever on the island.' Nevertheless, he felt that conditions were still favourable in these colonies, and in British Guiana, if 'concrete activities' were carried out. In Haiti there still remained a few contacts from the branch of the LAI organised by Rosemond, although the branch had itself collapsed. Ford cited language problems as one of the reasons for lack of contact between the ITUCNW and the Haitian workers but he felt that the strong 'national sentiment' in the

63. 'Re. Proposals on Initiating Activities in the British West Indies,' 26 February 1931, RGASPI 495/155/98/27-28.

64. 'Draft Proposals For Initiating Activities in the British West Indies,' RGASPI 515/1/2222.

65. 'To the TUUL,' 5 January 1932, RGASPI 534/3/730.

country could be channelled into a 'genuine struggle against imperialism and the native bourgeoisie.' However, Ford was still urging action by the TUUL and the Marine Workers Union in the US, as well as the CGTU in France, and demanding that the RILU sections 'radically change their attitude' towards 'the struggles of the colonial masses,' another clear sign that significant work in the Caribbean had yet to take place.[66]

The Caribbean Sub-Committee

When Padmore replaced Ford in Hamburg at the end of 1931 he immediately contacted the CPUSA to explain the priorities of the ITUCNW and indignantly enquired why, despite several letters, the Party had not implemented the proposals in regard to the Caribbean. By this time it had been decided by the RILU Negro Bureau that the Hamburg Committee would fully concentrate on developing its activities in Africa and the Caribbean. It was not expected to take responsibility for South America and 'was not expected to direct the Negro movement in the US,' since 'our Party and the TUUL as well as the LSNR [League of Struggle for Negro Rights] are making considerable headway in this field.'[67] However, the CPUSA was expected to assist with the work in the Caribbean, which included establishing a West Indian sub-committee of the ITUCNW, based in the US and composed of comrades of Caribbean origin such as Charles Alexander and Harold Williams. It was intended that this sub-committee would have responsibility for all the British colonies in the Caribbean region, including Honduras and British Guiana, as well as Haiti and 'the West Indian colony in Panama.' The CPUSA was specifically required by the CI to release Alexander and Williams from their other responsibilities so that they could proceed to the Caribbean and begin their work.[68] Padmore added that the matter was of some urgency not only because there were requests for assistance from workers in the Caribbean but also because the 'trade union reformists' of the Second Intern-

66. RGASPI 534/3/669/8-11.

67. Padmore to B.D. Amis, 2 January 1932, RGASPI 534/3/754. Padmore often could not resist giving advice to comrades in the US. See e.g. Padmore to E.L. Beone, 16 February 1932, RGASPI 534/3/754. Earlier ITUCNW reports had made a more critical assessment of work in the US. See e.g. 'Statement to the American Commission on Trade Union Work Amongst Negro Workers from the ITUCNW of the RILU,' n.d. RGASPI 495/155/77/85-87.

68. Both Alexander and Williams were leading black Communists based in New York, although both originated from the Caribbean. Williams had recently returned from study at KUTV in the Soviet Union. Both were regular contributors to *The Negro Worker.*

tional were planning a 'West Indian Labour Congress' and, 'it will be necessary for our comrades to help the opposition elements at the conference.'[69]

In January 1932, more extensive instructions were sent to the TUUL from the Secretariat of the RILU. These re-emphasised the importance of the work and the need to immediately send a comrade to Jamaica to make contact with the JTLU and other workers' organisations; to conduct propaganda work, as well as endeavouring to establish an 'International Club' for seafarers. Special emphasis was placed on the task of starting 'a small monthly trade union paper,' to be called 'The Workers' Voice,' which could be disseminated throughout the Caribbean to mobilise not only for the rights of workers but also for the 'fight for self-determination.'[70] Padmore also wrote to the sub-committee later the same month, enclosing literature for English-speaking workers in Cuba and explaining that he had established some contacts in Colombia and Honduras.[71]

However, the CPUSA decided not to fully implement the decision of the ECCI and the directives of the RILU. Instead, work in the Caribbean continued to be the responsibility of the Caribbean sub-committee of the CSLA, based in New York. The sub-committee appears to have had an extremely limited membership, although it managed to co-opt Cyril Briggs and Harry Haywood for some of its meetings, and was also poorly resourced. It included neither Alexander nor Williams, and there is no indication that it seriously took up the work required by the RILU before July 1932. Evidently the previous month Padmore wrote to the sub-committee again asking for contacts in Cuba and elsewhere in Latin America to whom he could send *The Negro Worker*. He also asked if articles could be written for the Negro workers in Honduras and Colombia and enquired how the ITUCNW might strengthen the sub-committee's work.[72] Somewhat belatedly the sub-committee acknowledged the weakness of its work 'amongst the toiling masses of the West Indies, as well as amongst the West Indian workers who in thousands work in the banana plantations of all the Central American countries, in the Canal zone in Panama, as well as in Cuba and other countries,' and resolved to implement the decisions of the CSLA and to assist the work of the ITUCNW. It initially planned to do so partly in line with the Resolution of the ECCI but without accepting the organisational forms required and therefore not under the direction of the ITUCNW.[73]

69. Padmore to R. Minor, 16 December 1931, RGASPI 534/3/668.

70. 'To the TUUL,' 5 January 1932, RGASPI 534/3/730.

71. Padmore to Caribbean Sub-Committee, 25 January 1932, RGASPI 534/3/754.

72. Padmore to Sub Comité del Caribe, 21 June 1932, RGASPI 534/3/755.

73. Secretary of the Caribbean Sub-Committee to ITUCNW, 23 August 1932, RGASPI 534/3/756 and Report of Caribbean Sub-Committee, 4 November 1932, RGASPI 534/4/427/29-30.

Its eventual effort was poorly planned and implemented and highlighted the fact that local activists, and even communist parties, sometimes openly defied, or were unable to implement, directives from Moscow. The reasons advanced for such defiance were that Jamaican workers were to be found working as migrants in such countries as Cuba, Honduras and Panama, where the CSLA had sections. It was therefore envisaged that they would be drawn into the work of the CSLA sections and by these means the revolutionary trade union movement would be developed. Based on the same logic it was suggested that the work in Trinidad might be developed in connection with the CSLA section in Venezuela since there were close economic ties between the industries of the two neighbouring countries.[74] What is apparent is that the sub-committee had very limited support from the CPUSA, which refused to release the comrades requested by Moscow, allegedly because of their other work commitments.[75] It was also unable to get any support from the TUUL, which, it reported, had no 'functioning Negro committee,' and it was apparently advised to take up the question of organising in the Caribbean 'directly with some of the Negro comrades.'[76] It also lacked financial resources, requesting these from the ITUCNW, and even admitted that for some five months it had no direct contact, nor secure line of communication, with the leadership of the CSLA in Montevideo. Indeed communications to Uruguay were sent via Berlin. In short the sub-committee was poorly equipped and resourced to begin work in the Caribbean, although it devised a plan to do so.[77]

Financial means were eventually found and the sub-committee sent Cecil Hope, a party member of Barbadian origin to the Caribbean with vague plans to establish a 'mass paper' in Trinidad. The mission was poorly planned and Hope spent most of his time in Barbados, finding it impossible to remain in Trinidad for more than a few hours. Although he brought back first-hand evidence of the extreme poverty and increased repression in these islands, the visit had no tangible results.[78]

74. Ibid.

75. In February 1932 Alexander had been heavily involved as 'defense counsel' in a case of a white member of the Furrier's union who was charged with racism and 'subjected to a trial' before his peers. See M. Solomon, *The Cry Was Unity: Communists and African Americans 1917-1936* (Jackson, 1998) p.143.

76. Secretary of the Caribbean Sub-Committee to ITUCNW, 23 August 1932, RGASPI 534/3/756 and Report of Caribbean Sub-Committee, 4 November 1932, RGASPI 534/4/427/29-30. The Negro Bureau of the TUUL was at this time led by James Ford.

77. Secretary of the Caribbean Sub-Committee to ITUCNW, 23 August 1932, RGASPI 534/3/756.

78. 'Report of Comrade Hope,' 31 October 1932, RGASPI 534/4/427.

Padmore and the Hamburg Committee

The ITUCNW had to find other methods of working in the Caribbean. It had on paper already established a differentiated approach to such work, based on the level of organisation of the workers' movement, in each country, whether unions existed, or were under 'reformist' leadership, and whether significant numbers of workers of Indian origin existed.[79] However its primary task was to establish contacts and during 1932 Padmore wrote to both individual activists and organisations in Jamaica, Haiti, Trinidad, St Lucia, British Guiana, Barbados, Bermuda, Grenada, the Dominican Republic, Panama, Honduras and Guadeloupe.[80] Those individuals he contacted were always sent copies of *The Negro Worker* for distribution and asked for the names of others who might be sympathetic. Contact with the Caribbean was also made through seafarers in the US, the NWA and its supporters in Britain, such as Jim Headley and Harry O'Connell, and through Kouyaté and the LDRN in France.[81] Some contact existed between the HC and workers from Curaçao based in Holland,[82] but there were also attempts, some of which were made public in *The Negro Worker*, to remind the Communists in Holland of the need for the 'organisation and extension of their work' in the Dutch West Indies.[83] The ITUCNW was mindful of the fact that the deteriorating economic conditions in the Caribbean, particularly large-scale unemployment, were contributing to an increase in strikes and other protest actions by the workers, that new organisations of the unemployed were emerging in such countries as Jamaica and British Guiana, and that therefore conditions were favourable for developing a militant trade union movement and organisations of the unemployed.[84]

79. 'Resolution on the Work of the Hamburg Committee,' 18 October 1932, RGASPI 534/3/669.

80. 'Report of the Work of the Hamburg Committee for the Period 1931-1932,' 9 January 1933, RGASPI 534/3/753. In this report Padmore claimed that groups had been organised in Guadeloupe, Haiti, Jamaica, St Lucia and Panama.

81. See e.g. Padmore to the Secretary, Seamen's Club, New Orleans, 6 February 1932, RGASPI 534/3/755; Padmore to Ward, 27 February 1932, RGASPI 534/3/754 in which Padmore encourages Ward to contact unions in Trinidad. Also J. Headley to Padmore, 15 June 1932, RGASPI 534/3/755.

82. International Seamen's Club, Amsterdam to Padmore, 4 January 1932, RGASPI 534/3/754/19.

83. 'The Plan of Work of the Negro TU Committee for February-July 1932,' 1 February 1932, RGASPI 515/1/3038 and O. Huiswoud, 'The Fight Against Starvation in Dutch Guiana,' *NW*, 2/1-2 (January-February 1932) pp.16-19.

84. See O. Huiswoud, 'Starving Workers Demonstrate in Demerara,' *NW*, 1/12 (December 1931) pp.15-17 and C. Alexander, 'For a Revolutionary Trade Union Movement in the West Indies,' *NW*, 2/3 (March 1932) pp.14-18.

In Guadeloupe, for example, a strike by sugar workers in 1930, led to clashes with the local gendarmerie in which several workers lost their lives. A group of workers, most probably a group led by Sabin Ducadosse, subsequently wrote to *The Negro Worker* and the *Cri des Nègres,* complaining of the terrible conditions they had to endure, explaining that the existing trade unions did not fight for their interests, and stating that they therefore wished to organise themselves, and even stand candidates in the election.[85] In this instance Huiswoud wrote to the CGTU in France to ask if it had provided advice and assistance to these workers and offering the help of the ITUCNW.[86] However, connections between the PCF/CGTU and the French Antilles were not well developed, according to the report submitted by Garan Kouyaté in 1931.[87]

In the case of Trinidad, Padmore wrote directly to Vivian Henry, secretary of the Trinidad Workingmen's Association (TWA), to apologise that no contact had been made sooner, to acquaint him directly with the work of the ITUCNW and to find ways in which the two might collaborate. Since the TWA was associated with the British Labour Party, Padmore took the time to explain the nature of this party and the British Trade Union Congress, and to expose the 'reformism' and 'social imperialism' of both. He also offered advice on particular issues, such as the recent banning of *The Negro Worker* under the Seditious Publications Ordinance, which Henry was campaigning against.[88] On this issue Bridgeman and the LAI in Britain had enlisted the support of sympathetic parliamentarians. James Maxton of the Independent Labour Party (ILP) had raised the matter in Parliament even before Padmore requested LAI

85. 'An Appeal from Guadeloupe,' *NW*, 1/10-11 (October-November 1931) pp.39-40, also 'Lettre à la Guadeloupe,' *Le Cri des Nègres*. 2/8-9 (March-April 1932) p.4 The 'Preliminary Verification of the Fulfilment of the RILU Secretariat Decisions on the Work of the Hamburg Committee,' 14 March 1932, RGASPI 534/3/730.

86. O. Huiswoud to la Commission Coloniale de la CGTU, 10 February 1932, RGASPI 534/3/754. Huiswoud's correspondence with Padmore makes it clear that the RILU Negro Bureau was drafting proposals for both Guadeloupe and Haiti. See Huiswoud to Padmore, 21 February 1932, RGASPI 534/3754. See also *Cri des Nègres*, October 1931, which merely suggested that the workers in Guadeloupe should contact the PCF and the CGTU.

87. 'Special Report by Kuyatte (sic),' n.d. RGASPI 534/3/753. According to Kouyaté the PCF did not respond to communications from Martinique.

88. *The Negro Worker* was banned by the Governor of Trinidad on 14 April 1932, although it remained legal in other British colonies in the Caribbean. When questioned in Parliament the British government offered no explanation for the ban. See *Hansard*, HC Deb 01 June 1932 vol. 266 cc1150-1. The ban also led to protests from the NWA in Britain. See A.R. '"Negro Worker" Banned by Imperialists,' *NW*, 2/6 (June 1932) pp.14-17 and C. Alexander, 'Free Speech and Press for West Indian Masses,' *NW*, 2/8 (August 1932) pp.9-10.

intervention and both and the LAI and the ILP made contact with Henry and the TWA.[89]

Henry agreed to work with the ITUCNW and Padmore adopted an approach that was both friendly and critical, inviting the TWA to the Tenth Anniversary of the ILD in Berlin and acknowledging that he had been a schoolmate of Henry's brother but at the same time writing: 'The question that stands before us is: Do we sincerely want our liberty, or are we satisfied to be the political, economic and social slaves of these European overlords? Your answer to this question will determine the relationship between ourselves and the Association.'[90]

In order to develop its work in the Caribbean the ITUCNW even published Albert Marryshow's 'Appeal to West Indians Overseas,' in *The Negro Worker.* Marryshow, an elected member of the Legislative Council of Grenada and President of the Grenada Workers' Association, was attempting to raise money for a delegation to Britain to lobby the Imperial government over the economic problems facing the colony. *The Negro Worker*, however, added to this 'Appeal' Padmore's commentary and denunciation of such methods, pointing out that a similar recent delegation from Trinidad had achieved nothing. Padmore declared:

> It is high time that West Indians who pose as leaders stop this kow-towing business of sending memoranda, petitions and deputations to England. It is no use kidding ourselves that we can at the same time fight our oppressors and beg them for favours...Furthermore this kind of humbug merely creates much harm, for it helps to support the illusion which missionaries and other so-called friends of the colonial peoples try to foster among the masses that the Secretary of State is different to the bureaucrats on the spot...They are all birds of the same feather... Workers, peasants and militant intellectuals of Grenada, organise your ranks into an anti-imperialist movement. Demonstrate on the streets, as you have recently done, in order to dramatise before the whole world the sufferings of a starving, bankrupt, ruthlessly crushed down and exploited people. If need be you must be prepared to call a general strike. Grenada will have the sympathy and the support of the working class throughout the world, especially the British workers, who after the bitter betrayal of the Labour Party, and their ever increasing misery are learning to realise that they will never be able to emancipate themselves unless

89. Padmore to R. Bridgeman, 2 June 1930, Bridgeman to Padmore, 14 June 1932 and Padmore to J. Maxton, 17 June 1932, RGASPI 534/3/755; *Hansard*, HC Deb 01 June 1932 vol 266 cc 1150-1.

90. Padmore to V. Henry, June 1932, RGASPI 534/3/755/127-130.

> they support the struggles of the colonial peoples for freedom and self-determination.[91]

It was through the NWA and the LAI, as well as through the work of the NMM in Britain that the ITUCNW hoped to gain support from British workers for the struggles in the colonies. However, the activities of the CPGB and the NMM were at best minimal in this regard and Padmore continually urged them support the struggles and the workers' movement that were developing in the Caribbean and other colonies. In one letter to John Mahon of the NMM he pointed out that, 'the Minority Movement can create a tremendous impression by corresponding with these less advanced colonial unions, helping them to draw up their programmes etc.'[92]

The ITUCNW continually put the greatest emphasis on organising the working people of the Caribbean, pointing out that the colonial system was one of exploitation and oppression and that only through class struggle could resistance be successful. It explained that history showed that the workers of town and countryside must rely on their own efforts and leaders, not on those like Garvey who posed as their leaders. Indeed in this period its attacks on Garvey, who had relocated to Britain, were just as numerous as in previous years.[93] It also called on the workers to struggle not just for economic reforms and their rights, such as the right to free speech and press freedom, but also for independence from colonial rule and for an 'independent West Indian Federated Republic.' In this connection, it also warned against harbouring any illusions about the nature of the British government, its agents in the colonies, or the various commissions that we sent to the Caribbean.[94]

It is difficult to assess the ITUCNW's impact in the Caribbean during this period. Certainly it had established contacts and received letters of interest sent to *The Negro Worker*. The banning of this publication in Trinidad, suggested that the colonial authorities felt that it was having some influence amongst sections of the workers. But the ITUCNW was still critical of the lack of support that was being received from the revolutionary organisations within the impe-

91. G. Padmore, 'Trouble in the West Indies,' *NW*, 2/5 (May 1932) pp.5-6.

92. Padmore to J. Mahon, 13 January 1932, RGASPI 534/3/754.

93. See e.g. C. Briggs, 'How Garvey Betrayed The Negroes,' *NW*, 2/8 (15 August 1932) pp.14-17 and 'A Garveyite Offended,' ibid, pp.22-24.

94. C. Alexander, 'Against Illusions in the West Indian Masses,' *NW*, 2/7 (July 1932) pp.12-15 and 'Free Speech and Press for West Indian Masses,' *NW*, 2/8 (August 1932) pp.9-10. Also G. Padmore, 'Nationalist Movement in West Indies,' *NW*, 3/1 (January 1933) pp.6-7.

rialist countries and it was unable to send its activists to directly organise in the Caribbean in the way that it had intended. [95]

Communism in Haiti

In some cases such intervention was unnecessary because local activists were successfully organising themselves. In Haiti during this period efforts to establish a communist party were being led by the well-known poet, writer and activist Jacques Roumain and were partly precipitated by the uprising against US occupation in 1929. In early 1932 Roumain and his comrade Christian Beaulieu travelled to the US and held discussions with the CPUSA but few details of this visit have emerged.[96] Within the country the struggle against the US occupation had intensified but so too had the efforts of the government to suppress opposition and several anti-imperialist organisations were banned. It therefore became even more difficult to organise from outside the country as Rosemond had attempted in previous years.[97] Padmore seems to have had no direct contact with Roumain but he did ask the Caribbean sub-committee in New York for a 'responsible friend' in Cuba to whom he could send literature for the Haitians.[98] In response the sub-committee supplied details of Haitians in the Dominican Republic, to whom he could send *The Negro Worker*, and also the name of Benjamin Peguero La Paix, who had formerly been one of the leaders of the Dominican Confederation of Labour, had worked with Junco in Cuba and had then been forced to move to Haiti in 1930 when Trujillo came to power.[99]

By 1932 the ITUCNW was in contact with an organisation referred to as the 'Ligue Haitain,' (perhaps the Ligue Patriotique or the Ligues des Ouvriers) which informed Padmore that it had been working to establish a workers' organisation in Haiti. He offered support and invited the Ligue to send delegates to the conference of the ILD. Indeed, it seems that Padmore had contact with several activists in Haiti and he was able to report that one of them was even

95. B. Jan, 'The Struggle of Seamen and Harbour Workers in British Guiana,' *NW*, 2/9-10 (September-October 1932) pp.27-28.

96. C. Fowler, *A Knot in the Thread: The Life and Work of Jacques Roumain* (Washington D.C., 1980) pp.14-1-145. Also Smith, *Red and Black in Haiti*, pp.13-23.

97. The Caribbean sub-committee reported to Padmore that Rosemond had 'totally gone to the other side.' A. Martes to the ITUCNW, 12 December 1932, RGASPI 534/4/372/11.

98. Padmore to Sub comité del Caribe, 21 June 1932, RGASPI 534/3/755.

99. A. Martes to the ITUCNW, 12 December 1932, RGASPI 534/4372/11.

ready to travel to Moscow as a student.[100] Communication with La Paix, who was in close contact with the CSLA, which sent him and others instructions in the pages of its publication *El obrero del Caribe* and probably by other means, was more difficult. This was particularly the case after his arrest by the Haitian government at the end of 1932. Many others were also arrested in the same period, including Roumain and those connected with the Ligue des Ouvriers en Générale d'Haiti, as *The Negro Worker* reported the following year.[101] The ITUCNW continued to maintain contact with activists in Haiti both directly and through the UTN in Paris, the CSLA and the Caribbean sub-committee in New York.[102] When Padmore was forced to move the work of the HC to Paris, early in 1933, he reported that he had become involved in the UTN's campaign to release La Paix from prison.[103] The work to establish the communist party in Haiti continued and culminated in the founding of the Parti Communiste Haïtien (PCH) by Roumain and others in 1934.[104]

The government in Haiti employed increasingly repressive methods against it opponents. The Haitian Scottsboro Defence Committee, led by Jacques Roumain was outlawed and many were jailed. Joseph Jolibois *fils*, the radical journalist and former president of the Haitian Senate was incarcerated and died in custody.[105] Roumain's arrest and imprisonment in 1934 was allegedly for distributing the UTN's *Cri des Nègres,* although actually was in connection with his activities to found the Haitian Communist Party (PCH).[106] Roumain's declaration 'I am a Communist...I have renounced my bourgeois origins,' and 'I am glad to stand beside the heroic proletariat which defends the Negroes of Scottsboro, Tom Mooney and so many other victims of class justice, rather than beside their murderers,' had been made public in 1932 but by 1934 the Haitian government had other incriminating evidence in its hands, including the manifesto of the Central Committee of the PCH, *L'Analyse schématique,* published in June of that year and bearing Roumain's signature.[107] His subsequent incarceration for three years led to an international campaign for his release in which

100. Padmore to Dear Comrades, 14 September 1932. RGASPI 542/1/54/92. Indeed it seems that Padmore had contact with several potential students in Haiti.

101. 'A wave of terror is sweeping over Haiti,' *NW*, 3/2-3 (February March 1933, pp.15-16.

102. Padmore to the Ligue Haitiain, 17 June 1932, RGASPI 534/3/755.

103. Padmore to Dear Comrades, 9 March 1933, RGASPI 534/3/895.

104. Fowler, *A Knot in the Thread*, pp.150-156; Smith, *Red and Black in Haiti*, pp.19-20.

105. 'Haiti-Wall Street Government Outlaws Scottsboro Defense,' *NW*, 4/3 (July 1934) p.25 and 'Poisoned in Prison?' *NW*, 6/5 (July 1936) p.26.

106. 'Haitian Revolutionary Writer Jailed,' *NW*, 5/4 (April 1935) p.28 and Fowler, *A Knot in the Thread* p.156.

107. Fowler, *A Knot in the Thread* pp.140, 149 and 'Poisoned in Prison,' *NW*, 6/5 (July 1936) p.26.

the African American writer Langston Hughes played a prominent part.[108] Roumain was then forced into exile in Europe, and for some time was based in France, where he worked more closely with the relocated ITUCNW and the UTN.[109]

The ITUCNW in Trinidad and British Guiana

Some of the most successful work of the ITUCNW was its attempt to work with existing workers' organisations in Trinidad and British Guiana. Padmore had made every effort to develop links with the BGLU and to disabuse Critchlow of any lingering illusions he may have harboured about the British Labour Party. He explained to him that 'the only way out of the crisis is the revolutionary way,' and that therefore there was a need to strengthen the organisation of the workers and the unemployed, to step up the struggle for their demands and to break with 'Macdonald and the reformists.'[110] He also invited the BGLU to send a delegate to the congress of the ILD and even claimed that the BGLU had 'accepted the leadership' of the ITUCNW.[111]

Both Vivien Henry and Hubert Critchlow attended and addressed the First Congress of ILD in Moscow in November 1932, and Henry addressed the Congress as a 'delegate from the West Indies Labour Movement.'[112] Both returned to the Caribbean with positive experiences in the Soviet Union and Critchlow addressed a public meeting in Georgetown, British Guiana, where a branch of the ILD was established, to recount not only his experience of the Soviet Union but also his reception by workers in Holland and German. He reported that in the Soviet Union he had even received medical treatment, completely free of charge, and from a woman doctor. He had many other wondrous things to relate about the country, including the fact that there was no unemployment. He told his audience that 'Labour was not a racial issue but a class issue, the rich versus the poor,' and declared that he wished to return to the

108. See 'An Appeal for Jacques Roumain,' reproduced in C.C. de Santis (ed.) *The Collected Works of Langston Hughes [vol. 9]* (London, 2002) pp. 554-555.

109. See e.g. 'Meeting commun du Rassemblement Coloniale et l'UTN,' 15 March 1938, SLOTFOM 2/2, ANOM.

110. Padmore to H.E. O'Connell, 5 January 1932, RGASPI 534/3/754.

111. Padmore to the Bureau of the ISH, 1 August 1932, RGASPI 534/5/231.

112. 'Class War in the West Indies,' *NW*, 3/2-3 (February-March 1933) pp.21-24 and 'Letters from Delegates,' Ibid., pp.29-30. Padmore had earlier invited delegates from Jamaica, British Guiana, Barbados and Haiti to the conference of the ISH held in Hamburg in May 1932. See e.g. Padmore to A.B. Alves, Stevedores' Union of Jamaica, 2 April 1932, RGASPI 534/3/754.

OTTO AND HERMINA HUISWOUD, 1940.
Hermina Dumont Husiwoud Photographs Collection, Tamiment Library, New York University

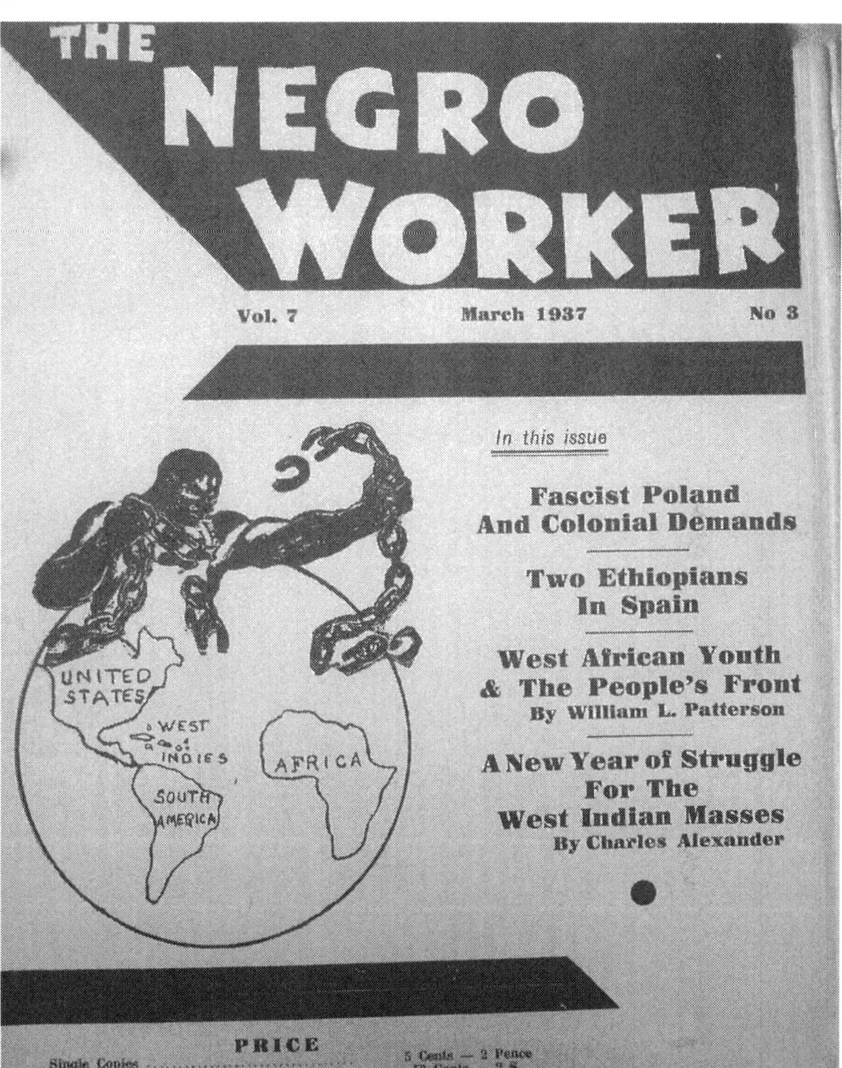

THE NEGRO WORKER

Vol. 7 March 1937 No 3

In this issue

Fascist Poland And Colonial Demands

Two Ethiopians In Spain

West African Youth & The People's Front
By William L. Patterson

A New Year of Struggle For The West Indian Masses
By Charles Alexander

PRICE
Single Copies .... 5 Cents — 2 Pence
Annual Sub. .... 50 Cents — 2 S.

THE NEGRO WORKER, 1937 – From the author's collection

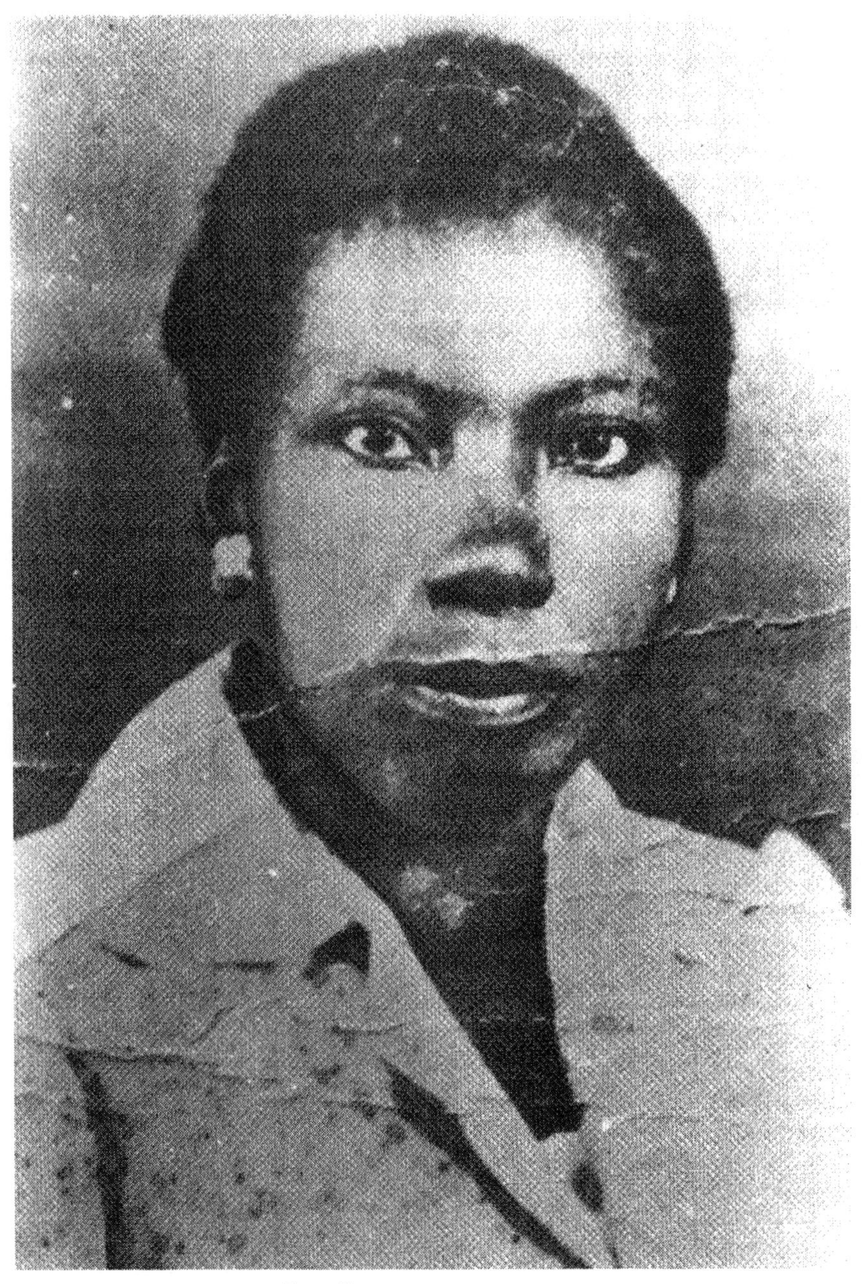

Elma Francois, founder of the
Negro Welfare, Cultural and Social Association, Trinidad.
Courtesy of Rhoda Reddock

Isaac Wallace-Johnson, founder of the West African Youth League.
from the author's collection

JOHNNY GOMAS OF THE CPSA FOLLOWING HIS RELEASE FROM PRISON, 1931,
Courtesy of Doreen Musson

Johnny Gomas speaking in 1932. Courtesy of Elizabeth Braggs and Jeanette du Preez

Soviet Union, if permitted by the government, and that he would take others with him.[113]

The ITUCNW promoted the BGLU as a model trade union engaged in 'an active struggle for the daily burning demands and interests of the working masses.' It reported how even the local press was forced to acknowledge the Union's successful organising of the workers and unemployed, as well as the wide support it had received on May Day. *The Negro Worker* commented 'this policy has our hearty support and we can only sincerely recommend its trial by the other millions of toilers in the West Indies and Africa who are being bled dry by the imperialists...Follow the example of the toilers of British Guiana! Fight against unemployment! Fight against wage cuts and long hours. For land, bread and freedom! For the right to live![114]

The difficulty of organising in the Caribbean from outside prompted Padmore to think of a radical solution. Early in 1932 he wrote to O'Connell encouraging him to contact his compatriot Critchlow in British Guiana and keep him informed him about events in Britain. In the course of his letter he explained that he had also promised Critchlow support and that 'we intend to send a West Indian comrade, a very capable young leader to help the West Indian workers to organise and build a real labour movement.' It seems very likely that this young leader was Jim Headley, who returned to the Caribbean at this time to reside in Trinidad. In 1933, in one of his first letters from Paris to the Negro Committee in Moscow, Padmore wrote that 'Comrade H has already left for Trinidad,' and added, 'he was sent from England as the Americans are not interested in this work.' Padmore even went as far a to ask for a monthly sum of $50 to be paid to Headley so that he could begin his work. He concluded by stating, 'we shall now concentrate upon Jamaica – then all will be well. Our organisation in Haiti has suffered a setback but we are taking up the question here with the local Haitians.'[115] However, Padmore's decision to despatch Headley led to severe criticism from Moscow.'[116]

The Negro Committee of the RILU had already made its own critical assessment of the efforts to further develop the activities of the ITUCNW in the British West Indies, acknowledging that this work was still at an embryonic stage. In particular it was critical of the Caribbean sub-committee in New York and its ill-fated attempt to send an activist to the region in 1932 and the fact

113. 'Report of Negro Workers' Leader on Soviet Russia,' *NW*, 3/4-5 (April-May 1933) pp.28-31.

114. 'Bravo, British Guiana!' *NW*, 4/8-9 (August –September 1933) pp.4-5.

115. Padmore to Dear Comrade, 6 March 1933, RGASPI 534/3/895. Padmore claimed that De Leon, who had attended the Hamburg Conference, had 'organised a union of 200 members,' and that therefore he was 'sending him directions.'

116. J[ackson?] to Dear Geo, 22 March 1933, RGASPI 534/3/895.

that it had ignored the proposals made by the RILU. In March 1933 the Negro Committee again proposed sending a comrade to the Caribbean under the direction of the RILU in order to establish a journal and groups of supporters of the ITUCNW. It again thought it necessary to involve the Marine Workers Union and called on the Caribbean sub-committee to organise groups of supporters amongst those from the Caribbean resident in the US, particularly in New York, that could be linked with any groups established in the Caribbean.[117] The Negro Department of the CPUSA and the US-based ILD had taken some initial steps to begin organising in the Caribbean and amongst Caribbean migrants in the US and the ILD even began to produce a publication entitled the *Caribbean Defender*. Possibly in response to demands from the Negro Committee, a New York-based West Indian sub-committee of the ITUCNW was belatedly established in 1933, but it and other US-based activity has not provided any evidence of a significant impact in the Caribbean.[118]

Huiswoud and the Caribbean

When the ITUCNW was re-established in 1934 by Otto Huiswoud and his wife Helen Davis, they had to re-establish communication with all the contacts in the Caribbean.[119] Although in early 1935 Huiswoud was able to report to Moscow that he had successfully re-established contact with Trinidad and British Guiana, after several months of silence, work in the Caribbean was slow to develop because communication was very difficult and new couriers had to be found, but also because Huiswoud had very little contact with or assistance from the CPUSA.[120] In regard to the BGLU, Huiswoud reported that 'while greatly confused, they are doing good work and to a good extent following our line.' However, he admitted that he was less successful in encouraging the Union to send its members to study in the Soviet Union,[121]

By this time the BGLU was again actively involved in the labour unrest that had broken out in British Guiana, which the colonial authorities blamed not only on the severe economic conditions but also the impact of the Italian inva-

117. A. Zousmanovitch to Secretariat of the RILU, 5 March 1933, RGASPI 534/3/895.

118. Stevens, 'The Red International and the Black Caribbean,' pp.212-258.

119. Huiswoud to Dear Friends, 9 June 1934, RGASPI 534/3/986.

120. Huiswoud to Dear Comrades, 23 August 1934, RGASPI 534/3/986. Also Huiswoud to Dear Comrades 11 April 1935,and Huiswoud to Dear Friends, 24 June 1935, RGASPI 495/155/102.

121. Huiswoud to Dear Friends, 24 June 1935, RGASPI 495/155/102. See also 'Monster May Day Rally in British Guiana,' *NW*, 5/7-7 (July-August 1935) p.28 and for Critchlow's letter to the ITUCNW dated 15 May 1935, ibid. p38.

sion of Ethiopia, and the renewed militancy of Critchlow and the BGLU.[122] In an earlier report sent to the Colonial Secretary in London from the Governor of British Guiana in 1933, Critchlow was identified as receiving instructions from the ITUCNW, while the BGLU, which was advancing demands in line with suggestions from the Hamburg Committee was credited with forcing several reforms from the colonial authorities. The Governor bemoaned the fact that he was unable to take any legal action against Critchlow, who was organising with some success amongst the unemployed and on the sugar estates but had issued a proclamation banning a major demonstration planned by the BGLU in August 1933.[123]

The Negro Welfare, Cultural and Social Association

Huiswoud was also able to re-establish communication with Headley in Trinidad, who explained that the 'Unemployed Workers' League' that he and others had founded with some two hundred members, had 'collapsed as a result of lack of support.' Headley declared that 'what is wanted is a sound revolutionary organisation here to school the masses along well defined and scientific lines.'[124] His article on conditions in Trinidad and the 'series of unemployed hunger marches' that the League had initiated subsequently appear in *The Negro Worker*.[125] Presumably with some guidance from Huiswoud, Headley was also engaged in the work to establish the Negro Welfare, Cultural and Social Association (NWCSA).[126]

The NWCSA was formed in 1934 and led by Elma Francois, who originated from St Vincent and was employed as a clothes washer, although Headley and Rupert Gittens, who had been deported from France for his activities with the

122. Geoffrey Northcote to H. Beckett, 18 October 1935, (TNA) CO 111/726/4.

123. Edward Denham to the Colonial Secretary, 17 October 1933, (TNA) CO 111/712/6.

124. 'Exerpts from Letter from Trinidad, Br. W. Indies,' *NW*, 4/5 (September 1934) p. 28. For more detail on the formation of what is referred to as the Unemployed Workers' Movement see R. Reddock, *Elma Francois: The NWCSA and the workers struggle for change in the Caribbean in the 1930s* (London, 1988) pp. 12-16.

125. In one report on Headley by the NWA in Britain he was referred to as 'our comrade' and actions organised by the League were reported to have 'compelled the government to concede the demands of the workers.' *Umsebenzi*, 31 April 1934, p.2.

126. J. H., 'Jobless Trinidad Toilers Demand Bread,' *NW*, 4/6-7 (October-November 1934) pp.4-6.

PCF, also appear to have played an important role.[127] The NWCSA, which may have had a membership of several hundred, worked within the Trinidad Labour Party and other organisations, as well as independently.[128] It established several local trade unions, including the Seamen and Waterfront Workers' Union and the Federated Workers' Trade Union, as well as three unemployed workers' councils and a tenants' organisation, and it played a prominent role in the strikes and other workers' protests that occurred in Trinidad from 1937-1938.[129] Huiswoud reported that it had a core of twenty Communists, four of whom formed a fraction within the Labour Party and others who worked in the oil industry.[130] The NWCSA was established with a clear focus on 'the Negro People of Trinidad,' but does not appear to have faced any problem dealing with the fact that many Trinidadian workers were of Indian origin.[131] The RILU Negro Bureau, well aware of the nature of the population in Trinidad, British Guiana and elsewhere in the Caribbean region, had issued directives stressing the importance of organising workers of both Indian and African origin. However there do not appear to have been any specific instructions to the NWCSA, or the BGLU on this issue. The reports of the speeches made by Francois show that she spoke about and to both 'the Negro and East Indian workers,' so the organisation's name, focus and aims are intriguing and may well have been influenced by the existence of the NWA and the ITUCNW.[132] The NWCSA aimed: 'to develop solidarity with the oppressed Negro of the West Indies and the entire world; to make known the conditions of the oppressed Negro people and their sufferings against oppression;' and 'to win the masses of the oppressed people the world over in struggle for the better welfare of the Negro people.'[133]

---

127. See Reddock, *Elma Francois*, R. Reddock, *Women, Labour and Politics in Trinidad and Tobago* (London, 1994) pp.108-111 and 135-140 and B. Rennie, *History of the Working Class in the 20th Century -1919-1956 – the Trinidad and Tobago Experience* (Toronto, 1974) pp.45-140. See also K. Yellington, 'The War in Ethiopia and Trinidad 1935-1936' in K. A. Yellington and B. Brereton (eds.) *The Colonial Caribbean in Transition: Essays in Post-emancipation Social and Cultural History* (Gainesville, 1999) pp.189-225. There are very few details of Gittens earlier activities but for some aspects of his career see S. Campbell, 'Kay Donnellan, Irishwoman and Radical in Trinidad, 1938-41,' *Journal of Caribbean History* 44/1 (2010) pp. 75-104.

128. 'Report of the Activities of the ITUCNW,' January 1937, RGASPI 534/3/1103.

129. Reddock, *Elma Francois*, p. 5. For the actions of the Dockers' Union in Trinidad which refused to load or unload Italian ships see *NW*, 5/11 (December 1935) p.28.

130. 'Extracts from Edward's Report,' 26 October 1935, RGASPI 495/14/36/42.

131. Reddock, *Elma Francois*, p. 5.

132. Ibid. p. 36.

133. Ibid. p. 58.

However, the NWCSA was also internationalist in its orientation. Francois spoke about the working class in Germany, Britain and the Soviet Union, the anti-fascist struggles in China and Spain, as well as the anti-colonial struggles in Kenya and Nigeria in her speeches. Clement Payne, who was President of the NWCSA also organised amongst the workers of Barbados, his parents' homeland, and is now recognised as one of the national heroes of that country.[134] The NWCSA played a major role in the political life of Trinidad during the late 1930s and even contributed to the drafting of a new constitution for the colony.[135] However, although Huiswoud reported that the NWCSA was one of the organisations with which he worked most closely, there seems to be very little information on the precise nature of their relationship. Nevertheless, the ITUCNW's work with the NWCSA was perhaps the most fruitful of all its activity in the Caribbean because of the important role that the latter played in the events preceding and during the labour rebellion of 1937.[136]

Ethiopia

Through the pages of *The Negro Worker*, the ITUCNW gave extensive coverage and attempted to give some political guidance to the workers' struggles and strikes that erupted throughout the Caribbean in the latter years of the 1930s. Particular prominence was also given to those colonies where workers' organisations existed and demands made such as Martinique, British Guiana, Dutch Guiana and Trinidad.[137] It is clear that as well as the consequences of the worldwide economic crisis and colonial rule, the workers' struggle in the Caribbean were also influenced by the Italian invasion of Ethiopia and the massive international campaign that developed to oppose it. Opposition to the Italian invasion existed on a global scale but was particularly evident throughout the African Diaspora. The Union of Surinam Workers in Holland, for example, sent a protest resolution to the Italian government and formed an Ethiopia support committee. While the 'crew of Negroes' on the *S.S. Holmlea*, sailing from England, declared that they were 'alive to the war threat of fascists and imperialists against coloured people in Africa,' and resolved, 'in the event of this ship being loaded with war material of any description to immediately approach the shore trade unions, dockers etc. to stop the ship from sailing.'[138]

134. For a report of one of Francois's speeches see R. Reddock, *Elma Francois* pp.35-38.

135. Rennie, *The History of the Working Class in the 20th Century*, pp.128-135.

136. O. N Bollard, *On the March: Labour Rebellions in the British Caribbean, 1934-19* (Kingston, 1995) p.88.

137. See e.g. 'Monster May Day Rally in British Guiana, *NW*, 5/7-8 (July-August 1935) p.28.

138. 'International Actions in Support of Abyssinia,' *NW*, 5/9 (September 1935) pp. 12-14.

In British Guiana, several organisations sent resolutions to the governor, the British government and the Emperor of Ethiopia, Haile Selassie. The BGLU sent a cable to the Emperor of Ethiopia, stating: 'The Negroes of British Guiana hail your declaration that you will defend your Empire to the last man against foreign aggression.' It is of note that the at the large May Day rally in Georgetown in 1935 the BGLU unanimously passed resolutions not only on the rights and demands of the workers in British Guiana but also in opposition to the fascist invasion of Ethiopia. [139] The BGLU had already played a key role in securing the removal of a ban on demonstrations and rallies of workers, which had been imposed by the colonial authorities, and had secured the introduction of a Workmen's Compensation Act.[140]

In Trinidad the NWCSA played a leading role in the protests over Ethiopia just as it would later in the labour rebellions. One of the key features of the NWCSA's approach was that it also linked the problems facing working people in Trinidad with the Ethiopian conflict and it worked alongside local trade unions.[141] Much criticism was levelled at the imperialist system and the nature of colonial oppression facing the people of both countries, including the prohibition against demonstrations that was introduced by the colonial government after one NWCSA-led demonstration.[142] In one leaflet advertising a mass meeting and addressed to 'all interested in the welfare of the Negro peoples,' the NWCSA pointed out that the preparation for fascist Italy's attack on Ethiopia came 'at the same time with the attack on the general living standards of the Negro peoples throughout the world. In the West Indies, in Trinidad Negro youth and adult walk the streets for months unemployed, with no unemployment relief, many existing in state of semi-starvation.' (sic) The leaflet concluded, 'the people of Trinidad must protest against this attack on the standard of living of the Negro people. Protest against any attack on the Abyssinian Negro peoples.'[143] Commenting on the prohibition on assembly another leaflet pointed out that ' In the eyes of Imperialists, this attack against our freedom of association, our social rights, goes hand in hand with the attack against our education, our living standards which are becoming daily like that of the natives of Africa.'[144]

139. See 'Monster May Day Rally in British Guiana,' *NW*, 5/7-8 (July-August 1935) p.28.

140. *NW*, 5/7-8 (July-August 1935) p.38. By this time the BGLU was reported to have a membership of some 2000 dockers, seamen, mechanics, miners, builders and other workers. RGASPI 495/14/36/42.

141. On the actions of the Docker's Union in Trinidad which refused to load or unload Italian ships see *NW*, 5/11 (December 1935) p.28.

142. Yellington, 'The War in Ethiopia and Trinidad,' p.207.

143. RGASPI 495/14/60/14.

144. RGASPI 495/14/60/16.

The NWCSA sent protest resolutions not only to Mussolini and the League of Nations concerning attacks on the rights of Ethiopians but also to the Colonial Secretary in London, complaining about attacks on the rights of Trinidadians.[145] It remained at the forefront of anti-colonial protests in Trinidad and later played a leading role in the labour rebellion that broke out in the summer of 1937.[146]

Towards the Labour Rebellions

In the late 1930s the work of the ITUCNW in the Caribbean underwent a change as a result of the changing international situation, the rise of fascism and such events as the Italian invasion of Ethiopia, but also as a consequence of the deliberations of the Seventh Congress of the CI held in 1935. By early 1937 Huiswoud was reporting that the ITUCNW's activities were much more connected with organisations rather than individual contacts and he specifically mentioned the NWCSA in Trinidad, the BGLU, the Dock Workers' and Bakers' Unions in Dutch Guiana, as well as the 'Negro workers' organisations' in Holland, France and Britain.[147] Using his own connections, and taking advantage of the temporary relocation of the ITUCNW to Antwerp and Amsterdam, Huiswoud had been able to make contact with several organisations and individuals from Dutch Guiana, including the exiled Anton De Kom, the author of *We Slaves of Suriname* and a future hero of the anti-fascist Dutch resistance. De Kom, who had been deported and banned from his homeland for his anti-colonial activities, contributed an article describing the terrible conditions in Dutch Guiana for *The Negro Worker*.[148]

As is evident from the reports in *The Negro Worker* of bloody clashes in Jamaica, St Kitts and Martinique, during the 1930s workers struggles in the

145. To Mussolini the NWCSA sent a resolution demanding 'Hands off Abyssinia,' to the League of Nations a resolution calling for the 'unconditional withdrawal' of Fascist Italy from Ethiopia and at the same time condemning 'the policy of World Imperialism for the dividing up of Abyssinia.' To the Colonial Secretary they sent a demand for the 'immediate withdrawal' of the prohibition on assembly which thy viewed as 'something unable to offer any solution towards the problems of the people.' RGASPI 495/155/101/42-44.

146. Reddock, *Elma Francois*, pp.28-50. Also A. Lewis, *Labour in the West Indies: The Birth of a Worker's Movement* (London, 1977) pp.31-33.

147. 'Report of the Activities of the ITUCNW, January 1937,' RGASPI 534/3/1103.

148. See A. de Kom, 'Slavery, Misery and terror in Dutch Guyana, NW, 4/2 (June 1934) pp.19-20; On de Kom see K.M. Kinshasa, 'From Surinam to the Holocaust: Anton de Kom a Political Migrant,' *Journal of Caribbean History*, 36/1 (2002) pp.36-68 and P. Meel, 'Anton de Kom and the Formative Phase of Surinamese Decolonisation,' *New West India Guide*, 83/3-4 (2009) pp.249-280.

Caribbean developed an increasingly militant character but these were contained by ever more ferocious acts of repression.[149] Nevertheless the workers' organisations and anti-colonial forces stepped up their struggles. In Martinique, the assassination of André Aliker led to protests in neighbouring islands and in Europe and did nothing to diminish the activities of the Groupe Jean Jaurès.[150] Indeed the assassination probably strengthened its links with the UTN, which kept in regular contact with Martinique through the distribution of the *Cri des Nègres*.[151] Following the merger of the *Groupe* with *Front Commun* several of their members announced that they wished to join the PCF and appealed for assistance that eventually led to affiliation, but there does not appear to have been any direct connection with the ITUCNW.[152]

By the late 1930s Communist organisations had been formed in several countries in the Caribbean region. However, there do not seem to have been any direct links between the parties in Venezuela, Panama, Puerto Rico and elsewhere and the ITUCNW. Most operated in conditions of illegality or extreme repression and the Communist Party in Haiti was actually disbanded by the Haitian government in 1936. The ITUCNW based in Europe with few resources at its disposal and with very limited assistance from the CPUSA became increasingly marginalised. When an activist from Guadeloupe studying in Moscow was asked to give his assessment of the ITUCNW he admitted that although its existence was known to a few 'even they are little informed of the real activity of the Committee.'[153] Despite its efforts the influence of the ITUCNW seems to have been mainly limited to a few British colonies and even the information it received about the communist movement in the region appears to have been extremely limited. *The Negro Worker* sometimes commented on events in Cuba but rather strangely seldom mentioned the PCC. Helen Davis's article 'The Negro Workers and the Cuban Revolution,' for instance, reported on the Cuban province of Oriente, where the majority 'Negro population' were, 'demanding the right of Self-Determination – the right to govern themselves and to determine their own affairs,' and 'the class-

149. See e.g. H. Eugene, 'The Fight For Bread,' *NW*, 5/5 (May 1935) pp.8-9.

150. RGASPI 517/1/1652. Protest actions were even organised by the NWCSA in Trinidad. See Rennie, *The History of the Working Class in the 20th Century*, p.49. See also the editions of *Cri des Nègres*, January, April-May and July 1934.

151. Report by 'L.S.' 3 December 1937, 2 SLOTFOM 2, ANOM.

152. 'Le Groupe "Jean Jaurès" et le Groupe"Front Commun" au Secrétaire du P.C.' 9 October 1935, RGASPI 517/1/1740. A. Nicolas, *Histoire de la Martinique* [vol.2] (Paris, 1996) p.241.

153. 'Special Discussion Material on the Negro Question,' 10 July 1936, RGASPI 495/14/36/32.

conscious white workers are supporting this demand,' without mentioning that this demand was the policy of the PCC.[154]

The PCC, which under the direction of the CI had developed a very definite policy on the Negro Question in Cuba, also exerted some influence outside its own borders, largely because of the large numbers of migrant workers from Jamaica and elsewhere based in Cuba. It was while living in Cuba that many of Jamaica's early Marxists received their formative training. Antonio King, a Jamaican tile maker was even reported to have been a member of the PCC. He was an associate of another Jamaican who had migrated to Cuba, Hugh Clifford Buchanan, who in 1936 founded the Jamaica Workers and Tradesmen Union. Buchanan was a master mason who migrated to Cuba in 1923 and is also thought to have had some connection with the PCC.[155] Buchanan and King appear to have been part of a preparatory committee formed in 1933 to organise a communist party in Jamaica along with B. Pequero La Paix and others, but there seems to be no evidence of the work of this body in Jamaica.[156] According to Richard Hart, the Jamaica Marxists operated without any strong connection with the CI even after they were first contacted by the CPGB in 1939.[157]

The ITUCNW evidently played some part in strengthening and providing some orientation for organisations such as the NSCWA and the BGLU and *The Negro Worker* continued to provide an analysis of the attempts of the colonial authorities to force the burden of the economic crisis on to the backs of the mass of people in the colonies.[158] But it faced a variety of complex problems, not least the repressive nature of colonialism, was based outside the region and its activities were handicapped by the inactivity of the communist parties of Britain, France and the US. In early 1937 Charles Alexander reflected on the

154. H. Davis, 'The Negro Workers and the Cuban Revolution,' *NW*, 4/1 (May 1934) pp.27-29. For a very brief report of the Second Congress of the Cuban Communist Party see 'Cuban Workers Strengthen Their Organisations,' *NW*, 4/3 (July 1934) p.18.

155. R. Hart, *Rise and Organise: The Birth of The Workers and National Movements in Jamaica 1936-1939* (London, 1989) pp.16-20. See also B. Carr, 'Identity, Class, and Nation: Black Immigrant Workers, Cuban Communism, and the Sugar Insurgency, 1925-1934,' *Hispanic American Historical Review*, 78/1, (February 1998) pp.83-116.

156. 'Acta De Constitucion Del Comite Pro-Organizacion Del Partido Comunista De Jamaica.' 4 April 1933, RGASPI 500/1/10. This document was written in Spanish and signed by La Paix.

157. Hart, *Rise and Organise,* pp. 137-138. Ben Bradley to R. Hart, 17 April 1939 and R. Hart to B. Bradley, 7 May 1939, (TNA) KV2/1824.

158. See e.g. 'British Imperialism's Hunger Drive in Trinidad,' *NW*, 6/8 (October 1936) pp.25-26. It is however noticeable that the distribution of *The Negro Worker* was somewhat limited in the Caribbean. In 1937 it was report that only about 145 copies were distributed throughout the Caribbean, whereas over 200 were sent to England and 425 to South Africa. 'Report on the Activities of the ITUCNW,' January 1937, RGASPI 534/3/1103.

previous year as a 'glorious one for the West Indian masses' in which workers had militantly fought for their rights in St Kitts, Trinidad, St Vincent, Barbados, Jamaica, British Guiana, Haiti and elsewhere. He predicted that these struggles would continue throughout 1937 and would embrace political as well as economic demands.[159] It is indeed ironic that at a time when the struggle for independence and for the rights of the workers was intensifying in the Caribbean, events reflected in the pages of the last edition *The Negro Worker* in the autumn of 1937, the ITUCNW was in the process of being dissolved and unable to provide the political leadership to events it had long agitated for and predicted.[160]

159. C. Alexander, '1937 – A New Year of Struggle for the West Indian Masses,' *NW*, 7/3 (March 1937) pp.10-11.

160. See *NW*, 7/7-8 (September-October 1937) for articles on the strikes and disturbances in Trinidad, Barbados and Jamaica.

Chapter 9

The Comintern and West Africa

First contacts and the League Against Imperialism

The first direct contact between the international communist movement and West Africa seems to have been the recruitment in Paris of Lamine Senghor, a Senegalese postal clerk and ex-serviceman, by the PCF and its trade union centre, the CGTU, in 1924. The following year Senghor stood as a PCF candidate in the municipal elections in Paris and subsequently became the leading figure in the CDRN, established in Paris in 1926. This organisation claimed to have hundreds of members in French West Africa. Certainly by early 1927 it was distributing its publication *La Voix des Nègres* in several of the French colonies.[1] So alarmed were the French colonial authorities that the

1. RGASPI 495/155/36/2.

publication's distribution was prohibited, recipients were placed under surveillance and Senghor was prevented from returning to West Africa.[2]

Subsequently, and with PCF assistance, Senghor founded the LDRN, with a French-based but mainly West African membership. The *Ligue* utilised African sailors to distribute its new publication *La Race Nègre*, as well as LDRN membership forms throughout French West Africa, and from its inception established a presence in Africa, much to the concern of the colonial authorities. It was reported that the LDRN attempted to establish branches in Senegal, Dahomey and Cameroon, had been responsible for demands for political independence and was even blamed for organising uprisings in French Congo and others parts of French Equatorial Africa.[3] Senghor's early death did not curtail the activities of the *Ligue,* which came under the leadership of another West African, Garan Kouyaté. In early 1929 it was reported that it had established branches in Dakar, Abidjan, Ouidah and some twenty other towns in the French colonies in West and Equatorial Africa.[4]

The colonial authorities continued to monitor the activities of Kouyaté, the LDRN, its successor the UTN and the PCF throughout the 1930s. The Communists in France maintained varying degrees of contact with the West African colonies throughout this period, supplying sympathisers with revolutionary literature by post, with the support of seamen as couriers and via local distributors.[5] In May 1932 the Ministry of Colonies in France warned of PCF attempts to establish unions throughout French West and Equatorial Africa, in which it was claimed Kouayté was also involved. At the same time there were reports that a workers' organisation with over two hundred and fifty members had been established in Dakar, Senegal and was requesting 'directives' to enable it to realise its aims from the CGTU in France.[6] Such links created the conditions for several students to be sent from Senegal to Moscow for political train-

2. E.T. Wilson, *Russia and Black Africa Before World War II* (London, 1974) pp.149-150.

3. J. Spiegler, 'Aspects of Nationalist Thought Among French-Speaking West Africans, 1921-1939,' D.Phil. Thesis, University of Oxford, 1968, pp.125-133 and B.H. Edwards, *The Practice of Diaspora: Literature, Translation, and the Rise of Black Internationalism* (London, 2003) p.254.

4. Report of the Trip in Interest of the Work of the ITUCNW of the RILU, the Negro Bureau of the CI and the Meeting of the Executive Committee of the LAI, 14 February 1929. RGASPI 534/3/450.

5. See, Report of Paul, 22 January 1934; Réunion de la fraction communiste Nègre, de l'UTN, 26 February 1934; Report on 'bureau de UTN,' 27 February 1934, 3 SLOTFOM 53, ANOM.

6. 'Le Ministre des colonies à le gouverneur general de l'Afrique occidentale francaise, 17 May 1932, SLOTFROM 2, ANOM.

ing, the beginnings of trade union organisation and for the later emergence of an openly communist organisation.

The Comintern's attempts to directly develop its influence in Anglophone West Africa began in earnest with the preparations for the founding congress of the LAI in Brussels in February 1927.[7] The organisers used the occasion to make contact with several prominent individuals in British West Africa, including those associated with the National Congress of British West Africa, the Sierra Leone Railway Workers Union, the Gold Coast Farmers' Association and organisations in Liberia. [8]

None of those invited to the congress from British West Africa were able to attend, although Lamine Senghor ably represented the French colonies. Senghor was subsequently elected to the executive committee and then promptly arrested by the French authorities on his return to France, which prevented his appointment as one of the joint secretaries of the LAI. [9] Although there was no representation from British West Africa, the LAI, the CI and the RILU tried to build on the initial contact that had been established. Shortly after the Brussels congress the International Secretariat of the LAI reported that it was endeavouring:

> To link up the different organisations of the African Negro movement in order to concentrate the forces of the African Negro fight for emancipation. The Secretariat is in touch through the CDRN with the Negro population of the French African colonies. A special secretariat has been established in Dakar (French Western Africa). The Gold Coast Farmers' Association, the Sierra Leone Railwaymen's Union and the Mozambique Railwaymen's Union are further important links in the chain of the organised Negro Labor trying to gain Africa(sic).[10]

The LAI was already placing most emphasis on the workers' movement in Africa, especially on the possibilities in South Africa, where it hoped that the ANC and the Industrial and Commercial Workers Union could 'become the centre of a continentally organised Negro Movement.'[11]

---

7. W. Munzenberg, 'For a Colonial Conference,' *International Press Correspondence (Inprecor)*, 26 August 1926, p.968.

8. The National Archives (TNA) CO 323/966/1 and CO 323/971/1.

9. See J. Nehru, 'Notes for the Working Committee,' 4 April 1927, British Library, India Office Records, (IOR) L/PJ/12/266.

10. L. Gibarti 'Report on the activities of the LAI in the different countries,' February-May 1927 IOR L/PJ/12/266.

11. Ibid.

Later in 1927 E.A. Richards, the President of the Sierra Leone Railway Workers' Union, was invited to Moscow for the tenth anniversary celebrations of the October Revolution. He was eager to make the journey but his movements were closely monitored by the British Colonial Office and security services as soon as he left Sierra Leone. In Moscow, Richards was feted and he even presided over a congress of the Friends of Soviet Russia alongside Clara Zetkin and Lenin's widow Krupskaya.[12] However, when he passed through Britain on his return to West Africa he was detained by the security services and found to be carrying the not insignificant sum of more than a hundred and twenty pounds, a revolver and ammunition apparently purchased in Berlin, as well as revolutionary literature and a diary detailing his activities in Moscow. On that occasion the British authorities had been unable to prevent his visit to the Soviet Union, which appears to have been paid for by the LAI.[13] Richards was subsequently unable to attend the meeting of the General Council of the LAI, held in Brussels in November/December 1927, but suggested asking another West African, Bankole Awooner-Renner from the Gold Coast, then a student at KUTV in Moscow, to attend on his behalf.[14] Richards's visit to Moscow facilitated a meeting with Lozovsky and the RILU, and he sought their aid for those of his comrades in the Railwaymen's Union who had been sacked following the strike that had taken place the previous year.[15]

It seems almost certain that it was the railway workers' strike of January and February 1926 that had first brought the union to the attention of the RILU. It was one of the first major industrial disputes in British West Africa and for some six weeks involved over 1000 workers in 'the locomotives, engineering, and traffic branches, and practically all the telegraph operators.' It was widely supported in Sierra Leone, assumed an anti-colonial character and prompted punitive action by the colonial authorities that were reluctant to even recognise the right of Africans to form trade union or to strike.[16] It also seems to have prompted the CI to begin organising amongst African labour unions

Ernest Alfonso Richards was born in Sierra Leone in 1885, although he travelled on a Nigerian passport. An ex-locomotive fitter, he was apparently no

12. Wilson, *Russia and Black Africa,* p.334 n.54.

13. The National Archives (TNA) CO 267/622/1, Special Branch to Lloyd, 24 November 1927.

14. E.A. Richards to the Secretary LAI, 12 November 1927, RGASPI 542/1/8/190.

15. E.A. Richards to Losovsky, 23 December 1927, RGASPI 537/7/79/7. It appears that Richards had also been dismissed for leading the strike.

16. D. F. Luke, 'The Development of Modern Trade Unionism in Sierra Leone – Part 1,' *International Journal of African Historical Studies,* 18/3 (1985) pp.425-454 and A.J.G. Wyse, 'The 1926 Railway Strike and Anglo-Krio Relations,' *International Journal of African Historical Studies,* 14/1 (1981) pp.93-123.

longer employed on the railway following the 1926 strike, but remained President of the Railwaymen's Union and was subsequently invited to the Fourth RILU Congress in 1928. However, the British authorities alerted to the connection which existed between Richards and the CI, refused to allow him to travel to Moscow and he only managed to reach as far as Liverpool, where he was detained and his subsequent movements closely monitored by the security services.[17] Richards remained in contact with the RILU and the LAI, despite such travel restrictions, and the Railwaymen's Union subsequently affiliated to both organisations. In later years, the ITUCNW tried to find ways to further develop the relationship with the Railwaymen's Union and other workers in Sierra Leone through the publication of several 'open letters.'[18]

Bankole Awooner-Renner, who Richards had suggested as his replacement, was one of the first African students to study at KUTV in Moscow, along with Kolli Seleh Tamba, a tailor from Liberia.[19] They were part of a group of African and African American students sent to the Soviet Union in 1925 by Fort-Whiteman, of the ANLC, under the auspices of the WP.[20] Born in the Gold Coast in 1898, Awooner-Renner went to the United States to study journalism in 1922. He was a student both at Tuskegee Institute and the Carnegie Institute in Pennsylvania and became secretary of the African Students' Association. How he came into contact with the ANLC is not clear but he evidently joined the WP in April 1925, just a few months before he was sent to the Soviet Union. Once there he became a spokesman for African interests, even openly challenging Zinoviev, the head of the CI, who had omitted to mention Africans, the 'most oppressed people,' as Awooner-Renner described them, in a lecture given at KUTV in April 1926.[21] It is, however, unclear whether Awooner-Renner subsequently represented Richards and the Railwaymen's Union at the Brussels

17. E.A. Richards to Losovsky, 23 December 1927, RGASPI 537/7/79/7 and TNA CO 267/622/1.

18. See e.g. 'An Open Letter – To the Workers of Freetown, To the Toiling Masses of Sierra Leone,' n.d. RGASPI 534/6/23/2-8 and 'What the Workers of Sierra Leone Should Do,' *NW*, 1/9 (September 1931) pp.17-19.

19. W. McClellan, 'Black Hajj to "Red Mecca": Africans and Afro-Americans at KUTV. 1925-1938,' in M. Matusevich (ed.) *Africa in Russia, Russia in Africa: Three Centuries of Encounters* (Trenton, NJ, 2006) pp. 61-83 and W. McClennan, 'Africans and Black Americans in Comintern Schools, 1925-1934,' *International Journal of African Historical Studies*, 26/2 (1993) pp.371-390.

20. L. Fort-Whiteman to Dear Comrades, 6 August 1925 RGASPI 495/155/33/24.

21. McClennan, 'Africans and Black Americans in Comintern Schools,' p.4.

meeting of the LAI, although he does appear to have been involved in the drafting of a Union 'Declaration' prepared for that meeting.[22]

In April 1927, while still a student at KUTV, Awooner-Renner wrote a lengthy report on economic and political conditions in West Africa at the request of the CI. He concluded that the growing discontent of the workers and peasants, of the Muslim population and the 'native bourgeoisie' suggested a 'bright prospective of a militant national movement which will embrace the whole of western Africa with a Bolshevik Party as its vanguard.'[23] It seems that Awooner-Renner considered that he might be part of such a vanguard, to judge from his requests to join the 'People's Revolutionary Army of China' and the Commanders' Academy of the Red Army after he had graduated from KUTV.[24] He also seems to have been involved in discussions that took place in Moscow in 1927 to establish an African Bureau in London, which could make the conditions of those oppressed in the colonies known to 'the class conscious workers.' These plans included a monthly publication, entitled *Colonial World,* and the possibility of convening an 'All-African Conference' in Africa. Certainly Awooner-Renner made the CI aware of the revolutionary potential of African and Caribbean seamen, workers and students in Britain, who he thought should have been drawn into the ranks of the CPGB. The following year he was more eager to return to West Africa in order to establish a workers' and peasants' party in both British and French colonies, which would 'be the basis of a Communist Party in tropical Africa.'[25] Although Awooner-Renner returned to West Africa in 1928 he appears to have achieved little of any note until he worked with Wallace-Johnson's WAYL in the late 1930s.

In the United States, Lovett Fort-Whiteman had himself been interested in developing links with West Africa in general, and Liberia in particular, when he led the ANLC during the mid-1920s. In 1926 he wrote to the Peasants' International, or Kresintern, to enquire if it was 'well disposed to taking up the work in West Africa and particularly the countries of French and British Nigeria (sic), Ashanti, Dahomey, Sierra Leone and Senegambia as well as Liberia.' Fort-Whiteman reported that the ANLC had recently received a letter from 'a very intelligent worker' in Lagos, Nigeria, 'who wishes to organise the peasants in that section of the country.' However, he appears to have mentioned this fact in order to demonstrate the 'very broad connections' of the ANLC throughout the

22. 'Declaration of the Sierra Leone Railwaymen's Union to the Brussels Conference of the LAI,' 14 November 1927, RGASPI 495/64/166/1-2.

23. B. Awooner-Renner, 'Report on West Africa,' 4 April 1927, RGASPI 495/64/166/9-22.

24. B. Awooner-Renner to Eastern Secretariat of the ECCI, 22 May 1927 and 30 March 1927, RGASPI 495/64/166. Also McClellan, 'Black Hajj,' pp. 61-83.

25. 'To the Anglo-American Secretariat of the ECCI on behalf of Comrade Bankole,' 1928, RGASPI 495/64/166/26.

African continent. Such connections led him to propose a 'program of action embracing America, West and South Africa,' but nothing more seems to have come of these proposals, or his plan for 'a Russian-Liberian Commercial Agreement,' which he claimed 'has as its prime motive the hidden purpose of spreading communist influence into the heart of Africa, and particularly West Africa.'[26]

THE HAMBURG CONFERENCE AND WEST AFRICA

The main impetus to heightened Comintern activity in West Africa was the founding of the ITUCNW, and the RILU Negro Bureau meeting in July 1928 and the deliberations on Africa that emerged from the Sixth Comintern Congress at the same time. The activity of the RILU was based on the new orientation of the CI, which was to give greater emphasis to the need for the development a 'united front from below' in which the workers should take the lead whether in the colonies or the imperialist countries. There was also a continued concern in the CI that a new war, especially a war against the Soviet Union, might be imminent and that black troops, especially those from Africa, would again be forced to play a significant interventionist role. During the late 1920s and 1930s the use of African troops against the Soviet Union, and against the interests of the workers in countries such as France, remained a constant concern and therefore efforts were continually made to combat the potential threat. Indeed, the last and most substantial point of the ITUCNW's 'A Trade Union Programme of Action for Negro Workers' was on 'The War Danger.' [27]

The founding of the ITUCNW placed special emphasis on the workers in colonial Africa but the early activities and programme of the ITUCNW had a limited impact on the continent outside of South Africa. Much of this initial work involved research and investigation and the turning point was the plan to hold an international Negro workers' conference in 1930.[28] The initial plans for what became the Hamburg Conference only envisaged three delegates from West Africa, from Sierra Leone, Dakar and Monrovia, as well as delegates

26. L. Fort-Whiteman to Acting General Secretary Dombal, International Farmers Council, 16 April 1926, RGASPI 495/155/37/1-2. J. Jackson (Fort-Whiteman), 'Project for a Russian-Liberian Commercial Agreement,' n.d., RGASPI 495/155/25/14-19.

27. See also 'Negro Toilers and the International Red Day,' 1929. RGASPI 534/3/450 and G. Padmore, *The Life and Struggles of Negro Toilers* (London, 1931) pp.111-120.

28. See e.g. 'Minutes of Meeting of the ITUCNW,' 1 December 1928. RGASPI 534/3/359. From 1928 both the CI and RILU Negro Bureaus carried out investigative studies on Africa. On some of the Negro Bureau's preparatory work with an African focus see e.g. 'Memo on Negro Work for Month of May,' 3 May 1929. RGASPI 495/155/74/8 and J. Ford, 'Significant and Outstanding Facts abut British West Africa and Liberia,' 4 June 1929. RGASPI 495/64/166.

from Central Africa, East Africa and the Belgian Congo.[29] Nobody participated from the latter three regions but a concerted effort by the ITUCNW, and a tour of West Africa by George Padmore, resulted in five delegates travelling to Hamburg from British West Africa, in addition to Bilé from Berlin. No West Africans resident in France or Britain participated at Hamburg, although it is evident that Kouyaté and others had originally planned to travel from France.

The convening of an international conference had long been planned and seemed to be particularly timely for western Africa in 1930 where the ITUCNW reported a major rebellion had erupted in French Equatorial Africa in addition to important struggles in the Belgian Congo and elsewhere. It particularly highlighted the recent strike in Bathurst, the capital of the Gambia, which had been suppressed by martial law, as well as the mass murder of over forty women by the colonial authorities in Nigeria.[30]

The strike in Bathurst, under the leadership of E.F. Small, had immediately received the support of the RILU, the CPGB's Labour Research Department, the NMM and the British section of the LAI. These organisations appealed for trade union support and some British workers even threatened to begin a solidarity strike in support of their Gambian comrades. This example of 'proletarianism internationalism' made a big impact in Gambia and may even have contributed to the success of the strike, leading to union recognition and agreement on a minimum wage.[31] The success of the Bathurst workers encouraged the local farmers to organise and the foundations of a 'peasant league' were also established with LAI support. As a consequence, Small soon succeeded Richards as the most prominent West African trade unionist in contact with the CI and was invited to attend the congress of the Farmers' and Peasants' International (Kresintern), held in Berlin in 1930, where he met William Patterson, one of the main organisers of the Hamburg Conference.[32]

It was with Small's assistance that Padmore subsequently managed to travel quite extensively in West Africa, visiting Senegal, Sierra Leone, the Gold Coast

29. 'List of Delegates and Agenda of Negro Workers International Trade Union Conference,' 14 November 1929.

30. Both of these incidents were reported in *The Negro Worker.* See G. Padmore, 'Africans Massacred by British Imperialists,' *NW*, (December 1929) pp.2-4 and J. Reed, 'The Strike of the Negro Workers in Gambia,' Ibid. pp. 6-7. See also G. Padmore, 'British Imperialism in Nigeria,' *International Press Correspondence (Inprecor)*, 7 August 1930, p.705.

31. 'Suppression of Trade Unionism in British West Africa,' *The Monthly Circular of the Labour Research Department*, XVIII/12 (December 1929) pp.265-267.

32. W[illiam]W[ilson] (Patterson) to Negro Bureau Profintern, 12 April 1930. RGASPI 534/4/330. It is interesting that Patterson later complained that in regard to Small's Bathurst Trade Union, the 'English comrades' took 'no steps to gain such influence over his organisation as would give us guidance of it; took no steps to send assistance there.' W. Patterson to Haywood, 10 April 1930. RGASPI 495/18/809.

and Nigeria, despite the constant attention of the British and French authorities. In the Gold Coast he found two delegates, J.A. Akrong, representing the Drivers' and Mechanics' Union and T.S. Morton the Carpenters' Union, while in Sierra Leone he re-established contact with Richards who was to be the delegate of the Railwaymen's Union. Small was subsequently selected to represent the renamed Gambia Labour Union and Nigeria was represented by Frank Macaulay, son of Herbert Macaulay – the 'father of Nigerian nationalism' – and a delegate of the Nigerian National Democratic Party (NNDP), at that time the most significant political organisation in the colony. Padmore was drawn into some of the ongoing political disputes within the NNDP while he was in Lagos and it appears that Macaulay was only finally selected with the support of the Muslim-led Ilu Committee of the NNDP, which was closer to the mass of Lagosians than most of the NNDP leaders.[33]

When the conference finally convened in Hamburg, Macaulay, Richards and Small were elected members of the 'presidium' and all three spoke during the event to highlight the particular problems that workers faced in their respective colonies. Amongst other things, Small declared that 'The Gambia workers regard the struggle of their Negro comrades everywhere as their own; they are in fact with the struggle of the oppressed millions of toiling workers throughout the world.' He concluded by stating, ' it is our hope that this Conference will go a long way to consolidate the forces of economic and industrial resistance against all forms of capitalist oppression not only among Negroes but among workers and peasants of the world.'[34] Following the speeches of all the West African and other delegates, Macaulay delivered a major presentation on 'The War Danger and its significance to the Negro Masses.'[35]

At the conclusion of the conference both Macaulay and Small were elected to the executive committee of the ITUCNW along with Kouyaté who was elected in his absence. Macaulay, Small and Bilé then proceeded to Moscow, where they were joined by Kouyaté, to attend the Fifth RILU Congress and for further discussions with the ITUCNW. The Hamburg Conference was strongly criticised by some of its principal organisers but Macaulay had his own evaluation of its significance for West Africa:

> The principle thing is for the Negro Conference to be regarded as the first step towards the formation of a trade union in West Africa. There is no trade union there, and it is for conference having made

33. Minutes of the meeting of the International Secretariat with the Negro friends, 14 October 1930. RGASPI 542/1/40/77.

34. A Report of Proceedings and Decisions of the First International Conference of Negro Workers (Hamburg, 1930) pp.21-23.

35. Ibid. pp. 35-37.

> contact in West Africa, not to allow the opportunity to slip by. It is for them to snatch every moment and all the time that is available, because the British Government will not be asleep...It is for the Negro Committee to see that the opportunity is not lost, that arrangements are being made for the formation of trade unions, and to see that the Negroes of West Africa are properly organised...If they do not organise the Negroes now the British government will be before them in passing laws that no one will be allowed to go and organise a trade union in West Africa.[36]

This was a theme that he reiterated in his address to the RILU Congress, where Small and Kouyaté also spoke, becoming the first Africans to address such an international gathering. Macaulay also took the opportunity to criticise 'white chauvinism' within the ranks of the workers' movement, an issue that had been stressed in an earlier speech by Lozovsky, and to suggest that black and white workers needed to be organised in unison. However, he concluded his speech with an appeal for more information to be disseminated in Africa about the Soviet Union, in order to counter the 'many anti-Soviet lies that are constantly being spread abroad.' In his presentation Small used numerous examples from the recent general strike in Gambia to show the importance of continuing to organise amongst the workers and peasant farmers as the economic crisis intensified and to demonstrate that the line of the RILU, 'the united front from below,' was indeed correct and would bring tangible results.[37]

Several other participants from the Hamburg Conference also addressed the RILU congress, which formulated a special resolution on work among 'Negro Workers,' stressing that organising these workers meant 'rallying the last remainders of the proletarian reserves to the international revolutionary movement.' It also devoted special attention to colonial Africa, although focusing particularly on South Africa, calling for the organising of urban and rural workers, the urgent need for political training of cadres and the uniting of the worker's struggles in the colonial and metropolitan countries. In regard to West Africa, the reactionary role of the British Labour government was highlighted and the need for the workers to struggle 'for the immediate evacuation by the imperialists of all Negro colonies and for complete independence.'[38]

36. Report on Negro Conference, 5 July 1930. RGASPI 534/3/490.

37. T. Marsh (Macaulay) and G. Miller (Small), 'Le Mouvement Nègre en Afrique,' *L'Ouriver Nègre* (1November 1930) pp.15-16 and 19-22. Also 'Report on the Economic Situation in the Gambia,' 16 August 1930. RGASPI 495/64/165; and 'Nigeria,' 28 July 1930. RGASPI 495/64/168.

38. 'Black Africa, ' and 'Work Among Negro Workers,' in *Resolutions of the Fifth World Congress of the RILU* (London, 1930) pp. 64-66 and 159-165.

The LAI and the Negro Friends

Macaulay, Small, Bilé and Kouyaté remained in the Soviet Union for some weeks after the RILU Congress, in order that they could travel throughout the country and have more discussions with representatives of the CI and the RILU, before they returned to Germany in mid-October 1930. The complete details of their stay are not available but documents show that Bilé travelled as far as Baku where he discovered a Togolese family, a mother and five children, the youngest of whom was 13 years old. The parents had originally been part of a visiting circus but had remained in the Soviet Union. Bilé and Kouyaté made proposals that the children, four of whom were workers who all spoke their parent's language as well as Russian, might be trained in Moscow so as to be involved in some way with work connected with Africa but it is unclear if these proposals were adopted.[39]

On their return the four West Africans were met in Kiel by Bohumir Smeral, a Czech Communist who was already a leading figure in the CI and a member of the International Secretariat of the LAI. Smeral escorted them to Berlin where they participated in five lengthy meetings with the International Secretariat. These meeting were designed to develop a programme of action for West Africa and were clearly undertaken under the guidance of the CI.[40] The LAI had by this time developed a detailed analysis of the 'World Negro Question,' based on the political line of the Comintern. In regard to the British colonies in West Africa it demanded 'complete independence,' and 'immediate and complete evacuation of these colonies by British imperialism.' In French West Africa, it pointed out the continuing dangers of the recruitment of African troops for the French army and opposed the imposition of 'various forms of slavery.' The LAI also condemned the suppression of the uprising that had occurred in French Congo and for all French colonies in West and Equatorial Africa it called for 'complete national independence.'[41]

Smeral, who chaired the first meeting in Berlin, acknowledged that relations with Africa had been somewhat neglected by the LAI in the past but stressed that 'this section of the anti-imperialist front is of extraordinary importance.' He therefore concluded, 'we have to give the same attention to the Negro question in Africa that until now we have given to the Negro question in America,' and explained that the meeting with the four Africans was held in order to

39. Kouyaté 'Rapport,' 30 September 1930. RGASPI 495/155/18/810/88-90.

40. The League Fraction to Dear Friends, 3 November 1930. RGASPI 495/155/90/78-81.

41. 'Draft Resolution on the World Negro Problem,' 4 June 1929. RGASPI 495/155/72/40-58. This document was almost certainly drafted by Ford who delivered a 19-page report on the 'Negro Question' to the Frankfurt Congress of the LAI. See J. Ford, 'Report of the Negro Question at the LAI Congress,' 3 October 1929. RGASPI 534/3/450.

discuss how the struggles in West Africa might be advanced. The LAI wanted to have first hand accounts of the situation in West Africa but also suggested that it might be possible to establish local branches of the League, and that it would also be able to assist with the training of cadres.[42]

In response Macaulay gave a detailed account of conditions in Nigeria, which suggested that recent events had made a significant impression on him. Amongst other things, he pointed out that he had known nothing about Soviet Russia, or even the independence struggle in India before his trip to Russia. He described the political parties in Nigeria as 'completely reformist,' and led by 'lawyers who were educated in the spirit of the English constitution and who want to act on the basis of that constitution.' He hoped that both leaders and parties might be better guided by joining the LAI. Recent experience had also taught him that the 'English Labour Party' was 'worse than the Conservatives,' and he concluded that 'we can gain our freedom and independence only with the help of Russia.'[43]

Small's comments were more ambivalent because he was critical of some of the speeches and members of the 'Negro delegation' that had travelled to Moscow. He considered that the 'Negro question' could not be solved 'until Negroes become conscious of their race not only conscious of their class.' At the same time he was clear that significant class differences existed between the 'Negro workers' and the 'Negro bourgeoisie,' and was also critical of reformist organisations such as the National Congress of British West Africa of which he was a leading member. He also made much of what were merely differences of emphasis between the LAI, the RILU and the CI but he too had returned from Russia with 'the conviction of how important the Soviet Union is for the Negroes.' He had also learned important lessons from the support that the Gambian workers had received from the Labour Research Department, the LAI and workers in Britain and pointed out that this 'international solidarity' had 'resulted in the victory of the Gambian workers.' Their experience he said, showed that 'they can conduct their struggle not on their own but as part of the international working class.' Small suggested that the LAI should establish itself and a special 'anti-imperial bulletin' in Africa, which could educate the masses of the people about economic and political issues and developments in the Soviet Union.[44]

Kouyaté had the most Pan-Africanist orientation of the four Africans. He championed the 'creation of a Negro African republic,' which would unite

42. Minutes of the meeting of the International Secretariat with the Negro friends, 14 October 1930. RGASPI 542/1/40/77.

43. Ibid.

44. Ibid.

Africans who had been separated by the borders imposed by the imperialists into a unified federation. However, this was a view that was not supported by the others, although Small was in favour of a united struggle of West Africans. Indeed it was difficult to find unity of opinion amongst them on how the anti-imperialist struggle in West Africa should be conducted, with both Small and Macaulay opposed to any demands for the expropriation of the imperialists. There was also discussion on the question of sending cadres to be trained. Here too both Small and Macaulay showed some reluctance to send workers and it was clear that on this issue there might well be practical difficulties. Kouyaté, however, had already selected five potential students and plans were made for their journey to Moscow.[45]

The meetings led to the drafting of a document 'The Anti-Imperialist Struggle of the West African People,' but as the four West Africans refused to put their names to it, both the LAI and the CI were uncertain about its usefulness. Its contents reflected many of the issues discussed during the five meetings and included the proposal that 'it is absolutely necessary, for the successful overthrow of imperialist exploitation, to establish a united front of the masses in all the colonies of West Africa, with the ultimate object of establishing a strong West African Federation of independent Negro States.' It also sought to establish unity between the LAI and 'all those classes in each colony that are the victims of imperialist exploitation and oppression,' and set out a clear list of immediate demands around which they might unite, including 'the right to bear arms for personal defence,' and the 'abolition of the system of tribal chieftancy.'[46] However, no branch of the LAI was organised in West Africa, Macaulay died shortly after returning to Nigeria, while Small failed to maintain his initial enthusiasm.

Kouyaté and the LDRN seemed to offer greater possibilities, although even here there were also difficulties to be overcome. Although the LDRN still claimed to have several branches in Senegal, Ivory Coast, Togo, Dahomey, and even French Equatorial Africa and the Belgian Congo, it was almost impossible for it to maintain contact, or successfully distribute *La Race Nègre* owing to censorship and the outright banning of the publication by the colonial authorities.[47] The initial inability of Kouyaté and other French-based activists to fully develop their contacts with the French colonies in Africa clearly had an impact

45. Ibid. The League Fraction to Dear Friends, 3 November 1930. RGASPI 495/155/90/78-81.

46. 'The Anti-Imperialist Struggle of the West African People,' November 1930. RGASPI 542/1/40.

47. Report on the League of the Defence of the Negro Race,' n.d. RGASPI 495/155/78/23-27 and Kouyaté, 'Report,' 30 September 1930. RGASPI 495/155/87/396-403.

on the work of the ITUCNW, which during most of its existence concentrated its work towards the British colonies.

Kouyaté and the LDRN also occupied an important role in Germany, where the Liga zur Verteidigung der Negerrasse led by Joseph Bilé had been established. Although the Liga was based at the Berlin offices of the LAI and received some LAI support it appears to have also received some political leadership from the LDRN in Paris. Although the Liga had established some connections in the former German colonies of Togo and Kamerun, in addition to its activities amongst 'Negro dock workers' in Hamburg, it was short of finance and very critical of the limited support it received from the LAI. The LAI had apparently even been unable to help with payment for the burial of one of its members and other members felt that its activities in West Africa could only advance if certain measures were taken. Amongst other proposals the Liga suggested that one of its members should be co-opted into the leadership of the Colonial Section of the German Communist Party and that young Africans should be sent as a group directly from Africa to Moscow for training.[48] Although Bilé was eventually sent for training in Moscow at KUTV in 1932, the Liga continued to face major difficulties. Unfortunately, the work of the Berlin-based LAI did not seem destined to make major advances in West Africa either and was later severely criticised by Padmore.[49] The British Section of the LAI did establish and maintain links in the region throughout the 1930s, often working in tandem with the ITUCNW.

The Hamburg Committee and West Africa

The Hamburg Committee (HC) of the ITUCNW, led by James Ford, was established in the German port in the autumn of 1930. The most important decision of the RILU was for the ITUCNW to 'make Africa the centre of gravity of its work' and initially there had also been a proposal to establish an 'African Secretariat' of the ITUCNW.[50] In general the ITUCNW was tasked with making contacts throughout Africa, especially amongst the workers, and encouraging the latter to organise themselves. Such a task was far from straightforward, since the colonial authorities took measures to prevent the formation of trade unions. In these circumstances therefore the activities of the ITUCNW

48. '*Kurzer Tatigkeitsbericht der Liga zur Verteidigung der Negerrasse*,' 30 November 1930. RGASPI 495/155/87/404-408.

49. See e.g. J. Ford to Padmore, 13 July 1931. RGASPI 534/3/668. Also Padmore to Dear Comrades, 16 June 1932. RGASPI 534/3/755.

50. Resolution on the Work of the Hamburg Committee,' 18 October 1931. RGASPI 534/3/668; 'On the Organisation of the ITUCNW,' 5 September 1930. RGASPI 495/18/810/77.

and its supporters in favour of the rights of the workers also had a decidedly anti-colonial and anti-imperialist orientation.

Ford and the RILU Negro Bureau made every attempt to develop their work in West Africa.[51] In several cases this meant consolidating those links that had already been established, especially those developed in connection with the Hamburg Conference, as well as by enlisting the aid of the British LAI and Kouyaté and the LDRN in France.[52] In April 1931, for example, the HC agreed to place a representative of the Sierra Leone Railway Workers' Union on the ITUCNW's Executive Committee, and attempted to strengthen its links with the Union and its activities through an 'Open Letter' in *The Negro Worker*.[53] However, Ford found it difficult to maintain contact with those from West Africa who had been placed on the Executive, such as Small, and even more difficult to establish new contacts or organise 'revolutionary trade union groups in Africa.'[54]

Ford was also charged with establishing contacts with seamen who could act as couriers for propaganda and carry out other work for the HC in Africa. He devoted considerable time and effort to this work and through it came into contact with several Anglophone West Africans including a Sierra Leonean seamen, Ernest Foster-Jones, a member of the executive committee of the 'United Kroomen's Club, which had been established in Sierra Leone in 1923. Although this was not a trade union, the seamen who congregated there had, according to Ford, put forward demands for improved working conditions and wages and achieved some success. Elder Dempster, the main shipping line between Britain and West Africa, had refused to negotiate further with the seamen unless they had some official connection with a trade union. Foster-Jones, who often resided in Liverpool, indicated that the Kroomen's Club might be prepared to affiliate to 'a militant seamen's union,' and Ford considered that it might be possible to work with the Club and even train some of its members.[55]

The HC and the RILU Negro Bureau also made some attempts to develop their activities in Liberia. Padmore published a major article 'American Imperialism Enslaves Liberia' in February 1931, in which he not only attacked the governments of Liberia and the United States, as well as the Firestone Corporation,

51. G. Padmore, 'The Agrarian Crisis in British West Africa,' *The Communist International*, 8/13 (15 July 1931) pp. 370-376.

52. G. Padmore to Ford, 8 February 1931. RGASPI 534/3/668.

53. 'Proposal,' 21 April 1931, and J. Ford to Executive Committee ITUCNW, 21 April 1931. RGASPI 534/3/668. Also 'What the Workers of Sierra Leone Should Do,' *NW*, 1/9 (September 1931) pp.17-19.

54. Concrete Proposals on Report of Work of Hamburg Committee, 10 June 1931. RGASPI 534/3/668.

55. J. Ford to Padmore, 20 April 1931. RGASPI 534/3/668. See also, Foster-Jones, 'Situation of Negro Workers in Sierra Leone,' *NW*, 1/4-5 (April-May 1931) pp.3-5.

but also managed to criticise various African American leaders such as Garvey and Du Bois. [56] The article appears to have been prompted by the increasing domination of Liberia, nominally one of only two independent states in Africa, by Firestone with the support of the US government. There were also increasing attempts by Britain, as well as the US with the connivance of the League of Nations, to place Liberia under European or international rule.[57]

In October 1931, just before he replaced Ford in Hamburg, Padmore held a meeting in Moscow with 'Comrade Smith,' one of the new Liberian students.[58] They discussed plans to establish a worker's organisation in Monrovia and it was evident that the CI already had contact with several Liberians, some of them students in Moscow, and that this facilitated a focus on that area.[59] Ford also reported that he had begun to train a young Liberian seaman in Hamburg, who he recommended for further training in the Soviet Union, and that he had contact with several other Liberian seamen in Germany. Yet another Liberian had contacted him from West Africa after receiving a copy of *The Negro Worker* and 'was very pleased and enthusiastic about our aims.'[60] It was in these circumstances that Ford had published a hundred copies of Padmore's article 'Hands off Liberia' in what he referred to as a 'little pamphlet.' The ITUCNW continued to take a great interest in Liberia, established several contacts and seems to have been able to send several students to Moscow.[61] In early 1932 the Liberia Workers' Progressive Association was founded with Kolli Selleh Tamba as its secretary.[62] The Association was presented in *The Negro Worker* as a branch

56. G. Padmore, 'American Imperialism Enslaves Liberia,' *The Communist*, 10/2 (February 1931) pp.133-146.

57. See M.K. Akpan, 'Ethiopia and Liberia, 1914-35: two independent African states in the colonial era,' in A. Boahen (ed.) *UNESCO General History of Africa VII – Africa under Colonial Domination 1880-1935* (London, 1985) pp.712-745. It was often in connection with Liberia that Padmore began to use the terms 'white imperialism' and 'white imperialist.' See e.g. G. Padmore, 'Hands off Liberia,' *NW*, 1/10-11 (October-November 1931) pp.5-11; 'Workers Defend Liberia,' *NW*, 2/1-2 (January-February 1932) pp.3-4.

58. Possibly Nathan Varne Gray but identified as originating in Liberia not the Gold Coast. See McClennan, 'Africans and Black Americans in Comintern Schools.'

59. 'Discussion on the Situation in Liberia,' 10 October 1931. RGASPI 534/3/668.

60. J. Ford to Padmore, 13 July 1931 and 25 July 1931. RGASPI 534/3/668.

61. See e.g. 'Workers Correspondence,' *NW*, 2/3 (March 1932) p.32 and Padmore to Dear Comrades, 14 September 1932. RGASPI 542/1/54/92.

62. K. Tamba, 'Liberia and the Labour Problem,' *NW*, 2/6 (June 1932) pp.5-8 and K.S. Tamba, 'Liberian Politicians Terrorize Workers,' *NW*, 2/9-10 (September-October 1932) pp.24-25. On Padmore's attempts to help a comrade, possible Tamba, leave Liberia see Padmore to Dear Comrades, 14 September 1932. RGASPI 542/1/54/92. Tamba had reported to Padmore that he feared for this life after the publication of the article in *The Negro Worker*. K.S. Tamba to Padmore, n.d. RGASPI 534/3/756/100.

of the ITUCNW, although officially such branches could not be formed. Padmore kept in close contact with Tamba, sent detailed correspondence on organisational matters and proposed to co-opt him onto the executive of the ITUCNW.[63] Tamba also contacted potential students but initially rejected Padmore's suggestion that he too should go to study in 'Europe,' arguing that if he did so the new Association would collapse.[64]

Certainly Padmore continued to take a great interest in Liberian affairs and the recruitment of potential students. In 1932 he wrote to one of his contacts in Liberia:

> You have a naïve faith in the League of Nations, which is wrong. They will never help Liberia, except to take away her sovereignty. The conditions of the masses will remain just the same... You Liberian politicians are just playing with fire. Don't you see what they do with China? And there are 400 million peoples...Liberia needs a group of young men who will go abroad and study the policies of imperialism and the methods of organising the masses to free themselves from the yoke of foreign oppressors. Perhaps you are in a position to recommend us some young men who are interested in such studies.[65]

Padmore's arrival in Hamburg in 1931 led to greater activity by the HC and he immediately sent out scores of letters in an attempt to establish and re-establish contacts throughout West Africa as well as the Belgian Congo.[66] There is some indication that the ITUCNW managed to establish direct links in the Congo, and the CI established contact, through the Communist Party of Belgium, with a clandestine group of Congolese workers in Leopoldville.[67] This group, which met regularly and were engaged in 'individual propaganda where they work as well as among the unemployed,' had originally tried to contact the LAI on two separate occasions but had not received a reply. The group also reported that it was extremely hazardous for its members to attempt to make contact with the Congolese insurgents.[68]

63. Padmore to K.S. Tamba, 3 February 1932 and 31 May 1932. RGASPI 534/6/23.
64. K.S. Tamba to Padmore, 19 July 1932. RGASPI 534/3/756.
65. Padmore to Dear Friend, 25 March 1932. RGASPI 534/3/754.
66. See e.g. Padmore to Small, 20 November 1931, RGASPI 534/3/668.
67. Letter from unknown correspondent in Leopoldville/Matadi to Cher Camarade, 2 June 1932, RGASPI 534/3/755.
68. 'Notes on the Situation in the Belgian Congo,' 1 January 1932. RGASPI 495/155/99/1-10 and 'Situation du travail colonial au moins de juillet en Belgique,' 29 July 1932. RGASPI 495/155/99/92.

Padmore also made efforts to strengthen the French and German sections of the LDRN and to develop work with Foster-Jones, who appears to have established a 'Sierra Leone Workers Association' in Freetown in late 1931 in addition to organising a seamen's committee on board at least one ship.[69] Padmore had nothing positive to say about the 'Kroomen's Club,' which he described as an 'openly mafiosi organisation,' and a 'branch of the police department,' but he encouraged the ISH to utilise the services of Foster-Jones while distancing itself from the club.[70] Indeed he wrote a lengthy report in order to persuade the ISH of the importance of developing its work in West Africa. He particularly stressed the need to strengthen the worker's movement, overcome its political isolation, and build organisations in Africa. However, he also emphasised the importance of work amongst West African sailors in London and the other European ports and the need for the 'training of cadres.'[71] The ISH appears to have been reluctant to work with Foster-Jones, a former policeman, and for a variety of reasons was unable to develop its work in the main ports of West Africa as it had intended. This also made it more difficult for the Hamburg Committee to develop its work in the region. According to Padmore, Foster-Jones had developed 'an opposition' in the Kru seamen's club, which had it been supported by the ISH, 'would give us a basis of organising sections of the African Union in all the other ports along this coast.'[72] Padmore was unable to get this support from the ISH, nor to get Foster-Jones to Moscow with help from the LAI, but he did subsequently became a 'contributing editor' for *The Negro Worker* and, for a time, a significant courier and disseminator of literature in West Africa. Both Foster-Jones and 'Comrade Smith' the Liberian who had been a student in Moscow, acted as go-betweens in the developing relationship between Padmore and Isaac Wallace-Johnson in Nigeria.[73]

69. Padmore to Dear Comrades, 16 November 1931; Padmore to Comrade B, 17 December 1931. RGASPI 534/3/668. Jo Bo Kami to Gentlemen, October 1931. RGASPI 534/7/74/22-23.

70. Padmore to Dear Comrade Adolph, 10 December 1931. RGASPI 534/3/668 and Padmore to ISH Secretariat, 8 February 1932. RGASPI 534/3/754.

71. Ibid.

72. Padmore to Fred Thomson, 5 January 1932. RGASPI 534/3/754.

73. I. Wallace-Johnson to Padmore, 17 December 1931. RGSPI 534/7/74/29. The inability of the LAI to expedite Foster-Jones's passage to Moscow led to a heated exchange with Padmore. See Padmore to LAI, Berlin, 5 June 1932; Padmore to Dear Comrades, 12 June 1932; C. to Dear Comrade, 15 June 1932, and Padmore to Dear Comrades, 16 June 1932. RGASPI 534/3/755.

The Hamburg Committee and Nigeria

Initially Padmore had attempted to make contact with the African Worker's Union of Nigeria (AWUN), which had been organised in June 1930 by a group connected with the Nigerian Press Ltd and the *Nigeria Daily Telegraph*, at that time one of the largest daily newspapers in the country.[74] Although it appears that Wallace-Johnson was involved with this group, its leading figures were T. A Doherty, Frank Macaulay, Julius Ojo-Cole, Adeoye Deniga and Dr Hamed Tinubu.[75] All were leading political figures in Lagos, Doherty being a member of Nigeria's Legislative Council, while Deniga had formerly been a member of the National Congress of British West Africa. The founders of the AWUN may have been concerned with the 'improvement of the condition of the working class,' but it seems likely that apart from Macaulay, and perhaps Wallace-Johnson, there was no general orientation towards revolutionary politics. The AWUN was, for example, also interested in forming a syndicate 'for the purpose of taking a directorship share in the Nigerian Mercantile Bank.'[76]

Following Macaulay's death, Wallace-Johnson became both acting editor of the paper and the secretary-general of the AWUN. It was in the course of his second letter to Padmore that he introduced himself and it is clear that the two men had not met before, although some historical accounts have suggested otherwise.[77] Wallace-Johnson claimed that he had formerly been a supporter of the Railway Worker's Union in Sierra Leone and then, working as a mariner, had travelled throughout Africa. Recently arrived in Nigeria, he had become involved with the AWUN. On the basis of his extensive travels he claimed that conditions in the Gold Coast and Nigeria were even worse than in South Africa and agreed to work with Padmore, who introduced him to the SMM, Arnold Ward, Jim Headley and others in London.[78]

Wallace-Johnson was initially pessimistic about the prospects for political activity in Nigeria and was generally despairing of Nigerians. He agreed to encourage the members of the AWUN to subscribe to *The Negro Worker*, 'a

74. F. Omu, *Press and Politics in Nigeria, 1880-1937* (London, 1978) pp.262-263.

75. L. Denzer, 'Isaac Wallace-Johnson and the West African Youth League: A case study in West African Nationalism' Ph.D Thesis, University of Birmingham, 1977, p.44.

76. J.S. Coleman, *Nigeria: Background to Nationalism* (London, 1971) p.458 n.17. On the political significance of the bank see A.G. Hopkins, 'Economic Aspects of Political Movements in Nigeria and in the Gold Coast 1918-1939,' *Journal of African History*, VII/1 (1966) pp.133-152.

77. E.g. L. Spitzer and L. Denzer, 'I.T.A. Wallace-Johnson and the West African Youth League,' [Part 1], *The International Journal of African Historical Studies*, VI/3 (1973) pp.413-452.

78. I. Wallace-Johnson to Padmore, 7 January 1932. RGASPI 534/7/74/31-34 and I. Wallace-Johnson to J. Headley, 8 January 1932. RGASPI 534/7/74/35.

prohibited journal' in Nigeria, but it appears that he was only able to personally distribute a few copies.[79] In one letter he complains about widespread illiteracy, the hostile activity of the Nigerian Democratic Party 'whose policy is to divide and exploit the mass,' as well as the state repression and 'police terrorism' that made political activity difficult, and he laments the fact that 'the majority of members have been scared away.'[80] In another he writes: 'the position of things in Nigeria is growing from bad to worse and the peasant class are the worse for it for it is apparent that the present policy of the powers that be is bent on nothing short of oppression. Of course when it comes to political administration Nigeria is the worst in West Africa.'[81]

The AWUN sought affiliation to the ITUCNW and was eager to send its members for training in Europe. Wallace-Johnson became a member of the executive committee of the ITUCNW, as well as a contributing editor of *The Negro Worker,* and proposed himself as the most suitable candidate to be sent abroad for training.[82] He was finally sent to Moscow in the autumn of 1932, probably via Germany where he may have attended the ILD conference, but he appears to have remained in Moscow only until March 1933 before returning to West Africa.[83] There is as yet little evidence that he achieved much in Nigeria and Padmore found it necessary to combat both his pessimism and the inactivity of the AWUN.[84] He certainly made plans to send other Nigerians to study in Moscow and later organised with some success amongst the women of Lagos in support of the Scottsboro campaign.[85] There were many obstacles that prevented the AWUN from advancing, including the hostility of the existing political organisations and press, police raids on its premises and eventually its effective banning in 1933.[86] It was in these circumstances that Wallace-Johnson, who was already in contact with Awooner-Renner and others, relocated to the Gold Coast at the close of 1933.

Padmore established many new contacts in West Africa not just through correspondence but also through the dissemination of *The Negro Worker,* which as he admitted, was freely distributed in the early part of 1932 in order to gain more subscribers. He also often resorted to presenting the opportunity to 'study

79. Wallace-Johnson's first article in *The Negro Worker* appeared in December 1931. See 'British Oppression in West Africa,' *NW*, 1/12 (December 1931) pp.20-24.

80. Wallace-Johnson to Padmore, 7 April 1932. RGASPI 534/7/74.

81. Wallace-Johnson to Padmore, 3 August 1932, RGASPI 534/3/756.

82. Ibid.

83. See RGASPI 495/154/512/83 and RGASPI 495/154/512.

84. Padmore to Wallace-Johnson, n.d. RGASPI 534/3/756/112.

85. See *NW*, 4/8-9 (August-September 1933) pp.12-13.

86. 'Regime of Terror in Nigeria,' *NW*, 4/3 (July 1934) pp.11-13.

in Europe' as a means to consolidate contacts in Africa. The extracts from the letter below to G. B. Baisie, a new contact in the Gold Coast, give some idea of both his style and technique:

> Dear Friend,
>
> Thank you very much for your letter of February 3rd. We are very glad to learn of your willingness to cooperate with us in spreading the ideals of our organisation through the 'NEGRO WORKER'.
>
> You will acquaint yourself with the objects of our committee by reading the announcement in our magazine on the cover page entitled 'What is the International Trade Union Committee of Negro Workers?' Herein you will recognise that our aim is to help the working class of Africa to organise trade unions, so that they will be able to get better wages, shorter hours, more education and cultural opportunities. As a sanitary officer you will immediately realise that the sanitary and health condition of a people depends on their economic condition. It is no use telling people to clean their teeth, to wash themselves and their homes and things of the sort. We all agree that these are good and necessary things, but they cannot be carried out, unless the people have the means whereby to do these things.
>
> The European capitalists and officials who come out to Africa and suck the life blood out of the masses, and then look down upon them as a set of dirty ignorant 'Niggers', would themselves be just in the same position if they had to maintain themselves and their families on 9 pence and 1/ per day. Furthermore, you natives are being taxed in order to build nice bungalos (sic) for them, pay them fat salaries and provide them with all the comforts of life. No reason why the masses are kept poor and ignorant.
>
> This is why our Committee appeals to the young men of Africa who have the advancement and welfare of their country at heart, to join us in arousing the masses, so that they will realise their true interests. Unfortunately the men who have had an opportunity of coming to Europe to study are amongst the greatest traitors in your country. When they return to Africa they forget the masses from when they have come. They play the role of agents of the European oppressors and exploiters, with the hope of being rewarded with some little petty government official stupid title, which the imperialists have created in order to corrupt them.
>
> The workers and peasants of Gold Coast can never hope to get any real help from these 'black Europeans'. They must provide their own leadership from the ranks of those who toil and who know the pangs of hunger and starvation.

> We would like to get connections with the sons of workers, so that we can help to train them to become the leaders of their class. Perhaps, if you were not already in the government service, you would have availed yourself of the opportunity of coming to Europe to study in our schools. Only by learning the art and science of organising the workers and peasants will Africa be able to follow the road of China in fighting for her independence. Until then you Africans will always be the 'underdogs' of British imperialism. While you do the work, they get the money. While your fathers grow the cocoa, they get the profits. While their women live in comfort and luxury, your mothers and sisters eke out a miserable existence.
>
> Young Africa, Awake! Organise and show your oppressors that you will no longer be slaves!
>
> We have sent you 10 magazines and will continue to send you this quantity until we hear from you. Give them to your friends and ask them to write us. A word of advise (sic); you should send us your home address or some private address. It is not good to correspond with you at your office. The white overlords will spy upon your relationship with us and this may bring you into trouble. However, if you have a private address it will be safe. You should also be careful to whom you give the magazine. Tell your friends the same. You must understand this clearly, that the British government don't want you Africans to have any connections with the outside world less your eyes might become too open. Later on we shall tell you many things that will astonish you in this connection.[87]

Similar letters were sent to many throughout Anglophone West Africa, where Padmore was able to utilise existing political networks.[88] During this period the HC was contacted by several West Africans who were linked to these networks, or who were reached through the distribution of *The Negro Worker* and the work of maritime activists such as E. Foster-Jones.[89] Some of these, such as Kobina Sekyi, a leading figure in the GCARPS and Gold Coast Farmers' Association, had come across ITUCNW literature, or were interested in the Hamburg Conference and the political orientation of the ITUCNW, even though they were normally more concerned with the narrow economic and political interests of the West African coastal elite.[90] Others appeared more interested in accessing

87. Padmore to G.B. Baisie, 26 February 1932, RGASPI 534/3/753.

88. See for example Padmore's circular letter to West Africans Frye, Wallace-Johnson, Akrong, Ashong, Morton, Quarcoopame and Small, 7 February 1932, RGASPI 534/3/754.

89. See e.g. J. Galba Bright to Padmore, 6 February 1932, RGASPI 534/7/74. Galba Bright mentions his own connections with Foster-Jones, Edward Small and Frank Macaulay.

90. S. Rohdie, 'The Gold Coast Aborigines Abroad,' *Journal of African History*, VI/3 (1965) pp.389-411. Sekyi had also previously had some contact with the LAI.

the resources of the international Communist movement, such as R.Benjamin Wuta-Ofei, the editor of the *Gold Coast Spectator* who, after having received no response from his letters to Marcus Garvey, wrote to Padmore asking if he and his friends might be supplied with 'a complete printing press for a fairly large newspaper to be published solely in the interests of the Negro Workers.'[91]

But whatever the class background or interests of these 'bourgeois nationalists,' Padmore responded positively and enthusiastically. By way of encouragement he wrote to Sekyi, 'we appreciate very deeply the interest which you, as a professional man, are taking on behalf of the oppressed people...and the help which you are rendering to the working class of your country.'[92] As Sekyi was preparing to visit London, Padmore put him in touch with Ward and Bridgeman. They too corresponded with Sekyi, who in turn made various contributions to the activities of the NWA and even chaired one of its public meetings during his sojourn in London in the summer of 1932. Wuta-Ofei and Padmore also remained in contact for some time. Padmore attempted to assist in securing information about a suitable press, while Wuta-Ofei distributed *The Negro Worker,* reprinted appropriate ITUCNW material in the *Gold Coast Spectator* and began searching for 'experienced workers' from the Gold Coast who might be likely candidates for political training in Moscow.[93] Eventually he proposed himself as a suitable candidate for training 'together with another friend who contributes powerful articles to the *Spectator*.' Wuta-Ofei, who was thirty-nine, acknowledged that both of them were 'above the age limit' but added, 'if you really wish to have candidates who can go about things properly and organise the people, you cannot do better than accept us.'[94]

There is no indication that Padmore accepted his candidature, but Wuta-Ofei did later became a leading member of the Gold Coast section of Wallace-Johnson's WAYL. What is most significant about the correspondence with these West Africans is the fact that the HC had to try and engage with them not just on the basis of organising the 'sons of workers' but rather more along the lines of appealing to their nationalist sentiments. In this regard Padmore wrote to Sekyi, 'we cannot understand why there is no organised national movement...There are occasional flare-ups...But when these are over everyone seems to go back to sleep...I think the trouble is Africans still have great illusions about Britain.' However, he made it clear that the HC was willing to help people orga-

91. R.B. Wuta-Ofei to Dear Gentlemen, 7 October 1931, RGASPI 534/7/74.

92. Quoted in Rohdie, 'Gold Coast Aborigines,' p.392.

93. R.B. Wuta-Ofei to Padmore, 23 April 1932, RGASPI 534/3/755.

94. R.B. Wuta-Ofei to Padmore, 15 August 1932, RGASPI 534/3/755.

nise themselves because, as he concluded, 'the Gold Coast people have a right to govern themselves as an independent nation.'[95]

Unfortunately, as Padmore observed, there was as yet no 'sustained organised movement,' as in India and China, that still required organisation. He certainly established many new contacts throughout West Africa, some of whom such as Tamba, and especially Wallace-Johnson, would become key activists in the region. However, Small and Richards, who had attended the Hamburg Conference, as well as the two delegates from the Gold Coast, do not appear to have remained in contact long after they returned to West Africa. They and their unions are last referred to and called to action in September 1933 in the unpublished 'To the Workers of Accra! To the Toilers of the Gold Coast.'[96]

Huiswoud and West Africa

The arrest of Padmore by the Nazi regime and his subsequent resignation and expulsion from the Communist movement led to major disruption in the work of the ITUCNW. Not until mid-1934 did Otto and Hermie Huiswoud managed to re-establish links with Anglophone West Africa, both through West African students in Moscow and direct contact with the Gold Coast.[97] Lists of contacts had apparently been lost, or had not been handed over, by the departing Padmore. The Huiswouds had been forced to operate from Belgium, where the CP had no contact with African seamen, therefore the distribution of *The Negro Worker*, which although banned in most colonies had hitherto been smuggled and distributed by couriers, also needed almost complete re-organisation.[98] Huiswoud reported that initially he was hopeful that, since several West Africans had recently returned home from Moscow, 'actual organisational work' especially in the Gold Coast, would soon commence.[99] It is interesting to note that the one of his first activities was the publication, as a pamphlet, of an 'Open Letter' to Liberian workers. Not only were political and particularly economic conditions worsening, but the 'Open Letter,' which was published in *The Negro Worker*, suggested that Tamba, Smith and what was now referred to as the 'very small and weak' Liberian Workingmen's Association, were expected

95. Quoted in Rohdie, 'Gold Coast Ablorigines,' p.394.

96. RGASPI 534/6/23. See also Padmore to Small, 20 November 1931. RGASPI 534/3/668.

97. Huiswoud to Dear Friends, 9 June 1934 and 26 July 1934. RGASPI 534/3/986. Huiswoud reported that in the near future 'two guests,' presumably two students were expected from the Gold Coast.

98. Some distribution was also continuing from the British ports although evidently not from France.

99. Huiswoud to Dear Comrades, 23 August 1934. RGASPI 534/3/986.

to activate themselves and organise the workers, unemployed and others sections throughout the country.[100]

However organising the embryonic workers' movement in West Africa from Europe was not a simple task, not least because communication was so problematic but also because the colonial authorities took measures to prevent or limit such activity. Several of the letters Huiswoud and the Negro Bureau in Moscow received suggested that even those who had been trained in Moscow, including Wallace-Johnson, found great difficulties when they returned to West Africa.[101] What was seen as the negative influence of Padmore was also being felt, and was allegedly corrupting both Wallace-Johnson and Joseph Bilé. In response to these perceived difficulties the RILU Negro Bureau encouraged Huiswoud to obtain from Wallace-Johnson more 'live people' from the Gold Coast and Nigeria who had not yet been 'contaminated.' Indeed in this new period Moscow seemed to be obsessed with securing new African students to be trained in Moscow and 'sent back' to Africa, and so Huiswoud was also encouraged to contact comrades in France and England and, in particular, to write to Tamba, in order to secure 'three or four people' from Liberia.[102]

Huiswoud did not place much hope of securing students from Wallace-Johnson, who had hitherto not provided any, and of whom he had a low opinion. Wallace-Johnson, he reported was, 'confused and apparently dabbling in all kinds of schemes which make one question his future usefulness and reliability.'[103] The ITUCNW had another Moscow-trained activist in the Gold Coast, known as 'Robert,' who provided at least one negative report on Wallace-Johnson's activities, while significantly inflating his own importance.[104] However, it is clear that the Negro Bureau in Moscow had a low opinion of 'Robert' just as it expressed a poor opinion of Wallace-Johnson and Bilé, who was described as 'an agent of Padmore.'[105]

Huiswoud had also expressed doubts about securing any African students from Britain, although in France, from where several students had previously been sent, he had personally met a prospective student from Sierra Leone who he reported had made a 'favourable impression' on him.[106] Indeed seven

---

100. 'To the workers and peasants of Liberia,' NW, 4/1 (May 1934) pp.10-16.

101. Anon. to Dear Friend, 11 May 1935. RGASPI 495/155/102/13; Anon. to Dear Friends, 2 January 1935. RGASPI 495/155/102/1; Charlie to Dear COM-ZYC, 20 April 1935. RGASPI 495/155/102/7; Ward to Dear Friends, 11 May 1935. RGASPI 495/155/102/13.

102. Anon. to Dear Otto, 21 February 1935. RGASPI 495/155/102/2-3.

103. Edward to Dear Comrades, 11 April 1935, RGASPI 495/155/102/4-5.

104. See Letter to 'Dear Friends,' 2 January 1935, RGASPI 495/155/102/1.

105. Letter to 'Dear Otto,' 21 February 1935, RGASPI 495/155/102/2-3.

106. Huiswoud to Dear Comrade, 11 April 1935. RGASPI 495/155/102/4.

years after the founding of the ITUCNW, established in order to address the lack of attention paid to the Negro Question by the British, French and other communist parties, Huiswoud was still very critical of their inertia. In Britain he blamed the leadership of CPGB for the weaknesses exhibited by both the NWA and the LAI, as well as the 'lack of attention' paid by the Party to colonial matters in Africa. This disregard, he reported, was 'bringing about a situation of discontent among the N[egro] comrades who continually complain to us about it.' In this regard, Huiswoud also noted that not one student had ever been sent from Britain, and urged Moscow to remonstrate with Harry Pollitt.[107]

He was initially more optimistic about Liberia, from where it was reported that Comrade Smith was working on the Firestone plantations and Tamba promised to send three students for training in Moscow. However, poor communication made discussion on that subject difficult. So too did the poverty faced by activists in West Africa, most of whom were unemployed. Tamba, for example complained that 'there is no avenue of securing sustenance,' and even asked if Huiswoud could help him acquire waterproof boots.[108] Tamba, who had been named a 'contributing editor' of *The Negro Worker*, appears to have been mainly occupied during 1935 with providing a lengthy report, detailing both the problems in Liberia and the difficulty of addressing them, which was subsequently published in three consecutive editions of *The Negro Worker*.[109] Liberia seems to have had the greatest concentration of Moscow trained activists, and the following year *The Negro Worker* carried a brief report of the distribution of the journal throughout the country and a celebratory poem from Samuel Freeman, or 'Charlie' the last of the trio of Moscow-trained Liberian activists.[110]

Wallace-Johnson and The West African Youth League

Wallace-Johnson had been in close contact with the NWA and LAI from October 1933 when his house in Nigeria had been raided by the colonial authorities. This relationship was consolidated in the following year when communication between him and Huiswoud was still being established. Indeed Wallace-Johnson became skilled at collaborating with his British comrades and utilising their contacts with MPs to raise questions in the British Parliament. Through the LAI he also made contact with the National Council for Civil

107. Edward to Dear Friend, 24 June 1935. RGASPI 495/155/102/8-9a.

108. Nel. (S.K. Tamba) to Anon., 10 June 1935. RGASPI 495/155/102/16.

109. M. Nelson, 'The Situation in Liberia,' *NW*, 5/2-3 (February-March 1935) pp.22-24 and 28; *NW*, 5/4 (April 1935) pp.21-24; *NW*, 5/5 (May 1935) pp.23-24.

110. *NW*, 6/1 (March 1936) pp.24-25.

Liberties and other campaigning bodies.[111] He also found more fertile territory in the Gold Coast for his political activities than he had in Nigeria. In part this was due to the increasingly harsh economic and political conditions existing throughout British West Africa, caused by the Great Depression, which contributed to increasingly exploitative and repressive measures by the colonial authorities and consequently widespread anti-colonial activity. In addition, there were several journalists and activists in the Gold Coast who had been in contact with the ITUCNW, who were readers and distributors of *The Negro Worker*, and who were broadly sympathetic with its views. Wallace-Johnson, and the Nigerian journalist and activist Nnamdi Azikiwe, may have been able to introduce a new style of radical journalism into the colony but they were considerably assisted by the attempts of the colonial authorities to muzzle the press and, in particular, to prevent the importation of what the colonial authorities viewed as 'subversive Communist propaganda.'[112]

In 1933 the colonial authorities had confiscated some 1750 pieces of 'seditious' literature and 1100 of these were copies of *The Negro Worker*.[113] This suggests that perhaps most of what was despatched by the ITUCNW was seised but the authorities were determined not just to seize literature but also to take action against those who distributed it, or who might be considered 'link subversives' or 'active seditionists.' The prime suspects were those who had been in direct contact with the ITUCNW, such as Sekyi and Wuta-Ofei, as well as Wallace-Johnson. However, the colonial authorities were also concerned with several others, who all had strong connections with a Gold Coast press, which was exhibiting increasing hostility to the colonial government.[114] The Criminal Code Amendment Ordinance, or 'Sedition Bill,' which was subsequently proposed by the colonial authorities, was vigorously opposed and condemned by Wallace-Johnson but it was not directly aimed at his activities. Rather it aimed to limit the perceived 'subversive' influence of *The Negro Worker* and other literature on a section of the population of the Gold Coast, as well being introduced as an attempt to stifle all opposition to the colonial government. However, the Governor of the Gold Coast admitted his satisfaction that it might also curb the activities of Wallace-Johnson.[115]

111. Spitzer and Denzer, 'I.T. A Wallace-Johnson and the West African Youth League'.

112. See Denzer, 'I.T. A. Wallace-Johnson and the West African Youth League,' p.64 and S. Shaloff, 'Press Controls and Sedition Proceedings in the Gold Coast, 1933-39,' *African Affairs*, 71/284 (1972) pp.241-263.

113. Denzer, 'I.T. A. Wallace-Johnson and the West African Youth League,' pp.64-65.

114. Ibid. pp. 65-66 and Shaloff, 'Press Controls,' pp.242-243.

115. Thomas to A. Fiddian, 27 February 1934, (TNA) CO 96/714/21639.

Wallace-Johnson began his political activities in the Gold Coast, in November 1933, with a widespread campaign to win support for the nine 'Scottsboro Boys,' ostensibly carried out on behalf of the NWA, for which he was arrested the following month and then released without charge. In the course of his activities he joined with Awooner-Renner and Benjamin Tamakloe, the leader of the Ex-Servicemen's Association. When the 'Sedition Bill' was announced Wallace-Johnson joined the opposition to it, alongside many others, and immediately despatched a telegram to the Scottsboro Defence Committee in Britain, warning that the proposed Bill 'completely neutralises liberty of Gold Coast Press and People.'[116] This Committee was linked to both the LAI and the NWA, and Ward and Bridgeman proceeded to advise Wallace-Johnson how to develop the growing protest campaign in the Gold Coast, as well as initiating their own agitation in Britain.[117]

The campaign against the 'Sedition Bill' was subsequently extensively reported in *The Negro Worker,* which in an editorial commented that it was proud of the fact that, despite all obstacles, its message was 'penetrating the slave pens of British Imperialism and is causing discomfort to the exploiters.'[118] In order to justify the introduction of the legislation, the Colonial Secretary, Sir Cunliffe Lister, had quoted from an article in *The Negro Worker*, which demanded that 'the Negro masses must therefore rise up as the tide of the revolutionary front and use the arms which the white oppressors put in their hands not to shoot down their class brothers in the Soviet Union.' He referred to this as 'filth' and *The Negro Worker* as a 'foul and obnoxious' tract, which could not be tolerated.[119] *The Negro Worker* commented that the introduction of the Sedition Bill could be explained by the 'colonial exploiters' fear of 'a revolt of the native toilers against their poverty stricken conditions,' and compared its introduction with the actions of the Nazis in Germany. The ITUCNW called for mass meetings and agitation and pointed out that, 'Only mass resistance can force concessions from the colonial rulers.'[120] Some of Ward's advice to Wallace-Johnson and views on organising opposition, particularly his call for local 'protest meetings against the ordinance,' were subsequently made public and published in the Gold Coast press, while in Britain, through the influence

116. LAI ' Scottsboro Trial,' 26 February 1934. Bridgeman Papers (DBN) 25/4 and Denzer, 'I.T. A. Wallace-Johnson and the West African Youth League,' p.74.

117. LAI ' Scottsboro Trial'.

118. 'The "Foul and Obnoxious" Tract,' *NW*, 4/5 (September 1934) p.1.

119. Quoted in Shaloff, 'Press Controls,' p.250.

120. *NW* 4/5 (September 1934) pp.1-2.

of the LAI, several Members of Parliament contacted the Colonial Office, or asked questions and proposed amendments to the Bill in Parliament.[121]

Agitation against the Sedition Bill became a *cause célèbre* in the Gold Coast, and to some extent in Britain, where two delegations from the Gold Coast arrived in 1934.[122] It seems that it was partly in response to the introduction of this legislation that the West African Youth League (WAYL) emerged. Wallace-Johnson's activities continued, in concert with the NWA and LAI, with a campaign following the Prestea mine disaster in June 1934, in which 41 miners lost their lives.[123] The campaign in response to the disaster was an important one, since it put Wallace-Johnson and the embryonic WAYL in contact with a significant section of the Gold Coast's workers. The WAYL demanded better working conditions, 'workmen's compensation' and condemned the indifference of the mine owners and colonial authorities, as well as the African members of the colony's Legislative Council. It consequently began to organise amongst the workers and in support of their interests.[124]

In July 1934 Wallace-Johnson, Awooner Renner, F.A. Bruce, J.J. Ocquaye and others held the first meetings of the WAYL, but it grew slowly over the next few years mainly by cooperating with the members of existing organisations such as the Ex-Serviceman's Association, the Aborigines Rights Protection Society and the Mambi Party.[125] The aims of the WAYL were not confined to the Gold Coast and it concerned itself with all four British colonies and what was referred to as 'other sections of Africa as well as with the Western world.' In the course of its activities the WAYL pointed out that 'only a united movement would save the country from the disastrous effect of capitalist exploitation and imperialist exploitation,' and amongst other aims claimed that it was established to 'develop a feeling of self-determination among the inhabitants of the country especially the Youth, with a view to drawing up a programme for their economic, social and political emancipation and for a higher standard and free education for the masses, for a drive towards the establishing of a foundation for national independence.'[126] Its first major victory came in October 1935 when the candi-

121. See I. Wallace-Johnson, 'The Gold Coast Independent and Myself (Part V),' *Vox Populi*, (5 October 1935) pp.8-9 and *Hansard* HC Deb, 30 October 1934, vol. 293 cc113-137.

122. 'The Gold Coast Delegation and the Anti-Imperialist Movement,' *NW*, 5/6 (June 1935) pp.14-15 and 13.

123. Denzer, 'Isaac Wallace-Johnson and the West African Youth League,' p.88.

124. 'Minutes of a General Meeting of the WAYL(Gold Coast Section), Held at the Palladium, Accra,' 4 July 1936. RGASPI 495/155/101/4-5. Denzer, 'Isaac Wallace-Johnson and the West African Youth League,' pp.87-90.

125. Denzer, 'Isaac Wallace-Johnson and the West African Youth League,' pp.90-91.

126. I. Wallace-Johnson, 'The West African Youth League – Its Origin, Aims and Objects' *NW*, 7/5 (May 1937) p.9.

date of the Mambi, or People's Party, was elected with WAYL support to what was effectively the governing body of the Gold Coast, the Legislative Council.[127] Although the colonial authorities subsequently declared that this result was invalid, the Mambi Party/WAYL candidate then won a second election.[128]

The WAYL subsequently played a significant role in agitating amongst the population of the Gold Coast in support of Ethiopia following its invasion by Fascist Italy. In October 1935, together with the Ex-Servicemen's Union, it held a rally at which over a thousand people gathered at the Palladium in Accra and at the end of which it was reported that over 500 had volunteered to go and fight in Ethiopia's defence. As a result, an Ethiopia Defence Committee was established and an appeal for funds was launched in the local press.[129] The Committee was itself organised to educate 'the masses' not only on all matters relating to the invasion but also in 'on matters of racial and national importance.'[130] The WAYL also conducted its own fundraising and declared 9-18 November 1935 an 'Ethiopia week.'[131] The funds raised 'in aid of distressed Ethiopians' were then forwarded to the Ethiopian legation in London. For its part, the Ex-Servicemen's Union addressed a resolution of protest to the secretary-general of the League of Nations, the House of Commons and the British Government's War Office. The Resolution was clearly designed to provide food for thought amongst Britain's rulers and stated: 'Unless Great Britain sees that justice is rendered to Ethiopia according to the Covenant, the Gold Coast Ex-Servicemen's Union will never take arms to defend European nations in conflicts which may arise out of their diplomatic bargainings.' *The Negro Worker* then called on other colonial ex-servicemen's organisations to emulate what it called this 'splendid example.' It concluded that they too must 'recognise the treacherous role played by the British Imperialists in the Abyssinian Affair, which has served to whet the appetite of Fascist Germany for colonies in Africa, and may be the cause of another war instigated by them.'[132]

---

127. 'Peoples Candidate Victor in Gold Coast,' *NW*, 5/11 (December 1935) pp.14-16. *The Negro Worker* commented that the election victory needed to become part of a 'peoples movement' that was organised against the 'imperialist exploiters.' See also R. Bridgeman, 'Fight Against Colonial Oppression: Election Methods in the Gold Coast Colony,' *NW*, 6/1 (March 1936) pp.13-15.

128. *NW*, 6/5 (July 1936) p.5.

129. Plans for such a committee were first discussed in July 1935. See Wallace-Johnson to Dear Sir, 10 July 1935. RGASPI 495/155/101/6.

130. Spitzer and Denzer, 'I.T. A Wallace-Johnson,' p.440.

131 Denzer, 'I.T.A Wallace-Johnson and the West African Youth League,' pp.113-116. Also *NW*, 5/11 (December 1935) p.17.

132. *NW*, 6/5 (July 1936) p.24.

Most importantly Wallace-Johnson used the invasion of Ethiopia as a means to attack the whole colonial system and to present the view that the African was the equal of the European. In articles in the local press and in his many speeches he attacked in particular what he regarded as the hypocrisy of so-called 'western civilisation.' He argued, for example, that 'The Italo-Abyssinian war is destined to prove to the African masses that Europe with all its civilisation is still enshrined in barbarism and that Western civilisation is sheer mockery. It is also destined to prove to the African masses that Religion, especially Christianity as it has been introduced by the whiteman to the blackman is a heinous mass of deception.'[133] His most famous article on this subject was entitled 'Has the African a God,' and was published in the *Morning Post* in May 1936.

'Has the African a God' was prompted by the Italian invasion of Ethiopia but again it raised more general issues about colonial rule and the religious ideas that seemed to accompany it. Wallace-Johnson wrote that what he referred to as 'the European' believed 'in the god whose name is spelt *Deceit*,' and he continued 'Ye "civilised" Europeans, you must "civilise" the "barbarous" Africans with machine guns. Ye "Christian" Europeans, you must "Christianise" the "pagan" Africans with bombs, poison gases, etc.' Wallace-Johnson exposed the 'civilising mission' not only of fascist Italy but also Britain by linking the invasion of Ethiopia with colonial rule and repressive legislation in the Gold Coast and elsewhere. In conclusion he called on Africans to 'follow his example and worship Ethiopia's God,' in other words to rely on their own traditions and reject Eurocentrism. It was what *The Negro Worker* called 'a frank and truthful exposure of the methods of imperialist rule.'[134]

The colonial authorities had been waiting for an opportunity to arrest Wallace-Johnson and took advantage of the publication of the article to raid his home, where they discovered incriminating material from the LAI and NWA and evidence that he was the author of the article.[135] He was arrested, charged with sedition and subsequently found guilty of this offence for which he was

133. Quoted in Denzer, 'I.T.A Wallace-Johnson and the West African Youth League,' pp.115-116 and Spitzer and Denzer, 'I.T. A Wallace-Johnson,' p.435.

134. Spitzer and Denzer, 'I.T. A Wallace-Johnson,' p.442. An extract from the article was also published in *NW*, 6/6-7 (August-September 1936) pp.1-2. See also *NW*, 6/5 (July 1936) p.27.

135. Colonial Office officials noted that Governor Hodson had initially felt that Wallace-Johnson's activities could be dealt with by 'broadcast propaganda' but subsequently become much more concerned. G. Creasy note, 27 February 1936, (TNA) CO 96/731/1.Hodson subsequently demanded more powers and voiced his concern that the press was 'controlled by the Red element.' Shaloff, 'Press Controls and Sedition Proceedings in the Gold Coast, 1933-39,' p.255.

fined fifty pounds.[136] The whole case became another *cause célèbre* both in the Gold Coast and in Britain where the LAI caused questions to be raised in Parliament and supported Wallace-Johnson when he decided to appeal to the Court of the Privy Council.[137] In the Gold Coast the case undoubtedly contributed to the rapidly growing membership of the WAYL, which stood at over five thousand organised in twenty-two separate branches by the end of 1936.[138] At the close of 1936 the WAYL launched its own publication entitled *The Dawn* but this does not appear to have survived beyond the first few editions.[139] The case, and the relationship between the WAYL and the international communist movement, contributed to an increasingly sharp critique of the illegality of British colonial rule in the Gold Coast, which was also evident in the pages of *The Negro Worker.*[140] The activities of the WAYL in the Gold Coast only declined following Wallace-Johnson's visit to Britain in 1937 to pursue his legal appeal.

Wallace-Johnson and the WAYL clearly became an important political influence in the Gold Coast during this period. But he seems to have been much closer to Ward and Bridgeman in Britain than he was to Huiswoud and the ITUCNW. In the Comintern archives there is little evidence of direct communication between Huiswoud and Wallace-Johnson, although it is clear that this took place.[141] The ITUCNW mainly attempted to direct political activity in the Gold Coast through the pages of *The Negro Worker*. An appeal was issued to the miners, railwaymen and other workers in the Gold Coast, for example, calling on them to get organised, to strengthen and unite the trade union movement, as well as the anti-colonial movement.[142] But although workers in the Gold Coast may have become more organised than those in other parts of West Africa, progress along the path indicated by the ITUCNW and the WAYL occurred slowly.

---

136. Spitzer and Denzer, 'I.T. A. Wallace-Johnson,' pp.442-445. See also 'Gold Coast Raid and Arrest,' *NW*, 6/5 (July 1936) p.27, 'Persecution on the Gold Coast,' *NW*, 6/6-7 (August-September 1936) p.1, and 'Wallace Johnson fined' *NW*, 6/9 (November 1936) p.27. Nnamdi Azikiwe, the editor of the *Morning Post* was also charged with sedition.

137. Wallace-Johnson ultimately lost the appeal but the Gold Coast government had to pay for it.

138. See Denzer, 'I.T.A Wallace-Johnson and the West African Youth League,' pp.145 for different figures which still indicate a significant increase.

139. *NW*, (December 1936) p.3 and Denzer, 'I.T.A Wallace-Johnson and the West African Youth League p.146.

140. 'Sovereign or Slave,' *NW*, 7/1 (January 1937) p.4 and Wallace-Johnson, 'Great Britain and the Bond of 1844: The Vision of a Youth,' *NW*, 7/6 (June 1937) pp.14-15.

141. It is also quite likely that Wallace-Johnson met with Huiswoud in Paris on his way to London early in 1937.

142. 'To the Gold Coast Unions,' *NW*, 5/6 (June 1935) pp.3-5.

Nevertheless, the achievements of the WAYL were impressive and, despite the initial reservations of Huiswoud and the Negro Bureau in Moscow, it was undoubtedly the most successful of the African anti-colonial organisations associated with the ITUCNW. In the course of its activities the WAYL pointed out that 'only a united movement would save the country from the disastrous effect of capitalist exploitation and imperialist exploitation.' Indeed Wallace-Johnson's 'Christmas letter' of 1936, written to the youth and people of the Gold Coast, was hailed by William Patterson as 'an inspiration to struggle against inequality to the Negro youth of the world.'[143] This view, and the estimation that the WAYL formed the basis for a 'People's Front in West Africa, undoubtedly reflected the changes that had occurred in the orientation of the CI since its Seventh Congress. It also reflected the importance attached to the advances in the anti-imperialist struggles in India, China and elsewhere, as well as the changing international situation, which led the CI to put more emphasis on uniting all the anti-imperialist forces in the colonies in the struggle to end colonial rule. It was, however, also a change that made the ITUCNW, with its narrow focus on the workers, increasingly anachronistic.

The ITUCNW had played a signifcant role encouraging the organisation of workers especially in British West Africa, but does not seem to have been able to make much direct impact on the French colonies. In 1936 when two Senegalese students in Moscow were asked to assess its influence and whether it had 'been a factor in radicalising the Negro people' in their country, they replied that they knew nothing of its existence and that it was generally unknown in Senegal.[144] Yet paradoxically it was in Senegal that a communist organisation closely linked with the PCF was formed in July 1936, with both European and African members. Some of the latter, it was reported, had formerly studied in Moscow.[145] The following year *Humanité*, the newspaper of the PCF, announced that a constitution had been approved for the creation of a communist party in Senegal and that over a hundred workers, both African and European, had applied to join.[146]

The origins of this communist organisation in Senegal seem to have developed out of the work of the UTN and the LAI some years before, work that may even have initially involved Kouyaté. According to one police agent Kouyaté founded an organisation called the Ligue du lutte des peoples du Sénégal et

143. W.L. Patterson, 'West African Youth and the People's Front,' *NW*, 7/3 (March 1937) pp. 8-9 and 13.

144. 'Special discussion Material on the Negro Question,' 10 July 1936, RGASPI495/14/36/31.

145. Sagna, 'Des pionniers méconnus,' pp.715-721 and RGASPI 495/155/102/75.

146. Quoted in P. Durant, *Cette mystérieuse section coloniale: Le PCF et les colonies 1920-1962* (Paris, 1986) p.184.

Soudan.[147] In 1933 and 1934 the *Cri des Nègres* published a manifesto from the Ligue that was distributed in French West Africa, much to the consternation of the French authorities. They believed that the activities of the Ligue were being directed by a special African sub-section of the PCF that was in contact with supporters in Senegal, Soudan, Guinée, Togo and Congo.[148] Although the French colonial authorities satisfied themselves that the Ligue did not actually exist in the colonies, they stepped up surveillance on known activists and supporters of the UTN in Dakar, such as Eugène Dubuc and Léopold Millered.[149] In 1935 the police in Dakar seised a hundred and fifty copies of a leaflet entitled *Appel fraternal aux Nègres du monde entier*. It was reported that this publication was already having some impact on the Senegalese press and the organisation of seafarers, the Amicale des marins du Senégal, with which Dubuc and Millered were connected. It appears that despite the best efforts of the French authorities the Communists, including the UTN were utilizing mariners as couriers and organising not just from France but within Sénegal, where they had some influence amongst sections of the seafarers as well as railway workers.[150] This and the creation of a communist organisation in Senegal was a major advance for the Comintern during the era of the Popular Front government in France, but yet another indication that the ITUCNW was becoming increasingly redundant.

147. Report of Moise, 20 February 1934, 3 SLOTFOM 3, ANOM.

148. Certainly the LDRN was in contact with supporters in Dakar. See letter from Dakar, 30 May 1930, in which a correspondent reveals that even his 'patron' bought *Humanité* and listened to Radio Moscow. RGASPI 495/155/102/10-11.

149. 3 SLOTFOM 3, ANOM.

150. Y. Person, 'Le Front populaire au Sénégal (mai 1936-octobre 1938),' *Le Mouvement Social*, 107 (April-June 1979) pp. 77-101.

Chapter 10
The ITUCNW and South Africa

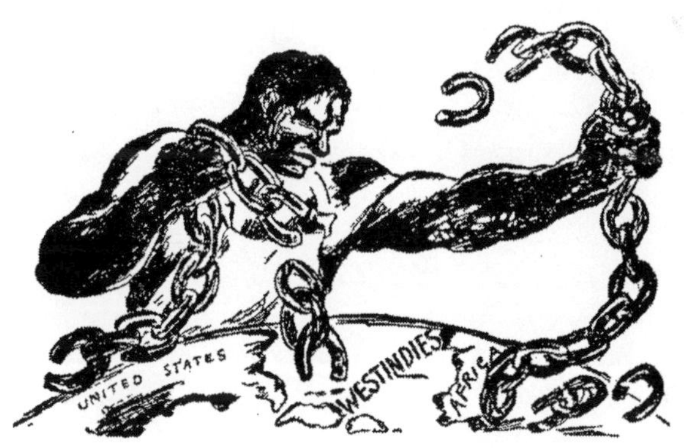

There is now a voluminous literature on the early history of the CPSA, much of it focusing on the consequences of the decisions taken at the CI's Sixth Congress. [1] However, although historians have often emphasised the fact that

1. Works on this subject include: S. Johns, *Raising the Red Flag: The International Socialist League & The Communist Party of South Africa, 1914-1932* (Belville, 1995); A. Drew, *Between Empire and Revolution – A Life of Sidney Bunting 1873-1936* (Pretoria, 2009); A. Drew, *Discordant Comrades: Identities and Loyalties on the South African Left* (Pretoria, 2002); A. Drew (ed.) *South Africa's Radical Tradition: A documentary history, [vol. one] 1907-1950,* (Cape Town, 1996); A. Drew, 'The New Line in South Africa: Ideology and Perception in a Very Small Communist Party,' in M. Worley (ed.) *In Search of Revolution: International Communist Parties in the Third Period,* (London, 2004), pp.337-360. A. Davidson et al (eds.) *South Africa and the Communist International: A Documentary History* [2 volumes] (London, 2003); Simons and Simons, *Class and Colour in South Africa, 1850-1950* (London, 1983); D. Musson, *Johnny Gomas – Voice of the Working Class: A Political Biography* (Cape Town, 1989); E. Johanningsmeier, 'Communists and Black Freedom

the congress decisions relating to South Africa were taken as part of a general internationalist approach to the Negro Question, there has been less interest in examining how one of the main instruments of that policy, ITUCNW, intervened in South African matters after 1928.[2]

One immediate consequence of the deliberations and resolutions of the Sixth Congress and the founding of the ITUCNW, in the summer of 1928, was that the latter began to intervene in South Africa on behalf of the RILU and consequently according to the decisions of the CI. It must be recalled that one of the main reasons for the founding of the ITUCNW was because of the alleged 'white chauvinism' and inactivity on the Negro Question of the relevant communist parties, including the CPSA. At the Sixth Congress, the CPSA had come under renewed scrutiny and was criticised for various weaknesses including its inability to send even one 'Negro' delegate to the congress.[3] At the founding conference of the ITUCNW, as well as throughout the Sixth Congress, the two South African delegates, Roux and Bunting, attempted to refute allegations of 'white chauvinism' and also objected to the ways in which the CI and RILU were intervening in the CPSA's work.[4] After the congress, intervention by the CI, the RILU, the CPGB and the newly formed ITUCNW increased in the wake of the exposure of the CPSA's political and organisational weaknesses.[5] In 1929 these were summed up by the CI's representative in South Africa, who referred to the CPSA as 'a feeble organisation' and added that 'the organisational forms already universally adopted in Europe, do not yet exist in Africa.'[6] Although the CPSA was beginning to attract significant numbers of African members, it was not viewed as a communist party with a consolidated membership and a strong grasp of revolutionary theory, nor was it yet based mainly amongst the African working masses. It was therefore not considered by the CI to be in a strong position to lead the revolutionary struggle in South Africa.

Movements in South Africa and the US: 1919-1950, *Journal of Southern African Studies*, 30/1, (March 2004), pp.153-180; S. Johns, 'The Comintern, South Africa and the Black Diaspora,' *Review of Politics*, 37/2, (1975), pp.200-234; R. Kelley, 'The Third International and the Struggle for National Liberation in South Africa, *Ufahamu*, 15/1-2 (1986), pp.99-120.

2. The work of Sheridan Johns is an exception in this regard.

3. Meeting of the Executive Bureau of the Profintern, 31 July 1928, RGASPI 534/3/306.

4. Minutes of Profintern Executive Meeting, 31 July 1928, RGASPI 534/3/306.

5. See e.g. Political letter from the Colonial Committee, CPGB, to CPSA, February 1929, RGASPI 495/64/85. Despite its poor record on the Negro Question the CPGB was given some responsibility to liaise with the CPSA.

6. Report of ECCI Representative in South Africa, 28 September 1929, RGASPI 495/155/77143.

The Negro Bureau of the Eastern Secretariat of the ECCI,[7] which included amongst it members Haywood, Ford, Patterson and Padmore, as well as the Negro Bureau of RILU, began to play important roles in the CI's intervention in South Africa. The aim was clearly to send 'detailed organisational instructions' to the CPSA, as well as to guide it politically in a period when its leadership appeared to be uncertain as to how to advance the Party's work. The ITUCNW assumed an especially important role as the instrument of the RILU because the main directive from the CI to the CPSA, in the period immediately following the Sixth Congress, was that 'the Party must orientate itself chiefly on the Negro labouring sections and address itself to them.' This required a focus on agricultural workers and peasant farmers, as well as the urban working class.

The ITUCNW regarded South Africa as a key area for its work, not just because it was the only sub-Saharan African country where a communist party existed but also because it was hoped that from this base the communist movement could expand into other parts of the African continent. The Fifth Congress of the RILU, held in Moscow in August 1930, made 'Africa the centre of gravity' of the ITUCNW's work. It recognised that increased economic exploitation of Africa by the imperialist powers, as a result of the global economic crisis, was leading to growing resistance by the 'toiling masses,' especially by the workers' movement. Here the RILU had in mind the strike struggles that had been waged in other parts of the continent, as well as those in South Africa. The RILU congress therefore resolved that the 'principal task' in all African countries was to 'organise the industrial proletariat which, in spite of its small numbers, is nevertheless, to be considered as the basis of the revolutionary anti-imperialist movement.'[8] The CPSA was also expected to be the 'ideological organisational leader of the revolutionary communist movement in the other parts of Black Africa.' It is to be noted that here too the CI, in keeping with its Pan-Africanist approach to such matters during this period, envisaged that the goal of this movement would be 'Independent Native Workers' and Peasants' Republics as a transitory stage towards the subsequent Union of Socialist Soviet Republics of Africa.'[9]

In regard to South Africa, the CI was also eager that the CPSA rapidly became a party led by and mainly consisting of African Communists, which could take up its tasks in South Africa as well as other parts of the continent. The CPSA was expected to play a leading role in 'Negro work' alongside the CP in the United States. It was the view of the CI that the CPSA's weaknesses, especially its 'underestimation of the role of the national revolutionary struggle

7. On the plans of the Negro Bureau of the Eastern Secretariat in regard to South Africa in 1929 see e.g. RGASPI 495/155/74/18-19.

8. *Resolutions of the Fifth World Congress of the RILU* (London, 1931) p.65.

9. Quoted in Johns, *Raising the Red Flag*, p.266.

in South Africa,' were hampering all its activities, especially in regard to recruiting African members and leaders, as well as in its work amongst African workers and peasants, the majority of the population in the country. It was this conception of the CPSA's tasks that was encapsulated in the slogan 'an Independent South African Native Republic with equal rights for national minorities as a stage towards the Dictatorship of the Proletariat.' [10]

The Sixth Congress of the CI and the Fifth Congress of the RILU also marked a change in emphasis for the international communist movement, since the Comintern presented the analysis that the post-war world was entering into a 'third period' during which there would be a major crisis of capitalism, increasingly fierce class and anti-colonial struggles and the likelihood of new wars of intervention against the Soviet Union, as well as wars between the major imperialist powers. The congresses therefore placed particular emphasis on the communists parties working to expose and limit the influence of what were seen as the 'reformism' and 'Social Democracy' of the Labour and Socialist International and the IFTU, while extending their own influence amongst the workers. Even in anti-colonial struggles the Comintern stressed the importance of organising the working class, which in many African and Caribbean countries was beginning to flex its political muscles. The communist parties were encouraged to approach this task by building the 'united front from below,' uniting workers at the workplace, or in particular struggles, outside of the influence of 'reformist' trade union leaders, as well as by establishing revolutionary trade union organisations directly under their political leadership. As a guideline for this approach the Sixth Congress put forward the slogan 'Class Against Class.' The decisions of these congresses were accompanied by an intensification of the struggle against 'reformism' in the workers' movement as well as what was referred to as 'national reformism,' such as politics of Garveyism. In South Africa, for instance, the aim was to counter the 'national reformism' of the ANC and the ICU. However, there were also fierce battles within many communist parties during this period against a perceived 'right danger' and those who were considered to be guilty of 'reformist' ideas and practices and this was certainly the case in the CPSA. The new orientation or 'New Line,' as it has sometimes been called, created the conditions for 'leftism,' and sectarianism within some parties, including the CPSA, which resulted in a failure to adequately work within existing trade unions, or other practices that served to isolate the Communists from the workers.[11] The

10. 'Draft Resolution on Revolutionary TU Work in South Africa,' 30 August 1930, RGASPI 495/18/810/64-66.

11. W.Z. Foster, *History of the Three Internationals – The World Socialist and Communist Movements from 1948 until the Present* (New York, 1955) See also Drew, 'The New Line in South Africa.'

ITUCNW therefore had significant problems to overcome and solve in its work with the CPSA.

The task of the ITUCNW in South Africa was to assist the CPSA's activities amongst African workers, but this had to be carried out from outside the country, by letter or by instructions in *The Negro Worker* and other publications. The ITUCNW had to overcome significant obstacles even to maintain contact with its supporters in South Africa, whilst the latter worked in extremely harsh conditions, often in a state of illegality and beset by the racial divisions that were already entrenched in the country, in order to organise some of the first African workers' organisations and trade unions.

The Federation of Non-European Trade Unions

One major task for the ITUCNW was to strive to strengthen the Federation of Non-European Trade Unions (FNETU), sometimes initially referred to as the South African Federation of Native Trade Unions, which was led by the CPSA and had been established with four affiliated unions in March 1928.[12] The first chairman of the FNETU was a white communist, Ben Weinbren, James La Guma was its first general secretary but its chief organiser was T.W. Thibedi, the first African to join the CPSA. The FNETU also worked in very difficult conditions but had some notable early successes. It led several strikes, including a strike of black and white workers at clothing factories in Germinston, near Johannesburg, and it even formed the beginnings of a united union of laundry workers.[13] It was also through the work of the Federation that some of the future African leaders of the CPSA were recruited, such as Moses Kotane, who joined the Bakers' Union in 1928. The following year he became a CP member and was soon elected vice-chairman of the Federation. In 1931 Kotane was sent to Moscow to study at the Lenin School.[14]

The ITUCNW was one of the main means by which the RILU aimed to assist the CPSA and the new Federation. At the founding of the ITUCNW it had initially been envisaged that La Guma, who was highly thought of in Moscow at the time, would play a leading role in its work.[15] This would no

12. 'Federation of Native Trade Unions,' *South African Worker*, 30 March 1928, p.6. Also Draft Letter to South Africa, 4 October 1929, RGASPI 495/155/67.

13. E. Roux, *Time Longer Than Rope – The Black Man's Struggle for Freedom in South Africa* (London, 1964) pp.207-210.

14. B. Bunting, *Moses Kotane – South African Revolutionary* (Belville, 1998) pp.49-52, 64-66.

15. On the RILU International Bureau of Negro Workers, see RGASPI 495/155/53/1. For an assessment of La Guma see Report of Comrade X (ECCI Representative in South Africa), 28 September 1929, RGASPI 495/155/77/146.

doubt have strengthened still further the role of the ITUCNW in South Africa. La Guma challenged the other leaders of the FNETU, Weinbren and Thibedi, who opposed the CI resolution on the 'Native Republic,' and he remained a leading protagonist in the CPSA's internal struggles. However, he was subsequently unable to take up a role in the ITUCNW, or the FNETU, because of his temporary expulsion from the CPSA in 1929 for 'political unreliability,' following his inexplicable support for an African nationalist opponent of the Party's candidate in the parliamentary elections of that year.[16]

The very first edition of *The Negro Worker,* published by the ITUCNW in July 1928, also focused on South Africa. It contained the article 'Colored Labor in South Africa,'[17] and included the Resolution of RILU'S Fourth Congress 'Regarding Negro Labor,' which pointed out that 'the central problem of the trade union movement in South Africa is that of COLOURED LABOUR and the relations which exist between the organisations of the white workers and those of the coloured workers.' (capitals in original) The Resolution also stressed that the amalgamation of 'white and coloured workers' into one trade union centre was 'the fundamental task of the revolutionary wing of the trade union movement in South Africa.'[18] By the end of 1928 *The Negro Worke*r had reached South Africa and the CPSA's *South African Worker* was recommending that 'the publication should be in the hands of every class conscious worker black or white.'[19] From then onwards *The Negro Worker* regularly carried articles on South Africa.

By the close of 1928 the FNETU decided to affiliate to the RILU, a decision that also further cemented its relationship with the ITUCNW.[20] Initially this relationship was affected by the continuing controversy over the Black Republic slogan. When Ben Weinbren wrote to James Ford in early 1929 in order to consolidate these links, it was also partly to complain about the 'bitter feelings' that the slogan had caused and to allege that the Federation's members

16. On La Guma's expulsion see *South African Worker*, 30 September 1939, p.2 and Simons, *Class and Colour*, p.412.

17. Balabushevich, 'Coloured Labor in South Africa,' *The Negro Worker (NW)*, vol.1 no.1, July 1928, pp.12-16.

18. 'Resolutions of the Fourth Congress of the RILU Regarding Negro Labor,' *NW*, 1/1, July 1928, pp. 6-7.

19. 'New Negro Workers' Publication,' *South African Worker*, 30 November 1928, p.8. During the CI's sixth congress, CPSA leader Sidney Bunting had even quoted from an article in *The Negro Worker* by Lozovsky, General Secretary of the RILU, in his efforts to oppose the adoption of the 'Native Republic' slogan. S.P. Bunting, 'Statement on the Kuusinen Thesis, reproduced in A. Drew (ed.) *South Africa's Radical Tradition: A documentary history, vol. one 1907-1950,* (Cape Town, 1996) pp.92-93.

20 'South African Native Federation of Trade Unions to affiliate to RILU.' *South African Worker*, 24 December 1928, p.8.

would not accept it.[21] However, Weinbren also signalled his readiness to accept directives from Ford, on this and other matters, and he subsequently submitted regular reports claiming that the FNETU was making steady progress.[22]

Through the ITUCNW the RILU's Negro Bureau sent several resolutions and proposals to South Africa in relation to the strengthening of the FNETU. It continually stressed the importance of work amongst the miners, railway workers and agricultural labourers, as well as organisational and political principles connected with this work. It also pointed out the necessity to organise and fight for specific demands, such as an end to forced labour and the right to strike. In short, the Federation was expected to build a revolutionary trade union opposition within existing 'reformist' trade unions, and work to implement the CI/RILU policy of establishing 'a united front from below.' This meant uniting workers to fight for their common demands even if they were in unions whose leaders did not fight, as well as establishing new revolutionary trade unions where none existed in a particular industry, or where existing unions excluded Africans. However, the Federation was also expected to organise so as to be able to 'transfer the economic struggles into political struggles.' It was left in no doubt that 'the trade unions must take a leading part in the struggle to achieve a native republic in South Africa.'[23] In its correspondence the RILU's Negro Bureau was often critical of the FNETU and its leaders, and of initiatives of the CPSA that involved the FNETU, such as the short-lived League of African Rights.[24]

The RILU's advice to the Federation was, of course also advice and direction for the CPSA. For the RILU, as for the CI, the communist party was the decisive factor to ensure the success of the peoples' struggles in South Africa, because only the Communists were considered to be in a position to organise the working class, make them conscious of their revolutionary tasks and leading role and present a programme which could unite both black and white workers and establish the way forward. But despite constant urging, the CPSA failed to

21. See e.g. Weinbren to Ford, 14 January 1929 and Weinbren to Dear Comrades, 19 January 1929, RGASPI 534/7/77/2-6. Similar letters of complaint were also written by Thibedi.

22. See e.g. 'Draft for Strengthening and Extending Trade Union Work in South Africa,' RGASPI 534/3/499 and 'Appeal to the Workers of South Africa for the United Front Struggle against the Capitalist Offensive,' RGASPI 534/3/546/10-13. G. Berns (Weinbren) to Ford, 7 August 1929, RGASPI, 495/155/80/47-48 and Weinbren to Ford, 9 October 1929, RGASPI 434/7/77/49-50.

23. The Executive Bureau of the RILU to the FNETU of South Africa,' *NW*, 2/2 (March-April 1929) p. 11, quoted in Johns, *Raising the Red Flag*, p.245.

24. RILU Negro Bureau to Dear Comrades, 25 October 1929, RGASPI 495/155/80/88-91; 'Draft Letter to the CP of South Africa, 17 January 1930,' RGASPI 495/155/83/38-51. For a view of the controversy surrounding the League of African Rights see Drew, *Between Empire and Revolution*, pp.189-199.

fully grasp its essential role and was unable to develop such a programme. The South African Communists were constantly urged to work within 'reformist' organisations, such as the ANC and Kadalie's ICU, as well as the trade unions including those that excluded Africans. The aim was to counter and criticise their political orientation, to educate rank and file members and to ensure that the workers did not remain under such influence and leadership, but instead took a revolutionary course.[25] In essence this meant leading a united struggle of all workers in South Africa and, as the RILU/CI kept pointing out, this required working within existing 'reformist' and 'traiterous'(sic) organisations of black and white workers, as well as building the FNETU, in order to create a united front of all.[26] The RILU/CI characterised this as 'fractional work' and pointed out

> In the SATUC[South African Trade Union Congress], in the Federation and in the ANC, the party members are not organised in a definite fraction and trained to ensure to exert the Party influence in these organisations, but everyone is allowed to carry on in the way he thinks best. The positive failures of the Party in the one time mass organisations of the ICU, in the reformist unions, in the ANC, are all due to lack of understanding of fractional work. This must be remedied immediately.[27]

It was an organisational approach that was maintained by the CI/RILU until the Seventh Congress of the CI in 1935 but which the CPSA and its members were slow to grasp.[28]

The ITUCNW and the Hamburg Conference

In keeping with this approach the ITUCNW worked with *Lekhotla la Bafo*, 'the council of commoners,' or 'League of the Poor,' an organisation established in Basutoland in 1919 'to champion the cause of the common people.' It appears that the CPSA first made contact with *Lekhotla la Bafo* in 1928 when Josiel Lefela, one of two brothers who had founded the organisation, sought information about Lenin and the Russian Revolution that might enlighten

25. See e.g. Report of Comrade X (ECCI Representative in South Africa), 28 September 1929, RGASPI 495/155/77/15-151.

26. See e.g. 'Draft Letter to South Africa,' 4 October 1929, RGASPI 495/155/67/31-42.

27. 'Fractional Work in Trade Unions and other Mass Organisations,' 24 August 1930, RGASPI 495/18/810/54.

28. Padmore to the South African Federation of Trade Unions, 10 April 1931, RGASPI 534/6/25/52-57.

the Basuto.[29] The organisation was then offered a regular column in the Party's paper, while Party members were often invited to attend and speak at its meetings, much to the displeasure of British colonial officials.[30]

Through the CPSA, *Lekhotla la Bafo* came into contact with the LAI, and other organisations associated with the CI, as well as the ITUCNW. In 1929 Maphutseng Lafela, the other joint founder, first wrote to James Ford asking for a subscription to *The Negro Worker*, which he found 'most needful and instructive.' He added that the publication would help to keep his organisation 'in close connection with the world's movement of Negro workers,' and explained that having affiliated to the LAI they were about to found an Agricultural Association 'to protect our people from local capitalist agents,' and that they now sought affiliation to the ITUCNW and RILU.[31] The RILU agreed to the affiliation and *Lekhotla la Bafo* remained in contact for many years, often receiving 'friendly criticism' from Moscow and from the ITUCNW.[32]

The Federation and South African Communists were also drawn into other aspects of the ITUCNW's work, such as distributing *The Negro Worker*, as well as other publications. They also participated in the preparatory work for the International Conference of Negro Workers, and Thibedi was officially a member of the preparatory committee.[33] In 1929 Bill Andrews represented the South African TUC at the meeting of the LAI in Frankfurt, at which James Ford organised a 'Negro delegation' to discuss the preparations for the conference.[34] In May 1930

29. D. Wolton, *Wither South Africa* (London, 1947) pp.62-63. For other versions of this initial contact see R. Edgar, *Prophets with Honour: A Documentary History of Lekhotla la Bafo* (Johannesburg, 1989) p.22.

30. Edgar, *Prophets With Honour*, pp.22-25. Some Notes for S.African Delegate's Report to Negro Sub-Commission, 9 August 1928, RGASPI 495/155/56/124. Also E. Roux, *Time Longer Than Rope: The Black Man's Struggle for Freedom in South Africa* (London, 1964) p.212.

31. M. Lefela to Ford, 9 October 1929, RGASPI 534/7/77/49-50 and 8 September 1929, RGASPI 534/3/527/5.

32. See Davidson et al (eds.) *South Africa and the Communist International* [vol.1] p.222 n.2. The Negro Section of the Eastern Secretariat also put the Kresintern in contact with *Lekhotla la Bafo*. For an example of such criticism see J.I Reed to Maphutseng Lafela, 16 May 1930, RGASPI 534/6/25/18-20.

33. *A Report of Proceedings and Decisions of the First International Conference of Negro Workers*, (Hamburg, 1930) p.1.

34. R. Cope, *Comrade Bill: The Life and Times of W.H. Andrews, Workers' Leader* (Cape Town, 1944) p.316. See also J. Ford, 'General Smuts and the Negro Native Masses of South Africa,' 15 January 1930, RGASPI 495/155/92/2. It should be noted that Ford was critical of Andrew's speech at Frankfurt, describing it as 'a social democrat speech,' in which 'he placed most emphasis on the question of the white workers in South Africa.' Ford added, 'while he did not declare it he seemed inclined against the slogan of native independence.' J. Ford, 'Report on the Negro Question in the LAI Congress,' 3 October 1929. RGASPI 534/3/450.

the Federation called all South African 'Negro organisations' to a conference in Johannesburg to prepare for the International Conference. It was reported that 'the South African natives' were glad to have the opportunity of meeting with other 'oppressed negroes' in 'order that all the forces may be united against imperialist oppression.'[35] Eventually E. S. 'Solly' Sachs (Albert Green) represented both the FNETU, Lekhota la Bafo and the 'left wing of the ANC' when the International Conference was finally convened in Hamburg.[36] Sachs's discussions in Moscow, where he had travelled after Hamburg to attend the Fifth RILU Congress, as well as his study of Lenin on the 'National and Colonial Questions,' seem to have convinced him of the correctness of the CI's Resolution on South Africa. When he returned he made several recommendations in regard to trade union work, which he reported Bunting and others leaders largely ignored.[37]

Initially the ITUCNW had requested 'as large a number of natives as possible' in the delegation from the FNETU to Hamburg, as well as delegates from the Johannesburg and Natal branches of the ICU, which by 1929 had split into three groups, and in which African Communists played a leading role.[38] Although three African delegates were elected to attend the Conference and the RILU congress, they were unable to make the journey from South Africa, due to passport and other restrictions imposed by the government.[39] Nevertheless the CPSA made a positive assessment of the significance of the Hamburg Conference for its work in South Africa.[40] Following the Hamburg Conference and the RILU's Fifth Congress, the ITUCNW took up in earnest its work to 'give directives' to the FNETU.[41] The RILU congress concluded that the Federation, although having achieved some advances, had 'still not succeeded in occupying any significant place in the native workers' movement.' In particu-

35. News Service, CPSA, 15 March 1930, RGASPI 495/155/87/117-118.

36. *A Report of Proceedings and Decisions of the First International Conference of Negro Workers*, pp.17-18.

37. Report of the South African Delegate to Hamburg, RGASPI 495/155/87/436. See also RGASPI 534/3/490 for Green's criticisms of the conference. Green also complained that he had been sent to Hamburg and Moscow against his will and that he had been forced to secretly remove money from his union's funds to finance the trip. RGASPI 534/7/77.

38. ITUCNW to RILU Secretariat, 2 February 1930, RGASPI 495/18/809/27. The ITUCNW had also initially hoped to send William Patterson to South Africa.

39. Report from A. Green, 2 July 1930, RGASPI 534/7/77/88-94 It seems that Josiah Gumede, President-General of the ANC, had also been prevented from attending the Conference. RGASPI 495/64/110/1; also 'South Africa's Secret Shame,' *Unsebenzi*, 23 May 1930, p.2. Green claimed that six other delegates were elected from South Africa and denied passports in his speech at the Conference.

40. See Davidson et al., *South Africa and the Communist International* [vol.1], pp.251-252.

41. A Plan of Work of the Negro Bureau of RILU, 31 December 1930, RGASPI 534/1/164/4-5.

lar it was charged with the task of organising amongst unorganised workers in farms, mines and transport.[42]

The African Federation of Trade Unions

In 1930 the FNETU came under the leadership of Albert Nzula, one of the first African leaders of the CPSA, and changed its name to the African Federation of Trade Unions (AFTU), following a proposal from the RILU's Negro Bureau.[43] Nzula, a former teacher and interpreter from the Transvaal, started his political life after being recruited by Kadalie into the ICU, where he became a local branch secretary. He then heard Douglas Wolton, the CPSA's general secretary, speaking at a meeting in the Transvaal and was apparently impressed by the idea of the 'Native Republic.' He began to investigate Communism for himself and subsequently wrote to *South African Worker*:

> I have come to the conclusion that every right-minded person ought to be a communist. I have hesitated all the time because communism has been misrepresented: I have been brought up on capitalistic literature, which is never satisfactory when it tries to explain working-class misery. I am convinced that no half-way measures will solve the problem...I am prepared to do my little bit to enlighten my countrymen on this point.[44]

Nzula joined the CPSA in August 1928 and, supported by Douglas Wolton, had a meteoric rise through the ranks at a time when the Party was attempting to Africanise its membership and leadership. A strong supporter of the 'Native Republic,' in 1929 he succeeded Wolton as the CPSA's general secretary and also became acting editor of *Umsebenzi,* (the new name for *The South African Worker*) and joint secretary of the League of Africans. In 1930 he was elected in absentia to the Executive Committee of the ITUCNW at its Hamburg Conference.[45]

---

42. *Resolutions of the Fifth Congress of the RILU,* p.66.

43. The AFTU was also known as the South African Federation of Trade Unions. Draft for Strengthening and Extending Trade Union Work in South Africa, n.d. RGASPI 534/3/499/103-104 and Amendments to South African Letter (Submitted by Haywood), 17 January 1930, RGASPI 495/155/83/52.

44. Quoted in Roux, *Time Longer Than Rope,* p.216.

45. R. Edgar, 'Notes on the Life and Death of Albert Nzula,' *International Journal of African Historical Studies,* (1983) 16/4, pp.675-679. For a longer but sometimes less accurate biographical account see R. Cohen, 'Introduction,' in A.Nzula, I. Potekhin and A.Zusmanovich, *Forced Labour in Colonial Africa* (London, 1979) pp.1-20. Also Simons and Simons, *Class and Colour in South Africa* p.414 and Wolton, *Wither South Africa,* pp.68-69.

The situation facing the AFTU and African workers was an extremely difficult one. Segregation, repressive and openly racist legislation, including the requirement for all Africans to carry passes, and vicious policing made organising extremely hazardous. Violence against Africans, and non-Europeans in general, was legally sanctioned and protest actions by African workers, and sometimes those of European workers, were routinely suppressed by state violence that often resulted in fatalities. Indeed, increasingly legislation was introduced that made any protest by Africans illegal. The divisions that existed between workers based on segregation and racism were encouraged and exacerbated by the ruling class and its governments. The Colour Bar Act of 1926 barred Africans from skilled occupation and the vast majority of white workers were organised in unions affiliated to the South African Trade Union Congress, which totally excluded African workers.

In opposition to the hardships facing African workers in 1919 Clements Kadalie, an African originally from Nyasaland, had founded the ICU, seeking to organise African and 'Coloured' workers.[46] A successful strike in the Cape Town docks and Kadalie's impressive oratory attracted many new members throughout the country and in 1920 encouraged further strikes in the mines. Although influenced by Garveyism, the ICU initially recognised the nature of the class struggle, declared that there could be 'no peace' between the workers and their exploiters, and in its paper *Workers' Herald*, called for a 'violent struggle' for social and national liberation. Tens of thousands of Africans, both in rural and urban areas, flocked to join the ICU.[47] Initially Kadalie also lavished praise on the Soviet Union and several Communists played a leading role in the ICU, including the two leading 'Coloured' members of the CPSA, John Gomas and La Guma, who became the ICU general-secretary.

In 1926, however, Kadalie took action to expel the ICU's leading communist members claiming that they belonged to a 'white man's party,' but also it seems in order to curry favour with 'reformist' trade union leaders in Britain and South Africa.[48] He then declared that strikes were 'wicked, useless and obsolete' and applied to affiliate to the British Trade Union Congress, the South African

46. C. Kadalie, *My Life and the ICU – The Autobiography of a Black Trade Unionist in South Africa* (London, 1970).

47. A. Nzula, 'The Struggle of the Negro Toilers in South Africa,' reprinted in Nzula et al, *Forced Labour in Colonial Africa*, p.206 and Simons and Simons, *Class and Colour in South Africa* pp.353-357.

48. 'The Communists and the ICU,' *South African Worker*, 24 December 1926, p.1; Drew, *Discordant Comrades*, pp.79-83. Kadalie presents the ICU's anti-communism partly as a result of the influence of Garveyism. Kadlie, *My Life and the ICU*, pp.98-101.

Trade Union Congress (SATUC) and the IFTU.[49] It was largely in response to the expulsion of Communists and what was seen as the 'decline of the ICU' that the FNETU was established in 1928.[50] In the same year the first major split occurred in the ICU with the secession in Natal of one of the largest and most important sections, led by the Zulu leader A.W. G. Champion. The following year Kadalie was succeeded in the leadership of the ICU by William Ballinger, the advisor sent from the Independent Labour Party in Britain to assist him. He then proceeded to form the so-called Independent ICU that soon floundered.[51]

The ITUCNW considered the ICU to be a prime example of 'Negro trade union reformism' and regularly denounced the speeches and activities of Kadalie and Champion, who were viewed as 'misleaders' of the African workers.[52] The AFTU therefore had to overcome not only the divisions between black and white workers, but also the fact that there were several different organisations competing for African members and creating confusion and disunity.[53] The disintegration of the ICU into three competing sections and the increasing militancy of African workers provided the conditions for advances in the AFTU's work but it proved unable to take full advantage of these favourable conditions, partly because of the repressive measures taken by the South African government but also because of its own political and organisational weaknesses.[54] State repression was a major problem. Legislation such as the Native Administration Act, which contained a section outlawing the promotion of hostility between Africans and Europeans, was used to attack the Communists, who were calling for the unity of all in opposition to the state. Communists were routinely arrested under this Act, simply for speaking or distributing literature, and under its terms could be sentenced to months of imprisonment and hard labour. African Communists and other activists could also be deported from one part of the country to their 'homeland' under the Urban Areas Act. A host of other repressive legislation, including the Riotous Assemblies Act, was routinely employed to 'banish, ban, or prohibit any person, public meeting or

49. Simons and Simons, *Class and Colour in South Africa,* pp.356-360. Even though the SATUC included Communists, such as Weinbren, amongst its leaders it rejected Kadalie's application. According to Weinbren 'we were all scared that he would swamp us.'

50. Roux, *Time Longer Than Rope*, p.175.

51. Johns, *Raising the Red Flag*, pp.188-194: Drew, *Discordant Comrades*, p.84.

52. See e.g. J.W. Ford, 'A Speech to the 2nd World Congress of the LAI at Frankfort, Germany,' July 1929, p.23.

53. See 'Open Letter of the South African Federation of Non-European Trade Unions,' *Umsebenzi,* 10 October 1930, p.2 in which James Shubin appealed for a united trade union movement.

54. In its edition of the 29 August 1930 *Umsebenzi* admitted that the FNETU had been suffering from internal problems and 'slack times.'

book' that the government considered a threat and to attempt to stifle any act of resistance.[55]

The CI and the ITUCNW were concerned that the AFTU and the CPSA were unable to provide the revolutionary leadership that the economic crisis of the period, the increasingly repressive measures of the government and the increasingly militant workers' struggles in South Africa demanded. It was a time when South African Communists such as Nzula were optimistically speaking of entering a new period, 'a period of mass action and conflicts against tyrannical laws, slave conditions and economic misery.'[56] The AFTU was accused of 'failure to win the leadership of the mass actions of the proletariat and peasantry...due to the underestimation of the role of the national revolutionary struggle in South Africa.'[57] In fact the activists of the AFTU were reluctant to work within the existing 'reformist' trade unions and to present demands that could unite the workers based on their everyday needs.[58] The RILU and the ITUCNW called for the AFTU to take measures to reorganise itself, to combat its isolation and those views associated with Sidney Bunting and others, which it was said, underestimated the revolutionary potential of the African masses, so as to be able to fully carry out its activities amongst the workers and lead them in a counter-offensive. The AFTU was of course dependent on the leadership of the CPSA that was beset by its own political and organisational problems. The CI issued many criticisms of the weaknesses and 'white chauvinism' of the CPSA[59] and several reports commented that the South African Communists had 'a poor understanding of the role and the tasks of the trade union movement in general.' Reporting back to Moscow in 1929 the CI's representative in South Africa had concluded that the Federation's 'weakest side is its complete disorganisation,' and he added it 'must become an object closely under the observation of the Profintern.'[60]

55. Simons and Simons, *Colour and Class in South Africa*, p.430.

56. A. Nzula, 'Native Workers Make Organisational Advances in South Africa,' *NW*, 1/2, (February 1931) pp. 14-15.

57. See e.g. 'Draft Letter to the CP of South Africa,' 17 January 1930, RGASPI 495/155/83/38-51 and 'Draft Resolution on Revolutionary TU Work in South Africa,' 30 August 1930, RGASPI 495/18/810/64-66.

58. 'Work in the reformist trade unions,' 14 August 1930, RGASPI 534/1/164/3.

59. See e.g. 'Letter from ECCI to CPSA,' 10 September 1930, in Davidson et al, *South African and the Communist International* [vol.1], pp.242-247.

60. Report of ECCI Representative in South Africa, 28 September 1929, RGASPI 495/155/77/150.

The Hamburg Committee and South Africa

The HC of the ITUCNW, established by Ford in October 1930, viewed South Africa as one of its main areas of work and planned that the first edition of its new monthly journal, temporarily renamed the *International Negro Workers' Review,* would feature an article 'to deal with the situation in South Africa.'[61] The HC also intended establishing sub-committees in various international ports and Cape Town was the designated port in South Africa.[62] Ford managed to make contact with Nzula who informed him that the AFTU was 'conducting the greatest part of its activities to the organisation of the Negro masses and for that reason I think it is just the body to form a sub-section of the ITUCNW.'[63] The ITUCNW envisaged that this sub-committee would not duplicate the work of the AFTU but would 'carry out activities in the surrounding countries' with the aim of establishing contacts in southern and eastern Africa. As George Padmore of the RILU Negro Bureau explained, 'it would be a dangerous policy to have the sub-committee in South Africa carrying on trade union activities in the Union itself because this will immediately bring it into conflict with the Federation, whose task is to lead and organise the economic struggle in South Africa.'[64]

Ford was also instructed to ask the South African comrades for lists of likely contacts, but this work developed slowly owing to Ford's inability to carry it out efficiently and the difficult of communicating with South Africa from Germany.[65] He did manage to regularly send Nzula a hundred and fifty copies of *The Negro Worker,* which carried several articles on South Africa, as well as other revolutionary literature. Ford reported that he was using Chinese seamen as couriers for this task and even getting mail posted from West Africa in order to avoid suspicion. Some new contacts were apparently established in the Portuguese colonies and in Rhodesia as a result of the work undertaken by Nzula and other South African activists.[66]

Acting on behalf of the Negro Bureau, in late 1930 Padmore then made contact with John Gomas, a leading figure in the AFTU and the CPSA, apparently after several months when the ITUCNW had no communication with

61. Plan of Work and Immediate tasks of the ITUCNW at Hamburg, 28 February 1931, RGASPI 534/3/668.

62. Ibid.

63. Report to European Secretariat of RILU on Activities of the ITUCNW at Hamburg, 31 January 1931, RGASPI 534/3/669.

64. Padmore to Ford, 17 March, 1931, RGASPI 534/3/668.

65. Ibid.

66. 'Report on Work of the ITUCNW (Hamburg), covering the period from December 1930 to September 15,' 1931, RGASPI 534/3/669.

South Africa. Gomas, a tailor by profession, had formerly been a leading figure in the ICU, and a leader of the ANC in the Western Cape. He had joined the communist movement even before the CPSA was formed and led its work in Cape Town.[67] Padmore corresponded with Gomas regarding trade union matters, demanding detailed reports on the situation in the Cape in particular.[68] He also employed him, as well several other South African Communists, as the means to distribute *The Negro Worker* and other literature. Mail was subsequently sent to several addresses so that it was less likely to be intercepted by the authorities.

In one of his first letters Padmore asked his opinion about the possibility of forming a Seamen's Club in Cape Town, and over a year later Gomas informed him that when the suggestion was put to the seamen they had decided to form a union.[69] This organisation, the Seamen and Harbour Worker's Union, was formed in 1932 under the auspices of the AFTU.[70] Gomas explained that over thirty seamen, 'mostly coloured and Negro workers,' had gathered to found the Union, which was seeking affiliation to the ISH. It was also asking the ITUCNW for financial support and appropriate literature for distribution. The workers had numerous grievances, many of them based on racial discrimination, as well as wage cuts, long hours and unemployment and Gomas had been able to unite them around specific economic demands, as well as around 'anti-war slogans' and in opposition to the colour bar.[71]

Padmore sent Gomas detailed directives on organisational matters, pointing out to him that, 'the success of the revolutionary movement depends not so much on "High Politics" than upon everyday work.' He also tried to clarify some of the confusion around the question of what distinguished the work of the CPSA from that of the AFTU, one of several key questions confusing the South African communist movement at the time. Gomas was also enlisted in the work of establishing a section of the ITUCNW in South Africa that could begin to 'make contact with workers in South West Africa and East African ports through the seamen who call in at Cape Town.'[72] Through his contact with Nzula, Padmore gleaned further information about the work and problems of the AFTU that he subsequently used to frame the directives sent from

67. See Musson, *Johnny Gomas.*

68. Padmore to Gomas, 12 February 1931, RGASPI 534/6/25/42-44.

69. 'Seamen and Harbour Workers Union Formed,' *Umsebenzi*, 25 May 1932, p1.

70. Gomas to Padmore, 6 May 1932, RGASPI 534/3/755 and 'Report on the Work of the Hamburg Committee for the period 1931-1932,' December 1932, RGASPI 534/3/753.

71. Gomas to Padmore, 6 May 1932, and Padmore to Gomas, 23 June 1932, RGASPI 534/3/755.

72. Padmore to Gomas, 12 February 1931, RGASPI 534/6/25/42-44.

the RILU but he also intervened directly in order to try to remedy some of the political confusion that existed in the CPSA.

At the start of 1931 Padmore received more regular news from Nzula who assured him that 'we are concentrating the greatest part of our activities on the organisation of the Negro workers of South Africa.'[73] He also provided some information on the bloody clashes that had taken place during the Dingaan's Day demonstrations in December 1930 in Durban, which led to many deaths including that of Johannes Nkosi, a member of the Executive Committee of the CPSA.[74] Nzula has indeed been vey active himself, taking part in the Dingaan's Day demonstrations, leading the pass burning in Johannesburg and, in January 1931, leading a strike of laundry workers.[75]

Padmore was also informed that the first steps had been taken to organise the agricultural workers and peasant communities and to establish a union amongst miners and transport workers.[76] It was on the basis of this and other information that the Executive Bureau of the RILU sent the AFTU a detailed 'letter of guidance' in April 1931, which was subsequently published in *The Negro Worker*.[77] The RILU remained critical of the AFTU's tendency to 'lag behind the developing struggles of the masses,' in other words its inability to make substantial progress organising amongst the urban and rural workers, and yet again called on the Federation to carry out the decisions of its Fifth Congress by developing and organising the struggles of the workers for economic reforms, strengthening existing unions, organising new ones and working within the 'reformist and reactionary unions, whether of European or non-European workers.' In particular the RILU called on the AFTU to remember that it was 'not a race but a class organisation,' and that it should pay attention to all the workers. However, it was also instructed to train and promote 'Native cadres' wherever possible and to focus on workers in mining, transport, and

73. *International Negro Workers' Review*, 1/2 (February 1931) p.23.

74. A. Nzula, 'Native Workers Make Organisational Advances in South Africa,' *The International Negro Workers' Review,* 1/2 (February 1931) pp.14-15. On Nkosi see Simons and Simons, *Class and Colour,* pp.435 and *NW*, 1/6 (June 1931) p.7 and A. Nzula, 'Comrade Johannes Nkosie, First African Revoutionary Martyr,' *Umsebenzi*, 9 January 1931, in *South African Communists Speak, 1915-1980* (London, 1981) pp.11-112. Also N. F. Ndlovu, 'Johannes Nkosi and the Communist Party of South Africa: Images of "Blood River" and King Dingane in the late 1920s-1930,' *History and Theory*, 39 (December 2000) pp.111-132.

75. M. Kotane, 'Coming Struggles in South Africa,' *NW*, 1/3 (March 1931) p.3.

76. A. Nzula, 'Native Workers Make Organisational Advances in South Africa,' *The International Negro Workers' Review,* 1/2 (February 1931) pp.14-15 and M. Kotane, 'Coming Struggles in South Africa,' *The Negro Worker (NW)* 1/3 (March 1931) p.3.

77. 'To the South African Federation of Trade Unions,' 14 April 1931, *NW*, 1/6 (June 1931) pp.14-18.

agriculture, as well as the unemployed. It was called upon to organise amongst the workers by encouraging them to advance and fight for specific demands and then leading their struggles, so as to make sure they were not betrayed by 'reformist leaders.'[78]

Padmore explained to Nzula that this 'open letter' should be published and widely discussed and he continued to press him to supply a range of information about the political situation in the CPSA and the AFTU, including information about the standing of individual comrades. It is clear from this correspondence that the CI/RILU wished to give as much direction as possible but found this difficult to do from such a distance. This was especially true of CI attempts to establish wider links within Africa, and hence as Padmore emphasised, the importance of establishing a 'sub-committee' of the ITUCNW 'which will be the connecting link between Europe and the African colonies in just the same way as the Hamburg Committee is the connecting link between RILU and the broad masses of Negro workers in different parts of the world who have not yet come into the camp of the revolutionary trade union movement.'[79] In subsequent letters similarly detailed directions, some of them based on the reports of the CI's representative in South Africa, were sent in regard to organising the unemployed.[80]

In the summer of 1931 Nzula arrived in Moscow as a student at the International Lenin School and was able to participate directly in the deliberations of the RILU Negro Bureau.[81] He subsequently played a leading role in the Bureau and the ITUCNW and remained in Moscow until his death in 1934.[82] He remained critical of the CPSA's lack of activity amongst the workers and the fact that AFTU had made relatively little progress. In 1931 the AFTU's affiliated unions were believed to have a total membership of five thousand but the Federation had barely begun to work amongst what were considered the most important sections of the workers, miners, railway workers and dockers.[83] Two years later at the start of 1933 the RILU was still calling for the setting up of a sub-committee in Cape Town and Padmore, who had succeeded Ford in Hamburg in late 1931, was lamenting the fact that in South Africa the AFTU

78. Ibid.

79. Padmore to Nzula, 16 June 1931, RGASPI 534/6/25.

80. See Negro Committee of the RILU To the South African Federation of Trade Unions, 30 September 1931, RGASPI 534/6/25/81-85.

81. During this period Padmore and the RILU Negro Bureau remained in contact with P.G. Moloinyane, the AFTU's Assistant Secretary. See Moloinyane to Padmore, 21 July 1931, RGASPI 534/7/78/1-2

82. Nzula suffered from alcoholism, which was a major contributory factor to his death from pneumonia. For a report of Nzula's drunkenness in Moscow see Helen Davis to Comrade Nikitin, 11 May 1932, RGASPI 495/279/52.

83. 'Protocol of the Meeting of the Negro Bureau,' 28 August 1931, RGASPI 534/3/668.

had 'not yet gone beyond the stage of promises.'[84] As a direct result of Nzula's presence in Moscow, the ITUCNW issued further directives with precise instructions on how to build revolutionary trade union groups within existing unions, as well as advice on the organisation of strikes, strike committees and pickets.[85] As well as providing such organisational advice and demanding regular reports from the AFTU, the RILU Negro Committee also attempted to develop the Federation as a separate organisation from the CPSA with its own headquarters, publication and leadership.[86]

The AFTU continued to face significant difficulties, not least the repressive conditions and legislation that forced African workers to exist as migrant labourers in their own land and criminalised the many unemployed as vagrants, as well as its limited human and other resources.[87] In the conditions of the Depression the government continued to exacerbate divisions between black and white workers, introduced a host of increasingly draconian laws, and sanctioned state violence against workers and Communists, which created some pessimism not only in the ranks of the workers but even amongst the activists of the AFTU. Such pessimism the ITUCNW did its best to combat, by pointing out that some victories had been won. There had, for example, been some joint demonstrations of African and European workers and the AFTU was encouraged to build on such manifestations of proletarian unity, and to recruit and train its own cadres especially from amongst the militant African workers.[88] However, as Gomas pointed out, they were also very short of experienced leaders. Constant arrests and imprisonment, including his own, meant that it was also very difficult to maintain continuity of leadership.[89]

The AFTU also had to contend with the expulsion of leading white Party members who were also key figures in the trade union movement, such as E.S. Sachs, C.B. Tylor, Weinbren and W. H. Andrews, who were accused of adopting 'white chauvinist' and 'reformist' positions. In July 1931, for example, P.G. Moloinyane, the assistant secretary of the AFTU and a member of the Political Bureau of the CPSA, wrote to Padmore complaining that Andrews and Wein-

---

84. 'Resolution on the Report on the Work of the Hamburg Committee,' n.d., RGASPI 534/3/753, also 'Report on the Work of the Hamburg Committee for the period 1931-1932,' December 1932, RGASPI 534/3/753.

85. ITUCNW to the South African Federation of Trade Unions, 6 October 1931, RGASPI 534/6/25/86-91.

86. Huiswoud to the AFTU, 17 November 1931, RGASPI 534/6/25/95.

87. See e.g. 'New Slave Law in South Africa,' *NW*, 2/11-12, (November-December 1932) pp.1-3.

88. Negro Committee of the RILU to the AFTU, 30 September 1931, RGASPI 534/6/25/81-85.

89. Gomas to Padmore, 4 November 1932, RGASPI 534/3/756.

bren were not genuine revolutionaries and that Andrews, one of the leaders of the new South African Trades and Labour Council (TLC), should be criticised for his activities within such a 'reformist' organisation which excluded 'Native' trade unions.[90] Andrews was also accused of spreading 'reformist' illusions amongst white workers.[91] Moloinyane also criticised Weinbren's Native Trades Assistants' Union for 'reformism,' complained that it was only a union of white workers rather than all workers, as Weinbren claimed, and was not affiliated to the AFTU.[92] Sachs had previously been accused of 'a very serious opportunist attitude' in regard to his alleged opposition to unions of white workers in Johannesburg affiliating to the AFTU.[93] These and other leading members were expelled alongside Sidney Bunting in September 1931.[94] The expulsions were justified and presented as being connected with the weaknesses of the AFTU, particularly as a necessary measure against those 'who held responsible posts in the independent white unions, who developed the theory that there was no basis for the rapprochement between the native unions and that of the white workers.' They were also seen as an important blow against 'Right opportunism' and 'Buntingism,' that is opposition to the full implementation of the 'Native Republic' thesis and therefore to the line of the Comintern.[95] The internal struggles took place in the context of the 'Africanisation' of the CPSA, the emergence of new African Communist leaders and a strong rejection of everything connected with 'white chauvinism' and 'disbelief in the native masses having the spirit to fight for their rights.'[96] However, personal rivalries and animosities also played a part and although there might have been some grounds for the criticism of individuals, the expulsions, which were organised from South Africa by the leaders of the CPSA but supported by the Comintern, cannot be

90. Moloinyane to Padmore, 21 July 1931, RGASPI 534/7/78/1-2.

91. Davidson et al., *South Africa and the Communist International* [vol.2], p.11 n.4; ITUCNW to the South African Federation of Trade Unions,' 19 April 1932, RGASPI 534/6/26/13-16.

92. Moloinyane to Padmore, 21 July 1931, RGASPI 534/7/78/1-2.

93. Negro Committee of the RILU to the AFTU, 30 September 1931, RGASPI 534/6/25/81-85.

94. The ECCI claimed that Bunting had merely been expelled from the Central Committee of the CPSA not as a CP member and carried out an investigation into the circumstances of his expulsion. Minutes of Political Secretariat of the ECCI, 15 July 1932, in Davidson et al. *South Africa and the Communist International* [vol.2], pp.27-28.

95. Negro Committee of the RILU To the South African Federation of Trade Unions, 30 September 1931, RGASPI 534/6/25/81-85; ' ITUCNW to the South African Federation of Trade Unions, 19 April 1932, RGASPI 534/6/26/13-16. Also see O. Huiswoud, 'The Revolutionary Trade Union Movement Amongst Negro Workers,' *RILU Magazine*, 2/3 (15 February 1932) pp.212-216.

96. Drew, *Between Empire and Revolution*, p.203.

said to have strengthened the CPSA nor the AFTU.[97] Others were subsequently expelled too, including La Guma and Gana Makabeni, a leading African trade unionist accused of supporting Bunting.[98] Such measures ushered in a period in which factionalism and sectarianism was rife, particularly amongst Party leaders such as the Woltons, Lazar Bach and Nzula, who from Moscow continued to play a significant role in developing the ITUCNW's approach to the AFTU.

Another major problem faced by the AFTU and Communist activists was the constant threat of arrest, imprisonment, usually with hard labour, and even death. Johannes Nkosi was the most well known martyr but other leading African comrades such as J.B. Marks and Edwin Mofutsanyana had barely escaped assassination. State repression not only had adverse consequences for individuals and their families but also disrupted the work of the Federation and the Party.[99] After a few months of imprisonment Gomas, who had several such experiences to draw on, provided this description for Padmore:

> Concerning my own imprisonment I happened to have survived it fairly well. You can see a photograph of mine, which I enclose herewith, that I look alright. However conditions are very bad in gaol, especially for all non-Europeans brutal. We are not treated under a special regime for political prisoners and therefore are treated just like ordinary criminals. I had to do all kinds of hard labour and was subjected to indignities and ill-treatment not meted out to dogs as a rule. The prisons are very crowded, conditioned no doubt by the severe economic crisis which has rendered large numbers of blacks out of work. [100]

It was in order to offer some support to activists and their families and following the death of Nkosi that the South African section of MOPR, Ikaka la Basebenzi (Workers' Shield), was created in early1931.[101] The MOPR seems to have existed in South Africa before this time but it was severely criticised for its 'absolutely unsatisfactory' work, the fact that it had 'not understood how to fulfil its prime task: the work among Negroes,' and because it had 'not developed the fight against

97. For conflicting views on the background to the expulsions and the condemnation of 'Buntingism see Simons & Simons, *Class and Colour*, pp.446-453; Drew, *Between Empire and Revolution*, pp.204-208; Drew, *Discordant Comrades*, pp.121-132.

98. Both La Guma and Andrews were later reinstated.

99. See B.R. Ndobe, ' Capitalist Terror in South Africa,' *NW*, 2/4 (April 1932) pp.13-15; 'New Slave Law in South Africa,' *NW*, 2/11-12 (November-December 1932) pp.1-3 and 'South African Imperialists Initiate New Terror Actions Against Natives,' *NW*, 3/2-3 (February-March 1933) pp.13-15.

100. Gomas to Padmore, 4 November 1932, RGASPI 534/3/756.

101. *Unsebenzi*, 9 January 1931, p.2.

white chauvinism and has even not been able to draw Negroes into its ranks.' As a consequence it was called upon to 'reorganise itself immediately in such a way that it becomes an organisation of the natives with Negro comrades occupying the majority in all leading positions.'[102] The organisation was established to 'assist to the utmost every revolutionary fighter and his family who may be arrested, deported, imprisoned, wounded or killed,' and also campaigned against the repressive measures taken in South West Africa, which was administered as a League of Nations mandate by the South African government.[103] Ikaka also participated in major international campaigns such as Scottsboro and in defence of the Meerut prisoners in India, and with the ITUCNW worked to establish a branch of MOPR in Madagascar.[104] Although it too suffered from some of the sectarianism of the CPSA, with which it was closely linked, it remained very active and for some time was led by Josie Mpama, one of the few black women members of the CPSA and the head of the CP's Women's Department.[105]

Padmore exerted every effort to keep in close communication with the leaders of the AFTU, such as Gomas and Moloinyane, as well as with Wolton, and even Gumede of the ANC.[106] He redoubled his efforts almost as soon as he arrived in Hamburg, complaining to Wolton that he had inherited a 'worthless South African mailing list' from Ford, composed mainly of 'East Africans, who he concluded were 'no doubt Gandhi'ists.' His efforts were not always reciprocated and he lamented the fact that South African comrades did not keep in contact and explained, 'our Committee has been organised in order to give assistance to you comrades in the colonies, but if you don't keep up contacts with us, it is no use raising hell that we do not help you.' He demanded detailed reports, pointing out that 'only on the basis of such reports will headquarters be able to formulate correct policies.[107] But such reports were not always forthcoming and there was also considerable difficulty concerning the despatch of *The Negro Worker* and other literature, which despite precautions and frequent changes of address was, as Gomas and others reported, often confiscated and destroyed by the authorities.[108] Those in South Africa also complained about a

102. Resolution on the I.R.A. Work Among the Negroes, RGASPI 495/18/810/97.

103. See 'Speech of A. Nzula at World Congress International Red Aid,' in Davidson, et al, South Africa and the Communist International, [vol 2], pp.63-65 and *South African Communists Speak*, p.112.

104. *NW*, 3/2-3 (February-March 1933) pp.27-28.

105. Meeting of Negro Department, 25 August 1933, RGASPI 534/3/895.

106. See e.g. J. Gomas to Padmore, 23 December 1931, RGASPI 534/7/78/11-12 and Padmore to Moloinyane, 28 February 1932, RGASPI 534/3/754.

107. Padmore to Wolton, 23 February 1932, RGASPI 534/3/754.

108. Gomas to Padmore, 4 November 1932, RGASPI 534/3/756.

lack of support from the CPGB and here too Padmore intervened, promising that he would complain directly to Harry Pollitt, its general secretary. He also wrote to the NMM in Britain, asking them to do more to support the work of the Federation in South Africa.[109]

In one area it appears that Padmore and the HC were considered to be intervening too far into South African affairs. In September 1932 Eugene Dennis, the representative of the ECCI in South Africa, wrote to complain about a recent cable from the Profintern that apparently instructed the Seamen and Harbour Workers' Union to apply for affiliation to the ITUCNW. The Union had itself initially applied for such affiliation but Dennis had encouraged it to merely maintain 'fraternal relations' with the ITUCNW, and instead to affiliate to the ISH. In justifying his approach Dennis explained that it was in line with the ECCI's decision that where sections of the RILU existed, trade unions 'shall not affiliate to the Hamburg Committee but to the respective RILU Centre, as well as affiliate to the respective International Trade Union.' Dennis therefore refused to implement the RILU directive, arguing that if it were 'universally applied,' it would 'lay the basis for building a Black International Trade Union.'[110] Consequently, the work that the Seamen and Harbour Workers' Union was starting to develop in other parts of southern Africa, Tanganyika, Nyasaland and the Portuguese colonies, which the ITUCNW hoped to develop through its South African section, would also being directed by the CPSA rather than by the ITUCNW.

The Huiswoud Mission

The RILU Bureau still considered that the AFTU could continue to make headway in the midst of the Depression that had 'shaken South Africa to its roots,' and along the lines set out by the Profintern. In February 1933 the Negro Bureau, now chaired by Nzula, and taking into account that previous interventions on the subject had led to 'no appreciable results,' issued a further directive on the importance of stepping up work amongst the miners.[111] This guidance was issued when the RILU was taking an even more direct interventionist approach. In 1932 it had taken the decision to send Otto Huiswoud, one of the leading members of its Negro Bureau, to South Africa. Huiswoud stayed in South Africa for several months from late 1932 to early 1933, visited Johannesburg, Durban

109. Padmore to J. Mahon, 13 January 1932, RGASPI 534/3/754.

110. E. Dennis to Dear Comrades, 13 September 1932, RGASPI 495/64/119.

111. 'To the AFTU – Work Among Miners in South Africa,' 7 February 1933, RGASPI 534/6/26/50-54. Nzula (T. Jackson) signed on behalf of the Negro Bureau and the Miners' International Committee.

and Cape Town and met with some of the leading comrades including Gomas.[112] It is not clear if he was sent specifically to clear up any confusion between ECCI and RILU directives, but he participated in some of the work to revitalise the AFTU during this period and on his return wrote a report for the RILU that was highly critical of the lack of progress that had been made.[113] 'When I arrived the AFTU practically did not exist as a national body,' he reported, adding,

> a number of local groups were attached to the Federation but there were even no local AFTU committees, no responsibility, directives from the AFTU as national organ were absolutely lacking. The main causes for this were 1) underestimation of TU work and generally of all mass-work...the last ECCI letter which was very good was practically neither discussed nor circulated among the members; and 2) the complete collapse of what was formerly the AFTU; the Federation was previously composed of different unions at least 5 or 6. The membership of 5000, which was then indicated, was greatly exaggerated. Very few attempts were made to revive the AFTU. The Federation was then exclusively composed of workers from secondary industries, the basic industries had been hardly touched. Today there is not one single union affiliated to the AFTU except the Seamen and Harbour Workers' Union in Durban and Fishermen's Union in Port Noloth.(sic) [114]

Huiswoud estimated that, as of February 1933, the Federation only had just over eight hundred members and small sections, rather than complete unions, of mineworkers, marine workers and agricultural workers. Few of the members paid regular dues and, apart from those who were paid officials, hardly any of the members did any work, or regularly attended meetings. Even newly formed unions, such as the Seamen and Harbour Workers' Union in Cape Town, had already collapsed.[115] This state of affairs was of particular concern because the

112. See Maria Gertrudis van Enckevort, 'The Life and Work of Otto Huiswoud: Professional Revolutionary and Internationalist (1893 - 1961),' Ph.D Thesis, UWI, Mona, 2001, p.108.

113. Huiswoud produced a detailed interim report that was published in *The Negro Worker*. See O.H., 'Problems and Tasks of the Revolutionary Trade Unions,' *NW*, 2/11-12 (November-December 1932) pp.6-17. This edition also contained detailed advice for the AFTU entitled 'How to build the Unemployed Movement,' ibid. pp.17-24. See also O. Huiswoud, 'The Tasks of the Revolutionary Trade Union Movement in South Africa,' *RILU Magazine*, 2/19-20 (1 November 1932) pp. 854-861.

114. Minutes of the Meeting of the Negro Bureau of the RILU of June 25th, 1933, RGASPI 534/3/895.

115. Huiswoud also had criticisms of the attempts of this union to organise dockers in Capetown. See O.H., 'Problems and Tasks of the Revolutionary Trade Unions,' *NW*, 2/11-12 (November-December 1932) pp.13-14.

workers were being forced to bear the brunt of the economic crisis in the form of wage cuts, longer hours, speed-ups and unemployment.

But Huiswoud's report also pointed out the great obstacles and difficulties that the AFTU had to overcome; state repression, including legislation against strikes, was a key consideration, in addition to the racially divided working class, which posed particular problems in the mining industry. In many areas and industries the AFTU could not organise legally, it also lacked trained cadres and in the mining industry found it almost impossible to organise in the compounds and amongst African miners who were temporary migrant workers.[116] In addition, Huiswoud concluded, the AFTU suffered from ' a left sectarian attitude on the question of TU work; utter confusion among the comrades leading the work on the question of TU work; no collective leadership, failure to take up specific grievances such as violence, bad food, cases of injury without compensation, etc.'[117]

Nevertheless, Huiswoud did point to few successes, notably the work starting amongst agricultural workers and 'peasants,' especially in Natal were they were organised against land evictions; the strike and organising connected with the transport workers in Cape Town, where a 'revolutionary trade union opposition' had been formed within an existing union, and work amongst the unemployed. It seems that Huiswoud's tasks had been to reorganise the AFTU and to encourage it to work in the existing 'reformist' trade unions and in key industries such as mining, as well as amongst agricultural workers. He had held several local conferences and established local committees to carry on the work 'to mobilise the workers for struggle against unemployment, wage cuts, etc' and on the basis of a programme of specific demands.[118]

The RILU Negro Bureau persisted with its plans to assist the AFTU, which by 1933 was led by John Gomas, and continued to encourage the Federation to develop its work amongst the miners and other sections of the industrial proletariat, as well as amongst agricultural workers and the unemployed.[119] It also continued to encourage the AFTU to work in existing 'reformist' unions, in the villages

116. Nzula had written to the AFTU to point out that not all miners were seasonal workers and that it should attempt to organise those that were not. J. Jackson{Nzula) to the AFTU, 2 March 1933, RGASPI 534/6/26/50-54.

117. Minutes of the Meeting of the Negro Bureau of the RILU of June 25th, 1933, RGASPI 534/3/895.

118. Ibid.

119. From 1932 the CPSA began to demand relief and an insurance scheme for the unemployed. See e.g. 'Against starvation and Unemployment – for the Unemployment Insurance Bill,' *Umsebenzi*, 27 May 1932, p.3.

in rural areas and in the ANC.[120] By the following year the RILU acknowledged some progress in these areas of work although it noted that the AFTU had failed to lead the workers' movement on the basis of the 'united front from below,' was still underestimating the importance of working in 'reformist' organisations, and still maintained a 'sectarian approach,' especially in regard to organising white workers. In short many of the weaknesses of earlier years persisted despite the continual intervention of the ITUCNW and the Negro Bureau of the RILU.[121]

The Crisis Within the CPSA

The weaknesses of the AFTU were a consequence of the problems that bedevilled the CPSA during the 1930s. In the main these arose from the lack of experience of the Party's leaders. Nzula, for instance, had only been a Party member for six months when he became general secretary. The CI tried to overcome this problem both by its intervention and by training fourteen of the leading South African Communists in Moscow.[122] However even in Moscow there were expressions of this inexperience as is clear from the letter of Moses Kotane, subsequently general secretary of the CPSA for nearly forty years:

> I being a Negro who the CI proposes to take the leadership, and despite the fact that I had no training and education prior to joining the revolutionary movement, I am only given one year's training in the [International Lenin School] ILS and shipped back to South Africa, with heavy responsibilities on my shoulders. The absurdity of this responsibility lies in the fact that I who have had no sufficient training (Theoretically and Politically) I am supposed to supervise the Communist Movement in South Africa. How can I? ...So my work in the AFTU can be nothing but subordinate to those above me. Not because I am a Negro but because theoretically they are super to me, of course due to historical reasons, for instance experience, education and environment (sic).' ...To consider me as a leader would be a mockery to Negro people and the Communist Movement in South Africa in particular.[123]

120. 'To the AFTU – On the Organisation of the Agricultural Workers Union,' n.d., RGASPI 534/6/26/86-98.

121. 'Letter to the AFTU,' 3 July 1934, RGASPI 534/6/26/116.

122. Davidson et al., *South Africa and the Communist International* [vol.1], p.6.

123. M. Kotane to the Comintern, 30 November 1933, in Davidson et al., *South Africa and the Communist International* [vol.2], p.67.

The CI had acted decisively during and after its Sixth Congress to reorient the CPSA, so that it was led by and took up the concerns of the majority in South Africa. Many attempts were also made to 'bolshevize' the Party so that it was properly financed, organised in a revolutionary way based on the principles of democratic centralism and built mainly amongst the workers. The reorientation of the CPSA and the adoption of the 'Native Republic' or 'Black Republic' slogan certainly created divisions in the Party but the main problem it faced was that lack of political clarity meant that it did not fully get to grips with the work of organising and leading the struggles that were breaking out in the country and the investigation into its shortcomings led to recrimination and factional infighting. The CPSA faced many difficulties, however, there was also an initial reluctance to fully base the Party's main activities amongst the African majority and to take up trade union work, especially work in the 'reformist' trade unions. The Party was also unable to overcome the difficulties involved in work amongst the rural masses, the majority in the country, as well as amongst the most important sections of the working class, such as the miners. For many years these problems were not satisfactorily resolved and attempts to solve them, or to combat 'sectarianism' and 'white chauvinism,' let to further factional divisions. Factional struggle even broke out over the actual meaning of the 'Independent Native Republic' slogan. This situation was a major impediment to the work to put forward a programme of concrete demands, and actions to realise them, in order to address the problems facing the masses of the people in South Africa.

The first African leaders of the FNETU/AFTU, Thibedi and La Guma were both expelled from the CPSA and the Federation for various misdemeanours and Thibedi's expulsion was used as the basis for disputes within the leadership. More damaging still were the factional struggles within the CPSA throughout the 1930s. Bunting and others were hastily removed from the leadership of the Party at the end of 1930, allegedly because they stood in the way of the full implementation of the decisions of the CI's Sixth Congress. But although 'Africanisation' of the Party continued and Africans such as Nzula and Kotane came into the leadership, the CPSA was initially dominated by the Woltons and by Lazar Bach, a recent migrant from Latvia. Wolton, Bach and their supporters appeared as the most zealous champions of the CI and Africanisation, in opposition to Bunting and the 'Buntingites,' but under this leadership the factional struggled intensified, expulsions continued and the CPSA became increasingly sectarian and in some areas almost stopped functioning.

The expulsion of Bunting and leading trade unionists in 1931 created further problems particularly within the AFTU.[124] The expulsion of E.S. Sachs and later Gana Makabeni, for instance, initially meant the loss of the Garment

124. 'The Fight Against the Right Danger,' *Umsebenzi*, 4 September 1931, p.3.

Workers' Union and African Clothing Workers' Union that they led.[125] Even La Guma, who had been readmitted to the Party, was expelled again in 1931 for further misdemeanours allegedly carried out in the course of his work for the AFTU.[126] Behind the expulsions lay a struggle over the political orientation of the CPSA but this struggle veered into factionalism and sectarianism, as well as undemocratic methods that severely handicapped the work of the Party and the Federation.[127]

The ITUCNW certainly opposed the CPSA's sectarianism, as did the CI most notably in Harry Pollitt's article published in *Communist Review* in 1932.[128] However, it is also evident that the factionalists utilised the Comintern's directives as well as more general campaigns against 'the right danger' for their own purposes. Despite this, and the efforts of representatives on the spot such as Huiswoud, the Comintern was unable to adequately deal with the factional struggle until the mid 1930s. Within the CPSA there were also attempts to overcome the obvious problems. Moses Kotane, who in 1933 became general secretary after Wolton returned to England, was one of the first to articulate some of the Party's problems, which he characterised as being 'too Europeanised.' However, his opposition to sectarianism, demands that the CPSA work amongst the masses and their organisations and actually build a united front, were also couched in the factional spirit and he was ousted from office.[129] Finally, in 1935, following the CI's Seventh Congress to which the CPSA did not send an official delegation, the Comintern was forced to step in and summon the leaders of the two major factions to Moscow in order to resolve the dispute.

A New Course

The ITUCNW also had its own internal problems, difficulties in realising its stated aims made worse by the resignation/expulsion of Padmore in 1934. Huiswoud who replaced Padmore in Europe then made efforts to rebuild

125. It should be noted that Sachs, Andrews and Makabeni subsequently worked closely with the CPSA and Andrews later became the Party's Chairman.

126. 'Against the Right Danger,' 30 October 1931, *Umsebenzi*, p.3.

127. Even in this period new forms of democracy were developed including the 'Mass trial' of four AFTU activists before their workmates. See 'Mass Trial of Disloyal Workers,' *Umsebenzi*, 10 February 1933, p.4 and 'Workers Court Tries Disloyal Workers,' *Umsebenzi*, 27 May 1933, p.2. There was also public self-criticism. See 'Laundry Workers Return to AFTU,' *Umzebenzi*, 1 July 1933, p.4.

128. 'The Work of the Communists of South Africa in the Trade Unions,' RGASPI 495/64/138/11-22.

129. M. Kotane to Politbureau, CPSA, 23 February 1934, in Davidson, et al., *South Africa and the Communist International,* [vol. 2], pp.80-82.

the work of the ITUCNW and re-establish contact with the AFTU. When communication was re-established with Gomas in early 1934, he reported a worsening situation in the country and in the CPSA. As for the AFTU, Gomas claimed it 'hardly exists,' and went on to confirm that in Cape Town the Seamen and Harbour Workers' Union had collapsed and that they had failed to re-organise the laundry workers. However, there was more positive news about work within the existing Bus and Tram Workers' Union, where the trade union opposition continued to grow and one of the comrades was going to be elected as shop steward. There were also apparently a few AFTU supporters amongst the dockers and transport workers in Durban and among the fishermen in Port Nolloth on the northwest coast. According to Gomas, the worsening situation was due to the increasingly repressive and fascist nature of the state. He reported that several comrades had been arrested and some deported and that in some places organising amongst Africans had become almost an illegal activity. But he also mentioned the Party's political weaknesses, the constant changing of leaders and what he referred to as the 'desertion' of Wolton.[130]

The RILU Negro Bureau continued to send advice to the AFTU, along the same lines as it had sent for several years, emphasizing the importance of combating sectarianism, especially in regard to white workers; the need to work in the 'reformist organisations;' the necessity of struggling for the workers' 'elementary demands,' building unity and working so as to build a 'united front from below.'[131] Zusmanovich, the Russian deputy chairman of the ITUCNW, wrote to Huiswoud that the situation in South Africa had become 'very sharp.' He concluded that 'an inner-party struggle is going on which is undermining the Party, there is also a noticeable turn to the Right – along the old lines of the mistakes on the National Question.' This apparent reference to the leadership of Kotane suggests that more than a hint of sectarianism also existed within the ITUCNW.[132]

Huiswoud reported that initially he heard very little from South Africa but in September 1934 *The Negro Worker* began a series of articles entitled 'Organisational Points,' which also appeared in pamphlet form, clearly aimed to assist the organising of workers in South Africa, as well as elsewhere.[133] The series began with a focus on 'organisational tasks amongst water transport workers,' and the need to establish a Seamen and Harbour Workers' Union, and

130. Gomas to Huiswoud, 17 May 1934, RGASPI 534/7/78/35-37. See also *NW*, 4/3 (July 1934) pp.16-17.

131. Letter to the AFTU from Johnson and Zusmanovich, 3 July 1934, RGASPI 534/6/26/116.

132. Zusmanovitch to Huiswoud, 5 September 1934, RGASPI 495/64/138/42.

133. Otto to Dear Comrades, 23 August 1934, RGASPI 495/64/138 and *NW*, 4/5 (September 1934) pp. 16-19.

in the following months there were articles on organising miners,[134] agricultural workers[135] and the unemployed,[136] as well as 'a few hints on how to carry on a strike.'[137] All this in addition to a 'special South African issue' of *The Negro Worker* published in January 1935, which included an article entitled 'What is the Independent Native Republic?' that addressed what had again become the main theoretical debate within the CPSA.[138] *The Negro Worker* subsequently also published an article entitled 'Is there a class of Native capitalists in South Africa?' another major bone of contention within the CPSA.[139] Both articles added more heat than light and, in the circumstances, were extremely unhelpful and only fuelled the internal struggle within the CPSA.

In March 1935, Gomas reported to Huiswoud that 'the position of the Party has gone tremendously back in many respects.' He complained about the removal of Kotane from the leadership and leaders who 'simply forced things down our throats.' He added, 'things are rotten up at the centre and the whole of the Party is suffering from this.' In regard to the trade union work Gomas explained:

> As far as trade union activities are concerned we are worse off than ever. We have nothing of our own, or Red Trade Unions. I think you have seen that whatever we have had consisted very much of paper members and was based on exaggerated reports. There was a good deal of dishonesty in these reports too. The leadership is keeping me and all districts in entire ignorance of the position of the Party and other revolutionary activities about the country. So I am not in a position to tell anything outside my own sphere...In Cape Town we have no organised following in the Trade Unions, particularly amongst the non-Europeans. Nothing at the Docks. In the Tram and Bus Workers Union our Militant Opposition, however, is organised on much stronger lines. The comrade who had to resign from the committee is now chairman of the Union. Otherwise we have nothing much to talk of.[140]

134. *NW*, 4/8 (December 1934) pp. 12-15.
135. *NW*, 5/1 (January 1935) pp.17-20.
136. *NW*, 5/4 (April 1935) pp.16-20.
137. *NW*, 5/7-8 (July-August 1935) pp.30-31 and 27.
138. H. Jordan, 'What is the Independent Native Republic?' *NW*, 5/1 (January 1935) pp.10-16.
139. *NW*, 5/5 (May 1935) pp.18-19 and 22.
140. 'Excerpts from Cape letter,' Gomas to Huiswoud, 18 March 1935, RGASPI 495/155/102/6. The Reference is to J.W. Emmerich, see *Umsebenzi*, 12 August 1931, p.1.

Gomas' assessment of the problems facing the AFTU prompted Huiswoud to suggest that the RILU should provide some 'personal guidance,' otherwise, he thought, 'very little headway, if any, will be made.'[141] In fact, in September 1935, Gomas, Kotane and Edward Roux sent a telegram to the CI asking for its intervention to stop further expulsions by the 'sectarian leadership.' They had evidently been emboldened by the decisions of the CI's Seventh Congress, at which Josie Mpama, at that time a student in Moscow, unofficially represented the CPSA and spoke at the congress.[142] In response the CI appointed a special commission, led by André Marty, the head of the Anglo-American Secretariat of the ECCI, to investigate the crisis within the CPSA and make recommendations for its future work.[143]

The Marty Commission, which continued to monitor the CPSA as late as 1937, demanded a new leadership and a reorientation of the Party's work.[144] In the period following the Seventh Congress, which recommended a reorientation of the entire communist movement, the CPSA was required to seek ways to build an 'anti-imperialist people's front' in South Africa, with the demand 'for bread, land and freedom.' The growing danger posed by the rise of fascism and the prospect of world war meant that the CPSA had to act in a new way to try to build a movement that could advance the interests of the majority of people in South Africa. This meant that greater efforts had to be made to work with a broad range of organisations, especially African bodies such as the new All-African Convention (AAC), founded in December 1935, but also those in which Europeans were dominant such as the League Against Fascism and War and even the South African Labour Party. At the same time the CPSA had to continue to focus on organising amongst and uniting the working class.[145]

For its part the ITUCNW continued to support the South African Communists in this new work, although it had noticeably less involvement in trade union matters, and particularly in regard to the struggle that had broken out in defence of Ethiopia. It also urged those in South Africa to make greater use of *The Negro Worker* and from 1935 onwards attempted to rebuild a network for its distribution.[146] This initiative was only partly successful, according to the report sent to the ITUCNW at the end of 1936 from a 'representative of Negro

141. Huiswoud to 'Dear Comrades,' 11 April 1935, RGASPI 495/155/102/4-5.

142. See *International Press Correspondence*, 15/60 (11 November 1935) pp.1474-1475.

143. A. Marty's Report to G. Dimitrov, 11 March 1936 in Davidson et al., *South Africa and the Communist International* [vol 2], pp.176-178.

144. For the first time the CPSA's Political Bureau included an African woman, Josie Mpama.

145. Draft Resolution Prepared by ECCI for Adoption by 9th Congress of CPSA, 25 February 1936, in Davidson et al., *South Africa and the Communist International* [vol.2], pp.173-175 and Resolution of Secretariat of ECCI on the Situation in the CPSA, 17 March 1936, ibid.

146. Huiswoud to 'Dear Friends,' 24 June 1935, RGASPI 495/155/102.

Worker in South African ports.' He reported that no copies were sold in Durban because so few Africans could read English fluently. However, this may reflect more the views of the representative than the reading ability of Africans, since according to another informed observer newspapers experienced an unprecedented boom in sales in the period following the Italian invasion of Ethiopia.[147] In Cape Town there were certainly more possibilities and it was agreed that the newly formed National Liberation League (NLL) would take over sales of *The Negro Worker* from the CPSA, increase distribution and provide two 'Worker Correspondents' who would send regular reports. However, here too language was a problem and it was suggested that some articles might be published in Afrikaans to encourage more 'Coloured' readers.[148] Despite such problems, in January 1937 Huiswoud reported that sales of *The Negro Worker* in South Africa exceeded over four hundred copies and that was where the best results were obtained in terms of distribution and payment.[149]

Ethiopia and National Liberation

Following its second appeal for action in June 1935, the ITUCNW reported 'the first mass response to the agitation and directives of the Committee was the huge "Hands off Abyssinia" demonstration of native and white workers held in Johannesburg, South Africa, on July 17th.'[150] Following this was a large united front protest meeting in August in Cape Town attended by representatives of twenty three Labour and other mass organisations of 'native, white, coloured and Malay workers.'[151] Apart from the protest resolution adopted, the meeting established a 'Hands off Abyssinia' Committee to develop counteraction against Italian fascism.[152] It is clear that the actions of the 'Hands off Abyssinia' Committee contributed to the CPSA's work to develop a united front in South Africa.

In September 1935 *The Negro Worker* publicised the 'Appeal to the Harbour Workers of South Africa,' from the Durban District Committee of the CPSA,

147. Roux, *Time Longer than Rope*, p.302.

148. R. Hurd to 'Dear Comrades,' 29 December 1936, RGASPI 534/7/78/91-92. The first Afrikaans article was W. Driver's 'Suid Afrikaanse Spoorweg En Hawer Werkers Unie,' *NW*, 7/5 (May 1937) p.7.

149. 'Report of the Activities of the ITUCNW,' January 1937, RGASPI 534/3/1103.

150. 'Hands off Abyssinia, *Umsebenzi*, 27 July 1935, p. 1.

151. 'Cape Town Workers Protest Against Italian Fascist Robber Plans,' *Umsebenzi*, 6 July 1935, p.1.

152. 'Activities of the ITUCNW on the Italo-Abyssinian Conflict,' n.d. RGASPI 495/14/60/10-13.

to 'defend the last independent Native state in Africa from the attacks of Italian imperialism,' which had appeared in *Umsebenzi* in June of that year. The Appeal claimed that plans were afoot to ship food supplies to Italian troops from Durban, Cape Town and other South African ports and called on both black and white workers to take a stand both against fascism and the preparations for a new world war. In particular it called on the 'Native dockworkers' to help their fellow Africans and demanded that any food supplies remained in the country to 'feed the starving people of South Africa.' The Appeal concluded by stating 'By defending Abyssinia you will be striking a blow against all the white robber imperialists of Africa and bringing nearer the day when the black man in South Africa shall be free.'[153] Three months later *The Negro Worker* was reporting that dockers in Durban, Cape Town and Luderitz Bay had refused to load Italian ships and that in Cape Town this action had been supported by a meeting of the Cape Federation of Labour, representing eighteen workers' organisations.[154] *The Negro Worker* also reported that protest meetings demanding 'Hands off Abyssinia' were held in Johannesburg and Cape Town. [155] Indeed news of the Ethiopian crisis was avidly followed in South Africa, sales of *Umsebenzi* are reported to have increased to seven thousand a week and a special 'Ethiopian edition' of the paper was published in Zulu.[156]

The CPSA was extremely active in the campaign against the invasion of Ethiopian and led many of the demonstrations and solidarity committees that were organised.[157] This campaign galvanised the country and contributed to a growing sense of political unity. The NLL was another attempt to organise an anti-imperialist front in South Africa and was first launched in Cape Town in 1935 by La Guma, Gomas and Cissie Gool with the slogan 'For Equality, Land and Freedom.'[158] The NLL was supported by the CPSA and Communists such as Johnny Gomas played a leading role within it. Its main aim was to unite black and white workers in a struggle for complete social and political equality but also for 'complete independence of South Africa from imperialist

153. 'An Appeal to the Harbour Workers of South Africa,' 22 June 1935, *South African Communists Speak*, pp.123-124.

154. See e.g. 'South African Native Dockers Again Take Action,' *Umsebenzi*, 21 September 1935, p.1.

155. *NW*, 5/9 (September 1935) pp.5-6 and 14.

156. Drew, *Between Empire and Revolution* p.220. *Umsebenzi*, 7 September, p.3 also Roux, *Time Longer Than Rope*, p.302.

157. See 'War in Africa' and 'Monster Anti-war Meetings in Capetown and Johannesburg –Thousands Demand "Hands off Abyssinia" – Communist Party leads Ethiopian movement,' *Umsebenzi*, 12 October 1935, p.1.

158. On the NLL see Drew, *Discordant Comrades*, pp.214-219 and A. La Guma, *Jimmy La Guma – A biography* (Cape Town, 1997) pp.58-59.

domination.'[159] Although the precise relationship between the ITUCNW and the NLL is unclear, *The Negro Worker* featured several articles on its activities.[160]

At the close of 1936 the ITUCNW reported that it was in close contact with several organisations in South Africa and particularly the South African Railway and Harbour Workers' Union,[161] the Cape Town Stevedoring Workers' Union, the NLL and the All-African Convention (AAC), which had been convened in 1935 to protest about the new discriminatory 'Hertzog Bills'.[162] The ITUCNW claimed to have been asked to give 'practical advice' to these four newly created organisations, 'on the concrete problems facing them and in suggestions as to methods of work.'[163] Full details of the ITUCNW's links with the AAC have not come to light but it is clear that it encouraged John Gomas and others to fight not just to make the AAC a permanent body representing all Africans and their organisations but also a body that established 'contacts with Africans and African organisations in other parts of the world.' In this regard it is interesting to note that the AAC passed a resolution calling for an 'International Conference of Africans and People of African Descent,'[164] at a time when the ITUCNW was itself considering organising a 'world Negro Congress'.[165]

When he was in Moscow before the Marty Commission in 1936, Kotane had been asked to evaluate the work of the ITUCNW, by a committee established by the ECCI, and also to indicate if he thought there was a need for a 'world Negro organisation' and an 'international Negro publication.' At that time the ITUCNW was itself facing the prospect of being dissolved as it was felt that the new international conditions required new forms of organisation. Kotane was in favour of such an organisation and publication. He recognised, perhaps also influenced by the impact of recent events in Ethiopia, that there was a 'deep rooted desire' in South Africa to establish 'international Negro connections.' He thought this desire should be utilised to establish an 'International Negro Congress and to build a united anti-imperialist front within the country.'

159. 'Programme of the NLL of S.A.' March 1937 in Drew, *South Africa's Radical Tradition*, pp.253-261.

160. W.D. Liverpool Matini, 'NLL of South Africa Active in Port Elizabeth,' *NW*, 7/5 (May 1937) p.4; J. Gomas, '2000 Protest Against New Anti-Colour Legislation, Spirit For Unity Grows,' *NW*, 7/6 (June 1937) p.4.

161. W. Driver, 'To the Editor of the Negro Worker,' *NW* 6/6-7 (August-September 1936) p.33. The Railway and Harbour Workers' Union decided to affiliate to the ITUCNW. 'Non European Workers Conference,' *NW*, 6/8 (October 1936) pp.7-14, 22.

162. On the ACC see Drew, *Discordant Comrades*, pp. 201-213.

163. 'Report of the Activities of the ITUCNW,' January 1937, RGASPI 534/3/1103.

164. J. Gomas, 'All-African Convention to be Permanent – Make it a Mass Liberation Movement,' *NW*, 6/6-7 (August-September 1936) p.36.

165. 'Report of the Activities of the ITUCNW,' January 1937, RGASPI 534/3/1103.

But at the same time he reported that the ITUCNW had not been an important factor in South Africa. As far as he knew, he said, 'the ITUCNW is not known in my country. Just a few individual Negroes have heard of it.' On this basis he was in favour of dissolving it and his views, as well as many other factors, contributed to the decision to terminate the ITUCNW and *The Negro Worker* at the end of 1937.[166]

The ITUCNW and *The Negro Worker* undoubtedly contributed to the political education of many activists in South Africa and in particular to developing an international perspective on the problems confronting workers throughout Africa and the African Diaspora. Reports from other parts of Africa and the Diaspora also regularly appeared in *Umsebenzi*, sometimes supplied by the NWA in Britain.[167] The ITUCNW also worked to overcome the problems within the CPSA and to assist the trade union movement in South Africa at a time when under the racist laws of the country African workers had few rights. It continued to play a role in the creation of the many new African industrial unions that were being formed in South Africa in the late 1930s, many of them led by the CPSA.[168] In the period after the CI's Seventh Congress the CPSA still aimed to encourage trade union unity but where this could not be achieved 'parallel trade unions of Native and Non-European workers' were being established. These were being encouraged not only to fight for economic demands but also for 'political social and democratic rights.' In this regard the call of the CPSA to the unions was to strengthen through the AAC 'the fight for National freedom and independence from the rule of imperialism.' [169] Increasingly some of these unions also affiliated to the South African Trades and Labour Council, which had decided to fully recognise their rights. It was these new unions including the African Miners' Union, African Iron and Steel Workers Union, African Tin Workers' Union, Chemical Workers' Union and others who sent their greetings to *The Negro Wor*ker in the last few months of its existence. The greetings of the Railways and Harbour Workers Union in 1937 were typical. With an unintended irony it declared 'May *The Negro Worker* grow from strength to strength in forging ahead the unity of the oppressed Negroes and their allies in their struggle for freedom.'[170]

166. 'Answers to June 16, 1936 Questionnaire,' RGASPI 495/14/36/28-29. Kotane's comments are rather strange as information about the ITUCNW had since 1928 regularly featured in the pages of *Umsebenzi*.

167. See e.g. *Umsebenzi*, 24 March 1934, p.2.

168. 'Native Trade Union Conference Meets with success,' *South African Worker*, 18 July 1936, p.1.

169. 'Native Trade Union Development in South Africa,' *NW*, 7/5 (May 1937) pp.3, 5.

170. See 'Voices from South Africa,' *NW*, 7/5 (May 1937) pp.10-12.

Epilogue

The Dissolution of the ITUCNW

The Committee on Negro Work

The future of the ITUCNW and the approach of the CI to the Negro Question remained under discussion in the period following the Seventh Congress of the CI in 1935. This discussion was necessary because for the CI the rapidly changing international circumstances necessitated building a united front against fascism as well as trade union unity, and this meant that the future of the RILU itself was also under discussion by a 'special commission' of the CI.[1]

1. W.Z. Foster, *Outline History of the World Trade Union* Movement (New York, 1956) pp.324-325; Dimitrov to Stalin, 27 January 1936, in A. Dallin and F.I Firsov, *Dimitrov and Stalin, 1934-1943. Letters from the Soviet Archives* (London, 2000) pp.24-25; and R. Tosstorff, 'Moscow Versus Amsterdam: Reflections on the History of the Profintern,' *Labour History Review*, 68/1 (April 2003) pp.79-97.

The ITUCNW had for some time been under the jurisdiction of the Negro Commission of the CI but that body was also under scrutiny following the dismissal of Zusmanovich, who had openly opposed the orientation of the Seventh Congress.[2]

It was in these circumstances that the Secretariat of the ECCI established a 'Committee on Negro Work' consisting of three Moscow-based members of the CPUSA, Charles Johnson, a member of the RILU Executive Bureau, Herbert Newton (Tom Sawyer) a leading African American Communist from Chicago, and S. Randolph (William Weinstone), who was the CPUSA's representative on the ECCI. They were asked to consult with 'other leading Negro comrades in Moscow' on a number of questions, including the effectiveness of both the ITUCNW and *The Negro Worker*; whether there was still a need for a 'world Negro organisation' and an 'international Negro publication,' and how effectively 'Negro work' was carried out by individual communist parties. The Committee only consulted with a few representatives who happened to be studying or based in Moscow at the time. The most significant figure consulted was William Patterson, the others were students from the US, South Africa,[3] Brazil,[4] Senegal[5] and Guadeloupe,[6] even though the three latter areas had very limited contact with the work of the ITUCNW or with *The Negro Worker*.[7]

Sawyer separately submitted his own recommendations to the ECCI, before the submission of the Committee's report, claiming that these reflected

2. I. Filatova, 'Anti-Colonialism in Soviet African Studies, 1920-1960,' in P. T. Zeleza (ed.) *The Study of Africa: Global and Transnational Engagements* (Dakar, 2007) pp.203-235.

3. Moses Kotane (alias Gurleigh), one of the leaders of the CPSA, responded that the ITUCNW was hardly known in his country and that in his opinion it should be liquidated. However he appeared to favour both an international congress and 'an international Negro body.' RGASPI 495/14/36/28-29.

4. Octavio Brandao, the representative of the Brazilian Communist Party at the ECCI, admitted that he could not comment on the activities of the ITUCNW 'because we do not know anything about its activities in Brazil.' RGASPI 495/14/36/17-18.

5. Both of the Senegalese respondents said that knew nothing of the ITUCNW. RGASPI 495/14/36/31.

6. Durant from Guadeloupe stated that the ITUCNW was only known to a few 'journalists, intellectuals and students' in his country but still thought it should be supported and developed. He also was in favour of an international congress and publication. RGASPI 495/14/36/32.

7. Special Discussion Material on the Negro Question, 10 July 1936, RGASPI 495/14/36/7-18. Sawyer admitted that he had not consulted with 'Spanish speaking Negro comrades from Cuba and Venezuela' and the relatively large number of African Americans at the International Lenin School. However, he concluded that the US was adequately represented and that even if he had consulted with the Spanish speakers ' it would not have changed the conclusions' he reached.

not just his views but also discussions between Randolph and Huiswoud in Paris, and Randolph, Patterson, himself and others in Moscow.[8] His submission to the ECCI's commission suggested that both the ITUCNW and *The Negro Worker* should be discontinued. Future international work, he wrote, should be based around the next National Negro Congress in the US, which it was proposed would convene in Philadelphia in 1937, and which should invite fraternal international organisations and establish a committee to convene a 'World Negro Congress'. This congress would then establish a committee to 'coordinate the activities of the Negro liberation movements throughout the world.' In the meantime, Sawyer suggested, the work of Huiswoud should be transferred to New York and could be based in Harlem. It seems likely that on the basis of Sawyer's evident interest in this matter he was subsequently asked to lead the work of the 'Committee on Negro Work.'[9]

The documents, or 'Special Discussion Material,' which Sawyer produced for André Marty and the ECCI came to very similar conclusion to those earlier arrived at by Otto Huiswoud. Sawyer argued that before the heroic example of Ethiopia, the struggles of 'Negro toilers' in the US and those outside it had very little impact on each other. His view was that the reason the ITUCNW had not been able to take advantage of the recent 'international Negro solidarity,' occasioned by the Italian invasion, was because of 'the narrow sectarian base on which the Committee was organised, because of its sectarian methods of work and consequently because of its lack of contact, prestige or influence among Negro toilers anywhere.'[10] In short, he concluded that the ITUCNW 'has not justified its existence,' but also that even at its founding 'there was no basis for such an organisation,' largely because it was an international trade union organisation with no solid roots amongst trade unions or workers. He added that the eight trade union organisations from the US that were involved at the time of the ITUCNW's founding no longer existed. Furthermore, he argued that 'any Negro organisation to be successful must above all be anti-imperialist but the ITUC cannot be an effective anti-imperialist organisation because its very structure and programme limits its activities to Negro workers and ignores the masses of Negro people who are ready to fight imperialism.' [11] (underlining in original)

Sawyer's report suggests that there was a growing awareness that if the CI was to continue to effectively answer the Negro Question it could not successfully do so through the ITUCNW. However, it also seems that in the few short

8. See Commission on Trade Union Reorganisation, 22 May 1936, RGASPI 495/20/428.

9. Commission on Trade Union Reorganisation, RGASPI 495/20/428.

10. Special Discussion Material on the Negro Question, RGASPI 495/14/36/11-12.

11. Ibid.

years of its existence at least part of the original *raison d'etre* of the Committee, to work with the communist parties and other organisations to encourage and facilitate their 'Negro work,' had been forgotten. The ITUCNW was now itself seen as the organisation for such work but was being declared unfit for purpose. Sawyer was even critical of the ITUCNW's inability to convene a 'world conference for defence of Ethiopia,' a task for which it had no responsibility. At the same time it is apparent that there were still differing views about whether the CI should organise an international organisation for Africa and the Diaspora, not least because it was argued that there was no 'common political basis' on which the 'separate Negro peoples' of the world could unite. In opposition to this view, Sawyer highlighted the significance of what he called 'Negro psychology' which, he claimed, was being exploited by Garvey and 'our class enemies.' He therefore proposed that a 'World Negro Congress,' organised on a broad basis and with Ethiopia as a focal point of its proceedings, should be convened and that it should include such organisations as the *Frente Negre* in Brazil, the South African National Congress and similar organisations elsewhere. He also proposed that such a congress would then be the basis for a new organisation, with its own monthly publication that could become 'an international centre of agitation and propaganda.'[12]

William Patterson submitted the most substantial response to the questionnaire issued by Sawyer and it seems apparent that many of the latter's conclusions were based on, or influenced by, Patterson's views. He was almost scathing in his criticism of the ITUCNW, especially its 'narrow trade union viewpoint,' claimed that it had little impact in Africa and suggested that in general 'it had no prestige or influence at the time of its creation and afterwards acquired extremely little.' For Patterson, one of the key figures in the initial work of the ITUCNW, 'the people of the black colonies were never able to answer satisfactorily the question; who or what is the ITUCNW?' In his view, the ITUCNW had been created in an arbitrary manner and those who had attended its Hamburg conference had been selected in a 'haphazard manner'. 'It should be,' he concluded, 'allowed to die a natural death. There should be no official liquidation and no noise made about it.'[13]

The views of Patterson who had worked so diligently to establish the ITUCNW and convene the Hamburg Conference are of considerable interest. But his claim that from the start the ITUCNW should have based itself on 'a broad anti-imperialist national-liberation front if it were to acquire either prestige or influence' was made retrospectively, and significantly after the Seventh

12. Sawyer envisaged that both Huiswoud and Ford would play a leading role in this organisation but also proposed that the Committee on Negro Work should be expanded and constituted as a permanent 'Negro Commission of the ECCI' with him as chairman.

13. W. Patterson (dictation) 'The ITUCNW,' 4 July 1936, RGASPI 495/14/36/19-20.

Congress of the CI, even if it may have been a view held for some time. But although he was critical of the nature of the ITUCNW, Patterson reserved similar criticism for the CPGB and 'its almost complete lack of Negro work' in regard to the African colonies. In other words, he levelled the same criticism as had been made before the creation of the ITUCNW and which had led to its founding.[14] To remedy the situation Patterson argued for a 'Negro comrade placed in the apparatus of the Comintern' who could 'follow trends in the Negro liberation movement,' and make concrete suggestions to the communist parties regarding how to develop the 'Negro work'. Patterson considered that this comrade might also write for the CI magazine, which he critically assessed as rarely containing an article on the Negro Question. However, he also pointed to the 'deep rooted desires' and feelings of international solidarity' existing amongst Africans and throughout the African Diaspora, evident in the movement to support Ethiopia but which 'Messrs Du Bois, Garvey and Padmore are seeking to lead either in utopian or reactionary channels.' He was therefore a strong supporter of an 'International Negro Congress,' not least because of the situation in Ethiopia, but also because of the threats which he perceived existed to Liberia and Haiti, and what he saw as the prospect of a new world war leading to a re-division of Africa. He was also in favour of 'an International Negro publication,' which he stressed, 'should be based upon the broadest anti-imperialist, anti-fascist, national liberation movement,' and which could be the organ of the international congress if it was convened.[15]

Patterson was not alone in stressing the need for an international congress. In April 1937, for example, James Ford, who had led the early work of the ITUCNW, was still advocating the convening of such a gathering. While recognising that there were important economic, linguistic and cultural differences among the 'Negro people,' Ford still asserted that they faced 'special and common racial oppression and hindrances.' and noted that there were organised movements and events in such countries as South Africa and Brazil in addition to the National Negro Congress organised in the US. He therefore argued that an international conference was necessary for the purpose of drawing the 'Negro people' into the international movement against fascism and war, 'developing a general attitude among advanced Negroes everywhere, leading towards unity in each country of Negroes with all anti-imperialist and anti-fascist forces,'

14. Patterson complained that the CPGB had ignored a plea for assistance from the British labour movement that had been made in *Labour Monthly* by a delegation from the Gold Coast that had visited Britain in 1935 to protest against the sedition laws in force in that colony. In his view a 'correct response' to the appeal would 'not only have been a stimulus to the development of the radicalisation of the Negroes in the colonies,' but would also have 'aided the struggle' against Padmore, Garvey and Du Bois.

15. W. Patterson 'The ITUCNW,' 4 July 1936, RGASPI 495/14/36/26-27.

and 'simultaneously developing the fullest possible expression of the feelings of solidarity held by all Negroes.' Ford also proposed more investigation of the existing conditions, especially those in Africa, and even suggested that 'Negro lecturers' should be sent 'from one country to another.' Also of interest was his proposal that *The Negro Worker* should be continued but 'broadened into a popular peace movement organ among the Negroes.'[16]

It seems clear that Huiswoud, Patterson, Ford and others involved with establishing the ITUCNW were determined to continue in some form the work they had begun even as the RILU's activities were being discontinued during 1936 and 1937. It is difficult to be precise about how the demise of the RILU impacted on them, and whether it influenced their enthusiasm for establishing a new body that was unencumbered by trade union roots. It is more likely that their proposals were more solidly rooted in their own experience of working within the limited boundaries of the ITUCNW and by the changing international situation, particularly in Africa and the Caribbean. Of course both the summation of experience and the changing world situation had contributed to the resolutions of the CI's Seventh Congress and its call for a people's front against fascism and imperialism. But what appears to have remained unchanged amongst these leading figures is a Pan-Africanist approach to the Negro Question, and the need to view it from an international perspective rather than solely as a question of a struggle for liberation in individual countries.[17]

Similar concerns were evident in a 'Memorandum on the International Negro Question' written in May 1937.[18] The document was clearly written in the context of the increasing likelihood of a new world war and the fact that the fascist powers were already employing black troops and demanding, and on occasions seizing, territory in Africa.[19] Its main focus, however, were the questions that had been perplexing the CI for many years and which were now expressed in this way: 'is it necessary to organise a movement among the Negro peoples according to race on an international scale or is it necessary to organise them according to country taking into consideration the concrete conditions, their traditions, etc., in each specific country? Is there a racial sympathy of an international character amongst Negroes which is of a revolutionary character?

16. J. Ford, 'Proposals for an International Negro Conference,' 15 April 1937, RGASPI 495/20/428.

17. Ford, Patterson, Huiswoud and also Harry Haywood were all involved in the final deliberations concerning the fate of the ITUCNW presided over by Dimitrov. A. Marti to Dimitrov, 27 May 1937, RGASPI 495/20/428.

18. 'Memorandum on the International Negro Question,' 3 May 1937, RGASPI 495/20/428.

19. See e.g. 'German Foothold in Morocco,' and 'An Appeal to All Negro Organisation,' *NW*, 7/2 (February 1937) pp.1-2 and 3.

What is to be done with the ITUCNW?'[20] The answer given was that both international and national movements were required and in some cases already existed. What was needed, it was argued, was to direct such movements into 'progressive channels.' The Memorandum highlighted the fact that 'certain dangers' might exist in regard to such 'international sympathy' and stressed that the CI must carefully guard its attitude towards it in case it became directed towards what was referred to as 'black internationalism.' The conclusion was that if the CI did not organise on the basis of 'international sympathy,' it would leave the opportunity open to 'reformists, fascists and other reactionary elements.'

The Memorandum suggested that such work could be organised through an international body made up of representatives from the National Negro Congress in the US, the WAYL, the All African Convention in South Africa, the NWSCA in Trinidad and the International Committee in African Affairs (later the US-based Council on African Affairs). *The Negro Worker,* which was to be 'enlarged and its name changed,' would be the organ of this committee. In addition however there would also be a new weekly 'international Negro News release.' Despite the fact that the proposal again stressed the vital role of individual communist parties and the fact that 'the work of the committee is by no means a substitute for the work of the Parties themselves,' it once again admitted that the parties were still weak in this area and argued that this was one of the main reasons why such internationally directed work was so necessary.[21]

By the end of May 1937 after further discussion a draft resolution on the 'International Negro Question' had been prepared for the secretariat of the ECCI. This document finally rejected the Pan-Africanist approach and unequivocally stated: 'All the questions concerning the Negro peoples must be examined and settled according to the concrete situation in each country. It is impossible to admit that there exists and must be developed a special international movement of the Negro race – despite the efforts of some of the Negro bourgeoisie to develop such a movement. The situation of the Negro people depends upon the situation in each country and upon the class relationships in the country and amongst the Negro peoples. For example, the situation in Guadeloupe and Martinique, in Brazil, in the USA, in South Africa, in Senegal, Cameroun and Congo is quite different and cannot be compared. Therefore: <u>the further existence of the International Trade Union Negro Committee working with the Profintern is not advisable and this committee is</u>

20. 'Memorandum on the International Negro Question,' 3 May 1937, RGASPI 495/20/428.

21. Ibid. The document made specific proposals in regard to the work of the South African, US, British and French parties in relation to work in Africa and the Caribbean.

liquidated.' (underlining in original)[22] However, the draft also recognised that the 'German and Italian fascists are developing increasing propaganda amongst the various strata of Negro peoples' and therefore directed each communist party to develop 'practical plans' to develop 'special work amongst all the Negro peoples.' Proposals for such work included building a 'solidarity movement' to support Wallace Johnson following his arrest in the Gold Coast and capitalising on the presence of Ghvet, the son of the captured commander of the Ethiopian army Ras Imru, amongst the Republican forces in Spain.[23] It was even proposed that Ghvet should be sent on a 'world tour' throughout the American continent, since it was believed that his story and example 'would prove one of the most dramatic events in the campaign to draw the Negro people in support of the Spanish Republic.'[24] Special responsibility for future 'Negro work' was placed on the parties in the US and Brazil, but chiefly on the French, British, Belgium and Italian parties, who were instructed to recruit colonial students and report directly to the ECCI.[25] The CPUSA was given responsibility, along with the CPGB, for the Anglophone Caribbean and Haiti. It was to establish a small committee of those of Caribbean origin based in New York and to begin training 'students' in the US and the Caribbean.[26]

But although the ITUCNW was to be 'liquidated,' it was still proposed that a new 'special committee' should be established in Paris in order to attract 'the Negro masses of Africa in to the Peoples' Front and to develop a progressive movement.' The new committee would be under the direction of the Secretariat of the ECCI and the New International Centre of MOPR, which would also be located in Paris. There it would gather information, publish a broad popular monthly journal and 'a semi-monthly press service', develop 'a campaign mainly on cultural questions' and function as 'a centre of propaganda and agitation,'

22. 'On the International Negro Question – Draft Resolution for the Secretariat,' 25 May 1937, RGASPI 495/20/428. It appears that Harry Haywood and William Patterson were responsible for making proposals on this issue to the ECCI Secretariat. See A. Marti to G. Dimitrov, 27 May 1937, RGASPI 495/20/428.

23. 'An Ethiopian Fights for Spain,' and 'Two Ethiopians Father Italian Captive – Son Fighting for Spain,' *NW*, 7/3 (March 1937) p.1 and p.7.

24. See 'On the Negro Question – Additional Resolution No.3 – For a Negro Correspondent in Spain,' RGASPI 495/20/428 and 'Negro Correspondent in Spain,' RGASPI 495/14/87/66-67.

25. For some reason the communist parties in Holland, Spain and Portugal were omitted from this list.

26. 'On the Negro Question – Additional Resolution No.2 - On the Work of the CPUSA,' RGASPI 495/20/428.

much as the ITUCNW had done. The new committee would also focus its activities mainly on Africa[27]

The final judgement on all the various proposals, including a report by Husiwoud, was given by the Secretariat of the ECCI in July 1937. It recognised the 'fundamentally different positions of the Negro masses' in various parts of the world and therefore that varied approaches were required to political questions depending on the concrete conditions in each country. It therefore suggested that 'the International Committee under these conditions and in its present form cannot render concrete assistance to the Negro worker's movement in individual countries.' At the same time, it recognised the importance of what was called 'the movement of sympathy which exists in various countries with the struggles of the Negro masses of the entire world for their equal rights and against racial oppression and exploitation' and that was particularly evident in 'the Negro movement in support of Abyssinia.' The key consideration was that the 'movement of sympathy' constituted 'a serious weapon in the struggle against fascism and imperialism.' However, the conclusion arrived at by the ECCI was that it considered 'the further existence of the International Negro Workers' Trade Union Committee inadvisable.'[28]

The onus, once again, was placed on individual communist parties, indeed it was their 'obligation' to 'develop special work amongst the Negroes,' in order to develop the struggles against racial oppression, fascism and imperialism. The emphasis was again to be on work in colonial Africa, which would be facilitated by a Paris-based 'special legal committee of as wide a character as possible,' that would work with the main western European communist parties. The committee was intended to 'assist the cultural development of the Negroes in Africa,' a task which remained undefined, and would comprise representatives from African countries and 'outstanding political figures of the imperialist countries.' In general the committee, which would publish a monthly journal, a more regular bulletin and other material, was envisaged mainly as a research and propaganda centre that would help the work of the 'European Labour movement in defence of Negro interests.' In this regard the 'Paris Committee in Defence of

27. 'On the International Negro Question – Draft Resolution for the Secretariat,' 25 May 1937, RGASPI 495/20/428. Although nobody was named as responsible for this work it seems like that it was envisaged that Husiwoud would continue to be based in Paris. In an earlier draft of this resolution it was proposed that the monthly journal would be called *The African Voice – A journal of African life and culture.* See 'Draft Resolution on the International Negro Question,' 21 May 1937, RGASPI 495/14/87/64-65.

28. 'On Work Among Negroes,' 3 July 1937, RGASPI 495/18/1206/37-39.

African Negroes' was more likely to continue the work of the LAI, which was also dissolved, rather than that of the ITUCNW.[29]

Evidence of the existence of the ITUCNW after October 1937, when the last edition of *The Negro Worker* was published, is difficult to find. The September/October edition of the publication issued a special 'Statement' of the ITUCNW directed 'to all our supporters' and 'to all readers of "the Negro Worker."'[30] This explained that in the seven years of the ITUCNW's existence the world had undergone a profound change and new tasks and struggles had arisen which were very different to those of 1930.[31] The ITUCNWC, it stated, had been established mainly to arouse 'worldwide sympathy and support for the Negro people;' to aid them in the organisation and development of a trade union movement;' and to 'connect them with the progressive and labour movements of the world.' In these aims, it was claimed, the ITUCNW had been partly successful, important links and contacts had been made and this was particularly the case in regard to support for the Ethiopian cause. Now that the world stood on the cusp of a new world war, the likelihood of a re-division of African colonies and the threat of fascism, the 'Statement' urged, 'everywhere Negro organisations must be linked with every movement, every expression of the democratic world against fascist reaction.' The ITUCNW therefore called for a united front not only in the colonies but also internationally and explained that 'in this unity lies not only the guarantee of defeat of fascism, but the hope of a full and complete democracy for Africa.' Some signs of a united front approach were already evident in the activities of the youth movements in West Africa and the All-African Convention in South Africa, it suggested, and the self-critical ITUCNW had 'already begun to appreciate the limitations of the approach to great issues solely along trade union lines.' So the result of the deliberations within the ITUCNW and the CI were presented publicly in this way, not a simple 'liquidation' but the possibility of working within a 'broad Committee,' unnamed but 'now in the process of formation.' The ITUCNW and *The Negro Worker*, taking into account the views of some supporters, were going to merge with this new committee and pass to it the details of supporters and subscribers. The ITUCNW therefore appealed to all the readers of *The Negro Worker* to give their full support to the new committee and its journal,

29. On Work Among Negroes, 3 July 1937, RGASPI 495/18/1206/37-39. Here again mention was only made of the British, French, Italian and Belgian communist parties. The Committee would be under the control of the Central Committee of the PCF.

30. *NW*, 7/7-8, (September/October 1937) pp.2-3. The Statement was signed by the Secretary of the ITUCNW, Charles Woodson, i.e. Otto Huiswoud.

31. The public founding of the ITUCNW at the Hamburg conference was chosen as the date for its anniversary.

which had as their aims 'the defence of the economic, political and cultural interests of the African peoples.'[32]

This was the last public statement of the ITUCNW. It is not yet clear if readers and supporters were contacted in any other way. At least two editions of a new publication *World Wide News,* a 'bulletin on world events and information concerning the Negro people,' did appear and were published in Paris in the autumn of 1937.[33] Beyond that there does not appear to be any further evidence of the activities of the ITUCNW. It is a rather poignant finale, the end of the ITUCNW for sound political reasons and the promise of something new, even if the rationale for the new was not fully elaborated. The new then appeared, fleetingly, only to disappear as mysteriously as it had arrived. It is also noticeable that in its final statement the ITUCNW concentrates almost totally on Africa, rather than the Diaspora, but the dissolution of the ITUCNW occurred just as major anti-colonial struggles were breaking out in the Caribbean.

The Negro Question after the ITUCNW

The ITUCNW can be seen as simply a creation of the 'Third Period' in the history of the Comintern that did not endure long after the Seventh Congress, but its demise was as much a rejection of the Pan-Africanist orientation that had hitherto been adopted, as it was of the trade union focus that had been so evident following the Sixth Congress in 1928. It must also be borne in mind that a concern to provide answers to the Negro Question dated back to the earliest years of the CI and marked it out as a unique international organisation in the inter-war years, certainly one that was easily distinguishable from the Labour and Socialist International, which took no positive measures in regard to Africa and the Diaspora, and in which the British Labour Party played such a key role.

The CI's concern with the Negro Question did not end with the dissolution of the ITUCNW, as has already been demonstrated, but the growing danger of fascism and world war impelled the Comintern to make this its main focus until it too was dissolved, partly as a consequence of war-time conditions, in 1943. In Britain, for example, the work of the NWA was further developed after 1937 and there was evidence of more support and commitment from the CPGB. The CPGB also exercised more responsibility for the work of the CPSA in this period, following the patient work of CI, and particularly the Commission led by André Marty that managed to point to a way to resolve the problem of factionalism and political confusion that had so weakened the

32. *NW*, 7/7-8, (September/October 1937) pp.2-3.

33. For a copy see (TNA) CO 323/1517/1. The second edition of *World Wide News* just contained an interview with Paul Robeson, previously published in the CPGB's *Daily Worker*.

CPSA in earlier years.[34] However, the CPSA still faced considerable difficulties, and these were not eased by the fact that many of the recommendations of the CI were not implemented and because its representative, the British Communist George Hardy, had little knowledge of South Africa.[35] The demand for a 'Native Republic' was not emphasised in the period following the Seventh Congress but it was certainly not abandoned and became the basis for all subsequent political programmes of the CP in South Africa over the next sixty years. As one informed commentator expressed it:

> The Native Republic thesis, it is now generally felt, registered a great advance in terms of class analysis of South African society. It concentrated the attention of the South African Party on the need to understand the national democratic struggle as a stage on the road to a socialist South Africa, and to recognise the enormous potential of the African National Congress as a mass revolutionary force. It laid the theoretical foundation for the Party's study of the national question, and its outline of the relationship which should exist between the forces of national and working class struggle was developed as a central feature of all subsequent Party programmes.[36]

In France, the very real danger of fascism concentrated the work of the PCF on support for the Popular Front government, and the strengthening of the peoples front against fascism and war. This orientation led the PCF to regard the demand for the total independence of the French colonies with some caution, since it was argued that if granted this would lead to their immediate occupation by Germany or the other fascist powers. Nevertheless, it was a view that sometimes led to an estrangement from the UTN and other former supporters. The period of the Popular Front government did, however, lead to the legalisation of trade unions and other workers' organisations in the African colonies and the emergence of a communist organisation in Senegal, as well as advances in the communist movement in the French Antilles.

34. See e.g. Programme of Action Proposed to CPSA, 19 March 1936, in A Davidson et al. (eds.) *South Africa and the Communist International: A Documentary History* [vol. II] (London, 2003) pp.200-210.

35. RGASPI 495/18/1185/150 and 'Minutes of Meeting of CPGB Colonial Commission,' 21 March 1936, RGASPI 495/14/360A/2. For Hardy's views on his mission see G. Hardy, *Those Stormy Years* (London, 1956) pp.229-236. For a brief assessment of Hardy by a member of the CPSA see R.A. Simons, *All My Life and All My Strength* (Johannesburg, 2004) p.87.

36. B. Bunting, 'Introduction,' in E. Roux, *S.P. Bunting – A Political Biography* (Bellville, 1993) pp.19-20 and A. Lerumo, *Fifty Fighting Years* (London, 1971) p.65.

In the US, which had largely been outside of the ITUCNW's jurisdiction, the CPUSA had extended its influence during the early years of the 1930s not only in the northern cities but also in many of the southern states such as Alabama.[37] This had been facilitated by the campaigns connected with Scottsboro and Angelo Herndon but also, by its efforts to unite sections of the major African American organisations, such as the NAACP, the National Urban League, and even Garvey's UNIA in defence of Ethiopia.[38] The efforts of the Communists and others culminated in a National Negro Congress (NNC) of over eight hundred delegates held in Chicago in 1936, which elected A. Philip Randolph, the African American labour leader formerly seen by the CPUSA as a 'great mis-leader,' as its president. As one historian has concluded concerning this period, 'the Communist Party's standing and acceptance among African Americans of all classes had reached unprecedented heights.'[39] In the CI the NNC was certainly seen as one of the great successes of the period following the Seventh Congress. A second NNC, held in Philadelphia in October 1937, had a similarly broad character and included over thousand delegates, representing trade unions, several Christian organisations and 'Negro universities,' as well as 'civil and community groups.' In his closing speech Randolph concluded:

> The NNC is neither Communist nor Socialist, neither Republican nor Democrat. It seeks to federate all existing organisations in the battle for Negro rights. It gives wholehearted support to the NAACP for the passage of the Anti-lynching Bill. It is confident that the strategy of the united front will free the five Scottsboro Boys, even as it has freed the great young Negro leader, Angelo Herndon.[40]

Such a united front, even if temporarily maintained, exemplified the successes of the new approach to the Negro Question in the US in the period leading up to the outbreak of war. The demand for self-determination in the Black Belt was not particularly stressed in the period immediately following the Seventh Congress but it was not abandoned and periodically revived during World War Two

37. See e.g. R. Kelley, *Hammer and Hoe – Alabama Communist During The Great Depression* (London, 1990); N.I. Painter, *The Narrative of Hosea Hudson – The Life and Times of a Black Radical* (New York, 1994) and G. E. Gilmore, *Defying Dixie: The Radical Roots of Civil Rights, 1919-1950* (New York, 2008).

38. H. Haywood, *Black Bolshevik – Autobiography of an Afro-American Communist* (Chicago, 1978) p.457.

39. M. Solomon, *The Cry Was Unity: Communists and African Americans, 1917-1939* (Jackson, 1998), p.304.

40. 'Information on the Second National NNC,' 3 January 1938, RGASPI 495/14/113/5.

and again when the CPUSA was reconstituted in the post-war period.[41] In 1945 Claudia Jones, a Communist of Trinidadian origin who was later deported to Britain for her political activities and membership of the CPUSA, was making an impression as one of those demanding that the right of self-determination for the 'Black Belt' be re-established as part of the programme of the CPUSA.[42]

The stand taken by the Comintern on the Negro Question, as well as the growing prestige of the Soviet Union, especially in regard to national and racial oppression, attracted many including some of the major cultural figures from the African Diaspora . Indeed even ten years after he parted company with the communist movement, George Padmore still felt compelled to write an entire book about 'how the USSR solved the National and Colonial problems which it inherited from Czarist Russia.'[43] Aimé Césaire in Martinique, Jacques Roumain in Cuba, Nicolas Guillen in Cuba were some of the most celebrated of those who joined the ranks of the international communist movement during this period, others such as Langston Hughes were clearly sympathizers.[44] Hughes and Guillen both travelled to Spain and wrote in support of the Republican cause, as did Roumain.[45] Perhaps the most well known 'Negro' supporter of the communist movement and the Soviet Union was Paul Robeson, who spent much of the 1930s living in London. It was not accidental that Robeson featured so prominently in *The Negro Worker*, and *World Wide News*, as well as a host of other publications. His politics and political stands were inspired by the positions adopted by the CI in the 1930s, as well as by his own experiences in the Soviet Union, and endured for the rest of his life. Robeson was clearly influenced by international events, such as the Spanish Civil War as well as activists in Britain, such as Arnold Ward of the NWA, he also had close links to the CPUSA and was a leading member of the Council of African Affairs.[46] Robeson made every effort to support the Republican government and the International

41. See e.g. J.W. Ford, *The Communists and the Struggle for National Liberation* (New York, c.1936); J.S. Allen, *The Negro Question in the United States* (New York, 1936); *The Communist Position on The Negro Question* (New York, 1947); H. Haywood, *Negro Liberation* (New York, 1948).

42. See C. Jones, 'Discussion Article,' *Political Affairs*, (August 1945) pp.717-720 and Haywood, *Black Bolshevik*, pp.548-559.

43. G. Padmore, *How Russia Transformed Her Colonial Empire* (London, 1946) p.ix.

44. For Hughes on the Soviet Union see C.C. De Santis (ed.) *The Collected Works of Langston Hughes* [vol.9] *Essays on Art, Race, Politics and World Affairs* (London, 2002) pp.56-102.

45. On Hughes travels to Spain with Guillen and his writing on the Civil War see L. Hughes, *I Wonder as I Wander* (New York, 1993) especially pp.321-400 and De Santis, *Collected Works of Langston Hughes*, pp.149-203; On Roumain see C. Fowler, *A Knot in The Thread: The Life and Work of Jacques Roumain* (Washington D.C., 1980) pp.177-180.

46. See M. B. Duberman, *Paul Robeson* (London, 1991) and P. Robeson with L. Brown, *Here I Stand* (London 1988).

Brigades, travelled to Spain and made large donations to support the families of the many African Americans fighting in the International Brigades.[47]

Not all those who came into contact with the communist movement or visited the Soviet Union had the same experiences, or drew the same conclusions as Robeson, but it is evident that the CI's approach to the Negro Question had a lasting impact not least on the wider Pan-African movement.[48] This was evident in the immediate post-war period with the political stands taken by the African and Caribbean delegates who participated in the founding of the World Federation of Trade Unions in Paris and London in 1945 and of course in the focus on the 'masses' as the key to the anti-colonial struggle so apparent at the Pan-African Congress held in Manchester the same year. These events featured many of those connected with the CI and the ITUCNW during the 1930s, including Padmore, Wallace-Johnson, Kenyatta, Small, Critchlow, Gittens and Desmond Buckle.[49]

What is perhaps most significant about the Comintern's approach was that it attempted to find answers to what was referred to as the Negro Question from its inception, at a time when those in Africa and the Diaspora were struggling to liberate themselves from colonial rule and other forms of exploitation and oppression and seeking the means of their empowerment. Moreover, representatives from Africa and the Diaspora played a leading role in developing the Comintern's approach. The founding of the ITUCNW illustrated that the communist movement itself had to overcome many weaknesses to address the question and pointed to the fact that those in Africa and the Diaspora needed to be at the forefront of discussing and finding solutions to such complex political problems. The Comintern's perspective, the whole experience of the inter-war period and the history of the ITUCNW showed the need for the organisation of the most oppressed sections of society and the vital role of the organised workers, if meaningful political advances were to be made in Africa, the Caribbean and elsewhere. It also established that the struggles that were taking place in the colonies, in the US and other imperialist countries were inter-related and required an internationalism that was most evidently displayed in regard to the Scottsboro case and in opposition to the invasion of Ethiopia, as well

47. Duberman, *Paul Robeson*, pp.215-220 and P.S Foner (ed.) *Paul Robeson Speaks: Writings, Speeches, Interviews 1918-1974* (London, 1978) p.118.

48. See e.g. R. Robinson, Black on Red: My 44 Years Inside the Soviet Union (Washington D.C. 1998) and H. Smith, *Black Man in Red Russia* (Chicago, 1964). Also W. McClellan, 'Africans and Black Americans in the Comintern Schools, 1925-1934,' *International Journal of African Historical Studies*, 26/2 (1993) pp. 371-390.

49. H. Adi, 'Pan-Africanism in Britain: Background to the 1945 Manchester Congress,' in H.Adi and M. Sherwood, *The Manchester Pan-African Congress Revisited* (London, 1995) pp.11-33.

as in support for the Republican government in Spain. What is evident is that the Comintern constantly evaluated and re-evaluated its approach, recognising the need not for dogma but a guide to action in ever-changing circumstances. The many years that have passed since the 1930s have perhaps contributed to obscuring certain aspects of this perspective and history, as well as the fact they reflected the experience, activism and conviction of those from Africa and the African Diaspora.

Bibliography

MANUSCRIPT COLLECTIONS

Britain

British Library, London
India Office Papers

Labour History Archive and Study Centre, Manchester
William Gillies Papers

London Metropolitan University
TUC Library Collections – Marjorie Nicholson Papers

The National Archives, Kew, London
Colonial Office (CO) Files
Foreign Office (FO) Files
Metropolitan Police (MEPO) Files
Secret Service (KV) Files

University of Hull Archives, Hull
Reginald Bridgeman Papers

Hodgkin Papers, courtesy of Michael Wolfers

France

Archives Nationales d'Outre-Mer (ANOM), Aix-en-Provence

Documents of the Service de Liaison des Originaires des Territoires Français d'Outre Mer (SLOTFOM)

Bibliothèque de Documentation Internationale Contemporaine, Paris

Le fonds Daniel Guérin,

Nigeria

University of Lagos, Gandhi Library, Lagos

Ladipo Solanke Papers

Russia

Russian State Archive of Social and Political History (RGASPI), Moscow

Documents of the Executive Committee of the Communist International (ECCI), Fond 495

Documents of Red International of Labour Unions (Profintern), Fond 534

Documents of the Caribbean Bureau of the ECCI, Fond 500

United States

Chicago Historical Society

Claude A. Barnett Papers

Columbia University, Rare Books and Manuscript Library, New York

Hubert Harrison Papers

Robert Minor Papers

Emory University, Manuscript, Archives and Rare Books Library, Atlanta

Theodore Draper Research Files

Howard University, Manuscript Division, Moreland-Springarn Research Center, Washington, D.C.

William L. Patterson Papers

Library of Congress, Manuscript Division, Washington, D.C.

Communist Party of the United States of America Records

International Committee for the Computerization of the Comintern Archive (INCOMKA)

New York University, Tamiment Library and Robert F. Wagner Labor Archives, New York

Communist Party USA Archives

James W. Ford Papers

Robert Minor Papers

Hermina Dumont Huiswoud Papers

Mark Solomon and Robert Kaufman Research Files

Princeton University, Firestone Library, Princeton, New Jersey

George Padmore Collection

Schomburg Center for Research in Black Culture, Manuscripts, Archives and Rare Books Division, New York Public Library, New York

Harry Haywood Papers

George Padmore Letters

Richard B. Moore Papers

St. Clair Drake Papers

University of Texas at Austin, Henry Ransom Humanities Research Center, Austin

Nancy Cunard Collection

NEWSPAPERS AND MAGAZINES

Amsterdam News

Baltimore Afro-American

Bulletin of the IV Congress of the Communist International

Chicago Defender

Colonial Information Bulletin

Colonial News

Communist Review

The Communist International

Cri des Nègres

Crusader News Agency

Daily Worker (Britain)

Hansard

International African Opinion

International Press Correspondence

L'Ami du Peuple

L'Humanité

L'Ouvrier Nègre
Labour Monthly
La Race Nègre
La Voix des Nègres
Les Cahiers du Bolchevisme
Negro Liberator
Philadelphia Tribune
Pittsburgh Courier
RILU Magazine
South African Worker
The Communist
The Crisis
The Keys
The Negro Worker
The International Negro Workers' Review
The Toiler
Vox Populi
Wood Green Sentinel
The Workers' Monthly
World Wide News
Umsebenzi

BOOKS

A Trade Union Programme of Action for Negro Workers (Hamburg, 1930).

Adi, Hakim. and M.Sherwood, *The 1945 Manchester Congress Revisited* (London: New Beacon, 1995)

Adi, Hakim. *West Africans in Britain, 1900-1960: Nationalism, Pan-Africanism and Communism* (London: Lawrence and Wishart, 1998)

Adi, Hakim, and Marika Sherwood. *Pan-African History: Key Figures from Africa and the Diaspora since 1787* (London: Routledge, 2003)

Akpan Ekwere O., and Violetta I. Ekpo, *The Women's War of 1929: A Popular Uprising in South Eastern Nigeria* (Calabar: Akwa Ibom State Government Press, 1998)

Alexander, Robert J., with Eldon M. Parker, *A History of Organized Labour in the English-speaking West Indies* (Westport: Praegar 2004)

Allen, James S. *The Negro Question in the United States* (New York: International Publishers, 1936)

Andrews, Geoff, Nina Fishman and Kevein Morgan, *Opening The Books: Essays on the Social and Cultural History of the British Communist Party* (London: Pluto, 1995)

Asante, S.K. B. *Pan-African Protest: West Africa and the Italo-Ethiopian Crisis, 1934-1941* (London: Longman, 1977)

Avery, Sheldon. *Up from Washington: William Pickens and the Negro Struggle for Equality, 1900-1950* (Newark: University of Delaware Press, 1990)

Bagshaw, Anne M., and Ederisu Sawyer, *Colour Bar* (London: Published privately, n.d.)

Baptiste, Fitzroy, and Rupert Lewis (eds.) *George Padmore: Pan-African Revolutionary* (Kingston: Ian Randle, 2008)

Bellamy, Joyce, and John Saville (eds.) *Dictionary of Labour Biography* [vol. Vll] (London: Macmillan, 1984)

Beloff, Max. *The Foreign Policy of Soviet Russia, 1929-41* [vol.2] (London: Oxford University Press, 1955)

Biondi, Jean-Pierre, and Gilles Morin. *Les anticolonialistes,1881-1962* (Paris: Robert Laffont, 1992)

Blakely, Allison. *Russia and the Negro: Blacks in Russian History and Thought* (Washington, D.C.: Howard University Press, 1986)

Boahen, A. Adu. (ed.) *UNESCO General History of Africa VII – Africa under Colonial Domination 1880-1935* (London, 1985)

Boesner, Dimitri. *The Bolsheviks and the National and Colonial Question* (Westport: Hyperion Press,1994)

Boittin, Jennifer A. *Colonial Metropolis: The Urban Grounds of Anti-Imperialism and Feminism in Interwar Paris* (London: University of Nebraska Press, 2010)

Bolland, O. Nigel. *On the March: Labour Rebellions in the British Caribbean, 1934-39* (Kingston: Ian Randle, 1995)

Bunting, Brian. *Moses Kotane – South African Revolutionary* (Belville: Mayibuye Books, 1998)

Burns. Emile. *Abyssinia and Italy* (London: Victor Gollanz, 1935)

Clark, John Hendrik and Amy J. Garvey (eds.) *Marcus Garvey and the Vision of Africa* (New York: Vintage Books, 1974)

Coates, W.P., and Zelda Coates. *World Affairs and the USSR* (London: Lawrence and Wishart, 1939)

Cohen, Robin (ed.). *Forced Labour in Colonial Africa* (London, Zed, 1979)

Coleman, James S. *Nigeria: Background to Nationalism* (London: University of California Press, 1971)

Cooper, Wayne F. *Claude McKay: Rebel Sojourner in the Harlem Renaissance* (Baton Rouge: Louisiana State University Press, 1996)

Cope, R.K. *Comrade Bill – The Life and Times of W.H. Andrews, Workers' Leader* (Cape Town: Stewart Printing Co., 1944)

Cross, Malcolm, and Gad Heuman (eds.) *Labour in the Caribbean: from Emancipation to Independence* (London: Macmillan, 1988)

Dallin, Alexander. and F.I Firsov, *Dimitrov and Stalin, 1934-1943. Letters from the Soviet Archives* (London: Yale University Press, 2000)

Daniels, Robert V. (ed.) *A Documentary History of Communism* [vol. 2] (New York: Vintage Books, 1962)

Davidson, Apollon, Irina Filatova, Valentin Gorodnov and Sheridan Johns (eds.) *South Africa and the Communist International: A Documentary History* [vol.1] *Socialist Pilgrims to Bolshevik Footsoldiers 1919-1930* (London: Frank Cass, 2003)

Davidson, Apollon, Irina Filatova, Valentin Gorodnov and Sheridan Johns (eds.) *South Africa and the Communist International: A Documentary History* [vol.2] *Bolshevik Footsoldiers to Victims of Bolshevisation 1931-1939* (London: Frank Cass, 2003)

Davidson, Basil. *Let Freedom Come – Africa in Modern History* (London: Little Brown & Co., 1978)

de la Fuente, Alejandro. *A Nation For All: Race, Inequality, and Politics in Twentieth Century Cuba* (Chapel Hill: University of North Carolina Press, 2001

Derrick, Jonathan. *Africa's 'Agitators' – Militant Anti-Colonialism in Africa and the West, 1918-1939* (London: Hurst, 2008)

De Santis, Christopher C. *The collected Works of Langston Hughes: Essays on Art, Race, Politics, and World Affairs* [vol.9] (London: University of Missouri Press, 2002)

Dewitte, Philippe. *Les Mouvements Nègres en France, 1919-1939* (Paris: L'Harmattan, 1985)

Draper, Theodore. *American Communism and Soviet Russia* (New York: Viking Press, 1960)

Drew, Allison (ed.). *South Africa's Radical Tradition: A documentary history – volume one 1907-1950* (Cape Town: Mayibuye Books, 1996)

Drew, Allison. *Discordant Comrades: Identities and loyalties on the South African left* (Pretoria: UNISA Press, 2002)

Drew, Allison. *Between Empire and Revolution: a Life of Sidney Bunting, 1873-1936* (Pretoria: UNISA Press, 2007)

Duberman, Martin B. *Paul Robeson*, (London: Pan, 1989)

Durant, Pierre. *Cette mystérieuse section coloniale: Le PCF et les colonies 1920-1962* (Paris: Messidor, 1986)

Dutt, Rajani Palme. *World Politics 1918-1936* (London: Victor Gollancz, 1936)

Edgar, Robert. *Prophets With Honour: A Documentary History of Lekhotla la Bafo* (Johannesburg: Ravan Press, 1988)

Edgar, Robert. *The Making of an African Communist: Edwin Thabo Mofutsanyana and the Communist Party of South Africa 1927-1939* (Pretoria: UNISA Press, 2005)

Edwards, Brent Hayes. *The Practice of Diaspora: Literature, Translation, and the Rise of Black Internationalism* (Cambridge: Harvard University Press, 2003)

Fifth Congress of the CI – Abridged Report of Meetings Held in Moscow, June 17 to July 8, 1924 (London: CPGB, 1924)

Foner, Philip S. *American Socialism and Black Americans: From the Age of Jackson to World War II* (London: Greenwood Press, 1977)

Foner, Philip S. *Organised Labor and the Black Worker 1619-1981* (New York: International Publishers, 1982)

Foner, Philip S., and James S. Allen (eds.) *American Communism and Black Americans: A Documentary History, 1919-1929* (Philadelphia: Temple University Press, 1987)

Foner, Philip S., and Herbert Shapiro (eds.) *American Communism and Black Americans: A Documentary History, 1930-1934* (Philadelphia: Temple University Press, 1991)

Ford, James W. *The Communists and the Struggle for National Liberation* (New York: Harlem Division of the Communist Party, c.1936)

Ford, James W. *The Negro and the Democratic Front* (New York: International Publishers, 1938)

Ford, James W. *World Problems of the Negro People -A Refutation of George Padmore* (New York: Harlem Section of the Communist Party, n.d.)

Foster, William Z. *Outline History of the World Trade Union Movement* (New York: International Publishers, 1956)

Foster, William Z. *History of the Three Internationals: The World Socialist and Communist Movements from 1848 to the Present* (New York: International Publishers, 1955)

Foster, William Z. *The Negro People in American Hist*ory (New York: International Publishers, 1982)

Fowler, Carolyn. *A Knot in the Thread: The Life and Work of Jacques Roumain* (Washington, D.C.: Howard University Press, 1980)

Franklin, John Hope, and A.A. Moss, Jr. *From Slavery to Freedom: A History of African Americans* (New York: McGraw-Hill, 1994)

Fryer, Peter. *Staying Power – The History of Black People in Britain* (London: Pluto, 1984)

Fyrth, Jim. (ed.) *Britain, Fascism and the Popular Front* (London: Lawrence and Wishart, 1985)

Garvey, Amy J. (ed.), *The Philosophy and Opinions of Marcus Garvey* (Dover, MA: The Majority Press, 1986)

Geiss, Immanuel. *The Pan-African Movement: A History of Pan-Africanism in America, Europe and Africa* (New York: Methuen, 1974)

Gilmore, Glenda Elizabeth. *Defying Dixie: The Radical Roots of Civil Rights 1919-1950* (London: W.W. Norton & Co., 2008)

Grimshaw, Anna. (ed.) *The C.L.R. James Reader* (London: Wiley-Blackwell, 1992)

Hardie, Frank. *The Abyssinian Crisis* (London: Batsford, 1974)

Hardy, George. *Those Stormy Years* (London: Lawrence & Wishart, 1956)

Harris, Joseph E. *African American Reactions to War in Ethiopia 1936-1941* (London: Louisiana State University Press, 1994)

Hart, Richard. *Rise and Organise: The Birth of The Workers and National Movements in Jamaica, 1936-1939* (London: Karia Press, 1989)

Haslam, Jonathan. *The Soviet Union and the Struggle for Collective Security in Europe, 1933-39* (London: MacMillan, 1984)

Haywood, Harry. *Black Bolshevik: Autobiography of an Afro-American Communist* (Chicago: Liberator Press, 1978)

Hill, Robert A. (ed.) *The Marcus Garvey and Universal Negro Improvement Association Papers*, [vol.I] (London: University of California Press, 2006)

Hill, Robert A. (ed.) *The Marcus Garvey and Universal Negro Improvement Association Papers,* [vol. 7[(London: University of California Press, 1983)

Hill Robert A. (ed.) *The Marcus Garvey and UNIA Papers,* [vol.10*] Africa for the Africans, 1923-1945* (London, 2006)

Hill, Robert A. (ed.) *The Crusader* (New York: Garland, 1987)

Hirson, Baruch, & Gwyn A. Williams. *The Delegate for Africa – David Ivon Jones 1883-1924* (London: Core Publications, 1995)

Hooker, James R. *Black Revolutionary: George Padmore's path from Communism to Pan-Africanism* (London: Pall Mall Press, 1967)

Hochschild, Adam. *King Leopold's Ghost: A Story of Greed, Terror and Heroism in* Colonial Africa (New York: Houghton and Mifflin, 2006)

Howard, Walter T. (ed.) *Black Communists Speak on Scottsboro* (Philadelphia: Temple University Press, 2008)

Howe, Stephen. *Anticolonialism in British Politics: The Left and the End of Empire 1918-1964* (Oxford: Clarendon Press,1993)

Hughes, Langston. *A Negro Looks at Soviet Central Asia* (Moscow-Leningrad: Cooperative Publishing Society of Foreign Workers of the USSR, 1934)

Hughes, Langston. *I Wonder as I Wander: An Autobiographical Journey* (New York: Hill and Wang, 1984)

Hutchinson, Earl O. *Blacks and Reds: Race and Class in Conflict* (East Lansing: Michigan State University Oress, 1995)

Institute of Marxism-Leninism, CC of the CPSU, *Outline History of the Communist International* (Moscow: Progress Publishers, 1971)

Ismael Tarek.Y., and Rif'at. El-Sa'id, *The Communist Movement in Egypt, 1920-1988* (Syracuse: Syracuse University Press, 1990)

Italiaander, Rolf. *Schwarze Haut Im Roter Griff* (Dusseldorf: Econ-Verlag, 1962)

James, Winston. *Holding Aloft the Banner of Ethiopia: Caribbean Radicalism in Early Twentieth-Century America* (London: Verso, 1998)

Jenkinson, Jacqueline. *Black 1919 – Riots, Racism and Resistance in Imperial Britain* (Liverpool: Liverpool University Press, 2008)

Johns, Sheridan. *Raising The Red Flag: The International Socialist League & The Communist Party of South Africa 1914-1932* (Belleville: Mayibuye Books, 1995)

Kadalie, Clements. *My Life and the ICU – The Autobiography of a Black Trade Unionist in South Africa* (London: Frank Cass, 1970)

Kelley, Robin. *Hammer and Hoe – Alabama Communist During The Great Depression* (London: University of North Carolina Press, 1990)

Kestleloot, Lilyan. *Black Writers in French: A Literary History of Negritude* (Washington, D.C.: Howard University Press, 1991)

Korniweibel Jr, T. *Seeing Red – Federal Campaigns Against Black Militancy 1919-1925* (Bloomington: Indiana University Press, 1998)

La Guma, Alex. *Jimmy La Guma – a biography* (Cape Town: Friends of the South African Library, 1997)

Langley, J. Ayo. *Pan-Africanism and Nationalism in West Africa 1900-1945* (Oxford: Clarendon Press, 1973)

Langley, J. Ayo. *Ideologies of Liberation in Black Africa, 1858-1970* (London: Rex Collins, 1979)

Lazitch, Branko, in collaboration with Milorad Drachkovitch, *Biographical Dictionary of the Comintern* (Stanford: Hoover Press, 1986)

Lenin, Vladimir I. *Collected Works*, Vol., 31 (Moscow: Progress Publishers, 1965)

Lenin, Vladimir I. *Lenin on the National and Colonial Questions* (Pekin: Foreign Languages Press, 1967)

Lenin, Vladimir I. *Lenin On the United States* (Moscow: Progress Publishers, 1975)

Lerumo, A. *Fifty Fighting Years: The South African Communist Party 1921-1971* (London: Inkuleko Publications, 1971)

Lewis, Arthur. *Labour in the West Indies: The Birth of a Worker's Movement* (London: New Beacon, 1977)

Lewis, David Levering. (ed.) *W.E.B. Du Bois: A Reader* (New York: Henry Holt & Co., 1995)

Liazu, Claude. *Aux Origines Des Tiers-Mondismes: colonisés et anticolonialistes en France 1919-1939* (Paris: L'Harmattan, 1982)

Litvinov, Maxim. *Against Aggression – Speeches* (London: Lawrence and Wishart, 1936)

Lunn, Kenneth. (ed.) *Race and Labour in Twentieth Century Britain* (London: Frank Cass, 1985)

Makalani, Minkah. *In the Cause of Freedom: Radical Black Internationalism from Harlem to London 1917-1939* (Chapel Hill: The University of North Carolina Press, 2011)

Martin, Tony. (ed.) *Message to the People: The Course of African Philosophy* (Dover, MA: The Majority Press, 1986)

Matusevich, Maxim. (ed.) *Africa in Russia, Russia in Africa: Three Centuries of Encounters* (Trenton, NJ: Africa World Press, 2006)

Marx, Karl, and Frederick Engels, *The Civil War in the United States* (London: Lawrence and Wishart, 1938)

Marx, Karl, and Frederick Engels, *Marx and Engels on Colonialism* (London: Lawrence and Wishart, 1960)

McDuffie, Erik. S. *Sojourning for Freedom: Black Women, American Communism and the Making of Black Left Feminism* (Durham: Duke University Press, 2011)

McKay, Claude. *A Long Way From Home – An Autobiography* (London: Pluto, 1985)

McLeod, Alan L. (ed.) *The Negroes in America/ Claude McKay* (London: Kennikat Press, 1979)

Morgenthau, Ruth S. *Political Parties in French West Africa* (Oxford: Clarendon Press, 1964)

Mortimer, Edward. *The Rise of the French Communist Party, 1920-1947* (London: Faber, 1984)

Murray-Brown, Jeremy. Kenyatta (London: Fontana, 1974)

Musson, Doreen. *Johnny Gomas: Voice of the Working Class – A Political Biography* (Cape Town: Buchu Books, 1989)

Naison, Mark. *Communists in Harlem During the Depression* (New York: Grove Press, 1984)

Ndiaye, Pap. *La condition noire: Essai sur une minorité française* (Paris: Gallimard, 2008)

Nicolas, Armand. *Histoire de la Martinique de 1849 à 1939* [vol. 2] (Paris: L'Harmattan,1996)

Nkrumah, Kwame. *The Autobiography of Kwame Nkrumah* (London: Panaf, 1979)

Nzabakomada-Yakoma, A. *L'Afrique central insurgée: La Guerre du Kongo-Wara* (Paris: L'Harmattan, 1986)

Omu, Fred I. *Press and Politics in Nigeria, 1880-1937* (London: Longman, 1978)

Padmore, George. *How Russia Transformed Her Colonial Empire - A Challenge to the Imperialist Powers* (London: Denis Dobson, 1946)

Padmore, George. *The Life and Struggles of Negro Toilers* (Hollywood: Sun Dance Press, 1971)

Padmore, George. *Pan-Africanism or Communism? The Coming Struggle for Africa* (London: Dennis Dobson, 1956)

Painter, Nell Irvin. *The Narrative of Hosea Hudson – The Life and Times of a Black Radical* (New York: W.W. Norton and Co., 1994)

Patterson, William L. *The Man Who Cried Genocide: An Autobiography* (New York: International Publishers, 1971)

Pennybaker, Susan D. *From Scottsboro to Munich: Race and Political Culture in 1930s Britain* (Princeton: Princeton University Press, 2009)

Perry, Jeffrey B. (ed.), *A Hubert Harrison Reader* (Middletown, Connecticut: Wesleyan University Press, 2001

Perry, Jeffrey B. *Hubert Harrison: the Voice of Harlem Radicalism, 1883-1918* (New York: Columbia University Press, 2009)

Polsgrove, Carol. *Ending British rule in Africa – Writers in a common cause* (Manchester: Manchester University Press, 2009)

Post, Ken. *Arise Ye Starvelings: The Jamaican Labour Rebellion of 1938 and its Aftermath* (The Hague: Martinus Mijhoff, 1978)

Rees, Tim, and Andrew. Thorpe (eds.) *International Communism and the Communist International 1919-1943* (Manchester: Manchester University Press, 1998)

Quinn-Judge, Sophie *Ho Chi Minh – The Missing Years* (London: Hurst, 2003)

Record, Wilson. *The Negro and the Communist Party* (New York: Atheneum, 1971)

Reddock, Rhoda E. *Women, Labour & Politics in Trinidad and Tobago – A History* (London: Zed Books, 1994)

Reddock, Rhoda. *Elma Francois – The NWCSA and the workers struggle for change in the Caribbean in the 1930s* (London: New Beacon Books, 1988)

Rennie, Bukka. *History of the Working Class in the 20th Century, 1919-1956: The Trinidad and Tobago Experience* (Toronto: New Beginning Movement, 1974)

Report of the Fourth Congress of the RILU (London, 1928)

Report of Proceedings and Decisions of the First International Conference of Negro Workers (Hamburg, 1930)

Report submitted to the 3rd Congress of the Labour and Socialist International, Brussels, 5-11 August 1928 (London, 1928)

Report of the Seventh World Congress (London, 1935)

Resolutions of the Fifth Congress of the RILU (London, 1931)

Rich, Paul. *Race and Empire in British Politics* (Cambridge: Cambridge University Press, 1990

Roberts, Geoffrey K. *The Soviet Union and the Origins of the Second World War: Russo-German Relations and the Road to War 1933-1941* (London: St. Martin's Press, 1995)

Robeson, Paul. with Lloyd Brown, *Here I Stand* (London: Cassell, 1988)

Robinson, Robert. with J. Slavin, *Black On Red: My 44 Years Inside the Soviet Union* (Washington D.C.: Acropolis Books,1988)

Rogers, Joel A. *World's Great Men of Color,* [vol. II] (New York: Simon & Schuster, 1996)

Rosen, Harold. *Are You Still Circumcised? East End Memories* (Nottingham: Five Leaves Publictions, 1999)

Roumain, Jacques. *When the Tom Tom Beats: Selected Prose and Poetry* (Washington, D.C.: Azul Editions, 1995)

Roux, Eddie, and Win. *Rebel Pity – The Life of Eddie Roux* (London: Rex Collins, 1970)

Roux, Edward. *Time Longer Than Rope: The Black Man's Struggle For Freedom in South Africa* (Madison: University of Wisconsin Press, 1964)

Roux, Edward. *S.P. Bunting – A Political Biography* (Belville: Mayibuye Books, 1993

Scottsboro Defence Committee, *"We Were Framed" – The First Full Account Published in England of the Trials of the Nine Scottsboro Boys,* (London: Scottsboro Defence Committee, 1934)

Seventh Congress of the CI – Abridged Stenographic Report of Proceedings (Moscow, 1936)

Sherwood, Marika. *Origins of Pan-Africanism – Henry Sylvester Williams, Africa and the African Diaspora* (London: Routledge, 2011)

Simons, Jack & Ray. *Class and Colour in South Africa 1850-1950* (London: IDAF, 1983)

Simons, Ray Alexander. *All My Life and All My Stre*ngth (Johannesburg: STE Publishers, 2004)

Smith, Homer. *Black Man in Red Russia: A Memoir* (Chicago: Johnson Publishing Co., 1964)

Smith, Matthew J. *Red and Black in Haiti: Radicalism, Conflict and Political Change, 1934-1957* (Chapel Hill: University of North Carolina Press, 2009)

Solomon, Mark. *The Cry Was Unity: Communists and African Americans, 1917-1936* (Jackson: University Press of Mississippi, 1998)

South African Communists Speak: Documents from the History of the South African Communist Party, 1915-1980 (London: Inkuleko Publications, 1981)

Stalin, Joseph V. *Marxism and the National and Colonial Question* (London: Lawrence and Wishart, 1936)

Stalin, Joseph V. *Problems of Leninism* (Pekin: Foreign Languages Press, 1976)

Tabili, Laura. *"We Ask For British Justice" Workers and Racial Difference in Late Imperial Britain* (London: Cornell University Press, 1994)

The Colonial Problem – Material submitted to the IIIrd *Congress of the Labour and Socialist Internationa*l (Brussels, August 1928)

The Communist Position on The Negro Question (New York, 1947)

The October Revolution and Africa (Moscow: Progress Publishers, 1983)

The Tasks of the International Trade Union Movement: Resolutions and Decisions of the Third World Congress of the RILU, July 1924 (London, 1924)

The Revolutionary Movement in the Colonies (London, 1929)

Turner, W. Burghardt, and Joyce Moore Turner (eds.) *Richard B. Moore, Caribbean Militant in Harlem: Collected Writings 1920-1972* (London: Pluto Press, 1992)

Turner, Joyce Moore. *Caribbean Crusaders and the Harlem Renaissance* (Chicago: University of Illinois Press, 2005)

Valtin, Jan. *Out of the Night* (New York: Alliance Book Corporation, 1941)

Van Diemel, Raymond. *'In Search of Freedom, Fair Play and Justice': Josiah Tshangana Gumede, 1867-1947: a biography.* Available at http://www.sahistory.org.za/archive/search-freedom-fair-play-and-justice. Accessed July 2012

Walters, F.P. *A History of the League of Nations, Vol. II* (London: Oxford University Press, 1952)

Weisbord, Robert G. *Ebony Kinship – Africa, Africans and the Afro-American* (London: Greenwood Press, 1973)

Weiss, Holger. 'The Collapse and Rebirth of the ITUCNW, 1933-1938. Part One - From Hamburg via Paris to Antwerp and Amsterdam, 1933-1935.' Comintern Working Paper 24/2011, pp.38-39 (https://www.abo.fi/student/en/media/7957/cowopa24weiss.pdf)

Wilson, Edward T. *Russia and Black Africa Before World War II* (New York: Holmes and Meier Publishers, 1974)

Wolton, Douglas G. *Wither South Africa* (London: Lawrence & Wishart, 1947)

Worley, Matthew. (ed.) *In Search of Revolution: International Communist Parties in the Third Period* (London: I.B, Tauris, 2004)

Yellington, Kevin A. and Bridget Brereton (eds.) *The Colonial Caribbean in Transition: Essays in Post-emancipation Social and Cultural History* (Gainesville: University Press of Florida, 1999)

Zeleza, Paul T. (ed.) The Study of Africa: Global and Transnational Engagements (Dakar: CODESRIA, 2007)

ARTICLES

Adi, Hakim. 'Forgotten Comrade? Desmond Buckle: An African Communist in Britain,' *Science and Society*, 70/1 (2002) pp.22-46

Aitken, Robbie. 'From Cameroon to Germany and Back via Moscow and Paris: The Political Career of Joseph Bilé (1892-1959), Performer, "Negerbeiter" and Comintern Activist.' *Journal of Contemporary History*, 43/4 (October 2008)

Berland, Oscar. 'The Emergence of the Communist Perspective on the "Negro Question" in America: 1919-1931 – Part Two,' *Science and Society*, 64/2 (Summer, 2000) pp.194-217

Berland, Oscar. 'Nasanov and the Comintern's American Negro Program,' *Science and Society*, 64/2 (Summer, 2000) pp.226-228

Boittin, J.A. 'The Language and Politics of Race in the Late Third Republic,' *French Politics, Culture and Society*, 27/2 (Summer, 2009) pp.23-46

Campbell, Susan. '"Black Bolsheviks" and Recognition of African-American's Right to Self-Determination by the Communist Party USA,' *Science and Society*, 58/4 (Summer, 1994) pp.440-470

Campbell, Susan. 'Kay Donnellan, Irishwoman and Radical in Trinidad, 1938-41,' *Journal of Caribbean History*, 44/1 (2010) pp.75-104

Carr, Barry. 'Mill Occupations and Soviets: The Mobilization of Sugar Workers in Cuba 1917-1933,' *Journal of Latin American Studies*, 28 (1996) pp.129-158

Carr, Barry. 'Identity, Class, and Nation: Black Immigrant Workers, Cuban Communism, and the Sugar Insurgency, 1925-1934,' *Hispanic American Historical Review*, 78/1 (February, 1998) pp.83-116

de la Fuente, A. 'Two Dangers, One Solution: Immigration, Race, and Labor in Cuba, 1900-1930,' *International Labor and Working Class History*, 51 (Summer, 1997) pp.30-49

Edgar, Robert. 'Notes on the Life and Death of Albert Nzula,' *International Journal of African Historical Studies*, 16/4 (1983) pp.675-679

Edwards, Brent Hayes. 'The Shadow of Shadows,' *Positions: East Asia Cultures Critique*, 2/1 (2003) pp.11-49

Elkins, W.F. '"Unrest Among the Negroes:" A British Document of 1919,' *Science and Society*, 32/1 (Winter 1968) pp.66-79

Filatova, Irina. 'Indoctrination or Schoarship? Education of Africans at the Communist University of the Toilers of the East in the Soviet Union, 1923-1937,' *Paeagogica Historica*, 35/1 (1999)

Genova, J.E. 'The Empire Within: The Colonial Popular Front in France, 1934-1938,' *Alternatives*, 26/2 (2001)

Harris, LaShawn. 'Running with the Reds: African American Women and the Communist Party During the Great Depression,' *Journal of African American History*, 94/1 (Winter 2009) pp.21-43

Hopkins, Anthony G. 'Economic Aspects of Political Movements in Nigeria and in the Gold Coast 1918-1939,' *Journal of African History*, VII/1 (1966) pp.133-152

Hughes, Arnold. and D. Perfect, 'Trade Unionism in the Gambia,' *African Affairs*, 88/353 (1989)

Joanniu, M. 'Nancy Cunard's English Journey,' in *Feminist Review*, 78 (2004)

Johanningsmeier, E. 'Communists and Black Freedom Movements in South Africa and the US: 1919-1950, *Journal of Southern African Studies*, 30/1, (March 2004), pp.153-180

Johns, Sheridan. 'The Comintern, South Africa and the Black Diaspora,' *The Review of Politics*, 37/2 (1975)

Johns, Sheridan. 'The Birth of the CP of South Africa,' *International Journal of African Historical Studies*, Vol. IX, No. 3 (1976) pp. 371-400

Jones, Claudia. 'Discussion Article,' *Political Affairs*, (August 1945) pp.717-720

Kanet, Roger E. 'The Comintern and the "Negro Question": Communist Policy in the United States and Africa, 1921-1941,' *Survey*, XIX no.4 (1973) pp.86-122

Kelley, Robin. 'The Third International and the Struggle of National Liberation in South Africa,' *Ufahamu*, 15/1-2 (1986) pp.99-120

Kinshasa, K.M. 'From Surinam to the Holocaust: Anton de Kom a Political Migrant,' *Journal of Caribbean History*, 36/1 (2002) pp.36-68

Klehr, Harvey and W. Thompson, 'Self-determination in the Black Belt: Origins of a Communist Policy,' *Labor History*, 30/3 (Summer, 1989) pp.354-366

Langley, J Ayo. 'Pan-Africanism in Paris, 1924-36,' *The Journal of Modern African Studies*, 7/1 (1969) pp.69-94

Legassick, Martin. 'Class in South African Protest: The South African Communist Party and the "Native Republic" 1928-34,' *Eastern African Studies* XV (July 1973) Syracuse University

Luke, D. F. 'The Development of Modern Trade Unionism in Sierra Leone – Part 1,' *International Journal of African Historical Studies*, 18/3 (1985) pp.425-454

McClennan, W. 'Africans and Black Americans in Comintern Schools, 1925-1934,' *International Journal of African Historical Studies*, 26/2 (1993) pp.371-390

Meel, P. 'Anton de Kom and the Formative Phase of Surinamese Decolonization,' *New West India Guide*, 83/3-4 (2009) pp.249-280

Ménil, René. 'Notes sur la développement historique du Marxisme à la Martinique,' *Action – Revue Theoretique et Politique du Parti Communiste Martiniquais,* 13 (1967) pp.17-30

Miller, J.A., S. Pennybacker and E. Rosenhaft, 'Mother Ada Wright and the International Campaign to Free the Scottsboro Boys, 1931-1934,' *American Historical Review*, 106/2 (April 2001) pp.387-430

Ndlovu, N.F. 'Johannes Nkosi and the Communist Party of South Africa: Images of "Blood River" and King Dingane in the late 1920s-1930,' *History and Theory*, 39 (December 2000) pp.111-132

Person, Yves. 'Le Front populaire au Sénégal (mai 1936-octobre 1938),' *Le Mouvement Social*, 107 (April-June 1979) pp. 77-101

Rhodie, Samuel. 'The Gold Coast Aborigines Abroad,' *Journal of African History*, 6/3 (1965) pp.385-411

Roth, Mia. 'Josie Mpama: the contribution of a largely forgotten figure in the South African liberation struggle,' *Kleio*, 28/1 (1996) pp.120-136

Shaloff, S. 'Press Controls and Sedition Proceedings in the Gold Coast, 1933-39,' *African Affairs*, 71/284 (1972) pp.241-263

Sherwood, Marika. 'Lascar Struggles Against Discrimination in Britain 1923-45: The Work of N.J. Upadhyaya and Surat Alley,' *The Mariner's Mirror*, 90/4 (November 2004) pp.438-455

Sherwood, Marika. 'Racism and Resistance: Cardiff in the 1930s and 1940s,' *Llafur*, 5/4 (1991) pp.51-70.

Sherwood, Marika. 'The Comintern, the CPGB, Colonies and Black Britons, 1920-1938,' *Science and Society*, 60/2 (Summer 1996) pp.137-163

Singh, K. 'Adrian Cola Rienzi and the Labour Movement in Trinidad, 1925-1944,' *Journal of Caribbean History*, 16 (November 1982) pp.11-35

Spitzer, Leo and LaRay Denzer, 'I.T. A Wallace-Johnson and the West African Youth League,' *The International Journal of African Historical Studies*, 6/3 (1973) pp.413-452

Squires, Mike. Communists and the Fight Against Racism During the Class against Class Period 1928-33,' *Communist Review*, (Summer 2000), pp.12-19

Stevens, Margaret. '"Hands of Haiti" Self-determination, Anti-imperialism, and the Communist Movement in the United States, 1925-1929,' *The Black Scholar*, 37/4 (Winter 2008) pp. 61-70

'Suppression of Trade Unionism in British West Africa,' *The Monthly Circular of the Labour Research Department*, XVIII/12 (December 1929) pp.265-267

Tillett, Lowell R. 'The Soviet Role in League Sanctions Against Italy, 1935-36,' in *The American Slavic and East European Review* (1956) Vol.15, pp.11-16

Tosstorff, R. 'Moscow Versus Amsterdam: Reflections on the History of the Profintern,' *Labour History Review*, 68/1 (April 2003) pp.79-97

Wyse, Akintola J.G. 'The 1926 Railway Strike and Anglo-Krio Relations,' *International Journal of African Historical Studies*, 14/1 (1981) pp.93-123

Zumoff, Jacob. 'The African Blood Brotherhood: From Caribbean Nationalism to Communism,' *Journal of Caribbean Studies*, 41/1-2 (2007) pp.200-226

THESES

Denzer, LaRay, 'I.T.A Wallace-Johnson and the West African Youth League: A case study in West African Nationalism.' (Ph.D dissertation, University of Birmingham, 1977)

Graham, J.L. 'Representations of Racial Democracy: Race, National Identity and State Cultural Policy in the United States and Brazil.' (Ph.D dissertation, University of Chicago, 2010)

Grossman, Jonathan. 'Class Relations and the Policies of the Communist Party of South Africa, 1921-1950.' (Ph.D dissertation, University of Warwick, 1983)

James, Leslie. E. '"What we put in black and white": George Padmore and the practice of anti-imperial politics.' (Ph.D dissertation, University of London, 2012)

Jones, Jennifer. E. 'The Anti-Colonial Politics and Policies of the CPGB: 1920-1951,' (Ph.D dissertation, University of Wolverhampton, 1997)

MacKenzie, Alan John. 'British Marxists and the Empire: Anti-imperialist Theory and Practice, 1920-1945.' (Ph.D dissertation, University of London, 1978)

Sagna, Olivier. 'Des pionniers méconnus de l'indépendence: Africains, Antillais et lutttes anti-colonialistes dans la France de l'entre-deux-guerres 1919-1939,' (Thèse de doctorat, Université Paris-Diderot, 1987)

Spiegler, James S. 'Aspects of Nationalist Thought Among French-Speaking West Africans 1921-1939,' (DPhil. dissertation, University of Oxford, 1968)

Stevens, Margaret. 'The Red International and the Black Caribbean: Transnational Radical Organizations in New York City, Mexico and the West Indies, 1919-1939.' (Ph.D dissertation, Brown University, 2010)

Van Enckevort, Maria C. 'The Life and Work of Otto Huiswoud: Professional Revolutionary and Internationalist, 1893-1961.' (Ph.D. dissertation, University of the West Indies, Mona, Jamaica, 2001)

Worsley, Matthew, 'Class Against Class – the Communist Party of Great Britain in the Third Period.' (Ph. D. dissertation, University of Nottingham, 1998)

Zumoff, Jacob A. 'The Communist Party of the United States and the Communist International, 1919-1929.' (Ph.D dissertation, University College, London, 2003)

Index